Latinos in New York

LATINO PERSPECTIVES

José Limón, Timothy Matovina, and Luis Ricardo Fraga,
series editors

INSTITUTE *for* Latino Studies
UNIVERSITY OF NOTRE DAME

The Institute for Latino Studies, in keeping with the distinctive mission, values, and traditions of the University of Notre Dame, promotes understanding and appreciation of the social, cultural, and religious life of U.S. Latinos through advancing research, expanding knowledge, and strengthening community.

LATINOS IN NEW YORK

Communities in Transition

SECOND EDITION

EDITED BY SHERRIE BAVER, ANGELO FALCÓN,
AND GABRIEL HASLIP-VIERA

University of Notre Dame Press
Notre Dame, Indiana

University of Notre Dame Press
Notre Dame, Indiana 46556
www.undpress.nd.edu

Library of Congress Cataloging-in-Publication Data
Names: Baver, Sherrie L., editor. | Falcâon, Angelo, editor. |
Haslip-Viera, Gabriel, editor.
Title: Latinos in New York : communities in transition /
edited by Sherrie Baver, Angelo Falcon, and Gabriel Haslip-Viera.
Description: Second edition. | Notre Dame, Indiana :
University of Notre Dame Press, 2017. | Series: Latino perspectives |
Includes bibliographical references and index. |
Identifiers: LCCN 2017018505 (print) | LCCN 2017018689 (ebook) |
ISBN 9780268101527 (pdf) | ISBN 9780268101534 (epub) | ISBN 9780268101503
(hardcover : alk. paper) | ISBN 0268101507 (hardcover : alk. paper) |
ISBN 9780268101510 (pbk. : alk. paper) | ISBN 0268101515 (pbk. : alk. paper)
Subjects: LCSH: Hispanic Americans—New York (State)—New York. | Hispanic
Americans—New York Region. | New York (N.Y.)—Social conditions. |
New York Region—Social conditions.
Classification: LCC F128.9.S75 (ebook) | LCC F128.9.S75 L37 2017 (print) |
DDC 974.7/100468—dc23
LC record available at https://lccn.loc.gov/2017018505

∞ *This paper meets the requirements of
ANSI/NISO Z39.48-1992 (Permanence of Paper).*

This book is dedicated to the memory of
our friend and colleague Juan Flores,
1943–2014.

CONTENTS

Introduction

Angelo Falcón, Sherrie Baver, and Gabriel Haslip-Viera

Developments in the Latino community of New York City have often served as a harbinger of things to come for this population nationally. As a leading global city, New York is subjected to powerful international forces as well as to the push and pull of local ones at a scale rarely seen elsewhere. Home to what is probably one of the most diverse Latino populations in the world, with the most complex settlement patterns, in many ways the city appears, in light of national trends, to represent the Latino future throughout the country. A close examination of the transitions taking place in New York's Latino community can provide clues about developments in the broader Latino and other similarly situated communities.

Since the first edition of *Latinos in New York* in 1996, the editors have witnessed continuities but also many dramatic changes in this community. In this second edition, we document, for a new generation of students and other interested readers, what has remained the same as well as what has changed. While we attempt a wide review of critical issues confronting the city's Latinos, the research agenda before us remains broader. Issues such as the role of race, culture and identity, health, the criminal justice system, the media, and higher education are but a few that require greater attention from both an academic and a policy perspective.

The impetus for the first volume was that while numerous works existed on Hispanics or Latinos,[1] we were surprised by the absence of a more comprehensive text on New York's Latino community. Studies that started

1

appearing in the 1960s often focused on particular national-origin subgroups such as Mexican-Americans, Puerto Ricans, and Cubans. They also often did so in specific US localities or regions such as Chicago, Los Angeles, New York, southern Florida, and the Southwest. By the 1980s, several volumes appeared examining the Hispanic or Latino community nationally,[2] spurred on by the rise in research interest in the issue of persistent poverty and the underclass, followed by the growth of immigration studies. Still, however, little research had been published on the New York Latino experience.

In comparison to the histories of migration between other localities and regions, the history of immigration from Latin America to New York differs in terms of its timing and the mix of its nationality groups. For example, "Spanish," "Hispanics," and "Hispanicized Native Americans" were already settled in southern California, Arizona, New Mexico, and Texas before those areas were ceded to the United States in 1848, at the end of the Mexican-American War. Small groups of Spaniards and Latinos were also found in Florida when that region was ceded to the United States by Spain in 1819. By contrast, the Hispanic presence in New York and other eastern and midwestern urban areas, such as Philadelphia and Chicago, became significant only in the early part of the twentieth century, although the origins of the migration, especially to New York and its environs, can be traced back earlier.[3]

Local and regional differences have been apparent in the mix of subgroups as well as in the socioeconomic status of Latino national-origin groups. In terms of the subgroup mix, Mexicans and other immigrants from Central America, for example, have been the predominant Spanish-speaking groups in the Southwest, while balanced but separate communities of Mexicans and Puerto Ricans were the pattern in Chicago. Cubans dominated in southern Florida since the early 1960s, while Puerto Ricans dominated in New York and other communities in the Northeast, most recently along with Dominicans, Cubans, Colombians, Ecuadoreans, Salvadorans, and Peruvians. In recent years, the growing immigration of Latin Americans to the United States and the migration of Latinos throughout the country have made all American urban areas much more diverse.[4]

On the issue of socioeconomic background, many immigrants and migrants in the first part of the twentieth century came from impoverished urban, rural, or mixed rural and urban backgrounds, such as Mexicans in the Southwest or Puerto Ricans and later Dominicans in New York and other parts of the Northeast. Yet other immigrant groups from South America were predominantly urban and middle class; and the first large wave of Cubans arriving in the early 1960s after the Cuban Revolution and mainly settling in Miami were, typically, well-off and well educated. This picture of the subgroups is now even more mixed, typified by the large migration of Puerto Rican professionals to Central Florida from Puerto Rico.

Aspects of the Latino presence usually overlooked are its scale and its geographic and sociopolitical complexity. In a city of more than 8.5 million residents, Latinos make up close to a third of the population spread over five counties, which are locally called boroughs. Geographically, Latinos live in as many as twenty or so *barrios*, each the size of a small to medium-sized city, with their own histories, national-origin makeup, political cultures, and community issues. Vertically, this community is embedded in a sociopolitical system with global as well as local elites and institutions that include Wall Street, the United Nations, and major media. Along with the national-origin diversity of New York's Latino population, this mix is, in many ways, unique even in comparison with similar cities like Los Angeles and Miami. However, the forces that have shaped this uniqueness are also effecting similar changes elsewhere; and this is where the New York example becomes most interesting to examine.

At present, the literature on Latinos nationally, in specific locales, or regionally is too large to cite adequately. This reflects the growth of this population in the United States, which is now at roughly fifty-four million people (fifty-eight million if one includes the US territory of Puerto Rico), or 17% of the total US population (2013).[5] In addition to monographs, there are now scholarly journals like *Latino Studies* that chronicle and analyze the US Latino experience generally and for particular subgroups.[6]

Since the first publication of *Latinos in New York*, several studies have appeared on this population and specific national-origin subgroups in New York City, and several authors of such studies have contributed chapters in this volume (e.g., Torres-Saillant and Hernández 1998; Hernández 2002; Morales 2003; Haslip-Viera, Falcón, and Matos Rodríguez 2004; Smith 2006; Torres 2006; Sánchez 2007; Noguera, Hurtado, and Fergus 2011). This also includes such works as Aparicio (2006), Dávila (2004), Dávila and Laó-Montes (2001), Hoffnung-Garskof (2010), Jones-Correa (1998), Remeseira and Delbanco (2010), Ricourt (2002), Thomas (2010), and Upegui-Hernandez (2014). Also since 1996, there has appeared a vast literature on immigrants and immigration in general that has informed and been informed by the Latino experience.

The significant changes in New York's Latino community since the first edition of this book appeared are in the size, diversity, and relative importance of the national-origin subgroups. At present, Latinos comprise 2.4 million New Yorkers, or 29% of the total city population; furthermore, they represent 23% of eligible city voters. Among Latinos, Puerto Ricans remain the largest subgroup (31%), followed closely by Dominicans (25%) and Mexicans (14%). No longer, however, are Puerto Ricans the majority of New York's Latinos as they were throughout most of the twentieth century. Despite this, given New York's location as major port of entry for the United States, there has always been a diverse Latino presence, with Cubans, Spaniards, and others playing significant roles in the history of this community.

In addition to the top three subgroups, Central and South American immigration has increased especially since the 1980s, making New York City the most diverse Spanish-speaking city in the world. What has not changed is that while great strides have been made in education, disproportionate numbers of Latino residents remain poor. Moreover, significant portions of these residents are undocumented and, therefore, remain without most basic rights, since comprehensive immigration reform, involving a legalization path for the undocumented, has been discussed but not addressed by Congress since the Immigration Reform and Control Act (IRCA) of 1986.

As noted in the introduction to the first edition of this text, the following chapters highlight, in part, what is unique about the Latino experience in New York, especially its breadth of diversity compared to other US cities. Still, recognizing the uniqueness of New York City as a leading global city, the editors intend that this volume will also have relevance for students, scholars, and policy analysts of the Latino experience throughout the United States. Each contributor, while focusing on the New York context, also understands that each Latino subgroup is transnational and, therefore, sensitive to the home-country context. Yet the contributors are also aware that each subgroup (especially as we move beyond the immigrant generation) is part of the larger Latino presence in the life of the United States. Scholars of the Latino experience will have more than enough work in continuing years to describe and analyze how these dual pressures, transnationalism and notions of *pan-latinidad*, play out for specific national-origin subgroups in different parts of the United States.

THE ESSAYS

The editors have grouped the essays into three broad sections. Part 1 examines the historical and sociocultural context of Latinos in New York. Typically, overviews of Hispanic migration to New York focused on Puerto Ricans in the twentieth century and especially post–World War II. In contrast, historian Gabriel Haslip-Viera's chapter covers the years 1613 to 2012 on the basis of his many years of tracing the city's Latino community. Although noting that the community evolved slowly before 1898, and especially during the periods of Dutch and English colonization, his pushing back the start of the immigration story of Spanish-speakers by more than two centuries enriches our understanding of the earliest nonindigenous settlers in Gotham.

In chapter 2, sociologist Clara Rodríguez focuses on Puerto Ricans, who had been the majority of Latino New Yorkers in the last century. While they are no longer the absolute majority, Rodríguez's point is they remain, in many ways, the predominant Hispanic group in the city. Rodríguez asks the novel question of how earlier ethnic communities in New York, especially Puerto Rican communities, provide a historical base for the more diverse Latino neighborhoods today. She places the Puerto Rican "great migration" of the mid-twentieth century into the larger context of "the long hiatus," roughly 1930–69, when few European or Asian immigrants were coming to the United States, and Puerto Ricans and Mexicans were arriving to supply America's low-wage labor. Rodríguez cites other Puerto Rican long-term contributions to newer arrivals to New York and America such as bilingual education, bilingual voting assistance, major contributions to the visual and performing arts, and the presence of Latino studies programs and departments in colleges and universities. She hypothesizes that immigration scholars do not capture the Puerto Rican contributions to US society because of their new focus on transnationalism. She argues, however, that immigration scholars should include the Puerto Rican case because Puerto Ricans are "migrants" as citizens but not "full-fledged US citizens." Finally, the contribution of Puerto Ricans as leaders in demanding multicultural recognition in New York City and the nation should be noted as demands for multicultural awareness have grown in the main urban centers in Europe and beyond.

Sociologist and historian of religion Ana María Díaz-Stevens focuses on Latino religious practice in New York. While she focuses mainly on the

Catholic Church and the especially Puerto Rican migration experience—which was especially difficult since Puerto Ricans were not accompanied by a native clergy—this is not the entire story. Díaz-Stevens injects diversity into her overview, focusing on newer Spanish-speaking immigrant groups to New York as well as other religious belief systems present in the community. She devotes a good part of her chapter to examining the influence of Afro-Caribbean rituals among Latino Catholics as well as the rise of Protestantism, especially Pentecostalism, among Latinos, and the recent increase in Muslim adherents among Latino New Yorkers.

Part 2 of the volume, titled "Under the Latino National Umbrella," examines the diversity constituting Latino New York. Although the chapters focus mostly on specific national-origin groups and do not follow a common format, each chapter notes (1) the factors that prompted emigration from the country of origin, (2) the socioeconomic status of the emigrants, (3) the extent of transnational ties with the home country, and (4) the immigrants' interaction with other Latino groups in New York. This last point should be highlighted since there is little research on how different Spanish-speaking national-origin subgroups interact and what the label "Latino" really means. This is because most people of Hispanic descent still identify in surveys first by national origin (e.g., Puerto Rican) and then secondly as Hispanic and/or Latino.

The beginning chapter in part 2 is presented by economist Andrés Torres and sociologist Gilbert Marzán. Given the decline in Puerto Rican numbers, Torres and Marzán reasonably ask, "Where have all the Puerto Ricans gone?" After an in-depth, quantitative study of the years 1985–90 and 1995–2000, they conclude that for the most part, New York Puerto Ricans have not gone very far. Some have gone to Puerto Rico or Florida, but most who have left New York City have gone to nearby suburbs or states. With the current massive movement of population out of Puerto Rico in the second decade of the new millennium, this issue of Puerto Rican migration patterns assumes greater importance. Therefore, this chapter's analysis of Puerto Rican population shift away from New York points to its changing role in the broader Puerto Rican migration circuits within the United States and Puerto Rico. The authors suggest that further research should be done on the characteristics of the out-migrants and the implications of these migrations for Puerto Rican identity and socioeconomic status.

Sociologist Ramona Hernández and humanities scholar Silvio Torres-Saillant, present and former directors of the City University of New York's

Dominican Studies Institute, focus on New York's large and growing Dominican community, projected to soon become the largest Latino group in the city. They note that in recent years, it is not only immigration but also births in the United States that explain the community's population growth. By the second decade of the twenty-first century, almost 50% of Dominican-Americans have been born in the States, which adds to the diversity of the Dominican experience. While most Dominicans initially chose to live in Manhattan, by 2010 more Dominican New Yorkers lived in the Bronx and thousands had moved to other boroughs and states such as Rhode Island, Florida, Massachusetts, and Pennsylvania. The authors conclude that while a majority of Dominicans still have a way to go to live the American Dream, they remain optimistic that these resilient immigrants and their children will contribute to this country as well as their Caribbean country of origin.

Political scientist Robert Smith continues his almost three-decade groundbreaking research of New York's dramatically growing Mexican community, the fastest-growing Latino group in the city. He notes that a major change from his 1996 essay for the first edition of *Latinos in New York* is that the community is much more rooted in a large US-born generation. Mexicans, at close to half a million people, are now the third-largest and fastest-growing Latino group in the city. Still, their path to incorporation and social advancement is not smooth because of the high rate of *indocumentados*, who suffer from legal exclusion. Smith then sketches out how specific city institutions, such as the Department of Education, the City University of New York, and the New York Police Department may help those excluded from social citizenship to attain more positive life outcomes than might otherwise be expected.

Veteran journalist Javier Castaño provides one of the first comprehensive overviews of Colombians and Ecuadoreans in New York, focusing on Corona, Queens. Two overarching problems Castaño highlights are (1) Anglo society's inability to distinguish one Spanish-speaking national-origin group from another and (2) the tensions among specific Latino subgroups. Castaño and his narrator in this chapter, Walter Sinche, offer particular details about organizational life in the Corona Latino community, including rivalries and inefficiencies among some groups but also the community's ability to mobilize, when necessary, to protest bias killings and media stereotyping. Furthermore, the chapter offers hope, with Castaño describing a growing number of community activists focusing on improving educational quality, reducing crime, and slowing housing foreclosures.

Finally, Walker Simon and Rosalía Reyes, both journalists, offer the first systematic overview of Central Americans in New York. They begin their essay focusing on US involvement in Central American civil wars of the 1980s, a fact that stimulated large-scale immigration to the United States. Next they concentrate on the specific national-origin groups in metropolitan New York, including Panamanians, Hondurans, Salvadorans, Guatemalans, Costa Ricans, and Nicaraguans, as well as the Garifuna community, coming primarily from Honduras but from other countries as well. Finally, they document the ongoing transnational ties among all these communities, a seeming commonality among Latino immigrant groups.

Part 3 focuses on politics and policy issues affecting New York's Latinos. In the first piece, political scientist José R. Sánchez addresses the inadequacies he sees in the theoretical approaches used to study local Latino power; more specifically, his concern is what is holding back Latino community power. Sánchez surveys the four most common social science approaches used to study the distribution of power in American society and then provides case studies to highlight the inadequacies of these approaches. One particularly detailed case study focuses on the struggle for public housing in the early 1970s. Sánchez also examines the concept of "identity politics" and tries to explain why "ethnic unity" doesn't always translate into political power for Latinos (or others). His answer is to offer a "social power" approach that is a "riff" on more traditional Marxist political-economy theorizing to examine power in American society. For Sánchez, Latinos' lack of power is now caused more by public sector than private sector institutions, along with activists' inability to draw on old civil rights concepts now in a seemingly "postracial" America.

In the next chapter, veteran civil rights attorney Juan Cartagena provides an overview of the Latino struggle for voting rights in New York City. As president and general counsel of LatinoJustice PRLDEF (formerly the Puerto Rican Legal Defense and Education Fund), Cartagena has been a leading participant in several of the key cases affecting the Latino community's ability "[to protect] voting rights writ large." His history and deep appreciation of the 1965 Voting Rights Act focuses on how activists successfully eliminated many of the discriminatory effects of both vote denial and dilution that had been used against Latinos and African Americans. This chapter highlights the many challenges in this area as we enter a new era in which the US Supreme Court has weakened voting rights in its June 2013 decision *Shelby County v. Holder*.

Political scientist Sherrie Baver updates her 1996 contribution to *Latinos in New York* by examining changes and continuities in US immigration policy in the last twenty years. The main continuities she finds are (1) that much of the American public remains ambivalent about immigrants, especially unauthorized immigrants—benefiting from their contributions but unhappy about living with them, and (2) that Congress had been unable to pass comprehensive immigration reform, especially since 9/11/2001, when reform efforts became tied to largely unrelated concerns about national security. Even before 9/11, the federal trend was to be less welcoming to immigrants, and in the last few years, deportations of the undocumented have risen dramatically. In the absence of federal policy-making, states and localities have carved divergent ideological paths in their treatment of immigrants, especially the undocumented. Fortunately, New York City (where two-thirds of the population is now made up of the foreign born or their children) has, for the most part, maintained immigrant-friendly policies.

Journalist and author Ed Morales focuses on housing politics in New York's Latino "core communities," as the administration of New York City mayor Bill de Blasio commits itself to the massive development of so-called affordable housing and the rezoning this will require. The main question explored in this chapter is how Latino core communities have been confronting disinvestment, reinvestment, and gentrification. These are forces affecting not only East Harlem / El Barrio but also the Lower East Side, Williamsburg, and Bushwick, among other neighborhoods. Morales notes that the challenges to the Latino presence in various areas intensified after 9/11, when shell-shocked New Yorkers elected Michael Bloomberg as mayor, and the new mayor's key pledge was to rebuild the city rather than reduce social and racial inequities. Morales critiques New York's feeble affordable-housing policies under Bloomberg and details activists' strategies to preserve at least some part of Latino core communities for the residents who have lived there for decades or generations.

Educators Luz Yadira Herrera and Pedro Noguera examine a central issue for Latino New Yorkers, the city's educational policies. In highlighting the challenges facing Mayor Bill de Blasio, the chapter examines the numerous reforms that occurred during the twelve years of the Bloomberg administration and their effects on Latino students, the largest demographic subgroup in the city's public school system. In 2002, Mayor Bloomberg abolished the Board of Education and assumed direct control of the schools to implement his new approach, called "Children First." Key features of his reform package involved implementing high-stakes testing to ensure teacher accountability, decentralizing the vast education bureaucracy to increase school autonomy, introducing charter schools into the mix of school choices, and closing schools that were seen as failing. Herrera and Noguera conclude that "Children First" has not been particularly helpful to New York's Hispanic community. The city's school system remains highly segregated, and "large concentrations of high-needs Latino students continue to be served by low-performing schools." The authors conclude that sixty years after the Supreme Court's *Brown v. Board* decision, New York should be doing a better job for its students.

Next, to provide some historical context to New York City's new emphasis on sustainability and environmental resilience, Sherrie Baver examines New York's environmental justice movement, and the leading role played by Latino, especially Puerto Rican, activists in creating a less toxic, greener city. Environmental justice activists pose two general questions: Why do poor neighborhoods face disproportionate environmental harm from polluted infrastructure, toxic and hazardous waste, and less green space than wealthy neighborhoods? and, How does this reality affect health and well-being in poor neighborhoods? Baver notes that the Young Lords grappled with these questions almost two decades before the country had an identifiable environmental justice movement, and, not surprisingly, several of the former Lords went on to help establish environmental justice organizations such as The Toxic Avengers in Brooklyn and the South Bronx Clean Air Coalition. Puerto Ricans and other Latinos were greening their New York neighborhoods with *casitas* and community gardens decades before community gardens became "hip." Even as we acknowledge that most successful environmental justice struggles in the city have been multiethnic coalitions, the Latino contribution cannot be overstated, especially as newer issues such as waterfront parks, green-collar jobs, food justice, environmental resilence, and climate justice are added to the earlier list of concerns.

A longtime "guerrilla researcher" and cofounder of the National Institute for Latino Policy (NiLP), political scientist Angelo Falcón provides the last essay in part 2, speculating on future trends in New York Latino politics. Falcón, the leading analyst of Latino politics in New York, identifies those elements affecting Latino politics in New York City that should be the basis of any analysis of the subject. He notes at least two competing themes in local Latino politics. While the hyperdiversity of New York's Latino community may impede easy development of a unified political agenda, the fact that Latino politicians need to appeal to more than their national subgroup for votes may push towards unity. In addition, the intense anti-immigrant and anti-Latino sentiment in the country in recent years has promoted a greater pan-Latino consciousness. Thus a unified political agenda may become a distinct possibility. Falcón ends the chapter with an overview of how these elements were playing themselves out at the beginning of the administration of New York City mayor Bill de Blasio.

Finally, a cultural studies scholar, the late Juan Flores, provides our concluding chapter. Flores focuses on *Nueva York*'s uniqueness as the major US city with the most diverse Latino diaspora, and he begins to explore the reality of Latino New York beyond its glossy image in popular culture. He is intrigued by both the awe and foreboding in the wider society about what the Latino "sleeping giant" will mean for "the presumed unity of American culture." Flores is especially interested in two themes: in the relation between Latinos and African-Americans and in Latinos' relations to their countries of origin, since return migration and circular geographical movement are common in the Latino story (as opposed to a one-way, permanent US immigration of earlier immigrant groups). This final "snapshot" of Latino New York nicely sums up several of the themes woven throughout the preceding essays.

CONCLUSION

Taken together, these essays reveal a great deal about the past and present condition of Latinos in metropolitan New York, especially about the transition from a majority Puerto Rican to a much more diverse Latino population in which no Latino subgroup is now in the majority. While Puerto Ricans still constitute the largest Hispanic national-origin subgroup in Gotham, and indeed one of the largest of all national-origin groups in the city, their numbers among Latinos and within the city as a whole have been steadily declining. Current trends indicate that by the end of the decade Dominicans are poised to become the largest Latino (and immigrant) group in New York City, if this has not already become the case.

The editors and authors understand there are differences both within and between the Latino national-origin groups. Race and class differences, for example, exist both within groups and among them. Real behavioral and attitudinal differences exist among the subgroups, and most of the Hispanic population still identifies first by national origin and only secondarily as "Latino" and/or "Hispanic." However, the forces that promote a pan-Latino consciousness are increasingly strong, both from within and outside of these communities. It is, as a result, still relevant to refer to a Hispanic or Latino community (some would prefer the plural, communities) in ways that connect it nationally and allows comparison with other settings. The Latino experience is complex and defined by the constant interaction between its national-origin and pan-ethnic identities within the context of US racial-ethnic dynamics.

Despite their distinct histories, many Latinos throughout the country share a similar life situation. First, they share a common language. Second, except for Puerto Ricans, large numbers are involved with immigration and citizenship status issues. Third, they are confronted with strong anti-immigrant and anti-Latino discrimination. Fourth, they find themselves racially segregated residentially and in the schools. Fifth, Latinos continue to experience great difficulty in placing their experience firmly in an "American" context, being continually viewed as "foreigners" and "the other," regardless of their history in the definition of a place called the United States of America. Sixth and finally, partially for bureaucratic expediency and to meet community demands, the federal government created and operationalized the category of "Hispanic" or "Latino" (Mora 2014). This fact has incentivized politicians and activists to embrace the concept, to view the community as united and increasingly vocal, and to work on issues of common concern such as immigration and education. This process is being aided, as well, by the efforts of corporations and their market researchers to create a malleable consumer group and the efforts of political parties and their pollsters to more efficiently create and influence this voting bloc.

Different contributors have asked in different ways if a new pan-Latino identity is emerging among immigrant children and grandchildren born in the United States. Are there several complementary or competing identities for young Latinos? A relevant question to which we do not have an answer is whether there is such a thing as a distinct "Latino vote" either locally or nationally, although it is widely accepted as a factor in general American political discourse.

Our ultimate goal is to pose provocative questions about the Latino experience and future in New York. Our hope is that these essays and the questions they pose stimulate a new generation of researchers. We also hope the essays will pose new thinking for promoting a social justice agenda for the City of New York and the rest of the country, in which Latinos are, at times, reluctantly seen as a part.

NOTES

1. As was the case in 1996, we still choose those terms interchangeably, reflecting everyday usage.

2. The authors provided an illustrative literature review in the first edition of *Latinos in New York* (1996); see nn 1–3, pp xx–xxi.

3. See, for example, chapter 1 by Haslip-Viera and chapter 5 by Hernández and Torres-Saillant in this volume; Sullivan (2010); Iglesias (1984); Falcón (1984).

4. Technically, "immigrants" are newcomers from other countries to the United States, while "migrants" are moving within the United States; hence Puerto Ricans are migrants, not immigrants. Still, in common usage, the terms are increasingly being used interchangeably, and we respect the choice of each author in this volume.

5. See "Data and Resources" from the Pew Hispanic Trends Project at www.pewhispanic.org.

6. *Latino Studies* has been published since 2003. Others include *Aztlán: A Journal of Chicano Studies*, since 1970; *Hispanic Journal of Behavioral Sciences* (*HJB*), since 1979; *Harvard Journal of Hispanic Policy*, since 1985; and *Centro: Journal of the Center for Puerto Rican Studies*, since 1987.

REFERENCES

Aparicio, Ana. 2006. *Dominican-Americans and the Politics of Empowerment.* Gainesville: University Press of Florida.

Dávila, Arlene. 2004. *Barrio Dreams: Puerto Ricans, Latinos, and the Neoliberal City.* Berkeley: University of California Press.

Dávila, Arlene, and Agustín Laó-Montes, eds. 2001. *Mambo Montage: The Latinization of New York.* New York: Columbia University Press.

Falcón, Angelo. 1984. "A History of Puerto Rican Politics in New York City: 1860s to 1945." In *Puerto Rican Politics in Urban America*, edited by James Jennings and Monte Rivera, 15–42. Westport, CT: Greenwood Press.

Haslip-Viera, Gabriel, Angelo Falcón, and Félix Matos Rodríguez, eds. 2004. *Boricuas in Gotham: Puerto Ricans in the Making of New York City.* Princeton: Markus Wiener.

Hernández, Ramona. 2002. *The Mobility of Workers under Advanced Capitalism: Dominican Migration to the United States.* New York: Columbia University Press.

Hoffnung-Garskof, Jesse. 2010. *A Tale of Two Cities: Santo Domingo and New York after 1950.* Princeton: Princeton University Press.

Jones-Correa, M. 1998. *Between Two Nations: The Political Predicament of Latinos in New York City.* Ithaca, NY: Cornell University Press.

Mora, G. Cristina. 2014. *Making Hispanics: How Activists, Bureaucrats, and Media Constructed a New American*. Chicago: University of Chicago Press.

Morales, Ed. 2003. *Living in Spanglish*. New York: St. Martin's Press.

Noguera, Pedro A., Aida Hurtado, and Edward Fergus, eds. 2011. *Understanding and Responding to the Disenfranchisement of Latino Males: Invisible No More*. New York: Routledge.

Remeseira, Claudio Iván, and Andrew Delbanco. 2010. *Hispanic New York: A Sourcebook*. New York: Columbia University Press.

Ricourt, Milagros. 2002. *Dominicans in New York City: Power from the Margins*. New York: Routledge.

Sánchez, José R. 2007. *Boricua Power: A Political History of Puerto Ricans in the United States*. New York: New York University Press.

Smith, Robert C. 2006. *Mexican New York: Transnational Lives of New Immigrants*. Berkeley: University of California Press.

Sullivan, Edward J., ed. 2010. *Nueva York, 1613–1945*. New York: New York Historical Society / Scala Publishers.

Thomas, Lorrin. 2010. *Puerto Rican Citizen: History and Political Identity in Twentieth-Century New York City*. Chicago: University of Chicago Press.

Torres, Andrés, ed. 2006. *Latinos in New England*. Philadelphia: Temple University Press.

Torres-Saillant, Silvio, and Ramona Hernández. 1998. *The Dominican Americans*. Westport, CT: Greenwood Press.

Upegui-Hernandez, Debora. 2014. *Growing Up Transnational: Colombian and Dominican Children of Immigrants in New York City*. El Paso, TX: LFB Scholarly Publishing.

Vega, Bernardo. 1984. *Memoirs of Bernardo Vega: A Contribution to the History of the Puerto Rican Community in New York*. Edited by César A. Iglesias. Translated by Juan Flores. New York: Monthly Review Press.

PART ONE

The Context

CHAPTER ONE

The Evolution of the Latina/o Community
in New York City

Early Seventeenth Century to the Present

GABRIEL HASLIP-VIERA

PHASE ONE: 1613–1898

It is, perhaps, quite accurate to say that interest in issues affecting Latina/os in New York has intensified steadily in recent decades. With greater frequency, journalists, academics, and government policy-makers have discussed the dramatic growth of a diverse Hispanic population and its impact on the city's employment, education, housing, crime, social services, and politics. In general, the increased scrutiny has continued to focus on Latinos as a contemporary phenomenon associated with the more recent waves of immigrants to the city; yet the origins and evolution of New York's Hispanic community may actually be traced as far back as the early seventeenth century.[1]

The first phase in the evolution of New York's Latino community as defined in this chapter (1613–1898) may appear much too long and unwieldy, but I adopt this chronology because this population remained consistently small and ethnically unchanged in comparison to other communities in the city throughout this period. Important historical events of relevance to the Latino community and the history of Latin America, in general, also took place during this period, but they were episodic for the most part and did not follow a clear linear progression, especially during the period of Dutch and English colonization.

A man named Jan Rodrígues was, perhaps, the first Latino to establish, at the beginning of the colonial period, what appears to have been a temporary residence in what became the city of New York. Described as a "free *mulato*" from the Spanish colony of Santo Domingo, Rodrígues was left somewhere in the area by Dutch merchants in 1613, with the authority to trade with local Indians before the formal establishment of the New Amsterdam colony eleven years later.[2]

Claims have also been made that the fifty-four Sephardic Jews who came to New Amsterdam from the Dutch colonies in Brazil in 1654 should also be listed as Latinos in New York, but this claim is controversial. It is not clear that the Sephardic Jews spoke Spanish or Ladino, and they were most probably the assimilated descendants of Jews who had fled persecution in Spain and Portugal 160 years earlier, in the 1490s.[3] It is clear, however, that the so-called Spanish negroes can be listed as Latinos in British New York during the eighteenth century. These were individuals of free or enslaved status who were captured by English privateers or the British Navy during wars with Spain in the early 1700s and sold to New Yorkers in the East River slave market that existed at the foot of Wall Street at that time. During the years of the Anglo-Spanish war of 1739–48, a series of suspicious fires and other disturbances broke out in the city, feeding rumors that the Spanish negroes were leading a slave population in a plot to take over New York and turn it over to the Spaniards. These rumors led to arrests, several sensationalized trials, and the execution of convicted prisoners, usually on trumped-up charges, in the immediate aftermath of the disturbances.[4]

Several decades of relative silence follow the disturbances of the 1740s, because of the tiny number of Spaniards and Latin American colonials living in the city, and because of the predominant anti-Spanish attitude that prevailed in the British colony during these years. However, reports of a Latino presence in the city began to increase with the establishment of an independent United States through the Articles of Confederation in 1781. A small group of Spanish diplomats and merchants led by Diego de Gardoqui, a Basque banker, became residents of New York in the 1780s. Francisco de Miranda, an early leader in the effort to end Spanish colonialism in Latin America, also came to New York to generate support during the same period.[5] Reports on the actual number of Latinos also began to appear by the mid-nineteenth century. A federal census enumeration of 1845 found that there were "508 persons from Mexico and South America" living in the city, but probably this was the start of a persistent undercount of Latinos that prevailed for this and other populations for the rest of the nineteenth century—an observation already made by Puerto Rican activist Bernardo Vega in the early twentieth century—a pattern that continues up to the present.[6]

In his important memoir, Vega refers to the large political gatherings of the 1880s and 1890s that were organized by advocates of Cuban and Puerto Rican independence and their supporters in the United States and other Latin American countries. He also refers to the 3,000 cigar factories that employed "many Puerto Ricans and Cubans" during the early 1890s. However, these claims are not confirmed by the official statistics for this period (see table 1.1). According to the census of 1890, the city had a Latino population of just under 6,000, which included 218 Mexicans, 1,421 Spaniards, 907 persons from Central and South America, and only 3,448 persons from Cuba, Puerto Rico, the Dominican Republic, and other parts of the Caribbean.[7]

In contrast to what developed later, Latino migration to New York continued to be quite small despite some growth in the later part of the nineteenth century. However, this growth was clearly outpaced by the increase in the city's overall population. Hispanic emigration was generally discouraged by the socioeconomic conditions that prevailed in Latin America throughout the nineteenth century. Most of the Central and South American republics and colonial possessions were underpopulated or were going through the first stages of economic modernization or industrialization. In Cuba, Puerto Rico, and Brazil, the importation of African slave labor continued into the 1850s and 1860s because of labor shortages in the expanding plantation sectors. As the economy of the Hispanic Caribbean changed during the late nineteenth century, slave labor was increasingly replaced by Native American and Chinese contract labor, and by an increased flow of mostly impoverished European immigrants who were attracted by the growth of the Caribbean sugar, coffee, and tobacco sectors. In the rest of Latin America, economic modernization and

Table 1.1 The Latino Population of New York City, 1870–1890*

	1870	%	1880	%	1890	%
Cuba & West Indies**	2,508	69.6	3,480	65.7	3,448	57.5
Cuba	1,565	43.4	2,073	39.1		
Mexico	86	2.3	170	3.2	218	3.6
Central America	22	0.6	29	0.5	184	3.1
South America	307	8.5	570	10.7	723	12.1
Spain	682	18.9	1,048	19.8	1,421	23.7
Total	3,605	100.0	5,297	100.0	5,994	100.0

*Total "foreign-born population" includes (before the creation of "Greater New York") Brooklyn, the Bronx, and Manhattan for the 1870 and 1880 census. For the 1890 census it also includes "Long Island City" (for all countries), Queens County, and Staten Island (for Spain, South America, Cuba, and the West Indies only).

**Probably includes many persons of Spanish origin or background who lived in Cuba and Puerto Rico, which were Spanish colonies throughout this period.

Sources: US Department of Interior, Census Office, *Compendium of the Ninth Census* (June 1, 1870) (Washington, DC: Government Printing Office, 1872), 387–91, 449; *Compendium of the Tenth Census*, Part 1 (June 1, 1880) (Washington, DC: Government Printing Office, 1882), 547, 551; *Census of 1890* (Washington, DC: Government Printing Office, 1892), 645–47, 670, 672, 674, 676.

industrialization contributed to a significant increase in European immigration, as was the case in North America during this same period. Argentina, Brazil, Chile, and a number of other countries or regions absorbed large numbers of immigrants from Spain, Italy, France, Germany, Portugal, Great Britain, Ireland, and Eastern Europe, and also from Lebanon, Syria, and other parts of the Middle East.[8]

Most of the immigrants who specifically came to New York from Latin America in the late nineteenth century were business people, professionals, white-collar workers, specialized artisans, and their dependents. It appears that a network of merchants and their subordinates were the predominant group during the early nineteenth century; however, after 1860, the Latino community became much more diversified and included the owners and employees of factories, artisan shops, grocery stores, pharmacies, barbershops, rooming houses, restaurants, and other enterprises. Skilled and semiskilled artisans and laborers also came to New York in increased numbers during the final decades of the nineteenth century. Most artisans and laborers were apparently employed in the city's tobacco-manufacturing sector, which expanded in the years between 1880 and 1920. However, in time, the artisans were also supplemented by a growing number of semiskilled and unskilled industrial laborers who came to New York in search of employment in factories and services.[9]

Political exiles also came to New York during the late nineteenth century. They included disaffected liberals, socialists, and anarcho-syndicalists from Spain and Latin America. They also included alienated labor leaders, writers, poets, artists, teachers, and intellectuals. In fact, New York became the headquarters for the exiled leaders and supporters of Cuban and Puerto Rican independence during this period. The Cuban patriots José Martí, Tomás Estrada Palma, and Dr. Julio Henna, an advocate of Puerto Rican independence, became residents of New York during the 1870s and 1880s. For a time, Martí worked for Joseph Pulitzer's *New York World*, which was one of the city's major newspapers, while Henna, a practicing physician, became one of the founders of Flower and Fifth Avenue Hospitals in upper Manhattan.

The importance of New York as a center for nationalist and revolutionary sentiment was reflected in successful efforts to raise funds, publish newspapers, and hold political rallies. It also was reflected in the frequent visits by important political and cultural leaders who came to New York to participate in various activities but were not residents of the city. These persons included Cuban revolutionary leaders such as Antonio Maceo and Máximo Gómez, who was actually a native of the Dominican Republic. They also included Spaniards, such as the labor leader Santiago Iglesias; other Dominicans, such as Enrique Trujillo, the author of the epic *El Enriquillo*; and educational and revolutionary leaders from Puerto Rico, such as Eugenio María de Hostos and Ramón Betances.[10]

The political exiles who lived in New York at least temporarily during this period became part of a small, vibrant, and growing community. In general, Latinos lived in scattered concentrations throughout Manhattan and downtown Brooklyn. Bernardo Vega suggests that there was relatively little housing discrimination against Hispanics during this period. However, he also acknowledges that the darker-complexioned or more "African"-looking Latinos were compelled to live in neighborhoods where African Americans predominated. Arturo Alfonso Schomburg, a Puerto Rican activist who later achieved fame as a Black bibliophile in the Central Harlem community, established his first family residence in an African-American neighborhood called "San Juan Hill," which was located in Manhattan, west of Amsterdam Avenue, between 60th and 70th Streets. Despite this and other instances of racial segregation and discrimination in housing, Hispanics were generally found in most working-class neighborhoods of the city during this period.[11]

Concentrations of working-class Latinos were found in Harlem, Chelsea, Yorkville, the West Side, and the Lower East Side of Manhattan. They were also found in the Columbia Street and "Navy Yard" districts of Brooklyn. In general, most Hispanics lived in the midst of larger immigrant communities, where Germans, Irish, Italians, Jews, Hungarians, and other groups from central and eastern Europe predominated. Bernardo Vega states that affluent Cubans lived in the largely middle-class section of south-central Harlem, north of Cathedral Parkway. He also notes that less-affluent Latinos were found in the midst of a working-class Jewish community, along Madison and Park Avenues, between 100th and 110th Streets. These last two concentrations were the nucleus of what later became known as Spanish Harlem or El Barrio.[12]

PHASE TWO: 1898–1945

In the final decades of the nineteenth century, Cubans, Puerto Ricans, and Spaniards were the predominant groups within the Latino population of New York City. This trend continued during the next phase of the migratory process, which began in 1898 and ended around 1945. It was during this period that Puerto Ricans became the largest Hispanic subgroup in the city, despite an island population that was very small when compared to Latin America as a whole. According to the estimates compiled at that time, the Latino population of New York had reached 22,000 by 1916, 41,094 by 1920, 110,223 by 1930, and 134,000 by 1940.[13] Of the 134,252 Hispanics enumerated by the US Census Bureau in 1940, 61,463 (45.8%) were Puerto Ricans, 25,283 (18.8%) were Spaniards, 23,124 (17.2%) were Cubans and Dominicans, 4,653 (3.5%) were Mexicans, and 19,727 (14.7%) were persons from Central and South America (see table 1.2).

The Antillean orientation of New York's Latino community between 1900 and 1945 reflected the socioeconomic and political changes that gripped Cuba, Puerto Rico, and the rest of the Caribbean during this period. Cuba and Puerto Rico were annexed by the United States as a result of the military victory over Spain in the War of 1898. Cuba was granted its independence in 1903, but Puerto Rico became and remains an "unincorporated territory" of the United States despite the granting of autonomous status in 1952. Direct political involvement by the United States had an impact on

Table 1.2 The Latina/o Population of New York City, 1920–1940*

	1920	%	1930	%	1940	%
Cuba & West Indies	8,722	21.2	19,774	17.9	23,124	17.2
Mexico	2,572	6.3	4,292	3.9	4,653	3.5
Puerto Rico	7,364	17.9	44,908	40.7	61,463	45.8
Central & South America	7,777	18.9	18,748	17.0	19,727	14.7
Spain	14,659	35.7	25,501	20.4	25,283 1	8.8
Total	41,094	100.0	110,223	100.0	134,252	100.0

*Includes "foreign born population" (except for Puerto Ricans) for the 1920 census, the "foreign born white population" for Cuba and the West Indies in the 1920 census, the "foreign-born white" and "native white of foreign or mixed parentage" population (except for Mexicans and Puerto Ricans) for the 1930 census, and the "foreign born white" and persons of "nativity and parentage of foreign white stock" (except for Puerto Ricans) for the 1940 census.

Sources: US Department of Commerce, Bureau of the Census, *Fourteenth Census of the United States . . . 1920*, vol. 3, table 6, p. 679, table 12, pp. 702 and 704; *Fifteenth Census of the United States: 1930*, vol. 3, part 2, table 17, p. 297, table 18, p. 301, and table 19, p. 303; *Sixteenth Census of the United States: 1940*, vol. 2, Characteristics of the Population, part 5, table 24, pp. 63–64, and Special Bulletin, table 7, p. 74; Walter Laidlaw, *Population of the City of New York, 1890–1930* (New York: Cities Census Committee, Inc., 1932), table 40, p. 247, and table 51, p. 253; and Ira Rosenwaike, *Population History of New York City* (Syracuse, NY: Syracuse University Press, 1972), 101, 121, 203.

emigration from Cuba and Puerto Rico in the years after 1900, but it was the relative geographical proximity to New York and the dramatic infusion of United States investment capital in the economies of both islands that had the greatest impact.

The United States also intervened actively in the internal affairs of the Dominican Republic during this period. The economy of the Dominican Republic grew substantially during the United States' military occupation of 1916 to 1924; however, with regard to Dominican migration, the impact of US-sponsored modernization was relatively less dramatic because the national economy was significantly less developed than that of Cuba or even Puerto Rico. Overall economic growth continued with the establishment of the Trujillo dictatorship after 1930, but the movement of Dominicans to the United States or elsewhere remained low because of the characteristics of the development and the rigidly restrictive policies that were imposed on emigration from that country during the entire period of the dictatorship from 1930 to 1961.[14]

In Cuba, United States investment capital further strengthened a sugar sector that was already dominant in the late nineteenth century. It also reinforced Cuba's economic dependence on the United States, which was the principal market for Cuban sugar. The expansion of the Cuban sugar sector created opportunities for some of its citizens, but it also led to economic and social misfortune for other segments of the population. Cubans were increasingly subject to the often dramatic and unpredictable effects of the volatile sugar market. Between 1900 and 1945 the Cuban economy experienced dramatic boom and bust periods that harmed many Cubans at each stage of the economic cycle. The result was increased Cuban immigration to southern Florida and the New York City area in the years after 1900. Cuban immigration to the United States rose because of economic dislocation and monetary inflation during periods of prosperity and growth. It also rose because of high unemployment, decreased wages, a decline in living standards, and increased political instability during periods of economic crisis and decline.[15]

Puerto Rico also suffered from US economic investment during this period, much more than Cuba. As in Cuba, North American economic investment in Puerto Rico was directed toward the sugar sector. There was also some investment in urban-oriented manufacturing; however, in contrast to Cuba, US investment in Puerto Rico brought disaster to the traditional, more labor-intensive coffee and tobacco sectors. The coffee industry, in particular, was extremely important to Puerto Rico's economy during this period. In the late nineteenth century it had been the dominant sector, providing most of the wealth and most of the employment for the island's population—especially in the mountainous interior region.[16]

As a result of the dramatic change in the investment climate and the shift in emphasis toward the sugar sector after the US takeover, the Puerto Rican coffee industry declined steadily between 1898 and 1930. The tobacco industry also began to wither away after an initial period of prosperity ended in the early 1920s. By the early 1930s, the labor-intensive coffee and tobacco sectors had ceased to be vital or even important components of the Puerto Rican economy. Thousands of rural and working-class Puerto Ricans were compelled to migrate from the coffee- and tobacco-growing regions of the island's interior to the coastal areas and the cities to seek employment in the sugar, manufacturing, and service sectors of the economy. The migration from the interior regions created enormous hardships for the populations that already lived in the cities and along the coast. Overall, wages fell, living standards deteriorated, and unemployment increased steadily between 1898 and 1930.[17]

This was only the beginning of a long and difficult period for the Puerto Rican economy. Commercial treaties between the United States and Cuba and the effects of the worldwide economic depression of the 1930s initiated a period of major crisis and decline for the Puerto Rican sugar industry. By 1935, the Puerto Rican economy had virtually collapsed, largely as a result of the crisis in the sugar sector and the impact that this had on manufacturing, services, and other sectors of the economy.[18] The increased migration of Puerto Ricans to New York between 1900 and 1945 reflected the deepening economic and social crisis that gripped the island throughout this period. It also reflected the ease of travel to New York, the relative prosperity to be found in the United States, and the fact that Puerto Ricans were granted US citizenship in 1917.[19]

Net migration from Puerto Rico to New York rose rather dramatically during the economic boom years of 1914–15, 1917–20, and 1923–30. After 1930, the pace of migration slowed considerably because of the global economic depression and the impact that World War II was to have on both Puerto Rico and the United States. Most of the Puerto Ricans and other Latinos who came to New York in the years between 1900 and 1945 were urban-oriented, working-class men and women. In contrast to the late nineteenth century, proportionally fewer immigrants were business oriented, well educated or middle class. Most of the newcomers were generally skilled or semi-skilled factory operatives, artisans, white-collar workers, and service-sector employees who found similar kinds of work in the New York labor market. A considerable number were skilled and semiskilled working-class women. By the late 1920s, large numbers of Hispanic women were employed in the labor-intensive service and industrial sectors. Many worked in the garment factories or performed piecework for entrepreneurs in that industry. Based on the figures compiled for Spanish Harlem in 1925, which are biased in favor of its mostly working-class population, 62% of all Latinos were employed in the industrial sector, 18% in services, 16% were engaged in commerce, and 4% were listed as "owners" and "supervisors."[20]

From 1900 to 1945, the burgeoning Latino population became identified with certain areas or neighborhoods of the city. According to Vega, the "barrio Latino" in East Harlem had already reached a mature stage of development by the late 1920s. Immigrants from Spain and their descendants were associated with the West 14th Street and Chelsea areas of Manhattan.

At the same time, other neighborhoods, such as parts of the Lower East Side of Manhattan, South Brooklyn ("Red Hook" and the Columbia Street area), the "Navy Yard," and the Williamsburg section of Brooklyn, also became identified with the Latina/o community by the late 1920s or early 1930s.

With some exceptions, Hispanics coexisted with the earlier immigrant populations, or they eventually displaced the earlier groups after a time. From 1900 to 1945, the Latina/o population of South Brooklyn more or less coexisted with the largely Italian-American residents of that neighborhood. In East Harlem, by contrast, the Hispanic population eventually replaced the predominantly Jewish population west of Park Avenue by the Depression years of the early 1930s.[21]

The housing stock available to working-class Latinos was among the worst that could be found in New York City during this period. The dwelling spaces were primarily "furnished rooms," "cold-water flats," and "railroad apartments" in the "Old" and "New Law" tenements and row houses that were found in most of the neighborhoods where Latinos lived. Most of this housing stock was already considered substandard soon after it was built between the 1860s and the 1890s. Overcrowding and the lack of maintenance had already turned many of these structures and their neighborhoods into what outsiders called "slums" by the time that they were populated by Hispanics.[22]

Despite the inadequacies of the housing stock and other serious problems, Latinos had a generally optimistic view of life in the city. This appeared to be the case even during the 1930s, when the community was forced to endure the hardships of high unemployment, decreased wages, and the diminished living standards associated with the Great Depression. Latinos worked hard, got married, gave birth to children, attended church, and participated in the rich social and cultural life that they created in their communities. They patronized grocery stores, barbershops, restaurants, tailoring establishments, and other businesses owned by Hispanics and non-Hispanics. They also organized social clubs, self-help groups, and political associations, and they debated the complex social, cultural, and political issues of the day. For the most part, Latino political concerns during this period were largely oriented toward the homelands that most still hoped to return to someday. At this stage in the evolution of the Hispanic community, a real commitment to life in the New York area had not yet emerged, although there were also political and organizational activities that focused on issues affecting the Latino communities of the city.[23]

PHASE THREE: 1945–65/70

The demographic composition and orientation of the Hispanic community in New York changed significantly during the next phase of the migration process. In effect, the Puerto Rican community became synonymous with the Latino community between 1945 and 1970. Thousands of Puerto Ricans began to leave their home island for New York City and mainland communities during the early part of the postwar period because of economic and social policies that were instituted at this time. After earlier efforts to revive the Puerto Rican economy had largely failed during the late 1930s and early 1940s, the US government developed an ambitious program for the industrialization of Puerto Rico in the postwar period. With the cooperation of Puerto Rico's political leaders, the federal government promoted the establishment of labor-intensive enterprises in an effort to reduce the island's rate of unemployment and underemployment. North American investors received tax benefits, free land, low-interest loans, and other incentives in an attempt to expand the number of enterprises, but all of this was considered insufficient to overcome a perceived problem of "overpopulation" and the negative effects of the economic collapse that continued to grip the traditional agrarian sectors. The result was the implementation of policies designed to encourage the unemployed and underemployed to leave Puerto Rico for New York and other mainland communities.[24]

Puerto Ricans were advised by government bureaucrats to leave the home island for those communities where, it was claimed, better employment opportunities could be found. Shipping companies, charter airlines, regular air-travel service, and reduced fares were established to facilitate the flow of migrants from Puerto Rico to New York and the other communities.[25] The result was a dramatic increase in the number of Puerto Ricans in New York City and its environs in the years after 1945 (see tables 1.2 and 1.3). The Puerto Rican population of New York rose from 61,463 in 1940 to 612,574 in 1960, and it continued to increase during the next decade, reaching 811,843 in 1970. The number of other Latinos who came to New York also rose during this period, but in contrast to the Puerto Ricans, the increase of other Hispanics was proportionally less dramatic. Between 1940 and 1970, the Cuban population rose from about 23,000 to 84,179, the Dominican population rose from an unknown figure to at least 66,914, and the population of persons from Central and South America increased from 19,727 to at least 216,120 (see tables 1.2 and 1.3).

Overall, the Latinos who came to New York during this period were overwhelmingly working class, and this was especially true of the Puerto Ricans. Most Puerto Ricans found employment in the labor-intensive manufacturing and service sectors of the New York economy. A significant number, mostly from the rural areas, also found employment on potato and vegetable farms in the surrounding suburban and rural counties. These individuals were brought to New York under a special agricultural contract labor program specifically created for this purpose. Puerto Rican farm workers normally traveled back and forth from their homes on the island to their jobs in the New York–New Jersey area. However, over time, many of these people settled in the city or the suburbs, where employment in the manufacturing and service sectors of the economy was considered more lucrative.[26]

The other Latinos who came to New York between 1945 and 1970 were of somewhat different socioeconomic backgrounds than the Puerto Ricans who came during the same period. Most of these other Hispanics were similar to the earlier group of Latinos and Puerto Ricans who came between 1900 and 1945. Many of the other Latinos were unskilled and semiskilled workers, but in contrast to the Puerto Ricans, they included a proportionally much larger group of persons who were well educated, urban oriented, and middle class. Overall, the Puerto Ricans who came between 1945 and 1970 were impoverished, unemployed, or underemployed persons from rural and urban areas of the island, with minimal education and few skills. However, some (though fewer) Puerto Rican migrants were better educated, business oriented, and middle class.[27]

A major transformation in the composition of the New York labor force enabled the city's economy to absorb enormous numbers of Puerto Ricans and other Latinos in the years after 1945. Returning World War II veterans of mostly European extraction were able to take advantage of new programs established by the federal government to promote upward economic and social mobility for this group in the early postwar period. For example, education programs enabled returning veterans to leave their jobs in the factories and low-grade services to become white-collar workers, managers, professionals, and entrepreneurs. At the same time, the federal housing and highway programs of the early and later postwar period enabled veterans and their families to leave the congested inner city for the greener, more open spaces of the suburbs. The earlier immigrant groups and their descendants were moving from the city to the suburbs continuously between 1945 and 1970. This movement was reinforced by the exodus of corporations and small businesses and by the establishment of new enterprises in the communities that proliferated in the suburbs and in other parts of the country.

The upward mobility of the earlier immigrant groups and the movement of people from the city to the suburbs created a vacuum in the manufacturing and service sectors of the urban economy. In fact, many enterprises in these sectors actually experienced labor shortages in the early postwar period and developed recruitment programs to attract workers from outside the city. As a result, labor was completely transformed in manufacturing and in services in the years after 1950. Persons of European extraction, such as the Irish, Jews, Italians, and Greeks, were increasingly replaced by Puerto Ricans, other Latinos, and by African Americans who came from the southern states.

Overall, Puerto Ricans and other Latinos worked in the garment industry, in paper box factories, in enterprises that manufactured dolls or plastic products, in restaurants, in grocery stores, in hotels, in office buildings, in residential structures, as cooks, dishwashers, "bus boys," messengers, elevator operators, custodians, and building superintendents. A smaller number were also employed in sales or as white-collar workers or lower-level managers in corporations or in public and private agencies and institutions.[28]

The massive influx of Puerto Ricans and other Latinos and the movement of the earlier immigrant groups and their descendants from the city to the suburbs permitted the growth and expansion of neighborhoods that were associated with the Hispanic population in the years after 1945. "El Barrio," or Spanish Harlem, expanded eastward from Park Avenue to the East River between 1948 and 1955. A huge new concentration of mostly Puerto Rican Latinos also emerged in the South Bronx during the same period. In the Lower East Side, Puerto Ricans continued to displace the earlier, mostly Jewish residents, and they also established themselves in new concentrations on the West Side and Upper West Side of Manhattan. The Puerto Rican–Latino neighborhoods of Brooklyn and Queens also grew during this period. The Puerto Rican enclave in the Navy Yard district of Brooklyn expanded northward and eastward into parts of Williamsburg, Greenpoint, and Bushwick. At the same time, the South Brooklyn enclave around Columbia Street expanded southward to include parts of Park Slope and Sunset Park.[29]

To some degree, the quality of the housing stock available to Latinos improved during this period, but overcrowding was a very serious problem, especially in the late 1940s and early 1950s, when severe housing shortages developed. In Spanish Harlem and the Lower East Side of Manhattan, the mostly Puerto Rican Latinos continued to occupy the same cold-water flats, furnished rooms, and railroad apartments that were considered substandard in the 1920s and even earlier. The same was also true of the housing stock in Red Hook, the Columbia Street area, and the Williamsburg section of Brooklyn; however, in other neighborhoods, such as the South Bronx, the West Side of Manhattan, and the Sunset Park, Bushwick, Brownsville, and East New York sections of Brooklyn, the housing situation was somewhat more complex. To be sure, tenement buildings were to be found in all of these neighborhoods, but there were also roomier multiple-family dwellings, row houses, brownstones, and the larger apartment buildings that were originally built for middle-class residents. There were also the low- and high-rise housing projects that were built by the city and state with increased frequency between 1935 and 1970. In general, apartments or accommodations in the privately owned buildings were more spacious, with larger rooms and full-size kitchens and bathrooms. However, in most cases, the landlords merely collected the rents and allowed their properties to deteriorate soon after they were occupied by Puerto Ricans and other Latinos. By contrast, the publicly owned housing projects were initially established and administered as ideal communities. In time, however, these structures were overwhelmed by the introduction of "problem," "negligent," or "welfare families" and allowed to deteriorate through disinterest or neglect.[30]

PHASE FOUR: 1965/70–90

The composition of New York's Latino population and the population of the city as a whole was again transformed between 1965/70 and the early 1990s as a result of major changes that took root in the migration process at the beginning of the 1960s. Starting as early as 1959, people from Cuba, the Dominican Republic, Colombia, Ecuador, Peru, and other countries in Central and South America began to arrive in New York in increasing numbers, and many of them came illegally. Cubans fleeing Castro's revolution were the first major group to settle in the New York area during this period, and they were soon followed by Dominicans who came in substantial numbers after the 1961 assassination of dictator Trujillo and the 1965 civil war. Most of the Cubans came as political refugees under a special program established by the federal government as part of its anti-Castro and "anticommunist" policies. The influx of Dominicans was made possible by a complex of factors, which included the aftereffects of political turmoil and civil war, the never-ending search for cheaper labor in New York, and the relaxation of Trujillo-era restrictions on emigration from the Dominican Republic. Some of these factors as well as other circumstances also set the stage for increased immigration from Central and South America during this same period. In the years after 1965, Colombians, Ecuadoreans, Peruvians, Salvadorans, and others arrived in New York in substantial numbers. New York's Latino population increased 135.5 %, from 757,231 in 1960 to 1,783,511 in 1990 (see table 1.3), and non–Puerto Rican Hispanics accounted for a substantial proportion of this increase. Although the Latino population was 80.9% Puerto Rican in 1960, Puerto Ricans accounted for only 50.3% of the Latino population by 1990.[31]

Economic and social forces were the most powerful contributors to Hispanic migration in the years after 1960. Overall, the peoples of Latin America and the Caribbean were profoundly affected by an accelerated process of development that, in many places, originated in the early postwar period. Economic modernization, industrialization, rapid population growth, and increased corporate investment from the United States and other industrial countries created economic, social, and political instability in most of the region during this period. As in Cuba and Puerto Rico between 1900 and the 1940s, rapid economic change produced economic and social opportunities for some groups and social dislocations or crises for others. By the late 1950s and early 1960s, many persons in countries such as Mexico, Colombia, Peru, and Ecuador began to migrate from rural areas to the urban centers because of unequal regional development and modernization. At the same time, the economies of the urban centers in most of these countries were not expanding rapidly enough to accommodate the mass of migrants coming to the cities from the countryside. The result was increased economic, social, and political insecurity for both rural and urban populations. Thousands of people were uprooted in the countryside by rapid growth, economic reorganization, and monetary inflation. These same forces often harmed significant sectors of the urban populations as well, especially when development was intense and migration from the countryside was substantial. Economic retrenchment, periods of high unemployment, government austerity programs, and high birthrates also hurt both rural and urban populations when economic growth periods suddenly stalled or ended. These same forces were also frequently associated with the rise of political instability, interpersonal violence, rebellions, and civil wars. The result was increased migration to the United

Table 1.3 The Latino Population of New York City, 1960–1990*

	1960	%	1970	%	1980	%	1990	%
Cuba	42,694	5.6	84,179	7.0	63,189	4.5	56,041	3.1
Dom. Rep.	13,283	1.7	66,914	5.6	125,380	8.9	332,713	18.7
Puerto Rico	612,574	80.9	811,843	67.5	860,552	61.2	896,763	50.3
Total Span. Caribbean	668,561	88.2	962,936	80.1	1,049,121	74.6	1,285,517	72.1
Costa Rica	1,761		4,429				6,920	
El Salvador	480		1,022		6,300		23,926	
Guatemala	1,019		2,036		6,323		15,873	
Honduras	2,516		6,785		14,100		22,167	
Mexico	8,260		7,893		25,577		61,772	3.4
Nicaragua	1,300		2,014				9,660	
Panama	8,377		15,225		17,700		22,707	
Argentina	7,789		13,327		14,009		13,934	
Bolivia	558		1,218				3,465	
Chile	2,516		3,328				6,721	
Colombia	6,782		27,657		45,160		84,454	
Ecuador	4,077		20,326		40,320		78,444	4.3
Paraguay	127							
Peru	2,297		5,438		11,640		23,257	
Uruguay	696		1,220				3,233	

Table 1.3 The Latino Population of New York City, 1960–1990*

	1960	%	1970	%	1980	%	1990	%
Venezuela	3,478		3,410				4,752	
"Other S. Am."	9,199		13,630		18,974			
Spain	27,438		23,225		11,825		20,148	
Other Hisp.	87,162		144,975		96,561			
Total/Non-Carib. Hisp.	88,670	11.8	239,345	19.9	356,903	25.4	497,994	27.9
Grand Total	757,231	100.0	1,202,281	100.0	1,406,024	100.0	1,783,511	100.0

*Figures include the total number of Puerto Ricans and total "foreign-born" and "native of foreign or mixed parentage" for other nationalities in the 1960 census; total number of Cubans, Mexicans, Puerto Ricans, and total number of "foreign-born" and "native of foreign or mixed parentage" for other nationalities in the 1970 census; number of Cubans, Mexicans, Puerto Ricans, and total number of "foreign-born" only for other nationalities in the 1980 census; and total number of Cubans, Mexicans, Puerto Ricans, and total number of persons of "Hispanic origin" by nationality for other groups in the 1990 census.

Sources: US Department of Commerce, Bureau of the Census, 1960 *Census of Population*, vol. 1, Characteristics of the Population, New York, part 34, table 99, p. 34/434; 1970 *Census of Population*, vol. 1, Characteristics of the Population, New York, part 34, table 119, pp. 34/607, 34/611; 1970 *Census of Population*, vol. 1, Detailed Characteristics, New York, part 34, table 141, p. 34/720; 1980 *Census of Population*, vol. 1, Characteristics of the Population, chapter C, General Social and Economic Characteristics, New York, part 34, table 59, pp. 34/100, 34/101; 1980 *Census of Population*, vol.1, Characteristics of the Population, chapter D, Detailed Population Characteristics, New York, part 34, table 195, p. 34/14; 1990 *Census of Population*, General Population Characteristics, New York, section 1, table 5, pp. 47, 49–51; 1990 *Census of Population*, Social and Economic Characteristics, New York, section 1, table 6, pp. 45, 47–49; John I. Griffin and Jean Namias, eds., *New York Metropolitan Regional Fact Book* (New York: New York Council on Economic Education, 1965), table T2.12; Population Division, New York City Department of City Planning, Puerto Rican New Yorkers in 1990 (New York: Department of City Planning, 1993), tables A and 8, pp. 13–14.

States and other countries from the increasingly troubled societies of Latin America in the years after 1960.[32]

In contrast to the largely rural and impoverished Puerto Ricans who came to New York between 1945 and 1970, the Latin Americans who came after 1960 were generally urban, better educated, and more highly skilled, and many came from middle-class, professional, or business-oriented backgrounds. In this sense, the new immigrants were comparable to the earlier group of Puerto Ricans and other Hispanics who came to New York between 1900 and 1945. Of course, the proportion of middle-class persons varied from one Latino subgroup to another. Immigrants from Argentina, Chile, and Uruguay, as well as the Cubans who came in the early 1960s, were more likely to be middle class than Dominicans, Hondurans, Ecuadoreans, or the Mexicans who began to arrive in substantial numbers at the end of the 1980s. However, as in the earlier period, middle-class orientation did not guarantee an easier transition to life in the city. Many of the better-educated arrivals, including quite a number with middle-class, professional, or semiprofessional backgrounds, fell to a lower social or economic status upon arriving in New York. Some were fortunate enough to find white-collar employment if they had an adequate command of English. Others started their own businesses in the neighborhoods where they settled, but most were compelled to accept working-class employment in the services and in manufacturing. As a result, Latinos of both working-class and middle-class backgrounds were employed in factories, restaurants, hotels, small businesses, and other enterprises; and to a significant degree, they replaced the largely Puerto Rican and African American labor force that had come to dominate these sectors in the previous period.[33]

The neighborhoods traditionally associated with the Latino communities also continued to expand after 1960—often dramatically. At the same time new enclaves were established throughout the city, and older ones were devastated due to increased problems with housing that involved the continued flight of earlier immigrants and their descendants, a dramatic slowdown in the construction of residential buildings for lower-income people, and the new phenomena of housing abandonment, vandalism, arson, and rising homelessness that came to characterize the 1970s. Certain neighborhoods also became associated with particular Hispanic subgroups or a combination of subgroups. For example, the Upper West Side and the Washington Heights section of Manhattan became increasingly associated with the Dominican community. For a time a Cuban community had emerged in this area as well; however, most Cubans eventually settled in other places, such as Astoria, the Elmhurst section of Queens, and especially Union City, Jersey City, and West New York, New Jersey. Colombians, Ecuadoreans, Peruvians, Dominicans, and other subgroups became identified with new enclaves that emerged in the Jackson Heights, Woodside, Elmhurst, East Elmhurst, and Corona sections of Queens. However, it also appeared that Mexicans and other newcomers from Central America were beginning to displace Puerto Ricans and other Latinos from their traditional enclaves in "El Barrio" or "Spanish Harlem" at the end of the 1980s.[34]

PHASE FIVE: 1990S TO THE PRESENT

The most recent change in the composition of New York's Latino communities began to take root in the late 1980s and early 1990s. Changing migration patterns, the 1986 federal immigration reform act (IRCA), and the political and economic problems that gripped certain Latin American countries during this period, as well as other factors, resulted in continued migration to New York from these countries, with a particularly dramatic surge from Mexico and Central America in the period from 1990 to 2010. Immigration of Dominicans to New York also continued to be important during this period, with dramatic spikes in their influx during periods of economic difficulty or crisis that gripped that country.

Despite attempts to curb immigration from Mexico and Central America through changes in US immigration laws and the implementation of new trade agreements between Mexico, the United States, and Canada (e.g., the North American Free Trade Agreement [NAFTA]), the economic difficulties that had plagued Mexico in the 1970s and 1980s continued unabated and, in some cases, became much worse. This was especially true in certain parts of the country, such as the rural Mixteca alta and baja regions of Puebla, Guerrero, and Oaxaca, which were gripped by droughts and other difficulties that battered their already beleaguered agricultural sectors.[35] Government repression and civil wars in Central American countries, such as Guatemala, El Salvador, and Nicaragua, also contributed to an exodus of people from these countries—first to Mexico, and then to the United States, and New York City in particular. The civil war in El Salvador (1980–92) and the intermittent attacks on or repression of the mostly native K'Iche and Ixil populations of rural highland Guatemala (1960–96) were particularly devastating and important contributors to emigration from those countries. US government policies against the post-Somoza "leftist" Sandinista government of Nicaragua (e.g., support for the "Contras," 1980–90) and the repression or economic difficulties that arose in the area around San Pedro Sula and elsewhere in Honduras also contributed to a surge in immigration from those countries. Immigration to New York from South America also continued in the years between 1990 and 2010; however, with the exception of Ecuadoreans and in contrast to the surge of immigrants from Mexico and Central America, this migration did not significantly affect the makeup of New York's Latina/o population.[36]

The figures in table 1.4 show how the composition of New York's Latino population changed from 1990 to 2010. Officially, the Dominican share of the population increased from 18.7% of the total Latino population in 1990 to 25.8% of the total in 2010. This resulted largely from a natural increase in a relatively young population, along with continued spikes in immigration from the Dominican Republic during this period. In a related trend, the total Spanish Caribbean population of the city became stabilized in the decade from 2000 to 2010 at almost 60% of total Latinos after a decline from 72% in 1990. This again resulted from the increase in the Dominican population during this period, which made up for the decline in the Puerto Rican share of the population, which fell to 32.4% of total Latinos in 2010 after constituting 50.3% of the total in 1990.

The Mexican population also grew dramatically during this period, increasing from 61,772 or 3.4% of the total Latino population in 1990 to 319,263 or 14.2% of the total in 2010. However, these official census figures were much too low given the large number of undocumented and uncounted Mexicans who also came to the city between 1990 and 2010. The same could also be said of the Guatemalans who also came to New York during this period. Their population doubled officially from 15,873 in 1990 to 30,420 in 2010, but again, these figures represent a significant undercount given the large number of undocumented Guatemalans who arrived during this period.

The socioeconomic characteristics of immigrants from the Dominican Republic and South America remained largely the same during this period, but the large influx from Central America and especially from Mexico, Guatemala, and El Salvador consisted of the overwhelmingly impoverished, or included those persons desperate to leave those countries because of economic crisis, political repression, or civil war. Impoverished Mexicans and Guatemalans, in particular, came to dominate the lowest levels of New York's

Table 1.4 The Latino Population of New York City, 1990–2010*

	1990	%	2000	%	2010	%
Cuba	56,041	3.1	41,123	1.9	40,840	0.1
Dom. Rep.	332,713	18.7	406,806	18.8	576,701	25.8
Puerto Rico	896,763	50.3	789,172	36.5	723,621	32.4
Total Span. Caribbean	1,285,517	72.1	1,237,101	57.2	1,341,162	59.9
Costa Rica	6,920		4,939		6,673	
El Salvador	23,926		24,516		38,559	
Guatemala	15,873		15,212		30,420	
Honduras	22,167		25,600		42,400	
Mexico	61,772	3.4	186,872	8.6	319,263	14.2
Nicaragua	9,660		6,451		9,346	
Panama	22,707		16,847		22,353	
Argentina	13,934		9,578		15,169	
Bolivia	3,465		2,942		4,488	
Chile	6,721		5,014		7,026	
Colombia	84,454		77,154		94,723	
Ecuador	78,444	4.3	101,005	4.6	167,209	7.4
Paraguay			1,658		3,534	
Peru	23,257		23,567		36,018	
Uruguay	3,233		1,907		3,004	
Venezuela	4,752		6,713		9,619	
"Other S. Am."			6,836		2,678	
Spain	20,148		44,365		30,838	
Other Hisp.	96,561		401,108		180,805	
Total/Non-Carib. Hisp.	497,994	27.9	937,453	42.8	894,914	40.1
Grand Total	1,783,511	100.0	2,160,554	100.0	2,236,076	100.0

Sources: US Census Bureau, 1990 *Census of Population*, General Population Characteristics, New York, section 1, table 5, pp. 47, 49–51; US Census Bureau, 1990 *Census of Population*, Social and Economic Characteristics, New York, section 1, table 6, pp. 45, 47–49. New York City Department of City Planning, Population Division, *US Census Bureau, 2000, Total Hispanic Population by Selected Subgroups*, Summary File 1, Part 1, P-8, http://www.nyc.gov/html/dcp/pdf/census/sf1p8p1 .pdf, http://www.nyc.gov/html/dcp/pdf/census/sf1p8p2.pdf; US Census Bureau, 2010, *Hispanic or Latino by Type: 2010*, Census Summary File 1, Table PCT 11, http://factfinder2.census.gov /faces/tableservices/jsf/pages/productview.xhtml?pid=DEC_10_SF1_QTP10&prodType=table.

labor market during this period; however, the large influx of Salvadorans found employment mostly in the New York suburbs, where they settled rather than in the city. Mexicans, Guatemalans, and others from Central America found low-level employment in construction and services—in restaurants, hotels, small convenience stores, and other similar enterprises of this type. There was some entrepreneurial activity which resulted in the proliferation of Mexican restaurants and of convenience stores specializing in the sale of Mexican products, and for a while, Mexican flower vendors worked the streets of the city.[37]

The new wave of immigrants also came to settle in the neighborhoods that were already associated with Latino populations. These continued to expand during this period. Dominicans continued to predominate in Manhattan's Washington Heights and in the Jackson Heights and Corona sections of Queens, and also, increasingly, in the South Bronx and in other sections of the city. South Americans continued to predominate along the "Number 7" subway line in the Woodside, Jackson Heights, Elmhurst, East Elmhurst, and Corona sections of Queens. The new wave of immigrants also settled in various neighborhoods in Brooklyn, such as Sunset Park. It was also clear by the beginning of the twenty-first century that Puerto Ricans were being displaced in the neighborhoods where they were previously dominant. For example, Mexicans were becoming the dominant group in "El Barrio" or East Harlem as upwardly mobile Puerto Ricans increasingly left this and other neighborhoods for the New York suburbs, central Florida, and Puerto Rico. The "gentrification" of certain neighborhoods by Anglo-American "pioneers" also had an impact—especially in Manhattan, but also in other parts of the city. East Harlem or "El Barrio" had become significantly gentrified by the beginning of the twenty-first century, along with what had been an important Puerto Rican enclave in the Lower East Side of Manhattan (called Loisaida for a time) and parts of the Williamsburg section of Brooklyn.[38]

CONCLUSION

This brief historical survey of New York's Latino population begins to reveal the differences among the numerous Hispanic communities that have settled in the city and in other parts of the United States since the middle of the nineteenth century. In one respect, dissimilarities can be seen in the composition of the Latino communities when these are broken down by national origin in various parts of the country. Puerto Ricans, Dominicans, Cubans, Colombians, Ecuadoreans, and Mexicans have been the most important subgroups in the evolution of New York's Latino community, with Puerto Ricans having played the dominant role for most periods during the twentieth century. In differing combinations, these same groups have been important to the evolution of other Hispanic communities throughout the Northeast and Midwest. By contrast, Mexicans and, more recently, Salvadorans, Guatemalans, and other immigrants from Central America have predominated in the Latino communities of Texas, California, and the Southwest. In southern Florida, Cubans and other expatriate groups such as the Nicaraguans have played the most significant role, while in Chicago, separate Mexican and Puerto Rican communities have developed in coexistence at different times since the early part of the twentieth century. In fact, and up until the late 1970s, a line could have been drawn in the middle of the country from Chicago south to New Orleans separating the Northeast, the Middle Atlantic states, Florida, and parts of the Midwest from the rest of the country. Although there was some overlap in the Midwest, Puerto Ricans, Cubans, Dominicans, and other nationals from South America and the Caribbean were the predominant groups east of the line, while Mexicans and people from Central America were the most important groups in the communities to the west of the line.

The chronology of Latino migration and settlement also differentiates the various communities that have evolved across the country. Mexicans, "Spanish Americans," and Hispanicized Indians already occupied various parts of Texas, California, and the Southwest prior to the takeover of these regions by the United States between 1836 and 1848. Florida also had a small Spanish-oriented population prior to the US takeover in 1819, but in the Northeast and the Midwest, most of the Hispanic communities emerged as actual communities only during the late nineteenth or early twentieth century and even later. Although the presence of Latinos in New York can be traced back to the Dutch colonial period, the actual emergence and significant expansion of the community did not begin until the later part of the nineteenth century. The development of Chicago's Hispanic community also began in the late nineteenth century, but it was not until the World War I period that Latinos first became a significant factor in the demography of that city. In contrast to what happened in Chicago and New York, most of the Hispanic communities in the Northeast and Midwest began to evolve in earnest only after the Second World War. This was the case in Philadelphia, Boston, Cleveland, and in Bridgeport and Hartford, Connecticut.

The geographical breakdown of Latino communities can be differentiated in other ways aside from chronology and country of origin. For example, the Hispanic populations of Texas, California, and the Southwest have been traditionally much more rural in their orientation than the Latino communities of the Northeast, Southeast, or Midwest. At the same time, the communities in southern Florida have attracted or absorbed proportionally larger numbers of the affluent from Latin America than the other Hispanic communities of the United States. At certain times, New York's Latino community has also been somewhat mixed in terms of its economic and social configuration; however, overwhelming poverty and working-class backgrounds have been the rule in Texas, California, and most parts of the Southwest.[39]

In the meantime, patterns of migration from Latin America to the United States began to change greatly in the early 1990s, especially in migration from Mexico and Central America. In addition to the surge of Mexican and Central American migrants to New York and surrounding communities, there was also a surge in Mexican and Central American migration to many other states and communities that had never experienced this kind of influx before. Based primarily on the desire of employers to obtain the cheapest labor possible, impoverished migrants from Mexico and Central America—legal and undocumented—were able to obtain low-wage employment in construction, in restaurants, in other services, in meat-packing plants, and in other enterprises in communities from Oregon and Washington in the northwest to Georgia, South Carolina, and Florida in the southeast. At times, it appeared as if most low-wage work in the United States was being performed everywhere by the new immigrants, resulting in a major political backlash that began against immigrants in general after the attack on New York's World Trade Center in 2001 and especially after the onset of the Great Recession in 2007.[40]

It was not clear what the future would be for the US Latino communities as the country entered the second decade of the twenty-first century. A real recovery from the Great Recession had not yet taken root as of 2013, at least in terms of significant job growth. Reports indicated that the severe economic downturn was disproportionately affecting the economic and social status of Latinos in general. Jobs were indeed scarce at all levels, and it seemed as if a major restructuring of the job market would be required to get the economy moving forward again. There were also reports that the flow of immigrants into the country from Latin America had stopped or had slowed to a trickle (with the exception of undocumented Central American minors in the summer of 2014). Nevertheless, anti-immigrant sentiment was still strong, with laws passed by a number of states and communities targeting "undocumented" immigrants, especially Mexicans and people from Central America, restricting their access to jobs, housing, education, and other public services.[41]

Although Latinos were generally preoccupied with the impact of the Great Recession at the beginning of this decade, it appeared that certain trends and realities that had emerged in earlier decades would continue into the future. For example, the economic, geographic, and social diversification of Latinos in US society will probably be a factor in the future if mass or significant migration from Latin America continues. However, the Latino communities as a whole, especially the offspring or descendants of the immigrants, will also drift toward cultural homogenization. At this point, total assimilation into US society over the long term does not seem very probable, because assimilation has failed as social policy or social reality for most racialized immigrant and minority groups during the past sixty years. Although theoretical acceptance of cultural pluralism and diversity has grown in US society in recent decades, the view that Latinos are a foreign racialized minority is still foremost, with the racial order of the country evolving but with a hierarchy that keeps so-called white people at the top, African Americans or Blacks at the bottom, and Asians and Latinos somewhere in the middle.

Otherwise, it seems certain that New York will continue to function as a major entry point for Latin Americans, Asians, Africans, and other immigrant and migrant groups in the future. At the same time, it also appears that no constitutionally acceptable policy or program will be able to completely stop or even significantly reduce the increased flow of foreigners into the country from other parts of the world if the economy is functioning well. Recent calls for a slowdown or for limits to immigration may have a short-term impact, but if the legislative experience of recent years is any guide, it is unlikely in the near term that comprehensive immigration reform will come to pass. This will be especially true if powerful economic interests, especially in the agricultural and service sectors, continue to be committed to relatively unfettered immigration as a means of reducing the costs of labor. These economic groups succeeded in their campaigns to weaken the Immigration Reform and Control Act of 1986, and they will probably lobby hard to stop or weaken any legislation that would significantly reduce the future flow of foreign workers into the country or the city. The New York City government has taken a consistently liberal position with regard to immigration over the years, even with conservative mayors. For example, conservative mayor Rudolph Giuliani made it clear on taking office in 1994 that he and city officials would not cooperate with efforts by the federal government to crack down on illegal immigration in the city. New York's Latino population continued to grow relative to the city's total population during this period. Latinos constituted 24.3% of the city's total population by 1990, 26.9% by 2000, and 27.3% by 2010. It seemed clear that Latinos would be a major presence in the city for many years to come.[42]

NOTES

1. The terms "Latina/o" and "Hispanic," which are used interchangeably in this chapter, refer to all persons living in the United States whose origins can be traced to Spain and the Spanish-speaking countries of Latin America and the Caribbean. Included in this category are all US immigrants who have come from these countries and their descendants who live in the United States, whether they are Spanish speaking or not.

2. Stevens-Acevedo, Weterings, and Álvarez Frances (2013); Dodson, Moore, and Yancy (2000, 19); Wallace (2010, 22n).

3. Wallace (2010, 22–24).

4. Wallace (2010, 24–25). The enslaved Spanish negroes always claimed that they were, in fact, persons of free status unjustly enslaved by the English. Also, see Berlin and Harris (2005); LePore (2005); McManus (2001).

5. Simón Bolívar also came to New York to generate support for the Latin American independence movement in 1807, but unlike Miranda, he did not become a resident of the city. See Wallace (2010, 27–28). Also see Wallace, Matson, Pérez, Manthorne, and others in Sullivan (2010) for other specific details on the relationship between New York and various parts of Latin America during the nineteenth century.

6. Rosenwaike (1972, 10). Historically, most undercounts in the census have been attributed to the existence of a significant number of immigrant and/or poor working-class people within a given population. It is said that such persons are generally reluctant to enter into any kind of contact with government institutions because of the perception that such contact will lead to obligations or future difficulties with the authorities. In recent years, the urban census enumerations have also become increasingly controversial because of the Census Bureau's inability to accurately count or estimate the foreign or impoverished population of the cities. This has led to congressional hearings, recounts, lawsuits, and other problems. For comments regarding the accuracy of the population estimates for New York City

for the years prior to 1930 see Thomas (2010, 47, 180, 256n5, 263nn4 and 6, 275n3) and Sánchez Korrol (1994, 57–58, 59, 62).

7. See *Census of 1890* (1892, 645–47, 670, 672, 674, 676) and Iglesias (1984, 12, 63–79, 102, 146–47) for the Latino population estimates articulated by Bernardo Vega and his discussion of Latino politics in New York during this period. Latina/o politics in nineteenth-century New York is also discussed in Mirabal (2001, 57–72).

8. For a general discussion of economic development in Latin America during the nineteenth century see Bulmer-Thomas (2003); Bulmer-Thomas, Coatsworth, and Cortes-Conde (2006); and Coatsworth, Taylor, and David Rockefeller Center (1999). There are also studies that deal with specific nation-states and regions during the same period.

9. Iglesias (1984, 45–46, 53, 57–58, 64, 73) and Sánchez Korrol (1994, 11–17). During the late nineteenth century, the price of sugar produced in Cuba, Puerto Rico, and the Dominican Republic was increasingly determined by refiners, importers, brokers, and bankers based in New York City. One of the most important brokers in this period was Manuel Rionda, a New York–based Cuban. In the early years of the twentieth century, Rionda merged his successful company with Czarnikow Ltd., a London-based firm, to create the Czarnikow-Rionda Company. Within a few years this company came to dominate the Caribbean sugar market to such an extent that it could act as sole broker for the entire Cuban sugar industry and for some 80% of the sugar produced in Puerto Rico and the Dominican Republic. See Moreno-Fraginals (1985, 10–13, 20).

10. Iglesias (1983, 39–79); Sánchez Korrol (1994, 10, 13, 167–72); Angelo Falcón (1984, 18–20).

11. Iglesias (1984, 12, 85–86); Sinnette (1989, 23).

12. Iglesias (1984, 7, 9, 12, 16, 33, 46, 74). Also, see Sánchez Korrol (1994, 51–62) and Chenault (1938, 89–109).

13. Iglesias (1984, 12). For the 1920, 1930, and 1940 estimates, see the sources listed in table 1.2.

14. For a discussion of economic development in Cuba, Puerto Rico, and the Dominican Republic during the first half of the twentieth century, see the relevant sections in Ayala (1999), Ayala and Bernabé (2007), Betances (1995), Clausner (1973), Dietz (1986, 2003), Le Riverend (1972), Moya Pons (2007, 2010), and L. Pérez (2003) among others. Also, see Sánchez Korrol (1994, 11–50) for another discussion of Puerto Rican economic development and its relationship to migration during the period from 1900 to 1945 and the present.

15. L. Pérez (2003); Le Riverend (1972, 187–256).

16. The importance of the nineteenth-century Puerto Rican coffee and tobacco sectors is discussed in Dietz (1986, 4–78). Also see Ayala (1999) and Ayala and Bernabé (2007).

17. See Dietz (1986, 79–135) and the relevant sections in Ayala (1999) and Ayala and Bernabé (2007).

18. Dietz (1986, 135–81); Sánchez Korrol (1994, 11–28); the relevant sections in Ayala (1999) and Ayala and Bernabé (2007).

19. For a discussion of economic opportunities for Puerto Ricans in New York, the relative ease of travel, and the role played by the 1917 citizenship legislation in the migration process, see the relevant sections in Acosta-Belén and Santiago (2006, 41–50, 54–71), Sánchez Korrol (1994, 17–47), and Thomas (2010, 23–36).

20. Acosta-Belén and Santiago (2006, 41–50, 54–57, 69–71), Sánchez Korrol (1994, 28–29, 30, 32, 34, 57, 89–96, 107–112), and Thomas (2010, 23–36). Other sources for the early migration experience of Puerto Ricans up to 1945/50 include Flores (2005), History Task Force (1982), and Iglesias (1984), among others.

21. See the comments on these issues made by Bernardo Vega in Iglesias (1984, 7, 9–12, 16, 28, 85–86, 91, 98, 103, 105, 151, 155). Also see Sánchez Korrol (1994, 53–62) and the relevant sections in Thomas (2010, 23–36).

22. Iglesias (1984, 119–20, 155, 184); Sánchez Korrol (1994, 57); Chenault (1938, 97–100, 106–7); relevant sections in Thomas (2010). Housing conditions in New York between 1900 and 1945 are also discussed in Jackson (1976) and Plunz (1990).

23. Sánchez Korrol (1994, 134–66, 172–203); Falcón (1984, 20–42); Estades (1978, 29–36). Also, see the comments by Bernardo Vega in Iglesias (1984) and the discussion by Thomas (2010, 36–132), who focuses specifically on the political and organizational activities of Puerto Ricans in New York with regard to issues affecting the communities in the city, as well as the island, during the 1920s and 1930s.

24. Dietz (1986, 182–310 and especially 206–21, 226–28, 247–55, 282–88). Also see Dietz (2003) and the many studies that have focused on Puerto Rican migration and the Puerto Rican experience in the mainland United States and New York for the years since 1945. These include, among others, Acosta-Belén and Santiago (2006, 75–105); Duany (2004, 177–96); Fitzpatrick (1987); Glazer and Moynihan (1970); Handlin (1959); History Task Force (1979); López (1980, 313–466); Maldonado-Denis (1980); Mills, Senior, and Goldsen (1950); Nieves-Falcón (1975); E. Padilla (1958); (Rodríguez 1989; 2004, 195–218); Sánchez Korrol (2004, 1–18); Senior (1965); Sexton (1965); Wakefield (1959); and Zentella (2004, 21–34), among others. There are also publications that deal specifically with the evolution of Puerto Rican communities in specific locations outside of New York City, such as Chicago and Philadelphia.

25. Fitzpatrick (1987, 18–20); López (1980, 314–19); Rodriguez (1989, 6–8); the relevant sections in Acosta-Belén and Santiago (2006, 75–105); Duany (2004, 177–96); Glazer and Moynihan (1970); Handlin (1959); History Task Force (1979); López (1980, 313–466); Maldonado-Denis (1980); Mills, Senior, and Goldsen (1950); Nieves-Falcón (1975); E. Padilla (1958); Rodríguez (2004, 195–218); Sánchez Korrol (2004, 1–18); Senior (1965); Sexton (1965); Wakefield (1959); and Zentella (2004, 21–34), among others.

26. Duany (2011, 81–103); Lapp (1991, 198–214); Fitzpatrick (1987, 24–25); Rodríguez (1989, 4–6, 26–48); Seidl, Shenk, and DeWind (1980, 417–32); United States Department of Labor (1975). Among other works, also see the relevant sections in Acosta-Belén and Santiago (2006, 75–105); Duany (2004, 177–96); Glazer and Moynihan (1970); Handlin (1959); History Task Force (1979); López (1980, 313–466); Maldonado-Denis (1980); Mills, Senior, and Goldsen (1950); Nieves-Falcón (1975); E. Padilla (1958); Rodríguez (2004, 195–218); Sánchez Korrol (2004, 1–18); Senior (1965); Sexton (1965); Wakefield (1959); and Zentella (2004, 21–34).

27. Evidence that demonstrates the differences in socioeconomic background between Puerto Ricans and other Latina/os is quite sparse for this period. Two examples of Hispanic subgroups that were clearly more middle-class in their orientation during the period 1958 to 1970 were Cubans and Colombians. See Rogg and Santana Cooney (1980, 35–40) and Urrea Giraldo (1982, 8–10).

28. On the transformation of the New York economy during the period from 1945 to 1970 and the role played by Puerto Ricans in this change, see Fitzpatrick (1987, 11–13, 92–103), Freidenburg (1995), Danielson and Doig (1982, 50–62), and Rodríguez (1979, 214–15; 1989, 31–35, 37–42, 44–45). Also see the relevant sections in Acosta-Belén and Santiago (2006, 75–105); Glazer and Moynihan (1970); Handlin (1959); History Task Force (1979); López (1980, 313–466); Maldonado-Denis (1980); Mills, Senior, and Goldsen (1950); Nieves-Falcón (1975); E. Padilla (1958); Rodríguez (2004, 195–218); Sánchez Korrol (2004, 1–18); Senior (1965); Sexton (1965); Wakefield (1959); Zentella (2004, 21–34); and the pamphlets and reports that were distributed during this period, such as Puerto Rico (1953), Monserrat (1953), and New York City Department of Commerce (1956) among other sources.

29. The expansion of Puerto Rican neighborhoods in the period 1945–70 is discussed in Kantrowitz (1969), Eagle (1960), E. González (2004, 99–100, 105, 109–29), Glazer and McEntire (1960), Jonnes (2002, 91–204, 219–362), Sánchez (1989, 202–20; 1990, 37–45), and US Department of Labor (1975, 30–41). Also, see the relevant pages in Dávila (2004, 27–58), Jackson (1976), and Plunz (1990).

30. See Eagle (1960), E. González (2004, 99–100, 105, 109–29), Jonnes (2002, 91–204, 219–362), Rodríguez (1989, 106–19), Sánchez (1989, 202–20; 1990, 37–45), and, for the more recent period, Dávila (2004, 27–58) and Vargas-Ramos (2003). Also, see the relevant pages in Jackson (1976) and Plunz (1990).

31. For a discussion of the migration and life experiences of Cubans and Dominicans in the United States and New York in the years from 1960 to 1990 and the present, see Baéz Evertsz and D'Oleo-Ramírez (1985); Brotherton and Barrios (2011); Current (2010); del Castillo and Mitchell (1987); Duany (1994); Eckstein (2009); Grenier and Pérez (2002); Grasmuck and Pessar (1991); Guarnizo (1993); Hernández (2002); Hernández, Rivera-Batíz, and Agodini (1995); Hoffnung-Garskof (2008); Méndez (2003); Paris (2002); Pedraza (2007); Pessar

(1995); Portes and Bach (1985); Prieto (2009); Ricourt (2002); Rogg and Santana Cooney (1980); Sagas and Molina (2004); M. Torres (2001); Torres-Saillant and Hernández (1998); and chapter 5 of this book, by Hernández and Torres-Saillant.

32. Many studies have focused on the relationship between investment capital, economic development, social change, and the reality of international migration from developing Latin American countries to the more advanced industrialized societies in recent decades. However, the volatility and the major changes that gripped the world economy during the Great Recession of 2007 generated a significantly high level of uncertainty with regard to this relationship and how it would impact international migration in the future. Nevertheless, the interested reader can consult the rather technical discussions that focus on Latin American emigrants, remittances by the emigrants to their home countries, and the impact of these remittances on the economic development of their home countries since and just prior to the onset of the Great Recession of 2007 in Acosta et al. (2012, 183–92), Cervantes and del Pino (2012, 193–214), and Fajnzylber and López (2008).

33. For a discussion of middle-class or working-class orientation and downward social mobility among specific Latino subgroups in the New York area for the period from 1965 to 1990, see the relevant sections in Hernández (2002), Julca (2001, 239–57), Mann and Salvo (1984), Rogg and Santana Cooney (1980, 35–46), and Urrea Giraldo (1982). Articles and book chapters dealing with the immigration and life experiences of Latina/os aside from Dominicans, Puerto Ricans, and Cubans in the New York area during the period 1965–90 are also found in Bogen (1987), Julca (2001, 239–57), Kyle (2000, 29, 31, 32, 35–37, 45, 64–65, 72, 109, 158–59), Sutton and Chaney (1987, 221–349), and Waldinger (1986).

34. Dávila (2004, 27–58); González (2004, 99–100, 105, 109–29); Jonnes (2002, 91–204, 219–362); Sánchez (1989, 202–20; 1990, 37–45); US Department of Labor (1975, 30–41). Also, see the relevant pages in Jackson (1976, 254–308), Plunz (1990, 313–40, especially 323–24), *Report of the Mayor's Commission on Hispanic Concerns* (New York: 1986).

35. On the North American Free Trade Agreement (NAFTA) and its impact on migration and the regional economy, see David Bacon, "How US Policies Fueled Mexico's Great Migration," *Nation*, January 23, 2012. Also see French (2010), Mize and Swords (2011), Mora and Dávila (2009), and Wise (1998), among other sources. On the 1986 immigration reform legislation and other attempts to reform US immigration laws, see chapter 11 in this book, by Baver.

36. On the turmoil and civil wars that gripped Central America during this period, see Booth, Wade, and Walker (2010); Jonas (1991); Landau (1994); LeoGrande (2000); Lynch (2011); and Rosenberg and Solís (2007), among other sources. Also see Smith (2006) and chapter 6 in this book, also by Smith.

37. On the Mexican flower vendors and their problems with housing and mere survival in New York City during the mid-1990s, see Lizette Álvarez, "Down from Poverty: Mexico to Manhattan," *New York Times*, October 9, 1996. On the Mexican flower vendors, see Smith (2006, 164, 215–16).

38. See Dávila (2004: passim); Jonnes (2002, 363–440); Marwell (2007); Morales (2009); Sam Roberts, "Region Is Reshaped as Minorities Go to Suburbs," *New York Times*, December 14, 2010; Vargas Ramos (2003), among other, mostly journalistic sources.

39. A number of studies have been written on Latino communities or specific Latina/o subgroups in various parts of the country outside of New York City or the northeastern part of the United States. These include García (1996), Gonzáles (2009), Mahler (1995), Martínez (2011), F. Padilla (1987), G. Pérez (2004), Ramos-Zayas and de Genova (2003), Silver and Duany (2010), A. Torres (2006), Whalen (2001), and Whalen and Vázquez Hernández (2005), among others. For a general overview of the Latina/o experience in the United States, see Bergad and Klein (2010); Davis (2001); Flores and Rosaldo (2007); Fraga et al. (2010); J. González (2000); Grosfoguel, Maldonado-Torres, and Saldívar (2005); Gutiérrez (2004); Mize and Peña Delgado (2012); Oboler and González (2005); Pérez, Guridy, and Burgos (2010); Shorris (1992); Suárez-Orozco and Páez (2002), among others.

40. See Gill (2010), Johnson-Web (2003), Murphy and Hill (2001), and Odem and Lacy (2009), among other sources.

41. Despite these laws aimed primarily at Latin Americans and Mexicans in particular, the migration from Mexico and Central America had actually declined from the start of the 2007–9 Great Recession and was calculated at zero or less in 2012. See Passel, Cohn, and González Barrera (2012) and Julia Preston, "Justices to Rule on Role of the States in Immigration," *New York Times*, April 22, 2012.

42. See figures in table 1.4, "The Latino Population of New York City, 1990–2010," in this chapter. Also note that every New York City mayoral administration since the mid-1970s has refused to cooperate with the federal government in its effort to have city police and other officials enforce the laws against undocumented workers in the city. The courts have consistently sided with the federal government in its attempts to enforce compliance, but these efforts have failed in reality. See the comments in David Firestone, "Giuliani to Sue over Provision on Welfare," *New York Times*, September 12, 1996; Sam Dolnick, "In Change, Bloomberg Backs Obstacle to Deportation," *New York Times*, September 30, 2011.

REFERENCES

Acosta, Pablo, Javier Béz, Rodolfo Beazley, and Edmundo Murrugarra. 2012. "The Impact of the Financial Crisis on Remittance Flows: The Case of El Salvador." In *Migration and Remittances during the Global Financial Crisis and Beyond*, edited by Ibrahim Sirkeci, Jeffrey H. Cohen, and Dilip Ratha. Washington, DC: World Bank.

Acosta-Belén, Edna, and Carlos E. Santiago. 2006. *Puerto Ricans in the United States: A Contemporary Portrait*. Latinos: Exploring Diversity & Change. Boulder, CO: Lynne Rienner.

Ayala, César J. 1999. *American Sugar Kingdom: The Plantation Economy of the Spanish Caribbean, 1898–1934*. Chapel Hill: University of North Carolina Press.

Ayala, César J., and Rafael Bernabé. 2007. *Puerto Rico in the American Century: A History since 1898*. Chapel Hill: University of North Carolina Press.

Báez Evertsz, Franc, and Frank D'Oleo Ramírez. 1985. *Emigración de dominicanos a Estados Unidos: Determinantes socio-económicos y consecuencias*. Santo Domingo: Fundación Friedrich Ebert.

Bergad, Laird, and Herbert S. Klein. 2010. *Hispanics in the United States: A Demographic, Social, and Economic History, 1980–2005*. New York: Cambridge University Press.

Berlin, Ira, and Leslie Harris, eds. 2005. *Slavery in New York*. New York: W.W. Norton.

Betances, Emelio. 1995. *State and Society in the Dominican Republic*. Boulder, CO: Westview Press.

Bogen, Elizabeth. 1987. *Immigration in New York*. New York: Praeger.

Booth, John A., Christine J. Wade, and Thomas W. Walker, eds. 2010. *Understanding Central America: Global Forces, Rebellion, and Change*. Boulder, CO: Westview Press.

Brotherton, David C., and Luis Barrios. 2011. *Banished to the Homeland: Dominican Deportees and Their Stories of Exile*. New York: Columbia University Press.

Bulmer-Thomas, Victor, ed. 2003. *The Economic History of Latin America since Independence*. Cambridge Latin American Studies. New York: Cambridge University Press.

Bulmer-Thomas, Victor, John Coatsworth, and Roberto Cortes-Conde, eds. 2006. *The Cambridge Economic History of Latin America*. Vol. 2, *The Long Twentieth Century*. New York: Cambridge University Press.

Census of 1890. 1892. Washington, DC: United States Government Printing Office.

Cervantes, Jesús A., and Alejandro Barajas del Pino. 2012. "Remittance Flows to Mexico and Employment and Total Earnings of Mexican Immigrant Workers in the United States." In *Migration and Remittances during the Global Financial Crisis and Beyond*, edited by Ibrahim Sirkeci, Jeffrey H. Cohen, and Dilip Ratha, 193–212. Washington, DC: World Bank.

Chenault, Lawrence R. 1938. *The Puerto Rican Migrant in New York City*. New York: Columbia University Press.

Clausner, Marlin D. 1973. *Rural Santo Domingo: Settled, Unsettled, and Resettled*. Philadelphia: Temple University Press.

Coatsworth, John H., Alan M. Taylor, and the David Rockefeller Center, Harvard University, eds. 1999. *Latin America and the World Economy since 1800.* Series on Latin American Studies. Cambridge, MA: David Rockefeller Center, Harvard University.

Commonwealth of Puerto Rico, Department of Labor, Migration Division. 1953. *The Jobs We Do.* New York: Commonwealth of Puerto Rico, Department of Labor, Migration Division.

Current, Cheris Brewer. 2010. *Questioning the Cuban Exile Model: Race, Gender, and Resettlement, 1959–1979.* El Paso: LFB Scholarly Publishing.

Danielson, Michael N., and James W. Doig. 1982. *New York: The Politics of Urban Regional Development.* Berkeley: University of California Press.

Dávila, Arlene. 2004. *Barrio Dreams: Puerto Ricans, Latinos, and the Neoliberal City.* Berkeley: University of California Press.

Davis, Mike. 2001. *Magical Urbanism: Latinos Reinvent the US Big City.* Expanded ed. New York: Verso.

Del Castillo, José, and Christopher Mitchell, eds. 1987. *La inmigración Dominicana en los Estados Unidos.* Santo Domingo: Editorial CENAPEC.

Dietz, James L. 1986. *Economic History of Puerto Rico: Institutional Change and Capitalist Development.* Princeton: Princeton University Press.

———. 2003. *Puerto Rico: Negotiating Development and Change.* Boulder, CO: Lynne Rienner.

Dodson, Howard, Christopher Moore, and Roberta Yancy. 2000. *The Black New Yorkers: The Schomburg Illustrated Chronology; 400 Years of African American History.* New York: John Wiley & Sons.

Duany, Jorge. 1994. *Quisqueya on the Hudson: The Transnational Identity of Dominicans in Washington Heights.* New York: Dominican Studies Institute, City University of New York.

———. 2004. "Puerto Rico: Between the Nation and the Diaspora, Migration to and from Puerto Rico." In *Migration and Immigration: A Global View,* edited by Maura I. Toro-Morn and Marixsa Alicea, 177–96. Westport, CT: Greenwood Press.

———. 2011. *Blurred Borders: Transnational Migration between the Hispanic Caribbean and the United States.* Chapel Hill: University of North Carolina Press.

Eagle, Morris. 1960. "Puerto Ricans in New York City." In *Studies in Housing and Minority Groups,* edited by Nathan Glazer and Davis McEntire, 144–77. Berkeley: University of California Press.

Eckstein, Susan. 2009. *The Immigrant Divide: How Cuban Americans Changed the U.S. and Their Homeland.* New York: Routledge.

Fajnzylber, Pablo, and J. Humberto Lopez, eds. 2008. *Remittances and Development: Lessons from Latin America.* Washington DC: International Bank for Reconstruction, World Bank.

Falcón, Angelo. 1984. "A History of Puerto Rican Politics in New York City: 1860s to 1945." In *Puerto Rican Politics in Urban America*, edited by James Jennings and Monte Rivera, 15–42. Westport, CT: Greenwood Press.

Fitzpatrick, Joseph P., S.J. 1987. *Puerto Rican Americans: The Meaning of Migration to the Mainland.* 2nd ed. Englewood Cliffs, NJ: Prentice Hall.

Flores, Juan. 2005. *Puerto Rican Arrival in New York: Narratives of the Migration, 1920–1950.* Princeton: Markus Wiener.

Flores, Juan, and Renato Rosaldo, eds. 2007. *A Companion to Latina/o Studies.* Malden, MA: Blackwell Publishing.

Fraga, Luis, John A. García, Gary M. Segura, Michael Jones-Correa, Rodney Hero, and Valerie Martínez-Ebers. 2010. *Latino Lives in America: Making It Home.* Philadelphia: Temple University Press.

French, Laurence. 2010. *Running the Border Gauntlet: The Mexican Migrant Controversy.* Santa Barbara, CA: Praeger.

Friedenberg, Judith, ed. 1995. *Anthropology of Lower Income Urban Enclaves: The Case of East Harlem.* New York: New York Academy of Sciences.

García, Maria Cristina. 1996. *Havana USA: Cuban Exiles and Cuban Americans in South Florida, 1959–1994.* Berkeley: University of California Press.

Gill, Hannah. 2010. *The Latino Migration Experience in North Carolina: New Roots in the Old North State.* Chapel Hill: University of North Carolina Press.

Glazer, Nathan, and Daniel Patrick Moynihan. 1970. *Beyond the Melting Pot: The Negroes, Puerto Ricans, Jews, Italians, and Irish of New York City.* 2nd ed. Cambridge, MA: MIT Press.

Gonzáles, Manuel G. 2009. *Mexicanos: A History of Mexicans in the United States.* 2nd ed. Bloomington: Indiana University Press.

González, Evelyn. 2004. *The Bronx.* New York: Columbia University Press.

González, Juan. 2000. *Harvest of Empire: A History of Latinos in America.* New York: Viking.

Grasmuck, Sherri, and Patricia R. Pessar. 1991. *Between Two Islands: Dominican International Migration.* Berkeley: University of California Press.

Grenier, Guillermo J., and Lisandro Pérez, eds. 2003. *The Legacy of Exile: Cubans in the United States.* Boston: Allyn & Bacon.

Grosfoguel, Ramón, Nelson Maldonado-Torres, and José David Saldívar, eds. 2005. *Latin@s in the World- System: Decolonization Struggles in the 21st Century U.S. Empire.* Boulder, CO: Paradigm Publishers.

Guarnizo, Luis Eduardo. 1993. "One Country in Two: Dominican-Owned Firms in New York and in the Dominican Republic." PhD diss., Johns Hopkins University.

Gutiérrez, David G., ed. 2004. *The Columbia History of Latinos in the United States since 1960.* New York: Columbia University Press.

Handlin, Oscar. 1959. *The Newcomers: Negroes and Puerto Ricans in a Changing Metropolis.* Cambridge, MA: Harvard University Press.

Hernández, Ramona. 2002. *The Mobility of Workers under Advanced Capitalism: Dominican Migration to the United States.* New York: Columbia University Press.

Hernández, Ramona, Francisco Rivera-Batíz, and Roberto Agodini. 1995. *Dominican New Yorkers: A Socioeconomic Profile.* New York: Dominican Studies Institute, City University of New York.

History Task Force, Centro de Estudios Puertorriqueños, ed. 1979. *Labor Migration under Capitalism: The Puerto Rican Experience.* New York: Monthly Review Press.

———. 1982. *Sources for the Study of Puerto Rican Migration, 1879–1930.* New York: Center for Puerto Rican Studies, Hunter College, CUNY.

Hoffnung-Garskof, Jesse. 2008. *A Tale of Two Cities: Santo Domingo and New York after 1950.* Princeton: Princeton University Press.

Iglesias, César Andreu, ed. 1984. *Memoirs of Bernardo Vega: A Contribution to the History of the Puerto Rican Community in New York.* Translated by Juan Flores. New York: Monthly Review Press.

Jackson, Anthony. 1976. *A Place Called Home: A History of Low-Cost Housing in Manhattan.* Cambridge, MA: MIT Press.

Johnson-Webb, Karen D. 2003. *Recruiting Hispanic Labor: Immigrants in Non-Traditional Areas.* El Paso, TX: LFB Scholarly Publishing.

Jonas, Susanne. 1991. *The Battle for Guatemala: Rebels, Death Squads, and U.S. Power.* Boulder, CO: Westview Press.

Jonnes, Jill. 2002. *South Bronx Rising: The Rise, Fall, and Resurrection of an American City.* New York: Fordham University Press.

Julca, Alex. 2001. "Peruvian Networks for Migration in New York City's Labor Market, 1970–1996." In *Migration, Transnationalization, and Race in a Changing New York,* edited by Hector R. Cordero-Gúzman, Robert C. Smith, and Ramón Grosfoguel, 239–57. Philadelphia: Temple University Press.

Kantrowitz, Nathan. 1969. *Negro and Puerto Rican Populations of New York City in the Twentieth Century.* Washington, DC: American Geographical Society.

Kyle, David. 2000. *Transnational Peasants: Migrations, Networks, and Ethnicity in Andean Ecuador.* Baltimore: Johns Hopkins University Press.

Landau, Saul. 1994. *The Guerrilla Wars of Central America: Nicaragua, El Salvador, and Guatemala.* New York: St. Martin's Press.

Laó-Montes, Agustín, and Arlene Dávila, eds. 2001. *Mambo Montage: The Latinization of New York.* New York: Columbia University Press.

Lapp, Michael. 1991. "The Migration Division of Puerto Rico and Puerto Ricans in New York City, 1948–1969." In *Immigration to New York,* edited by William Pencak, Selma Berrol, and Randall M. Miller, 198–214. New York: New York Historical Society / Associated University Presses.

LeoGrande, William M. 2000. *Our Own Backyard: The United States in Central America, 1977–1992.* Chapel Hill: University of North Carolina Press.

Lepore, Jill. 2005. *New York Burning: Liberty, Slavery, and Conspiracy in Eighteenth-Century Manhattan*. New York: Knopf.

Le Riverend, Julio. 1972. *Historia económica de Cuba*. Barcelona: Esplugues de Llobregat, Ediciones Ariel.

López, Adalberto, ed. 1980. *The Puerto Ricans: Their History, Culture, and Society*. Cambridge, MA: Schenkman Publishing.

Lynch, Edward A. 2011. *Cold War's Last Battlefield: Reagan, the Soviets, and Central America*. Albany: State University of New York Press.

Mahler, Sarah J. 1995. *American Dreaming: Immigration Life on the Margins*. Princeton: Princeton University Press.

Maldonado-Denis, Manuel. 1980. *The Emigration Dialectic: Puerto Rico and the U.S.A.* New York: International Publishers.

Mann, Evelyn S., and Joseph J. Salvo. 1984. *Characteristics of New Hispanic Immigrants to New York City: A Comparison of Puerto Rican and Non-Puerto Rican Hispanics*. New York: City of New York, Department of City Planning.

Martínez, Ruben O., ed. 2011. *Latinos in the Midwest*. East Lansing: Michigan State University Press.

Marwell, Nicole P. 2007. *Bargaining for Brooklyn: Community Organizations in the Entrepreneurial City*. Chicago: University of Chicago Press.

McManus, Edgar J. 2001. *A History of Negro Slavery in New York*. Syracuse, NY: Syracuse University Press.

Méndez, Antonio A. 2003. *La emigración dominicana hacia los EE.UU: Mitos y realidades*. Santo Domingo: Ediciones SURCO.

Mills, C. Wright, Clarence Senior, and Rose Goldsen. 1950. *The Puerto Rican Journey: New York's Newest Migrants*. New York: Harper and Brothers.

Mirabal, Nancy Raquel. 2001. "'No Country but the One We Must Fight For': The Emergence of an Antillean Nation and Community in New York City, 1860–1901." In *Mambo Montage: The Latinization of New York*, edited by Agustín Laó-Montes and Arlene Dávila, 57–72. New York: Columbia University Press.

Mize, Ronald L., and Grace Peña Delgado. 2012. *Latino Immigrants in the United States*. Malden, MA: Polity Press.

Mize, Ronald L., and Alicia C. S. Swords. 2011. *Consuming Mexican Labor: From the Bracero Program to NAFTA*. Toronto: University of Toronto Press.

Monserrat, Joseph. 1953. *Industry and Community—A Profitable Partnership*. New York: Commonwealth of Puerto Rico, Department of Labor, Migration Division.

Mora, Marie T., and Alberto Dávila. 2009. *Labor Market Issues along the U.S.–Mexico Border*. Tucson: University of Arizona Press.

Morales, Ed, and Laura Rivera, directors. 2009. *Whose Barrio: The Gentrification of East Harlem*. A documentary film. New York: Ed Morales. See http://www.whosebarrio.com/index.html.

Moreno-Fraginals, Manuel. 1985. "Plantations in the Caribbean: Cuba, Puerto Rico and the Dominican Republic in the Late Nineteenth Century." In *Between Slavery and Free Labor: The Spanish-Speaking Caribbean in the Nineteenth Century*, edited by Manuel Moreno-Fraginals, Frank Moya Pons, and Stanley L. Engerman, 3–21. Baltimore: Johns Hopkins University Press.

Moya Pons, Frank. 2007. *History of the Caribbean: Plantations, Trade and War in the Atlantic World*. Princeton: Markus Wiener.

———. 2010. *The Dominican Republic: A National History*. 3rd ed. Princeton: Markus Wiener.

Murphy, Arthur D., and Jennifer A. Hill, eds. 2001. *Latino Workers in the Contemporary South*. Athens: University of Georgia Press.

New York City Department of Commerce. 1956. *Puerto Ricans: A Key Source of Labor*. New York: New York City Department of Commerce.

Nieves-Falcón, Luis. 1975. *El emigrante puertorriqueño*. Rio Piedras: Editorial Edil.

Oboler, Suzanne, and Deena J. González, eds. 2005. *The Oxford Encyclopedia of Latinos and Latinas in the United States*. 4 vols. New York: Oxford University Press.

Odem, Mary E., and Elaine Lacy, eds. 2009. *Latino Immigrants and the Transformation of the U.S. South*. Athens: University of Georgia Press.

Padilla, Elena. 1958. *Up from Puerto Rico*. New York: Columbia University Press.

Padilla, Félix M. 1987. *Puerto Rican Chicago*. Notre Dame, IN: University of Notre Dame Press.

Paris, Margaret L. 2002. *Embracing America: A Cuban Exile Comes of Age*. Gainesville: University Press of Florida.

Passel, Jeffrey, D'Vera Cohn, and Ana González-Barrera. 2012. *Net Migration from Mexico Falls to Zero—and Perhaps Less*. Washington, DC: Pew Research Center.

Pedraza, Silvia. 2007. *Political Disaffection in Cuba's Revolution and Exodus*. New York: Cambridge University Press.

Pérez, Gina M. 2004. *The Near Northwest Side Story: Migration, Displacement, and Puerto Rican Families*. Berkeley: University of California Press.

Pérez, Gina M., Frank A. Guridy, and Adrian Burgos Jr., eds. 2010. *Beyond El Barrio: Everyday Life in Latina/o America*. New York: New York University Press.

Pérez, Louis. 2003. *Cuba and the United States: Ties of Singular Intimacy*. 3rd ed. Athens: University of Georgia Press.

Pessar, Patricia R. 1995. *Visa for a Dream: Dominicans in the United States*. Boston: Allyn and Bacon.

Plunz, Richard. 1990. *A History of Housing in New York City*. New York: Columbia University Press.

Portes, Alejandro, and Robert L. Bach. 1985. *Latin Journey: Cuban and Mexican Immigrants in the United States*. Berkeley: University of California Press.

Prieto, Yolanda. 2009. *The Cubans of Union City: Immigrants and Exiles in a New Jersey Community*. Philadelphia: Temple University Press.

Ramos-Zayas, Ana, and Nicholas de Genova. 2003. *Latino Crossings: Mexicans, Puerto Ricans, and the Politics of Race and Citizenship*. New York: Routledge.

Report of the Mayor's Commission on Hispanic Concerns. 1986. New York: Mayor's Commission on Hispanic Concerns.

Ricourt, Milagros. 2002. *Dominicans in New York City: Power from the Margins*. New York: Routledge.

Rodríguez, Clara E. 1979. "Economic Factors Affecting Puerto Ricans in New York." In *Labor Migration under Capitalism: The Puerto Rican Experience*, edited by the History Task Force, Centro de Estudios Puertorriqueños, 197–221. New York: Monthly Review Press.

———. 1989. *Puerto Ricans: Born in the U.S.A.* New York: Unwin and Hyman.

———. 2004. "Commentary: Forging a New, New York: The Puerto Rican Community, Post 1945." In *Boricuas in Gotham: Puerto Ricans in the Making of New York City*, edited by Gabriel Haslip-Viera, Angelo Falcón, and Félix Matos Rodríguez, 195–218. Princeton: Markus Wiener.

Rogg, Eleanor Meyer, and Rosemary Santana Cooney. 1980. *Adaptation and Adjustment of Cubans: West New York, New Jersey*. New York: Hispanic Research Center, Fordham University.

Rosenberg, Mark, and Luis G. Solís, eds. 2007. *The United States and Central America: Geopolitical Realities and Regional Fragility*. New York: Routledge.

Rosenwaike, Ira. 1972. *Population History of New York City*. Syracuse, NY: Syracuse University Press.

Sagás, Ernesto, and Sintia E. Molina, eds. 2004. *Dominican Migration: Transnational Perspectives*. Gainesville: University Press of Florida.

Sánchez, José Ramón. 1989. "Residual Work and Residual Shelter: Housing Puerto Rican Labor in New York City." In *Critical Perspectives on Housing*, edited by R. G. Bratt, C. Hartman, and A. Meyerson, 202–20. Philadelphia: Temple University Press.

———. 1990. "Housing from the Past." *Centro: The Journal of the Center for Puerto Rican Studies* 2 (5): 37–45.

Sánchez Korrol, Virginia. 1994. *From Colonia to Community: The History of Puerto Ricans in New York City, 1917–1948*. Latinos in American Society and Culture 5. Berkeley: University of California Press.

———. 2004. "Building the New York Puerto Rican Community, 1945–1965: A Historical Interpretation." In *Boricuas in Gotham: Puerto Ricans in the Making of New York City*, edited by Gabriel Haslip-Viera, Angelo Falcón, and Félix Matos Rodríguez, 1–18. Princeton: Markus Wiener.

Seidl, Tom, Janet Shenk, and Adrian DeWind, 1980. "The San Juan Shuttle: Puerto Ricans on Contract." In *The Puerto Ricans: Their History, Culture and Society*, edited by Adalberto López, 417–32. Cambridge, MA: Schenkman Publishing.

Senior, Clarence. 1965. *The Puerto Ricans: Strangers—Then Neighbors*. New York: Quadrangle Books.

Sexton, Patricia Cayo. 1965. *Spanish Harlem: Anatomy of Poverty*. New York: Harper & Row.

Shorris, Earl. 1992. *Latinos: A Biography of the People*. New York: W.W. Norton & Co.

Silver, Patricia, and Jorge Duany, eds. 2010. *Puerto Rican Florida*. Special Issue 22 (1) of *Centro: The Journal of the Center for Puerto Rican Studies*.

Sinnette, Elinor desVerney. 1989. *Arthur Alfonso Schomburg: Black Bibliophile and Collector*. New York: New York Public Library / Detroit: Wayne State University Press.

Smith, Robert C. 2006. *Mexican New York: Transnational Lives of New Immigrants*. Berkeley: University of California Press.

Stevens-Acevedo, Anthony, Tom Weterings, and Leonor Álvarez Francés. 2013. *Juan Rodríguez and the Beginnings of New York City*. New York: Dominican Studies Institute, City University of New York.

Suárez-Orozco, Marcelo, and Mariela Páez, eds. 2002. *Latinos: Remaking America*. Berkeley: University of California Press.

Sullivan, Edward J., ed. 2010. *Nueva York, 1613–1945*. New York: New York Historical Society / Scala Publishers.

Sutton, Constance R., and Elsa M. Chaney, eds. 1987. *Caribbean Life in New York City: Sociocultural Dimensions*. New York: Center for Migration Studies.

Thomas, Lorrin. 2010. *Puerto Rican Citizen: History and Political Identity in Twentieth-Century New York City*. Chicago: University of Chicago Press.

Torres, Andrés, ed. 2006. *Latinos in New England*. Philadelphia: Temple University Press.

Torres, María de los Angeles. 2001. *In the Land of Mirrors: Cuban Exile Politics in the United States*. Ann Arbor: University of Michigan Press.

Torres-Saillant, Silvio, and Ramona Hernández. 1998. *The Dominican Americans*. Westport, CT: Greenwood Press.

US Department of Labor, Bureau of Labor Statistics. 1975. *A Socio-Economic Profile of Puerto Rican New Yorkers, Regional Report #46*. New York: US Department of Labor, Middle Atlantic Regional Office.

Urrea Giraldo, Fernando. 1982. "Life Strategies and the Labor Market: Colombians in New York in the 1970s." Occasional Papers 34. New York: Center for Latin American Studies, New York University.

Vargas-Ramos, Carlos. 2003. *Centro Policy Brief: Housing Emergency and Overcrowding; Latinos in New York City*. New York: Center for Puerto Rican Studies, City University of New York.

Wakefield, Dan. 1959. *Island in the City: Puerto Ricans in New York*. New York: Corinth Books / Citadel Press.

Waldinger, Roger D. 1986. *Through the Eye of the Needle: Immigrants and Enterprise in New York's Garment Trades*. New York: New York University Press.

Wallace, Mike. 2010. "Nueva York: The Back Story." In *Nueva York, 1613–1945*, edited by Edward J. Sullivan, 18–81. New York: New York Historical Society / Scala Publishers.

Whalen, Carmen T. 2001. *From Puerto Rico to Philadelphia: Puerto Rican Workers and Postwar Economies*. Philadelphia: Temple University Press.

Whalen, Carmen, and Victor Vázquez Hernández, eds. 2005. *The Puerto Rican Diaspora: Historical Perspectives*. Philadelphia: Temple University Press.

Wise, Carol. 1998. *The Post-NAFTA Political Economy: Mexico and the Western Hemisphere*. University Park: Pennsylvania State University Press.

Zentella, Ana Celia. 2004. "Commentary: A Nuyorican's View of Our History and Languages(s) in New York, 1945–1965." In *Boricuas in Gotham: Puerto Ricans in the Making of New York City*, edited by Gabriel Haslip-Viera, Angelo Falcón, and Félix Matos Rodríguez, 20–34. Princeton: Markus Wiener.

CHAPTER TWO

Puerto Ricans

Building the Institutions for the Next Generation of Latinos

CLARA E. RODRÍGUEZ

In many analyses of migration and immigration, relatively little attention has been paid to the role that the characteristics of settled areas have played in the adaptation of immigrants and migrants. Rather, a long-standing tradition in urban analyses, exemplified by the early work of sociologists Robert Ezra Park, Ernest Burgess, and Roderick McKenzie (1925), has focused on how areas were changed by the entrance of "newcomers."[1] This focus on how newcomers have changed what existed has continued regardless of whether these newcomers were (1) of the "gentry" variety, (2) new immigrants replacing older immigrants—as in Dominicans and Mexicans overtaking formerly predominantly Puerto Rican and/or Black areas, or (3) new generations of the same immigrants or migrants settling in predominantly Mexican, Puerto Rican, or African American areas. Although this is an important and valid approach in understanding urban development and ethnic succession, my interest here is in how established ethnic communities have provided the historical base upon which newer communities have developed. Secondarily, I am interested in how these longer-term historical changeovers have created the New York City we know today. I focus particularly on the role that Puerto Ricans and the Puerto Rican migration played in contributing to (1) the Latino communities of today and (2) what New York is today.

COMMUNITIES IN CONSTANT CYCLES OF SETTLEMENT AND TRANSITION . . . AND THE DISCONNECT

It is generally acknowledged that New York has served as a port of entry for immigrants. But less clear in the public mind has been how these changes have created the city that we know today. Take, for example, the ever-present "bodegas" (i.e., local Mom & Pop grocery stores) of New York. This term no longer needs translation in New York. How did it become a part of the New York lexicon? Did Dominicans introduce the bodega? Puerto Ricans? The bodegas that came to populate not just Spanish-speaking areas but the city as a whole were not an invention of the Dominican community, or of the Puerto Rican community, but appear to have had their genesis in much earlier, perhaps less researched, Spanish-speaking communities in New York.[2] Historically, and contrary to what most (Latino and non-Latino) New Yorkers envision when they think of a "bodega," *Merriam-Webster's Collegiate Dictionary* indicates that the word actually refers to a warehouse in Spain or "a storehouse for maturing wine."[3] So, in the same way that the Puerto Rican communities of the 1920s–1930s[4] built upon the earlier patterns, structures, and accomplishments of preceding Spanish-speakers, so too have subsequent Spanish-speaking groups built upon the established Puerto Rican communities in New York. This, I suspect, will continue as new groups enter the ebb and flow of the city's development. In many neighborhoods, Puerto Ricans established bodegas where delicatessens—or delis, as they are universally known—previously stood. Then these businesses passed to more recent Puerto Ricans or Dominicans. Now, in some instances, Asians or Mexicans have taken over those same establishments.

THE ARRIVAL OF LATINOS DURING THE "LONG HIATUS"

However, in order to better understand the experience of Puerto Ricans and the role they have played in the development of New York and its constant cycles of settlement and transition, it is important to understand the temporal context during which most Puerto Ricans arrived. Although their numbers were few and their communities small, there were Puerto Ricans (and Cubans) who came to New York as political exiles, merchants, or skilled tobacco workers during the latter half of the nineteenth century.[5] More Puerto Ricans began to arrive after the annexation of Puerto Rico by the United States in 1898; then they came in substantial numbers after the passage of the Jones Act in 1917, which made Puerto Ricans citizens and sanctioned their service in the military and their participation in World Wars I and II. It was the post–World War II migration that is referred to as "the great migration," for this is when the largest numbers of Puerto Ricans arrived.[6] Indeed, this migration was so concentrated in New York that it spawned the now classic Broadway musical and then movie *West Side Story*, which came to frame the Puerto Rican experience for the American public.[7]

But this Puerto Rican (im)migration[8] took place in a larger temporal context, referred to by Doug Massey (1995) as the "long hiatus." This was the 1930–69 period when few European and other immigrants came to the United States, because of the restrictive federal immigration laws passed after World War I and during the 1920s. The Great Depression and the Second World War also curbed immigration to the United States. Countries in Europe restricted emigration from their countries during wartime and rebuilt their economies during the postwar period. However, during this hiatus period, many Puerto Ricans and Mexicans came. Many came to fill labor shortages occasioned by the decline in immigration, the war involvements, and the expansions of the economy. Indeed, so many Mexicans arrived that the US Census Bureau counted them in the 1930 census by adding a special category for them. It was also during this period that Puerto Ricans began to (im)migrate in larger numbers.[9] Although not often acknowledged, both these immigrations boosted the economies where the immigrants settled.[10]

The early (im)migrants entered a world where any departure from the white, nonethnic American—whether in language, accent, culture, or color—was often a basis for exclusion or discrimination. During this long hiatus, even movie actors of European extraction felt compelled to change their names to more bland—termed by some "harmonious"—English-sounding names in order to achieve their American Dream. Consequently, and for example, Bernard Schwartz became Tony Curtis, Natasha Nikolaevna Gurdin became Natalie Wood, and Joe Yule became Mickey Rooney (Jarvie 1991, 91).[11] Nevertheless, in New York, as elsewhere, these Latino immigrants persevered and built their communities, often upon the remnants of older and smaller Latino communities, or created new communities, as in the "West Side," the Lower East Side (which came to be known as Loisaida), the Bronx, and Brooklyn.

Those large numbers of Puerto Ricans who came after World War II also arrived during the McCarthy era, and entered a system that embraced the entrenched assimilationist ethics of an earlier period. The diversity, cosmopolitanism, and international flavor that is so much a part of New York today was present mainly as a dim historical antecedent, evident more in unread historical texts than in real-life classrooms. (This history of diversity was seldom acknowledged or taught during this hiatus period.)[12] The political conservatism—and McCarthyism in particular—created mistrust of Puerto Ricans' history of the struggle for political independence and influenced their reception. Some viewed Puerto Ricans suspiciously—as terrorists, even—because of the Nationalist uprisings in Puerto Rico protesting US control. There were also political acts that occurred in the States during the Truman administration; for example, four Puerto Rican nationalists opened fire on the US House of Representatives in 1954. Ironically, the cloud of distrust that these political acts cast upon these newcomers then is perhaps better understood from our post-9/11 vantage point, in the attitudes held by some toward Islamic communities today.

But these Latinos pushed ahead in spite of these reactions, and their children came together in the "Pa'lante," or "Forward," rallying call. In so doing, they carved out new cultural and social spaces for Latinos from a city that had become rather unreceptive to ethnic and cultural differences. Felipe Luciano, a New York Puerto Rican and one of the founders of the Young Lords Party, articulated this view of Puerto Ricans as trailblazers: "As the pioneers of Latino empowerment and pride, especially east of the Mississippi, we've paved the road for all Spanish speaking peoples coming to American cities, including Mexicans, Dominicans, Central Americans, etc." (Felipe Luciano, "A New Deal between Stateside and Island Puerto Ricans: The View from a New York 'Rican," guest commentary, NYC Latino Politics, March 30, 2011).[13] It is this history—of how these earlier waves of Latinos in New York contributed to and altered New York's cultural, political, and social landscape—that is often missing from analyses of contemporary immigrants in New York. This chapter, and this volume more generally, seek to address and fill in these views; for, as the title of this volume suggests, Latinos in New York are communities in transition. Then, again, New York has also been a place where communities are in continual transition.

THE DIFFERENCE BETWEEN TODAY AND THEN: SOME MAJOR CHANGES

Consequently, we also need to better understand that, in many respects, to-day's immigrants are not entering the same city that Puerto Ricans or immigrants encountered at the beginning of the twentieth century. They are entering a city that changed greatly during the sixties and seventies in terms of how diversity and immigrants were viewed and accommodated. The city changed in many ways during those decades because of the individual and collective action of Puerto Ricans and their allies. A few of such changes that were significant, impactful, and path breaking were bilingual education, bilingual voting assistance, removing accents as a barrier to employment in the school system and elsewhere, eliminating height and weight requirements for police officers and fire fighters, establishing the Latino arts and theatrical companies and institutions (still vibrant now), establishing institutions that facilitated high-school-to-college pathways, and founding the Puerto Rican studies programs that became the foundation for subsequent Latino and Latin American studies programs throughout the region.

Immigrants today enter a city where the law requires that bilingual education or ESL (English as a Second Language) must be provided to children who speak another language. This requirement came about when Aspira, a Puerto Rican agency (led by Antonia Pantoja) sued the Board of Education because it was not educating all of the city's children. This case was litigated through the courts and resulted in the 1974 Bilingual Consent Decree agreement with the Board of Education, which required that children in need of English instruction be provided with it.

Immigrants enter a city that provides bilingual voting assistance. The legislation that today requires this stems from the success of the Puerto Rican Legal Defense and Education Fund (PRLDEF—today known as Latino Justice PRLDEF), which went to court and, in 1973, won the argument that Puerto Ricans, as citizens—and some as former military personnel—should be allowed to register and vote in their own language. Soon after, Latinos who arrived with college educations from other countries could and did find jobs in the school system and elsewhere, because Puerto Ricans had argued that "accents" should not be a barrier to entering the teaching, social work, or other professions. Before this, some Puerto Rican, and likely other Latino, professionals raised in New York were rejected as possible teachers only because interviewers had detected an "accent" during their interviews for the job.

Today, the police and fire departments are more integrated than in the past; we can find police officers and firefighters who speak Spanish. This is, in part, because PRLDEF challenged the requirement that recruits had to meet certain height and weight measurements.

Spanish-speaking and bilingual theater and drama continue to flourish and nourish new talent both in acquired spaces and in public outdoor spaces, in large part because of many hard-fought struggles by Latinos to establish themselves and subsequently to survive as freestanding, quality institutions. Institutions like Teatro LATEA, El Repertorio (the Spanish Repertory Theater), the Puerto Rican Traveling Theater, and Pregones are places that continue to present dramas of particular interest to many Spanish-speaking communities, as well as to support and sustain the new (as well as the veteran) dramatic talents of actors within these communities and from other Spanish-speaking countries. These theaters continue the earlier New York traditions of other ethnic theaters, where plays were performed, for example, in Yiddish, in Italian, or bilingually.

It is not major news that the visual-art and performing-art works of aspiring Latin Americans from various countries are exhibited in New York. In the past, the works of globally acknowledged Latin American artists, such as Diego Rivera and José Clemente Orozco, were exhibited in major institutions. However, Latin American artists who were not so well known had difficulty having their works exhibited in New York. Puerto Rican artistic institutions that were established against great odds and with major sacrifices (e.g., El Museo Del Barrio and Taller Boricua) have, from their inception, sought to provide a space for artists from all Latin American countries when other museums were not interested in their work. And they have continued to expand this mission.

Aspira, one of the first organizations set up to help Puerto Rican students improve their educational attainments, has had wholly Dominican chapters for decades now. Hostos College, Boricua College, and various programs within other colleges have served and continue to serve as entry points for immigrants with limited English ability to receive a college education.

Finally, the Puerto Rican studies programs established thirty to forty years ago in institutions of higher education throughout the city—often against the resistance of the college administrations—have all branched out to include Latin American and Caribbean studies and have hired staff from all groups. In essence, the Puerto Rican community and its leaders and allies were directly responsible for these changes, and others, such as bilingual voting; Spanish-speaking priests, ministers, and services; and countless other small, community-based organizations that fought for the rights of new and older (im)migrants in a variety of areas and for all ages.

Again, this is not to say that the newer groups have not also established their own organizations; as with all new groups, they have done so and will continue to do so. In the same way that Puerto Ricans wished to write their own histories, so, too, have more-recent immigrants to New York. But immigrants today enter a city with a past, a city where they meet others who have come to expect and to provide these dimensions of New York life. Needless to say, these institutions and characteristics of New York life would not have come about without the efforts and hard-fought battles and struggles of the earlier waves of Latinos and others. Indeed, these earlier Puerto Rican accomplishments were in themselves also influenced and facilitated by African Americans' long-standing and contemporaneous struggles for civil rights and by the battles of prior immigrants who fought for better working conditions, education, and housing.

Our failure to place these new and emerging Latino communities within their historical contexts will limit our abilities to properly understand them and their unique circumstances, as well as their historical continuities. Puerto Ricans, arriving during and after the "Long Hiatus," found no organizations facilitating their entry into the United States. They fought long and hard to develop these and other institutions, which came to be redirected to serve the broader Latino and New York community. These organizations are not run only by Puerto Ricans today, but also by members of other Latino communities. And their orientations have also broadened to reflect the needs and cultural expressions of these groups as well.

NARROW TRANSNATIONALISM OFTEN MISSES THE PUERTO RICAN EXPERIENCE

One common perspective through which immigrants have recently been viewed is transnationalism. "Transnational" is defined by *Merriam-Webster's Collegiate Dictionary* as "extending or going beyond national boundaries," and the word's "first known use" was in 1921.[14] As an academic perspective that became popular during the nineties, transnationalism puts a positive spin on immigrants, seeing them as people who travel back and forth between their countries of origin and the one they immigrated to, and who thereby retain important associations to their countries of origin while also

gaining additional connections in their new lands. This perspective continues to offer a viable framework for studying new immigrant groups. Gone
within this formulation are the earlier, problematic references to the "circulating migrations" of Puerto Ricans and claims that such back-and-forth
movements prevented them from assimilating and setting down their roots
in the United States so that they could progress socioeconomically (see Rodríguez 1989, 1993).

Some transnational analyses, however, do not include Puerto Ricans as
a transnational group.[15] This tends to contribute to the "disconnect" in some
of the academic literature between the Puerto Rican experience and that of
more recent immigrants. The rationale for not considering Puerto Ricans to
be transnational is that they were not seen as emigrating from another, independent country. Rather, they were "migrants" because they were not "foreign born" but born in a territory of the United States and they did not have
to naturalize. Vargas-Ramos (2012) disagrees with this view but finds that
Puerto Ricans, in contrast to other groups, display low levels of transnational
practices. For example, they do not send remittances as much as other immigrant groups. However, this may reflect Vargas-Ramos's consideration of the
modern Puerto Rican community, which is dominated by second-, third-, or
even fourth-generation Puerto Ricans. It may be that as time has passed,
Puerto Rican transnationalism has declined with successive generations in
the United States.

Others, however, describe Puerto Ricans as immigrants (Aranda 2007),
and some include Puerto Ricans as a transnational group (Roth 2012, 9).
Torres and Marzán, in chapter 4 of this volume, state that "the transnational
character of Puerto Rican and other Latino communities reinforces the cultural ties to their homeland, abetting the retention of Spanish-language use
and sustaining participation in the political and economic life of their countries of origin." They add that "what has been noted as a distinctive quality
among recent immigrants from Latin America has been a longtime feature
of the Puerto Rican diaspora."[16] Duany (2010a) also compares the different
roles that remittances play in the transnational experiences of Puerto Ricans,
Dominicans, and Mexicans. Finally, DeSipio and Pantoja (2007, 120) refer to
the distinction often made—or the exceptionalism claimed—in the literature with regard to Puerto Ricans: "The fluidity of migration and the relative
ease of access of citizenship rights of Puerto Ricans in the United States often
[necessitate] an asterisk or a footnote in studies of Latino immigrant adaptation." However, they also note that "the failure of previous immigration

scholarship to theorize about and analyze Puerto Rican migrant adaptation represents a substantial gap in our understanding of the dynamics of immigrant transnational engagement in general." They further state that "in the study of ethnic politics in the United States, the experience of the Puerto Rican migration needs to be moved to a more central position within the immigration literature (and the asterisk needs to be removed from much of our analysis)."

The omission of Puerto Ricans from many transnational analyses differs from the way in which others have viewed Puerto Ricans, that is, as (im)migrants (Rodriguez 1989). That is to say that Puerto Ricans were both migrants, since they arrived as citizens, and immigrants, since they generally came speaking Spanish and not English, and with a different culture and historical experience. They were like more-recent immigrants to Britain, the Netherlands, or France (Rodriguez 1989), who come from "transnational colonial states" (Duany 2010a, 2010b) or "post-colonial colonies" (Jorge Duany, "Una Colonia Poscolonial," *El Nuevo Día, July 11,* 2012) with certain rights of citizenship.

Other trends have also contributed to the relative faintness of Puerto Ricans in the migration literature. For example, the focus on citizenship, particularly in Europe, has contributed to this invisibility, certainly in the past twenty years. Because Puerto Ricans are citizens, they are left out of the debate about citizenship and immigration. However, Vargas-Ramos contends that nominal US citizenship is not sufficient for a person to be considered a full-fledged member of the polity (personal conversation, July 17, 2012). Flores and Benmayor's (1997) concept of "cultural citizenship" was another theoretical construct in the literature that might have been more applied to the Puerto Rican experience. The argument, within this framework, was that despite the absence of formal citizenship, Mexicans had cultural citizenship in large part because of their long-term presence and their cultural, artistic, and linguistic transformations and appropriation of urban spaces. But, perhaps again because Puerto Ricans had formal "citizenship," this theoretical construct was not applied to Puerto Ricans to any significant degree. Nevertheless, Puerto Ricans, like Mexicans, also transformed and appropriated urban spaces in New York, making them established Puerto Rican neighborhoods.

Other authors have tended to view immigration from the policy perspective and have thus accepted the idea that there was an immigration hiatus. They, therefore, compare the post-1965 immigrants to the European immigrants that came prior to the passage (in the 1920s) of immigration laws limiting immigration. This also contributes to the disconnect between Puerto Ricans and newer Latino groups. The current era of substantial (non–Puerto Rican) Latino immigration to New York began with the passage of the 1965 immigration bill signed by President Johnson. The bill sought to lift quotas on southern and eastern Europeans but eventuated in facilitating the influx of many Asians and Latin Americans instead. In this "New Regime," which Massey (1995) dates from 1970 to the present, Latino immigrants, especially from the Dominican Republic and Mexico, began to arrive in greater numbers.

Many of these immigrants settled in areas where earlier groups of Latinos had established themselves. For example, Washington Heights was—until recent gentrification began—so solidly identified with the Dominican community that many referred to it as "Quisqueya Heights." ("Quisqueya" refers to Hispaniola.) Yet the Washington Heights area had previously been home to large groupings of working-class and lower-middle-class Cubans, Puerto Ricans, and white ethnics, including a strong Jewish community. The South Bronx, long identified as a large Puerto Rican community, also had, in earlier periods, substantial groupings of white ethnics and African Americans, and now has large numbers of Mexicans and Dominicans, as does the larger Borough of the Bronx, and Spanish/East Harlem. In areas in Brooklyn, like Williamsburg, and in Manhattan's Lower East Side, gentrification has also altered—in some cases, erased—these long-established Puerto Rican/Latino communities, and also their histories.

Gentrification has not been the only force altering these communities. As Torres and Marzán note in chapter 4 in this volume, many Puerto Ricans ("opportunity seekers") have moved of their own accord, seeking the suburban American Dream or new employment in areas outside of New York, while others were displaced "by shrinking employment opportunities and limited affordable housing" in New York.

In essence, and as Roth (2012, 8) has indicated, "Puerto Ricans are often excluded from research on immigration and thus tend to be understudied."[17] With notable exceptions, often at the dissertation level, few works have focused on a comparison of Puerto Ricans and other immigrant groups. Many works that analyzed the new Latino immigrants to New York placed them within a transnational framework from which Puerto Ricans were omitted. They viewed them within the first-time frame, or compared them to immigrants who came from Europe at the end of the nineteenth century.

Comparative work that included Puerto Ricans was rare. Work including Puerto Ricans was also less funded and less published in mainstream outlets.[18] This was very much in contrast to the earlier research period, when Puerto Ricans were the subject of much research (Rodríguez 1995; Rodríguez, Olmedo, and Reyes-Cruz 2003).

POPULAR CULTURE AND A JOURNALISTIC EXAMPLE: *NEW YORK MAGAZINE*

Curiously, during the period when New York's Latino population was overwhelmingly Puerto Rican, even popular culture and journalistic references tended to view Puerto Ricans—correctly or not—as immigrants and not migrants. A small, but interesting, reflection of this view of Puerto Ricans as immigrants can be seen in the text and lyrics written for *West Side Story*, for example, when Anita refers disparagingly to her Puerto Rican boyfriend as an "immigrant." However, in more recent times, this omission of the Puerto Rican experience in New York has not been limited to academia, but can also be seen in more journalistic or pedestrian circles. The debut of *West Side Story* in 1958 as a Broadway play, and then in 1961 as a major film, contested the arrival of the Puerto Rican "invaders," but it made clear that Puerto Ricans had arrived.

By 1972, there was a clear, and perhaps more positive, acknowledgment of the impact of Puerto Ricans on New York. *New York Magazine*, a (if not the) premier New York magazine of its time, led with a cover story on "the big mango" and focused on the "Latin impact on New York Style"; it provided a review of the best Latin restaurants, music, and nightclubs and published a special issue dedicated to "The City's Latin Soul" (*New York Magazine*, August 7, 1972). Twenty-seven years later, this same magazine placed Jennifer Lopez on its cover and retitled its September 6, 1999 issue "Nueva York"—thus implying or heralding another major transformation in the cultural life of the city. Its featured lead story was "The Latin Explosion," which asked whether Hispanic Heat was a fad or the future. It added in the description of this story that "this summer, the country went crazy for all things Latino; New Yorkers, of course, get the best of all 22 worlds." This wording acknowledged the multicountry reality of the then-Latino community in New York, but it ignored the long history of this community there. It was as if Latinos had just suddenly burst on the New York scene as the city was about to enter the twenty-first century.

ALL GROUPS HAVE THEIR OWN HISTORY

To acknowledge the early history of the Puerto Rican community in New York does not imply that all Latinos are the same. Each national-origin community in the city has its own history; and each group has to write its own history. But should these histories be written using the "first-time frame"? What is to be gained and what is to be lost in taking this approach? Another example from popular culture is useful in providing part of an answer to the question of what is to be gained. Drug addiction and gang violence are seen by many to have originated with the arrival of Puerto Ricans, Mexicans, or today Central American gangs. But Martin Scorsese's film *Gangs of New York*, set in nineteenth-century New York, helps a large audience see that these problems or lifestyles are not solely imported by new immigrants, but rather have clear economic, political, social, and historic underpinnings. By recognizing historical antecedents, we may also better understand the desire of the new Latino immigrants to have their own parades, and to create their own sports heroes, films, literature, music, leading entertainment personalities, and political leaders. It seems that democracy is strengthened and we all benefit from knowing the more comprehensive history of which we are all a part.

NEW YORK CITY AND IMMIGRATION

How has this history of (im)migration affected New York's view of immigrants and immigration? Across most of the country, immigration is often seen as a threat and worse, but not in New York. For example, seven hundred thousand letters from all over the country—almost all negative—were delivered to congressmen who played a large role in the defeat of the immigration bill in 2007. In other parts of the country, however, we have seen the immigration issue flare up and result in the passage of bills such as Arizona's SB1070 in six states and in the consideration of similar bills in at least twenty other states. Although all of these bills were eventually dropped or successfully challenged in the courts, anti-immigration views have persisted, and as of this writing, attempts at national immigration reform have not been successful (Lacayo 2012; Khan 2011). The US Supreme Court's 2012 decision on SB1070 moved immigration from the almost-permanent back burner status it had occupied to a central issue for the 2012 and 2016 national elections. In the tight economic times of 2007 to 2011, immigration became the third rail in national politics, with few national politicians wanting to address it and major pieces of anti-immigrant legislation appearing in many states. In New York, however, immigration has been less controversial; this is despite there being large numbers of immigrants in the city. In 2011, 37.2% of the population was foreign born (Lobo and Salvo 2013, 123), and in 2010 almost half of all New Yorkers spoke a language other than English at home; an estimated 200 languages were being spoken in New York. In contrast, in the country as a whole, only about 12% of the population was foreign born in 2010, with another 11% of the population having at least one parent who was not born in the United States.

NEW YORK—FOREVER AN IMMIGRANT CITY

Perhaps the New York nonchalance on the immigration issue is due, as these numbers indicate, to the fact that there are so many immigrants here; in 2010 over three million New Yorkers were foreign born. Indeed, according to one estimate from the head of the city's planning division, immigrants and their children made up approximately 60% of the New York City population (Lobo and Salvo 2013, 198).

Or does the city have this attitude because immigrants come from so many different areas of the world, that is, Europe, Asia, Africa, and of course, Latin America? Although it may appear to the uncritical eye that all immigrants in New York are from Puebla, Mexico, or the Dominican Republic, in 2011 just 32.1% were from Latin America (i.e., South America, Central America, Mexico, and the Spanish-speaking Caribbean). This leaves 67.9% who are foreign born but not of Spanish origin (Lobo and Salvo 2013).

Or has this attitude taken hold because—contrary to our media views of immigrants as illiterate, dirt-poor wetbacks—in New York, we see and experience the fact, often on an everyday level, that immigrants are actually a very diverse group in terms of education and occupations? But then, New York has always been a mecca for the rich and highly educated from other lands, as well as for those with fewer resources but seeking greater opportunities.

But perhaps it is because New York has historically been the entry port for so many immigrants and has developed a greater—for lack of a better word—"tolerance" for immigrants. Perhaps the earlier waves of immigrants have softened and eased the entry of subsequent immigrants by creating institutions and changing laws and policies—not just in the way noted above with regard to Puerto Ricans, but in the earlier efforts of immigrants who struggled to make sure that workers could unionize; make a decent wage; have lunch, rest and vacation periods, and overtime pay; and so on.

Whatever the reasons, we do not see New York passing, or even considering, the same legislation to curtail the influx of immigrants or the freedoms of those already here—legislation that makes headlines in other areas. Indeed, the role of immigrants—except when politicians are seeking immigrant votes—is often muted in the general running of the city.[19] Also subdued, however, is the general role that immigrants play in sustaining and servicing the city's middle- and upper-class life styles, for example, as nannies, repair technicians, restaurant workers, and workers in new construction and renovation projects, to name just a few. So, generally speaking, the New York view of immigrants is that they continue to contribute to making New York viable and livable.

To be sure, many Latina/o immigrants—and nonimmigrants—have paid, and continue to pay, a price in lower wages and poor working conditions to make the city livable. Indeed, we get a glimpse of this cost when we see the large proportion of Latinos in poverty as compared with white non-Hispanics. Nonetheless, Latino and other immigrants have historically made major contributions to the revitalization of the city and continue to provide many benefits to the economy. In essence, immigrants have always built this city and they will continue to do so.

MULTICULTURALISM WITHIN A GLOBALIZED WORLD: NEW YORK AND LONDON COMPARED

New York is not the only major city in the world containing immigrants whose history has often been disconnected from the history of the city's growth. This has happened in London as well. Although many US citizens may see the capital of the United Kingdom as having a history that is ethnically homogenous, London, like New York, has long been the "port of entry" for new immigrants and has historically been a city of immigrants. As a recent article in *The Economist* notes, London, like New York, was created by foreigners. The Romans invaded the Iceni tribe and established a colony in AD 43. Although this was burnt down seventeen years later, London became "a magnet for foreigners." But the entrance of foreigners was often contested, and conflicts often arose. "Riots occurred against the Jews in the 13th century, the Flemish in the 14th, and the Italians in the 15th, and so on until the Notting Hill riots against the West Indians in 1958" (Emma Duncan, "Special Report: London on a High," *Economist*, June 30, 2012, 5). So multiculturalism has strong roots in London—even though, as in New York, it has often been marred by violence when changeovers occur.

In the present, as well, London and New York are similar, though the public perceptions of them are different. Both are global cities today. Indeed, in 2010 the *Wall Street Journal* indicated that New York was the number-one global city and London was number two (Emily Peck, "The Top Ten Most Global Cities," blog in *Wall Street Journal*, September 9, 2010). What does it mean to be ranked highly as a global city? In addition to the standard methods of evaluating the global importance of cities, which include the size of the overall economy and the concentration of support services available for multinationals, such as financial and accounting firms and efficiency and access to capital and information, this study also includes the amount of foreign direct investment that cities have attracted; the concentration of corporate headquarters; the number of particular business niches they dominated; air connectivity (the ease of travel to other global cities); the strength of producer services; financial services, technology, and media power; and racial diversity (Kotkin 2014).

New York's growth as a global city parallels that of London, not just in the way we usually think of this, that is, in the financial, cultural, and political areas, but also in its growth as a multicultural center. We—or at least those of us who do not often visit London, and who follow its life only in briefly reading headlines about royal marriages and Queen Elizabeth's long reign—tend to think of London as the home of the British monarchy, where all is purely English. However, as the 2012 Summer Olympics intimated, and as the special report in *The Economist* cited above (June 30, 2012) stated, more than a third of today's Londoners were born abroad. Additionally, the earlier waves of West Indians in the 1950s and 1960s and South Asians in the 1970s and 1980s have altered the look, landscape, and language of London, giving rise to a language that has been termed a "multicultural London English"—"a mix of Cockney, Jamaican, and other languages spoken by the young of all ethnic groups" (Duncan 2012, 7). Doesn't this sound a lot like New York? The two cities resemble each other also in terms of socioeconomic stratification, with recent arrivals concentrated at the top as well as the bottom.

In the same way that the history of Puerto Ricans in New York is often disconnected from the growth of the city, so too the impact of immigrations to London in the 1960s and 1970s seems to be muffled. For example, in the case of Puerto Ricans, the critical labor that they provided to the New York economy in the post–World War II period is seldom acknowledged. Similarly, we hear little of the contributions of West Indians and South Asians who arrived in London during the latter part of the twentieth century.

As we learn about the history of London, more similarities appear. Although many of us are familiar with the idea of New York as a city built by immigrant labor and innovation, we tend not to think of London in this way. In the same way that London's history has contributed to its growth as a major multicultural center, so, too, the history and experience of previous immigrants (including Puerto Ricans) has contributed to the growth of New York as a similar multicultural city. In other words, the multiculturalism that many of us celebrate in New York today as a twenty-first-century innovation actually has been a dominant theme throughout its history.

A NEW, MORE GLOBAL VIEW OF MULTICULTURALISMS

In the past, many Puerto Ricans and others fought for a more open and accepting multicultural New York. We likely did so with little awareness of, acknowledgment of, or even, in some cases, interest in New York's previous multiculturalism, or its relevance to us. This disconnect from the past persists among the newest or latest immigrants from all countries and among some academics, who study the current immigration as if it were related only to great waves of immigration at the end of the nineteenth century and the beginning of the twentieth. As we have noted, the immigration of Puerto Ricans and Mexicans during the middle one-third of the twentieth century (i.e., during the immigration hiatus) is often forgotten, or covered as if they had no bearing on the contemporary communities that subsequent immigrants entered.

Occasionally, however, this multicultural history and its legacies to the present are acknowledged. In this regard, I am reminded of a conversation I recently had with a friend and colleague from Colombia, South America. He had already grasped a sense of the role that Puerto Ricans have played in the evolution of New York as a continually growing multicultural city. He told me he had gone to the bank and spoken with a bilingual teller and that he had Pantoja to thank for this. While Antonia Pantoja did not fight for bilingual bank tellers, she (and many others that she worked with) did fight for the rights of non-English-speaking students to be educated and taught in their language, so that they could retain this language and also learn English.

My friend's view makes the connection, as opposed to the more common disconnect discussed above. His view may also reflect an early, growing awareness of multiculturalism as a worldwide phenomenon in which cultures are absorbed and incorporated within or from a global perspective. In this globalized world, where many are exposed to an increased amount of diversity, people eat "mofongo"[20] in Puerto Rico or Miami, escargot in Paris or Chicago; and they eat mofongo not because it is Puerto Rican or escargot because it is French, but because they like to eat them. Because of changes in technology, communications, and travel, we are all part of this increasingly multicultural reality. People may reflect on the origins of these products, but the products are not being incorporated into diets because of their origins; rather, these tastes have been acquired because they are increasingly available and valued. For the same reason, tacos, wraps, and other "ethnic" foods are being eaten by people with cultural heritages different from those in which the foods evolved; they are part of a progressively more multicultural reality. This is a reality that we all gradually and inadvertently participate in, or will participate in, because of globalization.

In the past, becoming an American citizen may have been seen as discarding one's culture, language, and previous political loyalties. However, for my friend who recently became an American citizen, that experience was a validation of multiculturalism. How so, I asked? It was the presence of all these individuals from different parts of the world, he said, and the judge's words about how my friend and these other new citizens would now be able to contribute fully to the growth of the United States: this experience validated for him what he had come to know of multicultural New York and multiculturalism, more generally. For him, multiculturalism today was a worldwide phenomenon that allowed and acknowledged the contributions of all cultures. For me, this view that embraces the past and shows its connections to the global present may be the future that we seek and teach. Such a view highlights what is common to us—as opposed to what is different. It may also be what allows us to correct and bridge the disconnect noted above and to prevent disconnects in the future.

Not only must we acknowledge that without the new immigration, New York would not have recovered from its deep economic malaise starting with the fiscal crisis of the 1970s, a point often made in the press; we must also acknowledge how the early Puerto Rican communities, and the institutions they created and opened, significantly altered the social, cultural, and political fabric of the city.[21] These, too, are part of New York's cyclical existence. If we can do this, we will not only better understand the experience of new immigrants; we will also better understand how to prepare for the city's needs in the future—as well as how it should conduct itself in its relationship with an increasingly globalized world. Immigrants will continue to make New York viable, even as the city struggles with industry shifts, poverty, fiscal problems, and its place in the ever-evolving global economy.

NOTES

1. To some degree, it has also been generally acknowledged that immigrants were themselves changed and that they changed more broadly the culture and life of Americans. Commonly cited examples are the introduction of foods, such as pizza (Italian), hot dogs (German), tacos (Mexican; also perhaps burritos), and wraps (Middle Eastern) today. How many Puerto Ricans played handball before coming to New York? Who danced to salsa music before it was developed in New York?

2. References to a bodega, as a grocery store, and not as a warehouse for wines, do appear in late nineteenth-century Spanish ads.

3. http://www.merriam-webster.com/dictionary/bodega. The word likely has even earlier origins. The editors of *Merriam-Webster's Collegiate Dictionary*, 10th edition, note the word's entry into the English language in the mid-nineteenth century and that the word is also related to the word "boutique," which refers "to a small store or shop (and more recently to a small company) and came to English from French about a century before "bodega" entered English. Both "boutique" and "bodega" are derived from the Greek *apotheke*, meaning "storehouse," with "bodega" coming by way of the Latin word *apotheca*, also meaning "storehouse." "Origin and Meaning of 'Bodegas'; 'Fiasco'; How Pretzel Got Its Strange Name," Jewish World Review, July 6, 2006, http://www.jewishworldreview.com /0706/dictionary_men070606.php3.

4. See Sánchez Korrol (1983) for descriptions of these communities. See also Haslip-Viera (2010); Vega (2010).

5. By 1874, the first Puerto Rican newspaper in New York, *La Voz de Puerto Rico*, had already been published. By the same time, the Republican societies of Cuba and Puerto Rico had established offices in Philadelphia and New York, and the first Puerto Rican civic organization was established by 1892. Some of the travel to New York occurred through New Orleans during this early period.

6. "The great migration" refers to the period between 1946 and 1964 (Stevens-Arroyo and Díaz-Stevens 1982).

7. Sources for much of the historical overview that follows are Kullen (1992); Rodríguez-Fraticelli, Sanabria, and Tirado (1991); Sánchez Korrol (1983); and Olmo (1991).

8. The categorization of these Puerto Rican "newcomers" posed and poses a quandary for many observers (Handlin 1959). Are they immigrants (which means coming from another country?) or migrants (coming from another part of *this* country)? Legally, Puerto Ricans were "migrants" after the 1917 Jones Act, which made them citizens, but in practically all other important aspects—i.e., they spoke another language, came from a non–Anglo Saxon culture, and were mostly Catholic when Protestantism dominated the United States—they were more like "immigrants." That is why I refer to them as (im)migrants (Rodríguez 1989). See also Pérez y González (2000).

9. Other Spanish-speaking immigrants from the Caribbean and elsewhere also came during this period. This included some working-class Cubans and Dominicans, but they were fewer. During this hiatus, New York also was home to many African Americans who had migrated from the south and contributed to the Harlem renaissance along with immigrants from the West Indies and other parts (Watkins-Owens 1996). Given the segregated nature of life then, many tended to live in fairly segregated areas. After the Castro takeover in 1959, many middle- and upper-class Cubans arrived in the United States, but mainly settled in Florida and New Jersey. There were also smaller migrations of Colombians and other South Americans to New York during this period.

10. For reference to the contributions of Puerto Ricans to the New York City economy during this period, see History Task Force (1979, 1983).

11. Jarvie (1991, 91) examines the ethnicities and names of major stars during the thirties, forties, and fifties and finds that not only were the names WASP, but most of the stars were white Anglo-Saxon Protestants or Roman Catholics. He argues that in addition to euphony, people were trying to avoid the ordinary and the very fancy in these waspy star names.

12. The Puerto Rican migration of the fifties also coincided with a mass hysteria about juvenile crime and a national debate about the causes of juvenile crime and solutions. Again, as the lyrics to the song "Gee, Officer Krupke!," in *West Side Story* (1961) tellingly indicated, there was also a national debate about the causes of juvenile delinquency. Were JDs the result of life circumstances, like drunken mothers, abusive fathers, and general poverty? Or were individuals to be held responsible for their illegal behavior? By the administrations of Presidents Johnson and Kennedy, a shift had occurred to a more liberal perspective, and a war had been declared on poverty (see Pérez 1997).

13. In this column, Luciano was responding to negative views of Nuyoricans by Puerto Ricans in Puerto Rico. See http://nyclatinopolitics.com/2011/06/15/701/.

14. http://www.merriam-webster.com/dictionary/transnational. There are other definitions of "transnationalism." For example, Robert Courtney Smith (2005, 210) indicates that "transnational life includes those practices and relationships linking migrants and their children with the home country, where such practices have significant meaning, are regularly carried out, and are embodied in identities and social structures that help form the life world of immigrants or their children."

15. See Waldinger and Fitzgerald (2004) for an analysis of this literature.

16. See Itzigsohn (2009), Levitt (2001, 242–81); Smith (2005).

17. On this point, see also Oropesa, Landale, and Greif (2008).

18. Although mainstream publications focusing specifically on Puerto Ricans declined with the arrival of the newer Latino immigrants, publications on Puerto Ricans by Puerto Ricans and other Latinos increased greatly in other venues. For a review of some of the historical and social science research on Puerto Ricans, see Rodríguez (1995) and Rodríguez, Olmedo, and Reyes-Cruz (2003).

19. This is not to say that New York and its surroundings are without anti-immigrant sentiments. New York did reject a proposal to issue driver's licenses for the undocumented. There has also been anti-immigrant violence on Long Island. (On this, see the documentary *Farmingville*, http://farmingvillethemovie.com.) The DREAM Act was also rejected by the New York State Legislature at one point.

20. Mofongo is a Puerto Rican dish made of mashed yucca, plantains, and/or green bananas and pork crackling, garlic, and other spices. It can be eaten with a sauce, often of seasoned chicken broth; however, shrimp or other meats or seafood can also be served as part of it.

21. The present chapter has underscored some positives that can be derived from examining sociohistorical considerations. However, legacies may also be negative—as Diaz McConnell's (2010) work on "sundown towns" illustrates. Examining the racialized history of former sundown towns, where it was understood that after sundown, Blacks were not to be present, she asks whether, paradoxically, this history of excluding nonwhites may have played a role in the spatial configurations and continuing separation of Latinos and non-Hispanic whites. She notes, "Scholars investigating the contemporary processes of Latino population growth in 'new' destinations, both in metropolitan and nonmetropolitan areas, may want to explore the importance of socio-historical considerations, particularly localities' racialized historical contexts before the arrival of Mexican and other Latino immigrants."

REFERENCES

Acosta-Belén, E., M. Benítez, J. E. Cruz, Y. González-Rodríguez, C. Rodríguez, C. E. Santiago, A. Santiago-Rivera, and B. R. Sjostrom. 2000. *"Adiós, Borinquen querida": La diáspora puertorriqueña, su historia y sus aportaciones.*

Also published in English as *Adiós, Borinquen Querida: The Puerto Rican Diaspora, Its History, and Contributions*. Albany: Center for Latin American, Caribbean, and U.S. Latino Studies, State University of New York at Albany.

Aranda, Elizabeth. 2007. "Struggles of Incorporation among the Puerto Rican Middle Class." *Sociological Quarterly* 48: 199–228.

DeSipio, Louis, and Adrian D. Pantoja. 2007. "Puerto Rican Exceptionalism? A Comparative Analysis of Puerto Rican, Mexican, Salvadoran, and Dominican Transnational Civic and Political Ties." In *Latino Politics: Identity, Mobilization, and Representation*, edited by Rodolfo Espino, David L. Leal, and Kenneth J. Meier, 104–20. Charlottesville: University Press of Virginia.

Diaz McConnell, Eileen. 2010. "Racialized Histories and Contemporary Population Dynamics in the 'New' South." In *Being Brown in Dixie: Race, Ethnicity, and Latino Immigration in the New South*, edited by Cameron Lippard and Charles Gallagher, 77–98. Boulder, CO: Lynne Rienner / First Forum Press.

Duany, Jorge. 2010a. "To Send or Not to Send: Migrant Remittances in Puerto Rico, the Dominican Republic, and Mexico." *The Annals of the American Academy of Political and Social Science* 630: 205–23.

———. 2010b. "A Transnational Colonial Migration: Puerto Rico's Farm Labor Program," *New West Indian Guide / Nieuwe West-Indische Gids* 84 (3 & 4): 225–51.

Flores, William Vincent, and Rina Benmayor. 1997. *Latino Cultural Citizenship: Claiming Identity, Space, and Rights*. Boston: Beacon Press.

Handlin, Oscar. 1959. *The Newcomers: Negroes and Puerto Ricans in a Changing Metropolis*. Cambridge, MA: Harvard University Press.

Haslip-Viera, Gabriel. 2010. "The Evolution of the Latino Community in New York: Nineteenth Century to Late Twentieth Century." In *Hispanic New York: A Sourcebook*, edited by Claudio Iván Remeseira, 33–55. New York: Columbia University Press.

History Task Force, Centro de Estudios Puertorriqueños, ed. 1979. *Labor Migration under Capitalism: The Puerto Rican Experience*. New York: Monthly Review Press.

———. 1983. "Sources for the Study of Puerto Rican Migration, 1879–1930." New York: Centro de Estudios Puertorriqueños, Hunter College, City University of New York.

Itzigsohn, José. 2009. *Encountering American Faultlines: Race, Class, and the Dominican Experience in Providence*. New York: Russell Sage Foundation.

Jarvie, Ian C. 1991. "Stars and Ethnicity: Hollywood and the United States, 1932–1951." In *Unspeakable Images: Ethnicity and the American Cinema*, edited by Lester D. Friedman, 82–111. Urbana: University of Illinois Press.

Khan, Huma. 2011. "Politics Immigration Wars: More States Looking at Arizona-Style Laws . . . 2010 Saw Record Number of Immigration Laws, 2011 Projected to Surpass That." *ABC News*, March 4.

Kotkin, Joel. 2014. "The World's Most Influential Cities." Reinventing America, *Forbes*, August 14, http://www.forbes.com/sites/joelkotkin/2014/08/14/the -most-influential-cities-in-the-world/.

Kullen, Allan S. 1992. *The Peopling of America: A Timeline of Events That Helped Shape Our Nation*. Washington, DC: Americans All and the Portfolio Project.

Lacayo, A. Elena. 2012. *The Wrong Approach: State Anti-Immigration Legislation in 2011*. Washington, DC: National Council of La Raza. http://publications .nclr.org/bitstream/handle/123456789/1131/The_Wrong_Approach_Anti -ImmigrationLeg.pdf?sequence=1&isAllowed=y.

Levitt, Peggy. 2001. *The Transnational Villagers*. Berkeley: University of California Press.

Lobo, Arun Peter, and Joseph Salvo. 2013. *The Newest New Yorkers: Characteristics of the City's Foreign-Born Population*. New York: City of New York, Department of City Planning, Population Division. December. https://www1.nyc.gov/site /planning/data-maps/nyc-population/newest-new-yorkers-2013.page.

Luciano, Felipe. 2011. "A New Deal between Stateside and Island Puerto Ricans: The View from a New York 'Rican," *National Institute for Latino Policy Newsletter*, guest commentary, March 30, 2011.

Massey, Douglas S. 1995. "The New Immigration and Ethnicity in the United States." *Population and Development Review* 21 (3): 631–52.

Morris, Nancy. 1995. *Puerto Rico: Culture, Politics and Identity*. Westport, CT: Greenwood Press.

Olmo, José. 1991. "Puerto Rican History: 500 Years in Brief," part of the "Puerto Rican Heritage Month Cultural Guide" in a special supplement to the *Daily News* (New York), November 3, 1991.

Oropesa, R. S., Nancy S. Landale, and Meredith Greif. 2008. "From Puerto Rican to Pan-Ethnic in New York City," *Ethnic and Racial Studies* 31: 1315–39.

Park, Robert, Ernest W. Burgess, and Roderick D. McKenzie. *The City*. Chicago: University of Chicago Press, 1925.

Pérez, Richie. 1997. "From Assimilation to Annihilation: Puerto Rican Images in U.S. Films." In *Latin Looks: Latina and Latino Images in the U.S. Media*, edited by Clara E. Rodríguez, 142–63. Boulder, CO: Westview Press.

Pérez y González, María. 2000. *Puerto Ricans in the United States*. Westport, CT: Greenwood Press.

Roberts, Sam. 2006. "Immigrants Swell Numbers near New York." *New York Times*, August 15.

Rodríguez, Clara E. 1989. "The Circulating Migration Thesis." *Journal of Hispanic Policy* 3 (1988–89): 5–9.

———. 1993. "Puerto Rican Circular Migration: Revisited." *Latino Studies Journal* 2 (2): 93–113.

———. 1995. "Puerto Ricans in Historical and Social Science Research." In *Handbook of Research on Multicultural Education*, edited by James A. Banks, 223–44. New York: Macmillan.

Rodríguez, Clara E., Irma M. Olmedo, and Mariolga Reyes-Cruz. 2003. "Deconstructing and Contextualizing the Historical and Social Science Literature on Puerto Ricans." In *The Handbook of Research on Multicultural Education*, edited by James A. Banks and Cherry A. McGee Banks, 288–314. New York: Jossey-Bass.

Rodríguez-Fraticelli, Carlos, Carlos Sanabria, and Amilcar Tirado. 1991. "Puerto Rican Nonprofit Organizations in New York City." In *Hispanics and the Nonprofit Sector*, edited by Herman E. Gallegos and Michael O'Neill, 33–48. New York: The Foundation Center.

Roth, Wendy D. 2012. *Race Migrations: Latinos and the Cultural Transformation of Race*. Stanford, CA: Stanford University Press.

Sánchez, María E. and Antonio M. Stevens-Arroyo. 1987. *Toward a Renaissance of Puerto Rican Studies: Ethnic and Area Studies in University Education*. Highland Lakes, NJ: Atlantic Research and Publications, Inc. Atlantic Studies on Society in Change, Boulder, CO: Social Science Monographs (Distributed by Columbia University Press).

Sánchez Korrol, Virginia. 1983. *From Colonia to Community: The History of Puerto Ricans in New York City, 1917–1948*. Westport, CT: Greenwood Press.

Smith, Robert Courtney. 2005. "Globalization and Transnationalism." In *The Oxford Encyclopedia of Latinos and Latinas in the United States*, edited by Suzanne Oboler and Deena J. González, 2:209–15. Oxford: Oxford University Press.

Stevens-Arroyo, Antonio, and Ana María Díaz-Stevens. 1982. "Puerto Ricans in the States: A Struggle for Identity." In *The Minority Report: An Introduction to Racial, Ethnic, and Gender Relations*, edited by Anthony G. Dworkin and Rosalind J. Dworkin, 196–232. 2nd ed. New York: CBS College Publishing / Holt, Rinehart & Winston.

Vargas-Ramos, Carlos. 2012. "Chasing the Bandwagon: Puerto Rican Migration and the Pursuit of Transnationalism—Let That *Carreta* Go!" Paper presented at the 31st International Congress of the Latin American Studies Association, San Francisco, May 23–26, 2012.

Vega, Bernardo. 2010. "Memoirs of Bernardo Vega: A Contribution to the History of the Puerto Rican Community in New York." In *Hispanic New York: A Sourcebook*, edited by Claudia Iván Remeseira, 71–105. New York: Columbia University Press.

Waldinger, Roger, and David Fitzgerald. 2004. "Transnationalism in Question." *American Journal of Sociology* 109 (5): 1177–95.

Watkins-Owens, Irma. 1996. *Blood Relations: Caribbean Immigrants and the Harlem Community, 1900–1930*. Bloomington: Indiana University Press.

CHAPTER THREE

Latinos and Religion in New York City

Continuities and Changes

ANA MARÍA DÍAZ-STEVENS

With an estimated population of 8,550,405 persons, New York City is not only the largest city in the nation but a busy, complicated metropolitan center, whose diversity is reflected in terms of social class, racial composition, language preference, and the cultural and religious background of its inhabitants. It is a city of believers professing many religious faiths and traditions, but it is also a city with an increasing number of people who are either nonbelievers or religiously unaffiliated. Trying to accurately identify Hispanics with particular denominations or religious bodies within this city sometimes proves problematic, as some simultaneously practice and demonstrate adherence to more than one religious group. In the case of Puerto Ricans, for example, there is a common saying that Puerto Ricans are not so much a religious people but a people seeking a religious experience. It is not surprising, then, that religious shifting is common. Interestingly, the Bronx, where the largest proportion of Hispanics—the majority of them Puerto Ricans—live, is also the most Catholic borough. In general, however, Hispanics can be found in all Christian denominations as well as in non-Christian religions. They can be found worshiping in their own language in particularized parishes, congregations, or houses of prayer, or as integrated groups within the larger community of the faithful.

New York City is the US urban center with the highest number of foreign-born residents, surpassing Los Angeles and Miami. Among the immigrant population are people from all parts of Europe, Asia, and Africa along with a continuous flow of immigrants from the Caribbean and Latin America, especially from the Spanish-speaking parts. To these immigrants can be added a constant flow of "revolving-door" migrants from Puerto Rico who, though sharing some of the immigrant experience, are also US citizens (hence, technically migrants). Whether immigrants or migrants, the people known as Hispanics or Latinos in the United States come mostly seeking better economic, social, and political conditions; a few may have come for the adventure of a new setting. Among these immigrants and migrants are a large number of laborers from villages and large cities of the Hispanic world as well as a smaller but increasing number of professionals. The present migration from Puerto Rico, for example, represents what sociologists term "a brain drain"; that is, a large number of the Puerto Rican migrants of recent decades are highly educated individuals in contrast to early migration flows from the island, who overrepresented movement from the hinterland.

Not all Latinos are newcomers. The Puerto Rican migration began shortly after the United States took possession of the island in 1898. It picked up after the United States granted Puerto Ricans citizenship, and Puerto Rican men were inducted into the US army in 1917. The migration stream brought many thousands of Puerto Ricans as a floating labor force during the two decades between the end of World War II and the Voting Rights Act of 1965. Prior to the massive Puerto Rican migration, however, there were other Hispanic immigrants. Though fewer, Spanish immigrants from the European mainland as well as from the Balearic and Canary Islands took root in the city and were already actively engaged in commerce during the second part of the nineteenth century. Migration from Puerto Rico and immigration from Spanish-speaking Latin America, the Caribbean, Spain, and its islands have continued uninterrupted during the twentieth and twenty-first centuries with no sign of abating. For this reason, I prefer to use the term "Hispanic/Latino" rather than just "Latino,"[1] though occasionally I have used them interchangeably.

Although what I have called elsewhere a "Pioneer Puerto Rican Migration" can be dated back to the beginning of the twentieth century,[2] the "Puerto Rican Great Migration (post–WW II)," emptying approximately 40% of the entire Puerto Rican island population onto the shores of New York, would, in some ways, represent the greatest migratory flow of the twentieth century. It has been argued that it not only compares with but surpasses (if not in raw numbers at least in terms of percentage) the Potato Famine Irish immigration of the nineteenth century. The rapid commercialization of air travel made it possible for this Caribbean migration to be followed by considerable numbers of Dominicans, Cubans, and Central and South Americans who also came to New York escaping economic disaster or political upheaval. Because some who arrive are citizens (namely Puerto Ricans), some enter with student or worker visas, and still others enter illegally or do not return home after their visas have lapsed, it is difficult for census workers to count every person of Hispanic background. This, and other problems, often result in undercounts of the Hispanic population in the city and elsewhere in the United States. It is not surprising that when the 2010 official figure for the Hispanic/Latino city population was placed at 2,336,076, many contested this figure as well as the one for the entire city population. Even the mayor of New York, Michael R. Bloomberg, claimed an undercount of certain areas of the city. Figures for the total city population were placed at 8,244,910 and reestimated at 8,391,881 in 2011, making New York the most populous city in the nation. Even using the 8,244,910 figure, 28.6% or 2,358,044 were of Hispanic origin; thus, New York has one of the highest concentrations of Hispanics in the nation.[3]

Furthermore, the various cultures and nationalities represented in the city's eight-million-plus inhabitants make it one of the most ethnically rich and cosmopolitan cities in the world;[4] and that diversity is also represented within the Hispanic/Latino community in terms of racial composition, nationality, and economics. The city, for example, has the largest Puerto Rican population outside of Puerto Rico as well as the largest Dominican population in the United States. While increasingly large numbers of these two Hispanic subgroups are dispersing to other cities and states, more recent arrivals from Mexico and other Latin American countries are rapidly increasing in our area. In summary, people tracing their origin to every Spanish-speaking country can be found in New York City; and for more than 13% of the city's population, the language spoken at home is Spanish.[5] These facts strengthen the claim that if there is a Hispanic/Latino reality in the United States, New York is where that reality finds its most diverse expression.

RELIGIOUS MEMBERSHIP IN NEW YORK: QUANTITY AND QUALITY

According to the Maps and Reports section of the website of the Association of Religion Data Archives (ARDA), as of October 2, 2010, New York State is the fifth-most-religious state—surpassed by only Louisiana, Mississippi, Utah, and North Dakota. Both New York State and New York City's overall diversity extends to religious composition, with Christianity being the largest religious group. Claiming more than 40% of all religious adherents, the Catholic Church is not only the largest Christian denomination but the largest religious institution in New York. ARDA reports 30% for Protestants, 8.4% for Jews, 3.5% for Muslims, 1.0% for Buddhists and a significant 13% who prefer to identify as nonaffiliated. Within Protestantism, the three largest denominations are United Methodists (with 403,362), American Baptists (with 203,297), and Episcopalians (with 201,797).

The city differs from the nation and even the state in significant ways in terms of religion. With 62% of all religious adherents claiming to be Roman Catholics, the city contrasts sharply with New York State and the country as a whole. The city is also much more Jewish than all the other states, with 22% for New York City versus 4.3% for the entire nation. Even Muslims and the various Eastern Orthodox Churches are better represented in New York City. While the numbers indicate that only 0.5% of all people in the United States attend mosques, in New York 2.4% do—almost five times as many. More interestingly, the religious pattern varies throughout the city. The Bronx and Staten Island claim high proportions of Catholics, while Brooklyn, Queens, and Manhattan have the highest concentrations of Jews and Muslims. And while Manhattan leads in mainline Protestants, Brooklyn leads in Evangelical Protestants.[6]

Reflecting on the numbers listed above, scholars of religion in New York City know that any study of this metropolis must include the Catholic Church, the largest of the Christian churches in New York, and the Puerto Ricans, who have made the most significant of the mass migrations in the twentieth century. What is less certain is that most would begin that study of Latino religion with the 1511 papal decree *Romanus Pontifex* issued by Pope Julius II, authorizing the church in the Western Hemisphere.

The Roman Catholic bishop Alonso Manso arrived at the newly constituted Apostolic See in Puerto Rico in December of 1513, to create an institutional church on the American side of the world. Since Manso's arrival on that small Caribbean island preceded Martin Luther's split with the Catholic

Church and the beginning of the Protestant Reformation, Puerto Rico can claim the distinction of being the door through which the institution of Christianity officially entered the newly "discovered" territories,[7] when creating the first three New World dioceses.[8] If the importance of this event eludes us, we should recognize that by the time the Pilgrims landed at Plymouth Rock on the North American continent, the Christian faith had approximately a century to take root and grow in what was then a Spanish colony and is now a Caribbean territory under the US flag.

Furthermore, Catholic evangelization included the native peoples of America, whereas the Pilgrims professed a faith that generally excluded conversion and intermarriage with the indigenous peoples. The overtones of the English word "half-breed" are negative, while the Spanish word "*mestizo*," which means the same thing, has become a label of pride in many Latin American nations along with "*mulato*" and "*moreno*," which indicate an African component in the racial mixture.

The mixture of races in Latin America was accompanied by a mixture of culture and religious sentiment, since the people that Columbus and subsequent conquistadors and colonizers encountered were not a godless people. When Christianity was introduced to the New World, indigenous systems of belief were already in place. In fact, to varying degrees, characteristics of these systems have persisted either as a challenge or a complement to Christianity. More recently, groups of people within the Caribbean, Central and South America, and even Latinos in diaspora have reverted to or reconstructed these indigenous religious practices and worldviews, with the people calling themselves Neo-Taínos and those in the Southwest who have revived a host of religious practices and traditions traceable to Pueblo Indians, Aztecs, and other Native American groups.

With the importation of slaves, African-based beliefs and practices were introduced and transformed in the Americas, notably among Cubans, Brazilians, and Haitians. In the nineteenth century, French Spiritism, from the teaching of Allan Kardec, reached Puerto Rico and other areas of Latin America. In Puerto Rico, the mainline Protestant denominations[9] came on the heels of the Spanish-American War, and Pentecostalism was brought in by the first wave of returned Puerto Rican migrant workers from Hawaii around the period of the First World War. In the aftermath of the Cuban Revolution of 1959, the Afro-Cuban religion of *Santería* made an impact not only in Puerto Rico but among Puerto Ricans in the United States and other

Latinos in the diaspora. As Andrés Pérez y Mena documents, in New York, Santería and *Espiritismo* meshed to offer yet another religious expression to the Latino community, which some have called *Santerismo*.[10]

Among Latinos are also smaller numbers of followers of Judaism, particularly among Argentines and Cubans; there are also followers of various forms of neo-paganism such as WICCA and other New Age religious expressions and "earth religions." Latinos have also meshed the practices of *Curanderismo* from Central and South America with the *Santigüerismo* of the Canary Islands and other practices related to the use of herbs, foretelling the future, exorcising, and communication with the spirits of the dead. Buddhism, Hinduism, and other Eastern religions, though in smaller numbers, are also represented in the Latino community, along with the emergence of Latino Muslims as a significant religious group.

In summary, the religion that has been brought to New York by Spaniards, Puerto Ricans, and other Latinos over centuries has been shaped to be a special brand of Catholicism with admixtures from various sources. The diversity implicit in these religious expressions is a profoundly Latin American cultural product, reflecting centuries of interaction with different racial groups that produced a religious sentiment significantly divergent from the religious sentiment that rooted the Pilgrim origins of North American Protestantism. Because of its amazing porosity, Latino religion has continually been able to absorb new and varied expressions into its fabric of belief. The journey to New York City enhanced, rather than reversed this capacity; and this is the premise for the following review of Latino religion in New York.

THE ROLE OF CATHOLICISM IN THE FORMATION OF THE HISPANIC/LATINO COMMUNITY

Notwithstanding the diversity and complexity of religious affiliation among Hispanics/Latinos, Christianity in all its variants is the largest religious system to which they adhere, with Catholicism, as pointed out above, claiming the largest percentage; according to diverse surveys, figures range from 67% to 70%.[11] The historical strength of Catholicism among people of the New World in terms both of number and depth of spirituality is explainable in part by the nature of the Spanish missionary enterprise. As the late Fordham sociologist Fr. Joseph P. Fitzpatrick pointed out:

Emphasis on the conquest as a pursuit of gold and glory is sometimes exaggerated to a point that obscures the fact that the conquistadores also had God very much in mind. To a Spaniard, whether conquistador or not, the Catholic faith was the one true faith, the most important thing for which a man should live or die, and the most important gift he could give to another. The conquistadores had strange ideas about how the faith should be given to others, but they were determined to pass it on to the indigenous people they met in the New World. As a consequence, they created communities in which the Catholic faith was communicated together with the Spanish language, colonial organization, and economy.[12]

Further, with the onset of the Protestant Reformation, shortly after Christianity was introduced in the New World, the new followers were perceived by Catholic missionaries and the Catholic Church in general as the remedy to the consequences of the schism. In other words, the newly incorporated communities of indigenous Catholics would come to fill the vacuum left behind by those who had departed from the Catholic faith. Thus, the Caribbean and Latin America served both as a field for expansion and laboratory for experimentation not only in terms of commerce, technology, and governance but also in terms of religion. Christianity was transformed, acquiring new characteristics depending on regional and cultural particularities. This transformation continues, and continues to invigorate the established Latino communities in the United States as they are challenged and enriched by the new waves of immigrants.

AFRO-CARIBBEAN RELIGIONS

A number of religious traditions originating in Africa, brought and transformed in the New World, have also appeared in this country, particularly with the advent of the Cuban Revolution and the subsequent heavy influx of Cubans to Puerto Rico and the US mainland. *La Regla Lucumí*, *La Regla de Ocha*, Worship of the *Orishas*, Yoruba Religion, and Santería are names often given to Afro-Caribbean religious practices. To these can be added *Palo Mayombe*, which many have called "the darker side of Santería," *Voudou* from Haiti, *Gagá* from the Dominican Republic, *Candomblé* from Brazil, and other admixtures of these practices.

Recently, a number of scholarly works have been published on these religions, and it has been claimed that rather than viewing them as exotic or primitive, modern people have embraced and are embracing these religious practices.[13] It has also been claimed that Santería has been transformed in such a way as to constitute a new Afro-Caribbean religion in its own right. In New York, as Andrés Pérez y Mena points out, these practices are yet further transformed.[14] Once attached to Catholic beliefs and practices, at least among some followers of Santería in the United States, the religion now struggles to rid itself of any Catholic residues.

It is difficult to determine how many people actually practice Santería in the United States, particularly given that many of the followers maintain secrecy regarding their involvement. Migene González-Wippler claims millions of practitioners in Latin America and the United States,[15] but other estimates are more conservative.

The presence and strength of Santería and other African-origin religions is evident in the many *casas*, or houses of worship, and *botánicas* (herbal and religious paraphernalia shops) dispersed throughout the city as well as in a growing number of people who are initiated or at least dabble in the religion. Further, scholars and practitioners point out that Santería is no longer confined to the Cuban or Hispanic/Latino community, but it is also finding its way into the English-speaking community and claiming members from all the social classes.[16]

EARLY PRESENCE OF HISPANIC/LATINO CATHOLICS IN NEW YORK

Besides claiming both the largest portion of Christians and the largest segment of all religious followers in New York, the Catholic Church claims the faithfulness of the majority of the Latino/Hispanic community, though they are hardly represented in the hierarchical structures of the church.[17] Thus, this article will highlight the apostolate or ministry of this church to this community.

Hispanics/Latinos influenced New York Catholicism early in the city's postcolonial history through the administration of Fr. Félix Varela (1787–1853). Born in Cuba, Father Varela was in Spain as a representative of Spanish-ruled Cuba when King Ferdinand VII disbanded Parliament; Varela then fled Spain in 1823 after being sentenced to death for his support for independence and the abolition of slavery in Cuba. Sailing from Gibraltar, he came to the United States and resided in Baltimore and Philadelphia before settling in New York. Once in New York, he founded the Church of the Transfiguration on Mott Street in what now is Chinatown; and there he established the city's first parochial school. In 1837, Father Varela became the Vicar General for the Diocese of New York, which at that time covered all of New York State and the northern half of New Jersey.

In New York he worked both within the church and in social movements to improve the life of newly arrived immigrants from the Spanish-speaking world. He founded the first Spanish-language newspaper in the United States and used it as a vehicle for his ideas about religious tolerance, education, and human rights. During his tenure as Vicar General of the New York Catholic Church, the city was experiencing a large influx of Irish immigrants. So Father Varela, already fluent in Spanish and English, also learned Gaelic to better communicate with those Irish immigrants who were uncomfortable expressing themselves in the language of their colonizers. A well-educated man, Varela also served the church as professor of theology at St. Mary's Seminary when he lived in Baltimore.

EARLY RESPONSE OF THE CATHOLIC CHURCH TO HISPANICS/LATINOS

The Catholic Church the world over is divided into dioceses. In the United States each diocese is centered in a city or, in the case of New York, a group of boroughs within a city. The dioceses are composed of neighborhood parishes, often called territorial parishes. In practice, the territorial parishes in the Northeast were often dominated by the Irish, who had arrived in this country with experience of the Anglo-Saxon world and knowledge of the English language. They were also accompanied by priests from their homeland. While back in Ireland the English language and culture were most likely felt as an imposition, it is probable that they played a different role in the States, by giving the Irish an easier assimilation as "Americans" than was the case for most other groups. Irish clergy, who staffed many of the territorial parishes, outnumbered other ethnic groups both in terms of ordinary clergy and bishops, and thus held much control and political influence in their hands.[18]

Added to the territorial parishes were an ever-increasing number of national parishes, serving particular ethnic or language groups. These were most often ministered to by clergy from religious congregations or orders based in the group's homeland rather than by diocesan (also called "secular") priests from New York.[19] In 1902, the Archdiocese of New York (which does not include Brooklyn and Queens) had thirteen German churches, two French, one Bohemian, four Polish, one Maronite, two Slovak, one Hungarian, eleven Italian, and one Spanish.

The national parishes represented certain advantages and disadvantages both to the archdiocese and to the parishes themselves. On the positive side, the clergy assigned to them knew the language and customs of those they served. The diocese did not have to invest its diocesan priests or expend its financial resources, since the parishes were self-sufficient; they were supported by their members. What this meant in practice was that these national parishes were left to fend for themselves and with no direct participation in diocesan governance. While this gave them a certain level of freedom, on the negative side, they exercised far less influence in the institutional church and general society.

It was expected that over time, the national parishes would cease to exist as their members became Americanized and joined the territorial parishes. Most sociologists still maintain that the national parishes allowed the immigrants a continuity of cultural and religious expression while they integrated into the receiving society; hence, they did not have to sacrifice a cohesive group identity. It can also be argued that both territorial and national parishes aimed to provide for an Americanizing of Catholicism rather than allowing Americanization for the immigrants to mean becoming Protestants.

In the mid-nineteenth century, most of the Spanish-speaking immigrants in New York were exiles or merchants. The first Catholic parish that was to minister to them as an ethnic group would be founded in 1859 through a series of mergers including St. Peter, St. Paul, and Our Lady of Pilar. This last church, however, was located in Congress Street in Brooklyn, and thus was outside of the archdiocese since Brooklyn was made a separate diocese in 1853.

Pastoral attention towards Puerto Ricans included a synod, celebrated in Puerto Rico in 1917, also the year a unilateral act of Congress gave Puerto Ricans US citizenship. In New York, settlement houses administered by the Catholic Church were established. The best known among these was Casita Maria, which first opened in Harlem in 1934 and later moved to the Bronx.

Yet the first pastoral initiative directed toward the Spanish-speaking population was neither the 1917 synod nor the start of settlement houses. That first step towards ministering to the Spanish-speaking was taken in

1902 by Cardinal John M. Farley when Our Lady of Guadalupe Church on West 14th Street between 7th and 8th Avenues in Manhattan was designated as a Spanish National Parish. As with other national parishes in the archdiocese, La Guadalupe was intended as a temporary service under the control, but beyond the financial responsibility, of the archdiocese. With a number of Spanish merchants around 14th Street and a continuous Puerto Rican migration that was unaccompanied by native priests, it seemed proper to the archdiocesan authorities to assign the Augustinians of the Assumption, or Assumptionists, from Spain, to the chapel. According to Fr. Robert L. Stern, J.C.D., Director of the Archdiocesan Office of the Spanish-Speaking Apostolate in the early 1970s, at its beginning, the primary mission of La Guadalupe was to serve the Spaniards living in the vicinity, and secondarily it was to serve all other Spanish-speaking residents of New York.[20] What united these groups was not nationality but language. Thus, Puerto Ricans were not the specific focus of this archdiocesan initiative, a fact that highlights one of the key differences in the national parish of the Spanish-speaking compared to most other ethnic groups in New York. With the exception of the German-language parishes, which mixed Austrian with German nationals, virtually every other linguistic group was also a distinct nationality. Even if one could argue that the early Italian immigration before the establishment of the kingdom in the 1860s did not come from a nation, this circumstance was only temporary, whereas for Puerto Ricans, it would be permanent. In fact, for church purposes, Puerto Ricans, Cubans, Argentines, Mexicans, Dominicans, Spaniards, and so on are still lumped together as "Hispanics." As Father Stern rightly points out: "The concept of a Spanish 'national' parish is somewhat anomalous. For most nationalities, there is a coincidence between national and linguistic identity. In the case of Spanish speaking peoples there are twenty different nationalities."[21]

Though the Spanish-speaking population continued to grow in the first decades of the twentieth century, of the thirty-five national parishes serving different national groups in the Roman Catholic Archdiocese of New York in 1902, only one was Spanish, the aforementioned Our Lady of Guadalupe. As the Hispanic population grew, more parishes to minister to them were needed. Cardinals Farley and Hayes authorized Our Lady of Esperanza in 1912 (like La Guadalupe, served by the Assumptionists), La Milagrosa in 1925, and Holy Agony in 1930 (the last two served by the Vicentians of Madrid). The first two chapels were located in Upper Manhattan's West Side, and Holy Agony was located in East Harlem. The small Church of the Most

Holy Crucifix, built in 1925 for the Italian community, eventually also became home to the Puerto Ricans and Hispanics of the area and would continue serving them until June 15, 2005. On that date, Cardinal Edward Egan declared it the Roman Catholic Chapel of San Lorenzo Ruiz, the "Official Church of the Filipinos."

TOWARDS A NEW HISPANIC APOSTOLATE

In 1939, Cardinal Francis J. Spellman named Redemptorist priests to serve the largely Puerto Rican Catholic population at St. Cecilia's parish in East Harlem. This move was significant because the Redemptorists had previously worked in Puerto Rico. Since Puerto Ricans lacked their own clergy, the Redemptorists seemed to be the best choice for a new urban missionary approach to this group. The cardinal's decision to focus on the Puerto Rican experience was prescient because of the massive number of Puerto Ricans who began migrating to the city immediately following the end of World War II. This migration continued apace until the mid-sixties, when the new Civil Rights Act and immigration law radically altered the political power of minorities and reshaped immigration patterns. In fact, during the period between 1946 and 1964, "the Puerto Rican Great Migration" recorded a total exodus of more than six hundred thousand Puerto Ricans.[22] The pastoral measures adopted for the Puerto Ricans after 1940 may be said to have been the first innovative initiatives for Hispanic Catholics in New York history[23] and on a par with the church's response to the nineteenth-century Irish immigration and the changes that ensued.

The intent to use the national parishes as a springboard towards Americanization of European immigrants had been successful. By the 1950s, many of the national or linguistic parishes had lost their congregations to assimilation, age, and residential mobility. Cardinal Spellman and others after him expected the same would be true for the Puerto Ricans and other Spanish-language groups. It would be just a matter of time, they thought, when even the five Spanish-language parishes would cease and would be fully integrated as diocesan parishes with no need for special services in the Spanish language. However, having so many Hispanic/Latino nationalities under one roof meant conflicts of culture, history, and class which impeded the kind of unifying process around a national identity that had been part of the national-parish experience of other groups.[24]

The archdiocese faced a dilemma. One one hand, it saw the need to al-locate special resources and personnel to minister to the growing number of Hispanics/Latinos, yet on the other, it could ill afford to give each sub-Hispanic/Latino group special attention. To complicate matters for the arch-diocese, the period immediately following the Second World War made air transportation widely affordable and made migration now possible for thou-sands of hinterland Puerto Ricans and other Spanish-speaking people clearly in need of the church's services.

Well aware of this migration flow in the 1950s, the Archdiocese of New York decided to test a new ministerial approach rather than increase the number of linguistic parishes for the Spanish-speaking. While keeping the five Spanish-language parishes in place, after consulting with clergy (e.g., scholar-father Joseph P. Fitzpatrick, S.J., and scholar-activist Ivan Illich) and Spanish-speaking community leaders (among them a Puerto Rican poet who was one of the original organizers of the first San Juan Fiesta, Juan Avilés, and community organizer Encarnación Padilla de Armas), the then archbishop of New York, Francis Cardinal Spellman, introduced the notion of integrated parish. Basically, the integrated parish would use the existing territorial parishes to incorporate the Puerto Rican and Hispanic/Latino faithful as part of the overall congregation but offer them special ministries to serve their needs. As a first measure, Spanish priests, mostly from reli-gious congregations, were invited to join the parish staff, even if temporarily. The Puerto Rican and other Spanish-speaking faithful were invited to be-come members of these parishes and to contribute to their activities and maintenance by whatever means available. As members of the integrated parishes, they were allowed to use parish facilities, but preference was invari-ably given to the English-speaking group both in services and resources. This happened even when the numbers of Puerto Ricans and other Hispan-ics/Latinos were greater and their parish activities better organized, which increasingly was the case. In the first postwar decades, the Puerto Ricans in the archdiocese outnumbered all other Hispanic/Latino groups taken to-gether. Nationally, they were only outnumbered by Mexican Americans, who had become part of the United States when this nation took over their lands by armed conflict, through land purchase, or through other negotia-tions in the nineteenth century.

Without the benefit of a native Puerto Rican clergy, the archdiocese saw the need to train its own clergy in the Spanish language and in Puerto Rican culture. Thus was established the Institute of Intercultural Communications in Ponce, Puerto Rico, in consortium with the Catholic University in that city. However, by this time large numbers of other immigrants from the Spanish-speaking Caribbean and from Central and South America were rapidly settling in the Northeast; and the archdiocese continued to face the challenge of Hispanic/Latino diversity. One of the results of this diversity was an emerging dissatisfaction with the notion that when it came to the Hispanic/Latino community, "one size fits all." The emerging questions were as follows: Could North American clergy trained in Puerto Rican culture adequately serve the increasing numbers of Central and South Americans? Were the needs of newcomers the same as those who had been settled for years, even decades? What common characteristics might be used to bring the diverse Hispanic/Latino groups into one fold?

In terms of utilizing existing facilities and personnel, the integrated parish was an improvement over the national-parish approach. In many parishes, Hispanic/Latino parishioners learned to live and work with each other so that, in fact, a new Catholic Hispanic/Latino experience began to emerge. It could be argued that in the Northeast, particularly in New York, the most authentic "Hispanic/Latino" reality began to take root since it was here where the diversity of Spanish-speaking groups from Spain, Central America, South America, and the Spanish-speaking Caribbean was most clearly experienced. And it was the church that gave them a place to meet Sunday after Sunday and often during the week as well. Together these groups carved out a niche for themselves in the basements of churches where they worshiped and organized, unimpeded by English-speaking parishioners. In many cases, with even fewer resources, they became better organized and showed greater vitality than the English-speaking congregations. A by-product was greater participation of the laity in the work of the church, so that many of the mandates that would come later from the Second Vatican Council in the 1960s, had already been tried, by necessity, among the Spanish-speaking congregants in parishes throughout the city. But the problem persisted that the integrated parish ultimately meant preference in services and resources were invariably given to the English-speaking group. This was bound to happen in the absence of a strong Hispanic/Latino native local clergy and institutional ecclesiastical leadership to represent community interests.

Although they identified with the parish and worked assiduously to construct a strong community of believers, Puerto Ricans and other Hispanics/Latinos were often made to feel as if the parish truly did not belong to them. "Toleration" rather than "ownership" marked their "belonging." "Let's keep them in their place," was the prevailing sentiment of the other parishioners and the older clergy. In other words, the integrated parish failed to construct a church community. Instead it housed two separate religious congregations, one of English-speakers who were given preferential treatment and the other of Spanish-speakers who were often relegated to the church basement, where they would remain "out of sight and mind." For church officials, the English-speaking worshipers constituted the "real" parish.

Each parish in the city where Hispanics/Latinos have worshiped has its unique history. Some were national parishes (Italian, French, German) that were "taken over" by Puerto Ricans and Hispanics during "white-flight" periods. Others, as pointed out above, were officially designated as Spanish-language parishes; and still others were to function as integrated parishes where ministry to both the Spanish-language and the English-speaking congregations was to be imparted.

While some parishes have exhibited greater Hispanic/Latino diversity, in others what has taken place is a succession of Spanish-speaking parishioners from different parts of the Caribbean and Latin America. For example, Our Lady of Guadalupe Church, established in what at the beginning of the twentieth century was called "Little Spain," first served Spaniards working in the export-import business and immigrants from what then was referred to as Spanish America. Later came the Puerto Ricans, and more recently a Mexican immigrant community to settle in the 14th Street neighborhood. With the heavy influx of Mexicans in the first decade of this century, the original church, a baroque structure built at 229 West 14th Street, was closed, and the nearby parish of St. Bernard at 330 West 14th Street opened its doors to the congregation from Our Lady of Guadalupe. In order for the congregation to keep continuity (and presumably to honor the Mexicans with their patron saint), St. Bernard was renamed Our Lady of Guadalupe Church.

Perhaps one of the reasons why the integrated parish failed to fully serve Puerto Ricans and Hispanics/Latinos as successfully as Spellman had anticipated was related to the cardinal's conception of Puerto Ricans and Puerto Rico. He saw Puerto Rico as subordinate to the United States and anticipated the unqualified assimilation of the island into the federal union. Likewise, in ecclesiastical matters, Spellman viewed the Puerto Rican church as an appendage to that of the United States, a perception that persisted until his death. He urged Rome, at the time of Pope John XXIII, to place the island church directly under the jurisdiction of Washington's apostolic delegate. Thus the entire Puerto Rican church on the island would be to the Catholic

Church as the Puerto Rican and Hispanic parishioners were to any Catholic parish in the archdiocese—subordinate or "basement" Catholics.[25]

The shortcomings of the response of the archdiocese of New York to Puerto Ricans and other Hispanics/Latinos notwithstanding, to say that the archdiocese did not attend to their needs, in some measure, would be erroneous. It has, in fact, spent time, personnel, and resources in this apostolate. What it has not done, however, is successfully promote sufficient vocations to the priesthood and religious life among this community or elevate to the highest ecclesiastical post those who have been ordained within the Hispanic/Latino community.

THE IMPACT OF THE HISPANICS/LATINOS ON US CATHOLICISM

A 2000 study by The Pew Hispanic Center documents what scholars of Latino religion have been saying for decades and what the National Catholic Encounters have been claiming since 1972. With their growing numbers and their distinctive way of practicing Christianity, Hispanics/Latinos have been transforming the nation's religious landscape. The significance of this segment of the population is most evident in the Catholic Church, where, according to official church records, as confirmed by the Pew study, one-third of all Catholics in this country are Hispanics/Latinos.[26] In his classes at Fordham University, Fr. Joseph P. Fitzpatrick, S.J., having devoted his academic life to the study of mainland Puerto Ricans, was fond of repeating that the Puerto Ricans and other Hispanics were a breath of fresh air in the Catholic Church and that without them, the church would be in great peril.[27]

This will come as no surprise to Hispanics or Latinos themselves. They know by personal experience that in many places, the viability of the Catholic Church depends on their presence and work. Equally experienced by parishes and families is the exodus of Latino Catholics to Protestant denominations, which, no doubt, has a marked effect not only upon Catholicism but upon the denominations ex-Catholics are adopting. For the receiving Protestant congregations, that influence has to be measured not only in terms of numbers but also of Catholic-influenced Christian practices introduced with the newcomers.[28] Some Methodist churches, for example, are borrowing the "Quinceañera Manual" developed by the Catholic Church for the rite of passage of young Latinas into adulthood. Others are incorporating the placing of ashes on the foreheads of their congregants as initiation to the season of Lent, the Lenten devotion of the *Via Crucis* or Way of the Cross, and the reenactment of Jesus' passion during Holy Week. Added to these is the celebration of *Día de los Reyes* or Three Kings Day, also known as the Epiphany.[29] In some Protestant churches with large numbers of people of Mexican, Guatemalan, and other Central American descent, icons of Our Lady of Guadalupe and *El Cristo Negro de Esquipulas* are no longer uncommon. Mexicans and Dominicans who have left the Catholic Church still look favorably upon *La Virgen de Guadalupe* and *Nuestra Señora de la Altagracia*. Even the wearing of medals and recitation of the rosary is no longer exclusively practiced by Roman Catholics.[30]

Additionally, as many of the recent studies have documented, Pentecostal and Charismatic movements are a key attribute of Hispanics/Latino worship not only among Pentecostal congregations but among all mainline Protestant and Catholic Churches as well.

In an article published March 2, 2009, Paul Vitello expressed the hopes and aspirations of more than half of the Catholic Church in New York. The article, under the title "Hoping for a Latino Bishop, Eventually,"[31] points out what most New York Hispanic/Latino Catholics know by experience: that although they constitute the largest ethnic group within the Catholic Church, there is little hope for them in the near future to constitute a representative presence within the church hierarchy. As Vitello puts it:

> Latinos in New York today are almost the statistical twins of Irish New Yorkers of the late 19th century—[accounting] for 30 percent of the city's population and, by the archdiocese's estimate, 40 to 50 percent of its 2.5 million Catholics—an estimate that community advocates say probably misses large numbers of undocumented immigrants— . . . [though] their neighborhood churches are often filled to capacity. . . . Parishes originally named for Irish saints have been renamed for Hispanic ones . . . [and] Masses at St. Patrick's Cathedral honoring the feast days of their patron saints draw crowds so large and fervent that worshipers sometimes spill out onto Fifth Avenue to pray on their knees on the sidewalk. . . . They have not inherited the vast stake in the institution that their Irish-American forbears have.[32]

Although there was speculation from the community that with Cardinal Egan's departure a Hispanic/Latino candidate such as Roberto O. González Nieves, the archbishop of San Juan,[33] would be considered to head the

Archdiocese of New York, ultimately the post went to Timothy Dolan, yet another person of Irish descent.

HISPANICS/LATINOS AND PROTESTANTISM

Incorporating Hispanics/Latinos into the clergy and elevating them to high administrative and ecclesiastical posts is something the Protestant congregations have been more successful in doing than the Catholic Church. One could argue that it takes longer to educate a Catholic priest than to educate a Protestant minister, particularly one who is to serve a pentecostal and congregational church.[34] But the fact remains that from the very beginning, Protestantism has offered its adherents greater opportunity for ordination and administrative positions. And these opportunities also include the ordination of women, to which the Catholic Church remains adamantly opposed.

Allow me a brief digression on the present status of women in Christian churches. María Pérez y González's research demonstrates that the ordination of women in Protestant churches does not always ensure equality.[35] Oftentimes even with ordination, these women are relegated to second-tier positions within the church organization and made subordinate to male pastors and ecclesiastical leaders. In response to this situation, they resort to what Pérez y González calls "a heretical imperative," that is, subverting traditional ways of ministering, circumventing certain practices and expectations of ecclesiastical leaders, and creating new ministerial alternatives to tend effectively to the spiritual needs of those under their care.[36] As I have explained elsewhere, Catholic women, too, have a long history of "subversion" and appropriating vital religious roles to tend to the spiritual needs of their families and communities.[37] With the mandates of the Second Vatican Council, new possibilities were officially opened for Catholic women to take on additional roles or make official those they had always assumed unofficially. Thus in the PARAL Study, one of the findings which might have surprised many people, but not Hispanic/Latina Catholic women, was that in 19% of the Spanish-speaking Catholic faith communities, the person identified as the community "head" or "leader" was a woman. This was slightly higher than for all other denominations, which reported 18% of their "heads" as women.[38]

Mainline churches such as the United Methodist Church have made decisions at the highest levels to tend to the needs of their growing Hispanic/Latino community both nationally and locally. The Board of Global

Ministries, particularly through its National Division and its Women's Division, has contributed greatly to the advancement of Hispanic/Latino Methodism. The Women's Division is particularly active among the Hispanic/Latino community in developing specially focused program resources. The National Division, in conjunction with the diverse conferences (akin to Catholic dioceses)—particularly the Río Grande Conference and New York Conference—has been especially active in meeting the needs of an increasing Hispanic/Latino presence in this church.[39] The Episcopal Church and other Protestant churches, such as the Lutheran, Presbyterian, and United Church of Christ, have also stepped up their attention and employed their resources to respond to the growing spiritual needs of this population.

Drawing new Hispanic/Latino members from among both lapsed and nominal Catholics and mainline Protestant churches, Pentecostalism has become one of the fastest-growing Protestant denominations in terms of percentages. Those studying the phenomenon, however, advise caution not to confuse percentage growth with raw numbers of conversions. Furthermore, the sustained effort made in the Spanish-speaking Caribbean and in Central and South America by Pentecostal missionaries means that among the new immigrants from these areas, a number already have embraced this denomination before coming to the United States. Many also desert their congregations or switch from one to another.

In New York, however, there are Protestant congregations that have had a relatively long history of work and success among Latinos/Hispanics in diaspora. Such is the Antioch Church, founded in 1933 by Rev. Manuel T. Sánchez in Brooklyn. Tomás Alvarez was another pioneer sent from Puerto Rico to New York to begin Pentecostal missionary work. He founded the first predominantly Puerto Rican Pentecostal church, *Iglesia Misionera Pentecostal*, also in Brooklyn. By 1937, there were fifty-five Hispanic Protestant churches in New York, of which almost half, or twenty-five, were Pentecostal. By 1983, Latino Pentecostal churches had grown to 560.[40]

Just as in the Catholic community there were women such as Sister Carmelita Zapata Bonilla, a Trinitarian, who has the distinction of being the first Puerto Rican consecrated religious woman to work among the Puerto Rican community in New York, the Protestant Hispanic/Latino community had Leoncia Rosado Rousseau, otherwise known as Mamá Leo, who began her ministry in New York in 1935. Mamá Leo, like Sister Carmelita, was a groundbreaking missionary. Not only did she found the Bronx-based

Pentecostal-denomination Council of Damascus Churches in 1940; she was also the first Latina Pentecostal pastor in the city.[41]

In comparing the growth of the Catholic Church with that of the Pentecostals, one must remember that Pentecostal churches are usually small in membership. Furthermore, their pastors usually do not go through the rigorous training that the ordained clergy in Catholic and mainline Protestant congregations undertake in order to serve the community. Likewise, we should not confuse the label Charismatic with Pentecostal when gathering and interpreting survey information. Many Catholics, for example, identify themselves as "Charismatic" Christians because they belong to the Charismatic movement within the Catholic Church. This notwithstanding, Protestant Pentecostalism continues to grow and to offer a place for worship and community building to Hispanics in New York City.

THE RISE OF ISLAM IN THE HISPANIC/LATINO COMMUNITY

Perhaps the most recent proof of the continuing religious diversity among New York's Latinos is the rise of Islam as a religion of choice, either through the Nation of Islam or other Islamic religious groups in the United States. The Latino Muslim presence, claiming estimates ranging from twenty-five thousand to sixty thousand nationally, is more noticeable in metropolitan areas of Southern California, Chicago, and New York, where there are both large Latino and large Muslim communities. In these urban settings, one finds the largest number of mosques and organizations established to serve Latino Muslims exclusively. The Latino American Dawah Organization (LADO), a New York–based organization founded in 1997 and now with chapters around the country, has as its mission to introduce Islam to the Latino community through programs, services, and publications, not as a foreign or exotic religion but one that has historical roots in Spain. Another network is the League of Latino American Muslim Organizations (LLAMO), whose goals as stated in its website are as follows:

1) Educate ourselves and others on Islam, e.g., sponsorship to produce Latino Muslims Imams, unite Latino Muslims groups and organization; 2) Educate ourselves on community development; 3) Share resources that will benefit our membership [e.g.,] Islamic literature, sources of free

Qurans, training, and sponsorship programs available; 4) Cooperate and coordinate our effort with other Muslim groups, while seeking to reduce redundancy and duplication of effort; 5) Provide information to non-Muslims on Islam and its solutions to our society's problems.[42]

These organizations maintain active websites and send out newsletters containing not only doctrinal information but also news about current events in the community. More specialized organizations such as PIEDAD (*Propagación Islámica para la Educación y la Devoción a Alá el Divino*) are geared to specific populations, in this case women. *Alianza Islámica* was founded in East Harlem in 1975 by Puerto Rican converts close to the civil rights movement, but more recently, it has relocated to the Bronx. Besides religious activities, this organization seeks to provide the community with services including AIDS education. The Latino Muslim presence today has sufficient significance for the Islamic Society of North America to celebrate an annual conference on Latino Muslims and to have established a Latino Coordinating Committee.

The conversion of Hispanics/Latinos to Islam has begun to appear as a topic of discussion in scholarly circles. The 2010 annual meeting of the American Academy of Religion, for example, held its first panel on Latino Muslims. Among the findings were the following: (1) many conversions are brought about through the marriage of Latinas to Muslims; (2) Hispanic/Latino converts expressed satisfaction with Islam's strict monotheism and its simplicity of purpose and expression; (3) the absence of a hierarchical clergy was an added attraction; (4) some Hispanic/Latino converts were drawn to the African-American Muslim experience and its cultural outpouring; (5) some converts speak of "reversion" rather than "conversion." These Hispanic/Latino Muslims seek to identify with pre-1492 Islamic Spain (in a way similar to that of African-American Muslims identifying with Islam in Africa).[43]

Finally, at least some Hispanic/Latino Muslims claim for themselves a sort of underground or camouflaged religious experience akin to that of crypto-Jews. The repudiation of Christianity, viewed as an imposed religion, has a very important role in their embrace of Islam. There are others, however, who simply state that they were looking for a religion that made sense to them and gave meaning to the daily struggle of modern life. Islam offered them such a promise.

CONCLUSION

If religion, and in particular Christianity, has not fallen by the wayside, it is because it is deeply woven into the Latino culture. Tested by the crises of modern society in New York, the most complex contemporary metropolitan area in the nation, as well as by harsh deprivations imposed by a far-from-voluntary immigration process, faith and religious practices among Hispanics/Latinos have survived with remarkable vitality. Still, significant numbers have switched affiliation, just as others have opted for no religious affiliation at all as they adapt to life in the States. "No religion" as an identifier, however, does not always mean atheism or even agnosticism. While many of those choosing this identification do not want to be connected to one church or religious movement, often they continue to practice certain family, communal, and personal rituals and to hold to particular religious beliefs. This is done in answer to personal needs or loyalty to tradition or family values rather than to dogma or ecclesiastically prescribed practices.

Equally important, though, is to reaffirm the role that the Hispanic/Latino community plays to uphold the viability of the US Catholic Church and that of other Christian denominations today. Speaking of one group of Hispanics and the Catholic Church in New York, Glazer and Moynihan wrote several decades ago: "If the Puerto Rican mass should abandon Catholicism, or split on the issue, Catholics would shortly become a numerical as well as a political and cultural minority in the city."[44] If this was true for Puerto Ricans more than forty years ago, it is certainly true of the general Hispanic/Latino community today. There is no doubt that the Catholic Church needs to integrate more fully the Puerto Ricans and other groups of Hispanic/Latino origin if is to maintain its clout as a social institution and its viability as a faith community. To keep things in balance, it is not simply a matter of these groups keeping faith with the church but the church also keeping faith with this community. This is particularly true in the city of New York, where religion is a vibrant part of familial, communal, and social life, and where, amidst the highest levels of diversity and complexity, religious loyalty has become open to contestation. With a plethora of Christian denominations and religious belief systems, attachment to the Catholic Church is one among many options open to Hispanics/Latinos. Thus, while the Catholic Church still claims the adherence of the largest percentage of Hispanics/Latinos, at least some in the Catholic Church realize that their loyalty to the Catholic faith is not automatic. In fact, the city offers individuals the challenge and opportunity to choose rather than simply follow a particular religion, or to opt out of religion altogether.

Hispanics/Latinos, then, find themselves in a situation where their religious loyalty is tested and where they, as well, test the capacity of the religious institution to incorporate and maintain them as full members. Hispanics/Latinos report a rather impressive number who, at present, choose to associate with more than one religious family, claim no religious affiliation, or opt out of religion altogether; within the group, 17.9% nationally opted out of religion altogether.[45] Thus, the greatest challenge to Catholicism may not come from conversion to evangelical churches but rather from the reluctance to identify individual faith and spirituality with a single institutionalized religious group.

NOTES

1. The Catholic Church has opted for the term "Hispanic" or "Hispano" to refer to the faithful who can trace their origin to Spain, the Spanish-speaking Caribbean, and Latin America.

2. Díaz-Stevens, *Oxcart Catholicism on Fifth Avenue*.

3. Sam Roberts, "Filing Challenge to Census, City Says 50,000 Weren't Counted in 2 Boroughs," *New York Times*, August 11, 2011, A21, http://www.nytimes.com/2011/08/11/nyregion/ny-says-census-undercounted-brooklyn-and-queens.html.

4. As of the 2000 census, with 3,372,512 Italians, the New York metropolitan area became the home of the largest European ethnic group in New York. There are more Jews within the city limits of New York City than within the city limits of Jerusalem, making New York City's Jewish concentration the largest outside of Israel and the second worldwide after Tel Aviv. Nearly a quarter of US South Asians live in New York. The city is also home to the largest African American community in the United States.

5. Fifteen percent is Asian American, 20 to 25% African American / African. The city is in the most populated region in the United States, with an estimated twenty to thirty million in the eight-state megalopolis stretching five hundred miles from Boston to Washington, DC.

6. Data are taken from the *Religious Congregations and Membership Survey* and from Beveridge, "Religious City."

7. The significance of Puerto Rico as the first site for the initial institutionalization of Christianity in the New World is evident when one considers the

strong relationship that existed between three basic institutions instrumental in the colonization of the New World: the church, Audiencia (or Appeals Court), and the military. Given the geographic distance and isolation in which the island of Puerto Rico was kept, especially during this early colonization period, the geographic separation of the first official Apostolic See and the Audiencia established in Santo Domingo is noteworthy.

8. The dioceses were Concepción de la Vega, Santo Domingo, and Puerto Rico.

9. The Anglican Church is the only non-Catholic Christian church that predates the introduction of North American Protestantism on the island of Puerto Rico after 1898.

10. Pérez y Mena, *Speaking with the Dead.*

11. *Hispanic Churches in American Public Life* (HCAPL) National Survey, "conducted between August and October 2000 . . .[,] found that 70% of all Hispanic and Latino Americans are Catholic, 20% are Protestant, 3% are 'alternative Christians' (such as Mormon or Jehovah's Witnesses), 1% identify with a non-Christian religion, and 6% have no religious preference (with only .37% claiming to be atheist or agnostic)." No mention is made of Muslims, Buddhists, Jews, Espiritistas, Santeros, or membership in other non-Christian religions.

12. Fitzpatrick, *Puerto Rican Americans*, 116.

13. Among these are González-Wippler, *Santería*, and De La Torre, *Santería*. De La Torre's book is particularly valuable for a theological interpretation of this belief system.

14. Pérez y Mena, "Cuban Santería, Haitian Vodun, Puerto Rican Spiritualism."

15. González-Wippler, *Santería*, 10. González-Wippler writes: "The primitive beliefs and customs, with their 'barbarous words of evocation,' have found their way to the busy, sophisticated streets of New York, Chicago, Los Angeles, and Miami, where Santería flourishes now as powerfully as in the Caribbean islands."

16. The list of books and articles on Afro-based religions is extensive. Among them are Cabrera, *El Monte*; Pérez y Mena, *Speaking with the Dead*; Stevens-Arroyo and Pérez y Mena, *Enigmatic Powers*; Pérez y Mena, "Cuban Santería, Haitian Vodun, Puerto Rican Spiritualism"; Murphy, *Santeria*; Fernández Olmos and Paravisini-Gebert, *Art and Religion*; Fernández Olmos and Paravisini-Gebert, *Sacred Possessions*; De La Torre, *Santería*; González-Wippler, *Santería*.

17. Lipka, "Closer Look at Catholic America."

18. See Díaz-Stevens, *Oxcart Catholicism on Fifth Avenue*, 66–90.

19. Religious priests belong to religious congregations or religious orders such as the Dominicans (or Order of St. Dominic), the Benedictines (or Order of St. Benedict), the Carmelites (or Order of the Brothers of Our Lady of Mount Carmel), the Jesuits (or Society of Jesus), etc. In other words, they are members of a religious family, take religious vows of poverty, chastity, and obedience, follow a religious rule or guideline written for the particular religious order to

which they belong, and owe obedience to the head of that order, often called "Abbot" or "Father Superior." The diocesan or secular priests are trained for their ministry in seminaries belonging to their particular archdioceses or dioceses, do not take religious vows (although they practice celibacy), and respond to the head of the archdiocese or diocese to which they belong, usually a bishop, or an archbishop who can also be a cardinal. While religious priests are often sent to mission houses of the religious order that have been established throughout the world, a diocesan priest is ordained for a particular diocese and cannot leave that diocese without permission from his bishop. On the rare occasions that a secular priest is allowed to leave the diocese for which he was ordained, such priest may seek and be granted "incardination"—permission to minister as a priest—in a new diocese. After a review of his priestly credentials, his moral character, and religious commitment, the new bishop may grant him incardination.

20. See Stern, "Archdiocese of New York and Hispanic Americans." Additional information is found in Stern, "Evolution of Hispanic Ministry."

21. Stern, "Evolution of Hispanic Ministry," 7.

22. See Stevens-Arroyo and Díaz-Ramírez, "Puerto Ricans in the States."

23. Díaz-Stevens, *Oxcart Catholicism on Fifth Avenue*, 97–116.

24. Fitzpatrick, *Puerto Rican Americans*, 154, 155.

25. See Díaz-Stevens, *Oxcart Catholicism on Fifth Avenue*, 96–98.

26. Pew Research Center, *Changing Faiths*.

27. Fr. Fitzpatrick was the teacher at Fordham University under whose mentorship I completed my doctoral studies.

28. The term "convert" is not appropriate here, because this is a theological term which may or may not apply in this denominational switching.

29. Some years ago, I interviewed a Lutheran pastor whose family had left the Catholic Church when she was still a young woman. She remembers that Christmas Eve even her father could not resist the temptation of going back to the Catholic Midnight Mass. Without it, he did not feel it was Christmas.

30. One of my MDiv students at Union Theological Seminary had not only an icon of Our Lady of Altagracia, the Catholic patroness of her country, the Dominican Republic, but also a large wooden rosary. Another student, a Mexican Southern Baptist, wore a medal of La Guadalupana around her neck, while a third student, a Puerto Rican North American Baptist woman residing in Puerto Rico, not only learned the rosary but teaches it to Catholic women who have forgotten or never practiced this devotion before. The last case is an example of ecumenism in practice and also what could be described as a Catholic devotion making its way back home through "the back door." Taken as a whole, the above are also examples of Protestant women reclaiming Mary in their lives. From my personal experience both as a researcher and teacher, I have confirmed many more cases where Protestants have borrowed Catholic symbols and practices in spite of the official position of their churches. Admittedly, the Catholic Church

has also borrowed from Protestantism, as made evident in the choice of hymns sung any Sunday morning in Catholic Churches.

31. In "Hoping for a Latino Archbishop, Eventually," Vitello writes: "When the Vatican announced last week that the next leader of the Archdiocese of New York would be Archbishop Timothy M. Dolan of Milwaukee—the 10th in an unbroken line of Irish-American archbishops to hold that job since 1842—Latino Catholics in New York reacted as they would to news of another sunrise over the East River.

"The muted response did not reflect indifference to the new archbishop, whom many people seemed to like, or to the notion that appointing a prelate with a Hispanic name instead of a Celtic one might be smart: Latinos are not only ascendant in New York, but also likely to be the majority of Catholics in the United States within a decade. The archbishop of New York, with his pulpit in the media nexus of the world, has been called the pope of America. . . . There are still far more Irish-American priests than Latino ones in New York, as in most of the country. . . . Appointing a Latino archbishop in New York would not change the fundamental equation, but it would send a message, some community leaders said." *New York Times*, March 2, 2009.

32. Vitello, "Hoping for a Latino Archbishop."

33. González Nieves was a good candidate in the estimation of many. Besides being the present archbishop of San Juan, Puerto Rico, he also served in Boston, Massachusetts, and Corpus Christi, Texas. Thus, church officials could not disqualify him by claiming he was inexperienced in the mainland setting.

34. Ordinarily, studies to prepare for the priesthood in the Catholic Church can run from eight to ten years, and sometimes more, particularly if the priest is also a member of a religious community such as Dominicans, Jesuits, etc.

35. Pérez y González, "Latinas in the Barrio."

36. Ibid.

37. See Díaz-Stevens, "Saving Grace."

38. See *National Survey of Leadership in Latino Parishes and Congregations*.

39. In 1972 the United Methodist Church in Puerto Rico was given a measure of autonomy. It became fully autonomous twenty years later in 1992. As part of that autonomy a Puerto Rican, Juan Vera, was elevated to the post of bishop.

40. On Puerto Rican Pentecostalism, see Benjamín Alicea Lugo, "El Legado de Juan L. Lugo: El Pentecostalismo Puertorriqueño," http://agwebservices.org /Content/RSSResources/El%20legado%20de%20Juan%20L.%20Lugo%20(PDF) .pdf. See also Reyes, *Los hispanos en los Estados Unidos*.

41. Both Sister Carmelita and Mamá Leo lived long lives dedicated to the spiritual and corporeal needs of the Latino/Hispanic community in this city. Sister Carmelita dedicated herself to social and community work, and Mamá Leo to the pulpit as well as to work in the community, such as in a drug and alcohol rehabilitation program.

42. This information is provided by the League of Latino American Muslim Organizations, posted December 14, 2013, https://www.facebook.com/Latino AmericanMuslims/?fref=nf.

43. These points were summarized by Stevens-Díaz in "Muslim Narrative among Latinos/as."

44. Glazer and Moynihan, *Beyond the Melting Pot*, lxix.

45. See Mayer, Kosmin, and Keysar, *American Religious Identification Survey*.

REFERENCES

Beveridge, Andrew. "A Religious City." *Gotham Gazette*, February 12, 2008. http:// www.gothamgazette.com/index.php/demographics/3881-a-religious-city.

Cabrera, Lydia. *El Monte: Igbo, Finda, Ewe Orisha, Vititi Nfinda*. Miami: Ediciones Universal, 1995.

De La Torre, Miguel A. *Santería: The Beliefs and Rituals of a Growing Religion in America*. Grand Rapids, MI: Eerdmans, 2004.

Díaz-Stevens, Ana María. *Oxcart Catholicism on Fifth Avenue: The Impact of the Puerto Rican Migration upon the Archdiocese of New York*. Notre Dame, IN: University of Notre Dame Press, 1993.

———. "The Saving Grace: The Matriarchal Core of Latino Catholicism." *Latino Studies Journal* 4, no. 3 (1993): 60–78.

Fernández Olmos, Margarite, and Lizabeth Paravisini-Gebert, eds. *Art and Religion as Curative Practices in the Caribbean and Its Diaspora*. New York: Palgrave, 2001.

———. *Sacred Possessions: Vodou, Santería, Obeah, and the Caribbean*. New Brunswick, NJ: Rutgers University Press, 1997.

Fitzpatrick, Joseph P., S.J. *Puerto Rican Americans: The Meaning of Migration to the Mainland*. Englewood Cliffs, NJ: Prentice Hall, 1971.

Glazer, Nathan, and Patrick P. Moynihan. *Beyond the Melting Pot: The Negroes, Puerto Ricans, Jews, Italians, and Irish of New York City*. 2nd ed. Cambridge, MA: MIT Press, 1970.

González-Wippler, Migene. *Santería: African Magic in Latin America*. New York: Anchor Books, 1973.

Lipka, Michael. "A Closer Look at Catholic America." *Fact Tank: News in the Numbers*. Washington, DC: Pew Research Center, 2015. http://www.pewresearch .org/fact-tank/2015/09/14/a-closer-look-at-catholic-america/.

Mayer, Egon, Barry A. Kosmin, and Ariela Keysar. *American Religious Identification Survey (Key Findings)*. New York: Graduate Center of the City University of New York, 2001. http://www.gc.cuny.edu/CUNY_GC/media/CUNY -Graduate-Center/PDF/ARIS/ARIS-PDF-version.pdf.

Murphy, Joseph. *Santería: African Spirits in America*. Boston: Beacon Press, 1993.

The National Survey of Leadership in Latino Parishes and Congregations. A social science contribution to the PARAL Study, directed by Anthony M. Stevens-Arroyo. Brooklyn, NY: Brooklyn College, 2002. www.depthome.brooklyn .cuny.edu/risc/Acknow-Intro.pdf.

Pérez y González, María Elizabeth. "Latinas in the Barrio." In *New York Glory: Religions in the City*, edited by Anna Karpathakis and Tony Carnes, 287–96. New York: New York University Press, 2000.

Pérez y Mena, Andrés I. "Cuban Santería, Haitian Vodun, Puerto Rican Spiritualism: A Multicultural Inquiry into Syncretism." *Journal for the Scientific Study of Religion* 37, no. 1 (1998): 15–27.

———. *Speaking with the Dead: Development of Afro-Latin Religion among Puerto Ricans in the United States*. New York: AMDS Press, 1991.

Pew Foundation. *Hispanic Churches in American Public Life (HCAPL) National Survey*. 2nd ed. Washington, DC: Pew Foundation, 2003. http://www.hispanic churchesusa.net/hcapl-rpt-1.pdf.

Pew Research Center. *Changing Faiths: Latinos and the Transformation of American Religion*. Washington, DC: Pew Research Center, 2007. http://www.pew hispanic.org/2007/04/25/changing-faiths-latinos-and-the-transformation -of-american-religion/.

Religious Congregations and Membership Survey. University Park: Association of Religious Data Archives, Pennsylvania State University, 2010.

Reyes, José. *Los hispanos en los Estados Unidos: Un reto y una oportunidad para la iglesia*. Cleveland, TN: White Wing Press, 1985.

Stern, Robert L. "The Archdiocese of New York and Hispanic Americans." *Migration Today* 5, no. 6 (1977): 18–23.

———. "Evolution of Hispanic Ministry in the Archdiocese of New York." Prepared for the Archdiocesan Office of Pastoral Research. Monsignor Robert L. Stern's personal files. New York: Catholic Center, 1982.

Stevens-Arroyo, Anthony, and Andrés I. Pérez y Mena, eds. *Enigmatic Powers: Syncretism with African and Indigenous Peoples' Religions among Latinos*. New York: PARAL / Bildner Center for Western Hemisphere Studies, 1995.

Stevens-Arroyo, Antonio, and Ana María Díaz-Ramírez. "Puerto Ricans in the States: A Struggle for Identity." In *The Minority Report: An Introduction to Racial, Ethnic, and Gender Relations*, edited by Anthony Gary Dworkin and Rosalind J. Dworkin, 196–232. New York: Holt, Rinehart and Winston, 1982.

Stevens-Díaz, Adán E. "Muslim Narrative among Latinos/as." Paper Presented at the Latina/o Critical and Comparative Consultation at the Annual Meeting of the American Academy of Religion, October 20, 2010, Atlanta, Georgia.

ONLINE RESOURCES

http://www.hispanicchurchesusa.net/hcapl-rpt-1.pdf. Espinosa, Gastón, Virgilio Elizondo, and Jesse Miranda. *Hispanic Churches in American Public Life: Summary of Findings of Latino Religion.* The Interim Reports series. Notre Dame, IN: Institute for Latino Studies, University of Notre Dame, January 2003.

https://www.facebook.com/LatinoAmericanMuslims/?fref=nf. League of Latino American Muslim Organizations (LLAMO) website. December 14, 2013.

http://www.pewforum.org/2007/04/25/changing-faiths-latinos-and-the-transformation-of-american-religion-2/. Pew Research Center. Executive summary for *Changing Faiths: Latinos and the Transformation of American Religion.* Washington, DC: Pew Research Center, April 25, 2007.

PART TWO

Under the Latino National Umbrella

CHAPTER FOUR

Where Have All the Puerto Ricans Gone?

ANDRÉS TORRES AND GILBERT MARZÁN

Census data show that the United States Puerto Rican population has been growing steadily for a long time. From the beginning of the twentieth century to the beginning of the twenty-first, it grew from less than a thousand to 3.4 million in 2000; by 2010, it had grown to 4.6 million; and by 2013 it was estimated to have reached 4.9 million.[1] Several aspects of this trend have been well documented.[2] First is the rise in the US Puerto Rican population as a proportion of all Puerto Ricans, such that it now exceeds the population of Puerto Rico. Second is the end to New York City's dominant role as the center of the Puerto Rican population in the United States. As shown in table 4.1, the share of the New York City Puerto Rican population as a proportion of all US Puerto Ricans declined from 88% in 1940 to 23% in 2000, and 16% in 2010. Third is the phenomenon of a return migration to Puerto Rico; and finally is the emergence of Florida and other areas as new poles attracting Puerto Rican migrants, especially since the 1990s.

This chapter builds on the existing literature by broadening our knowledge of the outmigration of Puerto Ricans from New York City specifically. Working with Public Use Microdata Samples (PUMS) of the 1990 and 2000 censuses, we will:

Table 4.1 Puerto Rican Population of New York City, 1900–2010

Year	Puerto Rican Population of N.Y.C.	Percent of Total N.Y.C. Population	Percent of Total U.S. Puerto Rican Population
1900	300	*	**
1910	600	*	36.6
1920	7,400	*	62.4
1930	44,900	*	85.0
1940	61,500	*	87.8
1950	246,000	3.1	81.6
1960	613,000	7.9	68.6
1970	846,700	10.7	59.2
1980	860,500	12.1	42.7
1990	896,800	12.2	32.9
2000	789,200	10.0	23.2
2010	723,621	8.9	16.0

*Less than 1%.

**The first year in which the U.S. Bureau of the Census listed Puerto Ricans as a separate group in its publications was 1910. Thomas D. Boswell and Angel David Cruz-Báez, "Puerto Ricans Living in the United States," in Jesse O. McKee, ed., *Ethnicity in Contemporary America: A Geographical Appraisal* (Lanham, MD: Rowman & Littlefield, 2000), 183.

Note: Figures for 1910–1920 are for persons born in Puerto Rico; figures for 1940 include only persons born in Puerto Rico; the 1950 and 1960 data include those of Puerto Rican birth or parentage; the 1970–2000 data include all Puerto Ricans, irrespective of generational status.

Sources: Andrés Torres, *Between Melting Pot and Mosaic: African Americans and Puerto Ricans in the New York Political Economy* (Philadelphia: Temple University Press, 1991), 65, table 8; Carmen Whalen, "Colonialism, Citizenship, and the Making of the Puerto Rican Diaspora: An Introduction," in Carmen Whalen and Víctor Vázquez-Hernández, eds., *The Puerto Rican Diaspora: Historical Perspectives* (Philadelphia: Temple University Press, 2005), 3, table 1.2; Percent of Total U.S. Puerto Rican Population 1940–1990 from New York City, Department of City Planning, 1994, *Puerto Rican New Yorkers in 1990*, 9, table 1.1; US Bureau of the Census, 2000 Census Profile of General Demographic Characteristics: 2000, table DP-1. On 2000 and 2010 population: New York City, Department of City Planning, http://www.nycgov/hml/dcp/html/census/popdiv.shtml (accessed April 12, 2015).

Compare the socioeconomic background of all outmigrants to that of the Puerto Ricans who remained in New York (stayers). Do outmigrant characteristics differ substantially from characteristics of those who stay behind?

Describe the outmigration flows during the two periods 1985–90 and 1995–2000: what were the regional destinations of Puerto Ricans who left?

Compare, by region of destination, the socioeconomic background of out-migrants. For example, what are the differences in educational level, household income, and occupation between who moved to New England and those who migrated to Puerto Rico?

HISTORICAL TRENDS

In the mid-twentieth century, well before the current preoccupation with global migration, one of the most significant episodes in the history of labor migration began. A small Caribbean island, a territorial possession of a superpower, saw one-third of its population immigrate to the metropolis. Between 1940 and 1970, almost one million Puerto Ricans left their homeland for the agricultural fields and urban centers of the North. For every two persons added to Puerto Rico's population, one became a migrant.[3]

The story of that extended migration has taken twists, turns, and tangents. During the 1970s, although people continued to leave the island in large numbers, an almost identical number migrated back from US communities. These were middle-age workers and retirees of the pre–World War II and early post–World War II generations looking to resettle in their homeland. Also in this cohort of returnees were a significant number of unemployed and displaced workers, who had been sidelined by industrial restructuring and growing urban blight in northern cities, especially New York. The result was that the 1970s witnessed the lowest level of net outmigration from Puerto Rico since before World War II, some 66,000 people.[4]

In the 1980s, however, because fewer Puerto Ricans returned to the island while emigration from the island persisted at almost the same levels of the 1970s, Puerto Rico's net population exodus doubled compared to the previous decade. The prevailing view was that economic conditions in Puerto Rico were less favorable compared to those in the United States; this would explain why Puerto Ricans kept leaving and why potential return migrants tended to stay in the States during the decade.[5]

The large outmigration continued during the 1990s but with a twist. Migrants from Puerto Rico were leaving for other regions beyond the traditional destination points, accentuating a geographic dispersion that was already beginning to show up in the 1980s. By century's end, a major transformation had occurred in the population distribution of Puerto Ricans in the United States. Whereas in 1970 four out of five US Puerto Ricans lived in the Northeast (and two-thirds in New York State), this number had fallen to about 60% in 2000 (and just above a third in New York State). By 2009 this share had fallen to 54%.[6]

Meanwhile there was an ongoing pattern of individuals and entire households engaged in repeated trips back and forth between the US mainland and the island. This back-and-forth movement was variously termed "circular migration," "commuter migration," and "*el va y ven*."[7] Thus, it has been a half-century of intense multidirectional activity, during which everyone seemed on the move; now, major fragments of the population have lived in both Puerto Rico and the United States.

WHY PUERTO RICANS LEFT NEW YORK CITY

For as long as there have been large urban centers, there have been people leaving them, for reasons positive and negative. An ample body of research tracks the movement of these outmigrants, their destinations, and the underlying causes of their decisions to leave. The following brief survey reviews some of the key arguments in the literature that address either directly or indirectly the central concerns of this chapter. We conclude the survey with a typology of migrants that we think is helpful in understanding Puerto Rican outmigrants from New York City.

As shown in table 4.1, the Puerto Rican population in New York City grew explosively from 1940 to 1970. It grew steadily until 1990, then declined 19% over the next two decades. Until recently, it grew primarily because of births and not migration from Puerto Rico, which had been the case in the early postwar decades.[8] This pattern may have changed with the economic difficulties spawned by the recession of the late 1990s. More current data, unavailable at the time of this writing, may indicate a net positive inflow of island Puerto Ricans outweighing births from New York Puerto Ricans.

Another reason for the leveling off of the local population is the phenomenon of return migration among older Puerto Ricans who arrived in the city after World War II, the beginning of the "Great Migration." The elders want to reunite with family members, pursue dreams of a more tranquil and peaceful lifestyle, and spend their last years in their native homeland. Citizenship ensures ease of travel to visit children who stay behind in the States. And retirees can lead relatively comfortable lives with their Social Security and pension benefits. Puerto Ricans within this cohort are in the *retirement* stage of the life cycle (retirees) and are choosing to return to the island.

Another subset of those returning to the island do so in midlife for cultural reasons as well as to seek the tranquility of a slower-paced lifestyle.[9]

Over time, the size of the Puerto Rican middle-income segment on the mainland has gradually expanded, even as poverty has maintained its grip on a third or more of the population. Some of these middle class households benefited from rising educational levels that gained them entrée into higher-paying jobs and professions. This is especially the case for US-born Puerto Ricans, compared to their compatriots born on the island.[10]

Taking advantage of individual economic mobility, these sectors have pursued the traditional path of *suburbanization*. For suburbanites, residence in the suburbs enhances access to the amenities of good schools, decent housing stock, social services, and less crime.[11] Moving to the suburbs may or may not be tied to employment opportunity. Some individuals move to the metropolitan ring and continue to commute to their jobs in the city. Others leave the city following the growth of jobs in the suburbs. Since 1990 across the country, suburban employment growth has exceeded central-city employment growth in virtually all industrial sectors.[12] Suburbanization also seems to be influenced by household composition. Puerto Rican households composed of married couples had a greater propensity to leave the city than those of other types of marital status.[13]

Another measure of the suburbanization trend can be indirectly gauged by looking at the increase in Puerto Ricans within the Consolidated Metropolitan Statistical Area (CSMA). Despite a decline in Puerto Ricans of almost one hundred thousand within the five boroughs of New York City during the 1990s, the population within the broader area of the CSMA grew from 1,290,135 to 1,325,778. Theoretically this would imply a jump in Puerto Rican suburbanites of up to 135,000.[14]

Over the years, the booming economy in other states (in the Southeast and West, for example) seems to have induced significant numbers of Puerto Rican *opportunity seekers* to leave the city. Workers—unskilled or skilled, male or female, single or attached—identified industrial or occupational niches that would allow them to thrive, or at least make a modest living. During the later 1980s, blue-collar workers were the largest occupational group among males to leave New York City. Among females, it was professional and managerial types who had the greatest propensity to leave.[15] In this case, the motivating factor was primarily economic opportunity: the desire to relocate to a place where the possibility of upward mobility (or at least stability) was more favorable.

Another factor motivating these opportunity seekers has been the existence of affordable housing markets in the regions beyond metropolitan New York City. In New England and Pennsylvania, homeownership is within reach for working-class and middle-class Puerto Ricans who cannot purchase property in New York City.[16] In the Southeast, Midwest, and West, these conditions prevail as well. We may also suppose that opportunity seekers are generally younger and more-educated individuals pursuing better-paying jobs and career mobility. Responding to the pull of labor demand in other regions, they are willing to relocate over longer distances because of fewer family obligations (unmarried or married without children).

A fourth group of outmigrants were *displaced* from the city by shrinking employment opportunities and limited affordable housing. Since the 1950s, New York City's economic activity originally was production based; it was next transformed into service provision, and now into an information-based economy. Manufacturing and other lower-skilled industries have been in steady decline. This had a serious impact on Puerto Ricans, who were heavily concentrated in these low-skilled and low-paying jobs.[17] During the 1970s the principal outcome of the city's economic restructuring for Puerto Ricans was labor displacement, manifested in a sharp decline in labor-force participation and a rise in unemployment.[18] For this group of workers, other factors, such as poor housing and increased poverty, aggravated their plight and contributed to their dispersion to other cities.[19]

DATA

The data sets in this study consist of Puerto Ricans who, in the years 1990 and 2000, were living anywhere outside of New York City, but who had reported that they had lived in New York City in the years 1985 and 1995, respectively. These are *outmigrants* who left the city during 1985–90 and 1995–2000.[20] To track their migration pattern, we stratified this population into seven destinations to which scholars and journalists have suggested Puerto Ricans were moving.[21] Our attempt is to provide a more finely etched picture of outmigration patterns than prior studies that have tracked state-level or broader regional patterns. In particular, no previous study has decomposed these movements to isolate the New York City suburban area that crosses state lines. The samples of *stayers* are individuals who resided in New York City in 1990 and 2000, respectively.

The destinations are (1) the New York City suburban ring, (2) Florida, (3) Puerto Rico, (4) New England, (5) Pennsylvania, (6) other New York State counties, excluding counties in New York City suburban ring, and (7) all other states, excluding northern New Jersey counties in New York City suburban ring.[22]

Because of the way the US Census asks the questions about "residence five years ago," several issues should be noted. Some outmigrants may have moved more than once during the respective five-year intervals. Most variables discussed here generally refer to the individual's or household's status as of the census year, so a question about marital status, educational attainment, or homeownership refers to 1990 or 2000, and not necessarily to when the individual left New York City.

OUTMIGRANTS AND STAYERS

What are the key demographic and socioeconomic characteristics of outmigrants, and how do they compare to the characteristics of those who remained, the stayers? Table 4.2 presents comparative information on both groups for the periods 1985–90 and 1995–2000. (In the following sections, use of the terms "eighties" and "nineties" refers to 1985–1990 and 1995–2000, respectively.)

Gender, Race, Age, Birthplace

During the 1980s, females were a higher proportion of both those who left (52%) and those who stayed (54%). But these ratios are not very different from the gender split in general of all New York Puerto Ricans. As to racial identity, significantly more outmigrants defined themselves as white (52%) than was the case among those who did not leave (40%); and fewer outmigrants defined themselves as black (5%) or "some other race" (43%) than did stayers (7% and 48%, respectively). The 1990 census did not have a category for "two or more races" as did the 2000 census, to be discussed below.

Regarding age, outmigrants had a smaller senior cohort (16%) than did stayers (21%). The trend among the younger adult cohorts (age 20–39) indicates that outmigrants were younger than stayers. As to place of birth, a larger proportion of leavers were born in Puerto Rico (50%) than in New York (44%), and the opposite was the case for those who stayed in the city (45% to 50%).

Table 4.2 Puerto Rican Outmigrants and Stayers, 1985–1995 and 1995–2000

Variable	1985–1990		1995–2000	
	Outmigrants	Stayers	Outmigrants	Stayers
Gender				
Male	48%	47%	48%	48%
Female	52%	54%	52%	52%
Race				
White	52%	40%	53%	37%
Black	5%	7%	7%	8%
Other Race	43%	48%	32%	47%
Two or More Races	NA*	NA	7%	7%
Age				
20–29	31%	27%	29%	31%
30–39	30%	24%	30%	30%
40–49	16%	20%	16%	18%
50–54	6%	8%	6%	7%
55 and Older	16%	21%	19%	13%
Place of Birth				
United States	4%	1%	5%	9%
New York	44%	50%	57%	56%
Puerto Rico	50%	45%	36%	32%
Education				
Less Than High School	46%	54%	37%	39%
High School	24%	23%	25%	27%
Some College or More	29%	22%	38%	34%
English Language Ability				
Well or Very Well	77%	81%	86%	87%
Not Well or Not at All	23%	18%	15%	12%
Marital Status				
Married	58%	41%	50%	38%
Widowed	3%	6%	5%	3%
Divorced and Separated	18%	21%	18%	20%
Never Married	21%	32%	27%	38%
Employment Status				
Employed	54%	55%	61%	56%
Unemployed	14%	8%	8%	9%
Not in Labor Force	32%	37%	31%	35%

Table 4.2 Puerto Rican Outmigrants and Stayers, 1985–1995 and 1995–2000 (*cont.*)

Variable	1985–1990		1995–2000	
	Outmigrants	Stayers	Outmigrants	Stayers
Occupation				
White Collar	18%	17%	22%	21%
Service	50%	56%	54%	58%
Blue-Collar	32%	27%	25%	21%
Male				
White-Collar	13%	14%	19%	17%
Service	41%	47%	42%	49%
Blue-Collar	46%	39%	38%	34%
Female				
White-Collar	23%	20%	24%	25%
Service	61%	65%	65%	67%
Blue-Collar	16%	15%	10%	8%
Income	$23,660	$27,490	$45,185	$38,597
Home Ownership vs Rental				
Ownership	43%	13%	48%	20%
Rental	57%	87%	49%	78%
Poverty Status				
Below Poverty	41%	31%	31%	32%

Sources: 1990 IPUMS and 2000 PUMS. Authors' tabulations.

During the 1990s, most outmigrants were females; their proportion (52%) was slightly greater than that of males (48%). This is identical to the gender ratio among those who stayed in the city. Racial identification among outmigrants differed substantially compared to those who stayed. Fifty-three percent of outmigrants classified themselves as white compared to 37% among stayers. In the next-largest racial category (some other race), the pattern was reversed. Almost half of stayers (47%) defined themselves in this manner, while a third (32%) defined themselves as "some other race." There was little difference between the proportion of black stayers (8%) and black outmigrants (7%), as well as those who said they were of "two or more races" (7% in both groups).

The most significant difference in age is among outmigrants, who have a larger senior cohort: 19% of leavers are aged fifty-five and older, while only

13% of stayers are. For the rest of the age structure, stayers are slightly younger than outmigrants. This is a reversal of the pattern for the earlier, 1985–90 period. Regarding place of birth, a similar share of New York–born Puerto Ricans was to be found among outmigrants and stayers. This contrasts with the earlier period, when leavers were mostly Puerto Rico–born, and stayers tended more to be New York–born.

Education, Language, Marital Status

During the 1980s, there were differences in human capital between outmigrants and stayers. A higher percent of outmigrants (29%) than of stayers (22%) had "some college or more." At the lower end of the education-attainment spectrum, a larger group of stayers (54%) than of outmigrants (46%) had not completed high school. Differences in language use appear as well. A higher percentage of outmigrants (23%) than of stayers (18%) spoke English "not well or not at all." Looking at household structure, a higher proportion of married couples were in the outmigration stream compared to those who stayed (58% to 41%); among those never married, there was a larger group among stayers (32%) than among outmigrants (21%).

During the mid-to-late nineties, outmigrants had a higher level of education completed (38% with at least some college; 34% for stayers), but with respect to English-language fluency, leavers differed very slightly from their counterparts who remained behind. A relatively small group among both populations spoke English either "not well or not at all" (15% of outmigrants and 12% of stayers). This shift reflects the decline of return migration to the island compared to the earlier period, when Puerto Rico was the main destination for 40% of all outmigrants. As to marital status patterns, 50% of the outmigrant population consisted of married couples (38% of stayers); among leavers, a smaller segment had never married (27%) than of those who stayed (38%). This comparison implies that those who left the city were more likely to be traditional households than those who stayed, and this pattern held strongly for both periods.

Employment and Occupation

Estimates of employment and occupation patterns point to other differences between the two populations. During the earlier period, those who left New

York City tended to be more attached to the labor force (68% in the labor force) and face higher unemployment (14%) than those who stayed (63% and 8%, respectively).[23]

During the 1995–2000 period, outmigrants tended to be more connected to the labor market (61% vs. 56% for stayers) and to have a slightly lower unemployment rate than stayers (8% vs. 9%). Conversely, those who remained in the city were more likely not to be in the labor force (35% vs. 31%). Note that outmigrants were hit with significantly higher unemployment gaps (vs. stayers) during 1985–1990 than during 1995–2000. This may reflect the importance of return migration to Puerto Rico in the earlier period. Unemployment is more manageable for residents of the island, where extended family networks, the informal economy, and a more palatable climate ease the hardships of being without official work.

The occupational profiles of the two groups also differ rather markedly. During the 1980s, blue-collar jobs were more prevalent among outmigrants (32%) than among stayers (27%), while service occupations were more predominant among stayers (56%) than among leavers (50%). Service occupations were the largest category for both groups. Gender variations are part of the differentials. Blue-collar occupations were much more prevalent among male outmigrants (46%) than stayers (39%); for females, white-collar employees were a somewhat larger segment among outmigrants (23%) than among stayers (20%). Service occupations were the largest category for both groups.

Regarding occupational distribution patterns during the 1990s, outmigrants were distributed in the following pattern: service (54%), blue-collar (25%), and white-collar (22%). They tended to be skewed more toward blue-collar jobs and less to service jobs than is the case for stayers, who were 21% blue-collar and 58% service. White-collar workers displayed a similar representation among outmigrants and stayers. Also, comparing the two time periods, the share of white-collar workers increased moderately across all groups.

As to be expected, there was a sizable gender differential in the occupational distribution. For example, among outmigrants, males (38%) were three-and-a-half times as likely to be holding blue-collar jobs as females (only 10%). Also significant was the gender difference in service-sector jobs; 65% of female outmigrants had service-sector jobs, while only 42% of males held these jobs. A similar gender comparison held among stayers: 67% of female stayers were in the service sector, as compared to 49% of male stayers.

Income, Housing, Poverty

In the 1980s, household income was higher for those who stayed ($27,490) than for those who left ($23,660). This contrasts with the 1990s, during which household income was appreciably higher among outmigrants ($45,185) than stayers ($38,597). Furthermore, leavers had higher levels of homeownership. By 1990, at the end of the decision to move, a much higher fraction of outmigrants had their own homes (43%) than for stayers (13%). Conversely a much larger proportion of stayers rented their living quarters than did outmigrants (87% versus 57%). Similarly, in the 1990s, homeownership was a more prevalent status among outmigrants than among stayers (48% versus 20%), though homeownership grew appreciably among the stayers compared to the earlier period.

A comparison of hardship conditions can be gleaned by examining poverty levels between groups and over time. The data show that, for 1985–90, a larger cohort of outmigrants lived in poverty (41%) than did among those who stayed (31%). In the 1990s, there was not much of a difference between the two groups; about a third of both groups were affected by poverty.

Summary

Summarizing the 1980s, there were a smaller number of seniors among outmigrants than among stayers; this is a pattern at variance with the finding that the largest group of outmigrants were returning to Puerto Rico. Was retirement really the main driver of this stream? Did those leaving for Puerto Rico include a significant number of younger, perhaps second-generation Nuyoricans? Only a more sophisticated quantitative assessment (i.e., regression analysis) can shed light on this. Those who left in the 1980s were also more highly educated, yet tended to speak English less well than stayers. They also were more likely to be married-couple-householders. They were more likely to be attached to the labor force, including a larger segment of unemployed (these are officially designated as being part of the labor force, until they abandon job-seeking efforts). Incomes were lower, poverty higher, and yet homeownership higher among outmigrants during the 1980s.

In the nineties, there appears to be a degree of selectivity along dimensions of education, employment, income, and homeownership. Generally those who left the city during 1995–2000 were in a more favorable socioeconomic position than those who remained. This contrasts with the situation

Table 4.3 Destinations of Outmigrants, 1985–1990 and 1995–2000

	1985–1990	1995–2000
NYC Suburban Ring	18%	26%
Florida	16%	21%
Puerto Rico	40%	18%
New England	7%	8%
All Other States	13%	17%
Other New York State	3%	4%
Pennsylvania	3%	6%

Note: Sample sizes: 1985–1990: 124,933; 1995–2000: 114,537.

Sources: 1990 IPUMS file and 2000 PUMS file.

of outmigrants of the eighties, who had lower incomes and higher poverty than those who stayed in New York City.

WHERE PUERTO RICANS GO

We estimate that during 1985–90, some 125,000 individuals, about 17% of the city's Puerto Rican population, emigrated. For the 1995–2000 period, we estimate that 115,000 Boricuas, or 15% of the city's Puerto Rican population, left New York.

Table 4.3 disaggregates the leavers into seven destinations. It indicates that Puerto Rico was the single most popular destination of outmigrants during 1985–90. Following the 40% of outmigrants who went back to the Caribbean is the group that migrated to the New York City suburbs (18%); these two groups were followed by those leaving for Florida (16%) and those going to "all other states" (13%). In the 1990s, Puerto Rico and the New York City suburbs reversed position as destinations. Somewhat surprisingly, then, during the 1990s, when analysts had focused much attention on the "waning" of Puerto Rican presence in the city, the single largest outmigrant stream moved not to tropical Puerto Rico (19%) or sunny Florida (20%), but to the cooler New York City metropolitan ring (26%).

In what ways were migrants to the different regions similar, and how were they different? How do these comparisons change over time? Table 4.4

Table 4.4 Characteristics of Outmigrants by Destinations, 1985–1990 and 1995–2000

	NYC Suburbs		Florida		Puerto Rico		New England		All Other States		Other NY State		Pennsylvania	
	85/90	95/00	85/90	95/00	85/90	95/00	85/90	95/00	85/90	95/00	85/90	95/00	85/90	95/00
Gender														
Male	48%	48%	49%	48%	47%	50%	47%	46%	49%	49%	50%	47%	50%	47%
Female	52%	52%	50%	52%	53%	50%	53%	54%	51%	51%	49%	53%	50%	53%
Race														
White	59%	52%	69%	60%	NA	78%	41%	35%	37%	34%	42%	46%	39%	40%
Black	4%	6%	3%	5%	NA	7%	3%	6%	7%	10%	5%	8%	4%	4%
Other Race	37%	33%	28%	30%	NA	9%	56%	53%	56%	39%	52%	36%	57%	50%
Two or More Races	NA	45	NA	4%	NA	5%	NA	6%	NA	13%	NA	10%	NA	5%
Age														
20–29	32%	26%	26%	25%	23%	14%	46%	37%	45%	39%	50%	39%	41%	39%
30–39	41%	41%	26%	30%	27%	22%	27%	29%	29%	32%	24%	27%	32%	28%
40–49	16%	17%	21%	17%	17%	16%	16%	11%	13%	13%	13%	14%	12%	15%
50–54	4%	5%	8%	7%	9%	8%	4%	7%	3%	5%	3%	7%	3%	6%
55 and older	7%	11%	19%	20%	23%	40%	8%	16%	10%	10%	9%	14%	11%	11%
Place of Birth														
United States	4%	4%	5%	6%	3%	2%	6%	8%	9%	7%	1%	6%	6%	8%
New York	62%	73%	49%	58%	28%	23%	43%	54%	57%	69%	59%	65%	54%	60%
Puerto Rico	31%	22%	43%	33%	68%	74%	49%	36%	31%	23%	38%	29%	37%	31%
Education														
Less than HS	30%	22%	41%	39%	62%	53%	48%	51%	32%	24%	39%	43%	51%	41%
High School	25%	25%	29%	25%	22%	24%	17%	22%	25%	25%	29%	23%	25%	26%
Some College and more	45%	53%	30%	37%	15%	23%	35%	26%	43%	51%	32%	34%	24%	33%
Language Ability														
Well or Very Well	91%	92%	86%	91%	64%	69%	80%	83%	90%	92%	90%	93%	94%	86%
Not Well or Not at All	9%	8%	14%	9%	36%	31%	20%	17%	10%	8%	10%	7%	6%	14%

Table 4.4 Characteristics of Outmigrants by Destinations, 1985–1990 and 1995–2000

	NYC Suburbs		Florida		Puerto Rico		New England		All Other States		Other NY State		Pennsylvania	
	85/90	95/00	85/90	95/00	85/90	95/00	85/90	95/00	85/90	95/00	85/90	95/00	85/90	95/00
Marital Status														
Married	66%	58%	60%	52%	60%	49%	38%	33%	52%	49%	41%	29%	41%	42%
Widowed	2%	2%	5%	6%	4%	8%	2%	5%	3%	4%	2%	4%	1%	3%
Divorced and Separated	13%	15%	17%	19%	20%	22%	24%	25%	16%	15%	17%	19%	28%	14%
Never Married	19%	25%	17%	22%	15%	20%	36%	38%	29%	32%	39%	47%	29%	41%
Employment Status														
Employed	76%	74%	70%	68%	32%	34%	48%	43%	63%	68%	58%	49%	56%	56%
Unemployed	5%	5%	7%	6%	25%	12%	10%	14%	12%	6%	5%	8%	13%	15%
Not in Labor Force	19%	21%	23%	26%	43%	53%	42%	42%	25%	26%	37%	43%	31%	29%
Occupation														
White-Collar	25%	31%	16%	19%	12%	17%	14%	17%	14%	23%	21%	17%	12%	14%
Service	51%	50%	55%	59%	44%	50%	54%	50%	54%	56%	52%	56%	56%	48%
Blue-Collar	24%	19%	29%	22%	44%	33%	32%	33%	32%	20%	27%	26%	32%	38%
Male														
White-Collar	21%	26%	9%	17%	9%	15%	14%	11%	19%	19%	23%	15%	9%	16%
Service	41%	42%	44%	42%	38%	39%	40%	46%	49%	43%	63%	49%	38%	36%
Blue-Collar	37%	31%	47%	40%	53%	46%	46%	43%	32%	37%	15%	36%	53%	48%
Female														
White-Collar	30%	35%	24%	20%	17%	20%	14%	13%	26%	25%	23%	15%	15%	11%
Service	61%	57%	68%	74%	52%	60%	69%	67%	65%	68%	63%	72%	80%	68%
Blue-Collar	9%	8%	9%	6%	31%	20%	17%	20%	9%	7%	15%	12%	4%	21%
Income	$48,022	$74,206	$27,750	$44,498	$10,957	$18,264	$19,694	$31,117	$26,746	$46,515	$20,646	$26,490	$21,999	$30,386
Ownership versus Rental														
Ownership	48%	65%	45%	49%	55%	62%	7%	15%	23%	34%	23%	30%	21%	24%
Rental	52%	34%	55%	51%	44%	28%	93%	84%	77%	64%	77%	69%	79%	73%
Poverty Status														
Below Poverty	10%	13%	23%	19%	67%	59%	43%	42%	26%	25%	26%	54%	42%	42%

Sources: 1990 IPUMS and 2000 PUMS. Authors' tabulations.

presents the characteristics of the migrant streams that left for each of the seven receiving areas in the two periods under review. The following section highlights the key features of each group to show to what degree the profiles might correspond to the four outmigrant cohorts provisionally laid out earlier: *retirees, suburbanites, opportunity seekers,* and the *displaced.*

Puerto Rico

1985–90

Those who left for Puerto Rico, the largest single group, were generally older (32% were age 50+), were more typically Puerto Rico–born (two-thirds), had the lowest educational attainment (62% did not complete high school), and were heavily Spanish-speaking (more than a third did not speak English well, the largest fraction for any outmigrant stream). This group also experienced the highest unemployment (25%) and lowest labor-force attachment (43%) for any stream. Puerto Rico–destined outmigrants also were largely blue-collar workers (44%) and had the lowest income and highest poverty for any comparative group. On the positive side, the majority (55%) were homeowners once they settled on the island. This was the highest level of homeownership for all groups.

1995–2000

These trends basically held during the second half of the nineties. This cohort that migrated to Puerto Rico was (1) most likely to be fifty years of age or older (48%), (2) most likely to have been born in Puerto Rico (74%), (3) most likely to have less than a high school education (53%), (4) least likely to speak English well or very well (69%), and (5) most likely to be out of the labor force (53%).

In sum, these were relatively older movers, rural and working-class Puerto Ricans who generally came to New York during the period of the "Great Migration" of the 1940s and 1950s, and who decided to return to their place of birth. Another aspect of this population speaks to their vulnerable socioeconomic position. Three of every five persons who returned to Puerto Rico—and surely among these were a large number of retirees—lived in conditions of poverty. Poverty incidence is higher for this group than for outmigrants and stayers in general.

NYC Suburbs

1985–90

The next-largest stream of the 1980s, slightly larger than the Florida cohort, was composed of those who left for the suburbs. The suburban group is the mirror opposite of the Puerto Rico group. These were much younger than those headed to Puerto Rico and Florida (as measured by the 20–49 age category, which totaled 89%), were New York City–born (62%), had the highest educational attainment, and had higher-than-average English-language ability. They also faced markedly lower unemployment and displayed higher levels of labor-force attachment than the other groups. They had the highest composition of white-collar workers (25%), the highest income level, and by far the lowest poverty incidence. They were second only to the Puerto Rico group in the share of homeownership (48%).

1995–2000

Outmigrants to the New York City suburban area during 1995–2000 were (1) most likely to be middle aged (58% were of ages 30–49), (2) most likely to have been born in the state of New York (73%), (3) most likely to have had at least some college education (53%), (4) one of the most likely to speak English well (92%), (5) most likely to have white-collar jobs, and (6) most likely to be employed (74%). They also had the highest mean household income ($74,206) and the highest ratio of homeownership (65%). Paradoxically, those returning to Puerto Rico had a similarly high ratio of homeownership, 62%, though this is likely due to having inherited property that had been kept within their extended family, and also to the relatively less expensive real estate market on the island.

This profile describes the group of movers who left the five boroughs for the counties contiguous to the city, the destination of the single largest group of outmigrants during 1995–2000. These are the counties of northeastern New Jersey, Long Island, and southeastern New York.

Florida

1985–90

Puerto Rican New Yorkers who left for Florida displayed a few noteworthy characteristics. Their typical characteristics placed them in an intermediate range between the Puerto Rico and suburban streams. They were a sizable middle-aged cohort, given that they had the largest group of individuals in their forties and fifties (29%); but they also had the second-largest group, following the Puerto Rico cohort, of individuals in the 50+ age category (27%). They had the largest group of high school completion (29%), sharing this distinction with those who left for "other New York State" locations. They approached the employment level (70%) of labor-force attachment (only 23% were not in the labor force) and income level ($27,750) of the most economically successful group, the New York City suburbanites.

1995–2000

During 1995–2000, the group going to Florida displayed a profile that was most similar to that of those outmigrants going to Puerto Rico. They had a similarly high proportion of older-aged persons, individuals born on the island, and also of homeowners. A principal difference is in the area of English language fluency. Over 90% of outmigrants to Florida spoke English well or very well, compared to 69% of those going to Puerto Rico. This suggests that many of those retiring to Florida were either born or raised in the United States. Proximity to Puerto Rico, a tropical climate, and a vibrant Latino culture make seem to make Florida a natural alternative for those who wish to remain on the US mainland.

All Other States

1985–90

In both periods, the cohort going to "all other states" (encompassing the Midwest, West, and Southeast) was the fourth-largest stream. The distinguishing behavioral characteristic of the group is its willingness to relocate significant distances to areas of smaller Puerto Rican concentrations, Chicago being the most important exception. This would imply a younger, New York–born, dominantly English-speaking and fairly educated profile.

During the 1980s, these were some of the features describing this group. Especially significant is the high proportion of the "some college and more" population (43%); this is second only to the New York suburban group. Although not as successful in the economy as the New York suburbanites, this group displayed higher incomes and lower poverty than the *average outmigrant* (represented as all outmigrants in table 4.2).

1995–2000

During this period, those who left the city for regions westward and southward ("all other states") also ranked fairly highly along several of the dimensions that we have associated with suburbanite characteristics: education, English-language fluency, New York City birth, white-collar occupations, and household income.

Seventy-one percent (the largest proportion of any cohort) were age twenty to thirty-nine; 51% (almost identical to those going to suburban New York City) had some college or more; more than nine out of ten (similar to the Metro New York suburban group) spoke English well or very well; and two-thirds were employed (following the New York City suburbanites).

As mentioned above, outmigrants to Florida shared similar levels of these characteristics. There is a perceptible difference, though, regarding occupational distribution; those going to Florida had a greater representation of service workers, probably due to the higher proportion of women in this group than is the case for outmigrants going to "all other states." Although the "all other states" cohort displayed a higher household income than the Florida group, these outmigrants also faced higher poverty and lower homeownership. This suggests that the Florida group had a more homogeneous class structure than those migrating to the other distant regions.

New England, Pennsylvania, and "Other New York"

As noted in table 4.3, outmigrants to New England and Pennsylvania together composed 10% and 14% of all movers in 1985–90 and 1995–2000, respectively. During the eighties those moving to New England displayed lower labor-force participation and lower incomes and homeownership status than the typical outmigrant. They could boast a higher level of college education (35% vs. 29%). They were similar to the rest of outmigrants in terms of the percentage born in Puerto Rico, English-language proficiency, and the level of poverty. Aside from education, this group was not faring as well as the typical Puerto Rican who left the city.

During the 1990s, this group appeared to have lost even further ground compared to the rest of the outmigrant stream. A less-educated population, relatively speaking, was destined for New England, with the college-educated proportion falling to 26%, compared to 38% for the general group. Regarding the other indicators, this cohort remained less-integrated into the labor force, earned lower incomes, were much less likely to be homeowners, and were more likely to be in poverty. It is noteworthy that outmigrants to New England do not seem to have been relocating to take advantage of homeownership possibilities. During the eighties and nineties, they were overwhelmingly renters in their new places of residence. This would suggest that this cohort was responding to New York City's rental housing costs by relocating to a lower rental market, and not necessarily because they were in a position to invest in housing equity.

Those who moved to Pennsylvania during the 1980s were more likely to have been born in New York, to speak English well, and to work in service occupations. When compared to the reference group (all outmigrants), this stream was fairly similar in its characteristics along the dimensions of labor-force integration, income, and poverty. Homeownership among this group was less than the level for all outmigrants, but greater when compared to those who moved to New England.

Subsequently, during the 1990s, this group was faring less well with regard to labor-force attachment, incomes, and poverty. During this period, as in the case of outmigrants to New England, those leaving for Pennsylvania seem to have come from a stratum of Puerto Rican New Yorkers that was lower on the socioeconomic ladder.

The cohort that left for other parts of New York State, beyond the New York City metropolitan ring, had the following distinguishing characteristics. During the 1980s, individuals in this group were more likely to be New York City–born, speak English well, have attained higher education, be more integrated into the labor force, and be less affected by poverty than the reference group (all outmigrants). Partially offsetting these positive features, they displayed lower incomes and lower homeownership rates.

There were some changes for the worse regarding this cohort's relative status in the 1990s. These individuals sustained lower levels of labor-force integration, a larger gap in incomes, and a reversal in relative poverty. Comparing the two periods, the relative position of "outmigrants to other parts of New York State" compared to "all outmigrants" seems to have deteriorated in several key aspects. However, we are cautious in this assessment, since this is the smallest cohort of outmigrants, measuring only 3% and 4% for the two periods, respectively.

DISCUSSION

Suburbanization and Assimilation

The single largest group of outmigrants during 1995–2000 consists of those Puerto Ricans who moved to the New York City suburban ring. We have also noted that others appear to be pursuing suburban-style living in more distant places (such as Florida and "all other states"). This trend supports the argument that, for a significant fraction of the Puerto Rican diaspora, the classic pattern of assimilation has been taking place, at least in the conventional understanding of that term. However, some cautionary remarks are in order.

We question whether Puerto Ricans who relocate to the metropolitan ring are jettisoning their culture for the American "mainstream." Despite the greater adoption of English with the passing of generations, Puerto Ricans still sponsor their own parades and social organizations in a number of suburban towns and counties and continue to resist the hyphenated (Puerto Rican–American) identity.[24]

As has been the case with other middle class minorities, those moving to the suburbs often desire to congregate in areas populated by coethnics. It is quite possible that the tie between suburbanization and assimilation is not as strong as it once was in the mid-twentieth century when New York City's Irish, Jewish, and Italian residents were leaving. As long as suburban residential segregation persists for African Americans and Latinos, and as long as minorities still find themselves concentrated in the relatively lower-income suburban areas, the economic and social forces that historically "melted" Americans of European origin will be too weak to replicate the earlier assimilation process for non-European-origin minorities.

The transnational character of Puerto Rican and other Latino communities reinforces the cultural ties to their homeland, abetting the retention of Spanish-language use and sustaining participation in the political and economic life of their countries of origin. What has been noted as a distinctive quality among recent immigrants from Latin America has been a longtime feature of the Puerto Rican diaspora.[25]

Adding to the process that very likely will differ from the assimilation path of earlier immigrant groups is the pan-Latinization of Puerto Ricans and other Latinos in metropolitan areas. The emergence of a new umbrella identity offers an alternative to the gravitational pull of white or black identities. Whether the American racial order, still rigidly encased in the white-black divide, will continue to shape the assimilation process or will change due to the rise of a "third force" is one of the more interesting questions to be confronted by Puerto Ricans and Latinos in the future.

Suburbanization and the "Waning" of Puerto Rican New York

Another aspect of Puerto Rican suburbanization touches upon the alleged "waning" of the Puerto Rican presence in New York City.[26] It seems likely that a sizable part of the drop in inner-city Puerto Rican population during the 1990s is simply a relocation of population to the outer ring, a feature of all the "Great Migrations" to New York City. To what degree do Puerto Ricans living in the suburban ring commute to work as teachers, health-care employees, civil servants, and small business owners? To what degree do they continue to participate in the social, economic, and cultural life of the city's Puerto Rican community? To the extent that the metropolis continues to be a center of economic, cultural, and political activity for many of these suburbanites, are not the declarations of Puerto Rican decline overblown?

Perhaps the thought that shifting compositions in the Latino population are a zero sum game is the problem. We see a dramatic expansion of Dominican, Mexican, and Colombian communities, for example, deepening their imprint on the New York landscape. Perhaps some interpret this as coming at the expense of some other Latino group (i.e., Puerto Ricans). In reality, this speaks to the continuing enlargement of a Latino presence and contribution in the New York metropolitan context.

Displacement and the Poor

For those at the other end of the socioeconomic spectrum—the economically displaced—leaving New York has not freed them from poverty. During the 1995–2000 period, for example, outmigrants to New England, Pennsylvania, and the rest of New York State experienced poverty at greater rates (42%, 42%, and 54% respectively) than was the case for typical New York Puerto Ricans who remained behind (32% among stayers). For residents in smaller, deindustrializing northeastern towns and cities, who continue to face unemployment, crime, and poor housing, their decision to relocate did not deliver substantial improvements in socioeconomic well-being.[27]

This reality recalls the original Puerto Rican migration to New York City. During the postwar period, the newcomers arrived just as the city was beginning to transition from a manufacturing-based economy. Is the experience of the late 1940s and 1950s being repeated today in cities such as Waterbury, Bridgeport, Springfield, Allentown, and Bethlehem? These cities have steadily been losing their industrial base. Absent a serious regional effort to revitalize these local economies, there will be no viable prospects for stable livelihoods for these modern-day migrants of the Puerto Rican diaspora. It is also troubling that those who emigrate back to Puerto Rico encounter even higher rates of economic distress. Whether this represents predominantly seniors who are retiring or younger displaced families is not clear from our data.

As of this writing, the US economy has only recently emerged from the Great Recession of the first decade of the 2000s. Each additional year of tepid economic performance leaves a deeper mark on cities, families, and individuals. If the talk of a "lost decade" approaches reality, the effect on Puerto Ricans—still one of the most impoverished and vulnerable communities in the country—will be devastating. Migration patterns are likely to become more volatile and disruptive as people search for new ways and means of survival.

Racial, Cultural, and Gender Dimensions

Racial and cultural dimensions are other aspects deserving attention, especially if they *deter* outmigration. Black Puerto Ricans possessing the economic wherewithal and educational background to move to the suburbs will refrain from doing so if they fear discrimination and hostility in the new neighborhood. Anxiety about the potential for racial animosity may also deter relocation for opportunity-seeking individuals. Do those with language-dominance in Spanish behave similarly? We have seen evidence of differential racial self-identification among outmigrants. A much larger component of those going to Puerto Rico and Florida are white, in contrast to those going everywhere else (especially to New England and "other New York State"). How much of this difference reflects subjective self-identification mediated by generational differences in conceptions of race? How much of this difference is objective? How different are these comparisons among those who self-identify as "other"? These questions are worth exploring in further work.[28]

The gender dimension of the outmigration experience deserves analysis. "Job type" is an example. We have reported differential patterns with regard to occupational structures. Additional data, reported in an earlier phase of this study, indicate that females are slightly overrepresented among the flows to the high-poverty destinations (New England, Pennsylvania, and "other New York State"). Is there an association, yet to be discovered, between female single heads of households and poverty in this instance? On the other hand, males are slightly overrepresented among the cohort leaving for Puerto Rico, and Puerto Rico is where the highest rates of migrant poverty are to be found. It seems poor males tend toward Puerto Rico and females tend to stay in the Northeast. What might account for this?

FURTHER RESEARCH

Further research can proceed in a number of directions, including the following:

Examining the accuracy of the four reasons for Puerto Rican outmigration from New York City, as hypothesized here. Regression analyses can be conducted to assess the potential determinants of the outmigration decision. Since census data lack sufficient information at the individual level (for example, the census does not directly ask why a person left his/her previous residence), in-depth interviewing and qualitative studies can provide other approaches to this issue.

Extending the period of analysis to include 2010 census data to capture long-term patterns of outmigration from the city. Tracing changes in the city's economy and politics would help contextualize the forces driving outmigration. A look at the 2010 census permits a more current assessment of the trends examined in this chapter, including examining the "Great Recession's" impact on migration flows. In the final section of this chapter we offer some preliminary comments on post–2000 trends. Changes in the residence questions of the 2010 census complicate efforts to secure comparability between 2010 and prior decennial data.

Comparing the Puerto Rican story with Cuban, Dominican, and other Latino outmigration experiences. Are the reasons propelling other groups' movements the same, and are they going to similar regions? Similarly, it would be informative to compare Puerto Rican outmigration with the experience of African Americans, the non-Latino group whose experience is most commonly associated with that of Puerto Ricans.[29]

RECENT TRENDS

What can be said about post-2000 migration and population trends? Due to changes in some of the questions asked, the 2010 census does not offer comparable data on outmigration patterns. It is not possible to collect information about residence in the previous five-year period, and therefore we are unable to track Puerto Rican outflows from New York City during the 2000s in the same way examined in this chapter. However, research has been conducted on internal migration for Puerto Ricans on the mainland.[30] The largest flows still persist to the regions of the Northeast and South. While the Northeast continues to hold the largest number of Puerto Ricans, about 53% of all those living in the United States, Florida is the fastest-growing state of residence. According to García-Ellín, New York State's Puerto Rican population received a boost of 8.6% from internal migration during this period.[31] Continuing the pattern observed during the 1990s, Florida is the major destination for Puerto Rican internal migrants, as well as those coming from the island. A major draw is the economic opportunity this state provides, in terms of employment, higher income levels, and homeownership. Many reside in the Orlando area, which is a major service-based economy accessible to Puerto Ricans leaving the island. Another incentive is the low cost of living.[32]

Within the New York City metropolitan region, new developments have caught the attention of demographers. According to some recent counts, the New York City Dominican population has surpassed that of Puerto Ricans; although this remains contested at present, it will likely be a certainty by 2020. Meanwhile the Puerto Rican presence continues to increase in the counties outside of New York City, reflecting our earlier findings of Puerto Rican suburbanization since the 1980s. Puerto Ricans continue to be the largest Latino group within the metropolitan region.[33]

The 2010 census allows us to track population trends within the city. Table 4.5 presents data on the city's Puerto Rican population, including that of the boroughs, from 1980 to 2010. In 1980, 12% of New Yorkers were Puerto Rican. By 2010, Puerto Ricans constituted 9% of the city's population. At the borough level, Queens and Staten Island experienced modest increases, but the boroughs with the largest numbers of Puerto Ricans have experienced significant declines. Both Brooklyn and Manhattan have had a decline from 12% in 1980 to 7% in 2010. The biggest decline occurred in the Bronx, the borough with the largest Puerto Rican population. Over a quarter

Table 4.5 New York City Puerto Rican Population by Borough, 1980–2010

	1980	1990	2000	2010
New York City	852833 (12)	896763 (12)	789172 (10)	723621 (9)
Brooklyn	275758 (12)	274530 (12)	213025 (9)	176528 (7)
Bronx	318365 (27)	349115 (29)	319240 (24)	298921 (21)
Manhattan	166302 (12)	154978 (10)	119718 (8)	107774 (7)
Staten Island	11499 (3)	17730 (5)	28528 (6)	37517 (8)
Queens	80909 (4)	100410 (5)	108661 (5)	102881 (5)

Note: Number in parentheses represents Puerto Rican percentage share of total city-wide or borough population for that year.

Sources: Socioeconomic Profiles: A Portrait of New York City's Community Districts from the 1980 & 1990 Censuses of Population and Housing. New York City, Department of City Planning, 1993. On 2000 and 2010 population, Department of City Planning, retrieved on January 11, 2015, at: www.nyc.gov/html/dcp/html/cunsus/popdiv.shtml.

of the population was Puerto Rican in 1980, and this share reached a peak in 1990, at close to 30%. By 2010, 21% of the Bronx was Puerto Rican.

This breakout affirms that the long-term reduction that began in earnest during the 1990s persisted into the new millennium. And yet, in proportionate terms, the drop is not as dramatic in the post 2000 period, changing only one percentage point, from 10% to 9%.

A further perspective on long-term population change of Puerto Rican New Yorkers can be discerned by looking at key neighborhoods from 1980 to 2010. Table 4.6 shows five communities in which there have been large concentrations of Puerto Ricans since the mid-twentieth century. East Harlem (El Barrio) has been home to a Puerto Rican enclave since the 1920s. In 1980, 41% of the area was of Puerto Rican descent, and by 2010 the number fell to 25%. This turnover has been partially attributed to neoliberal policies of the times.[34] Similarly, the Lower East Side of Manhattan had maintained a robust Puerto Rican presence beginning in the 1940s. During the 1970s and 1980s, this area, renamed "Loisaida" by the locals, fell victim to severe disinvestment by real estate interests and city government.[35] The Puerto Rican presence declined from 28% in 1980 to 14% in 2010.

The Williamsburg and Bushwick sections were likewise affected by hyperdevelopment and gentrification, making it untenable for long-standing Puerto Rican neighborhoods to remain solidly intact.[36] In the former, the Puerto Rican proportion fell from 32% to only 12% during 1980–2010; in

Table 4.6 Puerto Rican Neighborhood Populations, 1980 to 2010

	1980	1990	2000	2010
Lower Eastside MN	43491 (28)	35819 (22)	26149 (16)	22826 (14)
East Harlem MN	47106 (41)	45582 (41)	35399 (30)	29979 (25)
South Bronx BX	42029 (54)	38550 (50)	33969 (41)	30075 (33)
Bushwick BK	40920 (44)	40869 (40)	30952 (30)	23934 (21)
Williamsburg BK	45321 (32)	42404 (27)	28274 (18)	21359 (12)

Note: Number in parentheses represents Puerto Rican percentage share of total neighborhood population for that year. Neighborhoods are defined from Community Planning District boundaries in the following manner: Lower East Side (Manhattan CPD #3); East Harlem (Manhattan CPD # 11); South Bronx (Bronx CPD # 1); Bushwick (Brooklyn CPD # 4); Williamsburg (Brooklyn CPD #1).

Sources: Socioeconomic Profiles: A Portrait of New York City's Community Districts from the 1980 & 1990 Censuses of Population and Housing. New York City, Department of City Planning, 1993. On 2000 and 2010 populations, Department of City Planning, retrieved on January 11, 2015, at: www.nyc.gov/html/dcp/html/cunsus/popdiv.shtml.

the latter, the population declined from 44% to 21% during the same period. The South Bronx is another case in point. Whereas more than half of the residents were Puerto Rican in 1980, only a third were in 2010. The Boricua presence in these traditional neighborhoods has continued to diminish. However, the declines in these once heavily Puerto Rican areas are far greater than the decline in the city overall. Between 2000 and 2010, the percentage drop in these five neighborhoods ranged from minus 11.5% (in the South Bronx) to minus 24.4% (in Williamsburg). These numbers well exceed the overall percentage fall of Puerto Ricans city-wide, which was minus 8.3% (or 65,551 individuals) as per table 4.5. What this suggests is that Puerto Ricans who remain in the city are gradually moving from the traditional *barrios* and resettling into other New York neighborhoods. Further neighborhood-level research is needed to confirm this conjecture.

Another population trend, wholly unanticipated, has emerged in recent years. Much has been said about the economic difficulties hurting the economy of Puerto Rico. The Great Recession that damaged the mainland starting in 2007 has left the island territory in much worse shape. Puerto Rico's finances, local labor market, and competitive condition were already fragile heading into the mid-2000s. By 2014 the losses to the economy were catastrophic: a 13% contraction in the economy, an 18% fall in the number of people employed, and an 11% decline in domestic investment. From 2006 to

2013, local government deficit rose to $2.2 billion, and total debt rose from $43 billion to $73 billion.[37]

It is unsurprising, then, that inhabitants of the island would begin a sizable outmigration, one not seen since the Great Migration of the post–World War II era. According to the Pew Research Center, by 2013, 4.9 million Puerto Ricans were living in the United States, and 3.5 million in Puerto Rico. Between 2010 and 2013 alone, there was a net outflow of almost 150,000 from the island to the US mainland. The bulk of emigrants were likely to move to Florida, Texas, and other southern states that islanders have shown a preference for since the 1990s. Nevertheless, a fraction (9%) of this flow appears to have settled in New York State. It is unknown what portion has settled in New York City or the metro region.[38]

To conclude, it is likely that Puerto Ricans will continue to be an important presence for the foreseeable future in the New York metropolitan area. In 2013, the inner city was still home to almost 720,000 Puerto Ricans, the longest-residing component of Latino New York City.[39] But if not now, within a very few years, they will no longer be the largest Latino population. That distinction will be held by their Caribbean cousins, the Dominicans. Future chapters in the history of New York will necessarily take greater notice of this dynamic and growing community.

Returning to the initial question posed in the title of this chapter, "Where Have All the Puerto Ricans Gone?," we are inclined to answer this way: in historical perspective, not all that many have left and many of the movers have not gone very far.

NOTES

This chapter is a revision and expansion of an earlier paper: Marzán, Torres, and Luecke, "Puerto Rican Outmigration from New York City." We thank Andrew Luecke for his assistance on the earlier paper, and to Juan de la Cruz for research advice on this chapter.

1. Acosta-Belén and Santiago, *Puerto Ricans in the United States*, 83 table 4.4. On 2010 population, see Ennis, Ríos-Vargas, and Albert, *The Hispanic Population: 2010*. On 2013 population, see Cohn, Patten, and Lopez, *Puerto Rican Population Declines*.

2. Falcón, *Atlas of Stateside Puerto Ricans*.

3. Rivera-Batiz and Santiago, *Puerto Ricans in the United States*, chap. 3.

4. Acosta-Belén and Santiago, *Puerto Ricans in the United States*, 81 table 4.2.

5. Ibid., 47.

6. For 1970–2000 comparisons see Acosta-Belén and Santiago, *Puerto Ricans in the United States*, 87 fig. 4.2, 90 fig. 4.4. For 2009, authors' compilation is based on the American Community Survey (ACS), published by the United States Census Bureau. See http://www.census.gov/programs-surveys/acs/.

7. On circular migration, see Marta Tienda and William Diaz, "Puerto Rican Circular Migration," *New York Times*, August 28, 1987; Rodríguez, "Circulating Migration," 5–9; Duany, *Puerto Rican Nation on the Move*, 32–33. On commuter migration (posited by its theorizers as a more intensive variation of circular migration), see Torre, Vecchini, and Burgos, *Commuter Nation*.

8. Acosta-Belén and Santiago, *Puerto Ricans in the United States*, 98.

9. On migrating from New York City to Puerto Rico, see Rivera-Batíz, "Puerto Rican New Yorkers in the 1990s," 110–11; Mireya Navarro, "Falling Back: A Special Report; Puerto Rican Presence Wanes in New York," *New York Times*, February 28, 2000.

10. On rising education levels and jobs, see Acosta-Belén and Santiago, *Puerto Ricans in the United States*, 124–26 table 5.7; Rivera-Batíz and Santiago, *Puerto Ricans in the United States*, 89 table 6.6, 90; Rivera-Batíz, "Puerto Rican New Yorkers in the 1990s," 119 table 9. On the US-born versus Puerto Rico-born comparison, see Sam Roberts, "Puerto Ricans on the Mainland Making Gains," *New York Times*, October 19, 1994. Roberts writes, "Puerto Ricans born in the 50 states made striking economic gains in the 1980s—so striking that, by one measure, their income now surpasses that of Hispanic residents generally and of American-born blacks. But those who migrated to the mainland from Puerto Rico lag behind mainland-born Puerto Ricans in income, education and employment."

11. New York City, *Puerto Rican New Yorkers in 1990*, 117.

12. Kasarda, "Industrial Restructuring and the Changing Location of Jobs."

13. Foulkes and Newbold, "Migration Propensities, Patterns, and the Role of Human Capital," 141.

14. US Census Bureau, *1990 Census of Population and Housing*; US Census Bureau, Census 2000.

15. New York City, *Puerto Rican New Yorkers in 1990*, 113.

16. Marzán, "Still Looking for That Elsewhere."

17. On Puerto Ricans and the decline of manufacturing jobs in New York City, see Acosta-Belén and Santiago, *Puerto Ricans in the United States*, 132; New York City, *Puerto Rican New Yorkers in 1990*, 109; Torres, *Between Melting Pot and Mosaic*, 66, 87.

18. Torres and Bonilla, "Decline within Decline," 96.

19. Acosta-Belén and Santiago, *Puerto Ricans in the United States*, 95; Baker, *Understanding Mainland Puerto Rican Poverty*, 172; Duany and Matos Rodríguez, *Puerto Ricans in Orlando and Central Florida*, 29.

20. Our thanks to Dr. Joseph Pereira, director of the CUNY Data Service, for providing us with a customized file of the 2000 census PUMS file. The data set for outmigrants contains records for 5,412 persons. These were weighted to generate a more representative sample of outmigrants, totaling 114,537. Thanks also to Dr. Juan Carlos Guzmán, director of research for the institute of Latino Studies, University of Notre Dame, for providing a file of the 1990 census IPUMS. This file contains records of 6,109 outmigrants, weighted to generate a sample of 124,933 cases. Dr. Gabriel Aquino, Westfield State University, also provided technical assistance for the 1990 IPUMS data set. The data set for stayers was compiled by the authors, drawn from the 1990 IPUMS and 2000 IPUMS. We would also like to thank Dr. Karen Tejada, University of Hartford, for her comments and suggestions on earlier versions of this chapter.

21. Foulkes and Newbold, "Migration Propensities, Patterns, and the Role of Human Capital," 134, 138–39 fig. 1; New York City, *Puerto Rican New Yorkers in 1990*, 111, 120 fig. 9.1. Also see Marzán, "Still Looking for That Elsewhere"; Duany and Matos Rodríguez, *Puerto Ricans in Orlando and Central Florida*; and Navarro, "Falling Back."

22. Our definition of the suburban ring includes the following counties: Nassau and Suffolk (making up Long Island), Westchester, Dutchess, Rockland, Orange, Putnam (in southeastern New York State), and fourteen counties in the northern half of New Jersey, stretching as far down as Mercer and Monmouth Counties. The city of Trenton, for example, is located in Mercer County. Excluded from this definition, and counted in standard definitions of the Consolidated Metropolitan Statistical Area (CMSA) for New York City, are two counties in Connecticut: New Haven and Fairfield. Our assumption is that these counties have a more logical association with the rest of New England. For discussions of how definitions of the New York City suburban boundary have evolved over time, see Andrew Beveridge, "Is There Still a New York Metropolis," *Gotham Gazette*, January 13, 2003, http://www.gothamgazette.com/index.php/city/1556-is-there-still-a-new-york-metropolis.

23. Labor-force attachment is defined as the population that is employed plus the population that is currently without work but still looking for work (the unemployed).

24. L. Torres, *Puerto Rican Discourse*, 3, 4; Allison Steele, "Annual Puerto Rican Parade Floats through Newark," *Star Ledger* (Newark, NJ), September 16, 2007; Steele, "Perth Amboy Names Street for Puerto Ricans," *Star Ledger* (Newark, NJ), January 24, 2008; Seth Kugel, "Traditional Puerto Rican Music Finds a Home in New Jersey," *New York Times*, November 23, 2003.

25. For examples see Itzigsohn, *Encountering American Faultlines*; Levitt, *The Transnational Villagers*, 242–81; Portes, Haller, and Guarnizo, "Transnational Entrepreneurs"; Smith, *Mexican New York*.

26. Navarro, "Falling Back"; for two vigorously dissenting views on the "waning" thesis, see the chapters by Angelo Falcón and Clara E. Rodríguez in Haslip-Viera, Falcón, and Matos Rodríguez, *Boricuas in Gotham*, 2004.

27. On socioeconomic conditions for Puerto Ricans in northeastern towns: Rivera-Batíz and Santiago, *Puerto Ricans in the United States*, 34, 35 table 3.7, 36, 47, 48 table 4.5, 49; Acosta-Belén and Santiago, 2006, 137 table 5.11, 138. Also see Marzán, "Still Looking for That Elsewhere."

28. For an analysis of patterns of concentration and segregation throughout the Puerto Rican diaspora, see Vargas-Ramos, "Settlement Patterns and Residential Segregation of Puerto Ricans in the United States."

29. McHugh, "Black Migration Reversal in the United States," 173, 178, 180–82.

30. Using the ACS, García-Ellín presents a profile of the internal migration (cross-state) of Puerto Ricans during the first decade of this century. His study differs from ours in two ways: first, that the outmigration stream of interest is from New York State (not New York City), and second, that it does not include Puerto Rico as a point of origin or destination. Also, his data are constructed from annual residence changes, in contrast to our (census-derived) five-year intervals of residential change. See García-Ellín, "Brief Look at Internal Migration of Puerto Ricans in the United States: 2000–2011," 26–28.

31. García-Ellín, "Brief Look at Internal Migration of Puerto Ricans," 28 table 2.

32. Silver, "Puerto Ricans in Florida"; Duany and Matos Rodríguez, *Puerto Ricans in Orlando and Central Florida*; Villarrubia-Mendoza, "Characteristics of Puerto Rican Homeowners in Florida."

33. Bergad, *Have Dominicans Surpassed Puerto Ricans?*

34. Dávila, *Barrio Dreams*, 8–15.

35. Mele, "Neighborhood 'Burnout.'"

36. Zukin, *Naked City*, 35–61.

37. Arturo C. Porzecanski, "Puerto Rico: Is This Any Way to Run an Island?" *Congress Blog*, May 29, 2014, The Hill, http://thehill.com/blogs/congress-blog/economy-budget/207436-puerto-rico-is-this-any-way-to-run-an-island; Errol Louis, "Crushing Debt Is Catching Up to the U.S. Territory," *New York Daily News*, July 17, 2014; Maryellen Tighe and Ellie Ismailidou, "Wall Street Waits While Statehood Debate Handcuffs Puerto Rico Decision Makers," *Forbes*, July 7, 2014; Federal Reserve Bank of New York, "Report on the Competitiveness of Puerto Rico's Economy."

38. Cohn, Patten, and Lopez, *Puerto Rican Population Declines*.

39. Bergad, *Have Dominicans Surpassed Puerto Ricans?*, table 2. Since these figures are estimates from the ACS, the source for Bergad's report, they are less reliable than the decennial census estimates. Until the 2020 census, we are not certain of the relative numbers; but there is little doubt of the long-term trend of Dominican growth. Nor is there much doubt that the number of Dominicans will surpass the Puerto Rican count in due time, and likely before 2020. This uncertainty concerning ACS-based counts applies also to endnote 39.

REFERENCES

Acosta-Belén, Edna, and Carlos E. Santiago. *Puerto Ricans in the United States: A Contemporary Portrait.* Boulder, CO: Lynne Rienner, 2006.

Baker, Susan S. *Understanding Mainland Puerto Rican Poverty.* Philadelphia: Temple University Press, 2002.

Bergad, Laird W. *Have Dominicans Surpassed Puerto Ricans to become New York City's Largest Latino Nationality? An Analysis of Latino Population Data from the 2013 American Community Survey for New York City and the Metropolitan Area.* Latino Data Project, Report 61. New York: Center for Latin American, Caribbean and Latino Studies, Graduate Center, City University of New York, 2014. http://clacls.gc.cuny.edu/files/2014/11/AreDominicansLargestLatino Nationality.pdf.

Boswell, Thomas D., and Angel David Cruz-Báez. "Puerto Ricans Living in the United States." In *Ethnicity in Contemporary America: A Geographical Appraisal,* edited by Jesse O. McKee, 181–226. Lanham, MD: Rowman & Littlefield, 2000.

Cohn, D'Vera, Eileen Patten, and Mark Hugo Lopez. *Puerto Rican Population Declines on Island, Grows on U.S. Mainland.* Washington, DC: Pew Research Center, 2014. http://www.pewhispanic.org/2014/08/11/puerto-rican-population -declines-on-island-grows-on-u-s-mainland/.

Dávila, Arlene. *Barrio Dreams: Puerto Ricans, Latinos, and the Neoliberal City.* Berkeley: University of California Press, 2004.

Duany, Jorge. *The Puerto Rican Nation on the Move.* Chapel Hill: University of North Carolina Press, 2002.

Duany, Jorge, and Félix V. Matos Rodríguez. *Puerto Ricans in Orlando and Central Florida.* New York: Centro de Estudios Puertorriqueños, Hunter College, City University of New York, 2006.

Ennis, Sharon R., Merarys Ríos-Vargas, and Nora G. Albert. *The Hispanic Population: 2010.* US Census Brief. Washington, DC: United States Census Bureau, 2011.

Falcón, Angelo. *Atlas of Stateside Puerto Ricans.* Washington, DC: Puerto Rico Federal Affairs Administration, 2004.

Federal Reserve Bank of New York. "Report on the Competitiveness of Puerto Rico's Economy." New York: Federal Reserve Bank of New York, 2012.

Foulkes, Matt, and K. Bruce Newbold. "Migration Propensities, Patterns, and the Role of Human Capital: Comparing Mexican, Cuban, and Puerto Rican Interstate Migration, 1985–1990." *Professional Geographer* 52, no. 1 (2000): 133–45.

García-Ellín, Juan Carlos. "A Brief Look at Internal Migration of Puerto Ricans in the United States: 2000–2011." In *Puerto Ricans at the Dawn of the New Millennium,* edited by Edwin Meléndez and Carlos Vargas-Ramos, 26–28. New York: Center for Puerto Rican Studies, Hunter College, 2014.

Haslip-Viera, Gabriel, Angelo Falcón, and Félix Matos Rodríguez, eds. *Boricuas in Gotham: Puerto Ricans in the Making of Modern New York City.* Princeton: Markus Wiener, 2004.

Itzigsohn, José. *Encountering American Faultlines: Race, Class, and the Dominican Experience in Providence.* New York: Russell Sage Foundation, 2009.

Kasarda, John. "Industrial Restructuring and the Changing Location of Jobs." In *Social Trends,* vol. 2 of *State of the Union: America in the 1990s,* edited by Reynolds Farley, 215–66. New York: Russell Sage Foundation, 1995.

Levitt, Peggy. *The Transnational Villagers.* Berkeley: University of California Press, 2001.

Marzán, Gilbert. "Still Looking for That Elsewhere: Puerto Rican Poverty and Migration in the Northeast." *Centro: Journal of the Center for Puerto Rican Studies* 21, no. 1 (2009): 100–117.

Marzán, Gilbert, Andrés Torres, and Andrew Luecke. "Puerto Rican Outmigration from New York City: 1995–2000." Policy report, vol. 2, no. 2. New York: Centro de Estudios Puertorriqueños, Hunter College, 2008.

McHugh, Kevin E. "Black Migration Reversal in the United States." *Geographical Review* 77, no. 2 (1987): 171–82.

Mele, Christopher. "Neighborhood 'Burnout': Puerto Ricans at the End of the Queue." In *From Urban Village to East Village: The Battle for New York's Lower East Side,* edited by Janet L. Abu-Lughod, 125–40. Cambridge, MA: Blackwell, 1994.

New York City, Department of City Planning. *Puerto Rican New Yorkers in 1990.* New York: New York City, Department of City Planning, 1994.

Portes, Alejandro, William J. Haller, and Luis E. Guarnizo. "Transnational Entrepreneurs: An Alternative Form of Immigrant Economic Adaptation." *American Sociological Review* 67, no. 2 (2002): 242–81.

Rivera-Batíz, Francisco L. "Puerto Rican New Yorkers in the 1990s: A Demographic and Socioeconomic Profile." In *Boricuas in Gotham: Puerto Ricans in the Making of Modern New York City,* edited by Gabriel Haslip-Viera et al., 107–29. Princeton: Markus Wiener, 2004.

Rivera-Batíz, Francisco L., and Carlos E. Santiago. *Puerto Ricans in the United States: A Changing Reality.* Washington, DC: National Puerto Rican Coalition, 1994.

———. *Island Paradox: Puerto Rico in the 1990s.* New York: Russell Sage Foundation, 1996.

Rodríguez, Clara E. "Circulating Migration." *Journal of Hispanic Policy* 3 (January 1988): 5–9.

Silver, Patricia. "Puerto Ricans in Florida." In *Puerto Ricans at the Dawn of the New Millennium,* edited by Edwin Meléndez and Carlos Vargas-Ramos, 62–80. New York: Center for Puerto Rican Studies, Hunter College, 2014.

Smith, Robert Courtney. *Mexican New York: The Transnational Lives of New Immigrants.* Berkeley: University of California Press, 2006.

Torre, Carlos Antonio, Hugo Rodríguez Vecchini, and William Burgos, eds. *The Commuter Nation: Perspectives on Puerto Rican Migration.* Rio Piedras: Editorial de la Universidad de Puerto Rico, 1994.

Torres, Andrés. *Between Melting Pot and Mosaic: African Americans and Puerto Ricans in the New York Political Economy.* Philadelphia: Temple University Press, 1995.

Torres, Andrés, and Frank Bonilla. "Decline within Decline: The New York Perspective." In *Latinos in a Changing U.S. Economy: Comparative Perspectives on Growing Inequality,* edited by Rebecca Morales and Frank Bonilla, 85–108. Newbury Park, CA: Sage Publications, 1993.

Torres, Lourdes. *Puerto Rican Discourse: A Sociolinguistic Study of a New York Suburb.* Mahwah, NJ: Lawrence Erlbaum Associates, 1997.

United States Census Bureau. *1990 Census of Population and Housing.* Accessed June 3, 2008. http://factfinder.census.gov.

United States Census Bureau. Census 2000. Accessed June 3, 2008. http://fact finder.census.gov.

Vargas-Ramos, Carlos. "Settlement Patterns and Residential Segregation of Puerto Ricans in the United States." New York: Centro de Estudios Puertorriqueños, Hunter College, City University of New York, 2006.

Villarrubia-Mendoza, Jacqueline. 2010. "Characteristics of Puerto Rican Homeowners in Florida and Their Likelihood of Homeownership." *Centro: Journal of the Center for Puerto Rican Studies* 21 (1): 155–71.

Zukin, Sharon. *Naked City: The Death and Life of Authentic Urban Places.* Oxford: Oxford University Press, 2010.

CHAPTER FIVE

Perspectives on Dominicans in New York City

RAMONA HERNÁNDEZ AND SILVIO TORRES-SAILLANT

Massive migration movements of Dominicans occurred in the last six decades. In the middle of the 1960s, thousands of Dominicans packed their luggage and left the Dominican Republic in search of a better life for themselves and their children. The overwhelming majority of those who left came to the United Sates, while some went to Europe and other parts of the world. The intensity and the volume of the exodus suggested that Dominican society had no room to accommodate those who were leaving. As with many immigrant groups, most Dominicans probably saw their migration as temporary; they planned to return to the Dominican Republic once they had reached the goals they had envisioned. But in accordance with the popular saying "una cosa piensa el burro y otra el que lo acarrea,"[1] many Dominicans ended up modifying or completely changing their plans to return to the home country.

In returning they faced numerous obstacles, including the fact that more than half of Dominican migrants were single, of prime marrying-age and able to start a family in the new location, and that more than one-third of the migrants were minors and susceptible to assimilation (Hernández 2011). In addition, researchers have found that in Dominican migrant families composed of married couples, women purposely delay the family's return to the Dominican Republic. Anthropologist Patricia Pessar's pioneering research suggested that Dominican women postponed returning because they preferred their lifestyle in the United States over the lifestyle assigned to women in the Dominican Republic, which, in their view, limits women's roles and places women under men's control (Pessar 1987, 120, 123). Homeland return was also affected by the socioeconomic reality Dominican migrants encountered both in the United States and in the Dominican Republic. In the former, many Dominicans joined the ranks of the very poor and were unable to meet the goals they had set before they migrated; in the latter, Dominicans found a society whose cost of living escalated alarmingly and which people continued to leave at a pace that made it seem as if no Dominican was going to remain in that country.

As indicated in figure 5.1 below, the number of Dominicans admitted with a Green Card to the United States continued to increase steadily during the 1960s–1990s period, reaching a peak in 1994, when more than fifty thousand Dominicans were granted permanent residence by the US government. Yet starting in 1995, the number of those admitted has been characterized by an irregular pattern, reflecting successive sharp declines followed by relative increases. When analyzing yearly admitted "Green Card" holders, one should keep in mind that the number of those admitted is composed of (1) migrants who have adjusted their immigration status while living in the United States and (2) newly-arrived immigrants or migrants who receive permanency status prior to residing in the United States. A look at the number of those admitted reveals that from 1996 to 2002, for instance, about one-third of all Dominican immigrants receiving Green Cards had *adjusted* their status (Hernández 2007), suggesting that immigration at the time was no longer the only driving force behind population growth among Dominicans in the United States and that natural births may have been already playing an important role in that population growth. In addition, a comparison of the flows through the last five decades reveals that, overall, fewer Dominicans have been admitted to the United States during the 2000–2010 decade than during the previous decade. In fact, in a previous publication, one of the authors of the current chapter suggested that the decline in Dominican migration to the United States was connected to a willful decision on the part of the US government to reduce the entrance of unwanted immigrants (Hernández 2002). Only time will tell whether the decline in the migration flow may reverse its course or whether the current trend will endure.

Table 5.1 Five Largest Hispanic/Latino Populations in the US, 2000 and 2010

Groups	2000	2010
Mexican	20,900,102	31,798,258
Puerto Rican	3,403,510	4,623,716
Cuban	1,249,820	1,785,547
Salvadoran	997,862	1,648,968
Dominican	1,041,910	1,414,703

Sources: 2000 US Census of Population; 2010 Census Briefs, US Census Bureau; and PUMS.

Despite the inconsistency in the volume of incoming migrants during the last decade, the Dominican population in the United States rose by a robust 26.35%, from 1,041,910 to 1,414,703 from 2000 to 2010. By comparison, the overall population of the United States increased by only 9.7% during these years. Dominicans now constitute the fifth-largest Hispanic/Latino group in the United States, following Mexicans, Puerto Ricans, Cubans, and Salvadorans (table 5.1).

ORIGINS OF THE EXODUS

During dictator Rafael Trujillo's thirty-two years of rule, international travel from the Dominican Republic was severely restricted, and only some people, particularly diplomats and well-to-do people who were not known to dislike the government, were permitted to travel abroad. Roberto Cassá, Frank Moya Pons, and Frank Canelo offer explanations for Trujillo's firm policy to keep Dominican borders closed. Justifications ranged from an established dictatorial policy that violently repressed political enemies and undermined people's social freedom to the implementation of strategies that encouraged economic growth via a labor-intensive industrialization process that depended on a frightened and constantly watched-over labor force (Canelo 1982, 41; Cassá 1982, 572; Moya Pons 1977, 516).

Trujillo's long reign ended abruptly when on the night of May 16, 1961, a Tuesday, the powerful dictator met his unforeseen death at the hands of a few brave Dominicans. Following Trujillo's *ajusticiamiento*,[2] Dominican society entered a period of political and social unrest that culminated in the 1965 Revolution, the second revolution in Latin America after the 1959 Cuban

Revolution. Juan Bosch was elected president in the country's first-ever constitutional elections after Trujillo, on December 20, 1962, with over 60% of the popular vote. Once elected to government, Bosch restored political freedoms and pushed for economic initiatives that irritated the Dominican oligarchy who had survived Trujillo as well as many conservative high-ranking officers in the armed forces. Bosch's new policies also redefined the entrance of foreign investments in the Dominican Republic by prohibiting foreigners from owning land in the country, by annulling a standing contract with Esso Standard Oil to install an industrial oil refinery, and by initiating a process of nationalization of large mass-producing companies (Faxas 2007). Bosch's new policies were perceived as "left-wing" by the United States and as a clear indication that he wanted to govern independently from the American government. Bosch's socioeconomic reforms and beliefs made him enemies within reactionary and very powerful sectors both in the Dominican Republic and in the United States.

On September 25, 1963, after being in office about seven months, Bosch's government ended through a military coup d'état. Collaborating in the coup were the various sectors of the Dominican elite, including merchants, the Catholic Church, landowners, and industrialists, who had not supported Bosch's candidacy, accusing him of being a communist. Bosch was replaced by a triumvirate whose cabinet was composed of right-wing corporate executives, entrepreneurs, business owners, and lawyers (Moya Pons 1995, 383).

The imposed triumvirate, largely unpopular, was the target of constant civil unrest and demonstrations of social discontent, ending in a civil war in 1965 headed by a number of groups, including the "constitutionalists," who demanded the return of constitutionally elected president Juan Bosch. But what had begun as an internal problem among Dominicans turned into an international affair when US military troops invaded the Dominican Republic on April 28, 1965. "In order to stop Bosch from returning to power and 'to prevent the emergence of a second Cuba in Latin America,' President Lyndon B. Johnson ordered forty-two thousand US soldiers to the Dominican Republic, under the justification of saving lives and protecting US interests in the country" (Moya Pons 1995, 388).

The civil war ended with the military defeat of the constitutionalists, a signed peace treaty, and the establishment of a provisional government under the watchful eyes of representatives of the Organization of the American States and the United States. Elections were scheduled for June 1966, and Joaquín Balaguer, a longtime official in Trujillo's dictatorship, whose

Table 5.2 Changes in the Distribution of Income in Santo Domingo, 1969 and 1973

Group of Income Percent of the Total Number of Families	Percent of the Total Income of the Working Sectors	
Year	1969	1973
20% (lowest)	2.9	1.4
50% (low-middle)	17.6	15.4
30% (middle)	27.6	30.2
20% (top)	54.8	54.4

Source: Lozano 1985, 160.

conservative and reformist politics the White House supported, would win these elections. Balaguer would remain in power for three consecutive four-year terms, from 1966 to 1978, during which the foundations of contemporary history of the Dominican Republic would be established, including massive migration to the United States.

In 1966, with the support of the United States, President Joaquín Balaguer put in place a plan to pacify and modernize the country within a capitalist model of development. During his first two terms, the Dominican economy grew remarkably compared to previous years and surpassed neighboring countries in Latin America and the Caribbean. From 1966 to 1974, for instance, the gross national product (GNP) averaged an annual growth rate between 12% and 13% (Ceara Hatton 1990, 64–65). The economic boom was fueled by special access to US markets given to sugar exports; by massive US foreign investments, particularly in industrial free-trade zones; by economic aid from the United States; and by successive international loans. Yet economic growth did not generate improvement for most Dominican people and further emphasized the gap between haves and have-nots. Table 5.2 compares income distribution in the city of Santo Domingo in two time periods: 1969 and 1973. As reflected in the table, the sector of the population with the lowest income experienced a reduction of shares in the total income, while the most privileged sectors of the population with highest income either maintained their shares or increased them.

In this scenario, Balaguer's political consolidation and control of the country was required if the economic plan was to be implemented. Consolidation involved the pacification of the population through political repression, killings, and incarcerations. Pacification also included expelling undesirable voices that questioned and attacked the regime and represented an immediate threat to the new political and social order. Through an undeclared agreement between the American and the Dominican governments, political dissidents were granted visas and surreptitiously dispatched to the United States. The number of Dominicans who were forced to leave their country this way still remains unknown; nor do we know what exactly happened to these Dominicans when they arrived in the United States. The story told in this chapter revolves around the hundreds of thousands of Dominicans who undertook the migration journey later and those who have followed them ever since.

Balaguer found an unforeseen ally that would enable him put in motion a Machiavellian plan to relieve Dominican society of the largest contingent of Dominican job-seekers in its history (see fig. 5.1). The unexpected ally was the United States' 1965 Family Reunification Immigration Act, a piece of legislation that facilitated the entrance of people into the United States who were related by blood or marriage to people who were already residents or citizens of the country. Overwhelmingly, most Dominican migrants during the period studied here have obtained their permanent residence through the Family Reunification Act. Contemporary migration has changed the character and nature of Dominican society and its people forever. Many Dominicans migrants would return for good one day; but most would end up staying in the United States. Those who returned would be permeated by the migration experience and would be treated differently by the rest of Dominican society; those who stayed in the United States would create a historical and cultural legacy different from the one they previously knew and different as well from the one that continued to evolve in the Dominican Republic after they left.

After Balaguer's first several governments (which were possible through elections that were often questioned) ended in 1978, Dominican society entered a period of political democratization, electing representatives of different political parties for government and running elections that most Dominicans and international observers deemed "clean" or whose results had not been altered or corrupted. The switch in political style was made possible largely by the appearance in the US government of a more prodemocracy administration, especially the administration of President Jimmy Carter. The changes in government, however, did not generate any remarkable social changes with regard to the provision and expansion of social services, for instance, or the reduction of social inequality among members of Dominican society.

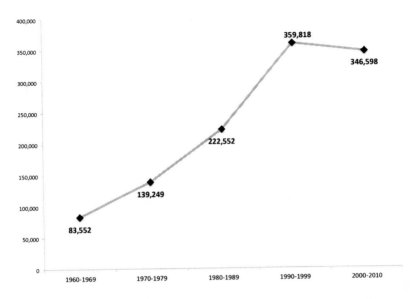

Figure 5.1 Immigrants Admitted from the Dominican Republic by Decade, 1960–2010

Sources: Annual Reports of the Immigration and Naturalization Services, Department of Justice, 1961–1978; Statistical Yearbook of the Immigration and Naturalization Service, Department of Justice, 1979–2003; Yearbook of Immigration Statistics, Office of Immigration Statistics, Homeland Security, 2008; Yearbook of Immigration Statistics, Office of Immigration Statistics, 2010. Homeland Security, 2004–2008; Yearbook of Immigration Statistics, Office of Immigration Statistics 2010.

THE 1980S AND THEREAFTER: THE NEED TO MIGRATE PERSISTS

By 1978, the import-substitution economic model, the leading developmental strategy implemented by Balaguer's governments, reached its limit. It was obvious that the country was importing much more than it was producing, and the number of unemployed continued to grow. Capitalists accumulated capital mainly on the basis of commercial trade (particularly through the import market), by means of activity that was subsidized by the government, and by reselling at high prices and paying extremely low wages. While inflationary prices affected most workers, the government increasingly borrowed money from foreign institutions to pay for capital goods, industrial inputs, and normal public expenditures and for the creation of nonproductive jobs. In the end, money was borrowed to repay interest accrued on these debts. By 1982, unable to pay its foreign creditors, the country was placed under an austerity plan by the International Monetary Fund—which, as one measure to repair the troubled economy, froze workers' wages.

During the 1980s, the Dominican government emphasized developing the tourist and agribusiness industries, both connected to a new economic orientation which sought to clean up the economic mess left by the failed import-substitution and export-driven economic models implemented over the previous two decades. But, as critics have argued, the problems of increasing poverty and unemployment remained. The new economic policies, like the others, continued to emphasize foreign investment, encouraged the use of foreign inputs in the process of production, and created economic enclaves without much connection to or impact on other economically productive sectors. Take, for instance, the tourist industry, now the country's most dynamic economic sector, which, since the mid-1980s, has become the single largest contributor to the country's GNP. The number of jobs generated in this area has increased only modestly, from 10,000 in 1980 to 17,258 in 1987 and 24,000 in 1989. By 1996, the number of direct jobs generated by the tourist industry had increased to only 35,000 (ENDESA 1996, 2).

Any accurate analysis of the performance of the Dominican economy must evaluate two distinct sectors: the people and the capitalists. For most Dominican people, the national economy has been in a constant state of crisis that has not improved their quality of life significantly. For capitalists, however, the economy has gone through stages reflecting the exhaustion of given economic modalities and reorientations as capitalists seek to accumulate capital faster.

During the 1980s, commonly known in Latin America as the lost decade, those who needed to work for a living suffered. Many were displaced from the process of production by an economy that systematically introduced technology into production and lacked the capacity to protect small farmers from large local and international agricultural production. In addition, many workers, uprooted from the countryside, began to move to cities in search of jobs. In 1950, less than 24% of the Dominican people were considered to be urban. During the following decades, however, the internal migration of people accelerated dramatically, and by 1985 the proportion of urban dwellers had already reached almost 58%.

In spite of the economic boom of the last years of the 1990s, unemployment in the Dominican Republic has remained consistently high. In 1993 the unemployment rate in the Dominican Republic was 26.2%; by 1996, it had increased to 37.6%. In a study conducted in 1998 by the International

Labor Organization it was found that the informal economy provided 50% of all urban jobs in the Dominican Republic. The same study found that among the seven countries studied, the Dominican Republic, with an annual average growth of 4.1% in GNP, experienced the highest economic growth since 1994 but the lowest growth in the labor force during the same years (Del Cid and Tacsan Chen 1999).

The migration flow that was unleashed when Balaguer took office in 1966 has not stopped. More Dominicans seek to leave today than ever before. Many now leave to reunite with loved ones who live abroad, but most continue to leave in search of a better life, dismissed from a society that has no room for them. The question, then, is whether their destinations, the societies Dominicans migrate to, have room for them once they get there.

SETTLEMENT IN THE UNITED STATES: PATTERNS AND CHANGES

Most Dominicans who came to the United States in the last four decades settled in New York, particularly in New York City. In 1980, over 65% of Dominicans in the United States resided in New York City; and the borough of Manhattan, particularly the neighborhood of Washington Heights / Inwood, was home to the largest Dominican concentration. Table 5.3 shows the distribution of Dominicans in New York City by boroughs from 1980 to 2010. As reflected on the table, Dominicans preferred Manhattan over any other borough, and that preference would remain strong until 2010, when the Bronx would emerge as the place with the largest Dominican population in the United States, with 240,987, a sharp increase relative to the 181,450 located there in 2000.

The 2010 US census shows that other geographical shifts occurred. While a little less than 50% of US Dominicans lived in New York State in 2010, the Dominican population had swelled in the state of Florida, from 100,000 in 2000 to 172,471; in Massachusetts, where Dominicans grew to 103,292; and in Pennsylvania, where the Dominican population rose to over four times its previous size, from 13,667 in 2000 to 62,348 in 2010. This growth is reflected in table 5.4. There are substantial numbers in other states as well, including Rhode Island, Maryland, and several other states—from Texas to Illinois—with budding Dominican communities. The geographical dispersal of Dominicans is reflected by the growth of their populations in or near major metropolitan areas of the eastern United States. Table 5.5 shows

Table 5.3 Distribution of Dominicans by New York City Boroughs, 2000 and 2010

Borough	1980	1990	2000	2010
Bronx	17,640	87,261	133,087	240,987
Manhattan	62,660	136,696	134,172	155,971
Brooklyn	21,140	55,301	65,693	86,764
Queens	23,780	52,309	69,841	88,061
Staten Island	160	1,146	1,860	4,918
Total	125,380	332,713	406,759	576,701

Sources: Ramona Hernández, Francisco Rivera-Batiz, and Roberto Agodini, *Dominican New Yorkers: A Socioeconomic Profile* (New York: CUNY Dominican Studies Institute, 1995); New York City, Department of City Planning, *Socioeconomic Profiles*, City of New York, March 1993; and 2010 US Census Bureau American Fact Finder (SF1).

Table 5.4 Geographical Distribution of Dominicans by State, 1990–2010

	1990	2000	2010
Total	511,297	1,041,901	1,414,703
New York	357,868	617,901	674,787
New Jersey	52,807	136,529	197,922
Florida	34,268	98,410	172,471
Massachusetts	30,177	69,502	103,292
Rhode Island	9,374	24,588	35,008
Pennsylvania	3,687	13,667	62,348
Connecticut	3,946	12,830	26,093

Sources: 2000 and 2010 Census of Population and PUMS. For 2010 Rhode Island and Connecticut numbers: 2010 US Census Bureau American Fact Finder (SF1).

the top cities of Dominican concentration in 1990, 2000, and 2010. Despite the intense shifting and aggressive growth of Dominicans in other places in the United States, New York City continues to be the top location of residence, with 576,701 Dominicans residing in the five boroughs/counties of the Big Apple in 2010.

The patterns of settlement reveal that Dominicans have preferred the Northeast over other regions in the United States. That preference shows two interesting patterns not yet studied. First, Dominicans tend to move to places

Table 5.5 Top Cities for Dominican Concentration, 1990–2010

	1990	2000	2010
New York City, NY	332,713	554,638	576,701
Lawrence, MA	11,095	22,111	30,243
Paterson, NJ	8,750	19,977	27,426
Providence, RI	8,138	19,915	25,267
Boston, MA	8,102	19,061	25,648
Jersey City, NJ	5,779	12,598	13,512
Passaic, NJ	6,422	12,481	12,340
Perth Amboy, NJ	5,272	11,431	14,773
Yonkers, NY	3,788	10,223	15,903
Union City, NJ	5,390	10,205	10,020

Sources: 1990 Census (STF4); 2000 US Census; author's tabulations; and 2010 Census (SF1).

with a large established Puerto Rican and/or Latino population. In most cases, Dominicans move into Puerto Rican neighborhoods, and in other cases, they move near Puerto Rican neighborhoods. Second, Dominicans tend to grow and expand within the same places where they live (i.e., the same neighborhood, the same county, etc.) rather than moving far away or outside from their original settlement. This pattern leads to the formation of Dominican neighborhoods that tend to grow in concentration and density, facilitating the development of areas that are distinctively "Dominican" not only because of the number of Dominicans but also because they become sites for the maintenance of Dominican cultural legacy. The implications of the geographical arrangement of the past fifty years, however, remain to be seen, particularly in New York City, where Dominicans are now moving into some of the politically strongest and oldest Puerto Rican neighborhoods in the Bronx, which boast a history of resistance and perseverance. In addition, in contrast to older populations, more and more Dominican neighborhoods are now composed of an increasing second generation who are homegrown and who may feel entitled to live in the places where they were born. This is in addition to the fact that the group are naturally inclined to accommodate themselves to the location they know best. For now one thing is clear: the Dominican population in the Bronx is positioned to continue to grow much faster than now.

LIFE IN NEW YORK CITY: THEN AND NOW

Most studies of Dominican migration to the United States have focused on Dominicans in New York City. Starting with the very first book published about Dominican migrants, Glenn Hendricks's *The Dominican Diaspora: From the Dominican Republic to New York City—Villagers in Transition* (1974), New York City has captivated the imagination of scholars and observers of Dominicans. Similarly, no other Dominican residential locality has received as much attention as the historic neighborhood of Washington Heights / Inwood, which still today has the largest concentration of Dominicans in the United States. Indeed, aspects of Dominican life in this neighborhood have been described by many, including former US Secretary of Labor Linda Chavez, sociologist Nancy Lopez, the popular television series *Law and Order*, and rapper, songwriter, and singer Jay-Z. The strong presence of Dominicans in New York and Washington Heights led to a widespread belief that all Dominicans living in the United States somehow resided in this city and this neighborhood alone. The first, most recognizable stereotype of the 1980s describing Dominicans who lived in the United States spoke specifically of Dominican New Yorkers: "the Dominican-york," portrayed as a hybrid specimen who did not speak English well and had a rudimentary Spanish; wore baggy pants below the waist and was unpolished and often impolite; walked with a big radio, listening to music; and wore a number of chains around the neck; the Dominican-york was also suspected of being capable of engaging in illicit dealings and was routinely stopped by police officers in the Dominican Republic (Torres-Saillant 1999). Dominicans who lived in other states and traveled to the Dominican Republic were not particularly enthusiastic about being taken as Dominican New Yorkers.

In 2010 one in two Dominicans residing in the United States lived in New York City. During the same year New York City was home to 576,701 Dominicans distributed throughout the five boroughs. As we noted earlier, referring to table 5.3, perhaps the most drastic change in distribution of Dominicans in New York City concerns Manhattan and the Bronx. While the Dominicans have continued to grow in Manhattan, overall the Manhattan Dominican population is now much smaller than the population of Dominicans in the Bronx. Within the Bronx, there are large Dominican settlements in University Heights–Morris Heights, Mount Hope, Van Cortlandt Village, the Concourse, Fordham, and Bedford Park. In Manhattan, the overwhelming focus of location remains Washington Heights / Inwood, from north to

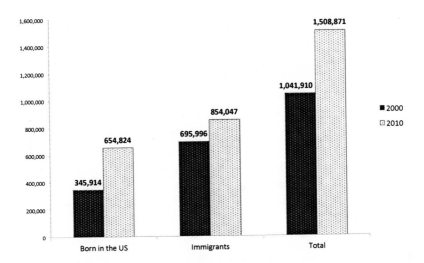

Figure 5.2 Dominican Immigrants and US-Born Dominicans, 2000–2010

Sources: 2000 US Census of Population, PUMS, and American Community Survey (ACS) 2010 1-Year Sample, table S0201.

south. In Queens, a significant community is located in Woodhaven, in Richmond Hill, and in South Ozone Park, while in Brooklyn the salient areas are Cypress Hills–City Line, East New York, North and South of Bushwick, North Side–South Side, South Williamsburg, and Sunset Park West and East.

The increased complexity of the Dominican experience is not only geographical; it also reflects changes in birth patterns, geographically speaking. In the past, studies on Dominicans focused almost exclusively on analyzing immigrants, or people born in the Dominican Republic. But this has also changed. US-born Dominicans now account for the largest proportion of Dominican population growth in the United States. There were 654,824 US-born Dominicans in the country in 2010, representing 43.4% of the overall Dominican population, up from 33.2% in 2000. Indeed, of the increase in the Dominican population of 466,961 in the period from 2000 to 2010, a total of 308,910 were born in the United States, accounting for almost three-quarters of the population increase. This means that a vigorously growing second generation is becoming a major demographic force, rapidly approaching the 50% mark, as reflected in figure 5.2. During the last decade in New York City, the largest number of babies of Dominican ancestry were born in the Bronx, followed by Manhattan. High birth rates in the Bronx among Dominicans partly explain the overwhelming surge in the Dominican population of this borough (see figure 5.3). As reflected in figure 5.4, the highest number of babies in New York City was born to Dominican immigrant mothers in 2005, 2009, and 2012.

The rise in the US-born Dominican population challenges generalizations and deterministic approaches about the identity of Dominican immigrants. The transforming nature of the composition of the Dominican demography makes us wonder about the different possible layers defining the contours of Dominican identity. Who is Dominican and what does it mean to be Dominican in this new context? Presumably, the longevity of the Dominican population in the United States and the growth of a substantial second and third generation create the spaces for the formation of identities that may evolve in different directions, toward different social practices. Similarly, the continued influx of new migrants from the Dominican Republic, the varying levels of adaptability exhibited by sectors of the community with different lengths of residence in the immigrant space, and the resulting differences in degrees of acceptance of the new abode as a permanent home make it exceedingly challenging to conceptually grasp a given identity with which to confidently classify and define the Dominican people in the United States. Undoubtedly, because of its volume and its age, more than any other Dominican settlement in the States, the New York Dominican community is likely to capture the complexities just described. The next section offers an overview of Dominicans in New York City. We particularly attend to their socioeconomic standing as an indicator of social mobility in their new home. The status of transnationalism among Dominicans, and how it unfolds once Dominicans settle, is also discussed.

THE VALUE OF MIGRATION

The general perception among researchers of Dominican migration is that the movement has been rewarding from a socioeconomic point of view. Invariably, the idea that Dominicans came to fill jobs that Puerto Ricans and native-born African Americans did not want to take prevailed in the minds of the first group of researchers (González 1970; Hendricks 1974; Sassen-Koob 1988) who undertook the task of writing about Dominicans in the

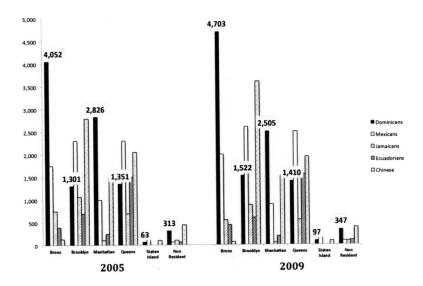

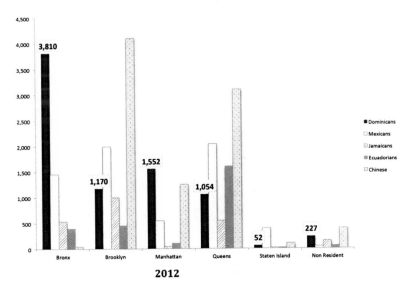

Figure 5.3 Live Births by Ancestry of Mother: 5 Highest Immigrant Groups in New York City by Borough, 2005, 2009, and 2012

Sources: Li, Wenhui, Swartz, Steven, and Zimmerman, Regina, *Summary of Vital Statistics 2005, The City of New York,* Bureau of Vital Statistics, New York City Department of Health and Mental Hygiene, New York, 2007; Li, Wenhui, Swartz, Steven, and Zimmerman, Regina, *Summary of Vital Statistics 2009, The City of New York,* Bureau of Vital Statistics, New York City Department of Health and Mental Hygiene, New York, 2010; Zimmerman, R., Li, W., Gambatese, M., Madsen, A., Lasner-Fratier, L., Van Wye, G., Kelley, D., Kennedy, J., Maduro, G., and Sun, Y., *Summary of Vital Statistics 2012, The City of New York, Pregnancy Outcomes,* Bureau of Vital Statistics, New York City Department of Health and Mental Hygiene, New York, 2013.

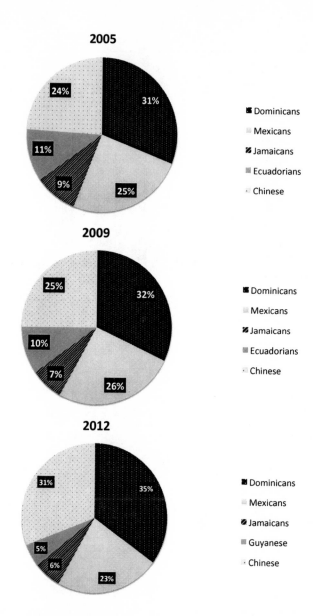

Figure 5.4 Live Births by Ancestry of Mother: 5 Highest Immigrant Groups in New York City, 2005, 2009, and 2012

Sources: Li, Wenhui, Swartz, Steven, and Zimmerman, Regina, *Summary of Vital Statistics 2005, The City of New York*, Bureau of Vital Statistics, New York City Department of Health and Mental Hygiene, New York, 2007; Li, Wenhui, Swartz, Steven, and Zimmerman, Regina, *Summary of Vital Statistics 2009, The City of New York*, Bureau of Vital Statistics, New York City Department of Health and Mental Hygiene, New York, 2010; Zimmerman, R., Li, W., Gambatese, M., Madsen, A., Lasner-Fratier, L., Van Wye, G., Kelley, D., Kennedy, J., Maduro, G., and Sun, Y. *Summary of Vital Statistics 2012, The City of New York, Pregnancy Outcomes*, Bureau of Vital Statistics, New York City Department of Health and Mental Hygiene, New York, 2013.

United States. The belief in jobs "waiting for Dominicans" and easily accessible, portrayed in the early research, continued to mature and become polished in the research that followed. Subsequently, scholars argued that Dominicans' social network enabled them to take control of "niches" in the labor market and pass on jobs to conationals (Portes and Guarnizo 1990; Light 1995). The penetration of immigrants into these labor markets had its negative consequences. Some argued that the network system was detrimental to native workers, particularly to African Americans, who were essentially shuttled off from growing job markets that functioned under the monopoly of immigrant labor (Waldinger 1986; Briggs 1992). Interestingly, even though the two sides of the argument seemed to agree in their depiction of immigrant jobs as poorly paid, lacking benefits, highly unstable, and undesirable, the general belief among Dominican migration scholars is that somehow Dominican immigrants in general could make a living out these jobs, have enough money to send remittances home, and even have money left to invest in the Dominican Republic for their return. This contradiction finds support in the complexity of the Dominican migration experience in New York City.

Empirical observation of the socioeconomic development of the Dominican community leads to a complicated picture of failures and triumphs. The community appears to be flourishing economically, as one can gather from a look at the northern part of Manhattan, where the majority of grocery stores, travel agencies, gypsy-cabs, clothing and shoe stores, restaurants, many pharmacies, beauty salons, barbershops, and liquor stores are owned and operated by Dominicans, whose economic presence extends also to small factories, bars, the finance sector, large supermarkets, and the elusive informal sector. At the same time, less-visible signs of economic distress such as persistent high levels of poverty and unemployment also plague the Dominican community, facts that quietly challenge its visible signs of prosperity (Hernández 2005 and 2011).

FORTUNE

The prosperity of Dominicans has been noted by various authors, who observe that this community has developed an important enclave economy in New York. Portes and Guarnizo were the first scholars to publish a study looking at the Dominican business sector in New York City (1990). Their research published in *Tropical Capitalists: U.S.-Bound Immigration and Small Enterprise Development in the Dominican Republic* portrayed the Dominican community as an enclave with an aggressive business sector that had a strong hold in bodegas and gypsy-cabs in the city, owned two television programs on local cable, and owned three supermarket chains (61). A decade after the publication of this study, the Dominican entrepreneurial sector had expanded considerably throughout New York City. The three supermarket chains, for instance, have transformed into the National Supermarket Association (NSA), a conglomerate of supermarkets located throughout New York City and in various other states with large Dominican concentrations. The president of the NSA in 2012, William Rodríguez, asserted that the association included a membership list of 400 supermarkets whose owners were of Dominican ancestry, and whose businesses were found in the five states with the largest Dominican concentrations, from New York to Rhode Island, as well as in other states where the Dominican population had just started to emerge, such as North Carolina. The president of the Association of Dominican Bodega Owners (ADB), Ramón Murphy, reported that there were over seven thousand registered bodegas owned and operated by Dominicans throughout New York City. The taxi companies, the beauty parlors, and a couple of franchises in service provision have also ventured into non-Dominican neighborhoods and succeeded. The finance sector mushroomed as well, with the NSA creating its own insurance company and with the rise of Benny Lorenzo, a second-generation Dominican who graduated from Cornell and Harvard Universities to become the chairman and CEO of Kaufman Bros., L.P., the nation's largest minority-owned/operated investment bank and broker-dealer.[3]

Prosperity may also be linked to a rising segment of middle-class Dominican skilled professionals. This is a group made up of college graduates and people with skills who hold well-paid jobs and whose household incomes range between $75,000 and $100,000 per year. Among this group we find executives in the private sector—from banks and insurance to real estate; lawyers in the private and public sectors; elected politicians; people who work in education and academia; appointed members in the city, state, and federal governments; and heads of community-based organizations (CBOs). Public statements by heads of Dominican CBOs suggested that the non-for-profit agencies account for almost one-third of all jobs generated in Washington Heights / Inwood. Similarly, as reflected in table 5.6, the comparison of per-capita household annual income of Dominicans indicates that this has improved significantly over the years. In 1990, for instance, the mean

Table 5.6 Mean Per-Capita Household Income in New York City, 1990–2010

Group	1990	2000	2010
Dominicans	$8,659	$10,032	$13,877.13
NYC Overall	$21,991	$24,010	$29,635.59
Non-Hispanic White	$31,026	$37,391	$47,866.45
Non-Hispanic Black	$14,573	$15,367	$20,769.95
Non-Hispanic Asian	$18,189	$19,533	$25,872.60
Hispanic/Latino	$11,515	$12,500	$17,313.32

Sources: 1990, 2000 5% PUMS; 2010 IPUMS ACS 1-Year Sample.

annual per-capita income of Dominican households was $8,659; by 2010 it had increased to $13,877.13.

Similarly, some may argue that the perceived prosperity is also linked to advancements obtained in education. In 1980, 72.0% of the Dominican population twenty-five years of age or older did not have a high school diploma. By 1990, the percentage of non–high school graduates had significantly declined, to 61.5%, and by 2007 it dropped to 52.8%. On the other hand, the percentage of those with "College or More" increased from 3.8% in 1980 to 6.1% in 1990 and to 9.1% in 2000. There are several explanations behind the positive gains in education in the 1990s. During the 1980s many Dominican professionals and technicians migrated to the United States. These were people displaced by the severe economic downturn that plagued most Latin American countries during the 1980s (Hernández 2002). In addition, gains in education are related to the high value poor Dominican families place on education, which they see as a safety valve to escape poverty, and to the educational performance of US-born Dominicans, who tend to do better in education than Dominican immigrants.

NOT THAT PROSPEROUS

But Dominican prosperity has its limitations. In 2000, over three in ten Dominican households in New York City lived below the poverty line. When compared to other racial/ethnic groups, Dominicans had that year the highest poverty rate in the city, including higher than Hispanics (see table 5.7). But poverty among Dominicans is hardly a new phenomenon. High pockets

Table 5.7   Poverty in New York City, 1980–2010

Population Group	Poverty Rate (%)			
	1980	1990	2000	2010
Dominican New Yorkers, overall	36	36.6	32	28.3
New York City Average	18	17.2	19.1	20.3
Non-Hispanic White Population	8.7	8.2	9.7	12.1
Non-Hispanic Black Population	28.3	22.9	23.6	22.4
Non-Hispanic Asian population			18.2	19.8
Hispanic/Latino Population	35	31.4	29.7	28.5

Sources: 5% Public Use Micro Data Sample; US Department of Commerce; 1980, 1990, and 2000 US Census of Population; 2010 IPUMS ACS 1-Year Sample.

of poverty have existed among this group throughout the last three decades. In fact, as reflected in table 5.7, in 1980, 36% of Dominican households lived below the poverty line. In 1990, the poverty rate had increased slightly among this group, to 36.6%, and by 2010, poverty still plagued a little less than one-third of the Dominican people living in the city.

The high level of poverty among Dominicans in New York City is the direct result of the group's low levels of income and high levels of unemployment. In 1980, for instance, more than 40% of Dominican households had annual income of less than $30,000; by 2009 the proportion of Dominican homes with a similar income remained the same even though the cost of living in New York City, particularly the price for rent, had escalated considerably in those years. Data on unemployment reveal similar distressing findings, showing that unemployment among Dominican men has fluctuated between 14.3% in 1980 and 11% in 2009, with a historic high of 18% in 1990.

Persistent above-average unemployment rates among Dominican workers suggest that unemployment rates among the group are not seasonal or frictional but *structural.* The loss of jobs among the group is caused by a contraction produced on the demand side of the labor market. The shifting of the economy from manufacturing to service produced a sharp decline of blue-collar jobs. Table 5.8 presents data on the decline of manufacturing and the share of the Dominican population employed in that sector. As reflected in the table, almost one in two Dominicans in New York City was employed in the manufacturing sector in 1980. By 2000, the proportion of Dominicans in the manufacturing sector had precipitously declined, to 12.4%, or one-quarter of the figure for 1980. In 2010, the proportion had continued to

Table 5.8 Persons in the Labor Force: The Decline of Manufacturing in New York City, 1980–2010

Share of Labor Force	1980	1990	2000	2010
Proportion of New York City Labor Force	18.0%	12.1%	6.6%	4.2%
Proportion of Dominican Labor Force	48.6%	25.7%	12.4%	5.5%

Sources: 5% Public Use Micro Data Sample; US Department of Commerce; 1980, 1990, and 2000 US Census of Population; 2010 IPUMS ACS 1-Year Sample.

decline, by approximately 7%. Unemployment among Dominicans resulted when displaced workers could not find jobs in the other, growing sectors of the economy, either because they did not have the educational or training qualifications required for those jobs or because there were not enough jobs available that Dominicans were qualified for.

The inability of the US economy to produce enough blue-collar, low-skilled jobs at a pace capable of matching the needs of the labor force seeking those jobs is an issue that seldom appears in the writings of scholars of migration studies. The lack of attention to this subject could be connected to a preponderance of scholarship that analyzes macroeconomic indicators and deemphasizes the examination of sectorial dynamics in the labor market, including issues of disparity. In addition, the fact that immigrant job-seekers continue to come and that the United States continues to create jobs simultaneously may obfuscate and contribute to undermining the importance of examining the relationship between migrants' skills and the needs of the labor market where immigrants are employed.

The mean per-capita household annual income distribution among groups disaggregated by race and ethnicity in New York City shows that in 2007, Dominicans lagged behind all the other groups compared (see table 5.6). It is equally important to add that Dominican households in the income bracket of $75,000 to $100,000 have accounted for less than 10% of all Dominican households since the 1990s, a decade when the number of Dominicans with "college and more degrees" had already significantly increased, as well as the number of those with US citizenship and the number of US-born Dominicans in the labor market.

Even the advancements made by Dominicans in education pale when compared to the advancements of other groups in the city. While 52.8% of the overall Dominican population did not have a high school diploma in

Table 5.9 Female-Headed Families in New York City, 1980–2010

Group	1980	1990	2000	2010
Dominican	34.0%	40.7%	38.2%	44.9%
Hispanic/Latino	31.5%	34.3%	32.0%	35.7%
Non-Hispanic Black	35.6%	38.8%	40.0%	40.1%
Non-Hispanic White	9.4%	9.2%	9.1%	8.4%
Non-Hispanic Asian	NA	NA	8.1%	10.0%
Total NYC	19.2%	21.7%	22.1%	24.0%

Sources: 5% Public Use Micro Data Sample; US Department of Commerce; 1980, 1990, and 2000 US Census of Population; 2010 IPUMS ACS 1-Year Sample.

2007, for instance, the corresponding figure for Hispanics was 37%, 20% for non-Hispanic blacks, 25% for Asians, and only 9% for non-Hispanic whites.

A high proportion of the Dominican population living under poverty consists of female-headed families. These families, headed by separated or divorced women as well as single women with children, tend to have lower income and higher poverty rates than other families, particularly married couple families. Families headed by single women are affected, in part, by the fact that women still receive less income in the labor market than men for similar jobs demanding similar experience and skills. The income inequality affects most salary levels and all racial and ethnic groups. This inequality impacts women's capacity as providers for meeting the needs of their families on their own.

The proportion of persons living in families headed by a single woman is substantially higher among Dominicans than among other groups, with the exception of non-Hispanic blacks, whose figures had been above Dominicans' both in 1980 and 2010. Table 5.9 presents the proportion of persons living in families headed by women, with no spouse present, for the major racial and ethnic groups for various decades. As reflected in the table, a little more than three in ten Dominican families were headed by a single woman in 1980; by 2010 the proportion of female-headed families jumped to four in ten.

ARE THEY BETTER OFF OR NOT?

When evaluating the benefits of migration, most scholars of Dominican migration to the United States begin from a perception which places Dominican migrants in the Dominican Republic, not in the United States. They evaluate the economic standing of Dominicans in the States as compared to the group's previous economic status in the native land. Scholars also think of social classes in the Dominican Republic and extrapolate those data to Dominicans in the United States. If middle-class Dominicans are associated with higher levels of consumption in the Dominican Republic, Dominicans who have furniture and access to foods and fashionable clothing would likely be thought of as obtaining a better life, an expectation supported by an underlying belief that living in the United States has afforded these Dominicans upward social mobility. Of course, the analogy is not accurate for one essential reason, which is that social conditions are contextual and historical: thinking of Dominicans in the Dominican Republic while they live here reveals very little, if anything, about how Dominicans actually do in the places where they live and what their chances (and those of their offspring) are in comparison to the likelihoods of other groups in these places.

The above discussion has not painted a rosy picture. As presented in the data, poverty has obstinately persisted, carried on from decade to decade as if the distressing phenomenon had acquired a life of its own. The facts are that as a people Dominicans are as poor as when they came and that they continue to struggle to move ahead. Yet some have done remarkably well, and their prosperity has penetrated all walks of life in New York City—from business to politics, from arts to education. Similarly, this prosperity has also impacted the perception of others, who have come to believe that Dominicans are moving too fast without paying their dues, with all the implications that such a view may entail, but that analysis escapes the scope of the present writing.

ATTACHMENT TO THE HOMELAND AND CITIZENSHIP IN THE UNITED STATES: A PARADOX?

The number of Dominicans who are becoming citizens of the United States has been rising. By becoming US citizens, Dominicans qualify for better-paying jobs, which are often reserved for citizens; these include low-end and intermediate jobs in the public sector, which do not require much formal schooling or educational degrees. Table 5.10 shows the proportion of Dominicans who have become citizens of the United States since time of arrival up to 2010, and compares the United States and New York City. Figure 5.5 uses both US and New York City averages and compares rates of US citizenship

Table 5.10 Dominican Naturalization Rate in the United States and New York City

United States	US Citizen by Naturalization	Not a US Citizen	All Foreign-Born Dominicans	Naturalization Rate
Arrived before 1980	116,617	28,969	145,586	80.1%
Arrived 1980 to 1989	113,195	56,068	169,263	66.9%
Arrived 1990 to 1999	122,349	129,735	252,084	48.5%
Arrived 2000 to 2009	47,568	222,127	269,695	17.6%
Arrived 2010	778	15,870	16,648	4.7%
Total Foreign-Born	400,507	452,769	853,276	46.9%

New York City	US Citizen by Naturalization	Not a US Citizen	All Foreign-Born Dominicans	Naturalization Rate
Arrived before 1980	53,328	14,357	67,685	78.8%
Arrived 1980 to 1989	52,083	28,188	80,271	64.9%
Arrived 1990 to 1999	46,497	59,974	106,471	43.7%
Arrived 2000 to 2009	17,407	92,024	109,431	15.9%
Arrived 2010	274	5,755	6,029	4.5%
Total Foreign-Born	169,589	200,298	369,887	45.8%

Note: Excluded are those born in Puerto Rico and born abroad of American parents.

Sources: 2010 IPUMS ACS 1-Year Sample.

with length of time living in the States. Both graphs help us understand Dominicans' view regarding becoming US citizens. The data show that the citizenship rate is at its lowest point among the most recent cohort, or people who have been living in the United States for less than five years. Conversely, rates of citizenship go up the longer Dominicans live in the United States. Such a revelation problematizes the long-held belief that Dominicans were not interested in putting down roots in the United States because they were too attached to the homeland and always treasured the idea of their return. Of course, such belief gains credence from the very way Dominicans recreate their cultural heritage, travel back home, stay connected to families through remittances, and so on.

As table 5.10 shows, Dominicans are increasingly becoming US citizens. It would be fair to think that there may be multiple factors motivating Dominicans to become citizens of the United States, including a pragmatic approach to life and a desire to increase access to the rewards of living in the

United States as full citizens. It is also possible that Dominicans are looking for ways to ensure some stability in a society whose leadership seems to hold an ambivalent politics of love and hate towards immigrants. And of course, the increases in naturalization may also be explained by the simple, inescapable fact that migration becomes, at the end of the day, a final destination for many who left home to secure a better life.

Despite systematic increases in US citizenship rates, Dominicans may indeed remain attached to their homeland, as argued by some observers. Furthermore, the same attachment may reveal transnational behavior among Dominicans as described by transnationalist researchers (Duany 1994; Guarnizo 1994; Levitt 2001; Levitt and Waters 2002; Pantoja 2005; Rodríguez 2009). Within the transnational framework, scholars have paid attention to what have been termed transnational practices exhibited by Dominicans in their everyday life in the receiving society. One of the first to describe Dominicans as transnational was anthropologist Jorge Duany, who defines transnationalism "as the construction of dense social fields across national borders as a result of the circulation of people, ideas, practices, money, goods, and information" (Duany 2008, 2). In Duany's view, though many immigrant groups can be characterized as transnational, "few immigrant communities have developed such a large number and variety of transnational ties to their country of origin, and have maintained such strong ties over several decades, as Dominicans in New York" (1994; 2008, 8). Today transnationalism has become a synonym for Dominicans in the United States. Proponents of this belief argue that Dominicans hold cultural values and social practices in the States that are associated with their home country, revealing their transnational identity and attachment (Levitt 2001; Bailey 2002; Kasinitz et al. 2002; and Sagás and Molina 2004; Guilamo-Ramos et al. 2007; Rodríguez 2009; Calzada et al. 2010).

It is obvious that scholars have found evidence of what they describe as transnational behavior and practices in the culture of Dominicans in New York City. While cultural maintenance may reveal attachment to home country, it may also reveal the very simple nature of a group's survival strategy: sharing and preserving a collective mentality that explains who they are and how they came to be, and then passing it on to their children so the process is repeated and their existence is ensured. Attachment may also camouflage the fact that most Dominican migrants remain responsible for the economic well-being of family members left in the homeland, and they either send remittance to support them or they don't. Choosing the first

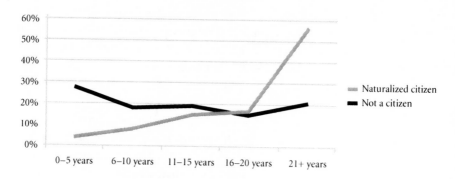

Figure 5.5 Dominican Naturalization by Length of Stay
Source: American Community Survey 2008.

option makes Dominicans good family members; choosing the second turns them into the opposite. The first option leads to transnationalism; the second option still begs for explanation. Two other considerations worth taking into account when thinking about Dominican transnationalism are the following: (1) Their desire to maintain cultural traditions and keep a commitment to family members in the homeland may not preclude Dominicans from developing sentiments of attachment to the immigrant abode that may be as strong and as solid as the ones they may feel for their ancestral land and what they left behind. Of course, Dominican immigrants do find hypernationalists and ethnocentrists in both societies who would question and challenge the legitimacy of their attachment and the loyalty to either place or, worse, their fidelity to both. (2) The cultural values and the social practices upheld by Dominicans in New York City reflect what Dominicans bring when they come, not the culture they leave behind; one does not remain static but is constantly transformed. In the end, the Dominican culture in New York is a combination of a memory—based on what Dominicans knew when they were back home—and their daily actions and thought as they live their lives in New York City.

CONCLUSION

The first version of this chapter, published in 1996, closed on an optimistic note, citing great baseball player Rojas Alou's laudatory remarks about the Dominican people and major-league players, in which he said Dominicans "'don't know fear,' because they dare to brave the Atlantic ocean in boats to come to the United States and with just one thing in their mind, 'to give it all they've got'" (Rains 1992, 37). We have no reason not to be cheerful today; most poor people, whether consciously or not, resist destitution and marginalization. Migrants in particular are perhaps the most resilient of the poor, since the very act of migration implies a willingness to begin again and build a new life—often from very little and in the most adverse circumstances. Dominicans are a remarkable people who built a community on what began as a foreign soil but which they turned into their own once their children were born on it and their dead were no longer taken back to the ancestral land. In the process, a clear pattern has emerged, and that is the rise of the US-born Dominican and a geographical dispersion of Dominicans in the United States. This development creates its own dynamics. In particular, the repercussions of the new development create the need, for instance, to see the Dominican people beyond the immigrant perspective and to consider the role of the US-born Dominican in shaping and defining who Dominicans are, what their goals are, and which roads the group will take to accomplish these goals. The rise of the US-born Dominican population also increases the group's sharing in the responsibility of forging the future of the Dominican people, in preserving its culture and its history, and in valuing its contributions. Whatever path they choose to take, in the end, this will certainly mark the Dominican people forever.

NOTES

1. "The donkey thinks one thing, but the one whom he carries thinks something else."
2. Execution.
3. This bank closed as of 2012.

REFERENCES

Bailey, Benjamin. 2002. *Language, Race, and Negotiation of Identity: A Study of Dominican Americans.* New York: LFB Scholarly Publishing.

Bray, David. 1984. "Economic Development: The Middle Class and International Migration in the Dominican Republic." *International Migration Review* 18 (2): 217–36.

Briggs, Vernon M., Jr. 1992. *Mass Immigration and the National Interest.* New York: M.E. Sharpe.

Calzada, E. J., et al. 2010. "Incorporating the Cultural Value of *Respeto* into a Framework of Latino Parenting." *Cultural Diversity and Ethnic Minority Psychology* 16 (1): 81–82.

Canelo, Frank J. 1982. *Dónde, por qué, de qué y cómo viven los dominicanos en el extranjero: Un informe sociológico sobre la e/migración dominicana, 1961–1962.* Santo Domingo: Alfa y Omega.

Cassá, Roberto. 1982. *Capitalismo y Dictadura.* Santo Domingo: Universidad Autónoma de Santo Domingo.

Ceara Hatton, Miguel. 1990. *Tendencias estructurales y coyuntura de la economía dominicana, 1968–1983.* Santo Domingo: Centro de Investigación Económica, Inc. (CIEGA).

Ceara Hatton, Miguel, and Edwin C. Hernández. 1993. *El gasto público social de la República Dominicana en la década de los ochenta.* Santo Domingo: Centro de Investigación Económica y Fondo de las Naciones Unidas para la Infancia.

Chávez, Linda. 1991. *Out of El Barrio: Towards a New Politics of Hispanic Assimilation.* New York: Basic Books.

Del Cid, Miguel, and Rodolfo Tacsan Chen. 1999. *Fuerza Laboral, Ingresos y Poder Adquisitivo de los Salarios en Centroamérica, Panamá y República Dominicana: 1998.* San José, Costa Rica: Organización Internacional del Trabajo, LIL, S.A.

Duany, Jorge. 1994. "El Impacto de la Inmigración Extranjera en el Mercado Laboral de Puerto Rico." *Homines* 17 (1–2): 241–52.

———. 2008. *Quisqueya on the Hudson: The Transnational Identity of Dominicans in Washington Heights.* 2nd ed., with a new preface. Dominican Research Monograph 1. New York: Dominican Studies Institute, City University of New York. First published 1994.

Encuesta Demográfica y de Salud (ENDESA). 1996. Santo Domingo: Centro de Estudios Sociales y Demográficos.

Faxas, Laura. 2007. *El Mito roto: Sistema político y movimiento popular en la República Dominicana, 1961–1990.* Romero de Terrenos, México D.F.: Siglo XXI: Fundación Global Democracia y Desarrollo: FLACSO Republica Dominicana.

Georges, Eugenia. 1990. *The Making of a Transnational Community: Migration, Development, and Cultural Change in the Dominican Republic.* New York: Columbia University Press.

González, Nancie L. 1970. "Peasant's Progress: Dominicans in New York." *Caribbean Studies* 10 (3): 154–71.

Guarnizo, Luis E. 1994. "Los Dominicanyorks: The Making of a Binational Society." *Annals of the American Academy of Political and Social Sciences* 533:70–86.

Guilamo Ramos, Vincent, et al. 2007. "Parenting Practices among Dominican and Puerto Rican Mothers." *National Association of Social Workers* 52 (1): 17–30.

Hendricks, Glenn L. 1974. *The Dominican Diaspora: From the Dominican Republic to New York City—Villagers in Transition.* New York: Teachers College Press.

Hernández, Ramona. 2002. *The Mobility of Workers under Advanced Capitalism: Dominican Migration to the United States*. New York: Columbia University Press.

———. 2005. "On Dominicans in New York City's Garment Industry." In *A Coat of Many Colors: Immigration, Globalization, and Reform in New York City's Garment Industry*, edited by Daniel Soyer, 169–91. New York: Fordham University Press.

———. 2007. "Living on the Margins of Society: Dominicans in the United States." In *Latinos in a Changing Society*, edited by M. Montero-Sieburth and E. Meléndez, 34–57. Westport: Praeger Publishers.

———. 2011. "The Dominican American Family." In *Ethnic Families in America: Patterns and Variations*, edited by Roosevelt Wright, 148–73. Englewood Cliffs, NJ: Prentice Hall.

Hernández, Ramona, and Francisco Rivera-Batiz. 2003. "Dominicans in the United States: A Socioeconomic Profile, 2000." Dominican Research Monograph Series. New York: Dominican Studies Institute, City University of New York.

Kasinitz, Philip, et al. 2002. "Becoming Americans / Becoming New Yorkers: Immigrant Incorporation in a Majority Minority City." *International Migration Review* 36 (4): 1020–36.

Levitt, Peggy. 2001. *The Transnational Villagers*. Berkeley: University of California Press.

Levitt, Peggy, and Mary C. Waters, eds. 2002. *The Changing Face of Home: The Transnational Lives of the Second Generation*. New York: Russell Sage Foundation.

Light, Ivan H., et al. "Ethnic Economy or Ethnic Enclave Economy?" 1995. In *New Migrants in the Marketplace: Boston Ethnic Entrepreneurs*, edited by Marilyn Halter, 23–42. Amherst: University of Massachusetts Press.

Lozano, Wilfredo. 1985. *El reformismo dependiente*. Santo Domingo: Ediciones Taller.

Moya Pons, Frank. 1977. *Manual de historia dominicana*. Santiago: Universidad Católica Madre y Maestra.

———. 1995. *The Dominican Republic: A National History*. New York: Hispaniola Books.

Pantoja, Segundo. 2005. *Religion and Education among Latinos in New York City*. Boston: Brill Academic.

Pessar, Patricia. 1987. "The Dominicans: Women in the Household and the Garment Industry." In *New Immigrants in New York*, edited by Nancy Foner, 103–30. New York: Columbia University Press.

Portes, Alejandro, and Luis E. Guarnizo. 1990. *Tropical Capitalists: U.S.-Bound Immigration and Small-Enterprise Development in the Dominican Republic*. Working Papers. Washington, DC: Commission for the Study of International Migration and Cooperative Economic Development.

Rains, Bob. 1992. "A Contender Is Exposed." *USA Today Baseball Weekly*, August 12–18.

Rodríguez, Tracy. 2009. *Dominicanas entre La Gran Manzana y Quisqueya: Family, Schooling, and Language Learning in a Transnational Context*. Chapel Hill: University of North Carolina Press.

Ruggles, Steven, J. Trent Alexander, Katie Genadek, Ronald Goeken, Matthew B. Schroeder, and Matthew Sobek. 2010. *Integrated Public Use Microdata Series: Version 5.0*. Machine-readable database. Minneapolis: University of Minnesota.

Sagás, Ernesto, and Sintia E. Molina. 2004. *Dominican Migration: Transnational Perspectives*. Gainesville: University Press of Florida.

Sassen-Koob, Saskia. 1988. *The Mobility of Labor and Capital: A Study of International Investment and Labor Flow*. Cambridge: Cambridge University Press.

Torres-Saillant, Silvio. 1999. *El retorno de las yolas: Ensayos sobre diáspora, democracia y dominicanidad*. Santo Domingo: Ediciones Librería Trinitaria y Editora Manatí, República Dominicana.

Waldinger, Roger. 1986. *Through the Eye of the Needle: Immigrants and Enterprises in New York's Garment Trade*. New York: New York University Press.

———. 1996. "The Jobs Immigrants Take." Editorial. *New York Times*, March 11.

CHAPTER SIX

Mexicans in New York at a Crossroads in the Second Decade of the New Millennium

ROBERT COURTNEY SMITH

Note: This chapter was written in 2013 and revised in 2014, when the federal policy of Deferred Action for Childhood Arrivals (DACA) held great promise and immigration reform seemed possible during a second Obama administration. I have added a coda at the end to discuss the current political context.

Mexicans in New York have reached a kind of crossroads. As a group, Mexicans seem suddenly more visible as the third-largest, and fastest-growing, Latino group in the city, but are changing from a mainly new-immigrant population to a more mixed population of new immigrants, long-term immigrants with US-citizen children, and US-raised young adults, each with distinct issues, opportunities, and challenges. Similarly, Mexicans have experienced a kind of bifurcated integration into New York, with much of the US-born second generation doing fairly well or better, while long-term exclusion from legal status has limited opportunities for an entire generation of young people. Furthermore, Mexicans as a group do not have any elected representatives in the city—as one would expect of a group with about half a million members—but are becoming more civically engaged and politically active. Over the coming decade, these changes will present new opportunities for strategic interventions that could promote fuller incorporation and advancement of Mexican immigrants and their children across a wide range of social, educational, and civic life. Moreover, there are important roles that can be played by major institutions in New York City (including the Department of Education [DOE], City University of New York [CUNY], New York Police Department [NYPD], and others) to promote positive outcomes. There will remain, however, the legacy of an entire generation of Mexican (and other) immigrants who have grown up from childhood to adulthood as undocumented immigrants, and whose life trajectories have been harmed by legal exclusion. In the chapter that follows, I describe and reflect on these themes and suggest interventions. This paper draws on data for my forthcoming book, tentatively titled *Horatio Alger Lives in Brooklyn, but Check His Papers* (University of California Press), and other research I have done over the last two decades.

DIMENSIONS AND IMPLICATIONS OF EXCLUSION AND INCLUSION

Mexicans in New York City offer an instructive case of the effects of public policies on the well-being of groups of people. In other research, I have used the concept of the "natural experiment" to describe the ways that immigration policy has created "target" and "control" groups consisting, respectively, of those who lack documents long term and those who can get them or are born in the United States. In social science, natural experiments happen when a policy affects one group but not a similarly, otherwise equivalent group. Classic natural experiments involved relocating some residents of demolished public housing to the suburbs, while others moved to other places in the city. Those who moved to the suburbs did better, because they had access to better schools, employment, and services and were away from problems in their old neighborhoods. The natural experiment here is in immigration inclusion. My own work on Mexicans in New York dates to 1987, when I first lived in the city, and has run until today. Over this period, my research has straddled a large *inclusionary* experiment—the 1986 IRCA amnesty program (which actually ran through 1988 as a program)—and the subsequent quarter century of an *exclusionary* experiment that I call a "moratorium period," wherein it was very hard for many undocumented people to adjust their status. Deferred Action for Childhood Arrivals (DACA)[1] and the promise of the DREAM Act or other more comprehensive immigration reform (CIR) offer the promise of yet another inclusionary experiment. The promise of this new inclusionary angle is yet to be determined, but the generosity or mean-spiritedness of the immigration fixes we adopt will have lasting consequences for the quality of our society and our democracy.

Mexicans in New York have experienced bifurcated integration primarily on the axis of legal status—those with access to it have done fairly well, while those without it have fared much less well. Estimates of the Mexican population in New York are somewhat complicated to make, because of the high percentage of Mexicans without legal status. The census estimates that the population increased from 56,698 in 1990 to 180,473 in 2000 to 324,349 in 2010. Research on census estimates (e.g., Smith 1996), however, indicate that Mexicans in New York fall into categories of persons who are particularly likely to be undercounted because they move around more than other populations and are more likely to be undocumented or to live in nonstandard housing. Their housing units may not show up on census lists, or may have more than one family living there or extra, nonfamily members; and so, the census will not seek to enumerate their presence, and they will be undercounted. The census will only seek to count you if it knows someone lives at a specific address. An undercount does not always occur because someone "hides" from the census; it also occurs because no one is looking for the person. Hence, I would estimate that the Mexican population increased from about 100,000 in 1990 to about 300,000 in 2000 to about 450,000 in 2010. It may have been as high as 500,000 in 2013, and could reach 600,000 by 2020. The higher growth rate between 1990–2000 and 2000–2010 reflects the bump that the amnesty program gave to Mexican immigration and settlement in the earlier period, and the slowing of the rate in the subsequent decade without it (Smith 2006).

The overall demographic profile of Mexicans in New York is changing. While there are still many new Mexican migrants to New York, the US-born (and New York–born) Mexican population is now nearly as big as the Mexican immigrant population. A recent report by Treschan and Mehrotra (2013) describes some of these statistics. Some 43% of the Mexican population in New York is native born, and the younger the age group, the higher the percentage. Some 92% of those under age sixteen are US born. Moreover, the Mexican population is very young, with 46% under the age of twenty-five and 30% under age sixteen. By comparison, 40% of Puerto Ricans and 41% of

Dominicans are under age twenty-five. This change can be seen in the changes in the population of sixteen- to nineteen-year-olds and its nativity. US-born Mexican New Yorkers in this age group numbered 2,694 in 2000, compared to 12,108 foreign born. In 2009, the US-born numbered 8,443 while the foreign born were 7,309 (Smith 2014).

While the US-born Mexican population is increasing, many of these youth are being raised in households whose heads are undocumented immigrants, as described by Hiro Yoshikawa in his 2010 book, *Immigrants Raising Citizens.* Undocumented Mexican parents in Yoshikawa's study are more likely to be recent arrivals, are more likely isolated from community supports, and are raising children in less-enriched educational environments; and their lack of knowledge and/or fear of American institutions make them especially unlikely to use institutional daycare prior to kindergarten. The use of such daycare is positively related to school readiness. Hence, the disadvantages of the undocumented immigrant parents impair the development of their US-citizen children. The longer the parents remain undocumented, the worse the harm. This has contributed to the bifurcated trajectories of Mexicans in New York.

Another point, insightfully developed by Treschan and Mehrotra (2013), is that the low incomes of Mexicans mean that as a population they become poorer as these youth become parents and have children of their own. While having multiple earners in a household keeps them above the poverty line as childless workers, the entire household falls into poverty as they have children. Indeed, 33% of Mexican New Yorkers are poor, and another 34% are near poor (less than 200% of poverty level), with 67% at or near poverty levels. (Rates are roughly similar for US and Mexico born.) Some 79% of those under age sixteen are at or near poverty levels (Treschan and Mehrotra 2013). A key reason is that many US-born Mexican children live in households where the adults are undocumented immigrants, who earn very little money. Incomes are higher for the US born who are raised in New York and for their subsequent US-born children (Smith 2012).

One concrete indication of the bifurcated trajectories of the Mexican population in New York comes in the differences between statistics for the US- and Mexico-born children of Mexican immigrants. A remarkable 41% of sixteen- to nineteen-year-olds born in Mexico were not in high school and had not graduated, while the number for US-born sixteen- to nineteen-year-old children of Mexicans is only 8%. (Stating the obverse, that means that 59% of the foreign-born and 92% of US-born of this age are in school.)

To give a sense of how high this 41% rate is, the next-highest rates were among island-born Puerto Ricans (19%) and Ecuadoreans (17%). The Chinese and Jamaican foreign-born rates were 6%. The story is similar with respect to college for 2005–9. Between 2000 and 2010 (2005–9 ACS data), nineteen- to twenty-three-year-old Mexican foreign-born youth attended or had graduated college at the same rate, at 6%, while rates bumped up dramatically for US-born Mexican youth, from 32% to 51% in the same period. This moved US-born Mexicans from an outlier for low attendance to right in the middle of other groups of US-born children of immigrants, such as Jamaicans (50%), Ecuadoreans (55%), and Dominicans (50%).

A significant part of this increase is due, I think, to the City University of New York's (CUNY) efforts both to disseminate information about college within the Mexican community and to forge tighter links between that community and CUNY. For the past decade, the CUNY Commission on the Mexicans and Mexican Americans and Education has worked to disseminate information about college attendance and to dispel myths among the Mexican community. Research I conducted in 2006 showed that most young Mexican immigrants had erroneous beliefs about access to higher education in New York—that one could not attend CUNY if undocumented, that one had to attend full-time, and that the cost was very high (many thought it cost over twenty thousand dollars a year to attend. In fact, in 2013, tuition was $5,730 per year). CUNY outreach targeted those myths, none of which were true. Dispelling the myths and promoting knowledge of how to apply and about CUNY's flexibility, plus its welcome of all students, have helped promote applications among Mexicans.

My research on Mexicans in New York has involved four surveys over the last twenty years that included questions about legal status and Mexican states of origin. The states of origin have remained consistent, with a trend of Puebla accounting for a slightly smaller percentage of the total, and of some new states beginning to show a notable presence. Each of these surveys was conducted partly in the waiting room of the Mexican Consulate in New York and partly in public places. In the latter, our strategy was to piggyback on natural concentrations of population, such as weekend soccer games in major parks, or 16th-of-September Mexican Independence Day celebrations. Surveys were anonymous. In the 1993 (N=561) survey (Valdes and Smith 1993), Puebla accounted for 47% of migrants in New York, Guerrero and Oaxaca together for 18%, and the *Distrito Federal* (D.F.) and state of Mexico for 11%. In 2011, Puebla accounted for 42% of migrants (N=729),

Oaxaca was 11% and Guerrero 10% (21% together), the D.F. was 8% and state of Mexico 9% (17% together), and Morelos 4% and Veracruz 3% (7% together). There are also differences between New York City and other areas. For example, New Jersey has more migrants from Oaxaca and fewer from Puebla than New York City.

My four surveys show that the percentage of migrants from Puebla has fallen slightly over time, but still accounts by far for the largest number of migrants of any state. This partly reflects the growth in migration from the other states, and partly an exhaustion of the migrant-sending population in Puebla. In many *municipios* in the migrant belt of Puebla and the Mixteca region of adjoining Oaxaca and Guerrero, so many migrants have left that the populations are significantly smaller than they were before. Hence, there are fewer new births, and fewer young men and women migrating. More-over, the legalization of many of these older migrants and their children re-sulted in a huge population shift to New York and the United States during the 1990s and the first decade of this century, further and permanently de-creasing the number of future migrants. Finally, other states have begun sending more migrants, though none has grown as large as Puebla itself. The number of migrants from Oaxaca has grown, especially, to New Jersey towns such as New Brunswick. The indigenous population among Mexicans in New York has also grown significantly, with 10% of the 2011 sample speak-ing an indigenous language. Mixteco is the most common, with 4% of the sample, followed by Nahuatl, with 3%.

LEGAL STATUS

The legal status of Mexican migrants is a key factor in the analysis of natural experiments. The 2011 *Seguro Popular* survey was performed with about half the surveys conducted in the consulate, and half outside it, including surveys conducted for the Consulate on Wheels, which sets up in commu-nity centers far from the consulate, for example, in New Jersey or Connecti-cut. The results did not differ significantly for those inside and outside the consulate. The results are probably still somewhat skewed because most of the people visiting the consulate are seeking documents—especially the *ma-tricula consular*, which certifies the identity of the person—either to travel back to Mexico or to use as identification while in New York. Undocumented people are more likely to seek such a document. Even allowing for this bias in the data, the statistics are still shockingly high. Our sample (N=724 for this question) shows that 85% of migrants surveyed lacked legal status in the United States, while 15% had it. What is more, illegal status persisted for a very long time. For example, 91%, or 152 of 166, people in our sample who had been in the United States for 0–5 years were undocumented. For those with 6–10 years of residency, 94%, or 206 of 220, were undocumented. For those with 11–15 years, the number was 92%, or 132 of 143. There is no significant drop-off in the rate of undocumented status until one has more than twenty years, when the rate falls to 49%, or 37 of 76. This rate reflects what I have called "the moratorium period"—the now quarter century since the amnesty program was passed and has made it increasingly difficult for undocumented immigrants to legalize their status.[2] We return to this point later. This long-term undocumented status is very significant in many ways including dampening the life chances of immigrants and their children; they are all excluded from opportunities by their unadjusted status.

Herein lie the roots of the bifurcated integration. In the two decades after IRCA, Congress made it increasingly difficult to legalize one's status. For example, it made it harder to fight deportations by raising the standard for relief, and made it necessary for some spouses to return to their country of origin to legalize even if they were marrying a US citizen and had children. Hence, in the quarter century since IRCA, Mexicans in New York, and in the country in many ways, have entered into bifurcated integration pathways. Many had access to legal status through immediate family members who were citizens, and fewer through work or investment channels. This group included people who had legalized their status through IRCA and become citizens. Another group that has grown dramatically in size has been unable to get a foothold in legal status for themselves and their families, and have lived as long-term undocumented people. This is a fundamentally new phenomenon in American immigration history—a very large class of persons who are unable to legalize their status over an extended time. The growth of this undocumented population has also increased because of tighter border enforcement and loss of faith that Mexico's economic situation will improve for people like them. This has led many to come to the United States and simply stay, and bring their families. Doug Massey's work with Jorge Durand and Nolan Malone (2003) has shown that before the tighter border security, circular migration meant that many undocumented workers kept their families in Mexico and simply visited them. Now, they are more likely to simply stay in the States and bring their families with them.

BIFURCATED INTEGRATION AND PROSPECTS OF DACA AND BROADER IMMIGRATION REFORM

What has this bifurcation meant for Mexicans in New York City? A primary impact has been to flatten the educational aspirations and life-course trajectories of many children of immigrants. I have seen this many times in my data, and in my work in the Mexican community. In many cases, even talented undocumented students will ask—Why should I work so hard to get a college education, when I will still be undocumented when I get out, with no chance of legalizing? It is a hard position to argue with. Their analysis was that it seemed like a rigged game: New York would support their ability to get an education, even to attend college at in-state tuition rates, but they were unable to work and convert that hard-won education into a middle-class lifestyle. This has led to a phenomenon I call the "sophomore/junior year crash." As other students begin to talk about their plans for college, undocumented students begin to think their status will hold them back, making it harder for them to focus on their schoolwork and leading many to seek other life courses, such as dropping out and working.

INCLUSIONARY AND EXCLUSIONARY PROJECTS

This is a particularly cruel irony, and shows how today's undocumented children of immigrants are caught between exclusionary and inclusionary projects in American law and society. The rationale for letting undocumented youth attend schools in the United States was most clearly expressed in Justice Brennan's majority opinion in *Plyler v. Doe* (1982), in which the Supreme Court overruled a Texas law preventing school systems that were educating undocumented youth from being reimbursed by the state for those expenses, as they were for other students. Brennan argued primarily that as children, these undocumented persons were not responsible for their unlawful presence in the United States, and that they were entitled to special protection as children; hence, they should be allowed to attend school. He also argued that the state had a compelling interest in preventing the formation of an underclass, which he saw as a logical consequence of excluding these youth from school. Finally, he argued that all persons in the United States are entitled to equal protection of the law—that the country had fought a civil war to eradicate invidious distinctions between classes of persons (e.g., slave vs. free)—and that Texas's statute hence violated the Fourteenth Amendment's equal-protection clause.

The cruel irony for long-term undocumented children is this. Their right to an education is constitutionally protected until grade twelve, and their right to in-state tuition (under certain conditions) is codified in New York State law (and the laws of about fifteen other states), but they become criminals when they try to get jobs of any kind. Those who do finish college can almost never find jobs commensurate with their educational levels. I have elsewhere called this a "cruel Cinderella moment"; they work hard as children, but once they become legally adults and try to work, they are transformed into criminals.

Let's go back to those Mexican youth I have interviewed, talked to, and worked with in the early 1990s. How would I answer their assertion that there was no point in going to college, because they would still be undocumented? I would usually say that having a college education should help with any legalization that comes down the road, and could help legalize in other ways, e.g., through a job. However, for most of the past twenty years, legalizing their status has seemed like a remote possibility, especially for teenagers, who are notoriously present-oriented. How compelling is it to tell a teenager to work hard for an achievement that might get rewarded, but probably will not; furthermore, it will require you to make huge sacrifices, likely for six years (because you're going to school part-time, while working full-time), when your family needs the income you could earn? Looking back at those conversations with teens in the early 1990s, who are now in their late thirties and, many, still undocumented, I have to conclude that *they were right*, in their time; the country that raised and educated them did not give most of them a chance to legalize their status, and hence changed the equation from "Work hard in school and you will have a better life" to "Work hard in school and you will end up in the same place, economically." Work hard in school, and you will be able to offer your own children the same economic standard of living as those who are dropping out of high school and going straight to work. It has the ring of a brutal joke. With a system rigged against them this way, was it any wonder so many children of Mexican immigrants went to work instead of school?

DACA, THE DREAM ACT AND BROADER IMMIGRATION REFORM AND EDUCATION

The likelihood of some kind of substantive immigration reform should be a cause for optimism. It should help immigrants, and American society as a whole, in the work of integrating newcomers. It should help make sure that everyone has a fair shot to turn their hard work into a reasonable reward for themselves and their families. Below, I discuss how some of these reforms would affect Mexican and other immigrant youth in New York.

DACA has the potential to quickly improve the lives of many undocumented children of immigrants. DACA allows those who were under age sixteen when they migrated to the United States and who have not passed the age of thirty-five, and meet certain other requirements, to gain legal status quickly. Before discussing these benefits, we must note the shortcomings of DACA. It was an executive decision by the Obama administration and hence will not extend beyond President Obama's second term if President Trump does not want it to. It also does not (and could not) offer a path to citizenship. However, it does offer legal status and work authorization. DACA, on its own, addresses one of the most fundamental problems Mexicans in New York, and other immigrants in the country, face—the link between educational effort and labor market rewards has been broken, but DACA largely restores that link. It is not a complete fix of immigration issues by any means, but it is a big step in the right direction.

DACA could enable very positive actions by civil society and government to promote positive incorporation. For example, New York City has the Young Men's Initiative (YMI), which combines a variety of incentives, programs, and services to support the educational effort and life chances of black and Latino New Yorkers. The program is thoughtfully constructed, including programs like peer mentoring and internships. In a panel at Baruch College, I urged former deputy mayor Linda Gibbs to consider bringing DACA into the YMI. While the YMI seeks to aid black and Latino youth as "youth of color," immigrant youth face distinct challenges related to legal status that have derailed the aspirations of many, and could largely be addressed with this program, at least in terms of educational and work possibilities. Among other things, DACA could help relink educational effort and improved future life chances for so many youth.

DACA could be useful in fighting the "sophomore/junior year crash" among undocumented students, by removing the structural obstacles that unlink school effort from future life chances. DACA can restore that link. DACA could also be used to help fight the growth of Mexican gangs in New York City, which has been partly fueled by this decoupling of school effort from future life chances.

The DREAM Act would be a further help to many immigrants, and Mexicans in New York especially. Depending on which version one considers, the DREAM Act would enable students who had graduated from high school or gotten a GED and gone to some college, or served in the US military, to legalize their status and get on a road to citizenship. The DREAM Act is strategically the most compelling immigration reform act available for several reasons, including that it resonates with American myths of bootstrap mobility and self-sufficiency. It seems to reward children who have grown to adulthood in the United States, who have been self-sufficient, not depended on the government, and who only want just rewards for their efforts, rather than some kind of "entitlement" (Abrego 2008). These are reasons I think that it has had the most political resonance. And I think that the youth who propelled this movement were politically and organizationally brilliant and brave, and deserve the success they have enjoyed.

The problem with the DREAM Act is that it leaves out so many people who are undocumented. First, it leaves out lower academic achievers—those who dropped out of high school, for example. The irony here is that many of these youth who dropped out of high school did so because they predicted—correctly—that there would not be a path for them to legalize. Second, it leaves out those who have aged out. If you came to the United States as a seven-year-old child with your parents in 1987, and have lived here your whole life, you would now be too old for DACA or the DREAM Act, in most of its possible forms. This seems unnecessary, and easily fixable.

The issue of all other Mexicans or other immigrants who are not covered under DACA or the DREAM Act is huge, since this group includes the large majority of the eleven million undocumented people in the United States. A key consideration here is that most families are mixed-status families—they may include undocumented parents, a DACA-eligible child, a non-DACA-eligible child, and a US-citizen child. How can we fix this kind of situation without a program that opens a road for many or most undocumented immigrants to legalize? A key dimension of American law is that it values families and seeks not to split them up where possible. This should be a guiding principle of immigration reform moving forward.[3]

A key issue involves the end status for undocumented immigrants who are legalized. Right now, America has the equivalent of an entire country living in undocumented status within its borders. The United States has eleven million undocumented people, while the Dominican Republic has a population of eight million, and the Republic of Ireland has five million. The long-term maintenance of a large population of permanently disenfranchised people, who cannot become citizens and hence formal members of the political community, is dangerous for our democracy. Among other things, it creates "civic deserts," neighborhoods where parents pay taxes, children attend schools, people work hard, but where most people cannot become politically active. As a result, they are not considered in the political process and their interests can be ignored, not given due consideration, or simply be unknown.

A final issue is one that we, as a nation, cannot easily address, and with which we will live in the future, namely, the legacy of twenty-five years of undocumented status for a large number of immigrants, many of whom are Mexican. In New York, a large percentage of the Mexican population is in this status. The bifurcated integration of Mexicans in New York makes the costs of this long-term exclusion clear. In my forthcoming book, *Horatio Alger Lives in Brooklyn, but Check His Papers*, I show how US-born or legal-status-possessing Mexicans did better in life in many ways than undocumented-born ones, and how those who came in without status but legalized before high school did as well as or better than US-born Mexican children. There is a large segment of this whole generation of youth that have already gone from early childhood through adolescence into early and even full adulthood without legal status. These are youth who went to American schools, listen to American music, speak English to their children and each other, and feel like "Americans." And they are, in all likelihood, here to stay. For a variety of reasons, including America's long-term economic self-interest, it makes sense to remove as many obstacles to their success as possible, and to welcome them more warmly and fully.

HOW?

Rereading that last paragraph, I feel compelled to offer concrete suggestions on how legalization could help, and how it could be implemented. Many of the positive effects of legalization could happen through DACA alone, though fuller forms of legalization with a road to citizenship could have even bigger effects. Below I reflect on some of the ways DACA and related programs might help now. As noted above, a key positive effect of DACA could be to restore the link between effort in school and future life chances. You study hard, graduate from high school, go to college, and your future life should be better. How could New York City help? There are many ways.

First, New York City has the Young Men's Initiative (YMI), which combines a variety of incentives, programs, and services to support the educational effort and life chances of black and Latino New Yorkers. The YMI could be retooled to include this focus on legal status as one of its key targets—one which can now actually be effected because of DACA or other legalization.

The New York Police Department (NYPD) could be an important partner here. While undocumented youth who have committed felonies are not eligible for DACA, the NYPD has a great deal of contact with youth who have *not* committed crimes, and even has programs targeting youth they want to keep *out* of trouble, such as the Juvenile Robbery Intervention Program or J-RIP (Ruderman 2013). Indeed, police gang units often seek to develop friendly relationships with gang members and their friends, who are actually not in a gang but may hang out with some gang members. The gang units do this in the hope of dissuading some from future crimes and to aid in investigations. The police, potentially, could help neighborhoods where, for example, there are gangs, if they would inform these youth about DACA or other legalization programs and offer information on how and where to apply. They would also warn the youth that they would be ineligible if they committed a crime. Removing the main structural obstacle, undocumented status, that seems to make a better future impossible to imagine should offer these youth strong, positive incentives. The NYPD might offer that help, which could reinforce a positive relationship between the police and the community, including these youth.

CUNY will continue its work with immigrant communities, including Mexicans. Its Citizenship Now Program has already started working with DACA-eligible students. It estimates that there are at least three thousand CUNY students eligible for DACA, and these three thousand are no doubt related to a much larger number in New York. Helping them through DACA would help give the community a deeper knowledge of how to negotiate the DACA program, or other legalization programs. CUNY's Mexican Institute could play a key role here, too.

The New York City Department of Education, or DOE, is ideally suited for this work. Many, if not most, long-term undocumented immigrants in the city have relatives in the New York City public schools (their own children, nieces/nephews, etc.). Studies have shown that students are helped by their parents having legal status (Yoshikawa 2012; Smith forthcoming). Hence, DOE could help promote its students' ability to learn by helping disseminate information about legalization through backpack notices. Such a policy would be appropriate in a city that is 37% foreign born, and where some two-thirds are either born abroad or children of immigrants.

Finally, the Mayor's Office, particularly its Office of Immigrant Affairs, could play an important role in promoting these programs. The Mayor's Office of Immigrant Affairs has quietly developed strong relationships with many immigrant communities in New York, which could be mobilized to help. The mayor should take to the bully pulpit (again) to make the commonsense case for why legalization makes sense for New York City, for all New Yorkers, and for America.

CODA—THE NEW POLITICAL CONTEXT AFTER JANUARY 20, 2017

Rereading this chapter in early January 2017, I find that it seems naively hopeful in its focus on how local institutions could collaborate to promote integration in the Mexican community and the city. It seems to presume that some positive, federal, immigration reform would happen. The reality we face in 2017 is grimmer, but we do not yet know how grim. The incoming president has promised to end DACA, and politically will very likely need to do that, but he has also promised to do something else that people will be "happy with." This small positive signal seems inconsistent with his appointing as attorney general Jeff Sessions, a Republican with a long record of anti-immigrant positions. The attorney general is very important for initiatives like DACA, because such positions are essentially prosecutorial discretion— they are a policy of deciding not to deport people, but not to give them full legal status, either. DACA is a legal status limbo, with the right to work legally, but it is a *revocable* right—unlike the rights of citizens, for example, to work, vote, or live their lives without fear of deportation—that can be taken back by the next president.

The 2016 presidential election has changed the immigration policy landscape and the work to be done. This work will depend largely on what the new administration actually does. My guess on what will happen is this. It seems less likely the new president will try to deport people who have applied for DACA—most Americans would see it as improper to go after youth who voluntarily tried to get legal status and just want to move on with their lives. But it seems likely he will end DACA, and it is unknowable what else he will actually do to replace it. There is one possible silver lining that the optimist in me hopes will matter. The new president owes nothing, politically, to the Republican Party, while it owes him a great deal. There is some chance that there will be a Nixon in China scenario—whereas immigration reform would have been blocked if proposed by a Democratic president, a Republican one who saved his party in the last elections could get them to act. It was, after all, the Republican icon President Ronald Reagan who supported one of the most important immigration reforms ever, who included a legalization program (Immigration Reform and Control Act of 1986). The shape of any future reform would likely be harsh and have negative downstream consequences.

I offer two examples of how a harsh reform could negatively affect America. Past reform proposals have included up to a seventeen-year process to become citizens, meaning one would be ineligible to vote or to participate in publicly, federally funded programs in that time. Imagine a four-year-old undocumented child growing up in a poor neighborhood, who got legal status but was ineligible for citizenship until he was twenty-one. He would thus never be eligible for any program with a citizenship test, even though investments in young children have been shown to be the most cost-effective, long-term, highest-benefit government programs (think Head Start). Secondly, there are about eleven million undocumented people in the United States in 2017—a population bigger than thirty-three of the forty-six countries in Europe. The continued presence of a country-sized population in the United States that has no legal status and no path to citizenship creates a civic and political desert within the country and harms American democracy. People in this status have no vote or voice in electing those who govern them, and live lives constricted by a structural master status they cannot change—their legal status (Gonzales 2016). America's first experiment with such a master status—slavery—should make all Americans very uneasy with the recurrence of another such large-scale exclusionary experiment with immigrants. It is our new American dilemma (Myrdal 1944).

NOTES

1. DACA grants temporary, two-year, renewable status to those who arrived before June 15, 2012, before turning sixteen, were no threat to the United States, had graduated from high school, or were in an adult education. It offers no road to permanent legal status and can be rescinded by a letter from the new president.

2. Mexicans accounted for the second-largest number of applicants for the 1986 IRCA amnesty program in New York City, a surprise at the time, but one which makes sense in retrospect. Mexicans were more likely to lack legal status than other groups, and, hence, more likely to apply for it (Smith 2006).

3. In November 2014, Democrats lost both houses of Congress in the mid-term elections. At that time, using his executive authority, President Obama sought to expand DACA and to create DAPA, Deferred Action for Parents of Americans and Lawful Permanent Residents (or Deferred Action for Parental Accountability), to protect more family members from deportation and allow them to work legally. Both the DACA expansion and DAPA were blocked by a Circuit Court judge in Texas and were never implemented.

REFERENCES

Abrego, Leisy. 2008. "Legitimacy, Social Identity, and the Mobilization of Law: The Effects of Assembly Bill 540 on Undocumented Students in California." *Law & Social Inquiry* 33 (3): 709–34.

Gonzales, Roberto. 2011. "Learning to Be Illegal: Undocumented Youth and Shifting Legal Contexts in the Transition to Adulthood." *American Sociological Review* 76 (4): 602–10.

———. 2016. *Lives in Limbo.* Berkeley: University of California Press.

Massey, Douglas, Jorge Durand, and Nolan Malone. 2003. *Beyond Smoke and Mirrors: Mexican Immigration in an Era of Integration.* New York: Russell Sage Foundation.

Myrdal, Gunnar. 1944. *An American Dilemma: The Negro Problem and Modern Democracy.* New York: Harper Brothers.

Ruderman, Wendy. 2013. "To Stem Juvenile Robberies, Police Trail Youth before the Crime." *New York Times,* March 4.

Smith, Robert Courtney. 1996. *Counting Migrant Farmworkers: Causes of the Undercount of Farmworkers in the Northeastern United States in the 1990 Census and Strategies to Increase Coverage for Census 2000.* Final Report to the Center for Survey Methods and Research, Statistical Research Division. Washington, DC: United States Census Bureau.

———. 2006. *Mexican New York: Transnational Worlds of New Immigrants.* Berkeley: University of California Press.

———. 2014. "Black Mexicans and Beyond." *American Sociological Review* 79 (3): 517–48.

———. forthcoming. *Horatio Alger Lives in Brooklyn, but Check His Papers.* Berkeley: University of California Press.

Treschan, Lazar, and Apurva Mehrotra. 2013. *Young Mexican-Americans in New York City: Working More, Learning and Earning Less.* Policy Brief. New York: Community Service Society, March. http://www.cssny.org/publications/.

Valdes, Luz Maria, and Robert Courtney Smith. 1993. *Report to El Colegio de la Frontera Norte: Perfil de la población Mexicana en Nueva York.* New York / Tijuana, Mex.: El Colegio de La Frontera Norte.

Yoshikawa, Hirokazu. 2012. *Immigrants Raising Citizens: Undocumented Parents and Their Young Children.* New York: Russell Sage Foundation.

CHAPTER SEVEN

Ecuadoreans and Colombians in New York

JAVIER CASTAÑO

"We Ecuadoreans are killed for being Mexicans," said Walter Sinche, who considers himself a messenger from the Inca Empire to the United States. His last name means "power" in Quechua, the language of the people of the Central Andes of South America. "I am not a common Ecuadorean living in New York City. I am a *Chasqui*, an athlete of the Andes, a general, a trusted man of pre-Colombian America that has evolved to this date." Sinche was born in the Andean city of Cuenca in 1968. His father was a military man, and his mother a music professor. He started working at the age of twelve. His biggest ambition was to become a pilot. In Ecuador, Sinche got his girlfriend pregnant, was forced to get married, and two days later decided to migrate to the United States. By then, he was a nineteen-year-old Ecuadorean in search of a new life. He crossed the border illegally via Aguascalientes, Mexico, in October 1988. For him it was a fast and easy journey, as easy as the other two times he entered this country without papers. His expertise in dealing with natural obstacles—mountains, rivers, deserts—came very handy during his arduous trek from Guatemala to the US border. It enabled him to zigzag through hundreds of miles of hostile terrain and avoid coyotes every step of the way.

Sinche is not only an immigrant who represents the Ecuadorean migration to New York; his story also illustrates the struggles that many Latino immigrants face in the United States. This chapter focuses on his life and the life of his countrymen, and will contain Sinche's commentaries. It will also include the vicissitudes of the Ecuadorean and Colombian communities in Corona, Queens. In 2013, Corona was deemed to have the most heavily Latin American immigrant community of any Queens neighborhood (Lobo and Salvo 2013). I have watched Sinche interact with his countrymen and immigrants from other Latin American countries, and I have interviewed him extensively for the purpose of this chapter. He has gained a reputation in the Latino community for being a progressive activist. Among South Americans, specially Ecuadoreans, Colombians, Peruvians, and Bolivians, Sinche is becoming a leader.

This chapter is not primarily a historical overview of Corona; it is a study of social similarities between the Ecuadorean and Colombian communities and of the journey of these communities through issues of overcrowding, lack of education or poor learning conditions, racial tensions, and assimilation into American society. In addition, I examine current issues such as foreclosures in housing, crime, and redevelopment. As with other communities that have resided in this area, history is bound to repeat itself if we do not learn from it. Throughout this chapter, the reader will notice that Latinos are disconnected from the political machinery and the distribution of public resources. Furthermore, they lack a civil rights movement capable of guiding them to empowerment. The Latino community of Corona and elsewhere in this city is looking for authentic leadership that can give them a second chance in life. Latinos came here to prosper; but for a great majority of them, the American Dream is elusive. (See table 7.1 with 2000–2010 population figures.)

I am a journalist and an editor who has worked in New York for almost thirty years. I have reported at length on education, housing, crime, immigration, politics, and other issues. Some of my reporting is being used in this chapter. My extensive work in the five boroughs of New York allows me to say that Queens is the most diverse of all, the real melting pot of America. Queens is a model for how the world is going to look in the future. Corona is definitely the neighborhood to study for how Latinos such as Ecuadoreans, Colombians, Dominicans, Mexicans, Peruvians, and Argentines are replacing Italians, blacks, Jews, and Irish residents in a place that they used to call home. This transformation process has ethnic and racial implications and high doses of animosity.

Table 7.1 Total Latino and Total Colombian and Ecuadorean Population in Queens, New York, 2000 and 2010

	2000	2010
Ecuadoreans	66,643	98,512
Colombians	66,192	70,290
Total Latinos	549,415	613,750

Sources: New York City, Department of City Planning, 2000, and National Institute for Latino Policy (NiLP, 2011).

According to the 2010 census, Ecuadoreans in Queens became the second-largest Latino subgroup after Puerto Ricans, relegating Dominicans to a third place (US Bureau of Census 2010). Colombians and Ecuadoreans are also fighting for recognition, and there are deep divisions among their incipient community-based organizations. Corona is also a neighborhood plagued with many problems, and those vicissitudes are mirrored by Latinos throughout the United States. Notably, by 2010, the Hispanics made up 73% of the Corona population, and blacks, whose presence had declined by 29% between 2000–2010, comprised only 9% of Corona's residents in 2010. Other relevant 2010 census data include the following: 70% of the population is foreign born, 30% is not fluent in English; up to 25% are undocumented; 21% live below the poverty level; only 56% have completed a high school degree, in comparison with 72% of all city residents; and only 8% have achieved a BA or greater.

Much has been written about the migration of ethnic groups through Corona, Queens. Geographically, the boundaries of Corona are delineated as Northern Boulevard on the West, the Long Island Expressway to the East, Flushing Meadows Corona Park on the North, and Junction Boulevard on the South. Many books about this area offer a wealth of information that helps us understand the history of the place, including the earlier relationship between blacks and Italians in Corona. However, these books provide little information about the now fifty-year-old migration of "newcomers" from South America. I embrace the concept of "inner city poverty"—based on complex socioeconomic issues such as joblessness and lack of access to the political machinery of power—instead of the "cycle of welfare dependency," as the theoretical framework of this chapter. The reality that Latinos are facing in Corona is the result of years of political negligence and isolation, and is reminiscent of the reality for blacks in Corona from 1920 to 1980, including their developing a civil rights movement to defeat their exclusion and isolation. This historical process is well explained in *Black Corona: Race and the Politics of Place in an Urban Community*, by Steven Gregory (1998). Latinos are now experiencing the same kind of bottom-up fight that takes time and effort from activists and community-based organizations. Through this chapter, I am hoping to take the "ghetto mask" off the face of the Latino community. The collective identity of the Latino community of Corona has an important and authentic role in the construction of this nation. Latinos have a voice and it must be heard, though, at times, it scares some more-established communities. I plan to go further in my defense of the Latino community as a group of people with deep roots and identity. Therefore, this chapter examines various community outreach events such as parades, demonstrations, and political rallies. Through these social engagements by Latino organizations and activists, I illustrate their struggle and the origin of their divisions as well as their cultural riches to show how these Latino community-based organizations (CBOs) interact (or sometimes do not) for the well-being of their people.

I embrace Gregory's concept of "community" and apply it to Corona, but not as a "ghetto." According to Gregory, "Community describes not a static, place-based social collective but a power-laden field of social relations whose meanings, structure and frontiers are continually produced, contested, and reworked in relation to a complex range of sociopolitical attachments and antagonisms" (Gregory 1998, 11). I also use the concept of "transnationalism" as utilized in "Colombian Immigration to Queens, New York: The Transnational Re-imagining of Urban Political Space," by Arturo Ignacio Sánchez (2003). According to Sánchez, "The study of transnationalism addresses how immigrants created and maintained multiple social relations that connect their societies of origin and settlement. By linking immigrant agency with societies of origin and settlement, the transnational approach opened a venue for analyzing how places in a socially constructed space are reconstituted across geographical boundaries" (6). This chapter will show many examples of this kind of transnationalism. The double citizenship mandates that were approved by the governments of Ecuador (1995) and Colombia (1991) are a good example of transnationalism. Ecuadoreans and Colombians living outside of their countries lose no rights when they become American citizens.

COLOMBIANS AND ECUADOREANS IN NEW YORK

Colombians and Ecuadoreans have been in New York for about eight decades and have a story to tell. The first wave of Colombian immigrants arrived in New York City in 1920 after enduring a three-week trip by boat from the port of Cartagena. Once the Korean War ended in 1953, a group of Colombian soldiers decided to stay and live in New York.[1] Those Colombians who entered the United States between 1945 and 1964 were professionals, technicians, and service workers trying to get away from the political violence taking over the big cities and the countryside of their nation.

In 1964 and due, in part, to the attractions of the World Fair at the Flushing Meadows / Corona Park, Colombians arrived en masse to the city and, more specifically, to the Corona section of Queens. At the time, all they had to do was apply for a resident visa at the American Embassy and consulates in Bogotá, Cali, Medellín, or Barranquilla, and they would receive it a few weeks after arriving in the United States. Changes in the immigration-law selection process also identified who could enter this country. The attractions of skilled-labor markets in the United States and the worsening of the political violence in Colombia (*La violencia*) fueled the Colombian migration to New York City from 1964 to 1990. Sánchez writes:

> During the decade of the 1990s, US-bound Colombian migration underwent important quantitative and qualitative changes. During the second half of the 1990s, changes in Colombian migration were framed by economic dislocations associated with the shift to models of neoliberal economic development and the escalations of the political and military crisis. New York City's role as an important site of Colombian immigration, on the other hand, was linked to a critical mass of co-nationals, economic restructuring, and the growth of formal and informal labor markets. (2003, 71)

During this period, drug trafficking also became an important factor in the Colombian community and migration process. At the end of the twentieth century and during the first decade of the twenty-first, Colombians in New York endured a complicated reality as a result of changes in technology, labor markets, and a national wave of xenophobia against minorities and immigrants in the United States.

These issues also impacted the Ecuadoreans who were also arriving in New York City in significant numbers during the same period. There are many similarities between the Colombian and Ecuadorean immigration to the city, and specifically to the neighborhoods where both groups reside. According to Ana Melo's "Transnationalism in New York City: A Study of Remittance Sending by Ecuadorean Migrants" (2006), it all started, perhaps,

> with the Panama Hat, which is actually made in Ecuador, in the southern region of the *sierra* known as *El Austro*. Almost a quarter of the workforce lost their jobs due to the collapse of the Panama hat trade in 1947. Former hat merchants and middlemen, who had become familiar with New York City due to the trade, started migrating to the city in the 1960s. In 1964, land-reform changes in Ecuador ended the centuries-old feudal system, but many peasants who were not experienced in owning land also left for New York. Later on, in the 1980s and 1990s, with an economy that overrelied on oil, plummeting oil prices led to an economic recession that placed 70% of Ecuadoreans below the poverty line in 1997. As a result, there was a mass migration of Ecuadoreans, and it consisted of both *serranos* [those from the mountains] and *costeños* [those from the coastal regions], as well as all strata of society. The primary migrant destination was New York City, although Madrid has also become a favored spot since the late 1990s. As evidenced by the countless Ecuadorean businesses along Roosevelt Avenue in Jackson Heights and Corona, over one-third of Ecuadoreans in metro New York live in Queens. Pockets of Ecuadoreans also exist in the Bronx, New Jersey, Westchester County, and Connecticut. (1)

Aida González-Jarrín, an Ecuadorean activist in New York City for more than forty-five years, and former director of cultural affairs for the Queens Borough President's Office, said that the Ecuadorean Sporting Club and Club Guayaquil were, perhaps, the first organizations created by her countrymen in the 1940s. She also noted that the Immigration Reform and Control Act (IRCA) of 1986 was important to the community in that it gave Ecuadoreans and other Latinos the opportunity to legalize their immigration status. González-Jarrín also mentioned that the two terrorist attacks on the Twin Towers, in 1993 and 2001, where some Ecuadoreans died, and the killing of US Army Captain Mario Fajardo on the last day of the Persian

Gulf War also contributed to the recognition of Ecuadoreans as part of this society—"a painful mark in the community, but an important part of the assimilation process."

As with other new immigrants from Latin America, Ecuadoreans endured major hardships. Juan Carlos Freile Franco wrote "Ecuadorean Migration: A Rough Road to Success" to describe this process of integration to the American way of life. He notes that in order to get to New York, "Ecuadorean migrants face a number of harsh physical and financial conditions as part of the process" (2009, 1). To emphasize his point, Freile Franco relies on the ethnographic research of David Kyle, who found that migrants, particularly those from the regions of Azuay and Cañar, often turn to human smugglers (Kyle 2000, 3).

"Undocumented Whites earn more money than documented Latinos," Walter Sinche said in the basement where the Centro Comunitario del Inmigrante was located. It is a new four-story building on 100–120 40th Road in Corona. The basement has two rooms with yellow walls and big white tiles on the floor. There is a single shelf with a few books, two photocopy machines, a computer, three tables, and some metal chairs. In the middle of the two rooms, the wall is covered with Latin American flags tied to one another. On one of the tables lie flyers with literature about GED classes, Peruvian folklore dance classes of *Marinera* and *Mosaicos*, traditional Mexican dance classes of *Mexihka* culture by the group *Yayauhki Tezcatlipoca*, embroidery workshops led by Leticia Hernández, and Andean gastronomy classes by Cristina Camacho to learn to prepare exquisite foods such as *quinua, kikwacha, cañigua,* and *tarwi (ceviche de chocho)*. They are traditional Andean products now arriving in America, full of nutrients and curative powers.

Sinche founded the Centro Comunitario del Inmigrante in March of 2011 to bring together the Latino community of Corona and other neighborhoods such as Flushing and Jackson Heights under one roof. This organization is part of the Alianza Ecuatoriana Internacional (International Ecuadorean Alliance), which was also created by Sinche in 2008 to promote Ecuadorean identity and to motivate the Ecuadorean community to defend itself from prejudice, discrimination, and even death. The first killing that motivated Sinche to react occurred in September of 1994, when Manuel Aucaquizhpi was killed in New York by a group of teenagers. *New York Magazine* reported on his death this way: "Manuel Aucaquizhpi was forty when he died. He had come to Brooklyn thirteen years ago from Ecuador. To the Italian kids who killed him, he was a Mexican—neighborhood shorthand for anybody who speaks Spanish and looks like an immigrant, as in 'You Mexican, get the f--- out of the park" (A. Pagnozzi, "When Good Kids Kill," *New York Magazine*, October 23, 1995, 24). Four teenagers were arrested and charged with his murder: Joseph Pennachio, Anthony Scarpati, John Tanico, and Steven Ruíz.

Then there was another killing of an Ecuadorean immigrant in Patchogue, Long Island, on November 8, 2008. Jeffrey Conroy and other teenagers stabbed Ecuadorean immigrant Marcelo Lucero to death. This case attracted national attention over anti-Latino violence. Conroy was found guilty of manslaughter as a hate crime, gang assault, and attempted assault. He was sentenced to twenty-five years in prison. Sinche was heavily involved in the case. Community leaders and Latino activists like Sinche criticized the Suffolk County Police Department for not investigating many attacks that took place against Latinos during the previous decade and before Lucero's murder. A federal investigation was initiated to study the way this police department handled reports of racial attacks targeting Latinos. A few weeks after the killing of Lucero came the violent death of another Ecuadorean, Jose Sucuzhanay. Sucuzhanay, hit in the head with a broken bottle and a baseball bat, died at Elmhurst Hospital in Queens from skull fractures, three days after he was declared brain-dead. His attackers, Keith Phoenix and Hakim Scott, were sentenced to thirty-seven years in prison.

As a result of these two killings, Ecuadorean movie director James García Sotomayor produced the film *Taught to Hate*, to teach tolerance among students and teenagers in the United States. García Sotomayor is from Long Island and has traveled around the country visiting educational institutions and community-based organizations to show his documentary. When the movie was shown at the Queens Museum of Art, some activists from the Ecuadorean community were there, and Sinche was part of the panel that discussed the killing of his countrymen. Sinche noted that as Lucero and Sucuzhanay were being beaten, the attackers called them "Mexicans," and that most Americans have no understanding of the differences within the Latino community. The broader society can only move beyond racial stereotyping through dialogue and education.

The money to start Sinche's Centro Comunitario del Inmigrante came from a two-year grant of $50,000 from the 2010 Union Square Awards. The grant to the Centro was intended to provide support to the affected families of the murdered men, to keep the issue of prejudice alive in the media, and to work with public officials and community members to develop a response. It has also been used for developing programs to meet long-term needs including immigrant rights, education, employment, sports, health, and culture.

As an immigrant in this country, Sinche has found nothing, including this grant, to be easy. When he came to New York for the first time in 1988, he was homesick; he cried for six months. Sinche worked in the textile industry in Manhattan's garment district, cutting and ironing clothes. One winter he met Tony Matron, an Italian businessman, who offered him a job in his factory, Volpe Electric. Sinche accepted the job; he also went to Brooklyn College to study English as a second language. He tried for a degree in electrical engineering but abandoned that dream for lack of residency papers and money. He married three times until he finally obtained his residency papers in 2005. Years later, while looking at the Manhattan skyline from Queens, he noted: "That day I said to myself, now I am a legal slave. Before as an undocumented immigrant, I always paid my income taxes and never received any help from the government. Every time I lost my job, I didn't collect unemployment insurance."

When Manuel Aucaquizhpi was killed back in 1994, Sinche looked for information and support from the Ecuadorean community of Queens. He went to the Ecuadorean Civic Committee of New York but found out that the most prominent Ecuadorean institution in the city was composed of folks who seemed to not care about civil rights. He also confirmed that Ecuadoreans remained divided between *serranos* and *costeños*.

At that time Sinche needed the help of his countrymen. He was working with the New York City Police Department and the US District Attorney's Office to identify some witnesses in the killing of Aucaquizhpi. Sinche went to the streets to talk to people and to ask questions; and for this, he was followed and received death threats from Italian-Americans. On several occasions, he was forced to run from attackers, and ultimately he decided to go to Miami for a short time to avoid being killed. For three years he followed Aucaquizhpi's case. When he returned to New York from Florida, he decided to change his approach as an activist, starting with moving from Brooklyn to Queens. In 1996 Sinche started the 3.1-mile Walkathon, *El Chasqui*, at Flushing Meadows / Corona Park in Queens. It is a race for all Latino families and athletes that resembles the one-hundred-mile run, a competition on top of the mountains of the former Inca Empire. Sinche's idea was to bring together all Latinos and especially those from South America. "The problem," he said, "is that each Latino community wants to work separately. It is difficult to integrate Ecuadoreans with Colombians or Peruvians with

Dominicans. We Latinos are one single community with five hundred different organizations" (personal interview with author, 2011). (See table 7.2 with census data on numerous groups in part of Queens.)

In 2011 Pablo Calle was an official representative of Ecuador's National Secretariat for Immigrant Affairs (SENAMI) in the United States, based in Queens, and was interviewed sitting next to a portrait of Ecuadorean president Rafael Correa Delgado. SENAMI is now called Casa Ecuatoriana. Calle noted that his community is growing and facing numerous obstacles, among them, blending, along with other Latino communities, into the fabric of New York City as a whole. Besides SENAMI, Ecuadoreans in New York have two consulates, one in Manhattan and the other in Woodside, Queens, on 67th Street and Roosevelt Avenue. According to Calle: "The difference between these organizations, the two consulates, and SENAMI is that the consulates' mission is more socially oriented. The consulates have programs in English as a Second Language and computers, have funds to help repatriate the dead, and work actively with community-based organizations in New York. In contrast, the fundamental goal of SENAMI is to inform and secure the rights of Ecuadoreans living outside of their country." SENAMI also has offices in Spain, Italy, England, Belgium, Chile, and Venezuela. This Ecuadorean agency also coordinates the *"Plan Bienvenidos a Casa"* (Welcome Home Plan), to help those who decide to return to Ecuador. When they return, the Ecuadorean government excuses Ecuadoreans from paying taxes for household goods and furnishings upon arrival. They may receive bonuses and low-interest loans to start businesses in Ecuador, and grants for first-time homeowners ($6,000). However, fewer than 1% of Ecuadoreans have decided to go back to their country of origin.

According to the report *Hispanics of Ecuadorian Origin in the United States, 2013*, about 61% of Ecuadoreans in the United States are foreign born, compared with 35% of Hispanics overall. About 35% of immigrants from Ecuador have been in the United States for over twenty years; and finally, about 42% of Ecuadorean immigrants are US citizens (López 2015, 2).

For the government of Ecuador, Ecuadoreans living abroad are important not only because their civic organizations are becoming more sophisticated, as in New York City, but also because the Ecuadorean community abroad is remitting large amounts of money to their country of origin. Data show a gradual increase in yearly overall remittances between 2005 and 2007 and then a slight decline in 2008 to $1.322 billion dollars. About 47% of all remittances originated in the United States, while 41% came from Spain. These remittances

Table 7.2 Latino Population in the Northwest Part of Queens, 2000 and 2010

| | 2000 Census Data | | | |
	North Corona	East Elmhurst	Jackson Hts	Total
All other Latino	**6,441**	**1,641**	**13,091**	**21,173**
Dominican Rep.	11,166	2,727	6,341	20,234
Ecuadorian	6,871	524	8,578	15,973
Mexican	7,438	1,105	7110	15,653
Colombian	1,233	851	12,052	14,136
Puerto Rican	1,061	798	4,322	6,181
Peruvian	525	280	2,323	3,128
Cuban	259	171	1,627	2,057
Spanish	599	151	1,258	2,008
Salvadoran	270	73	706	1,049
Argentinian	80	25	572	677
Bolivian	85	22	470	577
Honduran	154	41	382	577
Venezuelan	83	51	417	551
Guatemalan	208	32	237	477
Chilean	33	32	314	379
Spaniard	47	25	292	364
Spanish American	59	23	157	239
Nicaraguan	60	10	148	218
Paraguayan	35	18	164	217
Uruguayan	20	2	181	203
Panamanian	29	58	62	149
Costa Rican	28	5	73	106
Other Categories				
Central American	782	223	1,677	2,682
Other Central American	33	4	69	106
South American	9,048	1,840	25,553	36,441
Other So. Amer.	83	35	482	600
Other Latino	7,146	1,840	14,798	23,784

| | 2010 Census Data | | | |
	North Corona	East Elmhurst	Jackson Hts	Total
Ecuadorian	13,438	3,112	13,313	29,863
Mexican	14,739	2,978	10,786	28,503
Dominican Rep.	8,189	3,585	6,274	18,048
Colombian	1,217	1,536	13,441	16,194

Table 7.2 Latino Population in the Northwest Part of Queens, 2000 and 2010 (*cont.*)

	2010 Census Data			
	North Corona	East Elmhurst	Jackson Hts	Total
All other Latino	**2,495**	**1,002**	**4,145**	**7,642**
Puerto Rican	727	670	3,352	4,749
Peruvian	836	514	2,915	4,265
Salvadoran	468	294	817	1,579
Cuban	168	161	1,181	1,510
Guatemalan	708	86	571	1,365
Argentinian	91	71	739	901
Honduran	216	136	498	850
Bolivian	68	59	637	764
Spanish	348	57	248	653
Venezuelan	88	107	422	617
Spaniard	152	37	418	607
Paraguayan	92	89	285	466
Chilean	44	39	328	411
Uruguayan	30	26	230	286
Nicaraguan	56	31	182	269
Panamanian	30	64	109	203
Costa Rican	14	19	129	162
Spanish American	15	11	18	44
Other Categories				
Central American	1,502	603	2,314	4,446
Other Cent. Amer.	10	0	8	18
South American	15,928	5,560	32,385	53,873
Other So. Amer.	24	7	75	106
Other Latino	3,010	1,107	4,829	8,946

Source: New York City, Center for Urban Research, 2011. For more information see Boricua humanrights.org.

accounted for a peak of about 7.3% of Ecuadorean gross domestic product (GDP) in 2007, but this fell to 5.5% in 2009, presumably because of the global recession. Sixty-two percent of all remitters were children who were sending funds to their parents (CLACLS and SENAMI 2010, 47).

Jaime Buenahora is the Colombian congressman elected in 2010 to represent more than four million Colombians living outside of their country. His election was the result of the changes of the Colombian Constitution in

1991. Buenahora recognizes that his government has a lot to learn from the Ecuadoreans' government in terms of helping the diaspora and has acted on what he has learned. He introduced a bill in Colombia to expand the resources of the Foreign Ministry, reduce consular fees, create a social security system for Colombians living outside its borders, and also lengthen the voting process for a week to draw more Colombians to the ballot box in different countries around the world. According to Buenahora, the problem is that the government of Colombia puts less emphasis on diaspora issues such as these and human rights violations, to focus almost exclusively on remittances and real estate investments, the sectors that generate revenue (J. Buenahora interview 2011).

A 2010 report authored by Colombian Milena Gómez Kopp, *The Impact of Remittance on Colombia's Foreign Policy*, illustrates the importance of remittances for Colombia's government, as was shown above for Ecuador. In short:

> Like most developing countries, Colombia has seen a dramatic surge in remittances received in the last decades and these flows have captured the interest of the Colombian government. Prior to the mid-1990s remittances were not on the government's radar because their volume was minimal. . . . In the past decade, however, remittances have increased exponentially—from 745 million dollars in 1996 to over 4.8 billion dollars in 2008, making Colombia the third largest recipient in Latin America. (1)

The above-noted reports on Colombia and Ecuador underscore the importance of remittances as a transnational practice for the survival of many families in both countries. The stability of many community-based diaspora organizations that collect money to help families and friends is key to the development of many communities in Latin America as well as Latino communities in the diaspora. For example, Ecuadorean Pedro Calle's goal is to help those Ecuadorean organizations based in New York: Centro Cívico Ecuatoriano, Junta Cívica del Bronx, Alianza Ecuatoriana Internacional, Centro Ecuatoriano Internacional, Federación Internacional Pichincha, Juventud Ecuatoriana, Federación Ecuatoriana de Periodistas, Frente Unido de Inmigrantes Ecuatorianos, and Fundación Lucero de América, in honor of Marcelo Lucero, who was killed in 2008. These organizations are important both for the government of Ecuador and for the community in New York. Although they have internal squabbles, they support the yearly Ecuadorean

Parade on Northern Boulevard, the Ecuadorean Fair in Flushing Park, many religious festivals, and several soccer tournaments around the city. In this way, they are utilizing their cultural identity as a strategy to adapt to this society and prosper.

One example of transnational activities is the Ecuadorean Parade of New York, held every August since 1980 in Queens, to commemorate the independence of this South American country. Well-known politicians from Ecuador, representatives from the Ecuadorean Consulates in New York, businessmen, and local Ecuadorean activists, especially from religious and folkloric groups, participate in this event, which draws a big crowd. During the 2011 event, Walter Sinche and some 200 members of his organization were the first to march, with a large banner that combined all of the Latin American flags. Maria Fernanda Espinosa, the minister of culture of Ecuador, was also at the parade representing President Correa.

MEDIA AND PERCEPTION

Disunity is evident when one looks at the many newspapers each Latino community has in Queens. Ecuadoreans have several weekly publications, such as *Ecuador News*, in circulation for fifteen years, and *Orgullo Ecuatoriano*, in circulation for twelve years. The *Ecuador News* focuses on life and politics in Ecuador, and *Orgullo Ecuatoriano* has a more local focus, but lacks in-depth coverage and avoids controversy. Weekly, reporters at *Orgullo Ecuatoriano* interview politicians and activists. There are four other Ecuadorean publications, *Ecua Times*, *Noticiero*, *El Universo*, and *El Migrante Ecuatoriano*, but not one covers the issues affecting Ecuadoreans in New York City in-depth. At best, reporting is a process of copying and pasting items from the major newspapers in Ecuador. Community events may be covered with photos of someone receiving a plaque; but that's about it. Sports and entertainment are a constant in these media outlets. The Ecuadorean community of New York City also has two cable TV channels, *Ecuavisa Internacional* and *Teleamazonas*, and two radio stations, *Radio Impacto 2* via the Internet and *Radio Delgado Travel* as a subcarrier. They all play an important role in the construction of the Ecuadorean community in the Big Apple. All of these media, to a greater or lesser degree, serve as a cultural and informational bridge between Ecuador and Ecuadoreans living in New York City.

This rather superficial journalistic approach to news and events also affects *Ayllu Times* and *El Chasqui*, two Peruvian newspapers, as well as *De Norte a Sur*, a tabloid targeting the Argentinean and Uruguayan communities. The advertisements that run in all these Latino publications reflect the same territorial approach to the news. Ecuadorean businesses only advertise in Ecuadorean publications, Colombian restaurants and boutiques only place ads in Colombian newspapers, and so on. The same journalistic dynamic also prevails in the two print publications that focus on Colombians: *Noticiero Colombiano* and *La Semana Metro*. Colombians in New York have only one radio station, *La Nueva Radio Internacional*, as subcarrier, and two cable TV channels, *Caracol* and *RCN*. Latinos in Queens need to demand better media coverage.

A good example of the lack of depth in the Latino press in Queens was the coverage of the financial problems of the Colombian Civic Center of New York. The Colombian Civic Center was founded as Círculo Cívico Colombiano in 1974 to promote Conservative Party candidates for the Colombian presidency. In 1978 it changed its name to Colombian Civic Center, and in 1985 it took over the festival to commemorate Colombian independence at the Flushing Meadows / Corona Park. In 2011 the Colombian Civic Center could not raise enough money to celebrate the twenty-seventh anniversary of this festival, owing $17,000 dollars to the New York City Parks & Recreation Department from the previous year for items such as police and insurance. Not having the Colombian Independence Festival at Flushing Meadows Park on Sunday, July 24, 2011, as was planned, was devastating news for the Colombian community of Queens, and Colombians poured into local TV news and radio stations to express their disgust. This festival had drawn over half a million people annually for almost three decades. Unfortunately, the large sums of money required by the city for such events have forced many Latino organizations to cancel activities in public spaces.

Some top officials of the Colombian Civic Center tried to cut a deal with an Ecuadorean businessman who has helped organize other festivals in several city parks, to avoid canceling the Colombian Independence Festival. Their plan was to celebrate the Colombian Independence Festival on July 7, 2011, at an open space next to the Hall of Science at the Flushing Meadows / Corona Park without having to pay the $17,000 dollars to the city. This shows both a naiveté and an ethical lapse that need to be remedied. The Civic Center has played an important role in the development of the Colombian Community in New York City. Their members have raised money to help victims of natural disasters in Colombia and elsewhere in Latin America. The Center has its own building on Corona Avenue, which is used to teach computer, GED-preparation, and dance classes. However, in the last fifteen years, this not-for-profit organization has been plagued with internal conflicts and members' expulsions, especially around charges of nepotism and corruption. One of the twelve members expelled in 1997 from the Colombian Civic Center was Rafael Castelar, who, soon after his expulsion, created the Colombian Parade on Northern Boulevard in 2000; it is now the only public event that represents the Colombian community in New York City.

Yet the origin of the fragmentation in the Queens Colombian community runs deeper. According to Colombian American scholars Luis Eduardo Guarnizo and Arturo Ignacio Sánchez, in *Estados Unidos, Potencia y Prepotencia*, the problem may be that being Colombian in a foreign country is synonymous with "drug dealer" (1998, 325). This kind of stereotypical hostility has pushed many Colombians to hide their identity. Others prefer to live and work away from other Colombians, and many refuse to participate in Colombian organizations or activities. Other factors have contributed to the weakness of the Colombian community in New York. For example, the Colombian elite living in Manhattan look down on those Colombians residing in Queens. Historically, Jackson Heights, Elmhurst, and Corona have been under vigorous surveillance from the New York City Police Department, the Queens District Attorney's Office, the Drug Enforcement Administration (DEA), and community organizations such as the Jackson Heights Beautification Group. Some white members of Community Board 3, where many Colombians live, have pressed local and federal authorities to target the Colombian community. Regionalism and classism imported from Colombia further hamper efforts at community development.

For Guarnizo and Sánchez, this ideological and political fragmentation impedes cooperation between the old established Colombian immigrants and the new arrivals. They note: "This Colombian mistrust sentiment began to mark the isolation not only of Colombians, but other Latino-American ethnic groups. Colombians are trying to avoid unwanted problems, and other Latinos prefer to stay away from this stigmatization. This reduces the individual's Colombian networks to a small circle of relatives, friends, and neighbors" (1998, 327). Fear of stereotyping also explains why the Colombian community in New York reacted with such hostility to the film *Colombiana*, starring Dominican / Puerto Rican actress Zoe Saldaña. Colombians sent emails and used Facebook to condemn this movie. There were demonstrations outside of theaters on August 26, 2011, the night of the film's opening. Some Colombians stood in front of no less than ten theaters around the city to distribute booklets with a list of ten positive characteristics of Colombians and the Colombian nation. Their goal was to show "the other side of the coin." Their focus was on coffee, gold, and the well-known singer Shakira, instead of narco-traffic activity and violence. Jaime Buenahora, the Colombian congressman living in New York, sent a letter to María Angela Holguín, Colombia's minister of external affairs, protesting against the EuropaCorp and SONY Pictures companies for producing and distributing this offensive and violent movie (J. Buenahora interview 2011). Unfortunately, while the government of Colombia recognizes the importance of its diaspora, it has never been aggressive in supporting Colombian organizations or activists abroad, as in this case.

In the past, Colombians in New York have come together to protest films such as *Collateral Damage* (2002) with Arnold Schwarzenegger and the Colombian American actor John Leguízamo. However, this reaction against *Colombiana* showed the divisions and lack of leadership within the city's Colombian community. It also illustrates that the era of the old Colombian generation of activists such as Rafael Castelar, Orlando Tobón, Nayibe Núñez-Berger, Bernardo Duque, Humberto Suárez Motta, William Salgado, Gustavo Puerto, Gonzalo Peñaranda, Reinaldo Lindo, Jairo Casas, Daniel Jiménez, and Efraín Hernández is gone. Who will replace them? This is probably the most important challenge that the Colombian community in New York City is now facing. Colombian New Yorkers need to identify a new generation of activists that will connect to the community and potentially serve as the first Colombian American politicians to hold public office from Queens.

THE LEGACY OF EARLIER BLACK AND DOMINICAN ARRIVALS TO CORONA

Although this chapter has focused on Ecuadorean and Colombian organizational efforts in Corona, we need to note that Dominicans were the first Latinos in this neighborhood in the 1970s and, in some ways, paved the way for the later arrivals. Anthropologist Steven Gregory (1998, 60) sets the stage earlier, describing the transformation of Corona starting in the 1940s with the entrance of blacks and the corresponding "white flight" to understand the social conditions that paved the way for Latinos, especially Dominicans, to settle in the area.

Like Gregory, sociologist Roger Sanjek (1998) also details the history of prejudice and intolerance of earlier Corona residents toward the newcomers, first blacks and then Latinos. Particularly striking is the institutional racism that emanated from members of the Queens Community Boards (CB) 3 and 4 in the early 1970s, at the same time the fiscal crisis was gripping New York: "Much as white CB4 leaders mistakenly defined Lefrak City's growing black population as 'welfare cases,' they also mistakenly defined Elmhurst-Corona's immigrant population as 'illegal aliens.' But unlike 'welfare cases,' whose numbers might be contained but not eliminated, the phrase 'illegal aliens' suggested a law-and-order problem solvable by arrest and deportation" (70). In 2011, I interviewed Dominican-born Julio Ferreras, the father of Councilwoman Julissa Ferreras. Julio Ferreras arrived in Corona in 1976 and told me about early Dominican community-building efforts in the neighborhood. The Dominicans' first organization was the *Club Deportivo y Cultural Hermanos Unidos de Queens*, created by Salvador Brito, Radames del Río, Sucre Rivera, and Zoilo Céspedes. Although primarily a sports club, it was also involved in social and civic activities. Other early Dominican and Latino organizations were the Dominican-American Society (DAS), Mujeres Latinas de Queens, Acción Latina, and Festival 5 de Mayo. Ferreras said that he has never been discriminated against in Corona. He recalled that Dominicans and Cubans invested in the food industry in Corona, in bodegas and supermarkets, but he felt that these earlier Latino shopkeepers were now being pushed out by Ecuadorean and Mexican *bodegueros* and workers who were willing to accept lower wages. He also talked about the effort it took to finally get a space in the Flushing Meadows / Corona Park to play baseball, and how difficult it was to deal with the New York Mets baseball organization. He portrayed the National Tennis Center at the Flushing Meadows / Corona Park, site of the US Open every summer, as an "exclusive club not open to Latinos."

Yet others in the Dominican community of Corona had even fewer positive feelings about their early reception, and one mother's story is eerily reminiscent of the Ecuadorean experiences a decade later. Altagracia Mayí spoke bitterly about the 1991 killing of her son, Manuel, an eighteen-year-old Queens College student. Mayí insists that her son was murdered by a group of Italian-Americans because he was Latino. No one has been found guilty of his murder. Witnesses said that Manuel Mayí was chased sixteen blocks, from William F. Moore Park, also known as "Spaghetti Park," until he was beaten to death near his home. The New York City Police Department did not classify this murder as race related, but his family maintains it was racially motivated. Although Latinos are no longer in life-threatening danger in Corona, their presence still may be regarded as threatening in Nassau and Suffolk Counties on Long Island.

THE SLOW GROWTH OF PAN-LATINO CIVIC ORGANIZATIONS AND THE GROOMING OF NEW LEADERS

Latino Women in Action, on 103rd Street in Corona, and *Acción Latina*, on Roosevelt Avenue and 100th Street, are both dedicated to providing immigration and other services to Latinos for a small fee. Rubén Quiroz, founder of *Acción Latina*, with an office overlooking the Number 7 Flushing subway line, admitted that, at the moment, all Latino organizations in Queens are merely trying to survive and are doing a poor job in "preparing a new leadership to guide the new generation." Back in 2004, Quiroz helped to organize Queens Congregations United for Action, an interfaith organization to train leaders in Corona, Jackson Heights, Elmhurst, and Flushing. This organization is affiliated with the PICO (People Improving Communities through Organizing) National Network. "The goal of Queens Congregations and PICO is to create and mentor local leaders to fight for justice," but Quiroz opined that the Latino community is still lacking progressive leaders; in short, "Corona is suffering and nobody is paying attention" (Quiroz interview 2011).

Two non-Latino organizations trying to call attention to the plight of the Latino community are the Queens Theatre in the Park and the Queens Museum of Art. Both organizations are in the confines of the Flushing Meadows / Corona Park, surrounded by Latino neighborhoods, but they have not figured out how to get Spanish-speakers inside of their buildings. Still, they are trying. Every summer, the Queens Theatre in the Park holds a Latino Cultural Festival with groups and performers from Colombia, Ecuador, Mexico, the Dominican Republic, and other countries in Latin America. The executive director in 2011, Ray Cullom, recognized that the Queens Theatre had failed the Latino community, but he said, "We are re-examining what we have done to better serve this segment of the Queens population" (Cullom interview 2011).

The Queens Museum of Art is also trying to include more Latino artists and programming. This museum has partnered with the Immigrant Movement International, based in Corona, and is trying to use art as a weapon to generate cultural changes and new attitudes in and about his neighborhood. "Corona has been abandoned by the city of New York, and we can help to change this reality," said Tania Bruguera, director of the Immigrant Movement International, at a conference sponsored by the Urban Planning Program at Columbia University in September 2011. The goal of the Immigrant Movement International is to improve the quality of life in Corona by improving the health of residents through education, access, and lifestyle changes; by activating and beautifying Corona's public spaces, with a focus on culture; by creating a better climate for residents and businesses through marketing and networking; and by increasing communication and cooperation among community stakeholders.

The Latino activists of Corona interviewed for this essay consistently cited three issues as the most pressing concerns for community: the poor quality of education, crime, and economic woes including housing foreclosures.

Education

Make the Road New York (MRNY), originally started in Bushwick, Brooklyn, now has offices near Corona in Jackson Heights at Roosevelt Avenue and 92nd Street and in Port Richmond, Staten Island. (MRNY opened a fourth office in Brentwood, Long Island, in 2011.) MRNY is one of the most effective of the city's grassroots organizations, focusing on Latino immigrant rights and the concerns of working-class communities more generally. Although Ecuadorean activist Walter Sinche has felt MRNY is too focused on politics, "Make the Road" has organized significant campaigns to rectify deplorable working conditions and call unscrupulous landlords to account; it has also been effective in highlighting substandard city schools, which are attended overwhelmingly by immigrant youth. On May 9, 2011, Make the Road New York raised this issue once again as it launched its report *Too Crowded to Learn: Queens Schools Continue to Face Chronic Overcrowding Conditions.* At the press conference in front of Public School 19 on 98th Street in Corona, Democratic City Council members Julissa Ferreras and Daniel Dromm were there to support the organization. The MRNY report claimed that the Bloomberg administration allocated $486 million to new technologies and $200 million to charter schools, but zero dollars to alleviate overcrowding in Corona's schools. Javier Valdés, codirector of MRNY, said that educational problems in Corona have been around for more than thirty years. In short, the MRNY report found deplorable public school conditions, very similar to those of a third-world country. For example, in District 24, 63% of high schools are overcrowded, as are twenty-five out of thirty-five elementary and middle schools. In District 30, five out of eight high schools are overcrowded, as are twenty out of thirty-five elementary and middle schools. District 24 and District 30 serve the largest population of immigrant students in New York City, and these two districts were ranked first and second, respectively, in terms of having the highest average annual enrollment of recent immigrants. Presumably many of these new immigrant children need special attention to begin to acclimate to a new language and culture; overcrowded classrooms do not serve these students well.

Overcrowding in Corona's public schools gets worse every year. According to the New York City Department of Education, since 2005, student enrollment has increased 12% in District 24 while for the rest of the city it has been flat. Since 2003, the city has added 8,224 school seats. The city cannot keep up with new arrivals from Mexico, Ecuador, Colombia, and the Dominican Republic; however, the Department of Education plans to open 4,491 seats in Corona by 2014 (F. Santos, "In Queens Neighborhoods, Schools Are Bursting," *New York Times*, May 10, 2011). Politicians in the area are already aware of the problem. As City Councilman Daniel Dromm wrote bluntly to Schools Chancellor Dennis Walcott, in a letter dated May 5, 2011, "This means, that the schools with student populations that have the highest need of academic attention and language barriers are the schools that have the largest number of students per class and the least amount of space." On February 1, 2015, the *New York Times* reported that five new schools were scheduled to open in Corona in the coming years; but as of this writing, no construction has begun on any.

Crime

Crime remains a significant quality-of-life issue in Corona, and prostitution is a growing concern. State Senator José Peralta and Assemblyman Francisco Moya have focused on fighting the distribution of pimps' "chicas" business cards along Roosevelt Avenue. The cards Senator Peralta has tried to eliminate feature pictures of naked women along with phone numbers to call to acquire their services. Peralta saw his "chica card" legislation pass in June 2011, which made it illegal to hand out such cards, but business is still thriving. Queens ranks number one in prostitution arrests in New York City, and

Table 7.3 Crime in New York City and in the 110th Police Precinct in Queens, 2010–August 2011

NYC-Citywide	2010	2011 (to August)	
Murder	354	323	
Rape	872	969	
Robbery	12,166	12,143	
Felony Assault	11,371	12,235	
Burglary	11,910	11,643	
Grand Larceny	24,049	24,145	
Grand Larceny Auto	6,746	6,008	
110th Police Precinct	2010	2011 (to August)	NYC Precinct Average (to August)
Murder	2	2	4.25
Rape	15	14	12.75
Robbery	231	210	159.78
Felony Assault	170	179	160.98
Burglary	186	205	153.19
Grand Larceny	345	329	317.69
Grand Larceny Auto	103	76	79.69

Source: NYPD CompStat Unit (New York Police Department, 2011).

the 115th precinct, covering Jackson Heights, East Elmhurst, and Corona, accounts for the largest percentage of the arrests. In short, according to Peralta, "To reclaim the area, we need a level of commitment from city and state government, especially law enforcement, as strong and as determined as what we saw invested in the rejuvenation of Times Square" (interview 2011). (See table 7.3 with comparative crime data.)

Queens district attorney Richard Brown is trying to stop not only prostitution but also other kinds of crimes and gang activity. Brown and members of his staff have met with representatives of the Latino community in churches, in school auditoriums, and at the Elmhurst Hospital in Jackson Heights. The Latinos who attend these meetings are very few, around thirty on average. The language barrier, fear of authority figures, or simply trying to survive in a difficult economic climate is causing this low turnout. It is hard to integrate Latinos to the mainstream when they do not trust elected or appointed public servants.

The Fragile Economy (Unemployment, Redevelopment, Foreclosures)

Although the "Great Recession" of the first decade of the twentieth century is over, no one has informed Corona's Latino residents. For them, the unemployment rate remains high. The rate may well move higher with the planned redevelopment of Willets Point. Willets Point is located in Corona, in front of Citi Field, the new Mets stadium. For more than forty years, Willets Point was neglected by the city; however, in 2007, Mayor Bloomberg decided to take control of this land through eminent domain for what the city describes as a "historic redevelopment effort" (www.nycedc.com/project/willets-point-development). Still, many local Latino residents fear that this major effort will hold little promise for them. At present, more than 2,000 Latinos, some of them undocumented, work for the roughly 250 auto shops that will soon disappear.

The development of Willets Point will cost $3 billion, and is supposed to include building 2,500 housing units (with one-third considered affordable), a local convention center, hotel, and office space. Major real estate interests such as Macerich, Related Companies, Silverstein Properties, Avalon Bay Communities, and TDC Development have expressed interest in developing this sector of Corona. While some Latino activists have fought against the project, fearing that they will be priced out of the neighborhood, the odds are against them, as has been the case in numerous other New York City redevelopment battles. A lawsuit fighting this redevelopment plan was tossed out of court in 2014, so the project has "a green light" to move forward.

If education is the biggest problem facing Latinos in New York City, foreclosure is disrupting families in a way that nobody could have imagined several years ago. Franklin Romero, staff attorney for the Queens Legal Service Foreclosure Prevention Program, describes in detail how Corona got into this mess and the consequences of foreclosure:

> Many of the loans now in foreclosure were the result of predatory loans sold to homeowners during the height of the housing boom. We frequently see loans with adjustable rates and/or interest-only features that render the loans entirely unaffordable after the introductory "teaser" rate adjusts upward or the interest-only period expires. Many homeowners did not understand these features or were simply unaware of them. . . . Now that property values have fallen, there are thousands of homeowners in neighborhoods such as Corona that owe more money than their house is worth. . . . At the same time, many people have suffered

reductions in their income in recent years. While some homeowners are able to modify their existing loans, many others will face foreclosure. Widespread foreclosures are extremely damaging to communities, as the number of foreclosed homes cause property values to drop further, even for those homeowners who are current on their loans. It also has significant broader impacts, such as the loss of local business, increased crime rates due to vacant properties, the disruption of schooling for children in the community, and the possibility of homelessness for families actually losing their homes. (Romero interview 2011)

A 2010 report, *Mortgage Lending and Foreclosures in Immigrant Communities*, makes the same point with hard data: "In New York City, the number of foreclosure filings on 1–4 family homes increased from 6,873 in 2005 to 13,694 in 2008. The highest number of home foreclosure filings was in Queens County, where almost half the population (46%) is foreign-born. Among neighborhoods hardest-hit by foreclosure, many have higher shares of immigrants than N.Y.C. as a whole. In 2005, foreclosure actions in Queens were 2,666 and in 2008 that number reached 5,660" (Kirwan Institute 11). Foreclosure actions in Corona as of July 2011, according to RealtyTrac, were 1 in 1,968 housing units (RealtyTrac, Corona, NY 2011). Finally, as of 2015, Corona has become a prime candidate for gentrification in New York City (Thomas B. Edsall, "The Gentrification Effect," *New York Times*, February 1, 2015). While it is not entirely clear what this will mean for foreclosures, it likely means that poor Latino residents will be priced out of the neighborhood.

CONCLUSION: THE NEED FOR PAN-LATINO AND MULTIETHNIC SOLIDARITY

The Ecuadorean activist Walter Sinche dreams of a more holistic approach to problems that plague Corona's Latino community. He is always trying to connect with activists from other Latino groups in Queens, and often complains about the difficulty of the task. In some ways, Sinche wants to implement in the Latino community (or in a multiethnic coalition) the same bottom-up civil rights movement that Steven Gregory details in *Black Corona* (1998), when Corona and Jackson Heights residents successfully organized the multiethnic Cultural Awareness Council after the vicious Howard Beach attack on four black men in 1988 that left one young man, Michael Griffith, dead (Gregory 1998, 156).

For Sinche, it was a grueling, solitary journey to bring attention to the murders of his countrymen in the first decade of this century, but perhaps now he feels a bit more hopeful about greater solidarity among other Latinos and other progressive groups and individuals in the community. And plenty of issues remain to organize around. In addition to the three major issues previously mentioned, other "quality-of-life" issues such as subway crowding, inadequate numbers of parking spaces, housing code violations, sewing shop abuses, illegal dumping, gambling, drugs, homeless hotels, and lack of youth recreation facilities still rankle. Roger Sanjek detailed these issues in 1998, and they still remain of great concern to residents today.

One example of the kind of multiethnic organizing that Walter Sinche hopes will continue occurred in May 2011, when Queens Congregations United for Action (QCUA) and Make the Road New York (MRNY) demonstrated against the Queens Center Mall for "abusing" black and Latino workers. Fr. Darrell Da Costa represented QCUA, and Ana María Archila, a Colombian American, and Javier Valdés, an Argentine American, represented MRNY. The meeting took place at the Saint Paul the Apostle church in Lefrak City, Corona, but many activists came from nearby Rego Park to this black enclave, rich in history and community activism. More than five hundred people attended the gathering against Macerich, the company that owns the Queens Center Mall. It was an excellent example of Latinos and blacks fighting together for a cause. Archila and Valdés spoke about the three goals they wanted to accomplish: higher salaries for all workers, their right to unionize, and the creation of a community center inside the mall. A group of Democratic politicians were there to support QCUA and MRNY: State Senator José Peralta, City Councilman Daniel Dromm, Councilwoman Julissa Ferreras, and State Assemblymen Francisco Moya and Jeffrion Aubry. Councilman Dromm was the first openly gay politician who was elected in Queens and represents Jackson Heights and Corona. Senator Peralta and Councilwoman Ferreras are both Dominican Americans. Assemblyman Aubry is black, and Assemblyman Moya is the first politician of Ecuadorean origin elected to public office in the United States.

A second example of multiethnic solidarity in Corona took place on Sunday, July 31, 2011. That day, Dominican American Councilwoman Ferreras orchestrated the closing of the intersection of 104th Street and 46th Avenue to honor Nancy DeBenedittis, an Italian American woman whose family established the restaurant known as Mama's. Latinos and Italians celebrated the renaming of the street as "Mama's Way" joyfully with music and free food. Several local politicians were there, including former City Council Speaker Christine Quinn.

Finally, just one block to the east of Mama's Way, on 47th Avenue, is a street renamed "Marlon A. Bustamante Place," in honor of a Colombian-born soldier and father of three who was killed in Iraq in February 2006. His mother still lives in Corona in the same neighborhood where he was brought when he was a year old. This is yet another example of Latinos' growing organizational clout in Corona.

The Queens Center Mall demonstration, the "Mama's Way" street festival, and the naming of Marlon A. Bustamante Place are all events that nobody could have imagined a decade or two ago. Small steps have led the way to these meaningful episodes. Walter Sinche is correct in arguing, "When you see all these problems, it is easy to conclude that we Latinos must unite. There is no other option for us. We need to work as a team." Still, as a realist and fighter for social justice, he also understands the strength of numbers that multiethnic organizing provides. Sinche began to see the fruits of his organizing efforts when, in February 2013, the New York City Council honored Alianza Ecuatoriana Internacional and New York's Andean communities more generally.

NOTE

1. Roughly 5,100 Colombians fought in the Korean War. Colombian president Laureano Gómez saw this as a way to show support for the US war effort. Gómez's goals were to gain greater US economic support and to erase any lingering doubts among American policy makers about his previous anti-American sentiment during World War II. See Juliana Saldaña, "Colombia's Legacy with Korea," *The City Paper* (Bogotá), April 2, 2013, https://thecitypaperbogota.com/author/juliana-saldana.

REFERENCES

Bruguera, T. 2011. Director, Immigrant Movement International. Interview by J. Castaño, September 28.
Buenahora, J. 2011. Colombian congressman for New York. Interview by J. Castaño, May 13.
Calle, P. 2011. Representative of the National Secretariat for Immigrant Affairs of Ecuador (SENAMI). Interview by J. Castaño, July 28.

CLACLS (Center for Latin American, Caribbean & Latino Studies) and SENAMI (National Secretariat for Immigrant Affairs of Ecuador). 2010. *Ecuadoreans in the United States, 1980–2008.* New York: Graduate Center at the City University of New York.

Cullom, R. 2011. Executive director, Queens Theatre in the Park. Interview by J. Castaño, July 22.

Ferraras, J. 2011. Father of Councilwoman Julissa Ferraras. Interview by J. Castaño, August 15.

Freile Franco, J. C. 2009. "Ecuadorean Migration: A Rough Road to Success." Hanover, NH: Institute for Writing & Rhetoric, Dartmouth College.

Gómez Kopp, M. 2010. *The Impact of Remittance on Colombia's Foreign Policy.* Calgary, Alberta: University of Calgary, Latin American Research Centre.

González-Jarrín, A. 2011. Former Director of Cultural Affairs, Queens Borough President's Office. Interview by J. Castaño, May 11.

Gregory, S. 1998. *Black Corona: Race and the Politics of Place in an Urban Community.* Princeton: Princeton University Press.

Guarnizo, L. E., and A. I. Sánchez. 1998. *Estados Unidos, Potencia y Prepotencia.* Bogotá: Tercer Mundo.

Guzmán, O. 2011. President, Ecuadorean Parade in New York. Interview by J. Castaño, July 26.

Kirwan Institute for the Study of Race and Ethnicity. 2010. *Mortgage Lending and Foreclosures in Immigrant Communities: Expanding Fair Housing and Fair Lending Opportunity among Low-Income and Undocumented Immigrants.* Columbus: Kirwan Institute for the Study of Race and Ethnicity, Ohio State University.

Kyle, D. 2000. *Transnational Peasants: Migrations, Networks, and Ethnicity in Andean Ecuador.* Baltimore: Johns Hopkins University Press.

Lobo, Arun Peter, and Joseph Salvo. 2013. *The Newest New Yorkers: Characteristics of the City's Foreign-Born Population.* New York: City of New York, Department of City Planning, Population Division, December. https://www1.nyc.gov/site /planning/data-maps/nyc-population/newest-new-yorkers-2013.page.

López, Gustavo. 2015. *Hispanics of Ecuadorian Origin in the United States, 2013.* Washington, DC: Pew Research Center, September 15. http://www.pew hispanic.org/2015/09/15/hispanics-of-ecuadorian-origin-in-the-united-states -2013/.

Make the Road New York (MRNY). 2011. *Too Crowded to Learn: Queens Schools Continue to Face Chronic Overcrowding Conditions.* New York: Make the Road New York. www.maketheroad.org.

Mayí, A. 2011. Mother of Manuel Mayi. Interview by J. Castaño, November 20.

Melo, A. 2006. "Transnationalism in New York City: A Study of Remittance Sending by Ecuadorian Migrants." MA thesis. http://fletcher.tufts.edu/Research /Student-Theses-Archive/2005-2006.

Neira, M. 2011. Latino activist, Willets Point. Interview by J. Castaño, September 9.

Peralta, J. 2011. State senator. Interview by J. Castaño, April 3.

Quiroz, R. 2011. Founder of Acción Latina. Interview by J. Castaño, April 12.

Romero, F. 2011. Staff attorney, Queens Legal Services Foreclosure Prevention Program. Interview by J. Castaño, October 6.

Sánchez, A. I. 2003. "Colombian Immigration to Queens, New York: The Transnational Re-imagining of Urban Political Space." PhD diss., Columbia University. ProQuest.

———. 2011. Professor. Interview by J. Castaño, n.d.

Sanjek, R. 1998. *The Future of Us All: Race and Neighborhood Politics in New York City.* Ithaca, NY: Cornell University Press.

Sinche, W. 2011. Latino Community Activist and Founder of Centro Comunitario del Inmigrante. Interview by J. Castaño, June 30.

Taught to Hate. Directed by James García Sotomayor. Produced by Suffolk, County Long Island, New York, 2009.

US Bureau of Census. 2010. Census Summary File 1, table SF1-P8 NYC. "Total Hispanic Population by Selected Subgroups New York City and Boroughs." Washington, DC: United States Census Bureau.

Valdés, J. 2011. Codirector, Make the Road New York (MRNY). Interview by J. Castaño, May 10.

Walcott, Dennis. 2011. Chancellor of New York City Department of Education. Letter to D. Dromm. May 5.

CHAPTER EIGHT

Central Americans in New York

WALKER SIMON AND ROSALÍA REYES

Composed of seven nations, Central America is situated on an isthmus, which links Mexico to South America. For much of US history, the region remained on the fringes of American consciousness, except for the US building of the Panama Canal a century ago. Immigration from the area was negligible, but that began to change after Ronald Reagan took office in 1981 for the first of his two successive four-year presidential terms. Political violence in the isthmus deepened as Reagan escalated US military involvement in the region to counter Soviet and Cuban inroads. The widening unrest uprooted millions of Central Americans, initiating the first large-scale migration of Central Americans to the United States.

Reagan elevated Central America to the front ranks of US foreign policy, claiming that Moscow's engagement, particularly in Nicaragua, threatened vital US interests. Under the Reagan administration, Washington poured more than $6.5 billion in aid into Central America, of which over $3 billion went to El Salvador, which was beset by a leftist insurgency.[1]

The Soviet Union and its allies had sent arms to the recently established leftist Sandinista government in Nicaragua. Reagan said the Soviet bloc's military aid amounted to billions of dollars, and that the Sandinistas aided

the Salvadoran rebels.[2] He also warned that Nicaragua could become a second Cuba unless Washington stepped up its backing of anti-Sandinista rebels based in Honduras.[3] Seeing the Sandinistas as a threat, the Reagan administration imposed a trade embargo on Nicaragua.[4] For Reagan and his
advisors, Central America's proximity to the United States boosted the strategic stakes.[5] He warned that Nicaragua could become a privileged sanctuary
for terrorists and subversives that would only be a two days' drive to Harlin-
gen, Texas.[6] In a 1983 speech to Congress, he also said that "El Salvador is
nearer to Texas than Texas is to Massachusetts. Nicaragua is just as close to
Miami, San Antonio, San Diego, and Tucson as those cities are to Washington, where we're gathered tonight."[7] He struck a similar theme that year in an
Oval Office address when he said that "San Salvador is closer to Houston,
Texas, than Houston is to Washington D.C." and that "Central America is
America. It is at our doorstep."[8]

The United States also maintained a military presence in Honduras to
signal its resolve against Nicaraguan and Cuban involvement in the region,
and extensively equipped the Honduran military. In Guatemala, one of the
closest Central American countries to the United States, the Reagan administration reinstituted military aid to battle leftist guerrillas as a decades-old
civil war intensified; however, congressional human rights concerns checked
the scale of US aid to a tiny fraction of that which went to Honduras and El
Salvador.[9] According to a report by the office of the UN High Commissioner
for Refugees (UNHCR), "Nicaragua, El Salvador and Guatemala were caught
in a web of guerrilla warfare, sweeping counter-insurgency operations, widespread political and social unrest and sharp economic decline." The report
also stated that "individual and collective persecution was rife," and that "by
the mid-1980s, with the stakes raised by superpower involvement, the hos-
tilities in Central America were threatening to engulf the entire region."[10] In
geopolitical terms, the Reagan administration's intervention in Central
America and its civil wars coincided with the final effort to pressure and destabilize the Soviet Union into collapse. According to political scientist Jenny
Pearce, "Central America was one of the principal theaters of what some
analysts dubbed the second 'Cold War.'"[11]

However, in the final years of his administration, Reagan also feared
that masses of people from Central America would flee to the United States.
In a 1986 Oval Office address, he warned with much hyperbole that the Soviet Union and Cuba "could become the dominant power in the crucial corridor between North and South America." He added: "Should that happen,

desperate Latin peoples by the millions would begin fleeing north into the cities of the southern United States or to wherever hope of freedom remained."[12] He articulated his fears again at a 1988 White House briefing when he said, "It was not difficult to visualize a situation in which hundreds of thousands of Central Americans seek to escape violence by streaming towards the American Southwest."[13]

THE CENTRAL AMERICAN TIDE

With the end of the Cold War and the collapse of the Soviet Union in 1991, the red-hot anti-Communist rhetoric of the Reagan era faded. Peace accords signed in 1990 in Nicaragua, in 1992 for El Salvador, and in 1996 for Guatemala ended insurgencies; but by then the conflicts in Central American had uprooted up to an estimated 2 million people, with the UNHCR reporting that "some 80 per cent of those fleeing the Central American countries during this period headed north to the United States."[14] US census data demonstrate this upsurge. In 1980, the year of Reagan's election, the census counted 353,892 people in the United States that were born in Central America.[15] By 2010, that number had surged dramatically to 3.05 million immigrants—a more than eightfold increase over three decades.[16] According to Hugo Beteta, a former Guatemalan finance minister, "Large scale migration from abroad (Central America) started with the Nicaraguan, Salvadoran and Guatemalan civil wars of the late 1970s and early 1980s," but with the end of the wars, "migration continued due to a shortage of decent jobs and economic opportunities" in those countries.[17]

Demand for unskilled labor sustained subsequent flows of Central American immigrants to the United States, and this demand was coupled with an expansion of migrant networks in various parts of the country. The devastation wrought by Hurricane Mitch also sparked an outflow of Central American "environmental refugees in 1998."[18] Washington gave "Temporary Protected Status (TPS)" to Honduran and Nicaraguan immigrants due to the hurricane. Temporary Protected Status was also granted to Salvadorans as a result of earthquakes in El Salvador in 2001, and this kind of status has been given on and off to Central American immigrants since 1990.[19]

As Reagan predicted, communities in the southern United States were the major destination points for Central American immigrants. In 2010, California had the largest population of Central American immigrants, followed by Texas and then Florida. Collectively, these three states accounted for over half of all Central American immigrants, but New York State was also an important destination and ranked fourth, with 260,755 or about 8.5% of the total.[20] Identified by national ancestry, the population of Central Americans in the United States in 2010 was 3.998 million. This figure included immigrants and others identifying themselves with a Central American nationality, such as the descendants of immigrants.[21]

By metropolitan area, Los Angeles was number one in total population for Central Americans in the 2010 census.[22] By national ancestry, the US Census Bureau counted 830,891 Central Americans living in the Los Angeles region's "Combined Statistical Area" (CSA). At the same time, the New York City metropolitan area ranked second, with a total population of 531,593 Central American immigrants and their descendants residing in its CSA, which includes the city and suburban areas of New Jersey, Connecticut, Pennsylvania, and New York. In 2010, it had a population that included 206,475 Salvadorans, 131,244 Guatemalans, 107,241 Hondurans, 31,105 Panamanians, 31,961 Costa Ricans, and 19,609 Nicaraguans. Ranked by CSA metropolitan regions, New York had the most Hondurans, Panamanians, and Costa Ricans in the United States. It had the second-largest number of Guatemalans after Los Angeles, which was ranked first for this group. It also contained the third-largest concentration of Salvadorans after the Los Angeles and Washington, DC, CSAs. It also had the fourth-largest population of Nicaraguans in the United States, behind the Miami metropolitan area and the CSAs of Los Angeles and San Francisco.

Salvadorans are particularly numerous in suburban Long Island, New York, the 2010 census showed. By national ancestry, there were 97,128 Salvadorans in Nassau and Suffolk counties. In 2011, the Salvadoran Foreign Ministry launched a "diplomatic offensive" to protect Salvadoran immigrants and their working conditions on Long Island and strengthen ties with sympathetic local, state, and federal officials in the region. According to a statement provided by a ministry spokesperson, the Salvadoran community in Nassau and Suffolk counties has enjoyed relative stability and "limited persecution for their migratory status,"[23] a possible reference to undocumented workers in the area.

For its part, the US Department of Justice (DOJ) has been actively prosecuting the Long Island members of the transnational MS-13 gang (Mara Salvatrucha), based in El Salvador and other parts of the US. Composed primarily of immigrants from El Salvador and Honduras, the MS-13 is the largest street gang on Long Island, and it also has a significant presence in Queens, according to the DOJ's US Attorney's Office for the Eastern District of New York (EDNY). This office has said that it has secured federal felony convictions of more than 250 MS-13 soldiers and leaders since 2003, many on racketeering charges. Since 2010 alone, it convicted more than 35 MS-13 members in connection with more than 20 murders.[24]

OVERVIEW OF THE CENTRAL AMERICAN POPULATION IN NEW YORK CITY

According to the 2010 census, the total population of self-identified Central Americans in New York City was 151,378, or 6.5% of the estimated 2.336 million Latinos living in the city. They also accounted for about 1.8% of New York City's 8.175 million people. Overall, almost half of all persons of Central American ancestry spoke English, about one of every four had attended college, another sixth held a bachelor's degree or higher, and their median household income in 2010 was estimated at around $40,000 a year, with about one-fifth of the Central American population living below the poverty line. However, by comparison, a greater share of the city's Dominicans, Mexicans, and Puerto Ricans lived in poverty.

By national ancestry, the most numerous of the city's population of Central Americans were the Hondurans, with 42,400 people, followed by the Salvadorans, with 38,559 people and the Guatemalans with 30,420 people, according to the 2010 Census. Ranked fourth were the Panamanians, the longest-established group, with 22,353 people, followed by Nicaraguans with 9,346 persons, and Costa Ricans with a total population of 6,673. The remainder, a category called "other Central American" by the Census Bureau, totaled 1,627 persons and includes Native Americans and those saying they originate in the former US Canal Zone in Panama (also see table 8.1).[25]

Some demographers assert that a more accurate way to look at migration is by classifying population by foreign birthplace. They note that with the discontinuation of the long form in the decennial census of 2010, the US American Community Survey (ACS) became the sole source of data on the foreign-born population.[26] According to the 2011–15 ACS data, which reflect the most recent five-year estimate at the time of this publication and sampled approximately 6–7% of New York City's residents, a total of 117,188 New Yorkers were said to have been born in Central America. These included 32,271 Salvadorans, 29,653 Hondurans, 26,611 Guatemalans, 17,532

Table 8.1 Total Population of Central Americans in New York, 2010–2013

	2010 Census	Foreign Born, 2009–2013 ACS Survey
Costa Ricans	6,673	4,825
Guatemalans	30,420	22,497
Hondurans	42,400	30,022
Nicaraguans	9,346	6,157
Salvadorans	38,559	31,617
Panamanians	22,353	17,746
Belize	7,805	
Other Central Am.	1,627	776
Total	151,378	121,245

Note: The information on Belizeans as a national origin group is not available in the 2010 US census; however, the ACS survey for 2009–2013 tallied people from Belize as a foreign-born group.

Source: US Census, AmericanFactfinder. http://factfinder.census.gov/faces/nav/jsf/pages/index.xhtml.

Panamanians, 7,949 Belizeans, 5,964 Nicaraguans, 4,867 Costa Ricans, and 990 other Central Americans.

The ACS also provided 2011–15 estimates on Central American populations by ancestry, which have grown quickly since the 2010 census, led by the Salvadorans, who rank first among nationalities in the region. (Again, see table 8.1. Note that the difference separating the Salvadorans and Honduras falls within the ACS's margin of error.)

Several Central American immigrant groups are among the forty largest in New York City. Salvadorans ranked twentieth, behind Pakistanis but ahead of migrants from the United Kingdom and its Crown Dependencies. Hondurans were twenty-third, ahead of Ghanaians. Guatemalans ranked twenty-eighth, more numerous than those from Israel, and Panamanians ranked thirty-seventh, above those born in Cuba.[27]

By median household income and national ancestry, the Hondurans of the city were at the lowest end of the earning scale for Central Americans at $34,319 per year in 2013 dollars in the 2011–13 ACS. By contrast, the Panamanians earned a median household income of $43,526, which was also lower than that of Salvadorans at $44,070, and lower than that of Guatemalans at $47,523. The median household income of Nicaraguans was $43,839. That of Costa Ricans was the highest at $48,487 in 2010 dollars according to

Table 8.2 Median Household Income of Central American New Yorkers

	2006–2010 ACS Survey	2009–2013 ACS Survey
Costa Ricans	$48,487	
Guatemalans		$47,523
Hondurans		$34,319
Nicaraguans	$43,839	
Salvadorans		$44,070
Panamanians		$43,632
All New Yorkers		$51,526

Source: US Census, AmericanFactfinder. http://factfinder.census.gov/faces/nav/jsf/pages/index
.xhtml.

the 2006–10 ACS. These are the latest figures available for the last two groups. However, all these earnings lagged behind the $50,285 median household income of all New Yorkers in 2010 dollars, and $51,526 in 2013 dollars (see table 8.2).[28]

Despite being near the middle of the already low Central American earnings scale, Guatemalans in New York City sent home an estimated $230.2 million dollars in 2003, making Guatemalans the largest US source of remittances to their country; Guatemalans in New York were surpassed only by Guatemalans in Los Angeles, who sent $664.1 million in remittances.[29]

With the exception of the Salvadorans, there were also large gender imbalances in the Central American communities of the city. According to the 2010 census, there were about 40% more Guatemalan men than women though only 1.8% more Salvadoran men than women. Conversely, there were about 42% more Panamanian women than men, 40% more Costa Rican women than men, 17% more Nicaraguan women than men, and 11% more Honduran women than men. By comparison, 47.5% of all New Yorkers were men and 52.5% were women.

Overall, the median age for all Central American immigrants and their descendants was 35.6 years in 2010, but it varied widely by nationality, with the Panamanians being the oldest. The median age for Panamanians was 42.2 years, with the median for men at 38.4 years and the median for women at 44.6 years. The youngest were the Guatemalans, who had a median age of 30.2 years, with a median age for men at 29.3 years and a 31.7 median for females. In between were the Costa Ricans, who had a median age of 40.3 years, with a 43.7 median for women and 36.8 median for men, Nicaraguans

Table 8.3 Median Age of Central Americans in New York City, 2010

	Total	Male	Female
Costa Ricans	40.3	36.8	43.7
Guatemalans	30.2	29.3	31.7
Hondurans	32.0	30.1	34.1
Nicaraguans	35.8	33.8	38.4
Salvadorans	32.1	31.4	33.0
Panamanians	42.2	38.4	44.6
All New Yorkers	35.5	34.0	36.9

Source: US Census, AmericanFactfinder. http://factfinder.census.gov/faces/nav/jsf/pages/index
.xhtml.

at 35.8 years with a 38.4 median age for women and 33.8 for men, Salvadorans at 32.1 years with a 33-year median age for women and 31.4 for men, and
Hondurans at 32 years with a median age of 34.1 years for women and 30.1
for men. In comparison, the median age for all New Yorkers in 2010 was 35.5
years, with a 36.9 median for women and 34 years for men (see table 8.3).[30]

The larger Latin American communities of the city have overshadowed
the Central American immigrant population, which is rarely noticed as a
group in the cacophony of foreign-born New Yorkers. For example, the
Mexican foreign-born population was officially estimated to be 182,998—
much larger than the 117,888 persons constituting the Central American
immigrant population according to the 2011–15 ACS. This is a problem
connected to some of the Central American nationalities as well. While 24 of
New York City's 195 Neighborhood Tabulation Areas (NTAs) featured a
population of at least 2,000 Mexican immigrants, no single Central American nationality mustered enough foreign-born residents to break above the
2,000 threshold in any NTA, except for one instance for the Savaldoran-born,
who numbered 2,253 in the Queens neighborhood of Jamaica, according to
ACS 2010–14 data.[31]

The Mexican presence in restaurants and in Spanish-language media
has also become a prominent feature of life in the city. Locally, cable TV offers a host of Mexican-based networks, compared with one Miami-based
network, centroamericanatv, which targets Central Americans living in the
United States. The program *Honduras NY* has been presented sporadically
on Bronx public access television between 2010 and 2014. A Queens-based
monthly, *Enlace Centroamericano* (Central American link), publishes an

edition aimed at Central Americans in the tristate New York metropolitan area. Recently, New York–based country-specific periodicals have also appeared, including the monthly *Presencia Panama e Hispana News in the U.S.A.* (Panamanian presence and Hispanic news in the U.S.A.)—rechristened in March 2015 as *The International Panama Times / Presencia Hispana*—and *La Voz de Honduras* (The voice of Honduras).

At times, there is a collaboration or a recognition that the various Central American nationality groups have something in common. This was seen in November 2012 in the realm of folk arts when a newly formed Nicaraguan organization called ExpoNica NY organized a show of handicrafts, which included displays from Nicaragua's next-door neighbor, El Salvador, and also other countries in Central America. Held in a cavernous Brooklyn discotheque and called "Handicrafts from Central America and the Caribbean," the exhibit displayed not only Central American handicrafts but also folk art from the Dominican Republic and other Caribbean countries.[32]

IMMIGRANT NATIONALITIES: THE PANAMANIANS OF BROOKLYN, HONDURANS OF THE BRONX, SALVADORANS AND GUATEMALANS OF QUEENS, AND COSTA RICANS AND NICARAGUANS OF THE CITY AS A WHOLE

The Panamanians

For the most part, Central Americans are clustered in three population corridors, one bisecting Brooklyn, another the Bronx, and the third Queens, but these groups are also scattered throughout the city. The bulk of Panamanians live in predominantly black neighborhoods in Brooklyn, concentrated in an east-west ribbon, where many immigrants from the English-speaking Caribbean also live. Every Columbus Day weekend, there is a Panama Day parade along Franklin Avenue in the Crown Heights section of that borough. To the rhythm of drum groups, the parade also features local beauty queens who wave from convertibles. These are scantily clad sequined young women with elaborate plumed headgear reminiscent of Rio de Janeiro's carnival. There are also women, some with nose rings, attired as Cuna Indians from Panama. Ornamenting their dress are labyrinthine patterns sewn with images of flowers, plants, butterflies, and other animals. Some Cuna participants wear horned masks spiked with elongated fangs and topped by a small forest of feathers. In traditional Hispanic style, some contingents feature women wearing flowing white robes, trimmed with lace and elaborate blue, black, or red needlework.[33]

In 2010, the Panamanians tried to rename a section of Franklin Avenue as "Panama Way" but met resistance from other residents who claimed that the area was ethnically mixed and included many immigrants (along with their descendants) from countries that were once part of the British Empire in the Caribbean as seen in NTA data. According to the 2010 census, the following NTAs had at least 1,000 Panamanians actually born in Panama: Flatbush with 1,793 Panamanians, followed by 1,318 in Prospect-Lefferts Gardens-Wingate, 1,220 in Crown Heights North, and 1,054 in East New York. According to the 2010–14 ACS data, there were a total of 1,544 Panamanians in Prospect-Lefferts Garden-Wingate, followed by 1,226 in Flatbush, 1,199 in Crown Heights North, and 737 in East New York. In each of these neighborhoods, Panamanian-born residents were outnumbered by neighbors born in the English-speaking Caribbean, most notably from Jamaica, Trinidad and Tobago, and Haiti.[34]

According to Antonio Roberto Morgan, a former Panamanian diplomat in Latin America and consular employee in New York who in 1994 founded a New York–based Panamanian-focused periodical, whose latest name is *Presencia Hispana: The International Panama Times*,[35] the first waves of Panamanian immigrants had their roots in the English-speaking Caribbean, having worked on the Panama Canal and in the former US Canal Zone before coming to New York. Quite a number of migrants from the British West Indies were fundamental in the building of the canal, first started by the French in 1881 when Panama was part of Colombia. After meeting resistance from the Colombian government, the United States helped engineer Panama's independence in 1903, clearing the way for the decade-long US building of the canal and the continued influx into the Canal Zone of laborers from the British West Indies. According to Howard Dodson and Sylviane Diouf, Jamaica and Barbados alone supplied about 240,000 laborers for the Panama Canal between 1881 and 1915. That was more than double the 108,000 who emigrated from the entire Caribbean region directly to the United States between 1881 and 1932.[36] Between 1904 and 1914, 61 percent of the workers employed on the Panama Canal and its railroad projects were from the British West Indies, according to historian Velma Newton.[37]

Several factors eased the assimilation and migration process for Panamanian immigrants. According to Morgan, some of the Panamanians spoke English as a result of their British Caribbean roots, and others perfected their

English and familiarized themselves with American culture by working and living in the Canal Zone, a US territory straddling the waterway. The Canal Zone authorities also recruited Panamanians for the US armed forces, which also became a springboard for US-bound migration—a leading destination for all of these waves being New York. In 1964, student-led riots in the Canal Zone resulted in a nearly three-month-long break in US-Panamanian diplomatic relations. This led to a slowdown in the Canal Zone economy, spurring additional US-bound migration. Also facilitating the migration to New York were the frequent visits of middle-class Panamanians who came to watch championship fights in lightweight categories by celebrated Panamanian boxers, who were treated as national heroes. Many of these Panamanians settled in the city as a result.

According to US immigration statistics, the last surge of Panamanian immigrants began in 1977, when the leaders of the United States and Panama signed the Panama Canal Treaty under whose terms the Canal Zone was abolished in 1979. During the five-year span from 1977 to 1982, 6,322 Panamanians were admitted in New York as legal permanent residents. In all the other years since 1971, fewer than 1,000 Panamanians were admitted legally as permanent residents.[38] The impact of this immigrant bulge is seen in the 2009–11 ACS data. About 71.5% of the Panamanian foreign-born came to the United States before 1990, with 16.5% coming in the 1990s and 12% from 2000 onwards.[39] With the arc of Panamanian immigration being a century old, it's a challenge to quantify how many New Yorkers actually have Panamanian roots. Some of the descendants of the Panamanians immigrants are several generations removed from their forebears, and although many still identify as Panamanians, others may not. Among these are many naturalized and US-born citizens. Observers have noted that the Panamanian population could be 20,000, 50,000, or even 80,000 depending on whom you talk to and the standards used.

According to Carlos Russell, a former Panamanian ambassador to the United Nations and a Brooklyn College professor emeritus, the Panamanian community in New York is not contiguous. Cited in an article in an online publication, Russell noted that twentieth-century Panamanian immigrants with English last names, who were mostly black, moved to Brooklyn, while those with Hispanic last names settled in Queens or the Bronx. He used the term "visibly invisible" to describe the black Panamanian presence in Brooklyn. He noted that this problem often leads to a case of mistaken identity because Panamanians are frequently assumed to be African American, Afro-West Indian, or merely "black." He also noted that the key element in this issue is the concept of race. The usual assumption is that the individual who is "black" does not speak Spanish and is not a person of Hispanic culture.[40]

Over the years, some Panamanians have moved to the suburbs but return to Franklin Avenue on weekends to see friends and attend religious services. According to one community activist, Panamanians had settled in the area around Franklin Avenue by 1930, before the Jamaicans and other English-speaking West Indians settled in the neighborhood; and by 1960, they owned a wide variety of local businesses and were the majority population. According to the activist, "If you talk to someone in Panama about emigrating to the United States, they say they want to come to Franklin Avenue."[41] Another complication that arises with regard to Panamanian identity is the issue of their national origin. To this day, many of the city's Panamanians dispute their Central American origins by asserting the former status of their families as Colombian citizens. They therefore see themselves as South American in origin and not people from Central America, and this is especially true of Panamanians who originally came from the Canal Zone or migrated to the Canal Zone or Panama from Colombia after Panama was created as an independent nation-state.

The Hondurans and Garifuna

Most of New York City sprawls over islands surrounded by water, except for the Bronx, which is New York's sole borough connected to the US mainland. The main thoroughfare in the Bronx is the Grand Concourse, a broad boulevard modeled on the Champs-Elysees in Paris. On each side, within two miles of the Grand Concourse, live the bulk of New York's Honduran immigrants and their descendants, many of them Garifuna. Like most Panamanian New Yorkers, they also trace their Central American roots to the English-speaking Caribbean. Proud of their ethnic traditions, with their own dress, religion, music, and language, the Garifuna trace their ancestry to the island of St. Vincent, a British-held Caribbean possession before it became an independent country in 1979. In the years before effective British control was established at the end of the eighteenth century, shipwrecked or escaped African slaves were able to settle on the island and eventually mixed with the native Carib/Arawak Indians to forge a hybrid culture. The British called them Black Caribs to distinguish them from other defined native populations. After resisting British encroachment on their lands for decades, many Garifuna were sent into exile on the island of Roatan, off the coast of Honduras, which then became the springboard for further migration into Central America. Garifuna tradition holds that they departed from St. Vincent on March 11, 1797, and arrived in Roatan on April 12 of the same year.[42]

This voyage into exile, as described by the Garifuna, drew official recognition in New York in recent years when proclamations by Mayor Michael Bloomberg, Governor Andrew Cuomo, and the New York State Assembly and Senate commemorated Garifuna Heritage Month, which takes place from March 11 to April 12. Posted proclamations, framed prominently at the Bronx-based office of Garifuna Coalition USA Inc., include a 2010 declaration from Mayor Bloomberg, which states that the Garifuna peoples live in countries ranging from Belize and Nicaragua to the United States. According to the mayoral declaration, New York City is home to the largest Garifuna population outside Central America, with an estimated two hundred thousand living in the five boroughs; however, estimates for this population vary widely. Bloomberg also addressed a crowd of Garifuna on July 14, 2010, in an auditorium at Lincoln Hospital in the South Bronx under the auspices of the Garifuna Coalition USA and Hondurans against AIDS.[43] In his remarks, the mayor joked about his problem learning Spanish and stated that the Garifuna language would be much more difficult for him to learn.[44]

At Casa Yurumein, barely a mile from Lincoln Hospital, instructors teach classes in Garifuna, partly in an effort to keep the language and culture alive in New York. Yurumein is the Garifuna word for the island of St. Vincent. One Casa Yurumein-teacher, Milton Guity, said Garifuna is primarily derived from Arawak/Carib languages, spoken by Caribbean native Indians, with some Spanish and French. Some specialists say Garifuna's Arawak and Carib elements share commonalities with Amazonian Amerindian languages, and UNESCO has stated that the language has African elements. A US State Department background briefing paper on Honduras described Garifuna as "a mixture of Afro-indigenous languages."[45] In 2001, UNESCO declared the Garifuna language, music, and dance one of the world's masterpieces "of the oral and intangible heritage of humanity," a measure meant to help preserve its cultural legacy.[46] Less than half a mile from Casa Yurumein is the Garifuna Heritage Center for the Arts and Culture. One of its entities is the "Hamalali Wayunagu" (Voices of our ancestor) Garifuna Folkloric Dance Company. Its website displays dancers twirling to drumbeats in hoop-like skirts striped in yellow, black, fuchsia, and turquoise. In another dance, performers don long white robes with red embroidery, or they wear West African–like rectangular hats that are colored in gold.[47]

In its 2013 budget, the New York City Council allocated funds to help support Garifuna dance programs via a theater group. It also earmarked funds for the Bronx-based Garifuna Coalition USA to provide youth with "educational opportunities, guidance and validation."[48] In an October 2012 interview, Lilian Gómez, a Honduran vice-consul in New York, said that there were one hundred thousand Honduran Garifuna in New York; estimates vary widely. She also said that this community had a number of important leaders, including José Francisco Ávila, chairman of the Garifuna Coalition USA.

Ávila, also interviewed in October 2012, said the Bronx and Brooklyn were hubs of Garifunas. Overall, New York was home to more Honduran Garifunas than anywhere outside their native country, he said, noting they are concentrated in the Bronx. Ávila added: "The biggest Garifuna community of Belizeans is in Los Angeles, but the second-largest is in Brooklyn. The biggest Guatemalan Garifuna community outside of Guatemala is [in New York,] divided between the Bronx and Brooklyn." By country of origin, Garifunas from Nicaragua are the least numerous in the city. He added that Garifuna women tend to work mainly as home health-care workers and in other kinds of medically related employment, while most of the men are employed cleaning buildings or employed in other building services.[49]

According to the 2010 census, 18,679 Hondurans were living in the Bronx, with a notable Honduran presence in the Mott Haven, Melrose, Morrisania, Longwood, Van Nest–Morris Park, and Westchester Square sections of the borough, and also east and west of the Grand Concourse. The Mott Haven–Port Morris neighborhood, across the Harlem River from Manhattan, had 1,488 Hondurans, more than in any other NTA in the borough. In the Melrose South–Mott Haven North sections, the census reported 1,191 Hondurans, followed by 1,126 in Morrisania-Melrose. According to 2010–14 ACS data, the most important neighborhood for the Honduran foreign-born population of the Bronx was Mott Haven–Port Morris, with 1,025, residents, followed by 868 in Morrisania-Melrose, 783 in Melrose South–Mott Haven North, 769 in Hunts Point, and 718 in the Mount Hope. Another Bronx neighborhood with a significant Honduran presence was East Tremont, which abuts the Bronx Zoo and is located in the district's Southern Boulevard, where a traffic island memorial commemorates the victims of the tragic 1990 fire that destroyed the Happy Land social club, where many Garifuna died.

Many city residents were first made aware of the existence of the Garifuna community when, on March 25, 1990, a blaze swept through this social club, which is across from where the memorial now stands. This was one of deadliest fires in US history. Seventy-eight of the victims were Hondurans, with at least forty-five identified as Garifuna, according to Honduran Consul General Francisco Quezada, interviewed at a memorial ceremony in March 2013.

However, according to José Ávila, this tragedy set the stage for the emergence of new community organizations and a degree of social and political cohesion and activism. He notes, for example, that New York State records show that twenty-eight nonprofit Garifuna associations were founded in the 1990s, and twelve from 2000 to 2006.[50] Garifuna leaders have also attempted to obtain broader recognition for this community. According to Ávila, the Garifuna Coalition USA launched an educational campaign in 2010 to insert the term "Garifuna" in the "other" section of the US census as a category apart from traditionally recognized ethnicities. Ávila also noted that the Garifuna have had a tendency to identify themselves as black, but that they also fall into the Hispanic category because of their spoken Spanish, while the Belizean Garifuna fall into another category because they come from an English-speaking country. However, he also added that the Garifuna community in New York is the largest in the United States, but that the largest number of Belizean Garifuna are in Los Angeles. Anthropologist Nancie L. González has also noted that many Garifuna frequently traveled back and forth and many of them returned to their native villages upon retirement.[51]

Male Garifuna began arriving in New York in the 1930s as merchant seamen in vessels of the Standard Fruit and Shipping Company, a major US banana grower in the Honduran lowlands. This specific employment niche expanded in the 1940s as a result of a decrease in US civilian manpower during World War II. Some of the Garifuna joined the National Maritime Union, headquartered in New York City, where their paperwork was processed and where they were able to find employment with other companies when necessary. According to anthropologist Sarah England, "Some Garifuna men set up a residential base in New York City, forming the pioneer population of Garifuna migrants to the city."[52] The Garifuna at first lived in Harlem but kept their identity distinct from the African Americans and other Afro–West Indians in the neighborhood. The Garifuna were attracted to Harlem because it was considered the premier black neighborhood of the city, but they also stood apart because they spoke Spanish and also Garifuna, which was a language that few people understood. After the reform of US immigration laws in 1965, Garifuna men were able to bring their women and children to the city with greater ease because the new laws favored family reunification. Women were also able to come in increasing numbers by themselves with their children and other relatives. The result was an increase in the size of households as many Garifuna moved from Harlem, where they had lived in small "efficiency" apartments, to roomier apartments in the Bronx. This movement of the Garifuna increased in the 1970s because more large apartments in the Bronx became available as many long-time residents left the borough, particularly non-Hispanic whites.[53]

The current Puerto Rican political leadership in New York has built bridges to the Garifuna, especially in the Bronx. This includes the Reverend Rubén Díaz Sr., a state senator from the borough, and his son, Rubén Díaz Jr., the current Bronx Borough President. In an interview, Senator Díaz said that he organized annual banquets called "Abrazo al Garifuna" (Embrace of the Garifuna), noting that he had held these events since 2011. About five hundred Garifuna have come to these events each year, along with other local politicians. Díaz said that he also spearheads annual commemorations of the Garifuna Heritage Month in the State Senate in Albany, which hundreds of Garifuna attend. In the March 2013 Senate session, invocations were read both in English and Garifuna. He also said that Garifuna leaders are also starting to be active in registering voters, and predicted that "within the coming years, this community will have its own elected legislators because they are growing and many are becoming citizens."[54]

The growing importance of the Garifuna community has also been recognized by the Puerto Rican and Latino Caucus of the New York State Senate, which has bestowed honors on important leaders in the Garifuna community—especially some of the women. As recognized by Nancie González in her field research, Garifuna women in Central America became less reliant on their husbands because men frequently left their families for long periods as migrants and merchant seamen.[55] Today in New York, the leadership role of the women is also celebrated in events organized by the Garifuna themselves. Recently on October 13, 2012, female leaders in the Garifuna community were honored in a cavernous auditorium, one block from Times Square in Manhattan, with drum-dominated music and speeches and a lavish color publication with lengthy profiles of fifteen honorees, identifying five of them as immigrants from Guatemala and ten of them from Honduras. The national diversity of the Garifuna population has also been celebrated—for example, in the local Miss Garifuna contests, which feature contestants and performers from Guatemala, Honduras, and Belize, according to the booklets published for these events.

The Salvadorans

By landmass, Queens is New York's largest borough; it is also the city's most diverse in the number of immigrants. Nearly half the borough's population of 2.07 million people were born abroad.[56] By national origin, Queens has the city's largest Salvadoran and Guatemalan populations. According to the 2010 census, Salvadorans in the borough totaled 21,342, and Guatemalans 13,700. These two groups are concentrated in a five-mile-wide north-south corridor that begins, in the north, in the neighborhoods around Flushing Bay, an inlet off the Long Island Sound, and ends in Far Rockaway in the south. These districts include East Elmhurst (which abuts LaGuardia Airport) as well as Corona and Flushing (both close to Citi Field, the New York Mets' baseball stadium), and Jamaica in Central Queens, which is an important hub for subways and suburban trains. Jamaica by itself has 7,835 Central Americans by national ancestry, the most of any NTA in New York, and they account for nearly one of every seven residents in the Jamaica NTA with its total population of 53,571. Of that total, 3,449 are Guatemalans and 2,752 are Salvadorans, making Jamaica the neighborhood with the largest concentration of New Yorkers from Guatemala and El Salvador. The foreign-born population of Central Americans in the Jamaica NTA was also substantial. According to the 2010–14 ACS data, the neighborhood included 2,253 persons born in El Salvador, 1,942 from Guatemala, and 1,228 persons born in Honduras.

The Rockaway Peninsula is located in the southeastern part of Queens and juts westward into the Atlantic Ocean. The pounding waves on its beaches draw wet-suited surfers, and overhead, jets descend into nearby John F. Kennedy International Airport. According to the 2010 US census, the Far Rockaway–Bayswater NTA was home to 4,884 Central Americans as identified by national origin. This meant that about one in ten persons in the NTA's population of 48,344 residents were Central American. Of these, 2,499 were Salvadorans and 1,465 were Guatemalans, the second-largest concentration of each group in the city. The 2010–14 ACS data also showed that the NTA's foreign-born population included 1,809 persons from El Salvador, 1,797 from Guatemala, and 695 from Honduras.

The area is also among the poorest in Queens. About 16.7 % of households in the Far Rockaway–Bayswater NTA had a yearly income of less than $10,000, and according to the 2010–14 ACS survey, 37.9 % of households had an income of under $25,000 a year.[57] These low income levels were in part a result of the large concentration of subsidized public housing in the area, which tends to have a disproportionately high number of the city's poorest residents. In November 2012, the high-rise buildings in the public housing projects, along with their residents, were seriously impacted by Hurricane Sandy. Many individuals—especially impoverished senior citizens—were trapped in the buildings when they had difficulty walking, or could not walk, down ten, twelve, or more flights of stairs because buildings were flooded and had no electricity to power the elevators or the lights. At one point, the New York governor, Andrew Cuomo, commented that the Rockaways had the highest concentration of public housing in New York and said, "You have people in a crisis who don't have the resources to pack up the car and say go to their sister's house in suburban Long Island. So it made a bad situation worse."[58]

According to law enforcement authorities, Far Rockaway has also been plagued with gang violence. In 2010, eighty-four people were arrested in a police sweep of the area, and more than sixty handguns were confiscated from the so-called "Flocc" street gang, an amalgamation of young lawbreakers with ties to both the Bloods and Crips gangs, who are rivals elsewhere. Queens district attorney Richard Brown said the sweep struck "at the heart of a highly unified and criminally active street gang that turned the seaside Queens neighborhood of Far Rockaway into a war zone and threatened the lives and safety of innocent bystanders and law enforcement officers."[59]

Far Rockaway is a southern terminus on the Long Island Railroad for passengers going to Queens from areas such as Brooklyn as well as Nassau and Suffolk Counties. Some of the towns in these suburban counties are breeding grounds for gangs, such as the Mara Salvatrucha, or the MS-13, a Central American gang that has been able to expand into communities in Eastern Queens, such as Flushing and Far Rockaway.

The gang first emerged in southern California in the 1980s, but is now led from El Salvador as a result of the deportation of several of its leaders and many others who were undocumented. Evidence for the existence of the MS-13 in New York City first surfaced in 2000, initially in Flushing and later in Rockaway. At first, gang members were strictly Salvadorans, but they were soon joined by youths from Guatemala and Honduras, according to a New York City law enforcement official interviewed in November 2012. Other, smaller gangs in Queens, such as Salvadorans with Pride (SWP) and the Sureños-13 (Southerners-13), include youths with Central American ancestry. A 2011 database of gangs compiled by the New York City Police Department showed that overall, there were a total of 22,935 gang members split among some 235 gangs and crews in New York City.[60]

However, it has to be emphasized that the demographic data show Salvadoran immigrants to be more work-oriented than New Yorkers overall. They also stand out among immigrants in their labor-force-participation rate, that is, the proportion of those sixteen and older who are working or looking for work. Foreign-born Salvadorans have an 89% labor-participation rate, far above the 70% average for the city, according to the Department of City Planning (DCP). Among the 20 biggest immigrant groups, only Mexicans' labor-force-participation rate is higher, at 91%.

In addition, the proportion of Salvadoran immigrants receiving public assistance is relatively low, at 2.4%, despite their poverty rate of 27%, one of the highest among Latin American immigrants. The DCP notes that this goes against the general correlation of the level of public assistance with the poverty rate. Seventy percent of Salvadoran immigrants are service workers, higher than any of the other top twenty immigrant groups. Foreign-born Salvadorans also outrank the other nineteen in terms of working in the private sector and are least likely to be self-employed or be government employees.

Another distinguishing feature is the high number of employed persons per Salvadoran immigrant household. In 2011, it stood at 1.9 persons. Out of the twenty largest foreign-born groups in New York's civilian workforce, Salvadorans were matched only by Ecuadoreans and exceeded solely by Mexican households, at 2.1 workers on average.[61]

If one looks at New York's metropolitan CSA, the Salvadoran population is further outdistancing other Central Americans as the largest group by national origin.[62] According to the one-year ACS data for 2012, there were 267,678 Salvadorans versus 140,287 Guatemalans and 116,120 Hondurans, compared with aforementioned 2010 census data, which showed 206,475 Salvadorans, 131,244 Guatemalans, and 107,241 Hondurans in the CSA. The ACS's margin of error was narrow enough to have no bearing on the ranking.[63]

The Costa Ricans and Nicaraguans of New York

Costa Ricans represent the smallest number of New Yorkers from any of the six Spanish-speaking Central American nations. According to the 2010 census, the 6,673 Costa Ricans accounted for 4.4% of the 151,378 Central Americans in New York City. By borough, there were 2,576 Costa Ricans in Brooklyn, 1,749 in Queens, 1,095 in the Bronx, 987 in Manhattan, and 266 on Staten Island. As noted earlier in this chapter, the $48,487 median household income of Costa Ricans was the highest among Central Americans. Among occupations, about 29% of employed Costa Ricans were in management or had jobs in business, science, and the arts, more than any other Central American group. About 32.6% of Costa Ricans were involved in services, and 28.7% in sales. An additional 6.1% were also involved in transportation, and 3.5% in natural resources, construction, maintenance, and other occupations.

Among the more affluent Costa Ricans, the 2006–10 ACS data showed that in 2010 dollars, 18.9% of households earned from $50,000 to $74,999, 15.9% between $75,000 and $99,999, 9% between $100,000 and $149,999, 4.6% between $150,000 and $199,999, and 1.1% earned at least $200,000. On the lower end of the income scale, 11.3% earned less than $10,000, 4.1% between $10,000 and $14,999, 11.7% between $15,000 and $24,999, 12.7% between $25,000 and $34,999, and 10.6% earned between $35,000 and $49,999.[64] In 2010, Costa Ricans sent home an average of $437 a month in remittances, and according to a sample provided by the Costa Rican consulate, only 10% of them had university degrees, which compares unfavorably with the 66% of all persons surveyed elsewhere in countries like France, Britain, the Slovak Republic, Norway, Mexico, and Chile. Twenty-one percent of the Costa Ricans sampled also had some university education, but they still had not earned degrees. Thirty percent in New York had gone as far as attaining a high school degree, and the rest had fewer years of education.[65]

Unlike other Central American immigrant groups, the increase in the Nicaraguan population has not been an uninterrupted ascendancy. From 1,300 persons in 1960, Nicaraguans increased to 2,014 in 1970. However, the civil war in Nicaragua during the 1970s and the US-backed counterinsurgency that followed the establishment of the leftist Sandinista regime in 1979 led to a spike in the number of Nicaraguans entering the city and other parts of the country. A substantial number of these people, especially those of slightly higher socioeconomic standing, came to the United States because they prospered under, or were somehow otherwise connected to, the former Somoza dictatorship. Compared with other Central American immigrants, Nicaraguans enjoyed relatively higher success rates with their asylum applications to enter the country, especially in the years of the US-backed counterinsurgency and because of their political alienation from the Sandinista government.[66] The result was that by 1990, there were 9,660 Nicaraguans living in New York; however, with the end of the counterinsurgency at the end of 1980s, the Nicaraguan population dropped to 6,451 by the year 2000 before resuming its ascent to 9,346 in 2010.[67]

The narrative of a married Nicaraguan couple, interviewed in 2012 for this essay, illustrates these demographic trends. Rolando and Marlene González arrived in New York on July 4, 1980, after they felt compelled to close their travel agency in Managua because the new Sandinista government unionized their employees and began to interfere with their lives in other ways. However, in 1996, Rolando and his wife returned to Nicaragua and reestablished their travel agency because a new and presumably more liberal and supportive post-Sandinista government had come to power. Many other Nicaraguans also joined them in the aftermath of the civil war and counterinsurgency during this period. However, Rolando and his wife were again forced to close their business because union problems resurfaced along with other issues. They eventually came back to New York, where Rolando obtained employment as a limousine driver. In 2002, they were able to return to Nicaragua and open two restaurants; unfortunately, they were not successful, which brought them back to New York once again in 2006. In recent years, the couple has run a service to deliver packages to Nicaragua.

For the González couple and for many other Nicaraguans in New York, the paramount annual community event has been the festival of the Inmaculada Concepción de María (Immaculate conception of Mary), a Nicaraguan adaptation of the cult of the Virgin Mary, who is the patron saint of that country. The festival day itself falls on December 7, but the events in New York in 2012 were held on other days, and included the commemoration of Catholic Mass in the Rego Park section of Queens, in the Hamilton Heights section of northern Manhattan, and most notably, at St. Patrick's Cathedral in Manhattan, the seat of the Archdiocese of New York. Officiating at the December 2, 2012, event at St. Patrick's was Monsignor Sócrates René Sándigo, president of the Nicaraguan Episcopal Conference between 2012 and 2014, who noted that faith is what helped Nicaraguans abroad conserve their bonds with their home country. The funds for the prelate's visit were provided by the Comité Cívico Cultural Nicaragüense (The Nicaraguan civic cultural committee), one of the important US-based Nicaraguan community organizations. Over the years, it has raised funds to bring ecclesiastical representatives from Nicaragua to New York for these religious festivals.

The celebration in Rego Park at Our Lady of Angels Church, held on December 1, was organized by María Azucena Santos de Sándigo, in part to raise money for a charity based in Managua. Following Nicaraguan tradition, the Mass featured the *gritería*, which translates as the "shouting." The presiding clergyman cries out, "Who causes such happiness?," and the reply is "The conception of Mary." Call-and-response refrains are punctuated by noisemakers and rattles called *matracas*, which are brought to New York from Nicaragua for the occasion. Adults give out special Nicaraguan candy to children after they cry the standard refrain, and among the treats are coconut-flavored sweets and Nicaraguan staples like pork rinds and yucca and coconut-flavored milk. Santos de Sándigo noted that she was from Managua and came to New York about twenty-five years earlier in search of opportunities because these were lacking or were much diminished in Nicaragua during the final stages of the Sandinista regime in the late 1980s. Finally, she noted, "One comes to the United States to make a new life, but we always conserve our roots, and always try to conserve our traditions, above all the Catholic religion, which one does not lose, even when one is in a different country."

NOTES

Essay copyright © 2017 Walker Simon and Rosalia Reyes.

We want to give special recognition and gratitude to the following people for their valuable time and support to develop our research:

Escolastico Arzu, member of the Garifuna Coalition USA, Inc.
José Francisco Ávila, chairman, Garifuna Coalition USA, Inc.
David Brotherton, professor, Department of Sociology, John Jay College, City University of New York
Alejandro Cajina, Nicaraguan community activist
Javier Castaño, journalist
Erika Cháves Ramírez, economist, Central Bank of Costa Rica
Mirtha Colón, president/director, Hondurans Against AIDS, Inc., and president, Casa Yurumein
Lilian Gómez, former Honduran vice-consul in New York
Marlene González, president, Fundación Humanitaria Pro-Nicaragua
Rolando González, Nicaraguan community activist
Román Guerrero, chief editor of the newspaper *Enlace Centroamericano*
Milton Guity, Garifuna teacher
Lidia Hunter, Nicaraguan journalist and teacher
Donnise Hurley, official, Population Division, Department of City Planning, City of New York
Tulio Laboriel, Garifuna singer
Arturo Martínez, writer for *La Voz de Honduras*

Antonio Roberto Morgan, former Panamanian diplomat and founding publisher and editor of *The International Panama Times / Presencia Hispana*

Rubén Reyes, Garifuna teacher

Joseph Salvo, director, Population Division, Department of City Planning, City of New York

Irene Sánchez, former directora de comunicaciones (director of communications), Ministerio de Relaciones Exteriores, El Salvador

Sócrates René Sándigo, Nicaraguan bishop and former president of the Episcopal Conference of Nicaragua

Oscar Sandoval, president, Comité Cívico Cultural Nicaragüense (Nicaraguan civic cultural committee)

María Azucena Santos de Sándigo, Nicaraguan community activist

Aaron Terrazas, researcher, formerly of the Migration Policy Institute, based in Washington, DC

Ricardo José Valencia Pineda, former official of the Office of Communications and Public Relations, Embassy of El Salvador, Washington, DC

Juan Carlos Vargas, professor, Universidad de Costa Rica

Vicky Virgin, official, Population Division, Department of City Planning, City of New York

The authors also want to thank others, who cannot be identified, for their generous help and guidance.

1. US General Accounting Office (1986b, 2, 11; 1989, 2, 10).

2. Reagan (1988). Please note that estimates vary on the value of Soviet bloc military aid to Nicaragua. See US General Accounting Office (1989, 22), which says the US Department of Defense valued Soviet bloc military supplies to Nicaragua's Sandinistas at over $3 billion. Also see Klare and Adverson (1996, chap. 3), who say the US Arms Control and Disarmament Agency valued the Soviet bloc shipments to Nicaragua in the 1980s at more than $2 billion. Klare and Adverson also say that while the US government may have overvalued the dollar value of the shipments, it is safe to assume that that the Soviet light arms were supplied to all Nicaraguan soldiers and paramilitaries.

3. Reagan (1986b).

4. US General Accounting Office (1986b, 1989).

5. Reagan (1985).

6. See Reagan (1986b).

7. Reagan (1983).

8. Reagan (1984).

9. US General Accounting Office (1989, 2, 18, 25; 1986a).

10. UNHCR (1993).

11. Pearce (1988).

12. Reagan (1986a).

13. Reagan (1988).

14. UNHCR (1993, chap. 6).

15. Gibson and Lennon (1999), table 3.

16. Acosta and de la Cruz (2011, 2). This Census Bureau report defines Central American immigrants, outside of those from Mexico, as coming from what is termed "other Central America," which includes Belize, Costa Rica, El Salvador, Guatemala, Honduras, Nicaragua, and Panama. However, national ancestry data in the 2010 US census, which includes both immigrants and others identifying themselves from the region, do not include Belize.

17. Beteta (2012, 15).

18. Durand and Massey (2010, 25, 34).

19. Terrazas (2011).

20. Acosta and de la Cruz (2011, 5). Percentages of Central American immigrants by state were calculated by a coauthor of this chapter from Gibson and Lennon (1999), table 3.

21. Ennis, Ríos Vargas, and Albert (2011). This US Census Bureau Central American category, which excludes Mexicans, encompasses Guatemalans, Salvadorans, Nicaraguans, Hondurans, Costa Ricans, and Panamanians. It also has a category for "other Central Americans," and among them are those identified as Central American Indians, or others who are said to come from the former US Canal Zone in Panama.

22. The data on Central Americans in combined statistical areas and metropolitan areas are calculated from table DP-1, "Profile of General Population and Housing Characteristics: 2010," Census, Summary File 2, US Census Bureau. To search for Central Americans by national origin as a group and by major nationalities in CSA for New York and other urban areas, choose categories 221 to 226 from the drop-down menu in the following link: https://factfinder.census.gov/bkmk/table/1.0/en/DEC/10_SF2/SF2DP1/310M100US33100|330M100US288|330M100US348|330M100US408|330M100US488|330M100US548/popgroup~407|408|409|410|411|412?slice=GEO~330M100US408. Of the urban population clusters referred to in the text, all are CSAs except for Miami, for which metropolitan area data are featured. Search US Census, AmericanFactFinder, http://factfinder.census.gov/faces/nav/jsf/pages/index.xhtml. For a map of the New York CSA, please see New York-Newark-NY-NJ-CT-PA Combined Statistical Area, US Department of Commerce, Economics and Statistics Administration, US Census Bureau, AmericanFactFinder, http://factfinder.census.gov/faces/nav/jsf/pages/index.xhtml.

23. Statement from the Communications Office of El Salvador's Foreign Ministry, March 9, 2013, in response to the authors' questionnaire. For the visit by the vice president to Nassau County, see Whittle (2012).

24. US Attorney (2015).

25. New York (2010a, 14). Table SF1-P8 NYC: Total Hispanic Population by Selected Subgroups, New York City and Boroughs, 2010, 2010 Census Summary

File 1, Population Division, New York City Department of Planning, June 2012, http://www1.nyc.gov/assets/planning/download/pdf/data-maps/nyc-population /census2010/t_sf1_p8_nyc.pdf. See also New York (2010a, 14–16), https://www1 .nyc.gov/assets/planning/download/pdf/data-Dmaps/nyc-population/census 2010/pgrhc.pdf, and New York (2010b).

26. Passel (2012, 275). Passel notes that the 2010 US census was the first decennial census since 1850 that did not ask for place of birth. Instead, the annual American Community Survey is the US Census Bureau source for data on birthplace.

27. Table B03001, "Hispanic or Latino Origin by Specific Origin; Universe: Total Population," 2011–2015 American Community Survey 5-Year Estimates, https://factfinder.census.gov/bkmk/table/1.0/en/ACS/15_5YR/B03001 /1600000US3651000; table B05006, "Place of Birth for the Foreign-Born Population in the United States; Universe: Foreign-Born Population excluding Population Born at Sea," 2011–2015 American Community Survey 5-Year Estimates, https://fact finder.census.gov/bkmk/table/1.0/en/ACS/15_5YR/B05006/1600000US3651000. The Belizean national ancestry figure is from the 2015 ACS 1-Year Estimates, Summary File, as tabulated by the Population Division, New York City, Department of City Planning, November 2016, http://www1.nyc.gov/assets/planning/download /pdf/data-maps/nyc-population/acs/ancest_2015acs1yr_nyc.pdf. New York City's Department of City Planning provided the information on the percentage of New Yorkers sampled in the 2011–2015 ACS.

28. For income of Guatemalans, Salvadorans, Hondurans, and Panamanians, see table S0201, "Selected Population Profile in the United States," 2011–2013 American Community Survey 3-Year Estimates, for each nationality, https://factfinder.census.gov/bkmk/table/1.0/en/ACS/13_3YR/S0201/1600000 US3651000/popgroup~408|409|411|412. For the income by Central Americans in 2010, see table B19013, "Median Household Income in the Past 12 Months (in 2010 Inflation-Adjusted Dollars); Universe: Households," 2006–2010 American Community Survey Selected Population Tables, https://factfinder.census.gov /bkmk/table/1.0/en/ACS/10_SF4/B19013/1600000US3651000/popgroup~407|410. For New Yorkers' median household income as a whole, see table S1901, "Income in the Past 12 Months (in 2013 Inflation-Adjusted Dollars)," 2009–2013 American Community Survey 5-Year Estimates, https://factfinder.census.gov/faces/table-services/jsf/pages/productview.xhtml?pid=ACS_13_5YR_S1901&prodType =table. For 2010 median household income for all New Yorkers, please see again table B19013, cited above.

29. Lozano (2005).

30. See DP-1 Profile of General Population and Housing Characteristics: 2010, 2010 Census Summary File 2, US Census Bureau for the six main Central American national origin groups, search categories 22 to 226, AmericanFact-Finder, http://factfinder.census.gov/faces/nav/jsf/pages/index.xhtml.

31. Unless otherwise noted, data by neighborhood tabulation area (NTA) in New York City are compiled by the Population Division of the Department of City Planning (DCP). For a map of the Department of City Planning's 195 neighborhood tabulation areas, see http://www1.nyc.gov/assets/planning/download /pdf/data-maps/nyc-population/census2010/ntas.pdf?v=022016. ACS data by NTA data are available on the Population Division's American Community Survey tab, http://www1.nyc.gov/site/planning/data-maps/nyc-population/american -community-survey.page. For the 2010–14 ACS NTA data, choose the "social" tables and the year 2014 from the drop-down menu.

32. ExpoNica (2012).

33. Vaz (2010, 2011) and YouTube entries in Panamanian Day Parade (2011, 2012).

34. Bratu (2010) and Durkin (2010). Unless otherwise noted, all data on New Yorkers by ancestry and NTA are from the tabulation of the 2010 US Census in Table SF1-P8 NTA, produced by the Population Division of New York City's Department of City Planning and entitled "Total Hispanic Population by Selected Subgroups New York City Neighborhood Tabulation Areas, 2010," http:// www1.nyc.gov/assets/planning/download/pdf/data-maps/nyc-population /census2010/t_sf1_p8_nta.pdf. The 2010–14 ACS data for NTAs (see note 31) on foreign-born Panamanians in the Prospect-Lefferts Gardens-Wingate had a margin of error of plus or minus 471 persons, according to a chart drawn up by the Population Division of New York City's Department of City Planning, thus partly explaining why the figure of 1,544 for persons identified as foreign born in the neighborhood is substantially larger than the figure of 1,273 for Panamanians-by-national-origin listed by the US census for 2010.

35. Antonio Roberto Morgan, personal interviews, September 2011 and May 2015; Mora (2013, 38–39).

36. Dodson and Diouf (2005).

37. Newton (2004).

38. The source for legal permanent resident admissions for Hondurans and Panamanians is "Legal Permanent Residents Admitted by Year of Admission and Country of Birth, New York City, FY 1972–2011," Office of Immigration Statistics, US Department of Homeland Security.

39. Data on Panamanian immigration to the United States is found in US Census Bureau 2009–2011 ACS 3-year Estimates, AmericanFactFinder, http:// factfinder.census.gov/faces/nav/jsf/pages/index.xhtml.

40. Bratu (2010).

41. See "Fighting for Franklin" (2010).

42. England (2006).

43. "Civic Meeting with Garifuna Coalition USA and Hondurans against Aids Inc." (2010).

44. Ramos (2010).

45. There are diverse interpretations on the elements of the Garifuna language. Cayetano and Cayetano (2009, 239) identify the Garifuna language as being of South American and West Indian origin. They note in this regard that "it belongs to the Arawak language family, while including some lexical items derived from Carib and the European languages of the French, Spanish and English who attempted to colonize them." England (2006, 238) cites linguists who say that Garifuna is a mixture of grammars derived from Island Carib, Island Arawak, and African languages, and also that Garifuna has many loan words from English, Spanish, and French. The US Department of State (2011) described Garifuna as a mixture of Afro-Indigenous languages. The University of California at Berkeley in a news release (see Maclay 2012) states that the "intermingling of the Caribs, Africans and indigenous Arawaks resulted in the Garifuna language, which also was influenced by English, Spanish and French. Garifuna belongs to the Arawak linguistic family, whose members are mostly found in the Amazon Basin."

46. UNESCO (2006).

47. Solíz (2013).

48. On New York City's fiscal 2013 budget and its support for Garifuna, see New York City, Finance Division (2012, 120, 175).

49. José Francisco Ávila, interview, October 2012.

50. Ávila (2008).

51. Ávila, interview, 2012; Gonzalez (1988, 174–76); England (2006, 49).

52. England (2006, 44).

53. England (2006, 51–53) and Ávila, interview, 2012.

54. New York State Senator Rubén Díaz Sr., interview, March 2013. Also see Díaz (2011).

55. González (1979, 255).

56. According to the Population Division of the New York City Department of City Planning, the total population of Queens in 2010 was 2.23 million. See table PL-P1 NYC, "Total Population, New York City and Boroughs, 2000 and 2010," https://www1.nyc.gov/assets/planning/download/pdf/data-maps/nyc-population/census2010/t_pl_p1_nyc.pdf. According to estimates from the 2010 American Community Survey, the total foreign-born population of Queens was 1.066 million. See table B05006, "Place of Birth for the Foreign-Born Population in the United States; Universe: Foreign-Born Population excluding Population Born at Sea," 2013 American Community Survey 1-Year Estimates, New York City and Borough, https://factfinder.census.gov/faces/tableservices/jsf/pages/productview.xhtml?src=bkmk.

57. See ACS data, Profiles-Economic, 2014, Neighborhood Tabulation Areas, Population Division, New York City Department of City Planning, http://www1.nyc.gov/site/planning/data-maps/nyc-population/american-community-survey.page.

58. Maddow (2013).

59. See New York Police Department, "Sweeping Investigation of Queens Gang Members Results in Murder, Gun and Drug Charges Against 90+ Individuals," press release, April 16, 2010, http://www.nyc.gov/html/nypd/html/pr/pr_2010_ph28_gun_narcotics_takedown.shtml.

60. Joseph Goldstein, "Weekly Police Briefing Offers Snapshot of Department and Its Leader," *New York Times*, February 11, 2013.

61. Lobo and Salvo (2013, 104).

62. See table S0201, "Selected Population Profile in the United States," 2011–2013 American Community Survey 3-Year Estimates, US Census Bureau, AmericanFactFinder, https://factfinder.census.gov/bkmk/table/1.0/en/ACS/13_3YR/S0201/1600000US3651000/popgroup~408|409|411|412. No estimates were available for this time period for other Central American groups.

63. See table S0201, cited in the previous note. Within the table, see 2012 American Community Survey 1-Year Estimates. No estimates were available for this time period for other Central American groups.

64. For Central American groups by national origin by borough, see table SF1-P8 NYC, "Total Hispanic Population by Selected Subgroups: New York City and Boroughs, 2010," US Census Bureau, 2010 Census Summary File 1 Population Division, as tabulated by New York City Department of City Planning, June 2012, https://www1.nyc.gov/assets/planning/download/pdf/data-maps/nyc-population/census2010/t_sf1_p8_nyc.pdf. Also see DP03, table B19001, "Household Income in the Past 12 Months (in 2010 Inflation-Adjusted Dollars); Universe: Households 2006–2010," American Community Survey Selected Population Tables, US Census Bureau, in New York City, Finance Division (2012). Total percentage numbers exceed 100 because the percentages for income brackets are rounded.

65. Chaves et al. (2011).

66. See Riosmena (2010).

67. See Haslip-Viera's tables 1.3 and 1.4 (for 1960–90 and 1990–2010) in chap. 1 of this volume.

REFERENCES

Acosta, Yesenia D., and Patricia G. de la Cruz. 2011. "The Foreign Born, Latin America and the Caribbean: 2010." American Community Survey Briefs, ACSBR/10-15. Washington, DC: United States Census Bureau, September. http://www.census.gov/prod/2011pubs/acsbr10-15.pdf.

"Alcalde de Panamá cautivo a los panameños e invitados en Brooklyn el sábado 11 de octubre" (Panama City mayor captivated Panamanians and invitees in Brooklyn Saturday October 11), *The International Panama Times / Presencia Hispana*, year 21, no. 11, November, p. 29, http://www.elsoldata.com/Presencia/2014-11_files/Presencia%202014-11.pdf.

Ávila, José Francisco. 2008. "The Garifunas and Happy Land Social Club Fire." Bronx, NY: Garifuna Coalition USA. http://garifunacoalition.org/yahoo_site _admin/assets/docs/Happy_Land_Social_Club_Fire.243133832.pdf.

———. 2010. "Garifuna-American Heritage Month, 2010." Bronx, NY: Garifuna Coalition USA. http://garifunacoalition.org/yahoo_site_admin/assets/docs /2011_Garifuna_Heritage_Month.113170858.pdf.

———. 2012. "The Garifuna-American Community of New York." New York: National Institute for Latino Policy. http://archive.constantcontact.com/fs128 /1101040629095/archive/1111090139729.html.

Ávila, Tomás Alberto, ed. 2009. *Black Caribs—Garifuna Saint Vincent's Exiled People and the Origin of the Garifuna; A Historical Compilation.* Providence, RI: Milenio Associates.

Beteta, Hugo. 2012. *Central American Development: Two Decades of Progress and Challenges for the Future.* Washington, DC: Migration Policy Institute. https:// www.google.com/webhp?sourceid=chrome-instant&ion=1&espv=2&ie= UTF-8#q=hugo%20beteta%20central%20american%20development% 3A%20two%20decades.

Bratu, Becky. 2010. "Who Was First on Franklin Avenue? Local Organization and Panamanian Community Clash." *Brooklyn Ink,* October 19. http://thebrook-lynink.com/2010/10/19/16476-who-was-first-on-franklin-avenue-neighborhood -organization-and-panamanian-community-clash-over-avenue-name/.

Caribbean News Now! 2012. "Garifuna Trilingual Dictionary Released." *Caribbean News Now,* December 3. http://www.caribbeannewsnow.com/topstory-Garifuna -Trilingual-Dictionary-released-13618.html.

Casa Yurumein. 2013. Our Programs. Casa Yurumein website. http://www.casa-yurumein.com/our-programs.html.

Cayetano, Marion, and Roy Cayetano. 2009. "Garifuna Language, Dance and Music: A Masterpiece of the Oral and Intangible History of Humanity; How Did It Happen?" In *The Garifuna: A Nation across Borders; Essays in Social Anthropology,* edited by Joseph O. Palacio, 230–50. Benque Viejo del Carmen, Belize: Cubola Books.

Chaves, Erika, Patricia Barrantes, Evelyn Hernández, Yuliana Muñoz, and Walla Valverde. 2011. *Investigación de campo: Aspectos socioeconómicos de la remesas familiares en Costa Rica, 2010.* San José, Costa Rica: Banco Central de Costa Rica. http://www.bccr.fi.cr/publicaciones/politica_cambiaria_sector_externo /Remesas_2010.pdf.

"Civic Meeting with Garifuna Coalition USA and Hondurans against Aids Inc." Photos. NYC Mayors Office. N.d. Flickr.com. https://www.flickr.com/photos /nycmayorsoffice/sets/72157624372292639/.

Díaz, Rubén. 2011. "First 'Abrazo Garifuna in New York.'" Press release. Albany, NY: Office of Senator Rubén Díaz, March 17. http://www.nysenate.gov/press -release/first-abrazo-garifuna-new-york.

Dodson, Howard, and Sylviane Diouf. 2005. *In Motion: The African-American Migration Experience.* New York: Schomburg Center for Research.

Durand, Jorge, and Douglas S. Massey. 2010. "New World Orders: Continuities and Changes in Latin American Migration." *Annals of the American Academy of Political and Social Science* 630 (1): 20–52.

Durkin, Erin. 2010. "Neighborhood Split over Renaming Part of Franklin Ave. 'Panama Way.'" *New York Daily News*, October 21. http://www.nydailynews.com/new-york/brooklyn/neighborhood-split-renaming-part-franklin-ave-panama-article-1.190840.

England, Sarah. 2006. *Afro-Central Americans in New York City: Garifuna Tales of Transnational Movements in Racialized Space.* Gainesville: University Press of Florida.

Ennis, Sharon R., Merarys Ríos-Vargas, and Nora G. Albert. 2011. "The Hispanic Population: 2010." Census Bureau document C2010BR-04. Washington, DC: United States Census Bureau. http://www.census.gov/prod/cen2010/briefs/c2010br-04.pdf.

ExpoNica NY. 2012. "2DA Exhibición Artesanal Centroamericana y Del Caribe realizada por Exponica NY 2012." YouTube video, 7:33. Produced by ExpoNicaNY. Posted by "VisionLatinaNewYork," November 18, 2012. http://www.youtube.com/watch?v=3mpRiUGiYmQ.

"Fighting for Franklin." 2010. *I Love Franklin Avenue* (blog), September 23. http://ilovefranklinave.blogspot.com/2010/09/fighting-for-franklin.html.

Garifuna Coalition. 2010. Mayor Michael Bloomberg Declared a Garifuna Heritage Month. Bronx, NY: Garifuna Coalition USA, Inc.

Gibson, Campbell J., and Emily Lennon. 1999. *Historical Census Statistics on the Foreign-Born Population of the United States: 1850–1990.* Population Division Working Paper no. 29. February. Washington, DC: United States Census Bureau, Population Division. https://www.census.gov/population/www/documentation/twps0029/twps0029.html.

González, Nancie L. 1979. "Garifuna Settlement in New York: A New Frontier," *International Migration Review* 13 (2): 255–63. http://www.jstor.org/stable/2545031.

———. 1988. *Sojourners of the Caribbean: Ethnogenesis and Ethnohistory of the Garifuna.* Urbana: University of Illinois Press.

"History of Hamalali Wayunagu Garifuna Dance Company." 2013. Luz Solíz's Empower Network (blog). February 2. http://webcache.googleusercontent.com/search?q=cache:dDsNbz4vcrYJ:luzsoliz.empowernetwork.com/blog/history-of-hamalali-wayunagu-garifuna-dance-company&num=1&hl=en&gl=us&strip=0&vwsrc=0.

Klare, Michael, and David Adverson. 1996. *A Scourge of Guns: The Diffusion of Small Arms and Light Weapons in Latin America.* Washington, DC: Federation of American Scientists. https://fas.org/asmp/library/publications/scourgefl.htm.

Lobo, Arun Peter, and Joseph Salvo. 2013. *The Newest New Yorkers: Characteristics of the City's Foreign-Born Population*. New York: City of New York, Department of City Planning, Population Division, December. https://www1.nyc.gov/site /planning/data-maps/nyc-population/newest-new-yorkers-2013.page.

Lozano, Víctor. 2005. "Encuesta Nacional sobre Emigración Internacional de Guatemaltecos, 2002–2003." *Población y Salud en Mesoamérica* 2 (2): 1–35.

Maclay, Kathleen. 2012. "Graduate Students in Linguistics Leaving Legacy for Speakers of Endangered Language of Garifuna." *Berkeley News*, April 17. Berkeley: University of California. http://newscenter.berkeley.edu/2012/04 /17/students-study-document-little-known-central-american-language -of-garifuna/.

Maddow, Rachel. 2013. "Exclusive: Governor Cuomo on the Wrath of Superstorm Sandy." *Gotham Magazine*, January 15. http://gotham-magazine.com/person alities/articles/exclusive-rachel-maddow-interviews-governor-andrew -cuomo-on-superstorm-sandy.

Mora, Jorge Ivan. 2013. *Cronicas Panameñas en Nueva York*. Bogotá: Panamericana Formas e Impresos S.A.

Newton, Velma. 2004. *The Silver Men: West Indian Labour Migration to Panama, 1850–1914*. Kingston, Jamaica: Institute of Social and Economic Research, University of the West Indies.

New York City, Department of City Planning. 2010a. *NYC2010: Results from the 2010 Census; Population Growth and Race / Hispanic Composition*. New York: City of New York, Department of City Planning. http://www.nyc.gov/html /dcp/pdf/census/census2010/pgrhc.pdf.

New York City, Department of City Planning. 2010b. *NYC2010: Results from the 2010 American Community Survey; Socioeconomic Characteristics by Race / Hispanic Origin and Ancestry Group*. New York: City of New York, Department of City Planning. https://www1.nyc.gov/assets/planning/download/pdf /data-maps/nyc-population/acs/acs_socio_10_nyc.pdf.

New York City, Finance Division. 2012. *Fiscal Year 2013 Adopted Expense Budget: Adjustment Summary / Schedule C*. New York: City of New York. http://www .council.nyc.gov/downloads/pdf/budget/2013/FY%202013%20Schedule%20 C%20-%20Merge%20Final1.pdf.

New York State Senate. 2013. *Garifuna-American Heritage Month, in the NYS Senate, Tuesday, March 12, 2013*. Video, uploaded by Rubén Díaz, March 15. http://www.nysenate.gov/video/2013/mar/15/garifuna-american-heritage -month-nys-senate-tuesday-march-12-2013.

Palacios, Joseph O. 2009. *The Garifuna: A Nation across Borders; Essays in Social Anthropology*. 2nd ed. Benque Viejo del Carmen, Belize: Cubola Productions.

"Panamanian Day Parade 2011 in Brooklyn." 2011. YouTube video, 2:33. Posted by "industryhotel," October 9, 2011. http://www.youtube.com/watch?v=IoeD _ioUEMw.

Panamanian Day Parade. 2012. "Panamanian Day Parade~Brooklyn~2012~Pana-
manian Dancers~NYCParadelife." YouTube video, 3:08. Posted by "nycparade
life," October 7, 2012. http://www.youtube.com/watch?v=wXmICdGoPJk.

Passel, Jeffrey S. 2012. "Immigration." In *Encyclopedia of the U.S. Census, from the
Constitution to the American Community Survey*, edited by Margo J. Ander-
son, Constance F. Citro, and Joseph J. Salvo, 275–81. 2nd ed. Thousand Oaks,
CA: CQ Press.

Pearce, Jenny. 1998. "From Civil War to 'Civil Society': Has the End of the Cold War
Brought Peace to Central America?" *International Affairs Journal* 74 (3):
587–615. http://onlinelibrary.wiley.com/doi/10.1111/1468-2346.00036/abstract.

Popik, Barry. 2011. "Little Panama, Crown Heights, Brooklyn." *The Big Apple* website, September 29. http://www.barrypopik.com/index.php/new_york_city
/entry/little_panama_crown_heights_brooklyn/.

Ramos, Wellington C. 2010. "Commentary: New York City Mayor Bloomberg
Meets with Garifuna Community." *Caribbean Net News*, July 17. http://www
.caribbeannewsnow.com/caribnet/oped/oped.php?news_id=23985&start
=0&category_id=6.

Reagan, Ronald W. 1983. "Address before a Joint Session of the Congress on Central America." April 27. Public Papers of President Ronald W. Reagan. Ronald
Reagan Presidential Library, Simi Valley, CA. https://www.reaganlibrary.archives
.gov/archives/speeches/1983/42783d.htm.

———. 1984. "Address to the Nation on United States Policy in Central America."
May 9. Public Papers of President Ronald W. Reagan. Ronald Reagan Presidential Library, Simi Valley, CA. https://www.reaganlibrary.archives.gov
/archives/speeches/1984/50984h.htm.

———. 1985. "Statement by Principal Deputy Press Secretary Speakes on Economic Sanctions against Nicaragua." May 1. Public Papers of President Ronald
W. Reagan. Ronald Reagan Presidential Library, Simi Valley, CA. https://www
.reaganlibrary.archives.gov/archives/speeches/1985/50185c.htm.

———. 1986a. "Address to the Nation on the Situation in Nicaragua." March 16.
Public Papers of President Ronald W. Reagan. Ronald Reagan Presidential Library, Simi Valley, CA. https://www.reaganlibrary.archives.gov/archives
/speeches/1986/31686a.htm.

———. 1986b. "Remarks at a White House Meeting for Supporters of United States
Assistance for the Nicaraguan Democratic Resistance." March 3. Public Papers
of President Ronald W. Reagan. Ronald Reagan Presidential Library, Simi Valley, CA. https://www.reaganlibrary.archives.gov/archives/speeches/1986
/30386a.htm.

———. 1988. "Remarks to Civic Leaders at a White House Briefing on Aid to the
Nicaraguan Democratic Resistance." January 22. Public Papers of President
Ronald W. Reagan. Ronald Reagan Presidential Library, Simi Valley, CA. https://
www.reaganlibrary.archives.gov/archives/speeches/1988/012288d.htm.

Riosmena, Fernando. 2010. "Policy Shocks: On the Legal Auspices of Latin American Migration to the United States." *Annals of the American Academy of Political and Social Science* 630:270–75. http://www.ncbi.nlm.nih.gov/pmc/articles/PMC3172205/.

Small, Enrique. 2015. Photos of Desfile de Brooklyn (Brooklyn Parade). *The International Panama Times / Presencia Hispana*, year 21, no. 11/12, November/December, p. 13, https://issuu.com/presenciapanamena/docs/the_international_panama_times_-_pr_eb750834282c77/1?ff=true&e=1300778/31401106.

Solíz, Luz. 2013. "History of Hamalali Wayunagu Garifuna Dance Company, Feb. 2." *Luz Solíz's Empower Network*, blog.

Terrazas, Aarón. 2011. *Central American Immigrants in the United States.* Washington, DC: Migration Policy Institute, January 10. http://www.migrationinformation.org/usfocus/display.cfm?ID=824.

"Traditional Garifuna Dancers Perform during the Garifuna Heritage Celebration, March 12, 2013, Albany, NY." 2013. Photo posted by New York State senator Rubén Díaz. http://www.nysenate.gov/photos/2013/mar/28/traditional-garifuna-dancers-perform-during-garifuna-heritage-celebration-march-1.

UNESCO (United Nations Educational, Scientific and Cultural Organization). 2006. *Masterpieces of the Oral and Intangible Heritage of Humanity: Proclamations 2001, 2003 and 2005.* Paris: United Nations Educational, Scientific and Cultural Organization. http://unesdoc.unesco.org/images/0014/001473/147344e.pdf.

UNHCR (United Nations High Commissioner for Refugees). 1993. "Going Home: Voluntary Repatriation." Chap. 6 in *The State of the World's Refugees 1993: The Challenge of Protection.* New York: United Nations High Commissioner for Refugees. http://www.unhcr.org/cgi-bin/texis/vtx/home/opendocPDFViewer.html?docid=3eeedf3d5.

US Attorney, Eastern District of New York. 2015. "Additional MS-13 Gang Member Indicted for Murder of 19-Year-Old Man in Long Island." Press release. United States Attorney's Office, Eastern District of New York, March 5. http://www.justice.gov/usao/nye/pr/March15/2015Mar05.php.

US Census Bureau. 2008. *A Compass for Understanding and Using American Community Survey Data: What General Data Users Need to Know.* Washington, DC: United States Government Printing Office. https://www.census.gov/content/dam/Census/library/publications/2008/acs/ACSGeneralHandbook.pdf.

US Department of State. 2011. "Public Affairs Documents." In *Background Notes: Honduras.* Washington, DC: US Department of State. https://www.state.gov/outofdate/bgn/honduras/189476.htm.

US General Accounting Office. 1986a. *Military: The United States Continuing Munition Supply Relationship with Guatemala.* GAO/NSIAD-86-31. Washington, DC: United States General Accounting Office, January. http://www.gao.gov/assets/210/208114.pdf#page=1&zoom=auto,0,803.

———. 1986b. *Problems in Controlling Funds for the Nicaraguan Democratic Resistance.* GAO/NSIAD-87-35. Washington, DC: United States General Accounting Office, December. http://www.gao.gov/assets/210/208965.pdf.

———. 1989. *Central America: Impact of U.S. Assistance in the 1980s.* Washington, DC: United States General Accounting Office, July. http://www.gao.gov/assets/150/147879.pdf.

Vaz, Luís. 2010. "Décima Quinta Versión de la Gran Parada Anual Preambulo las Fiestas Patrias Panameñas en Nueva York." *Presencia Panameña e Hispana News in U.S.A.,* year 17, no. 12, September–December, pp. 7–8.

———. 2011. "Rotundo Éxito Desfile de los Panameños en Brooklyn el pasado 9 de Octubre." *Presencia Panameña e Hispana News in U.S.A.,* year 17, no. 11/12 November/December.

Whittle, Patrick. 2012. "Freeport Mayor Apologizes for VP's Visit." *Newsday,* August 20. http://www.newsday.com/long-island/nassau/freeport-mayor-apologizes-for-vp-s-visit-1.3916829.

PART THREE

Politics and Policy Issues

CHAPTER NINE

Puerto Rican and Latino Politics in New York

Still "Secondhand" Theory

JOSÉ RAMÓN SÁNCHEZ

*The first rule for understanding the human condition is that men
live in second-hand worlds. They are aware of much more than they have
personally experienced; and their own experience is always indirect.*

—C. Wright Mills, *Power, Politics, and People*

A legal complaint by the NAACP and Latino Justice in 2012 claimed bias in the admissions exams of New York City's specialized high schools.[1] Latino and African American children are woefully underrepresented in those schools. The NAACP claimed that this bias was by policy design. Was it intentional or structural? The Federal Department of Education, the New York State Legislature, the city council, city mayoral candidates, and the media debated a response. At the end, the exams remained as the sole criterion for admission.[2] The NAACP suit, however, raises theoretical issues about how we can best explain the deteriorated condition of the Latino community in New York City. This complaint is also, indirectly, a further disturbing comment about the low level of Latino power.

Reality does not speak for itself. Although some aspects of how we live are obvious, a lot more remain hidden and invisible. They are invisible because the social world is simply too complex, and the interconnections too many, to be easily captured by mere observation. What we mean by social interaction, in any case, takes place in language, perceptions, and the meanings we give to the things we do. We try to make sense of the shapes and contours of the social world that are otherwise invisible with concepts and theories. They provide an interpretative CAT scan of the social world.

How do we explain why otherwise intelligent, strong-willed, beautiful, and bighearted people, like Puerto Ricans and Latinos, find themselves so often mired at the bottom of the mucky sewers of a rich and successful city like New York? We will not find the whole answer in the historical and factual details of their life in this city. We can only find it by conceptualizing and theorizing well about the nature of the social world, the "facts" they inhabit.

While theories cannot be proven true or false, they can be more or less useful for explaining. Thus, we can say that the details of the Puerto Rican and Latino political experience have followed a certain trajectory and logic that can be better explained by some theories than by others. While there are no real empirical proofs to validate a theory, we can achieve conceptual validation. To do so, we must begin with acceptable, logical, and coherent assumptions in constructing a theoretical argument.

EXPLAINING LATINO POWER

A few theories about the distribution of power in American society dominate the study of Latino politics. At bottom, these theories are about power: who has it, how they got it, and how they use it. These approaches are the pluralist, the elitist, and political-economic. Each stakes out a certain range of political behavior for study, and each offers a very different vision about the nature of politics and power to answer the question most of us have about the Latino community: How do Latinos get power, and how have they lost it? As C. Wright Mills once suggested, these secondhand theories, like clothes, do not always fit the social reality they attempt to cover.

The pluralists suggest that political power is always "out there," readily available for different groups to compete for and to grab. Power is easily available and lands in the hands of those who are sufficiently motivated. For the elitist theorist, on the other hand, political power generally resides in the hands of only a few people who manipulate social conditions to keep it.

In contrast, the political-economist does not see political power as fruit that can be readily plucked from numerous trees or as the sole possession of a small group. It is instead an attribute of economic wealth or class standing, seen as structurally distributed in very uneven and permanent ways within society. Hard work and individual will are not enough to deliver wealth and power in this structured system. At the end of this essay, I introduce the "social power" approach. It provides the best account of the upward and downward movements in power for Latinos in the United States. It explains, for instance, why, despite the popular hype about this issue, population growth has not resulted in political power. Latinos have little to show for the over fifty million Latinos living in the United States as of 2010 (US Census Bureau, "2010 Census Shows America's Diversity," press release, March 24, 2011). It is not just that large population numbers alone have not automatically delivered political power. Voting has not done so either, even though, ostensibly, most Latinos have much to gain by voting.[3]

THE PLURALIST APPROACH

While the consensus in the literature on Latinos in the United States is that it is a mostly powerless community compared to other groups, the pluralist approach suggests that Latinos can always have power. It insists that if any people lack power, it must be because they lack political intelligence, legitimacy, and assertiveness or group organization. Can we explain Latino powerlessness this way?

As a founder of this approach, David B. Truman once claimed that groups gain power because there is "cohesion among members sufficient to give force to their claims" (1971, 269). A lobbying group, community-based organization, or professional association can, thus, be effective in the political arena to the extent that it has internal consensus, commitment, and leadership. The assumption is that political power originates, for the most part, in the intentional, purposeful activities of any middle-level social organization, that is, in the organizational "cohesiveness" of interest groups, such as labor unions, rather than in political parties or in larger social processes.

The pluralist position is partially true. New York City still has one of the highest levels of unionization in the United States. Latinos in general, however, have a lower rate of unionization than white or black New Yorkers. Puerto Ricans born in Puerto Rico are an exception. Probably as a result of higher levels of employment in government, Puerto Rican unionization rates are comparable to those of black New Yorkers (CUR 2010). But has such organizational capacity produced political influence? History shows that high levels of organization and mobilization have not always improved Puerto Ricans' ability to get what they need. The more interesting historical cases are, in fact, those where Puerto Ricans reached high levels of organization and yet remained essentially powerless.

CASE STUDY 1: THE STRUGGLE FOR PUBLIC HOUSING

Displays of political "firepower" may or may not impress those one is trying to influence. Voting and demonstrations may merely inform others about the intent to damage opponents or to shift the distribution of power; these activities are not, by themselves, enough to move others. One example was the struggle by Puerto Ricans during the 1972–73 period to expand the admission of Puerto Rican families to public housing in New York City.

As their housing conditions worsened during the early 1970s, Puerto Ricans turned their attention to public housing. Many community leaders drew notice to the persistently low level of Puerto Rican admission to public housing. Actually, much of the alarm, especially by Puerto Rican public officials, centered on evidence of the dispersal of Puerto Ricans within the public housing system. The concern was that dispersal would create lower geographic concentrations of Puerto Ricans and, thus, dilute the impact of the Puerto Rican vote. Though this was a legitimate worry for Puerto Rican politicians, Puerto Ricans themselves were more worried about getting into public housing in the first place. The Spanish daily *El Diario–La Prensa* articulated some of these fears.

> We are still the poorest among the low-income groups. We are therefore living in slums and are still at the tail end in being considered regarding our housing needs. Some people attribute this to an unwritten policy in the Housing Authority favoring one group against another. There are those who say this is the attitude of that agency toward the needs of the Puerto Rican families. What is true is that, though they have the smallest share of public housing, the tendency continues to reduce their share in that program even more. (1972a; author's translation of Spanish original)

Puerto Ricans became alerted to these inequities when they compared the proportional increase and decrease of blacks in public housing to that of Puerto Ricans. Blacks had increased as a proportion of the tenant population in 119 projects and decreased in only ten. Puerto Ricans, on the other hand, had increased their proportion in 85 but gone down in 44 (*El Diario–La Prensa* 1972a). Puerto Ricans protested these patterns and prodded the US Commission on Civil Rights to investigate their charge of discrimination. The commission held a public hearing in February 1972 to assess the civil rights of Puerto Ricans, particularly "the problem of access to public housing" (Buggs 1972).

This kind of attention to the civil rights needs of the Puerto Rican community appears unusual today given how much more the larger society ignores Latinos. But such attention was more frequent during the 1960s and '70s precisely because there was still a national mandate to expand the civil rights of minorities in the United States. That mandate began to seriously erode by the late 1960s, but still existed at some level in 1972.[4] It was the historical presence of a civil rights agenda that allowed Puerto Rican leaders to make legitimate demands to secure their own rights.

The Puerto Rican organizations that took a leadership role in protesting housing authority policies were primarily War on Poverty–funded groups with a smattering of private social and civic associations. At least nine Puerto Rican and South Bronx organizations, for instance, met with Housing Authority commissioner Aramis Gomez (the Puerto Rican leader of an earlier 1960s protest by Puerto Ricans against the West Side Renewal plans) and Amalia Betanzos, the commissioner of relocation, during 1971 and early 1972 to discuss Puerto Rican "community concerns."

Countless letters, petitions, mass sit-ins, and the actions of Puerto Ricans in official positions permitted Puerto Ricans to inject their case into the local policy agenda. They got new legislation and they used elected Latino officials to influence the housing authority. Puerto Rican tenants from the South Bronx, meanwhile, demonstrated at housing authority central offices in March of 1972 "to protest the nature of tenant selection at Betances Houses" (New York City Housing Authority 1972). Another demonstration in Seward Park, dubbed a "community upheaval" by the authority, also forced the housing authority to close an extension office of the housing authority's tenant selection division (Weiss and Tenner 1973, 12).

The housing authority appeared bewildered by the charges that it discriminated against Puerto Ricans. After one heated earlier demonstration at agency headquarters by a Puerto Rican group from the Lower East Side, a housing authority official casually dismissed the charges leveled against the authority as nothing more than "opportunism." The Lower East Side group, he said, had "apparently evaluated the housing authority as a [sic] most vulnerable public agency with which it has contact and intends to attack other elements of the official establishment through the Housing Authority" (Roye 1969).

In an effort probably intended to make sense of, as well as respond to, Puerto Rican protests, dazed officials at the housing authority began to issue internal weekly "Tension Reports" on the recurrent demonstrations. The authority also instructed the tenant selection division of the housing authority to warn its staff about the constant pressure they would face on the job since individual and mass sit-ins had become "the order of the day." The division's staff handbook further declared that "our atmosphere is so frequently charged with tension that although all Chiefs have had experience in the Division, none are anxious for an assignment here" (Weiss and Tenner 1973, 2).

Elected officials representing Puerto Rican areas also put pressure on the authority. Various local and state elected officials requested that Housing Commissioner Simeon Golar ask about the status of Puerto Ricans in public housing. In one case, state senators Luis Nine and Robert Garcia got a bill passed in the state legislature during May 1972 that prohibited discrimination by public housing "against women who have had children out of wedlock" (*El Diario–La Prensa* 1972a).

The housing authority's public response, at first, was to insist that its tenant selection process gave "fair and equal treatment for all applicants" (Weiss and Tenner 1973, 2). But the demonstrations and the mobilization of support from Puerto Rican elected officials lucidly expressed what Janeway once called the "ordered use of the power to disbelieve." The weak have the ultimate yet overlooked power to refuse "to accept the definition . . . that is put forward by the powerful" (1980, 167). Distrust, in some ways, empowered Puerto Ricans. They forced the housing authority to undertake a special study of its admissions procedures. This report concluded that "Puerto Rican families who file applications with the Authority . . . appear to be getting their fair share of available apartments." This denial of bias was secretly amended, however, in the form of a hidden caveat, consisting of a handwritten note by Aramis Gomez attached to the original draft of this study.[5]

The note questioned whether authority "procedures [were] such as to discourage Puerto Rican families in need of housing from filing applications"

(Gomez 1972). This carefully worded private note was an admission that a "fair" admissions policy could still be biased against Puerto Ricans. Though most of the recommendations in the report aimed at no more than further study of the problem, one recommendation appeared, on the surface, to suggest that the protests were successful.

The Gomez report to Housing Commissioner Golar advised the authority to "mount a special program to direct additional Puerto Rican families to apartments that become available in the following projects that have had marked changes in occupancy, particularly in the last two years: Douglas, Carver, Wagner, Mott Haven, Mitchell" (Gomez 1972, 3). The data on some of these projects in fact show that the Carver, Mott Haven, and Mitchell projects, as well as several others, experienced a drop in Puerto Rican residents prior to 1972 but experienced increases thereafter.

From 1972 to 1980, the Puerto Rican percentage in Carver Houses, for instance, increased by almost 3%. East River Houses gained almost 11% in Puerto Ricans in that same period. These gains in the percentage of Puerto Ricans in these specific projects, furthermore, continued into the 1980s. Clearly, whether or not the authority formally implemented the Gomez recommendation, the changes in tenant population intended by it were, in fact, achieved. The housing authority's response to Puerto Rican dissent resulted, however, in a mere redistribution of Puerto Rican families admitted into public housing as a whole. The percentage of Puerto Ricans in all public housing, then and now, has not changed. The protests had only a small impact.

There are fewer Puerto Ricans in public housing today than one would expect given their share of the population. The initial increase in the Puerto Rican proportion of tenants in public housing leveled off. Thus, whereas in 1975 Puerto Ricans constituted 24% of all families in public housing, in 1983 they were only 26%, and 28% in 2008.[6] The major accomplishment was to force the housing authority to maintain or increase the concentrations of Puerto Ricans in particular projects.

It is also clear that Puerto Rican protests, rather than generating independent changes in authority policies, produced these new admissions patterns. Records show that the authority did not abandon its general preference for admitting "submerged," or temporary poor, middle-class (generally white) tenants. Another internal management memo in the same year reaffirmed, for instance, that the authority's "immediate concern should be the continuation of a tenant selection process that will result in attracting higher income stable families" (Mattuck 1972).

The policy of rejecting housing-needy Puerto Rican and welfare applicants to public housing continued apace. Puerto Rican protests, mobilization, and organization did very little to change fundamental housing authority policies. The authority made some cosmetic changes. But, ultimately, they kept their long-standing policy as managers of public housing for the fallen middle class rather than as charity providers. Political will does not always deliver influence as pluralists assume. Group mobilization, organization, and action are simply not enough.

One possible response to this conclusion is that the relative power of opponents also plays a role. Latinos often find that their opponents include not only other groups. They are also up against political, economic, and cultural structures in the city and in the United States that make social life possible. These *structures* mediate and make possible some actions and not others. They also grant greater power to some groups than to others. The next case study shows how Latinos have even benefited from that process.

CASE STUDY 2: POLITICS IN THE 1950S

Latino political influence seemed to become possible when the larger society needed Latinos more than they need it. Puerto Ricans were both "incorporated" into and "excluded" from New York City's mainstream political system during the late 1940s. On September 12, 1949, New York City mayor William O'Dwyer established the Mayor's Commission on Puerto Rican Affairs (MCPRA) with a mandate to ease "the integration of US citizens from Puerto Rico into the life of the city" (MCPRA 195, 4). The most unusual aspect of this initiative was that Puerto Ricans in New York had not asked for or organized for it.

Practically all of the heads of the city's government departments, as well as a large representative sample of the Puerto Rican leaders from Puerto Rico, served as members of the MCPRA. The MCPRA also proved very effective in adapting the delivery of New York City social services to the special needs of Puerto Ricans. The Department of Welfare, for example, hired over 480 Spanish-speaking caseworkers and personnel in 1953 (Sánchez 1990, 59). The MCPRA undertook similar reforms in education and housing services.

The MCPRA gave Puerto Ricans unprecedented access to local government by incorporating them and their needs into the policy process. Puerto Ricans did not enjoy this level of access prior to 1949, nor have they since the dissolution of the MCPRA in 1955. What accounts for the creation of the MCPRA? The reasons are complex and, generally, have little to do with interest-group organizing by Puerto Ricans.

The most important catalyst for this local government attention was that Puerto Rican cheap labor had begun to play a major role in salvaging the city's eroding manufacturing sector during the late 1940s and early 1950s. This was made very clear by the expressed concerns of city officials and by the impact of Puerto Rican labor on city industries. City hall wanted to encourage and maintain this influx of cheap labor into the city.

Additionally, Mayor O'Dwyer was also motivated by his close relationship to Luis Muñoz Marín, the new governor of Puerto Rico. Puerto Rico initiated political and economic policies during the 1940s that demanded siphoning off "excess" Puerto Ricans from Puerto Rico. The MCPRA facilitated this goal by providing information, recruitment, and socialization programs to encourage Puerto Rican migration to New York.

The third reason was more political. Vito Marcantonio was a radical Italian-American US congressman who represented East Harlem. Throughout his long tenure in the Congress, beginning in the 1930s, he often embarrassed US officials by his repeated calls for Puerto Rico independence. Marcantonio was also a vocal supporter of Pedro Albizu Campos, the Puerto Rican Nationalist Party leader who was Muñoz Marín's major opponent on Puerto Rico. When Muñoz Marín became governor, Marcantonio set his polemical sights on the flaws of the new commonwealth structure and the Operation Bootstrap economic program in Puerto Rico.

Marcantonio's criticism of Puerto Rico's status with the United States and his support for Puerto Rican nationalists irritated Muñoz Marín, who conspired with O'Dwyer to ruin Marcantonio in New York. The MCPRA was, thus, used to undermine the support of Puerto Rican New Yorkers for Marcantonio by providing them with many of the same services they were getting from Marcantonio's office. This attack on Marcantonio eventually became part of a larger US government effort to exclude and eliminate radical leadership as well as to demobilize the Puerto Rican community in New York.

The city eventually killed the MCPRA in 1955 by creating a new agency, the Commission on Inter-Group Relations (COIR), when it became clear that cheap Puerto Rican labor could not keep manufacturing in the city. Unlike the MCPRA, the COIR worked for all groups in the city and had no Puerto Ricans on its board. COIR could subpoena witnesses and records as a defender of "minority rights," whereas the MCPRA could not. COIR was a big liability for Puerto Ricans, however. It was designed to be a nonpolitical body.

The MCPRA was, in many ways, reminiscent of the old party machine of the late nineteenth century, where working-class votes were exchanged for services. The COIR, however, reflected the rise of the new social-work orientation in the city. It emphasized the need for professionalism and "healing" as opposed to political representation and power as the way to solve the city's minority problem.

The shift from the MCPRA to COIR was a big step backward in political power for Puerto Ricans in the city. Puerto Ricans stopped being what Jennings (1984) called active "clients" and became passive "recipients." In the MCPRA, Puerto Ricans were able to *transact* benefits. In COIR, Puerto Ricans *received* them. The differences proved profoundly debilitating for Puerto Rican political development.[7]

The process of selective political exclusion and incorporation of Puerto Ricans described in Case Study 2 challenges the pluralist presumption that the process of interest-group action and competition neutrally allocates political power. Political power appeared a lot harder for Puerto Ricans to grab in part because "insiders" in local government and in the economy were determined to protect it. At the same time, Puerto Ricans gained some influence because of their political and economic importance to the city. Power, in this case, appears not as a low-hanging fruit but rather as something hidden, biased, and protected. But was it "elites" with power who created and dispensed that power to Puerto Ricans?

THE RULING-ELITE APPROACH

Ruling-elite theorists believe that only a few people control the political process. C. Wright Mills described the organization of power in the United States as a pyramid. At the top is a "complex" of rulers composed of top corporate executives, the joint chiefs of staff of the military and high-ranking politicians such as the president. This elite, he argued, has "the power to make decisions of national and international consequence" (Mills 1956, 27). Beneath this level is a sector, the "middle layers of power," consisting of interest groups, the Congress, the media, and judges. These people have some influence on the policy-making process but not like that of the ruling elite.

At the bottom of the pyramid sit the rest of the population. These "masses" have little political influence, and those above largely manipulate them, much like what happened to Puerto Ricans with the MCPRA. In fact, Mills admitted as much when he said "the bottom of this society is politically fragmented, and even as a passive fact, increasingly powerless" (1967, 38).

Despite its considerable merits, ruling-elite theory does not fit the Puerto Rican / Latino experience. Still, several studies on Puerto Ricans, at least at some point, subscribed to this model. Journalist Dan Wakefield's *Island in the City* (1959) is the best example. Wakefield attributed the political failures of Puerto Ricans in New York during the fifties, somewhat vaguely, to "those forces that no one could quite pin down but which were against the Puerto Ricans; those invisible forces of bitterness and disregard" (1959, 278).

Like most elitist theorists, Wakefield assumed a unity of purpose and action among these elites, especially in targeting Puerto Ricans for repression. But what's not clear is why Puerto Ricans were targeted. Why did elites spend their time and resources on Puerto Ricans? There are no clear answers from elite theorists. At other times, Wakefield blissfully underestimates the impact of particular government policies on Puerto Ricans. For example, he dismisses the MCPRA, discussed above, as a "harmless propaganda group" without asking the critical question: Why did positive propaganda about a poor and weak group become so important to the city's elites in the early 1950s (1959, 265)?

The exclusion of Puerto Ricans as a group from the policy process also can be read as an exclusion of Puerto Rican leaders. Indeed, the city hall decision to create the MCPRA, discussed above, was, in part, an attempt to discredit and exclude radical leadership elements within the Puerto Rican community, like Vito Marcantonio, from the political process.

Most of the other studies in this genre simply describe and identify Puerto Rican leaders with little if any reflection of what these leaders mean for the sources and shape of power in the Puerto Rican community. George E. Martin (1975), for example, used Floyd Hunter's "reputational" survey approach, in his book *Community Power Structure*, to identify those people Puerto Ricans themselves say are their leaders. Angelo Falcón conducted similar surveys during the 1970s and 1980s.

A big problem for elitist theory is that there is no one within the Puerto Rican community who is powerful enough to make "vital" decisions about government or the economy and, thus, to qualify as an "elite." Even the internal organization of Puerto Rican *barrios* was not in the hands of single individuals. Ramon Velez, Roberto Ramirez, and borough president Fernando Ferrer in the South Bronx were perhaps the closest any recent Puerto Rican leaders came to the elite label, but they were, at most, what C. Wright Mills would have called "middle-level" elites (Matos Rodríguez 2003).

Some analysts have attributed ruling-elite-type power to non–Puerto Ricans who are active or work in the Puerto Rican community. Luis Fuentes, for instance, made a case for the existence of a series of elite layers that culminate with the school system as the most immediate instrument of Puerto Rican oppression. Thus, his polemical attack on Albert Shanker, the head of the United Federation of Teachers during the late 1960s, claimed the existence of "a kind of piggy-back structure of American oppression . . . with each layer atop the other, and Shanker's union atop the schools of the poor, manipulated by the layers atop it, particularly the corporate-government interests that determine its contracts" (Fuentes 1980, 118).

What ruling-elite arguments such as Fuentes's ignore, however, is the extent to which significant changes in policy very often occur that conflict with apparent elite interests. The community movement to decentralize control of the New York City school system, which Fuentes helped lead, was generally successful despite Albert Shanker and the long and bitter teachers' strike called by his union in 1968. The community's victory appears hollow today since the local school boards became, first, a playground for corrupt and petty politicians rather than a true instrument of community control. Later, they were dismantled under Michael Bloomberg's mayoral administration. But they did once represent a real victory (Podair 2002). And it was not the only one. The interests and demands of the masses were, for example, also addressed by the enactment of minimum wage laws, unemployment insurance, civil rights laws, and other policies. The pluralists were wrong to assume that the American political system is totally open and accessible to any group. But it is also true that if there is a ruling elite, it does not always rule or rule in a unified way. Non-elites sometimes get their way.

What kind of elite is this then that permits followers to, even sporadically, decide policy? The ruling-elite theorist is quick to respond that particular elites support and sponsor such changes in order to appear flexible and satisfy public discontent without jeopardizing the mechanisms that allow them to rule. Social change for popular causes does not invalidate the notion of elite rule, according to this argument, because other factors point to an indomitable rule by elites even with some victories by the masses (Bachrach and Baratz 1963).

Pluralists respond to the elite model in several ways. They challenge the alleged dissimilarity between elites and the masses, the degree of access individuals are said to have to become members of the "elite circle," and the notion that elites are not accountable to the public. These responses by pluralists don't go very far in rebutting the ruling-elite thesis, however. They ignore the weakest link in the elite theorist's own argument, that is, the allowance recent elite theory makes for policy influence by the masses.

This allowance raises a number of issues. When do the masses have their way? Do elites measure the quantity or intensity of the demands by the masses to decide when to back off? Does the content of the demands make any difference? Do elites take action individually or collectively to fold under public pressure and to make victories by the public possible? Ruling-elite theorists generally can't answer these questions. They can't because they have never specified what, apart from the individual desire to rule, elites are really trying to protect.

CASE STUDY 3: VIEQUES PROTEST; ELITE POLITICS AND GHOSTS

What happens when Latino leaders try to influence the political process? The 1999 Vieques bombing protests showed, like no other moment, that Puerto Rican elected leaders, both in and out of Congress, are severely handicapped by the marginal status of their community in US society. The Vieques protest was a real-world lesson: a seat in Congress guarantees only the formal, and often limited, powers that result from becoming a representative. For most representatives that formal power turns out to be far from enough.

Puerto Ricans had attempted, since the early 1970s, to stop the US Navy's use of Vieques for target practice. Vieques is a small, partially populated island off the coast of Puerto Rico. In 1999, a stray bomb killed a Puerto Rican / Viequiese. The subsequent grassroots protests to get the Navy out of Vieques rose dramatically after that accident and attracted the attention of various Puerto Rican and non–Puerto Rican mainland political leaders.[8]

Months of nonviolent resistance produced arrests that heightened media attention. Almost all prominent and local Puerto Rican leaders from Puerto Rico and the United States as well as many Puerto Rican celebrities eventually got involved in this protest. This included political leaders from Puerto Rico's opposing political parties, the mayor of San Juan, labor leader Dennis Rivera, and local New York City Puerto Rican elected officials, as well as the entire Puerto Rican congressional delegation.

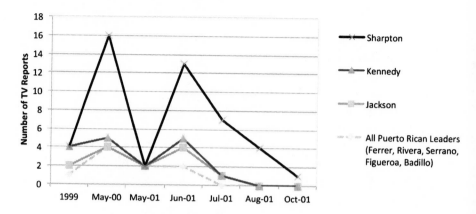

Figure 9.1 TV Reports on Vieques Issue by Political Leader, 1999–2001
Source: Vanderbilt University Television News Archive. http://tvnews.vanderbilt.edu.

This was an impressive political coalition and movement. The stout lineup of political and cultural leaders willing to expose themselves to public scrutiny, to stand up and speak for the weak, and willing to get arrested got plenty of media and political attention. Bronx Puerto Rican political leader Roberto Ramirez thought so.[9] He said: "What we did in Vieques, when we were willing to demonstrate, to go to jail, to make a statement on an issue that was morally correct is the greatest positive action we have made as political leaders."[10]

While all that was true, television media coverage suggests that the Puerto Rican leadership was important to the final victory but not critical to its success. The reason is that, for the most part, national television news hardly noticed the Puerto Rican leaders. Instead, as figure 9.1 shows, national news coverage on Vieques was repeatedly drawn to non–Puerto Rican political leaders.

US national television barely noticed long-term congressman José E. Serrano, New York City mayoral hopeful Freddy Ferrer, or Puerto Rican Legal Defense and Education Fund president Juan Figueroa. Instead, they hovered over the words and actions of African American political leader Jesse Jackson and political scion Joseph Kennedy Jr. Between 1999 and 2001, there were 61 national television newscasts concerning the Navy-Vieques protest.[11] Practically none of these broadcasts by ABC, NBC, CBS, CNN, and other networks bothered to feature or interview a Puerto Rican political leader.

Meanwhile, the television networks absolutely loved the minister and activist Al Sharpton. The coverage he received, as figure 9.1 shows, was greater than what was given to all Puerto Rican leaders combined. Thus, even on an absolutely Puerto Rican political issue spearheaded by grassroots and elected Puerto Rican leaders, the national media and the American public hardly noticed the presence and role of Puerto Rican political leaders.

This doesn't mean that the Puerto Rican leaders were not a factor in this protest. However, the key objective of these protests was to get media attention, in the hopes that television exposure would change public and government hearts and minds. Puerto Rican leaders protested towards those ends. It was non–Puerto Ricans, however, that actually reaped media coverage, while Puerto Ricans became nothing more than props for others on the national television stage.[12]

While the Vieques protest was important, it was the media coverage that most affected President Bush and the Congress. There were several possible pathways of influence. One was Bush's concern about the future Hispanic vote in 2004. Bush could not ignore the possibility that, as a possible swing vote in a close election, Hispanic voters might toss the election to the Democrats.

Even New York State Republican governor George Pataki was quick to demonstrate his alliance with Hispanic voters when he claimed that he wanted the bombing to stop immediately rather than in the two years Bush had planned.[13] In fact, some commentators attributed Bush's change of heart on Vieques directly to Pataki's position as well as to his political advisor Karl Rove's fear of a Hispanic voter backlash.[14]

Another argument is that Bush's response was simple political expedience, conceding what a popular referendum scheduled for 2002 in Vieques would have mandated anyway.[15] Any of these fears could have been what moved the president and Congress. The reality is, however, that whether they feared the Hispanic vote or the referendum or anything else, the *face* of that fear was essentially not Puerto Rican. The faces of the Vieques protest, as seen by the nation and the world, were those of white and black political leaders as well as religious leaders from the Baptist, Methodist, and Episcopal churches. They kept the issue alive before the national television public.[16]

It is important to remember that neither protest nor public opinion was enough to stop the Bush administration's "preemptive" policies in Iraq. In the end, Vieques may have been, as Juan Giusti-Cordero said, "a metaphor for something deeper."[17] Giusti-Cordero argued that Bush and the military were probably afraid that Vieques would lead, like the mythical falling dominoes, to future civilian efforts to throw out military bombing ranges and bases in other parts of the world.

At bottom, what is clear is that the president and the Congress didn't "see" Puerto Ricans and therefore could not possibly be scared by their protest. Puerto Ricans were and are mostly invisible on the national stage in the United States. The president was more likely afraid of awakening additional public protest against US military bases and power around the world. They were afraid that the Vieques protest could provide a historical precedent and give momentum to civilian efforts to weaken US military and state power.

The non–Puerto Rican political leaders who stood up against the Vieques bombing got most of the media attention. They were much more capable of using the media to discredit and undermine the military's national defense argument for keeping bases and practice facilities near other civilian communities. The Puerto Rican political leadership simply didn't pose a large enough threat. That was made clear by their invisibility.

Even if Latinos had members in the "elite," the theory has deep flaws. A better formulation is that power resides not in groups or individuals but in "social structures." One example is the institution of private property. The combination of laws, institutions, norms, and culture creates social structures that enable and limit actions of individuals, whether they are the masses or the elite. It is precisely those social structures involving private property, then, against which new social demands get measured, denied, or accepted.

Those structures do not exist by virtue of any specific actions and intelligence by individual elites. Social structures get built, maintained, repaired, or toppled by the interactions of countless actors in society, sometimes against their will or intent. And power gets perpetuated not just by the actions and decisions of all social actors, both elites and masses, but, in addition, by their inaction and nondecisions (Bachrach and Baratz 1963).

The possibility is that the foundation of power resides outside the framework of both the pluralist and ruling-elite perspectives. Ruling-elite theorists ignore the structural foundations of power because they view only individuals as important in the quest for and control of power. Pluralists, meanwhile, take social structures for granted as the "background" against which groups compete, neutrally, with each other for power.

THE POLITICAL ECONOMY APPROACH

The best example of a political economy approach in the study of Latinos in New York is the work of Alfredo Lopez (1973). Commenting (in a now classic work) on the development of Puerto Rican nationalism in New York City, he wrote that "as the question of political self-determination becomes important, the question of economic control rises. Economic control is the power to run, maintain, and, consequently, benefit from the means of production" (126). Lopez, thus, locates the sources of political power not in voting or representation but in the more general category of economic control. The control of substantial amounts of money clearly helps to create political power. But Lopez suggests that control over other institutions and resources is also important. Schools, workplaces, and government agencies are some examples.

In essence, for Lopez, "political power is the power to control all institutions that are basic to a people's survival" (1973, 267). If survival is not the primary aim in life, it is at least the means to all others. Control over basic sources of survival is, indeed, at a basic level a major source of power. Yet Lopez and others in the political economy tradition do not develop this idea of *control* very far.

What, for instance, accounts for the fact that Puerto Ricans usually don't control the social institutions necessary for their survival? How did this happen? Does a lack of such control mean that power is impossible for them? And what can Puerto Ricans do to get such control? Is this still true for other Latinos in New York today?

There are answers to these questions within the political economy perspective, especially in the reformulation outlined below. The political economy perspective has, however, lost traction recently within mainstream academia, in part because it could not fully answer the questions above. The structural and legal answer that the capitalist class controls the *means of production* just does not satisfy. It is both too narrow, limited to the economy, and too broad, explaining all political and cultural elements of capitalist society as mere *forms* of that class economic power.

Some Marxists explain the power workers sometimes have to get government to respond to their interests (e.g., minimum wage, public housing programs, etc.) as a function of the fact that capitalist societies need workers to exist if they are going to exploit and profit from them (Therborn 1982). This systemic need for workers translates into a "power capacity" that occasionally provides workers and their organizations (i.e., unions) with access and some influence over policy making.

In this argument, business or capital still enjoys a privileged position within policy-making circles, but its influence is not absolute. Workers must also have some ability to influence policy in order to protect their interests and existence. This is a good start. It is in this sense that the needs of corporations also get heard. *Too big to fail*, for instance, became the operative standard for the government bailout of corporations and banks during the 2008 recession.

All too often, however, both traditional and Marxist political economy treat power as a "thing," as something that individuals and institutions possess, carry, lose, or acquire. For traditional political economy, power is equivalent to money or the coercive dimension of state rule. Both money and arms are quantifiable, discrete, and transferable. Active individual and group agents are minimized if not eliminated from the explanation. The power of lower classes is explained as a function of how the class structures work.

One critique expands the Marxist claim that class power rests on control of the means of production. Thus, power is created from the relational interdependence of capital and labor rather than from a thing like money itself. Capitalists have power, in this sense, because they "own" the production process in social, cultural, and historical, and not just in legal, terms.

A "SOCIAL POWER" REFORMULATION OF THE POLITICAL ECONOMY APPROACH

A social power approach springs from the critique of the theories above. The critique of pluralist theory showed that political will is often not enough to produce results. And it also showed that political success can often come from doing little if other parties have deep interest in what Latinos have to offer. The alternative elite theory has little traction since Latinos have few elites and few leaders to whom others pay attention. And the idea that non-Latino elites control what happens in the Latino community fails from its inability to explain how it is possible for non-elites to occasionally get what they want.

The critique of elite theory points to the role played by social structures in making some things possible and not others. The problem with the structuralist position is that it does not easily account for Latino agency. Power becomes a thing that happens to Latinos. But it cannot show how Latino actions can create power. We are not automatons set in motion by larger forces. Somewhere between the extremes of total free will and total structural determination lies a valid account of power. The theoretical debate over the last two thousand years has been to find the sweet spot within those parameters. What can we do that others can't? Why can others do more? How can we be both free and constrained?

The way out of this morass is social power theory. Puerto Ricans are creative agents. They demonstrated consciousness and free will during the early 1970s campaign against the New York City Housing Authority. Yet they were not totally free. Puerto Ricans were limited by the power of elites and structures. They were constrained by social and natural laws, by institutions, by traditions and culture, and basically by each other.

The Puerto Rican and Latino experience teaches that the chains of domination are not just imposed from without. They also come from us. We set in motion, even if only partially, the restraints, the structures, as well as the powers of other people that block and channel our own actions. We are complicit in the power others have over us, even if we are mostly unaware of it.

The migration of Puerto Ricans and other Latinos to New York placed them in the hands of city political and economic leaders, institutions, and structural forces. In some historical moments, Latinos organized well and exerted political will, as in the public housing case study above. But those victories proved limited and temporary as the imperatives of existing social structures reasserted themselves.

At some moments Latinos also had unexpected influence. Those moments came mostly when the larger society developed a need for labor or votes, as Puerto Ricans discovered during the early 1950s. But that interest in Latinos by the larger community has not lasted over the years.

Puerto Ricans and Latinos never stopped striving to influence others. But these efforts, too, often fell flat. It's not just that elites or structures got in their way. They failed to move others because they could not find ways to build a sense of their own economic, political, or cultural value to elites and within existing social structures.

As social agents, we act and choose based on what we need, want, and desire. Unfortunately for us, sometimes what we choose comes back to haunt and even to dominate us. We choose to live on cake and find ourselves, much later, dominated by malnutrition if not by the ravages of diabetic disease. We seek careers in academia because we are drawn by the search for truth but find our careers warped by department chairs and deans with little regard for academic integrity. The payback is not moral but dialectical. It is our drives and interests that create and sustain power for others over us. We deliver ourselves into others' hands. It also works in reverse.

If power gets created or set in motion by desires and needs, it also gets reduced when we reduce or eliminate these drives. Almost every parent has witnessed how quickly most two-year-old toddlers learn to launch a gaggle of "no's" at gigantic control-freak adults determined to set the toddler's every agenda. Those "terrible" two-year-olds learn to thwart parental power by simply refusing (to desire) any snack, toy, or entreaty adults may offer them.

We take power back to the extent that we withdraw that need, that want, or that desire. Toddlers know this. So did the Stoics, poets, court jesters, nihilists, rebels, foot draggers, the sullen, and the lazy. They have all learned to detach from the world, as it is constructed, imagine a different one, mock it, despise it, or simply pretend to follow the rules while secretly subverting them. Each group, in its own way, rejects the values possessed by those on top. By doing that, they take power away from those on top. If they go far enough, these various "nay-sayers" can succeed in toppling those on top, bringing them down to their own level.

We can increase our power by increasing the degree to which others need or desire us as well as what we can offer. This is one reason why we go to school. We become educated and acquire degrees because we know that these are desired and required by those who have the jobs and salaries we seek. We hope to influence their hiring decisions by a display of our knowledge, skills, and degrees. To the extent that we can present ourselves as what the interviewer or the "dominant" seeks or imagines, we can increase our power. Images and imagination are often vital tools in this process. This is why the poet Percy Bysshe Shelley once said that "poets are the unacknowledged legislators of the world" (quoted in Stamm 1984).

The relationships that create power can take any form. They can be between capitalists and workers or between romantic partners. And for an individual or group to have power over others, there needs to be more than a relationship between them. The former must possess resources, actions, or relations that the others value. Power cannot come into being without the connections of a relationship.

What society, the state, or individuals value, therefore, is not limited to productive activity, however important this might be in a capitalist society. Public opinion in a media-saturated and media-valuing era is a source of influence that may supersede the power that comes from ownership of the means of production. Similarly, government employees have become more "valued" and thus powerful as government has become larger and a more integral component of how the economy works.

CONCLUSION

This reformulated political economy or social power approach also has distinct advantages over pluralist and ruling-elite approaches. It overcomes the structural blindness of the ruling-elite model. It does not make power merely a "thing" possessed by individuals. It provides some answers to the question "what do elites try to protect when they rule?" The social power model suggests that elites may or may not be motivated or equipped to protect social structures. But what's important for elite rule is whether those social structures and social relations get perpetuated. How that happens depends often on non-elites getting, but sometimes not getting, what they want.

Against the pluralist model, the political economy approach presented above recognizes the basic uneven distribution of power in this society. Power is not a fruit tree that all members of society have equal access to. Nor can power be manufactured simply by the bulldogged assertion of will. Wanting and striving are not enough. Power, in fact, comes to those who are wanted and desired.

Existing social structures certainly contribute greatly to making some things more valuable than others. This does not mean, however, that an individual or group cannot also make itself valuable. A pauper with the only camel in an empty desert has decidedly more power than the millionaire loaded only with credit cards and money in his pocket.

Voting and campaign contributions can be a source of power for individuals and groups to the extent that a politician needs and wants those votes and funds to win election. These needs deliver power to voters and political financiers. Once elected, however, politicians won't need votes again until the next election. Politicians can always use more campaign funds, however, especially since they can be banked for the next election. That makes money much more powerful than votes in our political system. The pluralist model is blind to all of this.

The outline of the social power approach presented here provides insight into some of the issues in the Puerto Rican and Latino political experience in the United States. It provides a good explanation for why Latinos have such a poor record of admittance to the selective public high schools in

New York City. It also explains why this failure seems to have been so easily tolerated by the Latino community and its leaders. As the *New York Times* reported, in 1971 one of these schools, Stuyvesant, "was mostly White, 10 percent Black, 4 percent Puerto Rican . . . and 6 percent Asian" (Kyle Spencer, "For Asians, School Tests Are Vital Steppingstones," October 27, 2012); but by 2012, Stuyvesant was "72 percent . . . Asian and less than 4 percent . . . Black or Hispanic" (ibid.).

One can debate the merits of the admissions exam, whether parents have a large role in test preparation, and the comparative educational desires of different racial/ethnic applicants. What's more important is what it reveals about Latino community power. The Latino community addressed this issue only in legal terms and mostly through a non-Latino organization, the NAACP. LatinoJustice PRLDEF (Puerto Rican Legal Defense and Education Fund) was a party to the lawsuit but largely missing in public discussion about the issue.[18] A quick search on Google shows that the NAACP had at least 125 web hits in the two months following the announcement. By comparison, LatinoJustice was mentioned in 7 results.

Then Mayor Michael Bloomberg responded to the NAACP lawsuit with blunt dismissal. "You get the highest score, you get into the school" (Spencer, "For Asians, School Tests," *New York Times*, October 26, 2012). Most telling was that the Latino community issued no protests, rallies, or calls for meetings. It was extraordinarily quiet and passive. Why? The answer would probably explain why LatinoJustice was also missing in action.

One possibility is that Latinos have come to grudgingly accept the idea that there is little the Latino community can demand of their mayor and of this city. Historian Steve Fraser argues in his new book *The Age of Acquiescence* that this lack of political will has become a general condition of the American public. This may be true. But Latinos have more to lose from remaining so quiet. In addition, this quiet and passivity may simply represent a shortage of leadership, organizations, and unity in the Latino community. But, ultimately, it also represents something else. The national calculus of power has changed so dramatically that it might be that the Latino community does not have enough capacity to speak the new language of power in this city.

The larger society seems to now see the Latino community less, and place even less value in it, than in the past. Latinos are no longer even remotely connected to the mainsprings of the present city's success, nor are they a vehicle of hope for what will help determine its future. No one is hitching economic or political wagons to Latino horses. Of course, this is not unique to Latinos. But Latinos have more to overcome.[19] The education and skills required for economic success in the present technological, fractured economy are simply too high and risky for Latinos to take on or overcome easily on their own. And given the global nature of New York's economy, Latinos offer no special benefit to the city's high-skill labor needs. This was not true of Puerto Ricans in 1949.

At the same time, other (ethnic, racial, and immigrant) groups appear much better prepared to meet the requirements for success in the present and future economy. The NAACP complaint about New York City's specialized high schools is an indirect admission of the advantage that other minorities, like Asians, have attained by their high rate of admissions to those schools.[20] Asians, for instance, constitute 72%, 63%, and 69% of all students at Stuyvesant, Bronx Science, and Brooklyn Technical high schools, respectively.

A more important liability may be the shift in contemporary political rhetoric. The Latino community cannot easily voice its demands in a language that draws upon old civil rights concepts (Lang 2015). The only policy issue on which Latinos have been heard and have been effective, to some extent, is immigration.[21] And that has been possible only by framing immigration as a civil rights issue.[22]

Nor can Latinos demand government attention when the pervasive view is that government cannot solve social problems. The "postracial era" many claim we are in means there is limited space within public discourse to deal with issues of racial equality and justice. Latinos, as African Americans have already learned, can be best heard mainly by offering paths aimed at achieving universal goals rather than specific Latino goals.

This resetting of the dominant political discourse creates an impossible and contradictory dynamic. How can Latinos, or any racial-ethnic group, launch a movement for and mobilize around universal goals and still address their own particular needs? The answer appears impossible at this point.

Thus, the transformation of the national political framework from civil rights to individual rights and the emergence of a neoliberal state have actively devalued the mechanisms and language that, in the past, helped make some power possible for the Latino community in New York City. In the long run, the emerging attention to reducing class inequality and to greater advocacy for the middle class in some places could help to address the many problems that beset the Latino community. But this is not guaranteed.

The limited success of the new (founded in 2014) Latino organization the Campaign for Fair Latino Representation, aimed at improving the Latino hiring record of the progressive Mayor Bill de Blasio administration, demonstrates this dialectic of social power. Latinos, as in this campaign, organized broadly, demonstrated leadership and media savvy and yet failed in their attempt to advance Latino interests. Fair Latino's primary request has been for a meeting with the mayor to discuss Latino needs. But as of December 2016, this progressive mayor, elected with over 85% of the Latino vote, has ignored them.

Gaining power for Latinos in New York City will take more than just increased numbers. It will take the kind of broad unity with which Latinos have little experience up to now. And it will take a radical adjustment in what is valued, by both Latinos and the larger society. Research shows that recent immigrant Latinos are more likely than US-born Latinos to persist in school and jobs and to move into the middle class (Crosnoe and Turley 2011). This suggests that Latinos must also find ways to minimize the impact of a racist culture that often causes them to turn to an "oppositional culture" and jeopardize their desire for a place in the larger society.

Gaining power will also depend on whether Latinos can attract greater interest in the (economic, political, and cultural) values Latinos can offer this city. Latinos may have to lower or change expectations in what they can demand or expect from the society, while raising interest from the larger society in what the Latino community can offer. Neither seems likely or practical, at least any time soon. The percentage of Latinos in the specialized high schools will likely remain lower than it was in 1970.

NOTES

1. See NAACP website reference for December 3, 2016, at http://www.naacpldf.org/case-issue/new-york-city-specialized-high-school-complaint. As of this writing (2016) the suit had not produced any legal remedy.

2. The exam remains. But Mayor Bill de Blasio put together a broad program of outreach and preparation for the city's minority students to improve their chances in the exam. See Miranda Katz, "NYC Will Spend $15 Million to Increase Diversity at Elite Public Schools," Gothamist, June 9. 2016, http://gothamist.com/2016/06/09/specialized_high_schools_diversity.php.

3. For more on the social power approach, see Sánchez (2007).

4. See Leadership Conference (2009).

5. A document I discovered decades after the fact in the New York City Municipal Archives.

6. US Census Bureau (2011).

7. Shortly after the creation of COIR, Antonia Pantoja, a young social worker at the time, joined the agency's staff as its only Puerto Rican.

8. See McCaffrey, Katherine T. 2002. *Military Power and Popular Protest: The U.S. Navy in Vieques, Puerto Rico*. New Brusnwick: Rutgers University Press.

9. The Bronx is one of five counties that constitute the City of New York.

10. Matos Rodríguez (2003, 206).

11. Vanderbilt Television News Archive.

12. There may have been more local television news coverage of Puerto Rican leaders in places like New York City. Since there is no archive to document this, local coverage was not analyzed.

13. See Deborah Ramirez, "Three Changing Places with Local Impact," *South Florida Sun-Sentinel*, June 30, 2001.

14. See David E. Sanger and C. Marquis, "U.S. Said to Plan Halt to Exercises on Vieques Island," *New York Times*, June 14, 2001.

15. See Angelo Falcón, "Liberating Vieques," comment, *The Nation*, July 9, 2001.

16. National Council of the Churches of Christ in the U.S.A., "11 U.S. Religious Leaders Ask Bush to Get Navy Out of Vieques," press release, April 18, 2001, National Council of the Churches of Christ in the U.S.A., http://archive.wfn .org/2001/04/msg00157.html.

17. See Juan Giusti-Cordero, "Vieques after September 11: KO'ed in the 12th round?," *The American Prospect*, December 19, 2001, http://www.prospect.org/web /view-web.ww?id=540.

18. The LatinoJustice PRLDEF press release on this complaint is at http://latino justice.org/briefing_room/press_releases/latinojustice_prldef_the_naacp_legal _defense_fund_and_the_center_for_law_and_social_justice_at_medgar_evers _college_file_complaint_challenging_admissions_process_at_nyc_public_specia lized_high_schools/index.html.

19. As the Federal Reserve argued in 2012, "While technological advances and globalization have created new jobs for workers at the high end of the skill spectrum and largely spared the service jobs of workers at the low end, these forces have displaced many jobs involving routine tasks—traditionally the sphere of middle-skill workers" (Abel and Deitz 2012, 1).

20. See, for instance, Katrina Shakarian, "The History of New York City's Special High Schools," *Gotham Gazette*, October 23, 2014, http://www.gothamgazette .com/index.php/government/5392-the-history-of-new-york-citys-special-high -schools-timeline.

21. The Latino organization that has captured the imagination of foundations, political leaders, and other organizations in New York is the Make the Road group. They appear to focus primarily on immigration and have had some success addressing these issues at the national and local level. See MTRNY: http://www .maketheroadny.org/whoweare.php.

22. See Esther J. Cepeda, "The Mirage of the Rainbow Coalition," *Desert Sun*, March 14, 2015 (first published in the *Washington Post*), http://www.desertsun .com/story/opinion/columnists/2015/03/15/cepeda-rainbow-coaltion-just -mirage/24797479/.

REFERENCES

Abel, Jaison R., and Richard Deitz. 2012. "Job Polarization and Rising Inequality in the Nation and the New York–Northern New Jersey Region." *Current Issues in Economics and Finance* 18 (7): 1–7. http://www.newyorkfed.org/research /current_issues/ci18-7.html.

Alt, James, and K. Alec Chrystal. 1983. *Political Economics*. Berkeley: University of California Press.

Bachrach, Peter, and Morton S. Baratz. 1963. "Decisions and Nondecisions: An Analytical Framework." *American Political Science Review* 57 (3): 632–42.

Buggs, John A. 1972. Staff director of Aspira, Inc. Letter to Luis Nieves, executive director of Aspira, Inc. LaGuardia Archives, New York.

Center for Urban Research (CUR). 2010. *The State of the Unions: A Profile of 2009– 2010 Union Membership in New York City, New York State, and the USA*. New York: City University of New York.

Crosnoe, R., and R. N. L. Turley. 2011. "K–12 Educational Outcomes of Immigrant Youth." *Future of Children* 21 (1): 129–52.

Dahl, Robert. 1956. *A Preface to Democratic Theory*. Chicago: University of Chicago Press.

El Diario–La Prensa. 1972a. "Poor Participation of Puerto Ricans in New York's Public Housing." February 14.

———. 1972b. "Nine's Law Eliminates the Last Vestiges of Discrimination in Housing Projects." May 25.

Falcón, Angelo. 1980. "Puerto Rican Political Participation: New York City and Puerto Rico." Paper presented at the American Political Science Convention, Washington, DC, August 28–31.

———. 1988. "Black and Latino Politics in New York City: Race and Ethnicity in a Changing Urban Context." *New Community* 14 (3): 370–84.

Fuentes, Luis. 1980. "The Struggle for Local Political Control." In *The Puerto Rican Struggle: Essays on Survival in the U.S.*, edited by Clara E. Rodríguez et al. New York: Puerto Rican Migration Research Consortium, Inc.

Gomez, Aramis. 1972. "Complaints of Puerto Rican Community-Tenant Selection and Apartment Assignments." Report by housing authority staff to Simeon Golar, housing commissioner, July 5. LaGuardia Archives, New York.

Harrigan, John J. 1989. *Political Change in the Metropolis*. 4th ed. Boston: Scott, Foresman and Company.

Janeway, Elizabeth. 1980. *Powers of the Weak*. New York: Knopf.

Jennings, James, and M. Rivera, eds. 1984. *Puerto Rican Politics in Urban America.* Westport, CT: Greenwood Press.

Lang, Clarence. 2015. *Black America in the Shadow of the Sixties: Notes on the Civil Rights Movement, Neoliberalism, and Politics.* Ann Arbor: University of Michigan Press.

Leadership Conference. 2009. "The 70s: School Desegregation and an Expanded Mandate." Chap. 4 in *Restoring the Conscience of a Nation: A Report on the U.S. Commission on Civil Rights.* March. http://www.civilrights.org/publications /reports/commission/the-70s.html.

Lopez, Alfredo. 1973. *The Puerto Rican Papers: Notes on the Re-emergence of a Nation.* New York: Bobbs-Merrill.

Martin, George E. 1975. "Ethnic Political Leadership: The Case of the Puerto Ricans." PhD diss., Fordham University.

Matos Rodríguez, Félix V. 2003. "Puerto Rican Politics in New York City: A Conversation with Roberto Ramirez." *Centro Journal* 15 (1): 196–210.

Mattuck, Joseph. 1972. Acting director of research. August 3 Memo to Marcus Levy, General Manager of the NYCHA. LaGuardia Archives, New York.

Mayor's Committee on Puerto Rican Affairs (MCPRA). 1953. "Interim Report of the MCPRA in New York City: September 1949 to September 1953." New York City Municipal Archives.

Milkman, Ruth, Laura Braslow, and Graduate Center. 2010. *The State of the Unions: A Profile of 2009–2010 Union Membership in New York City, New York State, and the USA.* New York: New York City Labor Market Information Service (NYCLMIS) / City University of New York.

Mills, C. Wright. 1956. *The Power Elite.* New York: Oxford University Press.

———. 1967. *Power, Politics, and People.* Edited by I. Louis Horowitz. New York: Oxford University Press.

New York City Housing Authority. 1972. "Tension Report for March 31." LaGuardia Archives, New York.

New York State Comptroller. 1976. "Audit Report on Tenant Selection by the New York City Housing Authority." Albany: New York State Comptroller.

New York Times. 1975. "Increasing Numbers of Problem Families in Public Housing." June 29.

———. 1975. "New York City Housing Authority Raising Maximum Income." January 22.

Podair, Jerald E. 2002. *The Strike That Changed New York: Blacks, Whites, and the Ocean Hill Brownsville Crisis.* New Haven: Yale University Press.

Roye, Wendell. 1969. Director of community affairs, New York City Housing Authority (NYCHA). Memo to Albert Walsh, chair, NYCHA. LaGuardia Archives, New York.

Sánchez, José Ramón. 1986. "Residual Work and Residential Shelter: Housing Puerto Rican Labor in New York City from WW II to 1983." In *Critical Perspectives on*

Housing, edited by Rachel Bratt, Michael Stone, and Chester Harmon. Philadelphia: Temple University Press.

———. 1990. "Housing Puerto Ricans in New York City, 1945 to 1984: A Study in Class Powerlessness." PhD diss., New York University.

———. 2007. *Boricua Power: A Political History of Puerto Ricans in the United States*. New York: New York University Press.

Shefter, Martin. 1994. *Political Parties and the State: The American Historical Experience*. Princeton: Princeton University Press.

Stafford, Walter. 1985. *Closed Labor Markets*. New York City: Community Service Society.

Stamm, Liesa, and Carol D. Ryff, eds. 1984. *Social Power and Influence of Women*. Boulder, CO: Westview Press.

Subvervi-Velez, Federico, ed. 2008. *The Mass Media and Latino Politics: Studies of U.S. Media Content, Campaign Strategies and Survey Research, 1984–2004*. New York: Routledge.

Therborn, Goran. 1982. "What Does the Ruling Class Do When It Rules?" In *Classes, Power, and Conflict*, edited by A. Giddens and D. Held. Berkeley: University of California Press.

Torres, Andres. 1989. "Labor Segmentation and Political Power: African American and Puerto Rican Labor in New York City." Unpublished paper. Center for Puerto Rican Studies, Hunter College, New York City.

Truman, David B. 1971. *The Governmental Process*. New York: Knopf.

Vanderbilt Television News Archive. http://tvnews.vanderbilt.edu/.

Vargas-Ramos, Carlos. 2003. "The Political Participation of Puerto Ricans in New York City." *Centro Journal* 15 (1).

Vega, Bernardo. 1984. *Memoirs of Bernardo Vega: A Contribution to the History of the Puerto Rican Community in New York*. Edited by César A. Iglesias. Translated by Juan Flores. New York: Monthly Review Press.

Wakefield, Dan. 1959. *Island in the City: The World of Spanish Harlem*. New York: New York University Press.

Weiss, Mel, and Ester Tenner. 1973. "Everything You Wanted to Know about Tenant Selection." Internal training manual for employees of the New York City Housing Authority. LaGuardia Archives, New York.

Wilson, Catherine E. 2008. *The Politics of Latino Faith: Religion, Identity, and Urban Community*. New York: New York University Press.

CHAPTER TEN

Latina/o Voting Rights in New York City

JUAN CARTAGENA

In June 2012, New York City witnessed a congressional primary election that crystallized decades of voting rights struggles and the promises of the Voting Rights Act of 1965 (VRA) for Latino voters. For the first time in New York, a third Latino congressional district was created, reflecting the growing demographic change in the city when Latinos went to court to force the issue. For the first time, a credible candidate who was Dominican, not Puerto Rican, had a decent chance at securing the sued-for Democratic Party nomination for Congress. For the first time in a long time, the debate over whether Latino communities are better off being represented by a Latino than by an incumbent African American was a subtext in the larger campaign debate. For the first time in a long time, serious questions were raised about the lack of sufficient bilingual assistance for Spanish-speaking voters that may have decreased the turnout in favor of the Latino candidate.

In short, Adriano Espaillat's challenge to the incumbency of Charles Rangel ushered in a new era of Dominican politics while reflecting the established, successful tools that Puerto Ricans used to gain their own footholds in New York City politics. Eventually Espaillat was successful in 2016 defeating Rangel's hand-picked successor and becoming the first Dominican elected to Congress in the nation. Latino political history is intertwined with Latino voting-rights history in New York City. Those tools, anchored in the Voting Rights Act, are also responsible for the election of the first Ecuadorean in New York, Assemblyman Francisco Moya from Queens, and years earlier, the first Dominican elected official in the country, Guillermo Linares from Manhattan.

As important as it is to study the political history of emerging Latino communities, their candidates for public office, and their interactions with the partisan political machinery, and given the role of law and civil rights enforcement in the city, it is equally important to study the role of the Latino voters and how Latino communities converted the struggle for civil rights into the protection of voting rights writ large.

Central to that analysis is the development and implementation of the Voting Rights Act of 1965 and its amendments. Considered the most effective of the civil rights acts passed in the heyday of the 1960s civil rights movement, the Voting Rights Act addresses two interrelated methods of discrimination in voting: *Vote denial* categorizes the set of laws and policies that impede equal access to voter registration and the voting booth. Poll taxes, literacy tests, white primaries, and grandfather clauses were successfully outlawed in the first wave of voter denial claims. Yet the vexing issue of how felon disfranchisement, which in New York dates back to 1821, still exists today and operates to thwart full Latino voting strength is a living example of vote-denial policies. In other parts of the country, voter photo-identification requirements are also modern-day vote-denial practices. *Vote dilution* refers to the minimization of the relative political strength of racial- and language-minority voters when their votes are aggregated. Where Latino voters coalesce around certain candidates and white voters coalesce to stop the election of minority-preferred candidates, certain election structures, such as at-large elections or unfair redistricting plans, can operate to cancel out the collective strength of protected minorities.

The Voting Rights Act has numerous provisions to eliminate the discriminatory effects of both unlawful vote denial and vote dilution. Section 2 of the VRA applies nationally and prohibits laws and practices that deny racial- and language-minority voters an equal opportunity to elect candidates of their choice. Section 5 applies to a small number of jurisdictions with a history of voter-related discrimination and requires them to get preapproval, called preclearance, from the federal government before implementing any change in election laws and policies. Section 203 also has a limited geographic scope in jurisdictions that contain citizens of certain language-minority background (such as, Spanish, Native American, or Asian languages) who need bilingual assistance because of their inability to fully and meaningfully cast their votes in an English-only system. And section 4(e) applies nationally, but only to voters from Puerto Rico who achieved at least a sixth-grade education there but have difficulty participating in the electoral process without assistance in Spanish.

Latino voting rights in the city can only be understood in the context of this forty-plus-year history, because New York City stood at the forefront of developing those laws and protections for marginalized voters throughout this time. And Latino voting rights in the city can only be assessed by focusing foremost on Puerto Rican voters, because for over forty years, they led the way in securing what we now take for granted in the many parts of the United States: the elimination of English-only election structures and the establishment of bilingual voting systems. It is to that history that we now turn.

PUERTO RICANS AND THE EMERGENCE OF LATINO VOTING RIGHTS

The migration of Puerto Ricans to the United States and their impact on the political framework of local politics in this country is neither of recent vintage nor of limited geographical scope. But what has not garnered enough attention is the role of the Puerto Rican community in the development of voting-rights protections for all Latinos in the United States. It all begins in New York City.

New York City enjoys a long history of Puerto Rican progressive electoral activism, starting in the first half of the twentieth century. In the period between the two World Wars, Puerto Ricans in New York had thirty-six vibrant political and social organizations and a voter registration rate of 50%.[1] The Puerto Rican population, which quadrupled from 1940 to 1950,[2] easily gravitated to Vito Marcantonio, an Italian congressman from East Harlem who became a tireless advocate for the working poor and the oppressed and a champion of Puerto Rican independence. Recognized as the "de facto Congressman for Puerto Rico,"[3] Marcantonio's politics proved too much for the entrenched power elite of the city and led to concerted efforts to defeat him and in turn destabilize the burgeoning Puerto Rican voting bloc in the city.[4] This newfound political strength that began with Marcantonio spilled over into the subsequent election of the first Puerto Rican official in the

United States in 1937, Oscar García Rivera to the New York State Assembly on the Republican and American Labor Party line. Eventually, the Liberal Party, the political arm of the garment workers union (ILGWU), along with the Tammany (Democratic) political machine, made it a point to block Puerto Ricans from leadership positions and stem the activism of Puerto Rican voters.[5]

Decades later Herman Badillo, a Democrat, became the first Puerto Rican elected to Congress in 1971. Badillo's congressional legacy was significant for the Puerto Rican community, because it coincided with the development of the Voting Rights Act, resulting in the surge of Puerto Rican elected officials, especially in Bronx County (a section-5-covered jurisdiction), and created an effective voice for Puerto Rican causes in Washington. That voice won VRA protection as well as federal sponsorship of bilingual education. By the 1990s, Puerto Rican political activism solidified in New York with the election of a second Puerto Rican to Congress,[6] Nydia Velázquez from Brooklyn, along with the emergence of the Bronx and Upper Manhattan as the base of Puerto Rican, and later, Dominican, electoral success.

None of these inroads would have been made, however, without the VRA, and these inroads, in turn, were presaged by a little-known provision of the original VRA, section 4(e), which was directed exclusively to benefit the Puerto Rican community: In 1965, literacy tests impeded the full enfranchisement of African Americans and were a clear target of the VRA. Despite the Supreme Court's pronouncement that literacy tests were constitutional,[7] the danger of the tests in the Deep South was in their discriminatory application. As a result, the coverage formula for section 5's protections specifically included literacy tests among the "tests or devices" that were used to trigger the VRA's most exacting provisions. Section 5's initial geographic scope was limited to a small number of states and jurisdictions, all of them in the South. In 1965, however, the discriminatory use of literacy tests as a prerequisite for voting went beyond the domain of southern states to include New York.

New York's literacy test requirement was the ultimate target of section 4(e), and it already had a history of discriminatory use against vulnerable populations in the state. In general, southern and eastern European immigrants had been the targets for literacy tests' exclusionary function.[8] In New York, the 1921 state constitutional provision mandating literacy tests for voting was equally exclusionary. As early as 1915, the debates by constitutional delegates established its clear racial purposes.[9]

By mandating English literacy exclusively, New York's literacy test impeded the full participation of Puerto Rican migrants, who used the courts to challenge its discriminatory nature. In 1961 in *Camacho v. Rogers*,[10] Puerto Rican voters tested the limits of the state's literacy test when applied to citizens from Puerto Rico. José Camacho was schooled in Puerto Rico in Spanish. He voted in Puerto Rico before migrating to New York but was unable to demonstrate literacy in English under New York law. Camacho was unsuccessful in his Fourteenth and Fifteenth Amendment constitutional challenge. But the issues raised in *Camacho v. Rogers* became the focal point of Puerto Rican political activism for years to come.

As the VRA was winding its way through Congress, the Puerto Rican community in New York was intent on finding a federal legislative solution to the issues raised in *Camacho v. Rogers*. The ultimate result of this effort was section 4(e), which states in part:

> 1. Congress hereby declares that to secure the rights under the Fourteenth amendment of persons educated in American-flag schools in which the predominant classroom language was other than English, it is necessary to prohibit the States from conditioning the right to vote of such persons on ability to read, write, understand, or interpret any matter in the English language.
>
> 2. No person who demonstrates that he has successfully completed the sixth primary grade in a public school in, or a private school accredited by, any State or territory, the District of Columbia, or the Commonwealth of Puerto Rico in which the predominant classroom language was other than English, shall be denied the right to vote in any Federal, State, or local election because of his inability to read, write, understand, or interpret any matter in the English language.[11]

With bipartisan support from Senators Robert Kennedy and Jacob Javits, section 4(e) was touted as an important remedy to the exclusion of Puerto Rican voters, who, through Congress's deliberate policies, were schooled substantially in a language other than English, but who were also required under New York constitutional law to demonstrate proficiency in English before exercising the franchise.

Puerto Rican activists also participated in this debate and testified before Congress in support of section 4(e) including Herman Badillo, Irma Vidal Santaella, and Gilberto Gerena-Valentín. Badillo, as noted above, became the first Puerto Rican elected to Congress and represented the Legion of Voters before Congress in 1965. Vidal Santaella subsequently became a judge of the New York County Supreme Court and was the first Puerto Rican woman admitted to the bar of New York State. She also represented the Legion of Voters in 1965 before Congress. Gerena-Valentín was a renowned community activist and became a New York City councilman from the Bronx in the 1970s. In the 1965 testimony, he represented the National Association of Puerto Rican Civil Rights. Their testimony[12] was clear: New York's English-only literacy test requirement was discriminatory on its face and as applied to Puerto Ricans in the city. They estimated that of 730,000 Puerto Ricans in New York of all ages, 150,000 registered to vote, but close to 330,000 were prevented from registering. Literacy test certificates would "suddenly disappear," causing delays of hours, if not the entire day, to replace them, or pencils would be missing whenever Puerto Ricans sought to take the test.[13] Collectively, the witnesses defused the "myth in [the] State of New York that a citizen can be an intelligent, well-informed voter only if he is literate in English."[14]

New York State fought back and challenged the constitutionality of section 4(e) all the way to the US Supreme Court. The court, in 1966 in *Katzenbach v. Morgan*,[15] upheld section 4(e) as valid, and in doing so, it unequivocally highlighted section 4(e)'s protection for Puerto Rican voters: "[Section] 4(e) may be viewed as a measure to secure for the Puerto Rican community residing in New York nondiscriminatory treatment by government—both in the imposition of voting qualifications and the provision or administration of governmental services, such as public schools, public housing and law enforcement."[16] Section 4(e)'s significance in the area of civil rights in general, and voting rights in particular, cannot be overstated. Rarely does the US Supreme Court rule on matters exclusively affecting the Puerto Rican diaspora. Rarely does Congress pass a law that applies only to Puerto Ricans to ensure their equal protection when they arrive in the United States. And rarely do any of these federal branches of government address discrimination against Puerto Ricans precisely because of their language background, thus implicitly equating language discrimination with national-origin discrimination in civil rights enforcement.

All told, the 1965 version of the VRA contained vigorous limitations on state power embodied in section 5's coverage of the Deep South, nationwide prohibitions on voting discrimination under section 2, and discrete protections against discrimination against Puerto Rican voters because of their unique language-minority status. Section 4(e) is often overlooked in the analysis of the VRA's impact on Latino voting strength by various commentators who erroneously conclude that the act's 1975 amendments expanding section 5 coverage to Latino citizens in English-only electoral systems and establishing section 203 bilingual assistance were the act's first targeted provisions to assist Latino voters.[17] In fact, section 4(e)—the Puerto Rican provision of the VRA—provided the means to extend the VRA's strongest protections under section 5 to New York, and in doing so extended the act's best tools to the only major metropolis outside of the Deep South. In 1970, Congress amended the threshold formula, and in 1971, three counties, Bronx, Kings, and New York, met the criteria for section 5 coverage. New York State again resisted and initially succeeded in stopping the application of section 5 in New York City.[18]

Simultaneously, a handful of federal court decisions in New York under section 4(e) underscored how New York's literacy test and English-only elections worked to discriminate against Puerto Rican voters. Lawyers at the Puerto Rican Legal Defense and Education Fund litigated these cases. In *Lopez v. Dinkins*,[19] Puerto Rican voters used section 4(e) to secure assistance in Spanish at the polls and the printing of ballots in Spanish. In *Coalition for Education in District One v. Board of Elections*,[20] a federal court overturned a school board election because, in part, of the city's failure to provide adequate bilingual assistance to Puerto Rican voters. Both of these cases paved the way for the wholesale provision of bilingual assistance in the case of *Torres v. Sachs*.[21] There, the court made two important findings. First it established that the city's English-only election system constituted a condition on the right to vote contrary to both section 4(e) *and* the 1970 Voting Rights Amendment. This conclusion effectively supported the construction that English-only elections were a "test or device" under the VRA—a critical legal interpretation at the time. Second, the court concluded that the right to vote requires meaningful access: "Plaintiffs cannot cast an effective vote without being able to comprehend fully the registration and election forms and the ballot itself."[22] As a result of the *Torres* decision, the United States reopened the court decision that exempted New York from section 5 coverage and successfully recaptured Bronx, Kings, and New York Counties under section 5.[23]

Thus, section 4(e) of the VRA, the Puerto Rican amendment, and the litigation that it engendered resulted in the act's strongest provisions to protect, first, African American and Puerto Rican voters, and, subsequently, all Latino and Asian voters in the city. The impact of section 5 coverage and protection of minority voters in New York City cannot be overstated. And all of that was due to the unique Puerto Rican provision of the Voting Rights Act.

But section 4(e)'s impact did not just stop in New York City—it had national import as well by demonstrating the viability of creating comprehensive, bilingual alternatives to English-only electoral systems, and on a large scale. With over 668,000 Puerto Ricans in New York City in 1960 and close to 812,000 in 1970, section 4(e) litigation worked to the benefit of hundreds of thousands of other Latinos in the city alone.[24] *Torres v. Sachs* and the other section 4(e) cases outside of New York City[25] created the template for full bilingual assistance above and beyond voter registration, to reach language access to the ballots and access to bilingual assistance at the polls. By the time the 1975 language-assistance amendments to the VRA were enacted, Puerto Rican voters were enjoying increased access to the political process through these alternative systems. These electoral reforms, forged by the continuous struggle of Puerto Rican activists and lawyers going back to the 1950s with *Camacho v. Doe*, justified the full expansion of bilingual voting assistance to all language minorities in the 1975 VRA amendments that created section 203. As the House Judiciary Committee noted at the time: "There is no question but that bilingual election materials would facilitate voting on the part of langauge [*sic*] minority citizens and would at last bring them into the electoral process on an equal footing with other citizens. *The provision of bilingual materials is certainly not a radical step.* . . . Courts in New York have ordered complete bilingual election assistance, from dissemination of registration information through bilingual media to the use of bilingual election inspectors."[26]

Section 4(e)'s national footprint went even further. The litigation it generated established the legal foundation to extend section 5's coverage to language-minority citizens in all section 5 jurisdictions. In 1975, the principal voting-rights advocates who urged Congress to amend section 5 to incorporate protections for Latino voters were Mexican American lawyers and activists.[27] The Mexican American Legal Defense and Education Fund (MALDEF) argued, "Federal courts have held that where Spanish-speaking Americans reside, the conducting of an election only in the English language is a 'device' which abridges or denies the right to vote of such citizens."[28] Congress agreed. In short, the construction of section 5's coverage formula to capture English-only election systems was won in large part by relying upon the only section 5 jurisdiction at the time that contained language-minority voters and that used the courts to assert their voting rights, specifically, the case of Puerto Ricans in New York City.

CREATING LATINO LEGISLATIVE DISTRICTS,
DEBATING WHO BEST REPRESENTS LATINOS

New York is unique in the way the Voting Rights Act operates on multiple levels and on such a large scale. On Election Day in New York City, over six thousand election districts with over three thousand electronic scanners and thirty-three thousand poll workers are in operation in a city of 8.5 million residents. The interconnection between the requirements of the VRA is an important element in the VRA's reach in the city. Federal observers—deployed pursuant to the VRA—provide information that is then used by the US attorney general in assessing the fairness of election changes for language-minority voters. Litigation under section 2 of the act is used to bolster denials of preclearance under section 5. And section 203 compliance issues become the focus of section 5 inquiries by the Department of Justice. Thus, despite its coverage of only a few counties in the state of New York, section 5 and section 203, in tandem with litigation, have addressed a breadth of voting-rights issues in the city. Besides language assistance, another staple of VRA protections in New York City is the creation of fair redistricting plans.

When it comes to elected officials, Latino communities have historically been excluded, and continue even now to be excluded, from American political spheres. In 2007, the census reported only 4,954 Latino elected officials in the United States, or *less than 1%* of the universe of over 500,000 elected positions in the country.[29] Despite this canyon of disparity, there is still a debate over the fate of majority-minority districts, a debate that began in earnest with the Supreme Court's decision in 1993 in *Shaw v. Reno*.[30] This is a debate that has benefited to some degree by concerns over its consequences for Latinos.[31]

Latino voters, like other protected minorities under the VRA, often face a polemic regarding race/ethnicity and political representation: the tension between having Latinos directly represent Latinos in a legislative body and having non-Latinos willing and able to adequately represent Latino interests. Much of this turns on what political scientists call descriptive versus substantive representation.[32] Descriptive representation is achieved when the representative comes from the same social or demographic group that she represents in an elected body. Substantive representation is obtained when representatives get results consistent with, and responsive to, the political needs of their constituents, regardless of the representatives' race, ethnic background, or social background. Adherence to descriptive representation would result in the creation of safe minority districts, that is, districts with high minority concentrations, in order to maximize the electoral success of the minority group. Conversely, distributing minority voters throughout more "influence" districts presumably increases the opportunities for minorities to elect candidates of choice who may not be of their race but would represent their interests.

The question for Latinos nationally is whether at this point of their political development they must be descriptively represented in their respective legislatures in order to be fairly represented. In other words, there are few places like Bronx County or Dade County, Florida, where the voting strength of Latinos is mirrored in the halls of their local legislative bodies. Yet when compared to the inroads made by African American elected officials, Latinos' progress has failed to reach parity in many jurisdictions. While Latinos share many attributes, opportunities, and lessons learned with African Americans in over forty years of VRA protection, the debate must still account for them separately in order to address their unique needs today and before the rules of the game are inexorably changed.

For decades, the VRA has been interpreted by the courts to require majority-minority districts in spite of some of these recent criticisms. In New York City majority-Latino districts have been created to comply with both section 2 and section 5 of the VRA. On multiple occasions, the Department of Justice has denied preclearance to unfair redistricting plans precisely because they failed to give Latinos an equal electoral opportunity by failing to create Latino majority districts. The classic example in this regard is the redistricting of the New York City Council in the 1980s.

In 1981, Mayor Edward Koch signed into law a city council redistricting ordinance with barely any protest from the eight minority members of the council. While African Americans and Latinos rose to 47% of the city's population at the time, the city council plan created only eight minority districts in a forty-five member council. The city's leadership explained its inability to create additional electoral opportunities for black and Latino voters by heralding a pervasive integration of the city's residents on a scale never seen before. In the Bronx, at that time two-thirds black and Latino, the council created only two minority districts out of six, claiming it could not find enough minority concentrations since the minority population was allegedly diffused throughout the borough. The city submitted its new plan to the Department of Justice for approval but would only provide it with additional information in a piecemeal fashion after the Puerto Rican Legal Defense and

Education Fund disclosed the pressure placed on minority council members to support the discriminatory plan. Citing an affidavit from Councilman Gilberto Gerena-Valentín, which described how the leadership threatened to draw his residence out of his district if he failed to support the plan, PRL-DEF charged that the plan violated section 5 because it purposefully failed to provide Latino and black voters with an equal electoral opportunity. [33]

Arrogantly, the city continued its preparations for a September 10 city council primary election without having secured the necessary federal pre-clearance in advance. PRLDEF attorneys filed *Gerena-Valentín v. Koch*, one of three VRA suits filed to stop the elections, and on September 8, 1981, the federal courts canceled the elections in the wake of the city's failure to comply with the VRA. The city responded by trying to hold citywide and city council at-large elections on September 22, 1981. But again, at PRLDEF's urging, the Department of Justice denied preclearance for the request to include at-large council races in the newly scheduled primary precisely because of the "uniquely disparate impact on Spanish-speaking voters."[34] By October 1981, the Department of Justice denied preclearance of the original council redistricting plan, noting as well that Latino communities in the Bronx were fragmented illegally, with the result that their voting strength was diluted. A remap was now required, and the city council reluctantly ceded to the demands of black and Latino voters. By February 1982, new minority districts were added in the Bronx and in Brooklyn, and minority districts in Manhattan were strengthened. The new plan was ultimately pre-cleared by the Department of Justice that year.

The 1981 city council redistricting battle was a watershed moment in securing voting rights for Latinos and blacks in New York City. It generated the beginnings of a minority-voting-rights bar in the city as the attorneys who worked on those cases (*Gerena-Valentín v. Koch*, *Herron v. Koch*, and others) would continue to counsel black and Latino voting-rights activists in the city for decades to come. It put teeth into the VRA as a federal court showed no hesitation in stopping an election at the eleventh hour in the country's largest city for its failure to get permission, in advance, to implement changes in a redistricting plan. And it provided Latino and black communities with a game plan to address their concerns directly to a responsive Department of Justice, a plan also emboldened by the courts' willingness to faithfully enforce the mandates of the VRA. Section 5's administrative vehicle to address concerns of minority voters provides a way for communities to directly relay their concerns about voter discrimination without going to court and without the need for an attorney. Because section 5 encourages jurisdictions to reach out to minority voters in advance of preclearance, Latino voters had an additional tool to stop discriminatory laws.

Afterwards, subsequent redistricting plans were successfully challenged because they failed to provide for Latino-majority districts. In 1991 the New York City Council redistricting plan was denied preclearance, and subsequently redrawn, because of the discriminatory effect it would have on Latino voters in at least two separate areas of the city: Williamsburg/Bushwick in Kings County (Brooklyn) and East Harlem / Bronx in New York and Bronx counties. The Department of Justice objected to unnecessary packing of Latino voters in the Williamsburg district while denying a fair chance of electing candidates of choice in the adjacent Bushwick district. In East Harlem, the objection centered on the failure to create a district that crossed county lines that would give Latino voters a chance to elect candidates of choice. In Queens, the Department of Justice commented that Latino voters were also not given an equal opportunity to elect candidates of choice because a majority district was not created.

In 1992, New York State was taken to task for its assembly redistricting plan. Faced with an identifiable, compact community of Latino voters in Washington Heights in Northern Manhattan, many of them from the Dominican Republic, New York State authorities attempted to fracture the community between two assembly districts (71 and 72), but were stopped. The objection letter highlighted the existence of racially polarized voting in that area. It also found that the state knowingly proceeded to fracture the Latino community and reduce its ability to elect candidates of choice: "The proposed district boundary lines appear to minimize Hispanic voting strength in light of prevailing patterns of polarized voting. Moreover, the state was *aware* of this consequence given its own estimates of likely voter turnout in Districts 71 and 72."[35] As a result of this enforcement of voting rights for the Latino community in 1996, Adriano Espaillat won election in Assembly District 72, becoming the first Dominican ever elected to the New York State Legislature.

These examples evidence the need to use Voting Rights Act protections and majority-Latino districts to create the electoral opportunities necessary to ensure equal access to political representation. But they beg the question: Are Latino-majority districts required to provide equal electoral opportunity? One social-scientific phenomenon, the existence of racially polarized voting, would tilt the answer in the affirmative.

Whether or not voting is characterized by racial polarization is a critical indicator of discrimination. Racially polarized voting ("RPV") is an indispensable element of proof in redistricting cases and others where structural impediments are challenged as preventing full and fair participation of the country's racial and language minorities. The data—a comparison of election returns at the election district level with demographic data at the smallest geographical unit—are analyzed using sophisticated statistical methods to prove the correlations between the race of the voter and the race of the candidate, while controlling for other factors. Two related phenomena are thus described: the level of political cohesion that may exist within the racial- or language-minority group (i.e., do minorities tend to support minority candidates? Or are there clearly identifiable minority-preferred candidates, irrespective of race?) and the presence of white bloc voting that tends to defeat minority-preferred candidates. In short, RPV describes voting behavior where Latinos significantly support Latino candidates and where whites behave correspondingly and, by and large, defeat Latino candidates.

New York City has had numerous episodes where RPV has affected the outcome of its elections. Not all the data have been put to rigorous, court-tested analysis, but there are enough episodes, in and outside of the realm of statistical significance, that speak to a continuing problem.

One of the earlier documented analyses of RPV—under more rigorous regression standards—was conducted by Richard Engstrom and led to a district court's finding of significant racially polarized voting in the 1985 case *Butts v. City of New York*.[36] Engstrom analyzed the1982 Democratic primary for lieutenant governor, where H. Carl McCall, an African American, ran against white candidates and also analyzed the 1984 Democratic presidential primary, where Jesse Jackson ran against Walter Mondale and other white candidates. Engstrom, using regression analysis, documented significant cohesion by African Americans and Latinos for McCall and by African American voters for Jesse Jackson. White voters, on the other hand, only gave McCall 24% of their vote and virtually no support to Jackson in 1984 (4%). Coupled with an analysis of the 1973 runoff election between Herman Badillo (Puerto Rican) and Abraham Beame (white), the court in *Butts v. City of New York* found that "racial and ethnic polarization and bloc voting exists in New York City to a significant degree."[37]

The Department of Justice has justified, in part, a number of its objections to preclearance under section 5 in New York City on the prevalence of racially polarized voting. For example, the 1992 state assembly plan was denied preclearance when it minimized Latino voting strength in Upper Manhattan by fracturing an identifiable community that was already suffering the effects of RPV. The 1991 elections for New York City Council and the 1990 elections for New York State Assembly have been identified as having evidence of RPV by at least two federal courts, in *Puerto Rican Legal Defense & Education Fund v. Gantt*[38] and *Diaz v. Silver*.[39]

The 2004 case of *Rodriguez v. Pataki* offers a limited analysis of RPV in a portion of Bronx County in a case that challenged the redistricting of the state senate. Despite its conclusion that the VRA was not violated, the court found that Bronx Latino voters in State Senate Districts 34 and 35 were politically cohesive and also concluded that white bloc voting defeated the Latino-preferred candidate.[40] While the evidence is limited—and ultimately the court denied the section 2 claim—the findings of the court are relevant here.

The *Rodriguez* case also offers a glimpse of additional evidence of political cohesion within black and Latino communities in the city. In the 2001 mayoral primary, where Fernando Ferrer (Puerto Rican) ran against Mark Green and other white candidates, Latinos and blacks coalesced behind Ferrer—the only election cited by the court where there may have been cohesion between the two groups. In other contests, African American voters demonstrated cohesion in the 1997 mayoral primary (63% voting for Rev. Al Sharpton) and in the 2001 city comptroller race, where William Thompson, an African American, defeated a white candidate, Harold Berman. However, there was no apparent cohesion behind Larry Seabrook's candidacy, at the same time that the Latino-preferred candidate was rejected both in the 1994 congressional district primary (the Puerto Rican, Willie Colon) and again in the 2001 citywide race for public advocate (Willie Colon, again). Similarly, Latino voters showed levels of political cohesion for Willie Colon on two occasions (the 1994 congressional Democratic primary and the 2001 public advocate race) but rejected the African American preferred candidates in the 1997 mayoral primary (Rev. Al Sharpton) and the 2001 city comptroller race (William Thompson).

Another comprehensive analysis of RPV in New York City was performed in 1991 by James Loewen for the Community Service Society regarding the viability of the city council redistricting plan after the 1990 census. The study, subsequently expanded and published in 1993,[41] analyzed a number of elections in the city where a minority candidate ran against a white candidate. The highlights include two primarily Latino-white races, for the citywide position of president of the city council. In 1985 three Latino candidates faced off against two white candidates (the African American candidate was not considered a major candidate in the analysis), and there was high cohesion among Latinos for the Latino candidates and high cohesion by white voters for the white candidates. Using regression analysis, Loewen concluded that in 1989 Andrew Stein, the incumbent, captured 90% of the white vote, Ralph Mendez captured 75% of the Latino vote, and blacks split among the two, but generally supported the white candidate.

Loewen also found that in general, white voters were the "most polarized group" among the voters he analyzed.[42] For Latino voters, he generally found the presence of RPV in the elections analyzed—both in their cohesion for Latino candidates and in the failure of white voters mostly, and to a much lesser extent, Black voters, to support Latino candidates. The study concluded with the admonition that "levels of political mobilization and racial bloc voting in New York City change constantly, due to registration drives, new candidacies, and changes in the underlying age structure and citizenship rate in the city's various ethnic and racial groups."[43] In short, racially polarized voting is a phenomenon in flux—and a phenomenon often used to justify the creation of majority-Latino districts, which in New York City paved the way to integrating city, county, and federal legislatures with Latino elected officials.

ENSURING COMPLIANCE WITH SPANISH-LANGUAGE ASSISTANCE COMES FULL CIRCLE

By the time of the 2012 primary election contest between Adriano Espaillat and Charles Rangel in the new 13th Congressional District, which covered El Barrio, Harlem, Washington Heights, Inwood, and a portion of the West Bronx, Spanish-language assistance to Latino voters had been a feature of court-ordered mandates for nearly forty years. *Lopez v. Dinkins* in 1973 and *Torres v. Sachs* in 1974 consolidated the promises of section 4(e) of the Voting Rights Act, and not just for Puerto Ricans. Instead, every Latino citizen who needed bilingual assistance reaped the benefits of this early litigation. But those court orders still required vigilance in 2012 as numerous complaints poured into the office of LatinoJustice PRLDEF about the lack of sufficient bilingual assistance in Dominican communities and about inadequate deployment of Spanish interpreters overall. Clearly both the need and the benefits of such assistance are still topics that require attention in Latino communities.

Aside from the value of promoting an open, accessible democracy, research conducted in six section-203-covered New York counties points to the salutary effects of providing bilingual assistance for Latino voters, namely, the positive correlation between section 203 language assistance and increased voter registration. One such study for New York concludes that after controlling for other factors that affect registration (e.g., education levels, nativity, residential mobility, etc.), analysts found that the use of ballots and registration materials in the covered language was significantly correlated to increased registration levels at both the city and county level for both Spanish- and Chinese-speaking voters.[44]

Nonetheless, the language-assistance provisions of the VRA require constant oversight. After the 2000 general elections, the New York State attorney general investigated the failure of the New York City Board of Elections to provide appropriate language assistance to Latino voters. Documenting future complaints and evaluating "flaws in election administration that may affect voters on the basis of race or ethnicity" were among the recommendations made as a result.[45] Major problems in securing oral assistance in Spanish at the polls continued to plague subsequent New York City elections. In 2001, the board was short 3,371 poll inspectors—15% of the total need. It was also short 33% of the total number of Spanish interpreters it needed for that election.[46]

Even considering the longevity of the Latino population in the city—especially its Puerto Rican community—the prevalence of Spanish-language use at home and the corresponding lower proficiency in English ensure that bilingual assistance remains a challenge in New York City.[47] For Latinos nationally, the percentage of persons who speak English less than "very well" and who report that Spanish is spoken in their homes is 40.6%. In New York City, 51% of Latinos who speak Spanish at home report lower proficiency levels in English. It is important to note here that the measure of speaking English less than "very well" is the measure used by the Census Bureau, along with other indicators, to certify section 203 coverage. Family literacy centers in New York City—indeed, all places where adults can try to learn English—are in very short supply, with demand far exceeding supply.[48] The city's inability to fully comply with section 203 requirements for Latino voters resulted in the assignment of federal observers in a number of elections since the 1992 amendments to section 203. Of the multiple times federal observers were present, the following elections were identified as warranting federal oversight to ensure bilingual assistance: September 2001 (Kings and New York Counties); October 2001 (Bronx County); September 2004 (Queens County).

New York City continues to be the city with the largest number of Puerto Rican residents: a sizable force of close to 720,000, making them the city's largest national-origin group among the city's 2.4 million Latino residents, at least for the next few years.[49] The conditions that led to their ability to gain access to New York's political process through Spanish-language assistance—including their strong ties to the Spanish language, the circular migration between Puerto Rico and New York City, and the juridical foundation of the unique relationship between the United States and Puerto Rico—have not changed appreciably, thus making Puerto Ricans' need for language assistance in elections today as vital as it was in the 1960s and 1970s.[50]

The provision of bilingual assistance today inures to the benefit of Dominican and Ecuadorean voters as well—groups that have had some electoral success. Assuredly, they will benefit Mexican American voters in the near future as well. But as seen in the 2012 congressional primary election in Harlem and Washington Heights, providing assistance where it is most needed is still a challenge in New York City.

CONCLUSION

Voting-rights enforcement guarantees opportunities, not results. The elimination of unlawful vote-denial practices and of illegal vote-dilution schemes provides only a foundation for an equal opportunity for racial and language minorities to elect their candidates of choice. Indeed, section 2 of the Voting Rights Act clearly prohibits any mandate on proportionality—the mere disproportionality between the share of the minority electorate and the number of minority elected officials does not by itself evidence a violation of law. Once given an equal opportunity to participate and to vote, the Latino electorate is responsible, for example, for exercising its discretion among competing candidates.

Nor does voting-rights enforcement guarantee postelection results consistent with the needs of the Latino community even if it is successful in electing Latino officials. Whether these Latino officials can exercise political power, however defined, is not a concern under the Voting Rights Act. In short, no matter how successfully Latinos use the courts and the legislative branch to establish voting rights, the endgame says little about the effectiveness of its representatives or the existence and enhancement of political power. Newly elected Latino officials may become marginalized by the legislative or party leadership once in office, or they may be last in line for choice appointments to important committees. Or conversely, they may learn how to exercise their influence by other means and bring home important public works projects or necessary funding. Again, whether they are successful or not is not within the purview of the statutes and case law that define voting rights today.

What the Voting Rights Act has done very successfully is to integrate the halls of legislative power (and judicial power in many cases in New York, as well) with Latino faces. Their mere presence acts as a shield and a sword in important deliberations over budget appropriations and legislative reform. This chapter presents a short description of some of those integration success stories[51]—stories that have paved the way for a reformation of how language, ethnicity, and race are played out in the New York City political scene. A comprehensive analysis of Latino political power would shed light on whether Latino voting rights in the city have succeeded in securing an equal share of political strength and influence. But what remains clear is that without the opportunities created by voting-rights enforcement, and the significant role Latino voters and communities played in that enforcement, Latino political power would hardly be part of the discourse.

POSTSCRIPT

At present, it is too early to discern the full negative impact from the June 25, 2013, Supreme Court decision *Shelby County v. Holder*. This decision struck down section 4 of the Voting Rights Act, which required New York City to gain preclearance or approval from the Department of Justice for any voting-law changes it sought to implement. In eliminating section 4 the Supreme Court rendered the section 5 preclearance provision inoperable. While the loss of section 5 is keenly felt throughout the South and especially for Latinos in Texas and Florida, its absence in New York City would have arguably prevented a diminution in Latino voting strength in two subsequent, unrelated incidents: the closing of polling sites in Charles Rangel's congressional district, which Adriano Espaillat complained of in his second campaign in 2014, and Governor Cuomo's inordinate delay in calling for special elections to fill vacancies in numerous state assembly and state senate districts throughout

2013. The real test in determining the value of section 5 in New York City, however, will be in the next round of redistricting after the 2020 census. Redistricting maps significantly change Latino voting strength and routinely part of the previously-monitored changes subject to section 5 review.

NOTES

1. Edgardo Meléndez, "Puerto Rican Politics in the United States: Examination of Major Perspectives and Theories," *Centro Journal* 15, no. 1 (2003): 29. This is the journal of the Center for Puerto Rican Studies, Hunter College, City University of New York.

2. Andrés Torres, *Between Melting Pot and Mosaic: African Americans and Puerto Ricans in the New York Political Economy* (Philadelphia: Temple University Press, 1995), 65.

3. Gerald Meyer, *Vito Marcantonio: Radical Politician, 1902–1954* (Albany: State University of New York Press, 1989), 171.

4. José R. Sánchez, "Puerto Rican Politics in New York: Beyond 'Secondhand' Theory," in *Latinos in New York: Communities in Transition*, ed. Gabriel Haslip-Viera and Sherrie L. Baver (Notre Dame, IN: University of Notre Dame Press, 1996), 272.

5. Ibid., 271. Also see discussion of the exploitation of Puerto Rican workers by the ILGWU in Herbert Hill, "Guardians of the Sweatshop: The Trade Unions, racism, and the Garment Industry," in *The Puerto Ricans: Studies in History and Society*, ed. Adalberto Lopez and James Petras (Cambridge, MA: Schenkman, 1974), 384–416.

6. Nydia Velázquez, Democrat, was elected to Congress in 1992 and continues to serve. She is the first and only Puerto Rican woman to serve in Congress. José Serrano represents the Latino congressional district in the South Bronx, which went from Herman Badillo to Roberto García to Serrano.

7. Lassiter v. Northampton County Bd. of Election, 360 U.S. 45 (1959).

8. John Higham, *Strangers in the Land: Patterns of American Nativism, 1860–1925* (New Brunswick, NJ: Atheneum, 1985; first published 1955), 101.

9. *Record of the Constitutional Convention of the State of New York, 1915, Begun and Held at the Capitol in the City of Albany on Tuesday the Sixth Day of April* (Albany: J. B. Lyon Co., 1915), 3:2912.

10. 199 F.Supp. 155 (S.D.N.Y. 1961).

11. 42 U.S.C. §1973b(e).

12. *Voting Rights: Hearings on H.R. 6400 before the Subcommittee No. 5 of the House Committee on the Judiciary*, 89th Cong., 1st Sess. (1965) at 508–17.

13. Ibid., 511.

14. Ibid., 510.

15. 384 U.S. 641 (1966).

16. Ibid., 384 U.S. at 652.

17. Juan Cartagena, "Latinos and Section 5 of the Voting Rights Act: Beyond Black and White," 18 *National Black Law Journal* 201, 207, n. 36 (2005).

18. New York State on Behalf of New York, Bronx and Kings Counties v. United States, 65 F.R.D. 10, 11 (D.D.C. 1974).

19. 73 Civ. 695 (S.D.N.Y. Feb. 14, 1973).

20. 370 F.Supp. 42 (S.D.N.Y. 1974).

21. 381 F.Supp. 309 (S.D.N.Y. 1974).

22. Ibid., 312.

23. New York State on Behalf of New York, Bronx and Kings Counties v. United States, supra, at 12.

24. Gabriel Haslip-Viera, "The Evolution of the Latino Community in New York City: Early Nineteenth Century to the Present," in Haslip-Viera and Baver, *Latinos in New York*, 14–15.

25. In Chicago: *Puerto Rican Organization for Political Action v. Kusper*, 490 F.2d 575 (7th Cir. 1973); in New Jersey: *Marquez v. Falcey*, Civil No. 1447–73 (D.N.J. Oct. 9, 1973); in Philadelphia: *Arroyo v. Tucker*, 372 F.Supp. 764 (E.D. Pa. 1974); in New York State: *Ortiz v. New York State Bd. of Elections*, Civil No. 74–455 (W.D.N.Y. July 10, 1975).

26. *Voting Rights Act Extension: Report from the Committee on the Judiciary Together with Additional, Supplemental, Separate Views*, 94th Cong., 1st Sess. (1975) at 24–25 (emphasis added).

27. Rodolfo de la Garza and Louis DeSipio, "Save the Baby, Change the Bathwater, and Scrub the Tub: Latino Electoral Participation after Seventeen Years of Voting Rights Act Coverage," 71 *Texas Law Review* 1479, 1482 (1993).

28. *Extension of the Voting Rights Act: Hearings on H.R. 939, H.R. 2148, H.R. 3247 and H.R. 3501 Before the House Subcommittee on Civil and Constitutional Rights of the House Committee of the Judiciary*, 94th Cong. 800, 864–65 (1975).

29. US Census Bureau, "Hispanic Public Elected Officials by Office, 1985 to 2008, and State, 2008," in *Statistical Abstract of the United States* (Washington, DC: US Census Bureau, 2010), 262 table 421, ftp://ftp.census.gov/library/publications /2011/compendia/statab/131ed/tables/12s0421.pdf. Also, Kim Geron, *Latino Political Power* (Boulder, CO: Lynne Rienner, 2005).

30. 509 U.S. 630 (1993).

31. For a discussion of how the attack on majority-minority districts affects Latino voting power in New York and for questions about the need for majority-Latino districts in particular and their relationship to overall Latino electoral participation, see Cartagena, "Latinos and Section 5 of the Voting Rights Act," 215n101.

32. Hanna F. Pitkin, *The Concept of Representation* (Berkeley: University of California Press, 1967), 60–111.

33. Juan Cartagena, "The Role of the Puerto Rican Community in the Reapportionment of Legislative Bodies in the '80s," in *The Hispanic Community and Redistricting*, ed. R. Santillan (Claremont, CA: Rose Institute, Claremont McKenna College, 1984), 2:174–211.

34. Ibid., 194.

35. Letter of James P. Turner, acting assistant attorney general, Civil Rights Division, U.S. Department of Justice, June 24, 1992, Re: Submission No. 92–2184 (emphasis added), accessed June 8, 2005, www.usdoj.gov/crt/voting/.

36. Butts v. City of New York, 614 F.Supp. 1527, 1545 (S.D.N.Y. 1985). Engstrom's analysis was subsequently cited by James Loewen as one of the earliest probative examples of RPV in New York City. See Richard Engstom, "Polarized Voting in Citywide Elections in New York: 1977–1984," cited in James Loewen, "Levels of Political Mobilization and Racial Bloc Voting among Latinos, Anglos, and African Americans in New York City," 13 *Chicano-Latino Law Review* 38, 41 (1993).

37. Butts v. City of New York, 614 F.Supp. at 1547.

38. Puerto Rican Legal Defense & Education Fund v. Gantt, 796 F.Supp. 677 (E.D.N.Y. 1992).

39. Diaz v. Silver, 978 F.Supp. 96 (E.D.N.Y. 1997).

40. Rodriguez v. Pataki, 308 F.Supp 2d 346, 420, 425 (S.D.N.Y. 2004).

41. James Loewen, "Levels of Political Mobilization and Racial Bloc Voting," 38, 41.

42. Ibid., 48.

43. Ibid., 72.

44. Michael Jones-Correa and Karthick Ramakrishnan, "Studying the Effects of Language Provisions under the Voting Rights Act" (paper presented at a meeting of the Western Political Science Association, Portland, Oregon, March 11–13, 2004; on file with author).

45. Ibid.

46. Ron Hayduk, *Gatekeepers to the Franchise: Shaping Election Administration in New York* (DeKalb: Northern Illinois University Press, 2005), 190.

47. New York City data reported in this paragraph come from the 2000 census. See also Nina Bernstein, "Proficiency in English Decreases over a Decade," *New York Times*, January 19, 2005. National data are derived from Roberto R. Ramirez, *We the People: Hispanics in the United States; Census 2000 Special Reports* (Washington, DC: US Census Bureau, 2004).

48. Bernstein, "Proficiency in English Decreases."

49. New York City Department of City Planning, "2010 Demographic Profile Data," New York City and Boroughs, accessed November 28, 2016, http://www1.nyc.gov/assets/planning/download/pdf/data-maps/nyc-population /census2010/t_sf1_dp_nyc.pdf.

50. Juan Cartagena, "Testimony of Juan Cartagena, General Counsel, Community Service Society, Before the Subcommittee on the Constitution of the House Committee on the Judiciary of the United States House of Representatives," November 9, 2005 (on file with author).

51. For a comprehensive description of voting-rights enforcement in New York City for black, Latino, and Asian American communities, see Juan Cartagena, "Voting Rights in New York City: 1982–2006," 17 *University of Southern California Review of Law & Social Justice*, no. 2 (Spring 2008).

CHAPTER ELEVEN

Latinos and US Immigration Policy since IRCA

National Changes, Local Consequences

SHERRIE BAVER

In recent decades, it has become fashionable for social scientists to differentiate between "borders" and "boundaries." "Borders" connotes a more dynamic, sociocultural construct in an era of rapid globalization, but "boundaries" is reserved for the more specific domain of nation-states and control of their territories (Duany 2011). While several contributions in this volume look at the shifting nature of borders and new understandings of sociocultural citizenship, this chapter focuses on the explicitly political definition of boundaries, and who is legally or illegally within those boundaries in the United States.

At present, immigration policy is a hot-button issue, not only in the United States but, increasingly, throughout the developed world, arousing citizens' fears about cultural dilution, national security, labor competition, and use of taxpayer resources. Given the context of these heightened concerns, the goals of this article are to outline the changes in US immigration policy since the 1986 Immigration Reform and Control Act (IRCA), the lack of comprehensive immigration reform since then, and the consequences of piecemeal reform for the Latino community, especially in New York.[1]

Comprehensive immigration reform would involve two basic features, a path to citizenship for the approximately eleven million undocumented people in the country (about eight million of whom are in the workforce) and stricter enforcement at the national boundaries and at workplaces. The discussion presented here on why comprehensive immigration reform has stalled since 1986 builds on the work of others (e.g., Skrentny 2011) and involves the above-mentioned national anxieties. The consequences of blocked reform since the 1986 IRCA amnesty have meant, especially since the mid-1990s, specific legal changes that have largely rendered immigration policy more restrictive and have made the lives of millions of undocumented workers more difficult both nationally and locally.

This chapter will unfold as follows. Part 1, at the national level, examines why comprehensive immigration reform is primarily a Latino issue and why it is controversial. Part 2 looks at federal immigration policy changes since IRCA in 1986. Part 3 focuses on immigration policy making in several US states in response to inaction at the federal level along with policy moves at the New York State and City levels. We conclude with some final thoughts on why both immigrants and the nation as a whole would benefit from a comprehensive initiative on immigration.

WHY IS COMPREHENSIVE IMMIGRATION REFORM A LATINO ISSUE?

The answer to this question is rather straightforward: the majority of unauthorized workers in the United States are from Latin America. One study (McCabe and Meissner 2010), for example, estimated that of all the undocumented, about 59% were from Mexico, 11% from Central America, and 7% from South America, totaling 77%.

Crucially important for this discussion is that large numbers of Latino families in the United States have both members with legal status and members who are unauthorized; and the number of Latinos and their families is growing. Between the 2000 and 2010 census, the Latino population grew by 43%, or four times the nation's overall growth rate of 9.7%. This represents an increase of about fifty million people, or about 17% of the US population. In 2012, about 23.3 million Latinos were eligible to vote, although only 48% of eligibles actually voted in the November presidential election (Lopez and Gonzalez-Barrera 2013).[2] While Latinos and Latino voters live in all fifty states, according to the 2010 census, more than 50% lived in just three states:

California, Texas, and Florida. Seventy-five percent of Latinos lived in eight states: California, Texas, Florida, New York, Illinois, Arizona, New Jersey, and Colorado (Ennis, Rios-Vargas, and Albert 2011). That is why immigration and voters' views on the issue matter deeply in those states.

WHY IS COMPREHENSIVE IMMIGRATION REFORM CONTROVERSIAL?

What are the key issues making comprehensive immigration reform, especially legalizing undocumented immigrants, so controversial? Three themes stand out: economics, culture, and disrespect for the law. First, economic arguments are made both for and against immigrants; however, "regarding economics, the complexity of the causal chains makes definitive statements surprisingly difficult" (Skrentny 2011, 275). Also worth noting is that economic arguments for and against immigrants do not fall into a neat liberal/conservative divide. While, in general, liberals are more open to a generous approach to immigration, this is not uniformly true, and some groups associated with conservative policy positions also hold that immigrants are good for the economy.[3] The US Chamber of Commerce, for example, supports comprehensive immigration reform. The chamber represents many small and medium-sized employers who believe that immigrants are entrepreneurial, are exceptionally hardworking, and will do the jobs that most American citizens reject, especially in agriculture, construction, and hospitality. In New York City, for example, immigrants make up 44% of workers and 46% of the incorporated-self-employed (i.e., small-business owners). Since job growth typically starts with small businesses, at least in New York, immigrants can be seen as a motor of economic growth rather than a drain.[4]

Another pro-immigrant economic argument is that more workers mean more tax revenue; and, on this point, illegal immigration is even better than legal immigration. The 2008 annual report of the US Social Security Administration, for example, noted that the growing numbers in the category "other than legal workers" was expected to shore up the program over the coming decades. According to the report, the taxes paid by the undocumented (partly because they cannot collect Social Security when they retire) would close 15% of the system's projected long-term deficit. A *New York Times* editorial on the report suggested that this fact highlighted "yet another irony in the nation's complex relationship with undocumented workers" ("How Immigrants Saved Social Security," *New York Times*, April 28, 2008).

Anti-immigration economic arguments have often been part of populist political strategies that have played to citizen fears. The first fear is that immigrants (especially the undocumented) take jobs from citizens. Low-skilled native workers are most likely to be competing with low-skilled immigrants, especially the undocumented, who will work longer hours for less. Gordon Hanson (2009), for example, found that undocumented labor was regressively redistributing income from low-skilled native workers to employers. If undocumented workers gained legal status, however, their pay as well as pay for native-born workers would likely increase. It becomes understandable, then, that since the 1980s, American union leaders (if not all the rank and file) have supported legalization efforts, though typically with sanctions imposed on employers for hiring undocumented workers.[5] Organized labor also had been divided on whether or not to support guest-worker programs, but in early 2013, the AFL-CIO gave qualified support to a guest-worker initiative.

While the population at large debates the causality of immigration's economic effects on specific sets of workers, most social scientists agree that for the economy overall, immigrants "increase tax revenue, help finance social security, bring in new home buyers, and improve the business environment."[6] It is also likely that while employers and the federal government may benefit from immigrants (e.g., immigrant contributions to Social Security), states and localities bear the burden of immigrant services. This may have been a major factor driving anti-immigrant campaigns in several US states.

Second, fears of "cultural dilution," especially now a fear of Hispanics and the Spanish language, pervade much of the anti-immigrant rhetoric. Noting that demanding immigrant labor and at the same time demonizing the immigrants themselves has been a persistent theme throughout American history probably will do little to stop the present-day restrictionists (Martin 2011). This certainly was a theme in the 2016 Trump presidential campaign. One often-heard charge is that undocumented immigrant women come to the United States to have "anchor babies," prompting some conservatives to call for changes in the Fourteenth Amendment to the Constitution, which grants birthright citizenship. Contrary to that allegation, however, a 2011 Pew Hispanic Center report found not only that about two-thirds of illegal immigrant parents of newborns had been living in the United States for at least five years but also that the birthrate among Latina immigrant women is rapidly declining, similar to the decline among American-born women.[7]

What may be new in our immigration history is that so many of the present-day newcomers speak the same language, Spanish; and so to some, it may seem like a flood (e.g., Huntington 2004). Still, the data reveal no basis for fears of unassimilated groups persisting through generations. An optimistic 2008 study (Kasinitz et al.) of the post-1965 second generation of immigrant children in New York found them fully assimilated and generally doing well. While some academic researchers had posited that the new second generation, due to their specific ethnic/racial distinctiveness, might face barriers to full integration into American life (e.g., Portes and Rumbaut 2007), Kasinitz and his coauthors found that the second generation had educational and occupational achievement leading, in general, to greater socioeconomic success than their parents or than other native-born young adults achieved. Thus they found a surprising and robust "second-generation advantage." Rather than feeling torn between two worlds—and speaking fluent English—members of the second generation were taking the best of both worlds. While these findings may not be true for all groups locally and nationally, the authors' conclusions are optimistic, especially considering that, at present, children with at least one immigrant parent make up close to a quarter of the US population.

Finally, it is not entirely unreasonable for citizens to view 11 million undocumented immigrants who have entered illegally or have overstayed visas as disrespecting US immigration laws. Still, once here, the vast majority of the undocumented are law-abiding residents, fully aware of the possibility of deportation for not obeying laws.

BACKGROUND: RECENT ATTEMPTS AT FEDERAL POLICY REFORM

In Aristide Zolberg's (2006) nuanced analysis of two centuries of US immigration history, he posits that immigration policy has been a conscious part of American political development, and Latinos, especially Mexicans, the largest number of immigrants to the United States, are a central part of the story. Specifically regarding Mexican immigration, before 1965, the US-Mexican border was essentially unmonitored and workers moved rather freely back and forth to work in US agriculture, since there were no restrictions on Western-Hemisphere immigrants during the era of the national-origins system. The process was encouraged and regularized through the US Bracero Program between 1942 and 1964.

US immigration policy changed dramatically in 1965 with congressional passage of the Hart-Cellar Amendments; this legislation ended the national-origins quota system as a response to the emerging civil rights agenda. Yet the consequences of the 1965 reform were "contrary to the tacit agreement to maintain immigration as a minor feature of the American existence.... While legislators did intend to eliminate the immigration system's discriminatory features, ... they did not anticipate that the incoming flows would expand as much as they did, nor that non-European sources would become as dominant" (Zolberg 2006, 337–38). Under Hart-Cellar, each country in the Eastern Hemisphere received a 20,000-per-year visa quota while all Western Hemisphere nations combined (including Mexico) were given an annual quota of 120,000 visas. Congress upped but also capped the Western Hemisphere immigration in 1976 by extending a 20,000 visa quota to each nation in the region. As a result of the 1965 and 1976 changes, the nation and New York City became strikingly more diverse. In viewing changes among the city's Latin Americans during those years, growth in the Dominican community was most apparent (Mitchell 1992; Hernández 2002).

The next major change in US immigration policy, the Immigration Reform and Control Act (IRCA), occurred in 1986 and represented several years of protracted and intense congressional negotiation. The process began in 1979 when President Carter established his Select Commission on Immigration Policy, chaired by Notre Dame president Fr. Theodore Hesburgh. The most noteworthy feature of IRCA was the amnesty offered to undocumented immigrants, a feature that has become central to political discourse around immigration reform ever since. Although approximately three million people were legalized nationally, this was far below what the Immigration and Naturalization Service (INS) predicted at the time. The agency had projected that at least 3.9 million immigrants would legalize. While the gap between estimated and actual applications was considered wide at the national level, the gap in New York City was especially striking. Estimates for New York were that one million people were eligible and that five hundred thousand would apply. In fact, the actual number of applicants in 1986 was 125,701; ultimately, 105,905 were successful (Lobo, Salvo, and Virgin 1996).

In addition to the national reasons for underapplication (lack of documentation, fear of exposing other family members, the requirement of five years of continuous residence, employers' fear of providing documentation), at least one study suggested that a reason for New York City's low application rate might be that the undocumented felt protected, because of working in ethnic business enclaves or because of the city's relatively liberal political climate (Meissner and Papademetriou, 1988). My own study conducted in 1989 concluded that few undocumented residents in New York were complacent. Everyone wanted a Green Card if possible (Baver 1996, 311–14).

John Skrentny (2011) has provided a detailed history of attempts at immigration reform since IRCA in 1986. He argues that because IRCA's legalization program had no effect on stemming continued illegal immigration, Congress has found it difficult to consider comprehensive reform since then. The first post-IRCA immigration legislation was the 1990 Immigration Act spearheaded by Senators Alan Simpson and Ted Kennedy. One of this act's major goals was redressing the "Third World Bias" of the 1965 Hart-Cellar Amendments. Kennedy's call for immigration "from the old seed sources of our heritage" was, no doubt, tied to his large number of Irish American constituents in Massachusetts and the large number of undocumented Irish workers in the United States. Still, in hindsight, the 1990 law was a reasonable compromise on US immigration policy. The 1990 law maintained a generous family-reunification provision, a key means for immigrants from Latin America and the Caribbean to enter the country legally. The law reduced the lengthy waits typical for reunifying spouses and minor children of US permanent residents, gave a one-year extension to 1986 IRCA applicants to complete their requirements, and granted temporary protected status (TPS) to undocumented Salvadorans in the United States. Thus the 1990 act, although trying to rebalance immigration policy towards Europeans, high-skilled workers, and the wealthy, gave little indication of the legislative mean-spiritedness that would soon follow.

By 1996, two laws showed that while Americans understood theirs was a nation of immigrants, "there was concern over whether it was becoming a nation of illegal immigrants" (Skrentny 2011, 273). Furthermore, perhaps as a harbinger of growing inequality in the United States, immigration became linked to anxiety over "welfare cheats." Thus, the Personal Responsibility and Work Opportunity Reconciliation Act (PRWORA) of August 1996 restricted eligibility of even legal immigrants for means-tested welfare programs. The second law coming one month later, in September 1996, the Illegal Immigration Reform and Immigrant Responsibility Act (IIRIRA), linked welfare reform with national security concerns; both acts represented a major restrictive and punitive change in US immigration policy. IIRIRA highlighted border-enforcement measures; called for mandatory deportations for most crimes, even minor ones, and even those committed by legal permanent residents; and increased restrictions on welfare benefits and reporting requirements that US educational institutions had to impose on foreign students. IIRIRA also contained the highly controversial section 287(g), which authorized the INS (since 2003 the Immigration and Customs Enforcement, or ICE) within the Department of Homeland Security to train local and state police to identify, process, and detain immigrants suspected of being undocumented. Section 287(g) was considered controversial because it involved local and state law enforcement officials in carrying out federal immigration policy.

When former Texas governor George W. Bush became president in January 2001, he declared interest in pursuing comprehensive immigration reform. As a Republican, Bush was indicating that a degree of bipartisan support remained for both broad legalization and enforcement. Bush went to Mexico in April 2001 to begin a series of talks with President Vicente Fox on a guest-worker program and a "process" (but never an "amnesty") for undocumented immigrants to earn permanent legal residency (and ultimately citizenship) after learning English and paying a fine.

The attacks of September 11, 2001, however, firmly placed immigration policy in a national security framework, and the subject was essentially shelved until the second Bush term (Duany 2011, 228–29). Legalization proposals even for "worthy" undocumented immigrants were doomed, and immigration policy became tightly linked to border security; enforcement measures became the preeminent concern. In his second term, President Bush tried in both 2006 and 2007 to promote immigration reform. The 2006 bill had a legalization program and passed the Senate but not the House. In 2007, with Democrats now also in control of the House, it seemed possible for legislation to pass, but at that time it did not even get out of the Democratic Senate (Skrentny 2011, 280). Since the mid-2000s, given the extreme political polarization in Congress and the economic downturn starting in 2008, promoting immigration reform that would include a legalization provision along with enforcement appeared virtually impossible at least for a time.

In 2008, Barack Obama, who won 67% of the Latino vote, took office saying that immigration reform was important but that the economy, health care, and energy policy were higher priorities. Also in his calculations, he must have been considering that the deep economic recession would make the potential political battle over legalizing undocumented immigrants especially contentious. Indeed, President Obama, ever searching for elusive

Republican support, spent his first term following an "enforcement first" strategy that one analyst characterized as "showing off by toughening up" (Skrentny 2011, 280). The administration prioritized enforcement and deportation; comprehensive legalization for the undocumented was essentially removed from the discussion.

Still, in 2010, another attempt at bipartisan comprehensive reform was tried, but the formidable senatorial team of Ted Kennedy and John McCain, who had worked together on the issue since the beginning of the decade, was no longer present.[8] In March of that year, Senators Charles Schumer (D-New York) and Lindsay Graham (R-South Carolina) offered a new compromise that, among other features, would require workers to (1) admit they broke the law and (2) carry a government-issued biometric identity card to prove their work eligibility. Additionally, the proposal minimized visa access for blue-collar workers while expanding visas for high-skilled, highly educated workers. Only an enforcement package, however, passed in August 2010.

Thus, since the mid-1990s, the primary focus of US immigration policy had been enforcement and deportation. From 2009 on, President Obama continued Clinton- and Bush-era enforcement strategies that included, first, fortifying the US-Mexican border. Spending on border controls increased greatly in the 1990s, starting with President Clinton (Kanstroom 2007, 13). By 2010 the number of border agents had increased fivefold over the 1993 total. As if this were not enough, the border is now also secured with sections of physical fences as well as virtual fences involving cameras, drones, and three types of sensors. Yet increased spending on the 1,969 miles of border was only one of several reasons (and quite possibly not the main one) for lower numbers of undocumented crossers at least during the 2008–12 recession.

This discussion must focus first on the US-Mexican border because until recently, Mexicans had constituted the largest number of undocumented (approximately 59% in 2010) coming to the United States. In recent years, though, the numbers for Mexicans have declined. (In 2016, they constituted 52% of the undocumented.) The number of arrests at the border peaked in 2000, and in 2010 was down by 75%. While the border crackdown or the US economic slowdown may tell some of the story, another part involves Mexico with its expanding economic and educational opportunities, rising border crime, and shrinking families. In 1970, for example, a Mexican woman had on average 6.8 children, but by 2011, the rate was 2.1, close to the US average. Another reason for the decline in unauthorized Mexican border-crossers is the increase in the number of visas Mexicans receive, especially the increased number of temporary farmworker visas, making legal entry easier. Significantly, while undocumented immigration may be on the rise again, these border crossers are less likely to be from Mexico and more likely to be from other places such as Asia, Central America, and sub-Saharan Africa.[9]

A second element of enforcement strategy has been sanctions imposed on employers for hiring undocumented workers, which were mandated in the 1986 IRCA. Although President Obama initially promised tough enforcement at workplaces as well as at the border, his administration adopted a somewhat "quieter" strategy than that of President Bush at workplaces. Under Obama, Immigration and Customs Enforcement (ICE) stopped the dramatic immigration raids that had been conducted at factories and farms under the Bush administration, which also involved deportations. Rather, the Obama administration focused on employer hiring practices instead of the workers themselves. Between mid-2009 and mid-2010, for example, the Internal Revenue Service (IRS) audited 2,900 companies and levied numerous fines in what immigration advocates characterize as "silent raids." Although the workers were not immediately deported, they were fired from their jobs.

A third piece of President Obama's enforcement strategy involved not only continuing but expanding President Bush's "Secure Communities" initiative. Daniel Kanstroom (2007) has written that, in fact, starting in the mid-1990s under President Clinton, the United States began an experiment in large-scale deportations. Kanstroom additionally notes that deportation is more than an instrument of immigration policy; it is also a "powerful, discretionary tool of social control" (3).

Secure Communities represented a deportation program that involved federal as well as state and local law enforcement agencies and often deported people based on very minor offenses. Even after Obama won 67% of the Latino vote in 2008, for each of the first six years of his presidency, deportations increased. Until mid-2012, he deported roughly four hundred thousand immigrants per year, exceeding all deportation during President Bush's two terms. Deservedly, this earned Obama the epithet of "Deporter-in-Chief" among immigrants and their advocates.

Under the Secure Communities program, anyone booked after arrest by local law enforcement was checked against both FBI criminal databases and Homeland Security databases, which recorded immigration violations. For the first few years after its inception, Immigration and Customs Enforcement was rather tentative on whether or not states could opt out of the program. Still, by fall 2011, Secure Communities had been adopted by more than 1,300 jurisdictions nationwide, and at that time, Washington mandated that all 3,141 state, county, and local jurisdictions had to comply by 2013. A major problem with Secure Communities was that its procedures were not error free, and hundreds of US citizens were held under the program along with others who should not be deported. Notably, through 2011, Latinos made up 93% of immigrants arrested under Secure Communities, although Latinos constituted only about 66% of the undocumented population in the United States ("Latinos Said to Bear Weight of a Deportation Policy," *New York Times*, October 19, 2011).[10] A more general problem was that the program eroded trust between immigrant communities and local police; some communities became reluctant to report crimes, which could damage efforts at community policing and, ultimately, result in greater levels of crime. Notably, the New York City Council voted to limit its cooperation with ICE in February 2013, and President Obama ended Secure Communities entirely in November 2014.

What are the real-world consequences of deportation? First, as already noted, deportation breaks up families because, not infrequently, the undocumented have spouses and children who are US citizens. At least one-third of people deported since 2008 had spouses or children who were US citizens. Furthermore, it may be especially damaging when US citizen children are separated from their noncitizen parents. A 2011 study found that because of families separated by deportation, more than 5,100 children ended up in foster care.[11]

Significantly, even the seemingly most politically acceptable immigration proposal to slow deportations of young immigrants, the "Development, Relief, and Education for Alien Minors Act," or "DREAM Act," languished in Congress for years after it was first introduced in 2001. After further half-hearted attempts, the next forceful try to pass legislation was in late 2010. While a bill did pass in the House, it failed in the Senate. At its simplest, the proposed "DREAM" legislation would grant a legalization path to eligible young people who came to the United States with their parents as undocumented minors. It was estimated that 2.1 million immigrant youth could be eligible for the DREAM Act and that nationally about 65,000 undocumented students graduate from high school or get a GED each year. To demonstrate their good character and potential contributions to the nation, DREAMers would serve in the military or complete at least two years of college and meet other requirements such as passing a criminal background check. Their ultimate reward would be citizenship.[12]

Absent comprehensive immigration legislation, President Obama began taking some executive actions, which do not require congressional action. A first move was to slow the previous deportation avalanche.[13] As of mid-2011, ICE would use more discretion in deportation proceedings, easing up on children, students, and those who pose no threat to national security and have deep roots in the community, a move the president's Republican critics in Congress swiftly labeled "a stealth amnesty."

As the 2012 presidential election approached, President Obama used his executive authority in June of that year to institute the program of Deferred Action for Childhood Arrivals (DACA). The program was aimed at unauthorized young people who had been brought to this country before age sixteen, had lived here for five years, and had not yet reached age thirty-one by June 15, 2012 (www.uscis.gov/DACA). This would allow as many as eight hundred thousand undocumented "DREAMers" to avoid deportation; to apply for work permits, Social Security cards, and authorization to travel outside the country; and, in several states, to apply for driver's licenses. By mid-2014, roughly six hundred thousand young people had been approved for this temporary reprieve.

In the November 2014 midterm elections, the Democrats lost both houses of Congress, thus continuing the impasse on federal immigration reform. Therefore, President Obama, who had won 71% of the Latino vote in the 2012 presidential election, again used his executive authority. Not only did he broaden the DACA program; he added a new program, titled Deferred Action for Parents of Americans or (DAPA). This initiative was intended to lessen the misery for many of the unauthorized parents of children who were US citizens or legal residents. It was estimated that four to five million people might qualify ("Obama Moves Ahead on Immigration," *New York Times*, November 21, 2014). Unfortunately the DACA expansion and DAPA were temporarily halted in February 2015 by a Federal District Court judge in Texas; and in November 2015, the US Fifth Circuit Court of Appeals (in *Texas v. United States*) upheld the lower court's rejection of President Obama's executive actions. The matter ultimately went to the Supreme Court, and in June 2016, the halt to the DACA expansion and DAPA was upheld after justices ended debate in a four-to-four deadlock. A tie vote automatically affirms the lower court's ruling.

STATE-LEVEL POLICY-MAKING IN RESPONSE TO FEDERAL INACTION

In the absence of comprehensive national immigration reform, states began making their own policy moves in recent years. While some conservative states, notably Arizona, Alabama, and Georgia, adopted an "attrition through enforcement" strategy, progressive states such as New York, Massachusetts, Illinois, and California followed a more benign approach to dealing with undocumented immigrants. It is worth noting that there is little evidence that "attrition through enforcement" strategies push most people to leave (or "self-deport"), no matter how miserable their lives become.[14]

While Arizona has been, perhaps, the most notorious state promoting harsh anti-immigrant measures, it shares some of its notoriety with Alabama, South Carolina, Utah, and Georgia, among others. The draconian 2010 Arizona measure (S.B. 1070) prompted the Obama Justice Department to sue to block parts of the Arizona law as well laws from other states. Specifically, the Obama administration sued to stop Arizona from requiring state law enforcement officials to determine the immigration status of anyone stopped or arrested if officials reasonably believe that person might be undocumented—a "show me your papers" provision. Furthermore, the government challenged the Arizona provision that allowed the police to arrest people without warrants if the police had probable cause to believe those people might have committed acts that are cause for deportation under federal law. In other states, the Justice Department sued South Carolina for making it illegal to transport undocumented people anywhere—including to hospitals—effectively denying them critical care and putting emergency medical technicians or other "Good Samaritans" in an untenable situation.

In 2012, Alabama, considered the regional capital of xenophobia, began forcing school districts to determine the immigration status of students and their parents and report data to the state. Alabama's law seemed designed to challenge *Plyler v. Doe*, the 1982 US Supreme Court decision giving all children the right to attend public school regardless of immigration status.[15] As of 2011, federal courts had nullified parts of some of these state laws and prompted the US Supreme Court to take up the Arizona law. In April 2012, the court heard arguments in *Arizona v. United States* and rendered what analysts considered a mixed verdict in June of that year. Still, an April 2013 decision, when the Supreme Court refused to hear an Alabama appeal, and an October 2013 settlement between Alabama and civil and immigrants rights groups can be seen, at least for now, "as the final blow to a breed of multi-pronged state laws aimed at cracking down on illegal immigration."[16]

In contrast, an increasing number of states and localities took a progressive, "welcoming" approach to the undocumented. For example, unlike much of the rest of the state, Tucson, Arizona, declared that its police would not do the work of the border patrol. Chicago, through its Office of New Americans, highlighted the role of both its documented and undocumented foreign-born residents as essential to its future economic growth. Indeed, the National Council of State Legislatures noted that in the first part of 2013, forty-three states and the District of Columbia had passed laws or resolutions related to immigrants, with a majority deemed immigrant friendly ("On Illegal Immigration, More Cities Are Rolling Out a Welcome Mat," *Christian Science Monitor*, November 28, 2013). For decades, New York City and State have been part of the "immigrant-welcoming" locales.

LATINO IMMIGRANTS IN NEW YORK STATE

The data show that while overall, the ethnic makeup of New York State is changing, the state is not being flooded with newcomers. In fact, in the first decade of the twenty-first century, New York State lost 1.6 million residents, the greatest decline since the 1970s and one of the highest rates of outmigration in the country. As a result of the relative population decline, the state lost twelve congressional seats between 1980 and 2011 (McMahon and Scardamalia 2011). After 9/11, foreign immigration to New York dropped by 25%, reaching its lowest level since the 1960s. The overall New York State population increase (roughly four hundred thousand people) between 2000 and 2010 largely resulted from the natural increase of births over deaths.

Yet also relevant to New York's changing demographic portrait, the 1990s witnessed a dispersal of Mexicans from their traditional residences in Texas and the Southwest to points throughout the United States and from newer immigrant-sending regions of Mexico directly to New York. This movement, along with new national-origin groups from Latin America, meant new Spanish-speaking residents were coming to New York State and City. According to the 2015 Census Bureau data, New York State had approximately 3.7 million Latinos, or roughly 18.8% of the total state population, a community composed of both US-born citizens and immigrants.[17] Governor Andrew Cuomo, who took office in January 2011, has maintained the pattern of New York as an "immigrant-friendly" state. Therefore, it is not surprising that in October 2011, for example, he signed an executive order making it easier for the roughly 2.5 million immigrants whose primary language is not English to access state services in the six most common non-English languages spoken in New York—Spanish, Mandarin Chinese, Italian, Russian, French, and French Creole.

New York City is the most populous city in the country, with 8.5 million residents—so the size and changing composition of its Latino population matters. In 1990, 1.7 million New Yorkers were Latinos, constituting 24% of the population, and in 2010, 2.4 million Latinos lived in the city, making up 29% of all residents. The national origins of New York City's Latinos have also changed in recent years. Puerto Ricans had been 49% of all Latinos in 1990 but had dropped to 31% in 2010. One consequence is that now the Latino population of New York City is more likely to be composed of immigrants, since Puerto Ricans are born as US citizens. While in 2010 Puerto Ricans were still the most numerous Latino national-origin group, between 1990 and 2010, Dominicans increased from 20 to 25% of all Latinos and are expected to surpass Puerto Ricans in absolute terms by 2025 if not sooner (CLACLS 2016). At present, Mexicans are the fastest-growing Latino national subgroup in New York, having increased from 3% in 1990 to 14% of Hispanics in 2010; they now represent the third-largest Latin American community. The Central and South American population also grew appreciably from 1990 to 2010.[18] It was significant for their potential political impact that in 2013 Latinos made up close to 25% of New York City's registered voters.

NEW YORK'S REACTION TO AN INCREASED FEDERAL FOCUS ON THE UNDOCUMENTED

Given that New York City has always had a large immigrant population and at present, two-thirds of the city's population are immigrants or children of immigrants, the New York mayors have been sensitive to immigrant concerns. Over three million residents are foreign-born, and over one-quarter arrived in 2000 or later. In 2012, Mayor Michael Bloomberg described immigrants as "a precious resource," and the lack of movement on comprehensive federal immigration reform as "the most ruinous economic policy."

On the specific issue of undocumented immigrants, the city has had a relatively long history of downplaying federal concerns. At present, New

York has roughly five hundred thousand undocumented immigrants, many of whom are Latino. An important landmark in New York City's policy toward the undocumented was Mayor Edward Koch's 1989 Executive Order 124. The order stated it was in the city's interest for undocumented immigrants to report crimes, to use the public health system, and to keep their children in school without fear of being reported to the federal government.

Enforcing federal mandates regarding the undocumented has continued as a gray area in New York public policy. The Bush Administration's Secure Communities program, begun in 2008 and expanded under President Obama, met a cold reception in New York City. When former governor David Paterson signed on to Secure Communities in December 2010, Scott Stringer, then Manhattan Borough president, was one of forty New York City and State elected officials who urged the governor to block the program. At the city level, public officials continued following Mayor Koch's logic, arguing that Secure Communities (like earlier federal programs) was not necessarily a deterrent to undocumented immigration but did deter *indocumentados* from interacting with local public officials. For example, not reporting crimes to the police would undermine an important New York City policy of community policing.

In 2011, Puerto Rican city councilwoman Melissa Mark-Viverito, representing a district (8) that includes Manhattan Valley and El Barrio in Manhattan and part of Mott Haven in the Bronx and has a large Mexican population, introduced a bill to soften the reach of Secure Communities locally. The bill, informally known as "ICE Out of Riker's," was signed into law in November 2011 by Mayor Bloomberg and limited the city's collaboration with ICE's detainer orders. City officials consistently maintained that since immigration is a federal responsibility, the city should not have to subsidize federal enforcement efforts; also, not collaborating with the federal government would allow New York to save tens of millions of dollars every year. This became a "nonissue" at the end of 2014, however, when President Obama ended Secure Communities throughout the nation.

A second policy area, in which New York City has taken a more progressive position, in contrast to New York State, involves undocumented students graduating from high school. Estimates are that about sixty-five thousand undocumented students graduate from high school nationally each year. It was further estimated that in 2012, for example, about 5,500 undocumented were attending colleges or universities in New York State, most in New York City.[19] Given the lack of movement on the DREAM Act at the federal level, students and their supporters have tried to make inroads on the state and city levels. As early as 1996, the City University of New York (CUNY) made it possible for some classes of undocumented students to receive in-state tuition; and in 2002, the then New York governor, George Pataki, granted undocumented students in-state tuition at public colleges and universities. Many argued this was a logical extension of the 1982 *Plyler v. Doe* decision, allowing undocumented children to attend public schools in the United States. The overall idea of these legislative moves was, of course, to help young people raised in the United States to graduate from college. This would allow them to strive for more than menial jobs they often accept because of their status and to fully contribute to the national economy.

By 2007, then-governor Eliot Spitzer introduced a New York State DREAM Act that would give undocumented students access to both tuition assistance and driver's licenses. The proposal, however, met intense criticism. In 2011, officials at CUNY as well as the State University of New York (SUNY) Board of Regents proposed expanding educational opportunities to undocumented college students by allowing them to receive state financial aid and scholarships; the idea was again rejected by the state legislature. At present, at least eleven states allow undocumented students to pay in-state tuition at public colleges and universities; but California, Washington, New Mexico, and Texas have passed a version of the DREAM Act allowing high school graduates access to state financial aid. Illinois has a DREAM Fund, which solicits private contributions for college scholarships for DREAMers.

Notably, under the leadership of Bill de Blasio and Melissa Mark-Viverito, who took office as New York mayor and city council president, respectively, on January 1, 2014, local officials signaled their progressive stance toward the foreign-born. The city council passed two laws to show support for all of the city's newcomers regardless of immigration status, further cementing New York's reputation "as one of the most accommodating places in the world for immigrants" ("Council Expected to Approve 2 Plans Aiding Immigrants," *New York Times*, June 25, 2014). The first reform provided municipal identification cards to all New Yorkers, joining other cities such as Los Angeles, San Francisco, and New Haven, which already had this program. For the undocumented, these cards would provide proof of residence and could be used to use public libraries, sign leases, and open bank accounts.

Another city initiative involved earmarking $4.9 million to provide a lawyer for every poor, foreign-born New Yorker who has been detained by immigration authorities and faces deportation. The issue is serious since the poor who try to fight their removal often face "an epidemic of schemes" by people posing as immigration lawyers. The problem is so widespread that in mid-2011, the Obama administration directed the federal Citizenship and Immigration Services agency to advertise in immigrant communities in major metropolitan areas to warn of scams and to bring criminal cases against "schemers" as negative examples. Additionally, a group of immigration judges were so alarmed by much of the "lawyering" they witnessed in their own courts that they offered a scathing indictment of deportation proceedings and commissioned a report. This study sampled cases in New York City between mid-2010 and mid-2011, and found that if immigrants (who have no guaranteed right to counsel in immigration proceedings) received counsel, it was inadequate in 33% of cases and grossly inadequate counsel in 14% (Katzman 2011, 1–10). In implementing this 2014 law, called the "New York Immigrant Family Unity Project," the city became the first jurisdiction in the country to fully fund a public defender system for the poor in deportation proceedings.

Finally, it would be incorrect to suggest that within metro New York's generally progressive reception of immigrants, no pockets of xenophobia exist. In recent years, Suffolk County on Long Island earned notoriety as a center of hate mongering and mistreatment of Latino immigrants, especially *jornaleros*, or day laborers. Suffolk's anti-immigrant atmosphere was stoked by, if not created by, pronouncements from prominent public officials, including a former county executive and several top county police officials. A major incident occurred in Farmingville in 2000, when two Hispanic immigrant men were lured to an abandoned building and viciously attacked by two white men. The most disturbing case, though, occurred in 2008 when an Ecuadorean immigrant, Marcelo Lucero, was hunted down and murdered by a group of local teenage boys that considered it sport to prey upon Latino men, whom they called "beaners." Lucero was beaten and ultimately killed by a knife, crowbar, and shovel. After the incident, the US Attorney's Office for the Eastern District of New York started investigating police behavior in Suffolk County, and after a four-year investigation and a subsequent agreement with the US Department of Justice in 2013, the police agreed to make significant changes in their practices. In addition to the general pledge to provide services that were "equitable, respectful, and free of unlawful bias," they agreed to do a more thorough job of tackling hate crimes, assigning bilingual officers to precincts with large numbers of Latinos, and meeting regularly with Latino and other immigrant community leaders ("Suffolk Police to Make 'Significant Changes' in Dealing with Minorities in DOJ Settlement," *Newsday*, December 3, 2013).

While not sinking to the depravity of murder, Port Chester in Westchester County gained media attention for ongoing anti-Latino discrimination. In 2007, although 46% of the population was Latino, as was 21.9% of the voting-age population, no Hispanic person had ever held public office. After complaints, the US Justice Department stopped a 2007 election for village trustees, arguing the town was violating the 1965 Voting Rights Act. In 2012 in East Haven, Connecticut, several police officers were indicted for "tyrannizing Latinos." Finally, erring on the opposite side of the law and revealing the ambivalence about low-wage Latino workers in suburban communities, in the mid-2000s, the mayor of Spring Valley, New York, was reprimanded for hiring undocumented *jornaleros* for town projects. He justified his act by arguing, simply, that they were cheaper than employees of the town's Department of Public Works.

SOME CONSEQUENCES OF STALLED IMMIGRATION REFORM

In earlier sections of this essay we raised the issue of potential economic costs and benefits of immigration, including undocumented immigration. We hypothesized that one factor provoking an anti-immigrant mood in some cities and states is that while the national economy might benefit from immigrant contributions, specific cities and states might suffer from increased demands on public education and social services. One main consequence of stalled immigration reform in recent years has been a patchwork of state and local immigration laws that, until the end of the 2008–12 recession, tended toward the "anti-immigrant" but in recent years have tended to be more generous towards immigrants, including the undocumented.

Stalled immigration reform also has social and psychological consequences for immigrant families, and especially children. Many immigrant households have members with mixed immigration statuses—citizens, legal residents, and undocumented. The stress in such families with an undocumented member has been captured by Harvard professor Hirokazu Yoshikawa (2011) in *Immigrants Raising Citizens*. Everyday experiences of such families often involve limiting or avoiding social contacts with other parents and authorities and limiting their children's participation in public programs and recreational activities. Thus, parents do not access valuable resources that could help with early development such as child care or food subsidy programs. Furthermore, undocumented parents often face exploitative working conditions—meaning low wages and longer workdays—compared to parents who are citizens or in legal status. Factors such as parental stress, economic hardship, and avoidance of center-based child care are all associated with lack of early skill development in children—resulting in poorly developed cognitive skills that can be recognized in children as early as age two. Yoshikawa estimated there are four million preschool children of undocumented immigrants nationally, many with hindered development.

It is worth repeating, however, that even with these early barriers, thousands of students in such families do manage to complete high school and would like to attend college. Passing a national DREAM Act would be not only an act of generosity towards young people who have grown up in this country but also a smart financial investment in our economy. Public policy scholar Dowell Myers underscores this point, arguing that since the total number of immigrants (legal and illegal) arriving in the first decade of this century was only half as many as in the 1990s, and with the size of the illegal population peaking in 2007, all immigrants should be viewed as a vast untapped human resource. The United States should be actively supporting their incorporation into the social fabric, which would include easily available English classes and help with attaining high school and college degrees (Dowell Myers, "The Next Immigration Challenge," *New York Times*, January 12, 2012).

President Obama won the majority of the Latino vote in both of his presidential wins, and while he pushed for congressional reform on immigration, until mid-2012, his most significant move was ramped-up deportations. Only in June 2012 did the president use his executive authority to begin the DACA program, and in late 2014 he again used his executive authority to introduce a broadened DACA program and a new deferral program for undocumented parents. that was halted by the Supreme Court in June 2016.

On a hopeful note, polls consistently show that a majority of voters support a comprehensive approach to immigration that is tough but fair and includes a path for legalization of status for at least some of the undocumented (Lawrence Downes, "When States Put Out the Unwelcome Mat," *New York Times*, March 11, 2012). Therefore, the time for congressional action is long overdue.

CONCLUSION

While some scholars wonder whether the nation-state is the appropriate unit of analysis for studying migration processes in the modern world (Wimmer and Schiller 2002; Duany 2011), at present the nation-state remains the key site determining who does and does not have full citizenship rights in specific political jurisdictions. Whether or not citizens of specific nation-states support immigration or are unsettled by it, immigration is inevitable; it is the human side of economic globalization. Therefore, a focus on US immigration policy and its consequences for the Latino community is relevant to the general themes of this book.

Political scientists focus on the nation-state, and several, recently, have theorized about how the United States might craft a more just immigration policy, including what to do with the country's *indocumentados*. Rogers Smith (2011), specifically concerned about the large undocumented-Mexican population, based his proposals on the concept of "constituted identities." Smith's concern for Mexicans stems from the fluidity of the US-Mexican border and almost a century of US guest-worker programs with Mexico. Through these programs, the US government has coercively constituted the identities of noncitizens and has hindered their ability to lead free and meaningful lives. Through past policies, the US government (unintentionally) has fostered Mexican aspirations for dual economic, cultural, and political citizenships; therefore, now, America has an obligation to deliver on its promises, while also helping to defray costs to states in which these immigrants might settle.

Although Smith limits his thoughts to Mexicans, I believe a similar argument might be made about people of the Caribbean and Central American nations, especially nations where the United States has played a pivotal role. One obvious case is Puerto Rico, where the United States has coercively constituted identities. Although island Puerto Ricans have US citizenship, in many ways, it is a second-class citizenship. The federal government might address this reality at the same time that it might energize the status debate, perhaps by offering the option of dual citizenship if Puerto Rico chose to become an independent nation.

Finally, in his detailed study of US immigration policy, Aristide Zolberg (2006) concludes that in a time of economic globalization, rather than beefing up the border patrol, the United States should be beefing up consular staffing to issue more visas. Writing in a post-9/11 policy environment, he argued that while it is reasonable to worry about national security, it is more urgent to protect victimized minorities. He concluded that "immigrants who feel welcome rarely set out to destroy their new home" (459).

In my essay for the first edition of this book in 1996, I wrote that "immigration policy . . . offers a window into the national psyche and touches deep feelings about what kind of country the United States is" (322). When that was written, the country was still enjoying the dividends brought by the end of the Cold War. We had not experienced the 9/11 attacks, the 2008 economic downturn, nor the deep divide now apparent in partisan politics. Thus, the policy proposals I mentioned in 1996 would seem to have little relevance in the present context; and the recommendations I offer now are more measured.

Washington now seems far more concerned with the domestic economy than with events in other world regions. As part of a focus on the domestic socioeconomic context, though, there remains the need to address the plight of millions in our country who represent an underclass of people with minimal rights. This situation is deleterious not only to them but also to American democracy (Ness 2011). If America wants to remain as a symbol of fairness to the world, it needs an immigration reform, and preferably a comprehensive reform. New York has tried to maintain a welcoming attitude towards immigrants and has considered them an economic resource. While we would like our city to be a model for the nation, only federal action can make that a reality; but this seems unlikely given the present political context.

NOTES

I thank my former colleague Diana Gordon for her helpful comments on this essay.

1. Writers at both the *New York Times* and *Economist* periodically reflect publicly on the appropriate term for unauthorized immigrants—illegal, undocumented, unauthorized, irregular. See, e.g., "Unauthorised," *Democracy in America* (blog), *Economist*, December 14, 2011, http://www.economist.com/blogs/democracy inamerica/2011/12/immigration. For better or for worse, I have chosen to use the adjectives, except "illegal," interchangeably.

2. In the 2016 presidential election, approximately 79% of the national Latino vote went to Hillary Clinton, and Secretary Clinton received 88% of the vote in New York State. See Gabriel Sanchez and Matt A. Barreto, "In Record Numbers, Latinos Voted Overwhelmingly against Trump: We Did the Research," *Washington Post*, No-

vember 11, 2016, www.washingtonpost.com/news/monkey-cage/wp/2016/11/11
/in-record-numbers-latinos-voted-overwhelmingly-against-trump-we-did-the
-research.

3. See Matt K. Lewis, "5 Reasons Conservatives Should Favor More (Legal)
Hispanic Immigration," *Daily Caller*, May 11, 2011, http://dailycaller.com/2011/05
/11/5-interesting-reasons-conservatives-should-favor-hispanic-immigration/.
Also relevant is Partnership for a New American Economy et al. (2013).

4. See, for example, "Firing Up America: A Special Report on America's
Latinos," *Economist*, March 14–20, 2015, or Lobo and Salvo (2013).

5. Waldinger (2008) wrote that union leaders have been farther ahead than
their membership on this issue. One union, the Service Employees International
Union (SEIU), has been notable in its lobbying efforts to pass a legalization program for undocumented workers. See "Union Seeks to Turn Hispanics against
Romney," *New York Times*, January 25, 2012.

6. For example, Tyler Cowen, "How Immigrants Create More Jobs," *New
York Times*, October 30, 2010.

7. Passel and Cohn (2011).

8. By 2009, Senator Kennedy had died and Senator McCain had joined his
more conservative Republican colleagues in Congress on this issue as part of his
2008 presidential bid.

9. The demographer Douglas Massey believes that Mexican immigration to
the United States correlates most closely with US economic growth and with the
number of visas handed out, not with increased policing of the border. He calls increased border enforcement "a colossal waste of money." See Damien Cave, "Better
Lives for Mexicans Cut Allure of Going North," *New York Times*, July 6, 2011; Jorge
Castañeda and Douglas Massey, "Do-It-Yourself Immigration Reform," *New York
Times*, June 2, 2012. The summer of 2014 witnessed an increase in the number of
unaccompanied, young Central Americans trying to enter the United States. See,
for example, "The Town Where Immigrants Hit a Human Wall," *New York Times*,
July 4, 2014. Finally, in late 2016, the Pew Research Center reported that the number of unauthorized immigrants in the U.S. had stabilized and that the countries of
origin had shifted. See Krogstad, Passel, and Cohn, "5 Facts about Illegal Immigrants in the U.S.," Pew Research Center, Fact Tank, November 3.

10. See also Kohli, Markowitz, and Chavez (2011).

11. Applied Research Center (2011).

12. For general background on The DREAM Act see several articles in
NACLA Report on the Americas 44, no. 6, *Latino Student Movements: Defending
Education* (November/December 2011).

13. See Lopez, Gonzalez-Barrera, and Motel (2011).

14. Jeffrey S. Passel and D'Vera Cohn (2011). Yet a few families do leave.
On the hardships caused by one family's euphemistic, "self-deportation," see "Do-
It-Yourself Deportation," *New York Times*, February 2, 2012.

15. In *Plyler*, the US Supreme Court held that children of undocumented aliens in Texas had the right to go to public school. The court rejected "creating a permanent caste of undocumented residents given that such an underclass represents difficult problems for a nation priding itself on adherence to principles of equality under law" (Kanstroom 2007, 16).

16. On the October 2013 Alabama lawsuit settlement see Muzaffar Chishti and Faye Hipsman, "Alabama Settlement Marks Near End of a Chapter in State Immigration Enforcement Activism," Policy Beat, website of Migration Policy Institute, November 14, 2013, http://www.migrationinformation.org/USfocus/display .cfm?ID=972.

17. Information about the Hispanic population of New York State in 2015 can be found by searching the QuickFacts section of the US Census Bureau's website: www.census.gov/quickfacts.

18. Search for population facts on the website of the New York City Department of City Planning: www.nyc.gov/planning. Also see CLACLS (2011).

19. Fiscal Policy Institute (2012).

REFERENCES

Applied Research Center. 2011. *Shattered Families: The Perilous Intersection of Immigration Enforcement and the Child Welfare System*. New York: Applied Research Center. https://www.raceforward.org/research/reports/shattered -families?arc=1.

Baver, Sherrie L. 1996. "New York's Latinos and the 1986 Immigration Act: The IRCA Experience and Future Trends." In *Latinos in New York: Communities in Transition*, edited by Gabriel Haslip-Viera and Sherrie L. Baver, 302–27. Notre Dame, IN: University of Notre Dame Press.

CLACLS (Center for Latin American, Caribbean and Latino Studies). 2011. *The Latino Population of New York City, 1990–2010*. Latino Data Project, report 44. New York: Center for Latin American, Caribbean and Latino Studies, November. http://opencuny.org/nlerap4ne/files/2011/11/The-Latino-Population-of -New-York-City-1990-2010.pdf.

———. 2016. The Latino Population of New York City 1990–2015. Latino Data Project, report 65. New York: Center for Latin American, Caribbean and Latino Studies, December. http://clacls.gc.cuny.edu/files/2017/03/Latino-Data-Project -Report-65.-The-Latino-Population-of-New-York-City-1990-2015-December -2016.pdf.

Duany, Jorge. 2011. *Blurred Borders: Transnational Migration between the Hispanic Caribbean and the United States*. Chapel Hill: University of North Carolina Press.

Ennis, Sharon, Merarys Rios-Vargas, and Nora Albert. 2011. *2010 Census Briefs: The Hispanic Population, 2010*. http://www.census.gov/.

Fiscal Policy Institute. 2012. *The New York State DREAM Act: A Preliminary Estimate of Costs and Benefits*. New York: Fiscal Policy Institute, March 9. http://www.fiscalpolicy.org/FPI-CostBenefitAnalysis-NYS-DREAM-Act-20120309.pdf.

Hanson, Gordon H. 2009. "The Economics and Policy of Illegal Immigration in the United States." Washington, DC: Migration Policy Institute. http://www.migrationpolicy.org/pubs/Hanson-Dec09.pdf.

Hernández, Ramona. 2002. *The Mobility of Workers under Advanced Capitalism: Dominican Migration to the United States*. New York: Columbia University Press.

Huntington, Samuel P. 2004. *Who Are We? The Challenges to America's National Identity*. New York: Simon and Schuster.

Kanstroom, Daniel. 2007. *Deportation Nation: Outsiders in American History*. Cambridge, MA: Harvard University Press.

Kasinitz, Philip, John H. Mollenkopf, Mary C. Waters, and Jennifer Holdaway. 2008. *Inheriting the City: The Children of Immigrants Come of Age*: Cambridge, MA: Harvard University Press.

Katzman, Robert A. 2011. "Foreword: Study Group on Immigrant Representation Symposium." *Cardozo Law Review* 33 (2): 1–10.

Kohli, Aarti, Peter L. Markowitz, and Lisa Chavez. 2011. *Secure Communities by the Numbers: An Analysis of Demographics and Due Process*. Berkeley: Chief Justice Earl Warren Institute on Law and Social Policy, University of California, Berkeley Law School. www.law.berkeley.edu.

Lobo, Arun Peter, and Joseph Salvo. 2013. *The Newest New Yorkers: Characteristics of the City's Foreign-Born Population*. New York: City of New York, Department of City Planning, Population Division, December. https://www1.nyc.gov/site/planning/data-maps/nyc-population/newest-new-yorkers-2013.page.

Lobo, Arun Peter, Joseph J. Salvo, and Vicky Virgin. 1996. *The Newest New Yorkers: 1900–1994*. New York: City of New York, Department of City Planning.

Lopez, Mark Hugo, and Ana Gonzalez-Barrera. 2013. *Inside the 2012 Latino Electorate*. Hispanic Trends Project. Washington, DC: Pew Research Center, June 3. http://www.pewhispanic.org/2013/06/03/inside-the-2012-latino-electorate/.

Lopez, Mark Hugo, Ana Gonzalez-Barrera, and Seth Motel. 2011. *As Deportations Rise to Record Levels, Most Latinos Oppose Obama's Policy*. Washington, DC: Pew Research Center, December 28. http://www.pewhispanic.org/2011/12/28/as-deportations-rise-to-record-levels-most-latinos-oppose-obamas-policy/.

Martin, Susan F. 2011. *A Nation of Immigrants*. New York: Cambridge University Press.

McCabe, Kristen, and Doris Meissner. 2010. "Immigration and the United States: Recession Affects Flows, Prospects for Reform." Washington, DC: Migration Policy Institute, January. www.migrationinformation.org/Profiles/display.cfm?ID=766.

McMahon, E. J., 2011. "Empire State's Half Century Exodus." Albany: Empire Center for Public Policy, September 16. www.empirecenter.org.

Meissner, Doris, and Demetrios Papademetriou. 1988. *The Legalization Countdown: A Third Quarter Assessment.* Washington, DC: Carnegie Endowment for International Peace.

Mitchell, Christopher. 1992. "U.S. Foreign Policy and Dominican Migration to the United States." In *Western Hemisphere Immigration and United States Foreign Policy,* edited by Christopher Mitchell, 89–123. University Park: Pennsylvania State University Press.

Ness, Immanuel. 2011. *Guest Workers and Resistance to U.S. Corporate Despotism.* Urbana: University of Illinois Press.

Partnership for a New American Economy, the Americas Society, and the Council of the Americas. 2013. *Immigration and the Revival of American Cities: From Preserving Manufacturing Jobs to Strengthening the Housing Market.* http://www.renewoureconomy.org/issues/American-cities/.

Passel, Jeffrey S., and D'Vera Cohn. 2011. *Unauthorized Immigrant Population: National and State Trends, 2010.* Washington, DC: Pew Hispanic Center, February 11. http://www.pewhispanic.org/2011/02/01/unauthorized-immigrant-population-brnational-and-state-trends-2010/.

Portes, Alejandro, and Rubén Rumbaut. 2006. *Immigrant America: A Portrait.* Berkeley: University of California Press.

Skrentny, John D. 2011. "Obama's Immigration Reform: A Tough Sell for a Grand Bargain." In *Reaching for a New Deal: Ambitious Governance, Economic Meltdown, and Polarized Politics in Obama's First Two Years,* edited by Theda Skocpol and Lawrence R. Jacobs, 273–320. New York: Russell Sage Foundation.

Smith, Rogers M. 2011. "Living in a Promiseland? Mexican Immigration and American Obligations." *Perspectives on Politics* 9 (3): 545–57.

Waldinger, Roger. 2008. "Will the Followers Be Led? Where Union Members Stand on Immigration." *New Labor Forum* 17 (2): 42–52.

Wimmer, Andreas, and Nina Glick Schiller. 2002. "Methodological Nationalism and Beyond: Nation-State Building, Migration, and the Social Sciences." *Global Networks* 2 (4): 301–34.

Yoshikawa, Hirokazu. 2011. *Immigrants Raising Citizens: Undocumented Parents and Their Young Children.* New York: Russell Sage Foundation.

Zolberg, Aristide R. 2006. *A Nation by Design: Immigration Policy in the Fashioning of America.* New York: Russell Sage Foundation.

CHAPTER TWELVE

Latino Core Communities in Transition

The Erasing of an Imaginary Nation

ED MORALES

There was still no central heating
in the tenements
We thought that the cold was
the oldest thing on the planet earth
We used to think about my uncle Listo
Who never left his hometown
We'd picture him sitting around
cooling himself with a fan
In that imaginary place
called Puerto Rico.

—Song 3, from "Three Songs from the 50s,"
by Victor Hernández Cruz

The slow erosion of spaces constructed by Puerto Ricans and other Latinos in New York City is often rumored or otherwise supported by anecdotal evidence of people leaving. Places that used to signify these spaces are noticeably changing. Yet despite all the talk, and the mounting evidence that stickball and salsa no longer seemed to permeate all of Spanish Harlem, Loisaida, and Williamsburg, the hard evidence was missing. Now, however, the census mapping that began to surface in 2011 and 2012 is telling an explicit and unavoidable story. In their color-coded simplicity, the maps show marked decreases in the Latino population of each neighborhood that has been associated with Latinos for almost a century, and their increase in the outer periphery. The same is true for African Americans. A major shift, or rather flip, in the racial and ethnic segregation models for our far-from-multicultural city is shaping up to be the biggest migratory trend since the postwar suburbanization era climaxed with "White Flight" in the 1970s.

Aside from considerations of how the urban core of New York City is being transformed to offer high-end goods and services in areas long associated with poverty, this radical alteration of our urban landscape is erasing the cultural fabric of neighborhoods that coalesced precious components of what we have come to know as New York's urban Latino identity. Like Central Harlem's once impregnable identity as Ground Zero for the Black cultural renaissance, with its political organizing and church-based influences, the symbolic meaning of El Barrio / Spanish Harlem is being discarded for a neoliberal project of investment meant to favor big real estate, corporate hegemony, and a tourism-driven economy; this project wants to turn Barrio dreams into safe, exotic fantasies for curious, moneyed spectators.[1]

Before we can determine whose barrio Spanish Harlem and the other Latino neighborhoods will be in the future, we need to know whose barrio it has been in the past. The evidence goes back as far as Bernardo Vega's classic texts[2] about the origins of Spanish Harlem / El Barrio. Puerto Ricans and other Latinos were drawn there in part because of the existence of Sephardic restaurants that served food somewhat familiar to Vega and his fellow Puerto Rican migrants. They were also drawn, in part, because it was Uptown African American, Italian, and, perhaps most importantly, on the margins of the New York real estate market—the inevitable magnet for working-class settlement. El Barrio / Spanish Harlem has been codified as a homeland (both real and imagined) for Puerto Ricans, and by extension, for many other Latino immigrant groups, not only through demographic and sociological analysis, but also through a tropicalization[3] process transmitted through literature, music, and visual art.

This kind of imprinting of a community and its culture onto a physical neighborhood space is a necessary requirement for such a community to become a "core community" for an ethno-racial group. The space is marked by a living language of culture and commerce and becomes imbued with the home country's spiritual and emotional energy, which attempts to transform the migrant's original identity in the homeland to a new one constructed and imagined for the neighborhood. Of course, much of what makes a neighborhood a "core community" is the physical presence of small businesses that sell the mangos and coconuts that not only create the tropicalized illusion but make concrete the presence of sellers and buyers, manifesting the community's "flavor."

But the work of creating such a "core community" is grounded in the construction of a collective identity. Luis Aponte-Parés's 1998 essay "Lessons from El Barrio—The East Harlem Real Great Society / Urban Planning Studio: A Puerto Rican Chapter in the Fight for Urban Self-Determination" begins with a discussion of how Antonia Pantoja located the forming of "community consciousness" in a constructed political-cultural environment called El Barrio. "Puerto Ricans, like other ethnic groups before them, began reshaping and appropriating the otherwise ordinary industrial city landscapes by building and claiming enclaves that *looked like them*,"[4] notes Aponte-Parés about the period between 1945 and 1960. El Barrio, he continues, became a paradigmatic "representational space" for the place where New York Puerto Ricans and other Latino migrants constructed their lived experiences.

However, the well-documented historical tragedy of Puerto Rican settlement in large US cities is a tale about how the migration peaked at a time when urban industrial economies were in decline,[5] dooming them to declining fortunes just as they were carving out this "representational space." But there was a silver lining in this cloud. The convergence of these historical factors with an ideological shift in the American character engendered by both the civil rights movement and the questioning of US foreign policy contributed to the formation of a Puerto Rican and Latino consciousness that allowed for the creation of El Barrio as both a populist, self-aware multicultural community and a crucible for an imaginary nation: the much-debated Nuyorican nation.

Of course, El Barrio has never been a neatly contained community with clearly defined borders and a homogeneous population. Several constituencies are clearly represented in the neighborhood, including the vestigial presence of the Italian American community in its northeastern corridor, the politically energized and populous African American community, predominantly in the northwest triangle but maintaining a presence in all of the neighborhood's territory, and in recent years additional immigrants from the Dominican

Republic and Mexico. The neighborhood's diversity only reinforces its importance, rather than diminishing El Barrio as a symbolic core community for
Puerto Ricans in New York. Its demographic face has never been as salient as
the iconographic importance of its street life and institutions.

The changes in the neighborhood over the last twenty years have reflected
a process that can adequately be described as gentrification, reflecting the para-
digms established by writers like Neil Smith and Jason Hackworth (2001),[6]
which identify various "waves" of the phenomena that more or less coincide
with the way capital becomes available for widespread investment in real estate. Much of this process originates with efforts by federal and state governments and their attendant agencies and urban planning apparatuses, while, as
is the case with trends in the economy in general, large-scale development fueled by concentrated capital in the private sector plays an increasing role.

The response to the forces that attempt to reshape the neighborhood
(often with the rationalized goal of creating "mixed communities," whose
desirability has not been universally agreed upon) often comes from various
community organizations who have historically played the role of fulfilling
mandates from their governmental-public sector origins and from individuals or small-business entrepreneurs who try to counterbalance the imperatives mandated "from the top down." This was the case in El Barrio during
the 1990s and first decade of this century when various organizations began
to try to shape a kind of renaissance in the neighborhood by combining
community advocacy and tourism-driven cultural spaces. These groups included housing provider Hope Community, the Upper Manhattan Empowerment Zone (generally recognized as a fiefdom under the control of US
Representative Charles Rangel), the Julia de Burgos Community Center, and
various small businesses, most notably, La Fonda Boricua restaurant.

In "Dreams of Place," a 2003 article by Arlene Dávila[7] published before
her definitive 2004 book *Barrio Dreams*, she quotes Mark Alexander, who
was director of Hope Community early in the first decade of this century:

> I recognize El Barrio's importance for Puerto Ricans, but I don't recog-
> nize it as the rightful home of only Puerto Ricans. Middle class Puerto
> Ricans themselves have chosen to vote with their feet, they've become
> upwardly mobile and are gone. That shapes my view of what we should
> do in our community. The intelligentsia has for long focused on the
> lower class and they're not focused on the middle class and those who
> went up the ladder because they've nowhere to go.

Although Alexander is no longer director of Hope Community, and the organization itself has scaled back much of its active participation in acquiring buildings in the neighborhood, the sentiment here epitomizes the neoliberal narrative that drives a new conception of "ethnic succession." According to this logic, the diminishing presence of Puerto Ricans in the neighborhood follows a natural pattern of migration among the group, some members of which are "succeeding," that is, moving to the suburbs; moving to Orlando, Florida (the preeminent relocation site of choice for both Puerto Ricans and Nuyoricans at the turn of the twenty-first century);[8] or retiring back home to Puerto Rico. But while this is in many cases true, there is also evidence that the poorer segment of a largely poor community[9] are being forced to peripheral areas in the outer boroughs and even rural Pennsylvania and urban Connecticut.

The neoliberal idea of urban redesign embraces depopulation and disinvestment followed by the private reinvestment model of most gentrification theorists,[10] without regard to the idea that an ethno-racial group's "well-being" can be affected by the evisceration of its core neighborhoods. In fact, the attention that is focused on Spanish Harlem / El Barrio as a site of gentrification and displacement over the last ten years is in part engendered by significant losses of core communities in the Lower East Side, Williamsburg, Bushwick, and to a lesser extent Washington Heights, Morningside Heights, Sunset Park, and Hell's Kitchen. If current trends continue, the erosion of *Latinidad* in Spanish Harlem will leave some stretches of the "South Bronx" as the Puerto Ricans' only remaining core community.

Aside from the South Bronx, whose landscape is changing even now as the housing market recovers from damage inflicted in the 2008 recession, Spanish Harlem / El Barrio was one of the last Puerto Rican core communities to be affected by the gentrification waves that began in the 1980s and 1990s. There has been much speculation about the reason for that. The housing stock is relatively unenticing to classic gentrifiers, who look for glamorous brownstones that, when renovated, create the feel of a "return" to a "classic" New York lifestyle. Another reason is El Barrio's proximity to the Upper East Side, which, because it is one of the wealthiest neighborhoods in Manhattan per capita, does not attract young students and artists who might live there first and probe northward in search of lower-priced rental apartments as rents rose, as happens in Brooklyn. Finally, an explanation popular with sociologists and urban planners is the concentration of housing projects in the neighborhood—the most dense in the city.[11] Public housing is often the most difficult obstacle to private developers looking to change demographics in an urban area, since such housing is associated with an urban underclass that is more difficult to romanticize as carriers of an urban ethno-racial culture attractive to gentrifiers. Furthermore, public housing would be practically impossible to privatize.

We can focus on three neighborhoods whose populations have changed considerably and identify a "stage"[12] pattern of gentrification based on "risk taking" that first involves artists and ultimately results in the creation of a youth-oriented lifestyle associated with one originally created by artists but no longer necessarily driven by it. The Lower East Side or East Village / Alphabet City / Loisaida has been almost completely gentrified in the last twenty-five years, and the resulting lack of affordable housing there has driven a migration across the river, starting in the late 1980s, to the Williamsburg section of Brooklyn, eventually extending to neighboring Bushwick in the first decade of the century.

Bushwick is now such a cutting-edge destination for young pseudo-bohemians that it has been featured in such entertainments as the controversial HBO series *Girls*, which has attempted to update *Sex in the City* for a younger generation. The art galleries, clubs, and entrepreneurial spaces that are popping up there now are almost completely removed from the original slash-and-burn aesthetic that once fueled the pioneering of Loisaida. The displacement of Puerto Ricans and other Latinos in this neighborhood during the 1980s has taken on such an impersonal air that it almost annihilates the memory of the at-times-awkward attempts of the Loisaida artists to engage the community, with some measure of success, in the 1980s.

As documented in Christopher Mele's *Selling the Lower East Side* (2000), the original artist incursion into the Lower East Side / Loisaida / Alphabet City began in the 1950s when abstract expressionist painters like Willem de Kooning and Franz Kline created what was known as the Tenth Street School; the area soon attracted beat poets like Frank O'Hara and Leroi Jones, who ultimately changed his name to Amiri Baraka (and later was a frequent guest at the Nuyorican Poets' Café). "Our showing up on Cooper Square . . . was right in tune with the whole movement of people East, away from the West Village with its high rents and older bohemians."[13]

The eventual flood of bohemians and, later, hippie counterculturalists in the 1960s involved messy and sometimes violent conflicts with the neighborhood's Puerto Ricans,[14] who had fought hard to maintain turf and found the cultural manifestations of "free living" somewhat contradictory to their notion of culture. But as the countercultural movements waned and the infamous city fiscal crisis of the mid-1970s took hold in Manhattan and the rest of the city, the neighborhood solidified its status as a stronghold for the Puerto Rican and other Latino communities (as well as African Americans, but to a lesser extent than in El Barrio / Spanish Harlem), enshrining its identity at once as a core ethnic and underclass community despite sporadic incursions from artists and bohemians and the tenacious presence of Ukrainians and Eastern Europeans.

In the 1980s, the Lower East Side / Loisaida / Alphabet City became a classic example of a community that attracted left-of-center artists who were interested in critiquing the transformation of the Reaganomics and social conservatism that have strong-armed the United States' political narratives into submission over the last thirty years. In the words of Allan Moore and Marc Miller, "The state of the Lower East Side of New York City provides pictures for painters, operas for actors and poets from an urban shambles of a slum where monstrous inequity is met with savagery, a nearly perfect specimen of malignant city life delivering itself up as subject for memorial before it is pushed off the local map by the contented belches of a bourgeoisie riding the wave of gentrification that has been called recession-proof."[15]

Many of the artists of the Loisaida scene were motivated by antigentrification activism and made alliances with some sectors of the Puerto Rican community, particularly at spaces like CHARAS, headed by activist Chino Garcia, a veteran of an earlier group called Real Great Society, which actually tried to empower the community by taking over neglected spaces. It was Garcia's CHARAS space that would become one of the most contested spaces in the neighborhood, and its sale to a private developer in 1998 (who has still not developed the space) was one of the pivotal events in the final surrender of the neighborhood.[16]

Some of the early "risk takers" used a bit of a camouflage game in that many of the names of the early art galleries had Spanish-sounding names like No lo Contendere (actually Latin, a legal term), No Se No, Aztec, and so on. This strategy also had a dark or flip side, as in a club that opened on Houston and Avenue C called the S.I.N. Club, an acronym that stood for "safety in numbers"—the flyers distributed for the club urged patrons to approach only from Houston Street and not the risky side streets. While many of the artists who arrived in the neighborhood at least promoted a worldview that was respectful and celebratory of Puerto Ricans and other people of color in the neighborhood, the resulting art explosion tended to obscure the contributions of Puerto Ricans and other Latinos in the downtown art scene from Soho to 14th Street.[17]

For example, in many glowing remembrances of the East Village heyday, the Pyramid on Avenue A is cited as a classic neighborhood performance art hotspot, and it was a gender-bending breakthrough for the neighborhood. But almost no one seems to remember that the Pyramid was earlier the home of New Rican Village, one of the most important clubs of the 1970s for the New York Latino music scene, practically the birthplace of Latin jazz, as well as the home of alternative theater promoted and created by the late Eddie Figueroa. The bar on 7th Street and Avenue B, once a strangely beautiful shared space between old Ukrainians and Puerto Ricans with polka and salsa on the jukebox, became one of the linchpins of Avenue B's hipsterization.

One can view the story of the East Village in the '80s as the story of a "mixed community" that ultimately could not stand success, which inevitably caused its resegregation. The mixed-community theory[18] holds that gentrification can be an antidote to the intense segregation that exists in New York. Yet Bridge, Butler, and Lees argue that "mixed communities policy" (1) is a top-down strategy that is seldom advocated in wealthy, equally homogeneous communities, (2) is a transitory strategy designed to disguise the eventual gentrification that will produce a new segregated community, and (3) advocates the ideal of social mixing, which is rarely achieved in a meaningful way.[19] If gentrification can be viewed as a sociopolitical urban phenomenon that takes place in stages, then 1979–87 can be viewed as a prolonged "risk-taking" stage, in which the leading edge of gentrification were artists and activists whose mere presence made the neighborhood palatable to more adventurous "middle-class" professionals. (The "risk-taking" professionals were looking for cheap rents, a stimulating night life, and a mixed-race living experience.)

The maturing of the mixed-community stage began symbolically with the death of iconic Nuyorican poet Miguel Piñero in 1988. At Piñero's funeral, Nuyorican Café owner Miguel Algarín decided to reopen the café, which had been closed for years for renovations.[20] Like the New Rican Village, just half a block away, the Nuyorican Poets Café was originally a space created by and for Nuyorican poets, immortalized in the 1975 anthology *Nuyorican Poetry: An Anthology of Puerto Rican Words and Feelings*,[21] which featured, among others, Algarín, Piñero, Sandra María Esteves, and Lucky Cienfuegos. In the words of the introduction to this anthology, "The poet juggles every street corner east of First Avenue and south of Fourteenth Street ending at the Brooklyn Bridge. Poetry is full of the act of naming. Naming states of mind."[22]

But when the café reopened after a long absence, it had bigger ambitions, attracting the "mixed community" already forming in the neighborhood as well as drawing in a torrent of multicultural poets, actors, and musicians. The primary vehicle for this new audience and school of writers was the poetry slam, imported from Chicago, which transformed the café from a place where a neighborhood- or barrio-specific bilingual literary movement was nurtured into a freewheeling experimental space for '90s multiculturalisms.

But the slam was a classic postmodern device, where poetry often moved away from substance and toward overindulgence in form. The most positive thing I can say about the slam is that it offered a platform for hiphop poetry, a space where the four elements of hiphop could flourish even as gangsta rap began to eat away at hiphop's idealism. But until a new wave of young Nuyoricans emerged in the mid-'90s, it meant the obscuring of "Puerto Rican" from the Nuyorican Poets Café.

By that time the slam and the popularity of the café were playing a significant role in the gentrification of the neighborhood. While many of the original artists from the East Village Days had fled across the Williamsburg Bridge to yet another seminal Puerto Rican neighborhood, a new set of multicultural hipsters stretched in long lines down 3rd Street, waiting to see what they had seen on MTV's first season of Real World, which starred emerging café poet Kevin Powell. Things would never be the same.

This is not to discount the scores of activists and artists who remained in the neighborhood and fought unbridled development either by directly confronting the tanks Mayor Giuliani sent into the neighborhood to evict squatters from buildings,[23] or by steadfastly defending community gardens, or by starting grassroots legal organizations like Good Old Lower East Side. But the process that tipped the neighborhood in favor of it becoming a playground for, first, middle-class hipsters and, finally, the high-rent children of the financial elite seemed inevitable. Twenty-five years after Nuyorican poet Bimbo Rivas had coined "Loisaida," a name for the neighborhood that honored the name of a Puerto Rican town (Loiza) and the way Puerto Rican migrants mispronounced the English name for the neighborhood, it had been transformed into a fantasy world for a generation of young people who had seen the Broadway play *Rent*.

Once a place so ugly and dangerous that it provoked Miguel Piñero to write a landmark poem about his affection and attachment to a place where "stabbing and shooting" were a call to nostalgia, the Lower East Side has become a site for understanding "the new urban form of globalization." Where once suburban white youth scurried to the S.I.N. Club, now young women of color offer reactions of shock and disorientation when they see yuppies jogging through the projects on the East River Drive—the last bastion of Puerto Rican presence in the neighborhood—on their way to the park along the river.

In her perceptive article "Negotiating Grit and Glamour: Young Women of Color and the Gentrification of the Lower East Side,"[24] Caitlin Cahill examines the reactions of young women in the neighborhood who feel tension between living up to "the grittiness of the ghetto life" and enjoying the "the glamour of the club, café and boutique life."[25] She examines the problematic of how young people, who previously could draw from their identity as being part of a core community, now grapple with living in a neighborhood in "transition," whose new residents seem willing to stereotype them.

Cahill identifies the dynamic of disinvestment, reinvestment, and gentrification that allows young people to see clearly how goods and services enter the neighborhood to benefit new residents and elide them. These forces are represented, for example, by the pattern of closing public schools that serve poor communities while increasing the number of pricey restaurants and banks. The reaction documented by the author, expressed by naming the group involved in her research project the "Fed Up Honeys," offers an interesting lesson for future resistance to the erosion of core communities, a lesson that in some ways challenges the original presupposition for the communities themselves. The critique is female driven, as the Fed Up Honeys are composed of young local women from varied ethnic backgrounds not necessarily loyal to a boundaried "imaginary nation" of Puerto Ricans, or by extension Latinos, and whose paradigmatic critical framework centers on class and gender, as well as ethnicity and race.

TROUBLE IN HIPSTER HEAVEN: WILLIAMSBURG

The central factors in the demographic shift, or displacement, of Latinos in Williamsburg were (1) the early trickle of artists who left the Lower East Side / Loisaida / Alphabet City in the early to mid-1990s during the long struggle between activists, politicians, and community-based organizations in the neighborhood over rezoning and development of affordable housing[26] and (2) the implementation of a series of initiatives by Mayor Michael Bloomberg's administration in the years following his election in the fall of 2001. (In general there has been a trend of decreasing Puerto Rican population in New York for reasons as varied as ascension to the middle class and suburban life, failure of small businesses like bodegas, or migration to Central Florida and back to Puerto Rico.)

The movement of artists and musicians to Williamsburg that began in the early-1990s was precipitated by the real estate machinations that were played out at a relatively glacial pace in the 1980s in the East Village. Their movement to Williamsburg was in part an attempt to reestablish the "authenticity"[27] of the alternative art experience in the Lower East Side / Loisaida / Alphabet City neighborhood in a new setting. The ethnic setting of the new neighborhood was also fairly parallel to that of the Lower East Side, in some ways more clearly demarcated by a physical boundary, Grand Street, which bisected the neighborhood into the "north" streets, where Eastern European ethnics predominated, and the "south" streets or "Los Sures," where Puerto Ricans and other Latinos had established a community.

The process accelerated more quickly than it had in the Lower East Side / Loisaida /Alphabet City neighborhood. The area quickly became a bohemian zone north of Metropolitan Avenue that led to a kind of popular culture codification of its residents as "hipsters." At once immortalized and satirized in a widely distributed tome called *The Hipster Handbook*,[28] the new Williamsburg residents seemed to represent an evolution (or devolution, if you will) of the politically concerned or the active artist or musician of the Lower East Side / Loisaida / Alphabet City neighborhood into a pleasure-seeking yuppie in tattered punk or beatnik clothing in the Williamsburg neighborhood.

While the dwindling Puerto Rican / Latino community was beset by subtle and nonsubtle methods to encourage their displacement, Puerto Ricans and other Latinos fought battles through institutions such as (1) El Puente (founded by an original Young Lord, Luis Garden Acosta), which charged itself with protecting and promoting cultural unity among Latinos while engaging in a panoply of educational and advocacy programs, and (2) Los Sures, a planning / legal advocacy organization that directly confronted apparent inequities in government-funded housing that favored the neighborhood's Hasidic Jewish population.[29]

The common thread in this neighborhood, as earlier demonstrated in other Latino barrios or core communities, was a policy of disinvestment, which caused depopulation and significantly diminished conditions and decreased services for remaining residents, along with new investment, geared toward gentrifying residents. This dynamic allowed for the gradual succession of a gentrification stage that allowed for some resistance and preservation of core community needs over a number of years; however, the first decade of the new millennium brought two unexpected market changes that accelerated the process of displacement and the erosion of the core Latino community.

The first was a nearly unprecedented real estate boom that sent housing prices soaring around the country, and was felt particularly strongly in New York. Just as community groups were beginning the transition between advocating for low-cost housing and encouraging home ownership for lower-middle-class families, the cost of both renting and owning began to skyrocket. In New York in 2006, the median home price was near $500,000, and in Manhattan, it approached $800,000. The deregulation of banking and lack of regulation of federal programs like Freddie Mac and Fannie Mae helped accelerate subprime mortgage lending to people of color, ultimately resulting in foreclosure for many. But the high prices also acted to keep aspiring minority homeowners out of the market altogether.

In addition, policies pursued by the administration of Mayor Michael Bloomberg, aided in part by the aftermath of the World Trade Center attacks, also played a significant part in the erosion of Williamsburg as a core Latino neighborhood. While the non-Latino white population increased by twenty-four thousand from 2000 to 2010, the Hispanic population fell by ten thousand, and now Latinos make up only 33% of the neighborhood population.

In 2011, I interviewed Jaime Estades, a lawyer and community activist who has lived in Williamsburg for twenty-four years. Estades felt the effects of gentrification hit home when it began to affect Public School 84, the school his children attended. "About four or five years ago, when I began sending my children there, it was about 95% black and Latino," he said. "Then all these parents started coming from the Midwest. Then they hired a lawyer to sue that we shouldn't have the Three Kings' celebration because of separation of church and state."

"The South Side of Williamsburg, what we used to call 'Los Sures,' is completely gentrified, nothing like what you saw five years ago," said Estades.

How does he interpret gentrification? "The pressure from landlords is intense. It's not like something where people have time to think for a while to figure out where to move."

The advocacy group Community Preservation at St. Nick's Alliance in Brooklyn gave me access to one of their clients, Mercedes Miranda, a thirty-six-year-old single mother from the Dominican Republic with a disabled child; Miranda claimed to being harassed by her landlord to leave her section 8 apartment on Meserole Street in East Williamsburg. "They told me that I have to leave, that they don't want any Hispanics here anymore," she said. "I've been living here for twenty-five years, but one by one my neighbors have moved away."[30]

Despite rhetorical flourishes from a city government that seeks to reconcile housing development with diversity, local residents often report being under siege. Rolando Guzmán, assistant director at St. Nick's, said an increasing number of Latinos in Williamsburg have relocated to East New York and beyond. "The landlords begin with harassment like not repairing their apartments," he said. "Once you give up a rent-stabilized apartment it's impossible to get another one in the neighborhood."[31]

Observers like Clara Irazábal Zurita, professor of urban planning at Columbia University, argued that the Bloomberg administration engaged in "a top-down approach that shifted resources and attention from the areas that would benefit Latinos the most, like education, housing, and job creation."[32]

The impact of large-scale development on neighborhoods like Williamsburg is one of the hallmarks of the Bloomberg administration, which oversaw a massive rezoning of the city to allow for new housing construction intended to accommodate an influx of population designed to resuscitate its economic base.

Over the course of her tenure, Bloomberg director of city planning Amanda Burden managed to rezone about 40% of the city.[33] Rezoning a neighborhood can have different effects: "upzoning" a neighborhood allows for larger buildings to be built, usually resulting in high-rise development, while "downzoning" limits development to preserve the architectural or historical quality of a neighborhood. Neighborhoods where blacks and Latinos live have mostly been upzoned. While policies like rezoning go back on a national scale to the 1970s, the Bloomberg administration aggressively implemented this policy on a large scale as a result of the 9/11 attacks. For Latinos—the vast majority of whom rent in New York City—this has had significant consequences.

The very election of Michael Bloomberg as mayor was the result of a rapid change in the city's political landscape. Political scientist John Mollenkopf argues in his book *Contentious City*[34] that in the aftermath of the attacks, traumatized New Yorkers became more interested in electing a mayor who was capable of reconstructing the shattered city than in being led by someone like Fernando Ferrer, who wanted to bridge the gap between the wealthy and what he called "The Other New York."

Ferrer ultimately lost a runoff primary to Mark Green, largely because of a sudden shift in priorities of an electorate shell-shocked by a terrorist attack on US soil. Addressing social inequities and a racial divide exacerbated by the brusque style of Mayor Rudolph Giuliani paled in importance to a need to rebuild and restore damaged parts of the city. Green, in turn, lost to Bloomberg, who until then had been perceived as an outside shot to win but who capitalized on his image as a business and development expert.

One of Bloomberg's first moves was to hire Dan Doctoroff as deputy mayor of economic development. Doctoroff had been pushing since the mid-1990s to organize New York City's bid for the 2012 Olympic Games. Doctoroff commissioned urban planner Alex Garvin[35] to develop a plan for using the Olympics as a catalyst for redeveloping blighted areas across all five boroughs.[36]

In the months after 9/11, businesses and the residents of the immediate area around the World Trade Center were clearly harmed. In the first year after the attacks, the population decreased by 50%, from twenty thousand to ten thousand. There was a buzz in East Harlem that younger apartment seekers were looking to move uptown, scared off by the general uneasiness about downtown.

In addition, the fact that the land to be used for World Trade Center reconstruction was controlled by the Port Authority meant that development would be controlled by the state and then-governor George Pataki, not the city and Bloomberg. Although the shift away from downtown was temporary, and the area would eventually rebound strongly, the shift in focus created a massive momentum to push development out to northern Manhattan and the outer boroughs.

At the time, many believed that investing in downtown real estate was the most problematic of propositions—the area around the attacks remained a frozen zone for months, and the trauma of the event discouraged visitors and pushed residents to move out.[37] This accelerated a trend toward developing other areas of the city, and this trend was pushed along by Burden's massive rezonings.

By 2005, when London won the bid for the 2012 Olympics over New York, a new development agenda had been adopted by the city. The intense interest the Bloomberg administration displayed in the Olympic bid morphed into developing the Far West Side into a mixed-use commercial office district.[38] From there, the city embarked on a massive rezoning plan that focused on neighborhoods like Williamsburg and Greenpoint.

The development in Williamsburg and Greenpoint hinged on a new twist in rezoning, called inclusionary zoning—demanded by community advocates and opposed by Doctoroff—which would offer financial incentives to developers to build permanent affordable housing. As a result, a series of towers sprung up along the Williamsburg waterfront, with names like Northside Piers and the Edge, developed by wealthy developers like Jeffrey Levine of Douglaston Development and the Toll Brothers.

The implementation of inclusionary zoning has created far less affordable housing than promised (only 2800 units as described in a 2014 report by the Association for Neighborhood & Housing Development),[39] and many community advocates say the effect of the increase in property values in the neighborhood has accelerated displacement. The effect has been to transform Williamsburg from a working-class neighborhood into a playground for the young and relatively well-off, some of whom are raising families; in contrast, estimates range up to 39.9% for the Latino population that has left.[40]

In his perceptive article, Brian Paul argues that the "public-private, affordable-luxury model of development has not produced enough affordable housing to meet the needs of longtime, working class residents. The flood of new luxury units has far outpaced the trickle of affordability."[41]

Paul points out that groups like the Community Preservation Corporation (CPC), which according to Paul had the blessing of Los Sures, is a consortium of over eighty banks and insurance companies that receive subsidies for affordable housing while at the same time it is involved in luxury housing development. The CPC operates in Brooklyn through its heavy involvement in luxury housing in Williamsburg, an involvement that produces inadequate affordable housing, contrasting with its production of affordable housing in peripheral areas like East New York and Brownsville. This amounts to a resegregation of the city when the purported goal is to create "mixed communities."

The irony of what has happened in Williamsburg in particular and other Latino neighborhoods in general is that community groups like Guzmán's argued for ways that the rezoning would not have an adverse impact on their neighborhoods. Over Doctoroff's objections,[42] community groups and the city worked out an "inclusionary rezoning" plan that would retain affordable housing and therefore some of the original character of the neighborhood.

Inclusionary housing is defined by the New York City Department of Planning as a program that "is designed to preserve and promote affordable housing within neighborhoods where zoning has been modified to encourage new development."[43]

But inclusionary zoning has been strongly criticized as ineffective. "First of all, the recession has made it very hard to construct high rises. Then you have thousands of people applying for 100 apartments at places like the Edge in Williamsburg," said Rolando Guzmán. "The city promised 30% affordable housing but by our estimates they have only provided about 15%. The city has failed on its promise."[44]

A 2009 report by John Petro with the Drum Major Institute said, bluntly, that the neighborhoods of Greenpoint and Williamsburg grew tremendously and witnessed the construction of new high-rise residential developments. However, the median price for a housing unit increased 140% between 2000 and 2007, while the median price in the city as a whole increased at the lesser rate of 87%.[45]

Further complicating the issue and shedding an important light on the contradictions in city policy is the formula used to determine affordable housing. An "affordable housing unit" is intended to be filled by a resident whose income is calculated to be 80% of the area median income (AMI).[46] However, the AMI as determined by the US Department of Housing and Urban Development (HUD) is drawn from the larger New York / New Jersey / Long Island metropolitan area,[47] which in 2016 was $90,600. In New York City, the figure is closer to $50,000, and in poor neighborhoods it hovers around $30,000.[48] This obviously means that affordable housing units by definition do not fit the needs of local residents; residents can easily be found for these units, but they are not those who are in most need in the area.

This dynamic, undoubtedly an underlying cause of an unfortunate outbreak of violence at a newly reopened McCarren Pool in Williamsburg—an incident that Mayor Bloomberg responded to with disgust as being "out of context" during a press conference—is part of an evolving dynamic that continues to exacerbate the problem of the erosion of Latino core communities in New York City. A public pool that had been neglected for years, lowering the quality of life of the neighborhood when it had more minority residents, reopened after years of gentrification. Tension soon arose when residents of the nearby Marcy housing projects clashed with lifeguards objecting to the backflips of men from this public housing complex located in Williamsburg's periphery.[49] As David Harvey put it, "What is at stake here is the power of collective symbolic capital, of special marks of distinction that attach to some place, which have a significant drawing power upon the flows of capital more generally."[50]

WHOSE BARRIO?

In her book *Barrio Dreams*, Dávila's contention is that El Barrio is a site of contradictions that illuminate problems with neoliberalism because it is an intersection between a long historical development of efforts to claim the neighborhood as a space of "collective symbolic capital" at the same time that large capital investment is focusing on tourism and development around an idealized version of the neighborhood's cultural capital. One strong clash is between El Barrio's embodiment of the Puerto Rican / Nuyorican cultural experience and "neoliberal capital's" agenda to promote a sanitized Latino cultural value and identity in the area to attract tourism.[51] Another contradiction has been the attempt by local Puerto Ricans / Nuyoricans to encourage home ownership as a way of buying into the neighborhood and the explosion of the housing market, making home ownership largely unaffordable to aspiring local homeowners.[52] Finally, the contradictions of inclusionary zoning came into play as a contentious struggle over the fate of a rezoning project (the East 125th Street project) was judged to be a step forward in the interests of the "community" by a seemingly progressive politician (see discussion of the film *Whose Barrio?*, below).

There has to be full disclosure here: My personal interest in El Barrio / Spanish Harlem has been forged by the fact that it became the place of residence for my parents after their arrival from Puerto Rico during the great migration after World War II. They arrived separately and lived just a few blocks apart until introduced by members of my father's family. Sometimes I go to Jefferson Park on 114th Street and First Avenue—a place now deeply entrenched in the nascent Mexican community in the neighborhood—and imagine my father arriving at the walkup where he lived with my grandmother and aunt, his lightish complexion allowing him to dodge the threat of Italian street gangs bent on stemming the tide of Puerto Rican migrants moving into the neighborhood. When I write about El Barrio / Spanish Harlem as a receptacle of cultural imprints, a site of tropicalization and unwavering New York Puerto Rican identity, it's a firsthand feeling, despite never having lived there.

My interest in El Barrio / Spanish Harlem as a writer and investigator was, however, stimulated by my recognition of the cues I'd been hearing all along during my residence in the Lower East Side / Loisaida / Alphabet City neighborhood. I had been hearing from acquaintances that trickling into the neighborhood were students and artists, suddenly prowling streets that had been consistently steeped in barrio ways since the 1950s. However, there were two interesting differences that distinguished El Barrio / Spanish Harlem from the Loisaida.

First, there was a growing narrative, led naturally by the *New York Times*,[53] that the Puerto Rican presence in New York was diminishing, something that rankled many feathers among community leaders. An 11% decline in the Puerto Rican population of New York was set against the backdrop of the displacement of storefronts on 116th Street by Dominican and Mexican businesses. The *New York Times* writer laid out the usual "culture of poverty" arguments about the "bad timing" of the Puerto Rican entry into the US industrial workforce, and the systematic discrimination and poor educational opportunities experienced by the group. However, Miguel Algarín of the Nuyorican Poet's Café, who seemed to follow the rhetoric of change that was affecting his own home in Loisaida, fell more on the side of "missed opportunity": "They [Puerto Ricans] should have stayed on 116th Street, fixed up the apartments like whites are doing now and maintained their political base in the United States," he said in hindsight.

This analysis was not entirely fair or accurate—many bodega owners were just happy to have survived a socioeconomic holocaust and sold their business to enjoy what was left of their golden years. Most Puerto Ricans had no incentive (e.g., dealing with hostile slumlords, lacking inherited wealth) to "fix up the apartments like whites are doing now." However, Algarín's words seem to have set off a response.

A growing cadre of young Nuyorican idealists were beginning to move into the neighborhood,[54] becoming involved in Community Board 11 and Representative Charles Rangel's Upper Manhattan Empowerment Zone to assert the Puerto Rican's "right to stay put"[55] in a systematic, progressive way. I began to visit and interview neighborhood residents and activists increasingly in 2002, amassing testimonies. On one summer afternoon in the ballroom of the Julia de Burgos Center, longtime residents Aurora Flores, a publicist and musician, and Fernando Salicrup, cofounder of the artists' collective Taller Boricua, spent hours telling me how strongly they felt about preserving the community ethos. "I learned how to be Puerto Rican in El Barrio, not in Puerto Rico," said Salicrup.[56]

A rhetoric calling for the need to support local cultural institutions and find ways to bring in new residents as renters or buyers resulted in the appearance of short-lived art galleries (Mixta), art-driven cafés (Carlito's), and a relatively longer-lasting restaurant (La Fonda Boricua). These new spaces seemed to signal that Puerto Ricans were "making a stand" in El Barrio / Spanish Harlem.

When I first began to investigate El Barrio / Spanish Harlem, there was still a narrative in the air about the neighborhood being an escape from downtown for those newer residents made skittish by the World Trade Center attacks. An interview with a middle school student of Mexican origin voiced the concern that "ever since 9/11 there's all these people from downtown around here."[57] Artist and El Barrio / Spanish Harlem native James De la Vega, who abandoned his Hope Community–owned artist storefront a couple of years later, had expressed the point of view of many of the new cadre of young "right to stay" types with a painting consisting of this scrawled, graffiti-style legend: *Don't think for a moment that we haven't noticed that the 96th Street boundary has moved further north.*

As documented in Dávila's *Barrio Dreams* (2004), important parts of the narrative included two other skirmishes that affected the idealized view of El Barrio / Spanish Harlem that the newly invigorated neighborhood leadership wanted to protect. The first was the fight over El Museo del Barrio, a museum that had begun as a community-oriented space run by native Nuyoricans in the 1960s and '70s. This was a paradigmatic example of one of Dávila's theses. It was a clash between "the goals and objectives of a marketing culture for economic development that favors ethnicity cleansed from ethnic memories and politics" and "those that are part of larger assertions of El Barrio's identity of place in resistance to gentrification."[58]

The "We Are Watching You" campaign, put together by local activists, made several demands of El Museo del Barrio,[59] whose location on the northernmost part of Manhattan's "Museum Mile" seemed to force it into competition with more-established museums, something that required professionalization of the staff and less of a community focus in curating the exhibitions. The board of the museum and its directorship had in recent years become increasingly devoid of New York–born Puerto Ricans or Puerto Ricans of any stripe, and the shows increasingly favored those of an internationally known Frida Kahlo over local artists.

According to Dávila, "The campaign sought a say in the institution's development, a reconfiguration in its board, as well as the development of policies . . . that would ensure the institution remained true to its Puerto Rican past and to its community mission."[60] The campaign, which famously held demonstrations across the street from the museum, had some effect on incoming director Julián Zugazagoitia, a Mexican who had spent most of his professional life in Europe.[61] He immediately assembled an advisory board[62] for the museum's education program that included members of the Nuyorican intelligentsia, and the permanent collection of the museum, which reopened after renovations to great fanfare in 2009 with a show that highlighted Nuyorican and Puerto Rican artists, was redeployed alongside artists who fit Dávila's "memory cleansing" hypothesis.[63]

While still not having a lot of New York–born Puerto Ricans in its highest administrative levels, and maintaining an "inclusive" pan-Latino agenda in its exhibitions, El Museo still holds several Nuyorican-celebrating events, such as those held by El Comité Noviembre, an older established institution, and a 2012 tribute to deceased poet hero Piri Thomas, author of the Barrio classic *Down These Mean Streets*.[64] Outside of a small skirmish over the titling of a poetry event as "Spic Up," which offended many local poets, El Museo seems not to have alienated the community entirely. In 2012, I attended an open house on a Saturday afternoon and found tables set up by local artisans who wanted their work sold in the Museo gift shop, and even though they were adamant about feeling excluded, they conceded that there was a dialogue with museum administrators to rectify that.

The ongoing dialogue between the community and El Museo del Barrio at least constitutes a negotiation between locals and an institution trying to maintain its viability in an increasingly competitive "big museum" art world scenario. But as happened in Williamsburg, a city government increasingly driven by a neoliberal plan for "reimagining" New York began to have a more pervasive impact. In a subsequent book called *Latino Spin*, Dávila captured a direct conflict between the corporate "Bloomberg way" of capitalizing on El Barrio / Spanish Harlem's cultural capital as a recognized Latino neighborhood and its Latino residents, who objected to its streamlining of Latino identity in order to more easily attract tourism.

The culprit was the Uptown New York project, part of a "river to river" development initiative, which would include a "Latino-themed mini-city featuring performance spaces, recording studios, entertainment spaces, and . . . housing for artists."[65] The problem with this project was that it was to be designed by a Los Angeles–based firm and amounted to a kind of "Disney-fication" of the neighborhood that would not include any input from residents. The form and function of the plan was directed by the Bloomberg-founded Latin Media & Entertainment Commission,[66] which Dávila says followed from the mayor's "penchant for mega-tourist events, such as national conventions [and] the failed Olympics."[67]

A sizable opposition arose, particularly at a meeting held at what was becoming the community space with the most authenticity, the Julia de Burgos Center on 106th Street and Lexington Avenue. A number of emerging voices were heard in opposition to the project, including media activist Marina Ortiz of eastharlempreservation.com, architect and community board member Gary Anthony Johnson, the African American Community Association of the East Harlem Triangle, and an activist who would eventually run for and ultimately lead the city council, Melissa Mark-Viverito.

The $1 billion Uptown New York project was canceled in May 2006 because of "community opposition that included concerns that the project would aggravate the area's high asthma rate."[68]

In 2007, while participating in the Revson Fellowship Program at Columbia University, I began to work, with codirector Laura Rivera, on a documentary about gentrification in El Barrio / Spanish Harlem called *Whose Barrio?*[69] In the film we tried to document the current state of gentrification in the neighborhood by interviewing various residents and capturing a few dramatic events, such as street protests, sleepy community board meetings, and calamitous confrontations at town halls.

Several spheres of contention were revealed in the process of the filmmaking. First there were the contrasting stories of José Rivera, a longtime resident of the neighborhood, and James García, a recently arrived young urban professional who was able to buy a condominium across the street from the Jefferson Projects on 112th Street between First and Second Avenues.

Rivera, who was born and raised in El Barrio / Spanish Harlem, had left briefly with his family to try to make a go of it in South Florida, only to have to return to El Barrio / Spanish Harlem and realize he was priced out of his own home neighborhood. García had moved uptown from Battery Park

City because he said El Barrio offered "more space for less money." Although the two never meet on camera, they provide classic narratives about their role in the gentrification drama.

José Rivera, who briefly had to double up with his family in a housing project apartment where his parents lived, was upset that gentrifiers could "pay more rent" than he could and that the "mom and pop stores" that he was accustomed to shopping in were closing and moving out of the neighborhood. He walked past the luxury Mirada, a condo project under construction, and complained, "Why can't they build something for us?"

James García, who was referred to me by then City Councilwoman Melissa Mark-Viverito, was indignant because the broker from the Corcoran Properties that sold him his two-bedroom apartment, which he bought for just under $600,000, told him that the housing projects across the street from him would eventually become privatized as co-op apartments. He was also very unsatisfied with the street crime in the neighborhood, the runoff of toxic chemicals from an auto body shop located on his block, and the general lack of amenities. Strikingly, even though he was a Latino himself (seventh-generation Mexican American from Texas), he felt no sympathy for the nationalist-oriented "right to stay put" crowd. "Some of these people say it should only be Latinos who move in, that the neighborhood should be Latino-only. They say to me, you're a Latino, why aren't you on our side? And I said 'why should I be on your side?'"

The documentary also depicts an evening where representatives of the Artemis Real Estate Partners make a presentation about a high-rise planned for a Fifth Avenue location in the neighborhood. Affordable housing is discussed, but the representatives stumble over both the projected prices of the apartments and their understanding of affordability measures expressed as a percentage of area median income (AMI). They interact with a bewildered and a sometimes cynical audience, with one member bringing up the common practice of the city, through the Cornerstone Program of New York City's Department of Housing Preservation and Development, to sell lots to builders of affordable housing at the cost of $1 per tax lot. This revelation sets off murmurs from the audience and sheds light on the lucrative advantages afforded to developers if they cloak themselves in a "housing development fund corporation."

Many contemporary studies of the El Barrio / Spanish Harlem neighborhood have drawn attention to the subliminal conflict between recent Mexican immigrants, who appear to many observers to have "taken over" the 116th Street commercial strip, and Puerto Ricans, who want to stake nationalist claims to the neighborhood. In *Whose Barrio?*, we contrasted two forms of confronting gentrification that seemed to fall along ethnic lines. We spent time documenting the efforts of a group called Movement for Justice in El Barrio (MJB), a Zapatista-style direct-action advocacy group that is primarily concerned with the Mexican tenants of a wide swath of buildings owned by an infamous slumlord named Steven Kessner.[70]

MJB has a radical working-class agenda that does not trust established political channels to effect change. Their main concession to working within the system has been connecting tenants with lawyers who sued Kessner for various violations including allowing apartments to deteriorate to unsafe conditions and using subtle and unsubtle practices to encourage tenants to move out. But besides this, they have often taken to the streets to protest, and one of their main targets was City Councilwoman Melissa Mark-Viverito. In the film, they even went as far to demonstrate in front of the house she owns in the neighborhood.

Mark-Viverito has long been associated with progressive causes, particularly during her time as a union leader at local 1199 and in the role she played in the student- and worker-led movement to force the US Navy out of Vieques, an island off the coast of Puerto Rico that had long been used for target practice.[71] During the time we filmed our documentary, she expressed the desirability of a mixed-income neighborhood while staunchly defending the existence of public housing and the "right to stay put" that was energetically created by the nationalist movement to defend the Latino character of the neighborhood.

With much chagrin, she accused Movement for Justice in El Barrio of being a group of outside agitators who refused to work with the established channels set up through her work with Hope Community and their tenant advocates. One of the early acts of her term as city councilwoman was to set up the East Harlem Anti-displacement Task Force, whose main partners are Hope Community and various tenant associations in local public and Mitchell-Lama housing, New York State's program to provide affordable housing, begun in 1955.[72] Another important partner, Picture the Homeless, stages events to try to highlight the warehousing of apartments, efforts that reveal to the public the highly visible spectacle of row upon row of empty apartments held by absentee landlords.[73]

The use of "East Harlem" rather than "Spanish Harlem / El Barrio" and "Anti-displacement" rather than "Anti-gentrification" seemed like political choices reflected in the interviews with Mark-Viverito and a representative of Hope Community in *Whose Barrio?* That is, as long as new investment is limited and preserves the Latino character of the neighborhood, new residents will find a welcoming environment. Although change is inevitable, a strong organization of local residents voicing their concerns would help ensure that this change is positive for the community in the long run, according to the councilwoman, who has been city council speaker since January 2014.

This is a rational enough position, but it was put to the test in the final sequence of *Whose Barrio?* To discuss the previously mentioned East 125th Street Project, Mark-Viverito called a town meeting at a Spanish Harlem school auditorium, during which she allowed input from the community. The new project was a scaled-down version of "Uptown New York," involving the construction of some high-rise buildings, a modest shopping center, and space for community organizations. As the sequence about the project in *Whose Barrio?* begins, City Councilwoman Melinda Katz talks about the availability of affordable housing in the proposal, but like the representatives of Artemis Real Estate Partners, lacks a critical analysis of the relative affordability of this housing based on the larger area's median income (AMI).

The film shows that it didn't take long before the meeting devolved into a shouting match between opponents of the project—a coalition of tenants, members of Community Board 11 (CB 11), small business owners threatened with eminent domain takeover of the land their businesses sat on, the Harlem Tenant Council and the Harlem Triangle Association—and Mark-Viverito. In one of the more dramatic confrontations, architect and CB 11 member Gary Anthony Johnson addressed Mark-Viverito: "This project is not going to create the level of affordable housing that we as a community envisioned. This project has been structured so that only large-scale developers can compete and get this. There is no way this project—three blocks—should have gone to one major developer." Mark-Viverito responded that Johnson was being "disingenuous in his objections, the project's wording had been agreed to every step of the way, and Johnson was grandstanding for political purposes."

Eerily enough, Dávila had opened her "Times Squaring of El Barrio" chapter of *Latino Spin* with the following quote from Johnson during the hearings for the Uptown New York project two years earlier: "We want a project, but a project that's planned by us, designed by us, and programmed for us. . . . Don't let this massive project be predetermined and solely given to one developer."[74]

Like the town hall meeting, the Community Board 11 meeting on the proposal also ends with the audience continuing to insist that they don't want the East 125th Street project. Still, Mark-Viverito joined the majority in the city council and voted it through. "These are actions which move the public policy further along," the councilwoman said, explaining her vote. "It's not going to get to the point where everybody is 100% happy. My job now as a public official is to balance those interests."[75]

But dire events in the US economy in 2008 had the effect of completely undermining this logic. Months after the vote, the main partner in the project, General Growth Properties, a firm that overextended itself by buying up massive malls around the country, lost 90% of its value and became an early victim of the quickly evolving recession.[76] The ambitious goals of the project have since been suspended or scaled back. The neighborhood had been granted a reprieve from impending destruction with a hope for a more rational, balanced development plan that can accommodate longtime residents.

These days, as I ride the number 6 subway train northward in the evening, I notice more and more white, middle-class riders exiting at 103rd, 110th, and 116th streets. New restaurants continue to spring up, while La Fonda Boricua, one of those anchors of the nationalist "right to stay put" folks, closed because of financial mismanagement. (It has since reopened.) A brief controversy flared in 2010 when Councilwoman Mark-Viverito engineered the ouster of Taller Boricua from control of the Julia de Burgos ballroom because they were allegedly misusing the space.[77] The space eventually came under the control of the Hispanic Federation, a major nonprofit with political ties, and a group of other, smaller organizations.

In the spring of 2012, I ran into Jerry Gonzalez, a Nuyorican trumpeter and conga player and one of the founders of Latin jazz; he had grown so fed up with New York and the limited possibilities he was experiencing that he had moved to Spain. He had just been at the Fonda Boricua lounge, a satellite of La Fonda Boricua that hosted his group, The Fort Apache Band, in a series of concerts that drew overflow crowds a year earlier. The lounge had recently been renamed "Sweet Jane's," and the menu offered "new American fare." According to Gonzalez, "It's a little place for non-Latino people to come in and have a drink with sofas and no music. . . . This is going to be a chi-chi bar so people could come in and say yeah, I been to Spanish Harlem and have had a couple of cocktails!"[78]

CONCLUSION

Patterns of disinvestment, reinvestment, and gentrification have had a clearly demonstrable effect on demographic realities in various Latino neighborhoods in New York that can be called "core communities." While these processes remain incomplete, there has already been much reaction to apparent changes in the character and cultural realities of these neighborhoods. Anti-gentrification movements have appeared in growing numbers, and awareness of displacement has become one of many interrelated issues, such as critiques of excessive use of force by police, the problem of mass incarceration, and, for Latinos specifically, advocacy of place-based cultural solidarity.

One thing that seems clear is that the effects of gentrification in Central Harlem and on El Barrio / Spanish Harlem have created a new awareness of Upper Manhattan that could conceivably coalesce into the label "uptown," one with no specific cultural, racial, or ethnic meaning other than a vague notion of "difference" symbolized by certain kinds of music, food, and street culture. The years ahead will probably see a new valorization of the South Bronx because of the increasing number of art spaces and a slow increase in rents.

We may look back on the second decade of this century as the one in which clearly defined Latino and other "minority" communities vanished from view. Bill de Blasio, who became mayor in January 2014, has pledged to create two hundred thousand units of affordable housing within ten years. His reliance on inclusionary zoning policy has been criticized as too much of a concession to large developers and as not creating enough affordable housing. Melissa Mark-Viverito, who became the powerful speaker of the city council, attempted to empower her East Harlem neighborhood by including them in the process of planning its predetermined, "up-zoned" development. Yet grassroots activists feel the process was nothing more than manufacturing consent for forces that will eventually require displacement.[79] This enduring dynamic between people-based movements and elected and community leaders will no doubt continue to shape efforts in the preservation of core communities for core communities' sake.

NOTES

The epigraph is reprinted by permission of Victor Hernández Cruz, *Maraca: New and Selected Poems, 1966–2000* (Minneapolis: Coffee House Press, 2001). Copyright © 2001 by Victor Hernández Cruz.

1. Arlene Dávila, *Barrio Dreams* (New York: New York University Press, 2004).

2. Bernardo Vega, *Memoirs of Bernardo Vega: A Contribution to the History of the Puerto Rican Community in New York*, ed. César A. Iglesias, trans. Juan Flores (New York: Monthly Review Press, 1984).

3. Frances Aparicio and Susana Chavez-Silverman, eds., *Tropicalizations: Transcultural Representations of Latinidad* (Lebanon, NH: University Press of New England, 1997).

4. Luis Aponte-Parés, "Lessons from El Barrio—The East Harlem Real Great Society / Urban Planning Studio: A Puerto Rican Chapter in the Fight for Urban Self-Determination," *New Political Science* 20, no. 4 (1998): 400.

5. Ramón Grosfoguel and Chloe Georas, "The Racialization of Latino Caribbean Migrants in the NY Metro Area," *Centro Journal* 1 and 2 (1996): 190–201.

6. N. Smith and J. Hackworth, "The Changing State of Gentrification," *Tijdschrift voor Economische Social Geographie* (Royal Dutch Geographical Society) 92, no. 4 (2001): 464–77.

7. Arlene Dávila, "Dreams of Place," *Centro Journal* 15, no. 1 (Spring 2003): 129.

8. Jorge Duany and Patricia Silver, "The Puerto-Ricanization of Florida: Historical Background & Current Status," *Centro Journal* 22, no. 1 (Spring 2010): 4–31.

9. Mark Hugo Lopez and Gabriel Velasco, *A Demographic Portrait of Puerto Ricans, 2009* (Washington, DC: Pew Hispanic Center, 2011), http://www.pew hispanic.org/2011/06/13/a-demographic-portrait-of-puerto-ricans/.

10. Neil Smith, *The New Urban Frontier: Gentrification and the Revanchist City* (New York: Routledge, 1996.)

11. Dávila, *Barrio Dreams*, 7.

12. Robert Kerstein, "Stage Models of Gentrification: An Examination," *Urban Affairs Quarterly* 25, no. 4 (June 1990): 620–39.

13. Christopher Mele, *Selling the Lower East Side: Culture, Real Estate, and Resistance in New York City* (Minneapolis: University of Minnesota Press, 2000), 143.

14. Mele, *Selling the Lower East Side*, 171–72.

15. Allan Moore and Marc Miller, eds., *ABC No Rio Dinero: The Story of a Lower East Side Art Gallery* (New York: ABC No Rio with Collaborative Projects, 1985), 5.

16. Yasmín Ramírez, "Nuyorican Vanguards: Political Actions / Poetic Visions: A History of Puerto Rican Artists in New York, 1964–1984" (PhD diss., Graduate Center, City University of New York, 2005).

17. Ibid.

18. Gary Bridge, Tim Butler, and Loretta Lees, eds., *Mixed Communities: Gentrification by Stealth?* (Chicago: Policy Press / University of Chicago Press, 2012).

19. See introduction to ibid. and Loretta Lees, "Social Mixing and the Historical Geography of Gentrification," in ibid., 53–68.

20. Ed Morales, *Living in Spanglish* (New York: St. Martin's Press, 2003), 104.

21. Miguel Algarín and Miguel Piñero, eds., *Nuyorican Poetry: An Anthology of Puerto Rican Words and Feelings* (New York: Morrow / Harper Collins, 1975).

22. Miguel Alagarín, introduction to Algarín and Piñero, *Nuyorican Poetry*, 10.

23. Mele, *Selling the Lower East Side*, 271–76.

24. Caitlin Cahill, "Negotiating Grit and Glamour: Young Women of Color and the Gentrification of the Lower East Side," *City & Society* 19, no. 2 (2007): 202–31.

25. Ibid., 203.

26. Nicole P. Marwell, *Bargaining for Brooklyn: Community Organizations in the Entrepreneurial City* (Chicago: University of Chicago Press 2007), 60–65.

27. Sharon Zukin, "Consuming Authenticity," *Cultural Studies* 22, no. 5 (2008): 724–48.

28. Robert Lanham, *The Hipster Handbook*, illustrated by Bret Nicely and Jeff Bechtel (New York: Anchor Books, 2003).

29. Marwell, *Bargaining for Brooklyn*, 76–78.

30. Mercedes Miranda, interview by author, published in July 2011 within an article in *El Diario–La Prensa*.

31. Rolando Guzmán, assistant director, St. Nick's Alliance, Brooklyn, interview by author, July 2011.

32. Clara Irazábal Zurita, professor of urban planning at Columbia University, interview by author, July 2011.

33. Julie Satow, "Amanda Burden Wants to Remake New York. She Has 19 Months Left," *New York Times*, May 18, 2012.

34. John Mollenkopf, ed., *Contentious City: The Politics of Recovery in New York City* (New York: Russell Sage Foundation, 2005), 11.

35. See Alex Garvin & Associates, Inc., "Visions for New York City: Housing and the Public Realm," report prepared for the Economic Development Corporation of New York City (New York: Alex Garvin & Associates, 2006).

36. Kathryn Wilde, Partnership for New York City, interview by author, 2011.

37. Mollenkopf, *Contentious City*, 3–21.

38. Hope Cohen, Regional Planning Association, interview by author, 2011.

39. Association for Neighborhood & Housing Development, *Inclusionary Zoning: Lost Opportunities for Affordable Housing* (New York: Association for Neighborhood & Housing Development, 2014), http://www.anhd.org/wp-content/uploads/2011/07/ANHD-2014-White-Paper-IZ-Opportunity-Lost.pdf.

40. US Census Bureau, 2000 and 2010 Censuses, Summary File 1, Population Division, New York City Department of City Planning. Map "Percent Change in the Hispanic Population by Neighborhood Tabulation Area, New York City, 2000

to 2010," https://www1.nyc.gov/assets/planning/download/pdf/data-maps/nyc-population/census2010/m_pl_p10a_nta.pdf.

41. Brian Paul, "Affordable Housing Policies May Spur Gentrification, Segregation," *Gotham Gazette*, February 22, 2011, www.gothamgazette.com.

42. Alyssa Katz, "Inclusionary Zoning's Big Moment," *City Limits*, December 15, 2004, http://citylimits.org/2004/12/15/inclusionary-zonings-big-moment/.

43. New York City, Department of Housing Preservation and Development, "Inclusionary Housing Program," accessed December 1, 2016, http://www1.nyc.gov/site/hpd/developers/inclusionary-housing.page.

44. Rolando Guzmán, interview by author, July 2012.

45. John Petro, *No More Delay: Proven Policy Solutions for New York City* (New York: Drum Major Institute, 2009), 14, www.community-wealth.org.

46. New York City, Department of Housing Preservation and Development, "Inclusionary Housing Program."

47. New York City, Housing Development Corporation, "Income Eligibility," within guidelines for applying for housing, December 1, 2016, http://www.nychdc.com/pages/Income-Eligibility.html.

48. Jenny Ye, John Keefe, and Louise Ma (WNYC Data News Team), "Median Income / NYC Neighborhoods," map produced on the basis of information from the US Census Bureau's American Community Survey, https://project.wnyc.org/median-income-nabes/.

49. Lisa W. Foderaro, "A Revived Pool Draws Tensions to the Surface," *New York Times*, July 4, 2012.

50. David Harvey, "The Art of Rent: Globalization, Monopoly and the Commodification of Culture," *Socialist Register* 38 (2002): 103.

51. Dávila, *Barrio Dreams*, 50.

52. Ibid., 29–30.

53. Mireya Navarro, "Puerto Rican Presence Wanes in New York," *New York Times*, February 28, 2000.

54. See Erica González's comments in Dávila, *Barrio Dreams*, 55.

55. See Chester Hartman, "The Right to Stay Put," in *Land Reform, American Style*, ed. Charles Geisler and Frank Popper (Totowa, NJ: Rowman and Allanheld, 1984), 302–18; Kathe Newman and Elvin K. Wyly, "The Right to Stay Put, Revisited: Gentrification and Resistance to Displacement in New York City," *Urban Studies* 43, no. 1 (2006): 23–57.

56. Ed Morales, "Spanish Harlem on His Mind," *New York Times*, February 23, 2003.

57. Morales, "Spanish Harlem on His Mind."

58. Arlene Dávila, *Barrio Dreams*, 11.

59. Ibid., 109–11.

60. Ibid., 109.

61. Ibid., 177.

62. Arlene Dávila, *Latino Spin: Public Image and the Whitewashing of Race* (New York: New York University Press, 2008), 133.

63. Deborah Sontag, "Beyond the Barrio, with Growing Pains," *New York Times*, October 9, 2009.

64. Piri Thomas, *Down These Mean Streets* (New York: Knopf, 1967).

65. Arlene Dávila, *Latino Spin: Public Image and the Whitewashing of Race* (New York: New York University Press, 2008), 101.

66. Ibid., 97–111.

67. Ibid., 103.

68. Timothy Williams, "Facing Neighbors' Concerns, City Kills Huge East Harlem Project," *New York Times*, May 4, 2006.

69. Ed Morales and Laura Rivera, directors and producers, *Whose Barrio?*, documentary film (New York, 2009). The film can also be viewed at https://www.kanopystreaming.com.

70. See Kavita Shah, "The New Gentrification," *Nation*, June 23, 2008; Taina Borrero, "Steven Kessner: All I Do Is Fix, and They Damage," *Village Voice*, June 27, 2006.

71. Ross Barkan, "The Unlikely Rise of City Council Speaker Melissa Mark-Viverito," *Observer*, June 7, 2014, http://observer.com/2014/06/no-2-and-trying-harder/.

72. Jason Sheftell, "Advocates Fight for Tenants, the Elderly and Low-Income Families in East Harlem," *New York Daily News*, December 28, 2007, http://www.nydailynews.com/life-style/real-estate/advocates-fight-tenants-elderly-low-income-families-east-harlem-article-1.276816.

73. Nick Pinto, "New York Has More Vacant Buildings and Lots Than It Has Homeless People," *Village Voice*, January 27, 2012, http://www.villagevoice.com/news/new-york-has-more-vacant-buildings-and-lots-than-it-has-homeless-people-6676558.

74. Dávila, *Latino Spin*, 97.

75. Morales and Rivera, *Whose Barrio?*

76. Michael J. Merced and Terry Pristin, "Heavy Debt Bankrupts Mall Owner," *New York Times*, April 16, 2009.

77. Ed Morales, "Art Space Furor Grows at the Julia de Burgos Cultural Center in East Harlem," *New York Daily News*, October 6, 2010.

78. Erica Y. Lopez, "New Life for G&G and Fonda Locations," *New York Daily News*, May 2, 2012.

79. Josmar Trujillo, "Rejecting the East Harlem 'Community' Plan," *City Limits*, November 21, 2016, http://citylimits.org/2016/11/21/op-ed-rejecting-the-east-harlem-community-plan/.

CHAPTER THIRTEEN

Children First and Its Impact on Latino Students in New York City

LUZ YADIRA HERRERA AND PEDRO A. NOGUERA

From 2001 to 2013, New York City's educational landscape was transformed dramatically. The election of Michael Bloomberg as mayor of New York City (NYC) marked the beginning of a major effort to reform what was widely seen as a troubled public school system. Bloomberg abolished the board of education, and with the approval of the state legislature, he assumed control over the public schools. In placing himself at the head of the largest educational system in the country, Mayor Bloomberg, a billionaire information/media executive, claimed that he would employ a business model to turn around the failing schooling system. His business-model approach to education centered on using high-stakes testing to ensure accountability, decentralizing the administrative apparatus to increase school autonomy, supporting the proliferation of charter schools, and closing those public schools deemed to be failing.

In this chapter, we first briefly describe the major reforms that were implemented during the Bloomberg era. We then analyze how Latino students were affected by these policies. We draw upon data compiled by a variety of organizations, including the New York City Department of Education (DOE), the Parthenon Study on secondary schools, and the New York City Charter School Center.[1]

MAYOR BLOOMBERG TAKES CONTROL: THE LAUNCH OF CHILDREN FIRST

Shortly after his first election in 2001, Mayor Bloomberg appointed former assistant US attorney Joel Klein to serve as chancellor for the city's public schools. Together, they unveiled the Children First reforms and launched a massive reorganization of the schools. The reform eliminated community school boards and established the Panel for Educational Policy (PEP; the majority of the board members were appointed by Mayor Bloomberg), which took on the oversight of the schools. Bloomberg worked with the former CEO of General Electric to create a corporate-style Leadership Academy to train new principals, and to further the goal of decentralization, he dismantled the vast academic support system (what he characterized as a failed bureaucracy) that previously assisted schools in the area of curriculum and professional development.

With central supports no longer available from the DOE or local school districts, schools were directed to purchase support services from newly created School Support Organizations (SSO's) or to become part of the "Autonomous Zone," later renamed the "Empowerment Zone." The goal was to provide principals with more autonomy in the operation of their schools. In exchange for greater autonomy, principals were expected to meet specific performance standards (O'Day et al. 2011). The organizational changes were designed to transform the city's public schools through competition and data-based decision-making (Fruchter and McAlister 2008).

Under Bloomberg, high-stakes assessments and rigid performance-based accountability became the drivers of the Children First reform strategy. The reforms revamped the instructional structures in schools, established a common literacy and mathematics curriculum, required that every school have a literacy coach and a math coach, and provided schools with additional classroom materials. The reforms also established a parent coordinator in every school and placed greater emphasis on school security, designating several chronically unsafe secondary schools as "impact schools" where additional security personnel were deployed (Beam, Madar, and Phenix 2008). To increase transparency and accountability, school progress reports were released annually to the public, and letter grades were assigned to schools based on how well a school performed in comparison to schools with similar demographics.

The reforms relied heavily upon state assessments, particularly the state English language arts (ELA) exam and state mathematics exam for grades 3–8 and the Regents exams for grades 9–12, to measure and monitor the performance of schools. To ensure that schools had access to student-level data, the DOE developed the Achievement Reporting and Innovation System (ARIS), an interactive online data tool that allows access to DOE assessment data to all stakeholders, including parents. Like several of the other measures that were implemented, ARIS was intended to significantly increase transparency and accountability system-wide.

Mayor Bloomberg and the DOE were committed to expanding school choice and creating a competitive marketplace that would force schools to compete for students. Hundreds of new, small schools were created, and 140 schools that failed to improve were closed (NYC Working Group on School Transformation 2012). Additionally, the DOE, the New York State Education Department (NYSED), and the State University of New York (SUNY) Board of Trustees were authorized to create several new charter schools. These new charter schools received public funding and had access to public school facilities but were managed by private organizations, some of which had strong ties to wealthy hedge funds and Wall Street investment firms. Since 2002, the number of charter schools created has risen dramatically; the New York City Charter School Center (2012) reported that there were 136 charter schools in the city.[2]

ASSESSING THE IMPACT OF CHILDREN FIRST ON LATINO STUDENTS

Since 2000, Latino students in New York City have constituted the largest demographic subgroup in the city's schools, making up 40% of the total student population (NYC Department of City Planning 2003; NYC Department of Education 2013). They are also the fastest-growing segment of the school-age population. Yet the Latino students in New York's population are extremely diverse, consisting of representatives from every country and territory in Latin America. Dominicans, closely followed by Puerto Ricans and a fast-growing Mexican population, constituted the majority of the Latino youth in the city in 2010, for example; what is more, most Latino youth in NYC were US-born (Treschan 2010).

As the demographic group with the youngest population in the city (according to the 2010 US Census, 35.5% of Latinos in New York are under the age of 18), Latinos have a vested interest in the performance of the city's schools (US Census Bureau 2010). In the first few years after the enactment of Children First, New York obtained what seemed to be overwhelmingly positive results. This was true with respect to notably higher test scores and graduation rates, which increased from less than 50% to 66% during the twelve years that Bloomberg was in office. Some skeptics have argued that some of the upward trends were actually the result of efforts already underway before Children First took effect (Fruchter and McAlister 2008; Kemple 2011). Data show that there was, in fact, an upward trend in performance a few years before Bloomberg took office, but they also clearly show a more rapid increase in performance after the enactment of Children First.

James Kemple, the director of the newly created Research Alliance, suggested that findings from his 2011 study showed that New York City was making significant progress in closing the gap in achievement between New York City and New York State before the start of Children First. The bulk of the credit for the apparent success being achieved in New York's public schools, however, went to Mayor Bloomberg and his chancellor, Joel Klein. In 2007, the city was awarded the heralded Broad Prize and designated the best urban school district in the United States (Eli and Edythe Broad Foundation 2007), and Mayor Bloomberg used the progress achieved in public schools as a central tenet of his campaign for an unprecedented third term as mayor.[3]

Unfortunately, the progress the city's schools seemed to be making ended abruptly in 2009. Following the release of several studies showing that large numbers of students throughout New York State were arriving in college unprepared academically, the New York State Board of Regents was compelled to acknowledge that student scores on fourth- and eighth-grade English language arts and math tests had been inflated, and the board recalibrated them downward. The action effectively negated most of the test score gains that had been recorded during the Bloomberg years. By 2010, the Regents reported that very few of the city's high school graduates—only 13% of black and Latino students who had entered ninth grade four years earlier—met the new college-ready standards established by the state.

In some respects, the news was hardly surprising because two years earlier, the City University of New York (CUNY) had reported that more than 50% of the city's public school graduates at four-year colleges, and nearly 80% at community colleges, were required to take remedial courses after

Table 13.1 Percent of ACT-Tested High School Graduates Meeting ACT College Readiness Benchmarks by Race/Ethnicity in 2013

Race/Ethnicity	English	Reading	Math	Science	All Four Subjects
African American	34%	16%	14%	10%	5%
American Indian	41%	26%	22%	18%	10%
Asian	74%	55%	71%	53%	43%
Hispanic/Latino	48%	29%	30%	21%	14%
Pacific Islander	55%	33%	37%	27%	19%
White	75%	54%	53%	45%	33%

Source: ACT 2013.

enrolling (Jaggers and Hodara 2011). In its 2013 Condition of College and Career Readiness report, the ACT showed Latino students among the least college-prepared in the nation, with only 14% meeting college readiness benchmarks in four core subjects. Moreover, despite the bold assertions by Mayor Bloomberg and the DOE, since 2003, there had been no significant reduction in the achievement gap separating New York City's African American and Latino students from white students on the National Assessment of Educational Progress (NAEP) testing program (see table 13.1).

In grade 8 mathematics, NAEP found that 51% of the city's black students scored at the lowest level (below basic), as did 50% of the city's Latino students, while just 11% of Asian and 16% of white, non-Hispanic students were in that group. Placing the New York State assessments side by side with NAEP revealed that substantial "grade inflation" had occurred under Mayor Bloomberg's leadership. In contrast to the sunny reports issued by the DOE prior to Mayor Bloomberg's campaign for a third term, New York State found that only 2% of black and Latino students scored at the highest level.

For Latino students, the recalibration of test scores proved to be devastating. Whereas 5% of the city's students achieved the highest level of mastery on the grade 8 English language arts assessment (level 4), when outcomes are sorted by racial/ethnic groups, 11% of Asian students are in level 4, as are 10% of White, non-Hispanic students but just 2% of black and 2% of Hispanic students (Schott Foundation 2012). In other words, it is five times as likely that a white non-Hispanic or Asian student will have a top score on the state's English language arts assessment as that a black or Latino student will.

Conversely, 15% of black and 16% of Latino students scored on level 1 on the 2010 eighth-grade ELA assessments. This means it is twice as likely that a Latino student will be in this lowest-scoring group as that an Asian student will be there, and three times as likely as that a white, non-Hispanic student will. Overall, 69% of the city's Latino students are in the two lower levels of achievement on the grade 8 English language arts assessment, while 60% of Asian and 59% of white non-Hispanic students score at the two upper levels. Why have such enormous disparities in educational outcomes persisted after ten years of reform? What the data suggest may be the under-lying cause of these large gaps in performance is the link between test scores and the geographic residential boundaries of school districts. In their 2012 report, *A Rotting Apple: Education Redlining in New York City*, the Schott Foundation describes the cause of these disparities as being the result of "the corrosive impact of redlining" (5).

Recently, the New York City Independent Budget Office confirmed that students eligible for free and reduced-price meals, the city's poorest children, do well in schools with relatively few poor students, and students ineligible for any subsidized lunch program do not do well in schools that predomi-nantly serve students living in poverty. Sadly, only 16% of Latino students have the opportunity to attend schools where the majority of students do not qualify for free or reduced lunch. In contrast, 31% of Latino students are in schools where over 90% of students qualify for free or reduced lunch. What is more, schools that serve mostly black and Latino students tend to attract teachers with the fewest years of teaching experience (Gandara and Contre-ras 2010; Darling-Hammond 2004). Gandara and Contreras (2010) found that in schools with the highest numbers of racial/ethnic minority students, a reported 88% of teachers scored in the bottom quartile for teacher quality; conversely, those schools with the lowest percentage of minorities had less than 11% of teachers who scored in the bottom quartile for teacher quality.

In addition to the lowered test scores and college readiness rates, the De-partment of Education's policy of using school closure as a means to further its reform agenda has taken a particularly damaging toll on Latino students. From the time Mayor Bloomberg took control of public schools in 2002, 140 schools were closed or scheduled for closure by 2012 (NYC Working Group on School Transformation 2012). The vast majority of school closings have occurred in Harlem, Washington Heights, the South Bronx, and parts of Brooklyn, all predominantly Latino and black communities. Furthermore, those schools closed during 2011–12 had a higher percentage of high-needs

Table 13.2 Schools on Closing List, 2011–2012

Student Type	High Schools on Closing List	All High Schools	Elementary and Middle Schools on Closing List	All Elementary and Middle Schools
Special Education	20.3%	12.8%	16.1%	15.0%
E.L.L.	13.7%	12.2%	8.4%	15.7%
Poverty	77.1%	67.2%	86.2%	78.1%
Black	40.4%	31.6%	63.2%	28.0%
Hispanic	55.4%	39.2%	31.1%	40.7%
White	1.1%	12.9%	2.0%	15.2%
Average	10.3%	6.1%	—	—

Source: Independent Budget Office, 2012.

students— including special-needs, poor, and Latino students—than the rest of the city's schools (see table 13.2).

A 2011 Urban Youth Collaborative study on twenty-one closed high schools further reveals a pattern of outcomes that have disproportionately affected the Latino community. The study revealed that these twenty-one schools had higher concentrations of students eligible for free lunch (74% versus 55%), had a much higher percentage of emergent bilingual students (21% versus 13%), and had a higher Latino student enrollment (47% compared to 36%) than the rest of the city's high schools (Urban Youth Collaborative 2011). In addition, the dropout and discharge rates spiked during the years of the phaseout in those schools, and most notably in the final year of the phaseout. For instance, in the former William Taft High School in the South Bronx, 70% of the students dropped out during the last year of the phaseout, compared to 25% during the three years prior to closure (Urban Youth Collaborative 2011).

In his analysis of nineteen transcripts from public hearings on school closures, Kretchmar (2014) provides the example of a traditionally well-performing high school whose principal disclosed that there were "deplorable learning conditions [in his high school in the aftermath of a nearby school closure] as a result of overcrowding, and . . . [that] the school was not provided any additional resources to deal with the overcrowding" (17). Since many of the more-poorly performing schools targeted for closure are predominantly in communities of color as shown above, there is a domino effect that occurs as those schools that previously performed well now deteriorate due to the influx of students phased out from schools. Fruchter (2011) describes the dilemma:

> If the DOE continues to invest in structural interventions while minimizing instructional initiatives, it will exacerbate the toxic cycle that closes struggling high schools instead of improving them, and sends their students to other vulnerable high schools, which then become additional targets for closure. As the current list of school closings indicates, new small high schools are also becoming vulnerable to this destructive strategy of musical chairs in which the losers are always the students who most need intervention and support to succeed. (para. 10)

The Parthenon Group, a Boston-based educational consulting firm, conducted an in-depth study on New York City public schools to determine the shortfalls, provide an improvement plan, and analyze the patterns of those schools that "beat the odds," that is, schools that have succeeded academically despite servicing a high-need student population. The 2006 study reported two major findings; those schools failing at higher rates (1) tended to be larger than other schools in NYC, and (2) had higher concentrations of low-level students (Parthenon Group 2006). Moreover, the study found that almost no secondary schools in New York City serving "high need" populations were beating the odds. The study also found that Latino students accounted for the largest percentage in high school dropouts for the 2004–5 school year. Meade et al. (2009a) found a similar pattern in the 2006–7 high school cohort. Although the percentage of high school dropouts in NYC has decreased since 1990, the percentage of high school dropouts is still alarmingly high, most notably among Mexican and Dominican youth. Additionally, Latino and Black students in secondary education were also more likely than their White and Asian counterparts to be over-age and off-track on the number of credits needed to graduate (Parthenon Group 2006). This is cause for further concern since those students who were more likely to drop out are those students who are over-age (Meade et al. 2009a).

In their improvement plan, the Parthenon Group suggested a system-wide reform that ensured a more equitable high school admissions policy, to prevent the concentration of low-performing students in a few schools and create smaller schools that could be devoted to serving low-level students.

THE IMPACT OF CHARTER SCHOOLS

As we mentioned previously, the number of charter schools in New York City has substantially increased since the Children First reforms were implemented. Their proliferation has been largely fueled by school closures in the city, creating the physical space in which to launch new schools, primarily charter schools. The charter school movement has seen its share of supporters, as well as its critics. Data compiled by the city's Charter School Center provide an insight into the composition and character of charter schools. Since Mayor Bloomberg launched Children First, charter school student enrollment has increased from under five thousand students in 2003 to an impressive forty-seven thousand in 2012 (NYC Charter School Center 2012). However, charter schools have consistently been criticized for enrolling a lower percentage of Latino students, particularly recent immigrants and English language learners (ELLs), than neighboring public schools. New York City charter schools disproportionately serve black students; in the 2010–11 school year the city's charter schools had a 62% black student enrollment, whereas district public schools accounted for only 28.6%. What is more, charter schools were serving 10% fewer Latinos than the surrounding district public schools, 30.9% compared to 40.4%. Charter schools reveal further disparities in enrollment in the emergent bilingual student population, another critical subgroup of students: district public schools in 2010–11 were nearly three times as likely as charters to enroll emergent bilingual students, 5.8% compared to 15%. According to the 2013–2014 DOE Demographic Report, 62% of emergent bilinguals are Spanish speaking; thus, most emergent bilingual students are also Latinos (NYC Department of Education 2015).

Enrollment disparities aside, charter schools have performed better than district schools by some measures and about equally well by others. Data from the New York City Charter School Center illustrate a higher percentage of students in charter schools than in district schools scoring at or above proficient levels on the 2011 New York State math exam. On the 2011 New York State English language arts exam (ELA), students in charter and district schools performed at comparable levels; notably, however, district school students in the fifth grade performed 8% better than charter school students. Nevertheless, Latino students in charter schools scored higher on both the ELA and math exams. The emergent bilingual student subgroup showed a similar trend, but to a lower extent (NYC Charter School Center 2012). Thus, 10% more Latino students in grades 3–8 scored at or above grade level on the math exam in charter schools than in district schools, and nearly 6% higher on the English language arts. Moreover, 10% more emergent bilingual students in grades 3–8 also performed at or above grade level on the math exam in charter schools than in district schools. It is important to note, again, however, Latinos and emergent bilinguals are two underrepresented student subgroups in the city's charter schools, and overrepresented in nearby neighborhood schools, as has been shown in the research of Suárez-Orozco and Sattin-Bajaj (2009). Critics have argued that since charter schools do not receive the extra public funding to service emergent bilingual students, they have no incentive to serve these students or immigrant families (Hoxby and Murarka 2009; Leal and Meier 2010). Nevertheless, there are specialized charter schools that serve only emergent bilingual students and that should not go unnoticed.

Charter schools have been at the center of controversy due to accusations that some are counseling certain student populations out of their schools. There are also concerns that some charter schools have alarming student attrition rates. In her study, Bennett (2010) has shown a disconcerting pattern of student attrition in New York City's highest-performing charter middle schools. She found that eight out of thirteen of these had an average attrition rate of 23%, with one charter school showing a 40% attrition rate; in contrast, the surrounding district schools showed a steady or an increase in student enrollment. She further notes that "as students disappear, the high-attrition schools record ever higher percentages of proficient students [in high-stakes exams]. This same pattern plays out in all thirteen schools. Schools with more than 20 percent attrition see their percent of proficient students rise to over 90 percent" (para. 1). Put differently, some schools have figured out that one way to raise test scores is to find ways to remove students that are likely to bring them down.

The New York City Charter School Center also compared the turnover rates for both teachers and principals in charter and district schools, and researchers found a striking difference in turnover rates between the two types of schools. While 26–33% of charter school teachers left their positions each year between 2006 and 2011, district school teacher turnover was between 13 and 16% during the same period. What is more, charter school principals were six times as likely to leave their positions at a charter school as were district school principals, 18.7% compared to 3.6%.

School closures have coincided with both the proliferation of charter schools and the increase in small schools. The Parthenon Group report (2006) cited small schools as one of the potential solutions to the problems confronting larger schools. Small schools in New York City have gained considerable support because they have outperformed larger schools. However, skeptics maintain that part of the reason for their improved performance is that they were shielded from serving large numbers of English language learners (ELL) and special education students during their first few years of operation, and more needs to be done to service the high-needs student populations. Michelle Fine (2005), for instance, has argued that small schools have served Latino students far better than large urban schools. In her study, students in small schools reported higher levels of satisfaction with their schooling experience, significantly higher levels of feeling academically challenged, and higher levels of feeling well prepared for college than their counterparts in large schools. Flores and Chu (2011) also studied how the rise of small schools has impacted Latinos in New York and found that small schools were more successful in keeping Latino students on track for graduation based on their accumulation of credits. Small schools also had overall higher graduation rates than larger schools. However, the authors question the quality of the programming available in the small schools; the small schools in their study were far less likely than large schools to offer bilingual programming, often only offering English as a second language (ESL) services to emergent bilingual students. Moreover, because of their size and limited resources, small schools are less likely to offer advanced placement courses or to provide comprehensive special education services and the broad range of electives offered at comprehensive high schools. And as Krashen and McField (2005) have shown, high-quality bilingual programming for emergent bilingual students is superior to English-only approaches (as cited in Flores and Chu 2010).

Another study on small schools revealed a problem with their pedagogical approach, which, according to some research, has frequently centered on test preparation. Shiller's (2010) study reveals the case of a large Bronx high school that was divided into three smaller schools, which she refers to as *Team Academy*, *Vision High School*, and *City Prep*. She found that there was an improvement in attendance and graduation rates (see table 13.3), a finding consistent with those studies cited above; nonetheless, Shiller also found that teachers were engaging in minimum-standards and test-centered pedagogical approaches. Furthermore, she found that students' critical thinking skills were not nurtured in these schools; instead, much class time was devoted to test preparation. She goes on to note that 90% of the schools' student population was black or Latino.

Table 13.3 Graduation Rates, Large Bronx H.S. vs. Three Smaller Schools

Schools	Graduation Rate
Bronx H.S.*	42%
Team Academy	86.8%
Vision H.S.	91%
City Prep	86.7%

* Bronx High School graduation rate is taken from the class of 2001.

Source: Adapted from Shiller 2010.

CONCLUSION: THE UNFULFILLED PROMISE OF CHILDREN FIRST FOR LATINO STUDENTS

More than sixty years after the Supreme Court's *Brown* decision, New York City continues to be segregated in many ways. Racial isolation is especially evident in the city's schools where Latino students are concentrated. In fact, the rate of racial/ethnic concentration in public schools is among the highest in the nation (Schott Foundation 2012). In neighborhoods such as the South Bronx, Bushwick, East New York, and Washington Heights, large concentrations of high-needs Latino students continue to be served by low-performing schools. Meade et al. (2009b) found that those schools with higher concentrations of Latino and black students were also the city's lowest-performing schools.

Undocumented status is yet another challenge facing the Latino community, further limiting higher education and employment opportunities.[4] According Motel and Patten's (2012) Pew Hispanic Center Report, forty million immigrants live in the United States, nearly half (47%) of them Latinos; and as of 2010, an estimated 11.2 million unauthorized immigrants were living in the country (Passel and Cohn 2011). In 2008, for example, the estimated percentage of undocumented immigrants in the United States by nationality showed that the majority of undocumented immigrants (59%) came from Mexico, with an additional 22% coming from other Latin American countries (Passel and Cohn 2008).

On numerous occasions, Mayor Bloomberg and former chancellor Joel Klein defended their reforms by asserting that "education is the civil rights issue of the 21st century." They also castigated their critics as defenders of failure and the status quo. Yet a close look at how the reforms initiated under their leadership have impacted Latino students reveals that two of the most important issues confronting Latinos, namely school segregation and the needs of undocumented students, were excluded from their reform agenda.

Finally, a new mayor, Bill de Blasio, and new chancellor, Carmen Fariña, took their respective offices in January 2014. At this point, and progressive rhetoric aside, it is too early to tell what the leadership change will mean for New York City's students. What is clear is that in the short term, the mayor will retain control of the public school system and retain the existing charter schools. Importantly, it is essential that Mayor de Blasio and Chancellor Fariña learn lessons from the past decade of reform. Latino students, in particular, cannot afford another period of experimentation that promises a great deal but delivers far less than is needed.

NOTES

1. For an early overview of de Blasio Administration reforms, see Chatterjee 2014. *Voices in Urban Education*, in which her article appeared, is published by the Annenberg Institute for School Reform, www.annenberginstitute.org.

2. By 2016, New York City had close to two hundred charter schools. See schools.nyc.gov.

3. In order to be allowed to run for a third term, Mayor Bloomberg persuaded members of the city council, who would also benefit from the change, to approve a change in the city's charter and allow for a one-time exemption to the two-term rule for mayor. Bloomberg claimed that such action was warranted due to the severe impact that the recession of 2008 had upon the city's finances. During a press conference announcing his bid for a third term, he declared, "Given the events of recent weeks and given the enormous challenges we face, I don't want to walk away from a city I feel I can help lead through these tough times." David W. Chen, "Bill Paves Way for a Third Term for Bloomberg," *New York Times*, October 3, 2008.

4. For an updated discussion of the undocumented in the United States and New York showing an overall decline, see Warren (2016).

REFERENCES

ACT. 2013. *The Condition of College and Career Readiness*. 2013. Various reports. Iowa City, IA: ACT. http://www.act.org/research/policymakers/cccr13/index .html.

Beam, John M., Chase Madar, and Deinya Phenix. 2008. "Life without Lockdown: Do Peaceful Schools Require High-Profile Policing?" *Voices in Urban Education*, no. 19: 27–37. http://annenberginstitute.org/sites/default/files /product/233/files/VUE19.pdf.

Bennett, Jackie. 2010. "Vanishing Schools, Rising Scores: Middle School Charters Show Alarming Student Attrition over Time." Accessed July 26, 2013. www .edwize.org.

Center for Latin American, Caribbean and Latino Studies. 2011. *The Latino Population of New York City, 1990–2010*. Latino Data Project, report 44. New York: Center for Latin American, Caribbean and Latino Studies, November. http:// clacls.gc.cuny.edu/files/2013/10/The-Latino-Population-of-New-York-City -1990-2010.pdf.

Chatterjee, Oona. 2014. "Equity-Driven Public Education: A Historic Opportunity." In "The Education Election," *Voices in Urban Education*, no. 39: 1–5.

Darling-Hammond, Linda. 2004. "Inequality and the Right to Learn: Access to Qualified Teachers in California's Public Schools." *Teachers College Record* 106, no. 10: 1936–66.

Eli and Edythe Broad Foundation. 2007. "2007 Broad Prize Winner." Los Angeles: Eli and Edythe Broad Foundation. http://broadfoundation.org/the-broad -prize-for-urban-education/.

Fine, Michelle. 2005. "High-Stakes Testing and Lost Opportunities: The New York State Regents Exams." *Encounter* 18 (2): 24–29.

Flores, Nelson, and Haiwen Chu. 2011. "How Does Size Matter? The Impact of the Rise of Small Schools on Latinos and Emergent Bilinguals in New York City." *International Journal of Bilingual Education and Bilingualism* 14 (2): 155–70.

Fruchter, Norm. 2011. "The Story behind the Parthenon Report." EdVoxNY. February 18. http://edvoxny.wordpress.com/2011/02/18/the-story-behind-the -parthenon-report/.

Fruchter, Norm, and Sara McAlister. 2008. *School Governance and Accountability: Outcomes of Mayoral Control of Schooling in New York City*. Providence, RI: Annenberg Institute for School Reform, Brown University, October. http:// annenberginstitute.org/pdf/MayoralControl.pdf.

Gandara, Patricia C., and Frances Contreras. 2010. *The Latino Education Crisis: The Consequences of Failed Social Policies*. Cambridge, MA: Harvard University Press.

García, Ofelia. 2009. *Bilingual Education in the 21st Century: A Global Perspective*. Malden, MA: Basil Blackwell.

Hoxby, Caroline M., and Sonali Murarka. 2009. "Charter Schools in New York City: Who Enrolls and How They Affect Their Students' Achievement." National Bureau of Economic Research Working Paper 14852. Cambridge, MA: National Bureau of Economic Research, April. http://www.nber.org/papers /w14852.

Jaggars, Shanna Smith, and Michelle Hodara. 2011. "The Opposing Forces That Shape Developmental Education: Assessment, Placement, and Progression at CUNY Community Colleges." CCRC Working Paper 36. New York: Community College Research Center, Teachers College, Columbia University. http://ccrc.tc.columbia.edu/Publication.asp?UID=974.

Kemple, James J. 2011. "Children First and Student Outcomes: 2003–2010." In *Education Reform in New York City: Ambitious Change in the Nation's Most Complex School System*, edited by Jennifer A. O'Day, Catherine S. Bitter, and Louis M. Gomez, 255–91. Cambridge, MA: Harvard Education Press.

Krashen, Stephen, and Grace McField. 2005. "What Works? Reviewing the Latest Evidence on Bilingual Education." *Language Learner* 1 (2): 7–10.

Kretchmar, Kerry. 2014. "Democracy (In)Action: A Critical Policy Analysis of New York City Public School Closings by Teachers, Students, Administrators, and Community Members." *Education and Urban Society* 46:3–29. http://eus.sagepub.com/content/46/1/3.short.

Leal, David L., and Kenneth J. Meier. 2010. *The Politics of Latino Education*. New York: Teachers College Press.

Meade, Ben, Frank Gaytan, E. Fergus, and Pedro Noguera. 2009a. *A Close Look at the Dropout Crisis: Examining Black and Latino Males in New York City*. New York: Metropolitan Center of Urban Education, August. http://steinhardt.nyu.edu/scmsAdmin/uploads/004/453/Dropout_Crisis.pdf.

———. 2009b. *Making the Grade in New York City Schools: Progress Report Grades and Black and Latino Students*. New York: Metropolitan Center of Urban Education. http://steinhardt.nyu.edu/scmsAdmin/uploads/004/450/Making_the_Grade.pdf.

Motel, Seth, and Eileen Patten. 2012. *The 10 Largest Hispanic Origin Groups: Characteristics, Rankings, Top Counties*. Hispanic Trends. Washington, DC: Pew Research Center, June 27. http://www.pewhispanic.org/2012/06/27/the-10-largest-hispanic-origin-groups-characteristics-rankings-top-counties/.

New York City Charter School Center. 2012. *The State of the NYC Charter School Sector*. http://www.nyccharterschools.org/data.

New York City, Department of City Planning. 2003. *New York City Public Schools: Demographic and Enrollment Trends, 1990–2002*. New York: Department of City Planning. Accessed July 15, 2013. http://www.nyc.gov/html/dcp/html/pub/school90_02.shtml.

New York City, Department of Education. 2013. *2013 Demographic Report*. Office of English Language Learners. http://schools.nyc.gov/NR/rdonlyres/FD5EB945-5C27-44F8-BE4B-E4C65D7176F8/0/2013DemographicReport_june2013_revised.pdf.

———. 2015. "School Year 2013–2014 Demographic Report." Department of English Language Learners and Student Support. http://schools.nyc.gov/NR/rdonlyres/FC0B4035-00DF-4318-A1F7-6EF23C15B7F6/0/20132014DemographicReportFinalWINTER2015.pdf

———. 2016. "New York State Common Core English Language Arts (ELA) and Mathematics Tests." ELA Data Files by Grade, 2013–2016, Excel Format. http://schools.nyc.gov/Accountability/data/TestResults/ELAandMath TestResults.

New York City, Independent Budget Office. 2012. "Statistical Profile of Schools on DOE's 2012 Closure List." New York: Independent Budget Office Education Research Team, February. http://www.ibo.nyc.ny.us/iboreports/2012school closing.pdf.

New York City Working Group on School Transformation. 2012. *The Way Forward: From Sanctions to Supports.* New York: New York City Working Group on School Transformation, April. http://annenberginstitute.org/sites/default /files/SchoolTransformationReport_0.pdf.

O'Day, Jennifer A., Catherine S. Bitter, and Joan E. Talbert. 2011. "Introduction to the Volume and Children First." In *Education Reform in New York City: Ambitious Change in the Nation's Most Complex School System,* edited by Jennifer A. O'Day, Catherine S. Bitter, and Louis M. Gomez, 1–14. Cambridge, MA: Harvard Education Press.

Parthenon Group. 2006. *NYC Secondary Reform Selected Analysis.* Boston: Parthenon Group. http://www.classsizematters.org/wp-content/uploads/2013 /05/parthenon-2006.pdf.

Passel, Jeffrey S., and D'Vera Cohn. 2008. *Trends in Unauthorized Immigration: Undocumented Inflow Now Trails Legal Inflow.* Washington, DC: Pew Hispanic Center. http://pewhispanic.org/files/reports/94.pdf.

———. 2011. "Unauthorized Immigrant Population: National and State Trends, 2010." Washington, DC: Pew Hispanic Center. http://www.pewhispanic.org /2011/02/01/unauthorized-immigrant-population-brnational-and-state -trends-2010/.

Schott Foundation for Public Education. 2012. *A Rotting Apple: Education Redlining in New York City.* http://schottfoundation.org/resources/education -redlining-new-york-city.

Shiller, Jessica. 2010. "It's Only Part of the Story: The Fallacy of Improved Outcome Data in New York City's Effort to Make Its High Schools Small." *Education and Urban Society* 42 (3): 247–68.

Suárez-Orozco, Marcelo, and Carolyn Sattin-Bajaj. 2009. "Charter Schools Fail Immigrants." The Blog, *Huffington Post,* November 30. Last updated May 25, 2011. http://www.huffingtonpost.com/carolyn-sattinbajaj/charter-schools -fail-immi_b_305338.html.

Treschan, Lazar. 2010. *Latino Youth in New York City: School, Work, and Income Trends for New York's Largest Group of Young People.* New York: Community Service Society. http://lghttp.58547.nexcesscdn.net/803F44A/images/nycss /images/uploads/pubs/LatinoYouthinNYCOct2010.pdf.pdf.

United Federation of Teachers. 2011. "School Closings Map: 97 Closed Schools." New York: United Federation of Teachers. http://www.uft.org/news/school -closings-map-closed.

United States Census Bureau. 2010. "Table PL-P3 NYC: Total Population, Under 18 and 18 Years and Over by Mutually Exclusive Race and Hispanic Origin, New York City and Boroughs, 2010." New York: New York City, Department of City Planning, Population Division." https://www1.nyc.gov/assets/planning /download/pdf/data-maps/nyc-population/census2010/t_pl_p3_nyc.pdf.

Urban Youth Collaborative. 2011. *No Closer to College: NYC High School Students Call for Real School Transformation, Not School Closings*. New York: Urban Youth Collaborative, April. http://www.urbanyouthcollaborative.org/wp -content/uploads/2011/05/No-Closer-to-College-Report.pdf.

Warren, Robert. 2016. "US Undocumented Population Drops below 11 Million in 2014, with Continued Declines in the Mexican Undocumented Population." *Journal on Migration and Human Security* 4 (1): 1–15.

CHAPTER FOURTEEN

Latinos and Environmental Justice

New York City Cases

SHERRIE BAVER

In recent years, several scholars have produced comprehensive studies of environmental justice activism in New York (e.g., Corburn 2005; Sze 2007; Angotti 2008). The point of this chapter, then, is not to cover the same territory but to highlight the Latino, especially Puerto Rican, contribution to this important social movement. While it has usually been multiethnic coalitions that have struggled and succeeded to create a less toxic, greener city, what is less known is that Latinos have been in the forefront of this activism.

WHAT IS ENVIRONMENTAL JUSTICE?

In its most basic formulation, environmental justice (EJ) proponents argue that poor people and people of color disproportionately suffer from the harmful impacts of environmental processes and policies (Faber 1998; Harvey 1999; Roberts and Toffolon-Weiss 2001; Agyeman, Bullard, and Evans 2003). The notion of environmental justice arose in the United States in the

1980s; and while arguments over its definition have existed since it was first used, more "takes" on its meaning have appeared as the concept has been adopted horizontally (to other nations) and vertically (from the local to the global level), for example, in documenting the negative effects of rich countries' consumption patterns on poor countries in terms of climate change.

The US Environmental Protection Agency's definition of environmental justice captures its essence as it is applied to the New York cases discussed in this chapter: "Environmental justice is the fair treatment and meaningful involvement of all people regardless of race, color, national origin, or income, with respect to the development, implementation, and enforcement of environmental laws, regulations, and policies. . . . It will be achieved when everybody enjoys . . . the same degree of protection from environmental and health hazards, and . . . equal access to the decision-making process to have a healthy environment in which to live, learn, and work" (US EPA 2016).

Environmental justice represents a new wave of environmentalism that differs markedly from its earlier, mainstream predecessor. Historically, mainstream environmental organizations have focused on conservation (green) issues at the national level and, in recent decades, at the global level. In contrast, environmental justice movements have been associated with remediation (brown) issues and demands for social equity, especially at the community level. For EJ activists, environmental injustice can be conscious or unconscious and can come in two stages. It can exist in the great disparity between the frequency with which polluting manufacturing plants, transportation hubs, hazardous waste disposal sites, and similar commercial developments (all with negative health and environmental consequences) are sited in minority and low-income communities and the frequency with which such facilities are sited in whiter, more affluent areas. Additionally, injustice can exist in the uneven enforcement of environmental laws and regulations, enforcement that tends to favor majority communities over minority/poor ones (Roberts and Toffolon-Weiss 2001, 9). Common strategies of the EJ movement are to (1) document the inequitable impacts of environmental harm, particularly on public health, and (2) advocate for measures to mitigate these documented negative impacts.

THE MOVEMENT'S HISTORY

In the late 1970s, many ordinary Americans began understanding they might be living near toxic chemicals and associated health risks, perhaps first widely noted in the case of Love Canal in upstate New York (Gibbs 1982).[1] This event and others rather quickly led to Congress legislating the Superfund Program in 1980.[2]

For some, the new understanding of the extent of pollution in old industrial communities dovetailed with a realization that a disproportionate number of harmful facilities were in low-income, minority neighborhoods, *and that these communities were continuing to be targeted.* The incipient movement to protest this reality took on various labels: "poor people's environmentalism," "environmental racism," and "environmental justice." "Environmental justice" is used here for two reasons. First, it focuses not merely on people's poverty and historical lack of political resources but also on their agency to seek justice. Second, writers and activists embracing the more specific label, "environmental racism," pinpoint the movement's beginning in 1982 with the African American struggle in Warren County, North Carolina; in this chapter, however, I argue that the movement first began to rumble earlier, with both African American and Latino contributions.[3]

In truth, the 1982 Warren County case was probably most directly responsible for the formal institutionalization of environmental justice concerns in the federal government. In that episode, more than five hundred activists gathered to protest the siting of a hazardous PCB landfill in a predominantly African American and low-income rural community. By 1987, the progressive United Church of Christ (UCC) had formed a Commission for Racial Justice, and in the same year it issued a report that gave the Warren County case and similar struggles wide national attention (Commission for Racial Justice 1987; Bullard et al. 2007). Then, in 1991, the UCC helped organize the "People of Color Environmental Leadership Summit" in Washington, which resulted in a declaration of 117 principles of environmental justice. The Summit also resulted in a pledge by participants to lobby the federal government to act on environmental injustice (Grossman 1994).

The US Environmental Protection Agency, aware of the EJ movement and its concerns even before the Washington summit, had established its own Environmental Equity Workgroup in 1990 to assess available evidence that environmental risks were not being shared equally across class and racial subpopulations. By 1994, environmental justice concerns gained additional, at least symbolic, recognition with President Clinton's Executive Order 12898, entitled "Federal Action to Address Environmental Justice in Minority Populations and Low Income Populations." The order created the Interagency Federal Working Group on Environmental Justice and gave

national importance to what had previously been a set of nonlinked struggles at the grassroots level. Thus by the mid-1990s, environmental justice was
seen as a civil right; and by the late 1990s, the EPA was issuing interim guidelines on how to proceed when environmental injustice was charged under
Title VI of the Federal Civil Rights Act (Abel, Salazar, and Robert 2015). Still,
winning EJ cases through litigation has not been easy, and the US Supreme
Court ruling in *Alexander v. Sandoval* (2001) likely made "EPA's ability to
rely on Title VI for environmental justice policy [even] less certain" (Mohai,
Pellow, and Roberts 2009, 421).[4]

ENVIRONMENTAL JUSTICE STRUGGLES IN NEW YORK: THE PREQUEL

Environmental Justice started as a local and national movement in the 1980s
and an international movement in the 1990s. Were there, however, precursors
in New York and a leading Puerto Rican role? In *Noxious New York* (2007),
Julie Sze asserts that the historical context in which environmental justice notions were first tied to cleanup and public health concerns was the Sanitary
Movement of the late nineteenth century and the Progressive era in the early
twentieth century. The more proximate context was the burgeoning civil rights
movement of the late 1950s and 1960s and the growing indignation about the
numerous injustices faced by racial and ethnic minorities in the United States.
One highly noticeable injustice in New York City, unequal garbage collection, was first highlighted in 1962 by the African American civil rights group
the Congress of Racial Equality (CORE). In "Operation Clean Sweep," the
Bedford-Stuyvesant chapter in Brooklyn dumped garbage on the steps of city
hall to protest the Sanitation Department's neglect of their neighborhood.

Yet it was, perhaps, the Young Lords, with their remarkable flair for pub-
licity, that drew attention to the same problem in East Harlem in 1969, at
least two decades before garbage and its disposal would become a key issue
for the city's environmental justice activists. In his study of "metropolitan
nature" in New York, geographer Matthew Gandy (2002) highlights the radical environmental politics of the Puerto Rican barrio in the late 1960s and
early 1970s. As former Young Lord, now journalist, Felipe Luciano has noted,
when they first began their activism, the Lords went to the community to
find out the biggest concern. While the Lords thought the answer would be
housing, the answer was, in fact, "la basura (garbage)." After a few Sundays
of sweeping with brooms "liberated from the Sanitation Department," the

Young Lords left the garbage in the middle of Third Avenue in El Barrio, launching the first "East Harlem Garbage Offensive" (Morales 1996).

Another basic issue for the Young Lords was inadequate community health services—inadequate, for instance, to prevent environmentally induced lead poisoning in children. They highlighted the inadequate state of health care for Latinos most notably in 1970 with their "liberation" of medical equipment and, ultimately, the takeover of Lincoln Hospital. Thus at the height of civil rights and antiwar activism, the Young Lords began to forge the link between public health and environmental hazards in the minds of poor New Yorkers.

Although the Lords were "Americanized" Puerto Ricans either born or raised from an early age in New York and other mainland cities, they became part of a link between Puerto Rico and mainland environmental activists that has not yet been fully explored. Due to the intensive industrialization of Puerto Rico since the late 1940s under Operation Bootstrap, Puerto Rico has been no stranger to toxic waste and pollution.[5] By the mid-1960s, particularly spurred by plans to develop a copper-mining facility in central Puerto Rico, a vocal island environmental movement arose with close links to progressive church groups on the island (Baver 1993; García Martínez 2006; Valdés Pizzini 2006). As young Puerto Ricans from the diaspora became more conscious of Puerto Rico's past and networked with homeland counterparts, they became increasingly aware of the effects of colonialism and pollution from rapid industrialization.

It is not, then, accidental that part of the Young Lords' legacy in New York has been the founding of environmental justice groups such as the Toxic Avengers in Brooklyn and the South Bronx Clean Air Coalition in the 1980s and 1990s. Environmental degradation in Puerto Rico and Puerto Rican neighborhoods in New York gained a special salience.[6] Furthermore, the networked activism continued in the late 1990s and early twenty-first century. New York Latino activists worked with Puerto Ricans in Puerto Rico to reframe the Vieques struggle as a cause of human rights abuse and environmental injustice and ultimately ejected the US Navy from Puerto Rico (McCaffrey and Baver 2006). A more recent struggle over the proposed *gasoducto*, or ninety-two-mile natural gas pipeline, in Puerto Rico is yet another controversy that reenergized island-stateside networked environmental activism begun five decades ago.[7]

A second way New York Puerto Ricans may have prefigured the national environmental justice movement was with their concern for urban greenspace, specifically by developing *casitas* and community gardens throughout the city. Sociologist Barbara Lynch (1993, 109) has posited a Hispanic Caribbean notion of environment, especially if "the environment" is understood as a social construction. While mainstream Anglo environmental discourse typically has been about pristine wildernesses and unpeopled frontiers, urban Latino environmental discourse (at least in New York) may be traced back to the Puerto Rican immigrant community of the mid-twentieth century and focused on recreational gardening and fishing. By the 1970s, the casita movement also became part of New York Latino environmental reality, as the right to control community space along with acts of resistance became more commonplace.

Casitas are an important part of this prequel, so they need a bit of discussion. Luis Aponte-Parés (1998) has provided the now-classic discussion of New York casitas. They are shacks, reminiscent of rural Puerto Rico: "Built on stilts, with land all around, frequently with a vegetable garden, you can identify them with their corrugated gable metal roofs, windows opening with shutters, bright colors, and ample verandas, so favored by Caribbean architecture.... They confer 'meaning' to the environment by building alternative landscapes on the devastated urban milieu. They are an architecture of resistance" (271–80). Casitas arose in Latino neighborhoods in New York—particularly El Barrio (East Harlem), Loisaida (Lower East Side), the South Bronx, and Brooklyn—that were experiencing some or all of the following pressures: population displacement, building abandonment, and incipient gentrification. Often the casitas were accompanied by vegetable gardens, sometimes even with chickens; the goal was to re-create family or neighborhood clubs and the milieu of the *jibaro*, the small independent peasant from the Puerto Rican hills. The casitas offered their builders a bit of green and new sense of social connection, a way to reconquer the city's hostile environment. Additionally, they have taught children (without the benefit of sleepaway camps or country homes) about nature in their own communities (Lynch 1993, 108–9).

THE GROWTH OF ENVIRONMENTAL JUSTICE ACTIVISM IN NEW YORK

What spurred the organized environmental justice struggles starting in the late 1980s? Analysts such as Sze (2007) and Angotti (2008) argue that the driving economic force of this new type of mobilization was the economic philosophy of neoliberalism beginning to take hold globally and in New York during the decade. New York City had experienced massive urban renewal in the 1960s, but this was over by 1973 when the city, essentially, went broke. For local officials and real estate developers, the answer to the city's ills in the 1980s was neoliberalism, with its emphasis on privatization and deregulation. A result of the rush of private real estate investment in several of New York's neighborhoods, especially in Manhattan and parts of Brooklyn with attractive housing stock and other amenities, was intensified gentrification. The result for other areas, those that were industrial or formerly industrialized, especially in the Bronx and Brooklyn and often with "locally unwanted land uses" (LULU's), was that the city wanted to locate even more LULU's (such as incinerators and power plants) in those communities.[8]

In *New York for Sale* (2008), Tom Angotti recounts that many of today's progressive community plans were constructed in response to neighborhood concerns about environmental justice and gentrification in the 1980s and 1990s. As Angotti tells it: "The city upzoned manufacturing land in wealthy neighborhoods to encourage new residential and commercial development but ignored the neighborhoods with LULUs. . . . Waterfronts in Manhattan and upscale neighborhoods in the outer boroughs were greened or promptly turned over to private developers, while waterfronts in working-class neighborhoods were left to languish. This was the context for the city's environmental justice movement" (133).

By the 1990s, with the city's economic and real estate boom in full swing, the pressures for more construction, more gentrification, and more potential environmental injustice became more intense; and New York continued its pattern as one of the most spatially segregated cities in the United States (Minnite and Ness 2006, 141; Frey 2010). It became ever clearer that struggles for a healthy environment and struggles against gentrification and displacement in poor neighborhoods were two sides of the same coin.

During this period, most of the New York neighborhoods battling for environmental justice had large numbers of Latinos.[9] Sze (2007), for example, studied several minority communities that struggled for EJ in the late 1980s and 1990s: Greenpoint-Williamsburg, Sunset Park / Windsor Terrace in Brooklyn, Melrose and Mott Haven, Hunts Point / Longwood in the Bronx, and West Harlem in Manhattan. Statistical data illustrate the large Latino presence in Sze's case studies. In the early years of this century, Brooklyn Community District (CD) 1 (Greenpoint-Williamsburg) was 37.7%

Hispanic, Brooklyn CD 7 (Sunset Park / Windsor Terrace) was 52.7% Hispanic, Bronx CD 1 (Melrose–Mott Haven) was 70.8% Hispanic, and Bronx CD 2 (Hunt's Point / Longwood) was 75.8% Hispanic. In Sze's last major EJ case, the North River sewage treatment plant, spearheaded by a predominantly African American group, West Harlem Environmental Action (WEACT), West Harlem actually was predominantly Hispanic. Manhattan CD 1 (West Harlem) was 31.3% African American and 43.2% Hispanic.[10] Angotti (2008), also researching EJ in New York City, agrees that Latino areas in the Bronx and Brooklyn were the epicenters of these struggles.[11]

THE ISSUES EJ ACTIVISTS EMBRACE

Generally speaking, environmental justice struggles involve (1) the siting and politics of dumping, (2) air quality and inequality, and (3) the uneven distribution of urban greenspace. As the EJ notion has spread globally through activist networks, additional concerns are (4) the environmental effects of mineral extraction and oil drilling on local communities; (5) the global waste trade, involving dumping in developing countries and electronics recycling with lax regulations; and (6) climate change and climate justice. On the last point, activists and scholars highlight the imbalance between residents in the developed world, with high consumption levels and large-scale electricity use, and residents in the developing world, who suffer the consequences of increased greenhouse gas emissions, such as farmers experiencing extremes of drought and flooding, and poor coastal dwellers dealing with sea-level rise (Clapp 2001; Walker 2012).

In New York City, while some similar issues resonate, others are more tied to urban life. Much activism is about economic decay and the attempted and actual siting of noxious facilities in decaying neighborhoods. Activists oppose potentially harmful infrastructure such as solid waste transfer stations, medical and municipal waste incinerators, sludge and sewage treatment plants, energy plants, and expressways and transportation hubs, not primarily on aesthetic grounds but because increased air pollution associated with this infrastructure seems responsible for the soaring asthma rates and other negative public health consequences in nearby communities.[12] Importantly, many environmental injustice issues overlap, as the following data on the South Bronx underscores:

The South Bronx has the lowest ratio of parks to people in New York City and takes in 40% of the city's waste, the handling of which is partly responsible for the 60,000 diesel truck trips into the Bronx each day. Rates for asthma in Bronx County, including for children, are eight times higher than the national average. In addition, the quality of the Bronx River water suffers from repeated combined sewer overflow events, which occur after rains, when overburdened waste treatment facilities release a mix of stormwater and untreated sewage into waterways (Ingram 2012, 279–80).

Before highlighting several major environmental justice struggles in New York, I offer a few general insights on why some protests succeed while other fail, based on earlier scholarly analyses. Mohai, Pellow, and Roberts (2009), for example, offer several hypotheses. First, it is easier to stop newly proposed projects than to close existing ones. Second, it seems necessary but not sufficient to garner support from well-known outside groups with experience fighting environmental battles. Third, communities do better, if they decide to sue, with support from public interest law clinics and firms rather than private injury tort lawyers. Finally, Peña (2010) reminds us that in all such battles, the challenge is much harder if the community is predominantly non–English speaking.

Garbage: Incinerators, Transfer Stations, Sewage and Sludge, Waste Storage

Julie Sze (2007, chap. 4) tells the complex saga of New York's garbage history in the 1980s and 1990s. While highlighting the city's economic push towards privatization, she also notes political factors, specifically mayoral promises to close Fresh Kills landfill on Staten Island[13] and the Manhattan district attorney's effort to end the commercial waste industry's mafia ties. The city's garbage crisis in the collecting and handling of waste began in the late 1980s when the tipping fees at Fresh Kills landfill were increased and commercial carters began building their own low-tech waste incinerators. The disposal crisis intensified at the end of the 1990s when Fresh Kills was closed. Throughout the 1990s, LULU's such as incinerators and transfer stations were proposed and sometimes built in low-income neighborhoods. As activists came to understand that the solid waste issue was too big for any one community group to handle, several groups coalesced in 1991 to form the New York City Environmental Justice Alliance (NYC-EJA).

While the goal of this essay is to highlight the Latino role in New York's environmental justice movement, the intent is not to play disadvantaged communities off against each other. Therefore, it is essential to restate that the city's EJ struggles are, typically, multiethnic efforts. No overview of EJ activism in New York would be complete without crediting the work of, for example, "MacArthur genius award winner" Majora Carter, founder of Sustainable South Bronx, and Peggy Shepard and Vernice Miller Travis of West Harlem Environmental Action (WEACT), or other activist groups, especially in the Bronx and Brooklyn, such as the Point Community Development Corporation, Mothers on the Move, Youth Ministries for Peace and Justice, and Make the Road by Walking.

Some of the first notable EJ garbage battles in New York involved the siting and closing of giant *incinerators*. One case occurred between 1991 and 1997 and resulted in the rare closure of a noxious facility in the South Bronx, the Bronx Lebanon Hospital Medical Waste Incinerator, built on private land with public monies. The neighborhood was low income, largely Puerto Rican / Latino in southwest Bronx, near a housing project and schools. (The project had originally been proposed for and rejected by suburban Rockland County.) Contrary to claims from the private operator and public authorities, the incinerator often discharged toxic emissions. The South Bronx Clean Air Coalition was the lead community group in this fight, and the facility was ultimately closed down in 1997 after a six-year struggle.[14]

A second, well-documented incinerator victory played out at the Brooklyn Navy Yard, which had been abandoned by the federal government in 1966. A giant waste incinerator was first proposed for this space in 1979 and ultimately defeated in 1995. The lead organization in this mobilization was El Puente, the community-based organization serving Los Sures, residents of the south side of Williamsburg, and headed by former Young Lord Luis Garden-Acosta. Ultimately the project was defeated by a multiethnic coalition (primarily Latino–Hasidic Jewish) that was so unusual that when Garden-Acosta first met with Hasidic Rabbi David Niederman of United Jewish Organizations, the El Puente leader felt "like Nixon coming to China" (Checker 2001; Gandy 2002).[15]

Siting waste-transfer stations has been a central part of environmental justice struggles in New York, and waste transfer stations (to ship garbage out of the city) were another feature of the garbage crisis starting in the late 1980s. The battleground was so large—involving eighty-five privately owned, commercial waste transfer stations located in working-class communities and communities of color, mainly in North Brooklyn and the South Bronx—that activists realized they needed to work for a citywide plan rather than fight numerous individual fights (Angotti 2008, 143–49). Thus, the Organization of Waterfront Neighborhoods (OWN) coalition was formed.

Key in this effort was activist and planner Eddie Bautista, for many years with New York Lawyers for the Public Interest (NYLPI) and later head of the NYC-EJA (with a stint as head of the Mayor's Office of Legislative Affairs). In 2002, OWN succeeded in persuading the newly elected mayor, Michael Bloomberg, to come up with a "fair share" citywide plan in which each borough would be responsible for handling its own waste. In addition to promoting increased recycling and reduced waste, the key to the "just" solid waste management plan was to retrofit existing marine transfer stations, located throughout the city. These stations would handle both domestic and commercial waste and would transport the garbage out of New York by barge rather than by diesel-spewing trucks emitting air pollution and foul smells.

Unfortunately, the "fair share" policy has faced years of litigation in Manhattan and a slow pace of retrofitting. The four outer boroughs, Brooklyn, Queens, the Bronx, and Staten Island, already have transfer stations, mainly in lower-income communities. At present, more than 60% of the city's garbage goes through plants in the South Bronx and along Newtown Creek in Brooklyn. (The South Bronx has thirteen waste transfer stations, and the area around Newtown Creek has nineteen.) For both areas, waste transfer still involves diesel-powered trucks.

Significantly, Manhattan, which produces 40% of the city's waste, has had no waste transfer stations.[16] Mayor Bloomberg, embracing EJ principles in his solid waste policy, insisted that each borough had to handle its own waste transfers. The Upper East Side of Manhattan refused to accept such a facility at 91st Street and the East River and began litigation 2006. The neighborhood, one of the wealthiest in the nation, argued "environmental injustice" because the facility would be near a public housing project. Because successful claims of environmental injustice involve *siting several* noxious facilities in one neighborhood, most activists regarded this argument as weak if not "ridiculous." Finally, the East 91st Street station received its permit to begin new construction in July 2012,[17] and, though it is still a contentious project, construction has continued under Mayor de Blasio.

Red Hook and Sunset Park in Brooklyn were at the epicenter of the *sludge* battles (Angotti 2008, 141–42). In 1988, New York was ordered to stop dumping its sludge (residue from treated sewage) from wastewater treatment plants into the ocean. The city's initial response was to propose building eight sludge-to-fertilizer plants throughout the city; all proposed plant sites were in low-income communities and communities of color with relatively low land values and with little land zoned for industry. Red Hook on the Brooklyn waterfront was to get two plants. The two-plant proposal was defeated, as was the next attempt by city officials to combine both plants into one larger facility on the Sunset Park waterfront. Both times, the sludge proposals were stopped by a multiethnic (Latino, Asian American, and Italian American) coalition; however, notably, both struggles were led by Elizabeth Yeampierre of UP-ROSE (United Puerto Rican Organization of Sunset Park), Brooklyn's oldest Latino organization. Yeampierre was acutely concerned because the proposed facility would be closest to a Puerto Rican neighborhood. Not surprisingly, this fight to "can the plan" received help from Puerto Rican officials, Congresswoman Nydia Velasquez, and then Bronx borough president Fernando Ferrer. While New York ultimately dropped the idea of a Brooklyn sludge-composting plant, about 40% of New York's sludge is now processed by a private firm in the South Bronx, with very noticeable odors.

An important hazardous waste storage victory in Williamsburg culminated after a sixteen-year fight against RADIAC. This struggle, too, was won with a multiethnic coalition, but Latinos and Hasidic groups were central to the effort. RADIAC was a radioactive waste storage facility on Kent Avenue and South 1st Street that periodically needed to renew its hazardous waste storage permit from the New York State Department of Environmental Conservation. RADIAC, New York State's only radioactive nuclear and toxic waste facility, was located one block from a city public elementary school. Only after the 9/11 attacks, however, did state officials recognize that the facility posed an unacceptable risk from terrorism or catastrophic fire. With help from Senator Charles Schumer, the operating permit was denied, and the facility closed down in 2005.[18]

We have already noted that a negative consequence of successful EJ struggles can often be intensified gentrification, and Williamsburg (adjacent to the Brooklyn Navy Yard) illustrates that this is not an idle fear. In Williamsburg, after the incinerator defeat and other neighborhood victories, fifteen acres of the Navy Yard were developed as the Steiner Studios in 2004, the country's most sophisticated film-production facility outside Hollywood. The Steiner Studios also hosts Abigail Kirsch's Stage 6, one of New York's most exclusive event spaces. Increasingly, longtime Williamsburg residents are finding themselves priced out of their ever-more-chic neighborhood.[19]

A second negative consequence of EJ struggles (even successful ones) can be a legacy of community infighting; and community infighting, perhaps, explains the story of the failed Banana Kelly project in the Bronx. The story of the Banana Kelly Community Improvement Association / Natural Resources Defense Council / Modo paper company project has been told several times (e.g., Herskovitz 2003, Harris 2003); but the key point here is that this was a potentially positive project advanced in the 1990s but defeated by community suspicion, rivalries, and fears resulting from earlier infrastructure fights (Soto-Lopez 2006). The project involved developing the Bronx Community Paper Company in the South Bronx to recycle the city's "urban forest (hundreds of thousands of tons of daily office paper waste)" into high-grade pulp for sale to international paper companies. It was also to generate new jobs and related local economic development and revitalize a brownfield site at the abandoned Harlem River Yards. This project would likely have been a win for the South Bronx, but beleaguered residents could not trust that this might be the case.

Energy Plants

In the mid-1990s, following the overriding logic of neoliberalism, New York governor George Pataki began pushing for the privatization and deregulation of energy provision. The governor's goal was to "promote competitive markets and streamline regulation in legislation passed in 1996 (Sze 2007, 157; Angotti 2008, 149). Because of favorable zoning laws and land values, new private and quasi-public power plants were developed in New York City, and, predictably, facilities were being concentrated in poor communities of color, especially Latino neighborhoods (Sze 2007, 162). In response to this next assault, community groups formed another broad-based EJ coalition, Communities United for Responsible Energy (CURE), to stop or at least mitigate the air pollution from these facilities.

As early as 2000, the New York State Power Authority (NYPA) admitted plants were being sited disproportionately in low-income areas.[20] As a result of protests and litigation by CURE, New York became the first state in the country to implement a special program to safeguard EJ communities from additional hardships from power plants. First, power plants now had to meet much stricter standards for particulate/soot pollution than before. Furthermore, for any power plant located in a poor neighborhood, the developer had to provide a pollution offset to reduce air pollution in that community (Sze 2007, 171–72; Eddie Bautista, personal interview, July 2012).

Transportation Issues

In the mid-twentieth century, many working-class communities in New York were split apart by Robert Moses's pharaonic expressways; since then, Latino and other poor communities have often had to live with the negative consequences—especially air pollution—of these projects (Caro 1974). UP-ROSE in Sunset Park, Brooklyn, has been a leader in advocating for a tunnel alternative to the city's plan to rebuild the elevated Gowanus Expressway, although at present, all plans for rebuilding have been tabled. EJ activists in the South Bronx have targeted the Sheridan Expressway, eventually hoping to have it torn down and replaced with homes and greenspace along the Bronx River. Moses's Cross-Bronx expressway, slicing through the South Bronx, is "now the most heavily traveled piece of interstate highway in the nation" (Angotti 2012, 177). It is also responsible for the largest number of trucks entering New York City daily, mainly traveling to the Hunt's Point Market; about twelve thousand diesel-emitting trucks per day use the expressway to reach the market.

In 2012, another transportation justice fight developed involving the upscale food delivery company FreshDirect. The company proposed moving its operations from Queens to the Harlem River Yards in the South Bronx. The proposal meant that some of the poorest New Yorkers would be accepting increased air pollution from hundreds more truck trips per day for the promise of low-wage jobs. Nor did the company help its initial public relations campaign when it announced it would not be delivering to most neighborhoods in the Bronx. Community opponents, with the help of New York Lawyers for the Public Interest, filed a suit to stop the project, arguing that in addition to the increased traffic and air pollution, the new facility would mean a loss of waterfront access and potential greenspace in the neighborhood.[21] As with the paper-recycling plan mentioned above, also destined for the Harlem River Yards, residents' memories of noxious infrastructure battles in the 1990s may prevent future large-scale projects in this environmentally overburdened area.

Lead-Based Paint

Although lead was banned from gasoline and paint in the 1970s, childhood lead paint poisoning remains a concern in poor neighborhoods with older housing stock. Lead from flaking paint and dust can cause neurological problems even in small doses. The Natural Resources Defense Council found that, nationally, twice as many Latino children as non-Latino white children are likely to have lead in their blood at levels higher than the action levels established by the federal Centers for Disease Control (Quintero-Somaini 2004).

Poor children are often exposed to lead inadvertently when cities plan infrastructure updates, as was the case when New York City proposed sandblasting the Williamsburg Bridge in the early 1990s. Jason Corburn, who studied this episode in *Street Science* (2005), noted that "compared to lead from peeling paint, the lead from lead-painted bridges is many orders of magnitude higher in lead content" (156). The coalition, Williamsburg around the Bridge Block Association (WABBA), spearheaded the community's case against bridge sandblasting, and one of the central players in WABBA was the Williamsburg community-based organization El Puente. Between 1992 and 1996, El Puente trained neighborhood residents as "street scientists," who would conduct epidemiological studies on lead exposure. Students at El Puente Academy, "The Toxic Avengers," also collected health data, and both groups adopted the Latin American tradition of participatory action research. The goal of such research is to educate communities and promote their empowerment (Freire 1974; Fals Borda and Rahman 1991). Ultimately, WABBA did not stop the sandblasting, but in 1999 the city agreed to proceed with much greater attention to mitigating lead dust. Thus, activists delayed the project until it could be done more safely and did bring more attention to the continuing health hazards from childhood lead poisoning. Another consequential victory stemming from this battle was that in 1997, the US EPA changed its risk assessment methodology from conducting traditional single-project assessments to considering the cumulative risks to which a community may be exposed (Corburn 2005, 80).

Greenspace and Community Gardens

Puerto Ricans have been in the forefront of fights for greenspace and community gardens in New York. Angotti (2012) relates the story of the group Nos Quedamos (We're staying), in the South Bronx; but he makes clear that contention can arise over the very definition of "greenspace." When New York's Housing Preservation Department proposed a planned suburbia in the South Bronx with individual houses, yards, and one large park, the residents of the Melrose section fought back, knowing these homes would be out of their financial reach. This was the threat that prompted forming Nos Quedamos in 1992. This community group successfully countered the city's plan with another vision of affordable residences and "multiple open greenspaces and their integration into the urban fabric" (Angotti 2012, 180). In addition to promoting affordable housing, Nos Quedamos remains in the forefront of developing greenspace in the borough.

The fight to preserve community gardens and casitas was taken up by the city's environmental justice movement in the mid-1990s. The idea of the gardens is not only to provide greenspaces, especially in poor neighborhoods, but also to teach children about nature in their communities. In the 1990s, the city's twenty-nine poorest community planning districts had less than 1.5 acres of open space per thousand residents.[22] What became known as "the community garden wars" began in 1998 when then mayor Rudolph Giuliani (1994–2001) wanted to auction off many of the city-owned lots to developers. Ultimately, the actress Bette Midler saved dozens of lots in 1999 through the New York Restoration Project, but many other community garden lots were the subject of litigation until 2002. At that time, the new mayor, Michael Bloomberg, and then state attorney general, Eliot Spitzer, agreed to a deal preserving 400 gardens while 150 other gardens would be turned over to private developers for low-income housing. While this clearly represented a victory for gardeners and greenspace advocates, many gardens have since been "sanitized" and "homogenized" to an extent, undoubtedly losing some of their *razon de estar* as places of national pride and cultural resistance.[23] Furthermore, this victory may be only the first round of a low-intensity war against community gardens and casitas, since the pressure to develop vacant land in New York City will only continue (Dávila 2004; Lynch and Brusi 2005; Martinez 2010).

EMERGING ISSUES FOR NEW YORK'S EJ ACTIVISTS

Waterfront Parks

A newer concern for New York's EJ activists is a more comprehensive vision of greenspace; in this vision, groups dealing with both air and water pollution plant urban forests and reclaim waterways in industrial areas. While Manhattan has had parks along the Hudson for decades, they have been absent from New York's poorer communities, for example, in the Bronx and Brooklyn.

In the Bronx, a total of sixty public and private organizations have formed the Bronx River Alliance; their goal is to establish ten miles of paths and parks along the southern end of the Bronx River near the Hunts Point market. At present, the Bronx is served by only pocket parks that are not interconnected, but city government and local community-based organizations are slowly cleaning the river and surrounding area.[24] In Brooklyn, Sunset Park's UPROSE created a "Greenway-Blueway design" that it has recently implemented. The plan, to promote expanded parkland (greenway) along the water (blueway) between 43rd and 50th Streets, resulted in the 2014 opening of the Bush Terminal Piers Park. This Greenway-Blueway added twenty-five acres of greenspace to the neighborhood.

Green-Collar Jobs

Green-collar jobs are well-paying jobs in the growing building-retrofitting industry. Torres-Vélez (2011) distinguishes between green jobs, traditionally associated with conservation issues, and newer green-collar jobs, involving redesigning buildings to lower greenhouse gas emissions (GHG's). Urban areas, and especially their buildings, are responsible for over 70% of US energy consumption and produce 48% of the nation's GHG's. New York City is especially problematic in this regard, since most of the city's buildings are considered energy inefficient (Gelman 2009). The energy efficiency sector is projected to grow more rapidly than any other green sector, yet disparities prevent training programs from targeting Latino workers. Torres-Vélez (2011, 97), troubled by this disparity, argues that since Puerto Rican community organizations have been at the forefront of environmental justice struggles in New York, they should play a central role in overcoming the green-collar jobs gap for Latinos.

One subset of the green jobs movement involves green co-ops as promoted by the Green Worker Cooperatives. This Bronx nonprofit, headed by longtime EJ activist Omar Freilla, not only wants to create environmentally friendly jobs in poor neighborhoods, but also wants the businesses providing the jobs to be established as cooperatives to empower the worker-owners. One such project was "Rebuilders Source," a short-lived cooperative to create building materials out of recycled construction waste; construction waste is a vast part of New York City's garbage. At present, the Green Worker Cooperatives is focusing on green retrofitting services, solar panel design and fabrication, and landscape design. The idea is to promote small, service-oriented businesses, especially in Latino neighborhoods.

Brownfield Redevelopment

The previously mentioned South Bronx Latino nonprofit *Nos Quedamos* continues its fight against community-displacing redevelopment but has branched out into other issues, including affordable housing and brownfield remediation and redevelopment. Indeed, many of their developments are on former brownfield sites. Eddie Bautista of NYC Environmental Justice Alliance (NYC-EJA) and Elizabeth Yeampierre of Brooklyn's UPROSE are also leaders in promoting brownfield redevelopment. These Latino-led organizations are in the forefront of creating standards and regulations on removing potentially hazardous materials in use at the city, state, and federal levels and making some of this cleaned-up land available for housing and businesses. Additionally, they are working on creating economic incentives for remediated brownfields that are consistent with progressive community development (meaning communities of color will not be displaced by gentrification).

Climate Justice

After the hurricanes and superstorms of recent years, New Yorkers are becoming more familiar with the negative effects of climate change and learning that the negative effects are often distributed unequally. Climate injustice has been examined at the global level, where it has been noted specifically that those countries consuming the most fossil fuels will not necessarily suffer most from the consequences of the change—such as extreme flooding and droughts. In the United States, especially in the aftermath of Hurricane Katrina in New Orleans in 2005, the scholarly literature on unequal vulnerabilities to climate disasters by race, ethnicity, and class has grown (Mohai, Pellow, and Roberts 2009, 420).

In New York City, the NYC-EJA is working hard to revitalize waterfronts in old industrial neighborhoods. The Waterfront Revitalization Program (WRP) aims to add newer areas of concern in the South Bronx, and also add Sunset Park and Newtown Creek in Brooklyn to the larger citywide effort of protecting ecologically sensitive areas.

A second concern of the WRP is to promote a citywide community resilience campaign, to raise awareness of potential risk that Significant Maritime and Industrial Areas (SMIAs) will be exposed to hazardous substances nearby, resulting from climate change impacts. Key questions activists ask are the following: How can these low-lying communities (e.g., in the South

Bronx or Sunset Park in Brooklyn) build resilience in case of storm surges and coastal flooding? How would people be evacuated? How would these neighborhoods rebound if chemicals used in industrial processes leaked and turned the neighborhood into a Superfund site? Hazardous materials in these communities need to be safeguarded to avoid "residents . . . wading through toxic water."[25] New Yorkers began to grapple with these issues seriously only after being hit by "Superstorm Sandy" in October 2012.

Still, a more complex problem is that activists want to protect environmental justice communities from the above scenarios, but at the same time retain good industrial jobs (Rosan 2012, 962). Therefore, any future heavy industrial-use projects in these vulnerable coastal locations would require risk assessments for storm surge, flooding, and sea-level rise in project planning and design. All facilities would need an adequate plan for pollution prevention and storing hazardous substances. Additionally, the city would need to rethink sewage infrastructure in these low-lying industrial neighborhoods. Such planning and action began in 2013, with the federal Department of Housing and Urban Development's "Rebuild by Design" competition to promote climate-resilient projects in "Sandy-affected areas" in New York, New Jersey, and Connecticut. Especially relevant to the present discussion is that in 2014 two South Bronx community and environmental justice groups, The Point CDC and Sustainable South Bronx, together with a major New York architectural design firm, were awarded a grant to provide community and climate resiliency for South Bronx residents. Finally, on each anniversary of Hurricane Sandy, NYC Environmental Justice Alliance head Eddie Bautista still worries that the city's most vulnerable residents living in industrial waterfront neighborhoods are not being fully considered in resiliency planning (e.g., OneNYC).

Food Justice

A final emerging issue for EJ activists both nationally and locally is "food justice" (e.g., Gottlieb and Joshi 2013). Devon Peña, a West Coast scholar and environmental justice activist, argues that at least one path to building community resilience is to "take back the garden . . . to sever capital's control over our food, nutrition, health and well-being" (2010, 151). UPROSE, for example, is working with the Brooklyn Food Coalition to connect local Latino communities with sources of affordable fresh food. These groups are developing urban farms, community gardens, food pantries, and farmers markets. UPROSE and others are also working in schools, with both parents and students, to provide education on culturally meaningful and nutritious food choices to counter the epidemic of obesity and diabetes in the community. Finally, food justice activists also advocate for the roughly twenty million food workers and farmworkers in the United States, many of whom are Latino, and who are frequently poorly paid and denied the rights and protections given other occupations under federal law.[26]

CONCLUSION

While Sze (2007, 88) claims there was only "a brief golden age of EJ activism in New York City," this essay argues that activism continues although activists may be taking up different and longer-term issues. While the threat of noxious-infrastructure siting in New York may have abated, other concerns remain, and the earlier activist struggles recounted here continue to shape the collective memory in Latino communities, both locally and nationally.[27] Asthma and air pollution remain a key concern, and greenspace and waterfront revitalization are seen as ways to combat the epidemic. More generally, EJ activists promote progressive community planning "to prevent displacement [by gentrification] and shape new development in ways that [preserve] existing affordable housing and community institutions" (Angotti 2012, 184).

Furthermore, EJ activists are at the forefront of defining "the community" broadly so that promoting environmental justice in New York City, for example, does not mean promoting injustice in poor communities elsewhere. EJ activists locally, nationally, and globally are increasingly moving from a Not in My Backyard (NIMBY) vision to a Not in Anybody's Backyard (NIABY) vision, or a "Just Sustainability Paradigm" (Agyeman, Bullard, and Evans 2003, 332). Ultimately, EJ activists understand that promoting social justice for all people with historically little access to political power and allowing them to speak in their own voices will contribute to long-term sustainability in policy making.

NOTES

1. In 1977, when residents of a working-class Niagara Falls neighborhood found their basements filled with noxious liquids, some soon linked this event to their children's serious health problems, especially cancers and birth defects.

They learned that their homes and local elementary school were built on top of a filled-in navigational canal that the Hooker Chemical Company had used for the first half of the twentieth century to dump its toxic wastes (Gibbs 1982). Soon after, residents in Woburn, Massachusetts, exposed another case of corporate negligence making their groundwater toxic. This case was widely covered in the press and detailed in the nonfiction account *A Civil Action* (Harr 1996).

2. The program is formally known as the Comprehensive Environmental Response, Compensation, and Liability Act (CERCLA).

3. Some Latino EJ scholars on the West Coast such as Laura Pulido (2000) and Devon Peña (2005, 132–33) use the concept "White Spatial Privilege." They have examined the racialized restructuring of spatial power in the Southwest in the 1890s, for example, how Mexican American communities were affected by the establishment of federal forests and national parks. The 1913 Supreme Court decision *US v. Sandoval* rationalized private and public enclosure of Mexican American property by rejecting the notion of communally held lands.

4. The case essentially took away a private right of action for racial or ethnic discrimination; people can enforce their civil rights only if they can prove that the discrimination was *intentional*, not merely that an action had a discriminatory impact based on race/ethnicity. Intentional discrimination is difficult to prove in court.

5. In 2012, Puerto Rico, a densely populated island two-thirds the size of Connecticut, had the dubious distinction of hosting seventeen EPA Superfund sites (personal communication with US EPA, Region Two, Public Information Office, New York City, www.epa.gov/enforcement/superfund-alternative-approach).

6. "For Latino Group, a Legacy Endures," *New York Times*, August 25, 2009; also, Iris Morales's 1996 documentary ¡*Palante, Siempre Palante! The Young Lords*. For information about viewing the film, see www.palante.org.

7. "Puerto Rico's Plan for Gas Pipeline Has Many Critics," *New York Times*, October 22, 2011.

8. Urban planner Ricardo Soto-Lopez (2006) points out the irony of postwar Puerto Ricans migrating from the island and moving into contaminated neighborhoods in the Northeast, just as those urban areas were losing their manufacturing base.

9. Latino community leaders continue to view environmental justice as a key issue facing their community as illustrated in the report they compiled for New York's incoming top officials. See Hispanic Federation (2013).

10. Census 2000 figures came from Sze (2007, 2). The 2010 figures for Hispanic population in the same CDs are as follows: Brooklyn CD 1, 27.2% Hispanic; Brooklyn CD 7, 45.5% Hispanic; Bronx CD 1, 70.9% Hispanic; Bronx CD 2, 74.8% Hispanic; and Manhattan CD 9 (West Harlem), 42.7% Hispanic. While two other Manhattan CDs with large Latino populations, East Harlem and the Lower East Side, were not fighting "classic" EJ facility-siting battles, they were

mobilizing over greenspace issues (casitas and community gardens). Manhattan CD 11 (East Harlem) had a Hispanic population in 2000 of 52.1%, and in 2010, a population of 49.2%. Manhattan CD 3 (Lower East Side) had a Hispanic population in 2000 of 26.9% and in 2010, a population of 24.6%.

11. While Angotti (2008) argued that EJ movements fighting LULU's mainly occurred in the Bronx and Brooklyn, Latinos in Manhattan experienced "wars" over casitas and community gardens, given the inexorable pressure to gentrify in the financial capital of the world. Notably, on the ability to organize predominantly Latino opposition movements in the other boroughs, Angotti notes that while Queens and (to a lesser extent) Staten Island are receiving newer Latin American immigrants, a pan-Latino identity is not yet emerging in these two boroughs. To date, "there are few place-based organizations . . . that deal in any substantive way with issues of housing, community development or environmental justice" (Agnotti 2012, 188).

12. While the public health community continues to debate the epidemiology of asthma extensively, air pollution is widely suspected as one of the triggers (Corburn 2005, 114–18). Few, however, doubt that in the United States, asthma hospitalization and morbidity rates for nonwhites are more than twice those for whites. New York City has one of the highest asthma rates in the country, and rates are especially high among Latinos and African American children.
A 2004 Natural Resources Defense Council study found that 91% of Latinos in the United States live in metropolitan areas where polluted air may increase the risk of illnesses, including asthma and cancer. Specifically in the New York City metro area, where traffic congestion is the second-worst in the nation, Latinos suffer the highest adult asthma rate of all ethnic groups, and Latino children are hospitalized for asthma at twice the national rate.

13. Although the widely held notion that Fresh Kills could be seen from Outer Space proved to be an "urban legend," at its busiest, the landfill *was* the largest manmade structure on earth, surpassing the Great Wall of China.

14. The Coalition was composed of local clergy and social justice organizations including National Council of Puerto Rican Rights and other Latino justice organizations. Also see "Bronx Lebanon Hospital to Shut Waste Incinerator," *New York Times*, June 27, 1997.

15. In the latter years of the Bloomberg administration a new battle brewed against high-tech incinerators that convert waste to energy and are used in parts of northern Europe. While the administration argued these plants were "state of the art," EJ activists countered that Europe was actually moving away from these facilities and moving towards more comprehensive recycling programs. See "Plasma Gasification Raises Hopes of Clean Energy from Garbage," *New York Times*, September 11, 2012.

16. Byerin Durkin, "Advocates: Give Manhattan Some Trash," *New York Daily News*, April 9, 2012.

17. "East River Trash Project Receives Federal Permit," *New York Times*, July 23, 2012. Despite opposition, an Upper East Side Transfer Station is slated to open in 2020.

18. "Schumer: Major Victory in 16-Year Fight against Nuclear Waste Storage Facility in Crowded Brooklyn Neighborhood," *States News Service*, June 15, 2005.

19. When Jason Corburn published his study of health risks in Brooklyn's Community District (CD) 1 (Williamsburg/Greenpoint) in 2005, he noted that the area was one of the poorest and most polluted in the city; the area was 42% Latino and had the largest percentage of its land (12%) devoted to industrial uses of any of New York's fifty-nine CD's. Since that study was published, Community District 1 has become a little less polluted and more unequal. Based on 2007–9 American Community Survey data, the area's two largest groups are whites and Latinos, and the white median household income ($44,000) is approximately double that of Latinos ($22,000). Puerto Ricans reported the lowest median household income ($18,000). In terms of pollution, an ongoing cleanup issue is the fifty-two-acre oil spill that occurred in Newtown Creek in the late 1970s; Newtown Creek was designated a federal Superfund site in 2010. See "Your Guide on a Tour of Decay," *New York Times*, June 17, 2012, New Jersey Section.

20. "State Admits Plants Headed for Poor Areas of New York City," *New York Times*, May 15, 2000.

21. "Suit Filed to Stop FreshDirect Plan for a South Bronx Complex," *New York Times*, June 13, 2012.

22. The nonprofit group New Yorkers for Parks published their Open Space Index in 2008, recommending there be a combined 2.5 acres of active and passive open space per thousand residents in community planning districts. See New Yorkers for Parks (2009).

23. "Ending a Long Battle, New York Lets Housing and Gardens Grow," *New York Times*, September 19, 2002.

24. "River of Hope in the Bronx," *New York Times*, July 22, 2012. Also, Ingram (2012). Committee organizations envision an interconnected park area, already designated as "the South Bronx Greenway."

25. "New York Is Lagging as Seas and Risks Rise, Critics Warn," *New York Times*, September 11, 2012. Still, it is notable that Mayor Michael Bloomberg promoted "the green city" (along with "the luxury city") as part of his legacy. During his time in office (2002–14), he committed to a long-term sustainability plan (PlaNYC2030) as well as the C40 Cities Climate Change Leadership Group, a worldwide network of mayors of megacities to address climate change by reducing greenhouse gas emissions. In April 2015, Mayor de Blasio announced OneNYC, his environmental initiative to focus on sustainability as well as income inequality. See Matt Flegenheimer, "New York City's Environmental Program Will Focus on Income Inequality," *New York Times*, April 21, 2015.

26. Two organizations that offer this kind of advocacy are the Brooklyn Food Coalition (www.Brooklynfoodcoalition.org) and UPROSE (www.UPROSE .org). See also Pellow (2002).

27. "Climate Is Big Issue for Hispanics, and Personal," *New York Times*, February 10, 2015.

REFERENCES

Abel, Troy D., Debra J. Salazar, and Patricia Robert. 2015. "States of Environmental Justice: Redistributive Politics across the United States, 1993–2004." *Review of Policy Research* 32 (2): 200–225.

Agyeman, Julian, Robert D. Bullard, and Bob Evans. 2003. "Towards Just Sustainabilities: Perspectives and Possibilities." In *Just Sustainabilities: Development in an Unequal World*, edited by Julian Agyeman, Robert D. Bullard, and Bob Evans, 323–35. Cambridge, MA: MIT Press.

Angotti, Tom. 2008. *New York for Sale: Community Planning Confronts Global Real Estate*. Cambridge, MA: MIT Press.

———. 2012. "Placemaking in New York City: From Puerto Rican to Pan-Latino." In *Diálogos: Placemaking in Latino Communities*, edited by Michael Rios and Leonardo Vazquez, 113–25. New York: Routledge.

Aponte-Parés, Luis. 1998. "What's Yellow and White and Has Land All around It? Appropriating Place in Puerto Rican *Barrios*." In *The Latino Studies Reader: Culture, Economy & Society*, edited by Antonia Darder and Rodolfo D. Torres, 271–80. Malden, MA: Blackwell.

Baver, Sherrie. 1993. *The Political Economy of Colonialism: The State and Industrialization in Puerto Rico*. Westport, CT: Praeger.

———. 2006. "Environmental Justice and the Cleanup of Vieques." *Centro Journal* 18 (1): 91–107.

Baver, Sherrie, and Barbara D. Lynch, eds. 2006. *Beyond Sun and Sand: Caribbean Environmentalisms*. New Brunswick, NJ: Rutgers University Press.

Bullard, R., et al. 2007. *Toxic Waste and Race at 20: 1987–2007*. Cleveland: United Church of Christ. www.ucc.org/environmental-ministries_toxic-waste-20.

Caro, Robert. 1974. *The Power Broker: Robert Moses and the Fall of New York*. New York: Knopf.

Checker, Melissa. 2001. "'Like Nixon Coming to China': Finding Common Ground in a Multi-Ethnic Coalition for Environmental Justice." *Anthropological Quarterly* 74 (3): 135–47.

Clapp, Jennifer. 2001. *Toxic Exports: The Transfer of Hazardous Wastes from Rich to Poor Countries*. Ithaca, NY: Cornell University Press.

Commission for Racial Justice. 1987. *Toxic Wastes and Race in the United States*. New York: United Church of Christ. http://d3n8a8pro7vhmx.cloudfront.net /unitedchurchofchrist/legacy_url/13567/toxwrace87.pdf?1418439935.

Corburn, Jason. 2005. *Street Science: Community Knowledge and Environmental Health Justice.* Cambridge, MA: MIT Press.

Dávila, Arlene. 2004. *Barrio Dreams: Puerto Ricans, Latinos, and the Neoliberal City.* Berkeley: University of California Press.

Duany, Jorge. 2011. *Blurred Borders: Transnational Migration between the Hispanic Caribbean and the United States.* Chapel Hill: University of North Carolina Press.

Faber, Daniel, ed. 1998. *The Struggle for Ecological Democracy: Environmental Justice Movements in the United States.* New York: Guilford.

Fals Borda, Orlando, and Muhammad A. Rahman. 1991. *Action and Knowledge: Breaking the Monopoly with Participatory Action Research.* New York: Apex Press.

Freire, Paolo. 1974. *Pedagogy of the Oppressed.* New York: Seabury Press.

Frey, William H. 2010. "Census Data: Blacks and Hispanics Take Different Segregation Paths." December 16. Washington, DC: Brookings Institution. https://www.brookings.edu/opinions/census-data-blacks-and-hispanics-take-different-segregation-paths/.

Gandy, Matthew. 2002. *Concrete and Clay: Reworking Nature in New York City.* Cambridge, MA: MIT Press.

García Martínez, Neftalí, et al. 2006. "Puerto Rico: Economic and Environmental Overview." In Baver and Lynch, *Beyond Sun and Sand,* 75–85.

Gelman, Emmaia, ed. 2009. *Green Jobs / Green Homes New York: Expanding Home Energy Efficiency and Creating Good Jobs in a Clean Energy Economy.* New York City: Center for Working Families.

Gibbs, Lois. 1982. *Love Canal: My Story.* Albany: State University of New York Press.

Gottlieb, Robert, and Anapama Joshi. 2013. *Food Justice.* Cambridge, MA: MIT Press.

Grossman, Karl. 1994. "The People of Color Environmental Summit." In *Unequal Protection: Environmental Justice and Communities of Color,* edited by Robert D. Bullard, 272–97. San Francisco: Sierra Club Press.

Harr, Jonathan. 1996. *A Civil Action.* New York: Vintage.

Harris, Lis. 2003. *Tilting at Mills: Green Dreams, Dirty Dealings, and the Corporate Squeeze.* Boston: Houghton-Mifflin.

Harvey, David. 1999. "The Environment of Justice." In *Living with Nature: Environmental Politics as Cultural Discourse,* edited by Frank Fischer and Martin Hajer, 153–85. New York: Oxford University Press.

Herskovitz, Allen. 2003. *Bronx Ecology: Blueprints for a New Environmentalism.* Washington, DC: Island Press.

Hispanic Federation of New York. 2013. *La Gran Manzana: The Road Ahead for New York City's Latino Community; Policy Blueprint for the City's Next Mayor and City Council.* New York: Hispanic Federation of New York. http://hispanicfederation.org/images/pdf/LaGranManzana.pdf.

Ingram, Mrill. 2012. "Sculpting Solutions: Art-Science Collaborations in Sustainability." *Environment* 54 (4): 24–34.

Lynch, Barbara D. 1993. "The Garden and the Sea: U.S. Latino Environmental Discourses and Mainstream Environmentalism." *Social Problems* 40 (1): 108–24.

Lynch, Barbara D., and Rima Brusi. 2005. "Nature, Memory, and Nation: New York's Latino Gardens and *Casitas*." In *Urban Place: Reconnecting with the Natural World*, edited by Peggy Barlett, 191–211. Cambridge, MA: MIT Press.

Martinez, Miranda J. 2010. *Power at the Roots: Gentrification, Community Gardens and the Puerto Ricans of the Lower East Side*. Lanham, MD: Lexington Books.

McCaffrey, Katherine, and Sherrie Baver. 2006. "'Ni Una Bomba Mas': Reframing the Vieques Struggle." In Baver and Lynch, *Beyond Sun and Sand*, 109–28.

Minnite, Lorraine, and Immanuel Ness. 2006. "Environmental Risk and Childhood Disease in an Urban Working-Class Caribbean Neighborhood." In Baver and Lynch, *Beyond Sun and Sand*, 140–57.

Mohai, Paul, David Pellow, and J. Timmons Roberts. 2009. "Environmental Justice." *Annual Review of Environment and Resources* 34:405–30.

Morales, Iris. 1996. *¡Palante, Siempre Palante: The Young Lords!* DVD. Directed by Iris Morales. New York: Third World Newsreel. www.palante.org.

New Yorkers for Parks. 2009. *The Open Space Index*. New York: New Yorkers for Parks. www.ny4p.org/research/osi/LES.pdf.

Pellow, David N. 2002. *Garbage Wars: The Struggle for Environmental Justice in Chicago*. Cambridge, MA: MIT Press.

Peña, Devon. 2005. "Autonomy, Equity, and Environmental Justice." In *Power, Justice and the Environment: A Critical Appraisal of the Environmental Justice Movement*, edited by David N. Pellow and Robert J. Brulle, 131–51. Cambridge, MA: MIT Press.

———. 2010. "Environmental Justice and the Future of Chicana/o Studies." *Aztlán* 35 (2): 149–57.

Pulido, Laura. 2000. "Rethinking Environmental Racism: White Privilege and Urban Development in Southern California." *Annals of the Association of American Geographers* 90:12–40.

Quintero-Somaini, Adrianna, et al. 2004. *Hidden Danger: Environmental Health Threats in the Latino Community*. New York: Natural Resources Defense Council, October. https://www.nrdc.org/sites/default/files/latino_en.pdf.

Roberts, J. Timmons, and Melissa M. Toffolon-Weiss. 2001. *Chronicles from the Environmental Justice Frontline*. New York: Cambridge University Press.

Rosan, Christina D. 2012. "Can PlaNYC Make New York City 'Greener and Greater' for Everyone? Sustainability Planning and the Promise of Environmental Justice." *Local Environment* 17 (9): 959–76.

Soto-Lopez, Ricardo. 2006. "Environmental Justice for Puerto Ricans in the Northeast: A Participant-Observer's Assessment." In Baver and Lynch, *Beyond Sun and Sand*, 131–39.

Sze, Julie. 2007. *Noxious New York: The Racial Politics of Urban Health and Environmental Justice.* Cambridge, MA: MIT Press.

Torres-Vélez, Victor M. 2011. "Puerto Ricans and the Green Jobs Gap in New York City." *Centro Journal* 23 (11): 95–112.

US Environmental Protection Agency. 2016. "Environmental Justice." Washington, DC: Environmental Protection Agency. https://www.epa.gov/environmental justice.

Valdés Pizzini, Manuel. 2006. "Historical Contentions and Future Trends in the Coastal Zones: The Environmental Movement in Puerto Rico." In Baver and Lynch, *Beyond Sun and Sand*, 44–64.

Walker, Gordon. 2012. *Environmental Justice: Concepts, Evidence, and Politics.* New York: Routledge.

Yu, Xue, et al. 2015. "Spatiotemporal Changes of CVOC Concentrations in Karst Aquifers: Analysis of Three Decades of Data from Puerto Rico." *Science of the Total Environment* 11 (April 1, 2015): 1–10.

CHAPTER FIFTEEN

Latino Politics in New York City

Challenges in the Twenty-First Century

ANGELO FALCÓN

As the Latino population in New York City grows, so does its potential role in shaping the politics of the city. However, the Latino political experience in New York raises serious challenges to the notion that demography is destiny. This chapter attempts to critically and comprehensively analyze the issues confronting the Latino community as it engages the city's political structures and processes. Much of the chapter is descriptive in an effort to provide some baseline data and identify elements that need to be incorporated in future research on the subject. It closes with some preliminary observations about the relationship of the Mayor Bill de Blasio Administration to the Latino community during his first term in office.

THE LATINO ELECTORATE IN NEW YORK

Much of the existing literature on Latino politics in New York focuses on one ethnic group or a specific neighborhood or borough and fails to examine the broader citywide community (Aparicio 2006; Cruz and Bloom 2009; Haslip-Viera and Baver 1996; Jones-Correa 1998; Laó-Montes and Dávila 2001; Marwell 2007; Muzzio and Cortina 2010; Remeseira 2010); Ricourt and Danta 2003; Sanchez 2007; Smith 2006; Torres 1995; Torres-Saillant and Hernández 1998). This essay aims to close that gap in the scholarship and thereby begin to connect some of the political dots of what constitutes Latino politics in New York.

Latino Voters in New York City

Although New York City's 2.4 million Latinos make up 29% its population, the 2005–9 American Community Survey (ACS) of the Census Bureau estimates that Latinos make up 23.1% of the Citizen Voting Age Population (CVAP) of New York City (CLACLS 2011), and it is estimated that they make up 21% of the city's actual voters (Roberts 2009). This is in comparison to 40.9% that is white, 23.7% that is black, 9.9% that is Asian, and 2.3% that is other. As a percent of the CVAP for the city's five boroughs (counties), Latinos represent 46% of eligible voters in the Bronx, 22% in Queens, 20% in Manhattan, 17% in Brooklyn, and 12% in Staten Island.

The national-origin composition of the Latino-citizenship voting-age population has changed dramatically over the last few decades. In 1990, Puerto Ricans made up 70% of the city's total eligible Latino voters in New York City, a proportion that declined to 44% in 2005–9. This resulted from the decline in the Puerto Rican population and increased US births and naturalization rates for other Latino groups, except Mexicans.

This Puerto Rican portion, 44% of the total Latino CVAP, is more than the 23% of eligible Latino voters who are Dominican and 33% who are from other Latino national-origin groups. However, Puerto Ricans remain a majority of the citizen voting-age populations in the Bronx, Brooklyn, and Staten Island; are the largest proportion in Queens; and in Manhattan, make up about the same percentage as Dominicans, the two being the largest groups of eligible Latino voters (CLACLS 2011).

Role and Impact of Local Races

The epicenter of New York Puerto Rican politics had long been the Bronx (where the majority of the city's Latinos reside) and the Bronx Democratic County Committee. However, in 2008, Puerto Ricans lost control of this key local party organization when a coalition of Puerto Rican and black legislators calling themselves the "Rainbow Rebels" (a group that some viewed as more of a split among the borough's Latino politicians) challenged the committee's leadership and appointed an African American as its head. This effectively divided the Bronx Latino elected officials and rendered the former Puerto Rican Democratic county leader weaker than ever before. This development has had the profound effect of significantly marginalizing the Bronx Latino political class, thereby affecting Latinos throughout the city and state. With other factors, it set the stage for the election of a renegade Puerto Rican state senator in the Bronx, Pedro Espada, who was to defect from the Democratic Party in a way that created political havoc in the state senate for that party and the governor, and who was sentenced to five years in prison for corruption (Hakim and Peters 2009; Gonzalez 2011). In March 2015, a Puerto Rican assemblyman, Marcos Crespo, resumed chairmanship of the Bronx Democratic County Organization as a result of the corruption charges that caused Assemblyman Stanley Silver to step down as assembly speaker; Silver was replaced as speaker by Carl Heastie, who had been the Bronx Party chair (Slattery 2015).

The Structure of Latino Politics in New York

As diverse as New York's population is, so have been its linkages to the city's Democratic Party in recent years. The power center of Latino politics is in the Bronx, where Puerto Ricans have been in control of the county's party committee; it is also the borough with the largest number of, and the most senior, Latino elected officials at all levels of government, including the office of the borough president. The next-strongest power center is in Brooklyn, which is represented by the second Puerto Rican congressperson and whose county organization was, until recently, headed by an Italian with a Spanish surname who presented himself at times as a Hispanic. The other two Puerto Rican power centers—East Harlem (El Barrio) and the Lower East Side—have lost much of their original Puerto Rican population and, in the process, lost influence, to blacks in the case of East Harlem (Dávila 2004) and to Jewish whites in the case of the Lower East Side.

The Dominican power center is in Manhattan's Washington Heights, which has Dominican elected officials in the city council, state assembly, and state senate. Dominican political influence has been moving away from Washington Heights to the western Bronx as the Dominican population has been increasingly shifting into that area; the Bronx now has the largest concentration of Dominicans in the city. In 2008, the first Dominican to hold elective office in the Bronx was elected to the state assembly. The Dominican population has also achieved elective posts in Brooklyn's Williamsburg-Bushwick sections and in Queen's Corona and East Elmhurst sections.

While as recently as 2008 all of the twenty-nine Latino elected officials in New York City were Puerto Rican or Dominican, by 2014 this had changed. The thirty Latino elected officials in the city in positions from the US Congress to city council included an Ecuadorean, a Cuban-Greek, and an Israeli-Argentinean. This reflected, in general, the size and length of residence of these national-origin groups in all of the boroughs that had Latino elected officials.

These Latino political power centers suffered major stresses during 2008. The Puerto Rican chair of the Bronx Democratic County Committee lost his post to an African American after a challenge by a new black-Latino coalition, the Rainbow Rebels. The Latino power centers in Manhattan, Brooklyn, and the Bronx were all experiencing different levels of internal conflicts. At the same time, political corruption began to take its toll as a good number of Latino elected officials throughout the city were under investigation, on trial, or in prison. In early 2012, for example, a major corruption trial of State Senator Pedro Espada and his son increased cynicism about the political process in the Latino community. In 2015, of thirty-five New York State legislators convicted of corruption, Latinos made up 17% although they constituted only 10% of state legislators (Craig, Rashbaum, and Kaplan 2015).

There were mechanisms beyond the Democratic county organizations to coordinate the efforts of these elected officials. The most high-profile is the New York State Puerto Rican / Hispanic Legislative Task Force, which sponsors statewide "Somos El Futuro" (We are the future) conferences in Albany, the state's capital, and Puerto Rico. This body was established at the initiative of white state assembly leaders, some have speculated, to weaken an earlier New York State Black and Hispanic Legislative Caucus, which was created in 1966 and which Latinos complained was too dominated by African Americans. The Puerto Rican / Hispanic Task Force was established at the initiation of a late Puerto Rican state assemblyman from East Harlem, Angelo del Toro, in response to this perceived Afrocentric predisposition of the state's so-called Black and Hispanic Legislative Caucus. In addition, the New York City Council has established a Black, Latino, and Asian Caucus (BLAC) (originally called the Black and Hispanic Legislative Caucus).

Despite the size of New York's Latino population and the number of Latino elected officials, the influence of this Latino component of the city political class is very limited. One indicator of this is the persistent legitimate

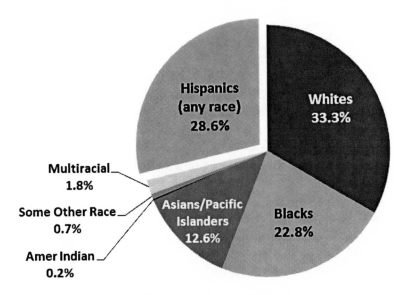

Figure 15.1 Racial-Ethnic Breakdown of New York City Population, 2010
Source: US Census 2010.

complaint among Latino political leaders that the Democratic Party has failed to groom and support Latino candidates for citywide and statewide office (Nahmias 2011). Another development that underscored what some saw as the unresponsiveness of the Democratic Party to Latino elected officials was the informal defection in the summer of 2008 of two Puerto Rican state senators from the party, a move that shifted power temporarily to the Republicans in the state senate, which previously had a one-vote Democratic majority (Hakim and Peters 2009).

CHARACTERISTICS OF THE LATINO POPULATION IN NEW YORK

The 2010 census conservatively counted 2,336,076 Latinos in New York City, representing 28.6% of the city's total population. Between 2000 and 2010, New York City's Latino population grew by 8.1%, considerably lower than its 21.1% growth in the previous decade. Together with the black and Asian populations, Latinos have been part of New York as a "majority minority" city since the early 1980s (Falcón 1988). (See figure 15.1.)

Political Party Linkages

While the Republican Party fielded the first serious Puerto Rican political candidates in New York City beginning in the 1920s, following World War II the Democratic Party became the dominant party among Latinos (Falcón 1984). While the relationship of the Democratic Party to the African American community was longer and deeper due to a different history and a more national political context that included the impact of the civil rights movement, the Latino relationship to that party was much thinner.

For most of the twentieth century, Latino politics in New York was defined as largely Puerto Rican, while at the national level it was dominated by Mexican Americans. This specifically Puerto Rican focus not only marginalized Latinos' relationship to the national parties because of the relatively small size and high poverty levels of the Puerto Rican population, but was further complicated by the role played by the politics of Puerto Rico, which until the late 1960s played an intermediate role in the relationship of New York's Puerto Rican community to American political elites (Sanchez 2007; Thomas 2010). It was in the context of the radical nationalist revitalization movements of the sixties and seventies that the New York Puerto Rican political leadership asserted its role as the representative of this community in opposition to the government of Puerto Rico (Falcón 1984). It did so in a manner that presented a highly cynical view of mainstream electoral politics and defined a division between an authentic community activism and a co-opted electoral politics of "poverty pimps" and the like.

Since the 1990s, the city's Latino community has begun to effectively use the federal Voting Rights Act of 1965, its continuing dramatic population growth, and other mechanisms to increase its representation in elected office significantly. By 2015, Latinos held two congressional seats, the Bronx borough presidency, six state senate seats, thirteen state assembly seats, and eleven city council seats, largely Democrats (one Republican) and mostly Puerto Rican and Dominican. By 2010, a Hispanic Republican had also been elected to the state assembly from Staten Island, as well as one elected to an upstate assembly district. This community had finally achieved representation in proportion to its share of the city's electorate, and had thus achieved parity. (See table 15.1 for 2014 representation.) However, this "parity" has proven to be of limited political impact. A recurring complaint among the Latino political class has been that despite their numbers and increasing seniority, the city's and state's political parties were not promoting Latino

Table 15.1 Number of Latino Elected Officials in New York City by Borough and Position, 2014

Borough/ County	2010 Latino Voting Age Population*	City Council	State Assembly	State Senate	Borough President	Congress	Totals
Bronx	51.2%	4	3	3	1	1	**12**
Brooklyn	18.8%	3	2	1	0	1**	**7**
Manhattan	23.3%	3	2	1***	0	0	**6**
Queens	26.0%	1	2	1	0	0	**4**
Staten Island	15.2%	0	1****	0	0	0	**1**
NYC Totals	**26.7%**	**11**	**10**	**6**	**1**	**2**	**30**

* per 2010 Census

** includes parts of Queens and Manhattan

*** includes part of the Bronx

**** the only Republican

Source: Compiled by the National Institute for Latino Policy (NiLP).

candidates for citywide and statewide office, with the exception of Fernando Ferrer, a Puerto Rican nominated by the Democratic Party as its unsuccessful 2005 candidate for mayor (Nahmias 2011). This reflected the marginal role that Latino elected officials played in the Democratic Party at both the state and local levels (as well as the absence of any significant role in the Republican Party).

This political marginalization was also reflected in the significant underrepresentation of Latinos in public-sector employment at both the municipal and state levels of government. Despite being 29% of the New York City population, Latinos only accounted for 20% of the city government work force (New York City 2013); at the state level, despite being 17.6% of the state's population, they were only 5% of state government workers (New York State 2014; Falcón 2009a). The relationship between a community's ties to the dominant political party and its representation in the public bureaucracy is historically an important indicator of power in New York.

Even with the election of the progressive mayoral administration of Bill de Blasio in 2013, this pattern continued in terms of his appointments. By the end of the first year of this new administration, Latinos had only accounted for 11% of de Blasio appointments, a figure that reflected an already declining rate of Latino appointments up to that point (Reyes 2014).

Besides resulting in a weak record of legislative accomplishments by Latino elected officials as a group, this marginalization had other negative effects. One is the high degree of official corruption that this Latino political class has exhibited, with a significant number behind bars or under investigation. The other is the growing pattern of political nepotism, practiced especially by the more senior Puerto Rican elected officials. In 2011, of the thirty-five Latino officials in New York City, eleven (31%) were related family members. Although this phenomenon, which I refer to as the "Boricua Game of Thrones" (Falcón 2012b), exists in other communities, it has appeared at a higher rate among the Latino political class. These characteristics have greatly undermined the legitimacy of New York's Latino politicians.

Hyperdiversity

The Latino population in New York City is perhaps unique nationally in being the most diverse in terms of national origin. (See table 15.2 for 2010 data.) Until the 1980s, Puerto Ricans were the majority of the city's Latino population, at one point representing 80% of the total; today, although still the largest Latino group, Puerto Ricans are about 30% of the total (Falcón 2004a). They are closely followed by Dominicans (who may have already surpassed them in size), and then Mexicans, Ecuadoreans, and Colombians. The growth of the Mexican population has been and continues to be dramatic, while that of Puerto Ricans, Dominicans, and Colombians has slowed or declined.

This ethnic "hyperdiversity" has important political implications. First, it relates to legal status, with the only group that arrives as US citizens, Puerto Ricans, becoming a smaller share of the total Latino electorate. Second, the various Latino national-origin groups have different political cultures, a different structure, and different priorities, all of which challenge the development of a unified Latino agenda, such as different key political institutions and the role and nature of homeland politics. Third, these various communities have developed to different degrees politically, based on their time of arrival, location in the city, settlement patterns, and other factors that affect intergroup communication and coordination. Fourth, the groups sometimes compete with each other politically and economically in different forms and levels, from church congregations to workplaces. These conditions certainly exist elsewhere, but not to the same extent or on the same scale as in New York City.

In terms of elected officials, this Latino population diversity has slowly begun to be reflected in their numbers. As recently as 2008, all Latino elected

Table 15.2 NYC Latino Population by National Origin, 2010

	Number	Percent
Total Hispanic	2,336,076	100.0%
Mexican	319,263	13.7%
Puerto Rican	723,621	31.0%
Cuban	40,840	1.7%
Dominican Republic	576,701	24.7%
Total Central American	151,378	6.5%
Costa Rican	6,673	0.3%
Guatemalan	30,420	1.3%
Honduran	42,400	1.8%
Nicaraguan	9,346	0.4%
Panamanian	22,353	1.0%
Salvadoran	38,559	1.7%
Other Central American	1,627	0.1%
Total South American	343,468	14.7%
Argentinean	15,169	0.6%
Bolivian	4,488	0.2%
Chilean	7,026	0.3%
Colombian	94,723	4.1%
Ecuadorian	167,209	7.2%
Paraguayan	3,534	0.2%
Peruvian	36,018	1.5%
Uruguayan	3,004	0.1%
Venezuelan	9,619	0.4%
Other South American	2,678	0.1%
Total Other Hispanic	180,805	7.7%
Spaniard	17,793	0.8%
Spanish	11,935	0.5%
Spanish American	1,110	0.0%
All Other Hispanic	149,967	6.4%

Source: 2010 Census.

officials in New York City were Puerto Rican and Dominican. By 2014, the first Ecuadorean, first Mexican, first Israeli-Argentinean, and first Cuban-Greek (the only Republican) had been added to the mix of thirty Latino elected officials. Of this current group of Latino elected officials, the majority (56.7%) are Puerto Rican, 30.0% are Dominican, and the others make up the remaining 13.3%.

Amidst all of this racial and national-origin differentiation within the Latino community of New York, strong pan-Latino forces are still at work, with a New York accent (Kasinitz et al. 2008). Current Latino elected officials (mostly Puerto Rican and Dominican at this point) need to appeal to broader Latino constituencies than those of simply their national-origin group. Then there is a growing array of Spanish-language media driven increasingly to a pan-Latino audience that it caters to and, in the process, helps to create (Subvervi-Velez 2008). Moreover, the increasingly intense anti-immigrant and anti-Latino sentiment in the country also promotes a greater pan-Latino consciousness. The degree of inter-Latino subgroup interaction is not as strong today as one would assume; and the eventual impact that these forces will have on the degree and nature of Latino political unity in New York City is not entirely clear yet.

Multiple Barrios/Regional Dispersion

New York's Latino population is unique in its spatial dimensions as well. In most other locations with large Latino populations, these populations are concentrated in one or a few *barrios* or *colonias*, usually under one local governmental structure. In New York City, in contrast, the Latino population is spread out in over twenty neighborhoods located in five different borough (or county) governments. Each one of these neighborhoods is the size of a small to medium city in population, and each has its political history, structures, and leadership, which are overlaid by state, city, and borough governments. This contributes to the problem of achieving some degree of political cohesiveness citywide and even at the borough level.

Another difference between Latino settlement patterns in New York and those in the Southwest and South Florida is the generally lower percentage of the population made up of Latinos in New York (and other parts of the Northeast and Midwest). Whereas 29% of the population of New York City are Latinos, that percentage is generally much higher in cities such as Laredo, Texas (94%), El Paso, Texas (80%), Santa Ana, California (79%), Miami (69%), and Los Angeles (48%). This obviously affects the nature of

Latino politics, which in New York City was in part compensated for by its large Puerto Rican population, which arrived in the city already as US citizens eligible to vote.

The scale and complexity of the Latino population's spatial configuration is generally ignored or downplayed in discussions of Latino politics at the citywide level, although some analyses at the neighborhood level have begun to emerge (Dávila 2004; Marwell 2007). For another perspective on how New York City's political structures affect participation of immigrants, in general, in comparison to Los Angeles, see Mollenkopf, Olson, and Ross 2001. The dispersal of the Latino population throughout New York City has historically been a political issue. Compared to other Latino settlements patterns, especially in the Southwest, the pattern in New York has been that the Latino population has been more dispersed and less concentrated. In the 1960s during the federal War on Poverty, when antipoverty programs were being designed in New York, Puerto Ricans had to make the case for the creation of citywide and ethnic-specific programs like the Puerto Rican Community Development Project (PRCDP) and Aspira (Fitzpatrick 1971, 68). This resulted in a structure of community-based organizations in the Puerto Rican community that was significantly different from a more neighborhood-focused and less explicitly racially organizational naming approach adopted by the African American community. Given the important role that these nonprofits played in the political development of these two communities, this difference had an effect on how each of these communities was organized politically.

New York City remains one of the more racially segregated cities in the country, a pattern replicated within the Latino areas of residence as well along national-origin group lines. Puerto Ricans and Dominicans are the major Latino groups in the Bronx, Brooklyn, and Manhattan. Queens has predominantly South and Central American populations. While in the black community large geographic areas are occupied by high concentrations of blacks, in Latino areas, the concentrations are generally lower and the level of segregation is more detailed in the sense that it exists in increasingly smaller spaces than standard segregation indices utilize—such as census tracts—and in smaller spaces than are seen in the black community. This relatively lower concentration of the Latino population in small areas as well as citywide also distinguishes it from much greater concentrations of Latinos in the Southwest.

The political effects of the regional dispersal of the Latino community have also not been adequately analyzed. Of the members of New York's

Latino population who have moved beyond the city's borders into Long Island, upstate New York, New Jersey, and beyond, many have been Puerto Ricans, whose departure decreases the number of the city's eligible voters. For a broader discussion of the regional aspects of urban politics, see Dreier, Mollenkopf, and Swanstrom (2001).

Racial Characteristics and Relations

Most Latinos in New York City, as in most of the Northeast, are Caribbeans with working-class origins, and as a result New York's Latino population differs in many respects from Latino populations in other parts of the country. The strong nonwhite influence among Puerto Ricans, Dominicans, and most Latino national-origin groups has a potentially significant impact on the racial aspects of the political process. In addition, the largest of these communities, the Puerto Ricans and the Dominicans, have largely grown in closer contact with African American and other black neighborhoods than have the Latino populations in many other cities with large Latino populations. Some advocates of stronger Afro-Latino identities have argued that these characteristics would create greater Latino solidarity with Caribbean and African blacks within the United States (Jiménez-Román and Flores 2010). Others have found that Puerto Rican racial self-identification affects levels of residential segregation in this community (Massey and Denton 1993). If this is the case, New York could be a major example of such an effect, more so possibly than in Latino communities in other parts of the country (Burns 2006; Foley 2010; Jennings 1994; June and Maynie 2008; Nelson and Lavariega Monforti 2005).

While most Latinos in New York identify racially as nonwhite, there is considerable variation among the Latino national-origin groups in this regard. (See table 15.3.) Those most not identifying as white are the larger Latino communities primarily from the Caribbean and Central America, while those most identifying as white are smaller groups largely from South America and Spain. However, the main nonwhite racial reference is to the "some other race" category in the census, while for Panamanians it is in the majority-black or African American (59.3%). Race is a major factor in the Latino community, but not for the most part in simple black-white terms. It is interesting, for example, to see that the least politically mobilized Latino subgroups appear to be the smaller South American communities (primarily in Queens), who most identify racially as white.

Table 15.3 Racial Self-Identification of Selected Latino National-Origin Groups, New York City, 2014

	Puerto Rican	Dominican	Mexican	Colombian	Ecuadorian	Honduran	Panamanian	Salvadoran	Argentinean
White	40.0%	22.4%	30.8%	55.4%	51.5%	27.2%	14.4%	32.9%	79.8%
Black	10.2%	9.0%	1.5%	1.6%	2.1%	20.5%	58.1%	2.0%	1.2%
Asian/Pacific Isl.	0.3%	0.1%	0.2%	0.2%	0.2%	0.0%	0.2%	0.2%	0.0%
American Indian	0.8%	0.5%	1.5%	0.7%	0.3%	0.5%	0.4%	0.0%	0.0%
Multi-Racial	5.3%	6.5%	3.4%	2.4%	6.1%	4.0%	2.6%	1.9%	9.9%
Some Other Race	43.4%	61.5%	62.7%	39.7%	39.8%	47.7%	24.3%	63.0%	9.1%
Total	100.0%	100.0%	100.0%	100.0%	100.0%	100.0%	100.0%	100.0%	100.0%

Source: 2014 American Community Survey (ACS).

The recent growing awareness of Latino nonwhite identities and long-term efforts at black-Latino coalition-building has helped define New York City politics in important ways. It played, for example, an important role in the election of David Dinkins, the city's first African-American mayor, in 1989 and in Jesse Jackson's primary run for president in New York in 1988, and it remains an important factor, both in its unifying as well as its competitive aspects. But this is an effect that is complex, as ambiguous racial-ethnic census categories like "some other race" and "more than one race" dominate the racial self-identification of Latinos as opposed to that of African Americans, Africans, and non-Spanish-speaking Caribbeans in the United States. Little research, however, has been done into this aspect of the effects of racial identification within Latino communities and their politics (Torres 1995; Opie 2014; Stokes-Brown 2012).

Socioeconomic Status and Integration

The Latino population in New York City has long been among the poorest in the country in a city with one of the largest indices of income inequality. Coupled with this population's youthfulness, this low Latino socioeconomic status has obvious effects that depress political participation in this community and affects the political priorities of this part of the city's electorate (Crissey and File [n.d.]). Latinos had the highest poverty rate in New York City in 2010 at 28%, compared to 24% for blacks, 19% for Asians, and 13% for whites. Among Latinos, Mexicans had the highest poverty rate at 33%, closely followed by Puerto Ricans at 32%, 30% for Dominicans, 18% for Ecuadoreans, and 15% for Colombians (census 2011). Although 29% of New York City's population, Latinos make up over 40% of the city's poor people. In addition, the median age for Latinos in the city was thirty-one years, compared to thirty-seven for Asians, thirty-eight for blacks, and forty-three for whites.

However, it is intriguing that it appears that levels of political participation among two similarly socially situated Latino subgroups, Puerto Ricans and Dominicans, appear to be different. While both communities exhibit relatively low levels of voter participation, this appears to be, counterintuitively, more the case with the one with the longest history of political involvement in the city, Puerto Ricans, than with the other, Dominicans, with a more recent political history in the city. Has the longer exposure to American politics by Puerto Ricans dampened their interest in participating? Is the greater nationalism of a first- and second-generation Dominican community promoting greater participation in this community? The basis of this difference and its implications clearly require further analysis.

The spatial concentration of Latino poverty in segregated neighbor-hoods and subneighborhood areas is a major obstacle to the social and polit-ical integration of Latino communities into the city's main structures. The phenomenon of so-called disconnected youth in these communities is a growing concern that recently prompted the former Bloomberg administra-tion to establish a Young Men's Initiative to address this problem specifically among black and Latino youth (Barbaro and Santos 2011). The lack of full integration by large segments of the Latino population into the city's labor and educational systems has very clear political consequences. It is ironic that this is more true of Puerto Ricans, who arrive with US citizenship and have the longest history in the city, than of other Latinos who have large numbers of undocumented and are more recently arrived (Treschan 2010). In some senses, this seems paradoxical, but it is quite possibly an ominous predictor for the broader Latino community.

In addition, the Puerto Rican case raises questions about the inevitabil-ity of the dampening effects of local socioeconomic status on political partic-ipation that defines Latino politics in New York. In Puerto Rico, the level of voter participation is significantly higher—consistently around 80% regard-less of socioeconomic status—than among Puerto Ricans and the general electorate in New York (Falcón 1983; Cámara Fuertes 2004). Explanations for this range from differences in electoral structures and practices to differ-ences in mobilization strategies. Since Puerto Ricans participate in both set-tings within the same general American political system, a full examination of the factors stimulating these higher political participation rates in Puerto Rico could yield important lessons for expanding the general American elec-torate as well as the number of active voters among stateside Puerto Ricans and other Latinos.

The other relevant demographic is sex. Among the five largest Latino nationalities in New York City, women predominate, except for Mexicans and Ecuadoreans (CLACLS 2011). This was largely the case among the for-eign born (and the Puerto Rico–born in the case of Puerto Ricans). How-ever, in terms of the Latino elected officials in 2014, of the total of thirty, eight were women (26.7%). What is striking is that Latina women were rep-resented well at the top and lower levels of representation. Of the two New York Latino congresspersons (both Puerto Rican), one is a woman, Nydia Velázquez. However, more impressive is Latina female representation in the city council, where of the eleven Latino council members, five were women (45.5%), and in 2013 a Puerto Rican woman, Melissa Mark-Viverito, was the first person of color to be selected by her colleagues to be city council speaker, and a Dominican woman, Julissa Ferreras, was appointed chair of the powerful finance committee. There was no Latina woman at the borough-president level or in the state senate, and of the ten Latinos serving in the state assembly, only two were women. The only study looking at the role of Latina women in New York City politics was by Ricourt and Danta (2003), which focused on Queens and how Latina politicians were more likely to promote pan-ethnic identity in their communities.

Transnationalism and Legal Status

With the rise in immigration, increasing attention has been paid to the transnational dimension of politics, an important feature of the Latino experience. Perhaps nowhere is this more important than in New York City, given the diversity of its Latino population. In a broad sense, the important role that immigration plays in defining the Latino experience in the United States introduces a certain complexity politically, but also has led to depictions of all Latinos as newcomers, despite the long presence of this community in the United States and New York City. This image, in turn, has reinforced the notion of "otherness/foreignness" as well as weakening Latino complaints of a significant history of discrimination within this country.

Besides New York's place as a global city with historically dynamic population movements, its location as the site of the United Nations—with its foreign consulates, missions, and other international organizations—and as the site of global market institutions makes the transnational nature of the city's Latino population a uniquely important feature of its politics. For example, the growing role of US-based Latino communities as important sources of remittances to their home countries has, over the last decade or so, transformed the relationship between home country governments and economies with these communities. Although Puerto Rico is not technically a foreign country, its government's establishment of an employment office in the 1920s and a migration division of its department of labor in 1948 in New York City prepared the way for a growing transnational relationship of later Latino communities to their homelands; the Puerto Rican model spurred the New York City government and other local institutions to negotiate the relations between local communities and their home countries in the Latino case (Thomas 2010; Sanchez 2007; Falcón 1984). Today, the active role that the governments of the Dominican Republic, Mexico, and Colombia play in the lives of their New York diasporas is relatively new and politically significant among these foreign countries.

Another way that international immigration directly affects the political situations of these Latino populations is in the different ways it defines their citizenship status. While most New York Latinos are US citizens, many are undocumented. According to the Census Bureau's American Community Survey, about three-quarters of Latinos in New York City (74%) are US citizens. Levels of citizenship status vary considerably between the different Latino national-origin groups: the noncitizenship rate among Mexicans is 51%, for Ecuadoreans 43%, Dominicans 34%, and Colombians 30%. Lack of citizenship status, of course, precludes their participation in the electoral process. Puerto Ricans, as already noted, are the exceptions to this because they arrive stateside in the United States as American citizens coming from a US territory; therefore, the decline in their numbers disproportionately impacts the number of eligible Latino voters.

This also has created a significant legal hierarchy within the Latino community: at the top, US-born citizens, then naturalized citizens, then legal immigrants, and, in the lowest tier, the undocumented of various kinds. This status hierarchy has profoundly affected the politics of the Latino community. It has made immigration a pervasive political issue, structured the ways that Latinos are integrated into and participate in the political process, and raised a whole host of policy questions that have transformed local government structures in pro-immigrant directions. The case of New York City also shows how the complexities of these status hierarchies in such a diverse Latino population both unify and complicate political agendas and strategies. While, on the surface, immigration appears to be a nonissue for Puerto Ricans as US citizens, Puerto Ricans are among the leaders in New York and nationally advocating comprehensive immigration reform and other pro-immigrant policies. This is but one indicator of the salience of this issue and the impact of the current citizenship-status hierarchy on the nature of Latino politics.

The debate continues about whether home-country political ties and loyalties affect the level of Latino political involvement and interest in the United States (Escobar 2004; Jones-Correa 1998). The increasing use of dual citizenship, home-country-absentee and local voting, local campaigning by home-country political candidates, and support of Spanish-language media and other bilingual practices by countries like Venezuela, the Dominican

Republic, and Mexico, as well as Puerto Rico, raise questions about whether these activities detract attention from local US politics and concerns, or, in fact, reinforce it (Aparicio 2006). This concern, for example, led to a campaign in the 1990s to promote the use of the term "Dominican American" as opposed to simply "Dominican" among Dominican citizen and noncitizen residents of the United States (Aparicio 2010). It is interesting to see what effect presidential elections in the Dominican Republic have on its diaspora's politics as the candidates campaign in Washington Heights and other Dominican communities in New York and other parts of the United States.

In 2008, the US political party primaries being held in Puerto Rico became surprisingly important when it was noted that because of their late date in the primary season schedule—June—they could potentially determine the outcome of the Democratic presidential primaries if the race were close (Barone 2008). Though this did not happen, it raised the profile of the Puerto Rican vote in general, as well as exposed the colonial paradox of a population without the right to vote for US president directly being in a position to influence the results through participation in a party primary (Falcón 2008). The "transnational" nature of Puerto Rican politics that year was also reflected in the controversial endorsement of Republican John McCain for president by Puerto Rico's *reggeatón* superstar Daddy Yankee, the counterendorsement of Obama by stateside rapper Fat Joe, and the widespread discussion of the presidential race that these endorsements generated among young people in Puerto Rican and other Latino communities in New York and elsewhere (Shear 2008).

The State and Structure of Local Latino Civil Society

As the city's Latino population has dramatically increased in size and diversity, its civil-society institutions have not developed at a scale that can address the needs of this growth. This situation has placed tremendous pressure on the limited social institutions that already existed in the Puerto Rican community and has resulted in a thin infrastructure in other, growing Latino communities (Falcón 2009b). The Great Recession of 2008 and, more recently, the federal budget sequester (especially during 2013), have further limited the resources available because of the governmental fiscal crises that these events have created, because of the limits on the role of private philanthropy, and because of the outflow of income from Latino communities in the form of home-country remittances.

Beyond the issue of scale, the nature of this nonprofit sector has also changed in the last three or four decades in ways that limit the political-advocacy and social-change roles of many of these institutions. With the growth of the government contracting with these community-based organizations as service providers, their political independence and their role as political actors have been compromised. In addition, as with the city's residential patterns, the functions of social agency and good-government advocacy in the city have been harmed by racial and ethnic segregation to the point where the role of the Latino community in the networks that carry out these functions has been significantly marginalized (Falcón 2009b). This has resulted in limiting this community's capacity to develop effective policy and political agendas as well as to adequately create effective city- and sector-wide advocacy networks. The fact that after decades, Latino social-service providers still need to prioritize improving education, integrating immigrants, expanding living-wage jobs, and increasing affordable housing in Latino neighborhoods underscores the Latino community's continued lack of political clout. In short, the growing numbers of Latinos in the city and in the electorate are not easily translating into policy-relevant results (Hispanic Federation 2013).

Finally, the role of the media has also changed in ways and become less supportive of Latino community interests. The Spanish-language media, once a major force in promoting Latino interests, has become less influential in New York politics, and Latinos continue to be underrepresented in the dominant English-language media. Within the Latino community, although ethnic newspapers have proliferated, their influence has been diffused with the waning of the role of the historically largest and most important, *El Diario–La Prensa*. After many changes in ownership, in 2012 it and impreMedia, its parent company, fell under the majority ownership of a conservative newspaper from Argentina, *La Nación*. After numerous controversies, including with the employees' union, *El Diario–La Prensa* lost a great deal of its historic influence, and no other Spanish-language paper has been able to replace it in this role (Falcón 2012a; Levy 2015). For the most part, Spanish-language radio and television news has also declined in influence after the largest of these, such as Univision and Telemundo, became owned by non-Latinos. The English-language media have made some gains in Latino staffing, but the lack of Latinos with editorial influence has resulted in largely superficial and sporadic coverage of the Latino community and its politics despite the community's size, growth, and increasing diversity. The general weakening of print media and the rise of social media have resulted in increasingly fragmented representations of this community.

LATINOS, NYC MAYOR BILL DE BLASIO, AND TRICKLE-DOWN PROGRESSIVISM

The election in November 2013 of Bill de Blasio as the 109th mayor of the City of New York seemed a hopeful sign that the return of Democratic Party control of city hall and the promise of a new progressive politics for the city after twenty years of the Michael Bloomberg and Rudolph Giuliani administrations would finally make city government more inclusive of Latinos. This impression was further supported at the start of 2014 by city council's selection of a Puerto Rican, Melissa Mark-Viverito, as that legislative body's speaker, the first person of color to hold that influential citywide position.

By the beginning of the de Blasio administration's second year, its relationship to the Latino community was, however, mixed. While many of its progressive policies did make the city more deeply immigrant friendly, questions remained about whether Latinos were being adequately incorporated into the administration and whether its policies would actually reach the Latino community, raising warnings of its trickle-down progressivism when it came specifically to Latinos.

Although the effects of this mayoral administration on Latino political influence require a more detailed analysis, at this point, a few initial, broad observations can be made about that administration's relationship with the Latino community:

1. Mayor de Blasio's election was carried by large majorities of Latino (87%) and black (96%) voters, while only a narrow majority of whites (54%) voted for him (*New York Times,* "Election 2013, Exit Polls: Mayor," n.d., http://www.nytimes.com/projects/elections/2013/general/nyc -mayor/exit-polls.html. http://www.nytimes.com/projects/elections/2013 /general/nyc-mayor/exit-polls.html). Subsequent polls on de Blasio's job approval also consistently reveal a sharp racial division, with large majorities of Latinos and blacks approving of the job he was doing while less than majorities of whites do.

2. The administration's progressive policies included the introduction of municipal ID cards available to the undocumented, paid sick leave, introducing living-wage requirements for certain jobs, and other policies

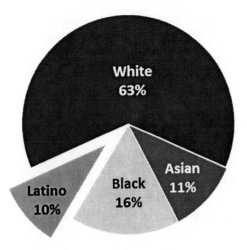

Figure 15.2 Racial-Ethnic Breakdown of New York City Appointments by Mayor de Blasio as of March 18, 2015

Note: N=269.

Source: "Share of NYC Mayor de Blasio Latino Appointments Continues to Decline, Now Only 10 Percent," *National Institute for Latino Policy & Politics Report*, March 19, 2015. http://www.nilp network.org/NiLP_Datanote_-_de_Blasio_Mar_2015.pdf.

that would benefit the city's immigrant populations. However, the benefits of the administration's policies—such as in terms of affordable housing and police-community relations—for the majority of Latinos who were already US citizens, earning a low income, and/or living in poverty are not at all clear (National Institute for Latino Policy 2015). With its strong focus on immigrant-friendly policies and programs, the city seems to be letting the needs of the more than seven hundred thousand Puerto Ricans in the city, who are entirely US citizens, fall between the cracks (Treschan 2010; Kasinitz et al. 2008).

3. The de Blasio administration has been strongly criticized by the Campaign for Fair Latino Representation (see http://LatinoRepresentation .org; Reyes 2014) for its extreme underrepresentation of Latinos in its appointments. Although Latinos are approximately 29% of the city's population, at the beginning of the second year of his administration they made up only 10% of his appointments. This made Latinos the most underrepresented group in the de Blasio administration, represented poorly even in comparison with blacks and Asians; meanwhile whites continue

to be greatly overrepresented, making up approximately 63% of his appointments but only 33% of the city's population (see figure 15.2). This public-sector employment underrepresentation is also an issue for Latinos at the state level, where Latinos make up 18% of the state population, but only 5% of the state government workforce (Campanile 2014).

4. Given that eleven Latinos sit on the fifty-one-member city council and a Puerto Rican serves as council speaker, it is assumed that Latino representation in city government is adequate. However, New York City has a strong-mayor system, where the executive sets the city's policy and budgetary priorities, and it is in this branch that Latinos are most underrepresented in policy-level positions. In addition, Mayor de Blasio's role in promoting the selection of Mark-Viverito as council speaker has further weakened the council's role given the resulting strong mayor-speaker relationship. One result of this close relationship between the city's executive and legislative branches in the case of the problem of Latino underrepresentation in mayoral appointments has been that the council speaker and ten other Latino city council members publicly defended the mayor over Latino community critics (Myles 2010).

5. When this new mayoral administration assumed office, it also sought to redefine the city political leadership. In the Democratic primary most of the Latino political establishment had supported one of de Blasio's opponents, Bill Thompson, an African American. Thus, the new mayor promoted a political realignment within the Latino community, catering to newer politicians in the Puerto Rican and Dominican communities while also cultivating newer players from Central and South American immigrant advocacy groups and labor unions. Over time more traditional political leaders from the Puerto Rican and Dominican communities, who hold the majority of Latino elected posts, have begun to reassert themselves. However, what the ultimate political configuration of Latino power distribution within the de Blasio administration will look like has not fully unfolded.

6. In this reshuffling of Latino political leadership, Puerto Ricans, as the largest number of Latino elected officials, continued to dominate in 2015. The ascendency of a Puerto Rican woman, Melissa Mark-Viverito, as the first person of color to assume the role of New York City Council speaker in 2014 was attributed largely to her early support of de Blasio's candidacy for mayor, and she is seen as his close ally and someone at least initially independent of the traditional Latino political leadership.

In March 2015, another rising Latino political leader, also Puerto Rican, is Bronx assemblyman Marcos Crespo, who became chair of the Bronx Democratic County Committee as well as chair of the Puerto Rican / Hispanic Legislative Task Force. He is a protégé of socially conservative state senator Rubén Díaz Jr. A third rising Latino political star, also a Puerto Rican, is Díaz himself, the Bronx borough president, who served as cochair of the Andrew Cuomo for Governor campaign in 2014. In 2015, Mark-Viverito, at age 45, Crespo, age 34, and Díaz, 41, represent a younger generation of Latino leaders.

7.   The de Blasio administration, the city's Democratic Party, and progressive players like the Working Families Party continue to take the Latino electorate largely for granted and appear comfortable approaching Latinos with a trickle-down progressivism (Falcón 2015). This approach continues to marginalize this community's role in city government while promulgating policies that, it is assumed, will flow down automatically to this community in a perverse version of what has come to be known as the Right's trickle-down economics of the Reagan years.

CONCLUSION: IMPLICATIONS FOR THE FUTURE

What is of concern from the analysis in this chapter is the marginalization of Latinos in the politics of New York City and State. The significant and growing Latino political class of elected officials appears increasingly fragmented and disproportionately beset by ethical problems. Its influence on Democratic Party structures is tenuous, limiting its upward mobility and general influence. On the other hand, in 2010, for the first time in New York State, Latinos were elected to public office as Republicans, and in other ways as well the state Republican Party is beginning to pay attention to this community, however slowly (Lindell 2011). Latino political marginality appears to be a function of the preservation of white privilege even when people of color are the majority of New York City's population.

While the impact of the 2012 presidential election on local Latino politics in New York City was minimal, the greater visibility it gave to Latino politics at the national level bestowed, perhaps undeservedly, increased credibility on local Latino political actors. One result was the beginnings of Republican Party interest in attracting local Latino support, but it did not change in any serious way the marginal relationship of Latino politics to the dominant Democratic Party structures.

Developing a coherent Latino political leadership and effective mecha-nisms for creating unifying political agendas for this community at city and statewide levels remain major challenges, leaving major gaps in the full inte-gration of Latinos in the city's and state's civic life. It is increasingly clear that an important unaddressed issue for New York's Latinos remains devising strate-gies to hold the Democratic Party more accountable for supporting political development of Latinos; at this point, the prospect of doing so with the Repub-lican Party is hard to imagine. We continue to live with the irony that Latino political power is problematic at a time when the size of the Latino population and its political class has never been greater in the city, state, and nation.

REFERENCES

Abrajano, Marisa A., and R. Michael Alvarez. 2010. *New Faces, New Voices: The Hispanic Electorate in America*. Princeton: Princeton University Press.

Aparicio, Ana. 2006. *Dominican-Americans and the Politics of Empowerment*. Gainesville: University Press of Florida.

———. 2010. "Transglocal Barrio Politics: Dominican American Organizing in New York City." In *Beyond El Barrio: Everyday Life in Latina/o America*, edited by Gina M. Perez, Frank A. Guridy, and Adrian Burgos Jr., 253–72. New York: New York University Press.

Barbaro, Michael, and Fernanda Santos. 2011. "Bloomberg to Use Own Funds in Plan to Aid Minority Youth." *New York Times*, August 3.

Barone, Michael. 2008. "Puerto Rican Poll Power." *US News & World Report*, February 6.

Beltran, Cristina. 2010. *The Trouble with Unity: Latino Politics and the Creation of Identity*. Oxford: Oxford University Press.

Burns, Peter F. 2006. *Electoral Politics Is Not Enough: Racial and Ethnic Minorities and Urban Politics*. Albany: State University of New York Press.

Cámara Fuertes, Luis Raúl. 2004. *The Phenomenon of Puerto Rican Voting*. Gaines-ville: University Press of Florida.

Campanile, Carl. 2014. "Latinos Under-Represented in Cuomo Administration: Study." *New York Post*, October 27.

Casella, Jason P. 2011. *Latino Representation in State Houses and Congress*. Cam-bridge: Cambridge University Press.

CLACLS (Center for Latin American, Caribbean and Latino Studies). 2011. *The Latino Population of New York City, 1990–2010*. Latino Data Project, report 44. New York: Center for Latin American, Caribbean & Latino Studies, Novem-ber. http://opencuny.org/nlerap4ne/files/2011/11/The-Latino-Population-of -New-York-City-1990-2010.pdf.

Center for Urban Research. 2008. "2008 Election Results in NYC." New York: CUNY Center for Urban Research, November 14. http://www.urbanresearch .org/news/2008-election-results-in-nyc/?searchterm=2008 election.

Cobas, José A., Jorge Duany, and Joe R. Feagin, eds. 2009. *How the United States Racializes Latinos: White Hegemony and Its Consequences.* Boulder, CO: Paradigm Publishers.

Craig, Susanne, William K. Rashbaum, and Thomas Kaplan. 2015. "The Many Faces of State Political Scandals." *New York Times*, January 22.

Crissey, Sarah R., and Thom File. N.d. "Voting Behavior of Naturalized Citizens: 1996–2010." Washington, DC: US Census Bureau, Social, Economic and Housing Statistics Division.

Cruz, José E., and Joel D. Bloom. 2009. "Latino Politics in the Northeast: Selected Findings from NYLARNet's 2008 Northeast Latino Survey—Executive Summary." A Project of NYLARNet's Latino Political Barometer. Albany: State University of New York.

Dávila, Arlene. 2004. *Barrio Dreams: Puerto Ricans, Latinos, and the Neoliberal City.* Berkeley: University of California Press.

de la Garza, Rodolfo O. 2004. "Latino Politics." *Annual Review of Political Science* 7:91–123.

de la Garza, Rodolfo O., Louis DeSipio, and David L. Leal, eds. 2010. *Beyond the Barrio: Latinos in the 2004 Elections.* Notre Dame, IN: University of Notre Dame Press.

De la Isla, Jose. 2003. *The Rise of Hispanic Political Power.* Los Angeles: Archer Books.

Dreier, Peter, John Mollenkopf, and Todd Swanstrom. 2001. *Place Matters: Metropolitics for the Twenty-First Century.* Lawrence: University Press of Kansas.

Duany, Jorge. 2002. *The Puerto Rican Nation on the Move: Identities on the Island and the United States.* Chapel Hill: University of North Carolina Press.

Equal Employment Practices Commission. 2008. *Workforce Analysis—Calendar Year 2008.* New York: City of New York.

Escobar, Cristina. 2004. "Dual Citizenship and Political Participation: Migrants in the Interplay of United States and Colombian Politics." *Latino Studies* 2:45–69.

Espino, Rodolfo, David L. Leal, and Kenneth J. Meier, eds. 2007. *Latino Politics: Identity, Mobilization, and Representation.* Charlottesville: University of Virginia Press.

Falcón, Angelo. 1983. "Puerto Rican Political Participation: New York City and Puerto Rico." In *Time for Decision: The United States and Puerto Rico*, edited by Jorge Heine, 27–53. Lanham, MD: North-South Publishing.

———. 1984. "A History of Puerto Rican Politics in New York City: 1860s to 1945." In *Puerto Rican Politics in Urban America*, edited by James Jennings and Monte Rivera, 15–42. Westport, CT: Greenwood Press.

————. 1988. "Black and Latino Politics in New York City: Race and Ethnicity in a Changing Urban Context." In *Latinos and the Political System*, edited by F. Chris Garcia, 171–94. Notre Dame, IN: University of Notre Dame Press.

————. 1993. "A Divided Nation: The Puerto Rican Diaspora in the United States and the Proposed Referendum." In *Colonial Dilemma: Critical Perspectives on Contemporary Puerto Rico*, edited by Edwin Meléndez and Edgardo Meléndez, 173–80. Boston: South End Press.

————. 1995. "Puerto Ricans and the Politics of Racial Identity." In *Racial and Ethnic Identity: Psychological Development and Creative Expression*, edited by Herbert W. Harris, Howard C. Blue, and E. H. Griffith, 193–208. New York: Routledge.

————. 2004a. *Atlas of Stateside Puerto Ricans*. Washington, DC: Puerto Rico Federal Affairs Administration.

————. 2004b. "'Pues, at Least We Had Hillary': Latino New York City, the 2000 Election, and the Limits of Party Loyalty." In *Muted Voices: Latinos and the 2000 Elections*, edited by Rodolfo O. de la Garza and Louis DeSipio, 194–212. New York: Rowman and Littlefield.

————. 2004c. "De'tras Pa'lante: Explorations on the Future History of Puerto Ricans in New York City." In *Boricuas in Gotham: Puerto Ricans in the Making of Modern New York*, edited by Gabriel Haslip-Viera, Angelo Falcón, and Félix Matos Rodríguez, 147–92. Princeton: Markus Wiener.

————. 2007. "The Diaspora Factor: Stateside Boricuas and the Future of Puerto Rico." *NACLA Report on the Americas* 40:28–31.

————. 2008. "Puerto Rico Vote an Enigma of Complexities." *Newsday*, June 3.

————. 2009a. *The More Things Change, the More They Stay the Same: Latino Underrepresentation in New York State Government, 1983–2009*. New York: National Institute for Latino Policy.

————. 2009b. "Latinos, Diversity and Racial Fatigue in the Age of Obama." *National Civic Review* 98:40–42.

————. 2012a. "The End of El Diario–La Prensa?" San Francisco: New America Media, July 21. http://newamericamedia.org/2012/07/the-end-of-el-diario-la -prensa.php.

————. 2012b. "A Boricua Game of Thrones? A Critical Review of the Rise of Puerto Rican Political Families in New York City." *The NiLP Network on Latino Issues*. New York: National Institute for Latino Policy, July 29. http://www.nilp network.org/NiLP_iReport_-_Boricua_Game_of_Thrones.pdf.

————. 2015. "Stop Pissing on Us! Trickle-Down Progressivism and New York's Latino Community." *The NiLP Network on Latino Issues*. New York: National Institute for Latino Policy, February 9. http://www.nilpnetwork.org/NiLP _Commentary_-_Trickle-Down_Progressivism.pdf.

File, Thom. 2013. "The Diversifying Electorate—Voting Rates by Race and Hispanic Origin in 2012 (and Other Recent Elections)." Current Population Survey Reports, P20–569. Washington, DC: United States Census Bureau.

Fitzpatrick, Joseph P. 1971. *Puerto Rican Americans: The Meaning of Migration to the Mainland.* Englewood Cliffs, NJ: Prentice-Hall.

Foley, Neil. 2010. *Quest for Equality: The Failed Promise of Black-Brown Solidarity.* Cambridge, MA: Harvard University Press.

Foner, Nancy, ed. 2001. *New Immigrants in New York.* New York: Columbia University Press.

Garcia, John A., Gabriel R. Sanchez, and J. Salvador Peralta. 2010. *Latino Politics: A Growing and Evolving Political Community.* Notre Dame, IN: University of Notre Dame Press.

Garcia Bedolla, Lisa. 2009. *Latino Politics.* Cambridge, MA: Polity Press.

Gonzalez, Juan. 2011. "New York Senate's 'Four Amigos' Down to Just 1: Only Ruben Diaz Sr. Remains." *New York Daily News*, December 20.

Grosfoguel, Ramon. 2002. *Colonial Subjects: Puerto Ricans in a Global Perspective.* Berkeley: University of California Press.

Hakim, Danny, and Jeremy W. Peters. 2009. "G.O.P. Regains Control of New York State Senate." *New York Times*, June 8, 2009.

Hardy, Carol, and Jeffrey N. Gerson. 2002. *Latino Politics in Massachusetts: Struggles, Strategies, and Prospects.* New York: Routledge.

Haslip-Viera, Gabriel, and Sherrie L. Baver. 1996. *Latinos in New York: Communities in Transition.* Notre Dame, IN: University of Notre Dame Press.

Haslip-Viera, Gabriel, Angelo Falcón, and Félix Matos Rodríguez, eds. 2004. *Boricuas in Gotham: Puerto Ricans in the Making of Modern New York City.* Princeton: Markus Wiener.

Heine, Jorge, ed. 1983. *Time for Decision: The United States and Puerto Rico.* Lanham, MD: North-South Publishing.

Hero, Rodney. 1992. *Latinos and the U.S. Political System: Two-Tiered Pluralism.* Philadelphia: Temple University Press.

Herzenberg, Michael. 2011. "NY1 Exclusive: Poll Shows Most New York Voters Disapprove of Obama but Prefer Him to Republicans." *NY1 News*, November 2.

Hispanic Federation of New York. 2013. *La Gran Manzana: The Road Ahead; Policy Blueprint for the City's Next Mayor and City Council.* New York: Hispanic Federation of New York. http://hispanicfederation.org/images/pdf/LaGranManzana.pdf.

Jennings, James, ed. 1994. *Blacks, Latinos, and Asians in Urban America: Status and Prospects for Politics and Activism.* Westport, CT: Praeger.

Jiménez Román, Miriam, and Juan Flores. 2010. *The Afro-Latin@ Reader: History and Culture in the United States.* Durham, NC: Duke University Press.

Jones-Correa, Michael. 1998. *Between Two Nations: The Political Predicament of Latinos in New York City.* Ithaca, NY: Cornell University Press.

——, ed. 2001. *Governing American Cities: Inter-Ethnic Coalitions, Competition, and Conflict.* New York: Russell Sage Foundation.

Judd, Dennis R., and Paul Kantor, eds. 2002. *The Politics of Urban America: A Reader.* New York: Longman.

Junn, Jane, and Kerry L. Haynie, eds. 2008. *New Race Politics in America: Understanding Minority and Immigrant Politics*. Cambridge: Cambridge University Press.

Kasinitz, Philip, John H. Mollenkopf, Mary C. Waters, and Jennifer Holdaway. 2008. *Inheriting the City: The Children of Immigrants Coming of Age*. Cambridge, MA: Harvard University Press.

Kuntzman, Gersh. 2008. "Zero-bama: Did Clinton Really Shut Out Obama in Some Districts?" *Brooklyn Paper*, February 23.

Laó-Montes, Agustín, and Arlene Dávila, eds. 2001. *Mambo Montage: The Latinization of New York*. New York: Columbia University Press.

Lehrer, Warren, and Judith Sloan, eds. 2003. *Crossing the Blvd: Strangers, Neighbors, Aliens in a New America*. New York: W.W. Norton and Company.

Levy, Nicole. 2015. "Newspaper Guild Reaches Tentative Agreement with El Diario." *Capital New York*, March 4.

Lindell, Sonia. 2011. "Upcoming Conference to Promote Latino Economic Growth." *Business Council Capital Business Blog*, October 13, 2011.

Marwell, Nicole P. 2007. *Bargaining for Brooklyn: Community Organizations in the Entrepreneurial City*. Chicago: University of Chicago Press.

Massey, Douglas, and Nancy Denton. 1993. *American Apartheid: Segregation and the Making of the Underclass*. Cambridge, MA: Harvard University Press.

Minnite, Lorraine C., and John Mollenkopf. 2008. "The University Collaborative / New Americans Exit Poll Project: Preliminary Results from the 2008 New York City Voter Exit Poll." New York: New York Immigration Coalition.

Mollenkopf, John, David Olson, and Timothy Ross. 2001. "Immigrant Political Participation in New York and Los Angeles." In *Governing American Cities: Inter-Ethnic Coalitions, Competition, and Conflict*, edited by Michael Jones-Correa, 17–70. New York: Russell Sage Foundation.

Murray, Shailagh. 2008. "A $20 Million Plan: Obama and the DNC Target Hispanics in Swing States." *Washington Post*, July 29.

Muzzio, Douglas, and Jeronimo Cortina. 2010. "New York in 2004: Political Blues for Hispanics." In *Beyond the Barrio: Latinos in the 2004 Elections*, edited by Rodolfo O. de la Garza, Louis DeSipio, and David L. Leal, 221–47. Notre Dame, IN: University of Notre Dame Press.

Myles, Rebecca S. 2010. "Top Ranking New York City Government Latina Defends De Blasio Administration On Latino Hiring." *Latin Post*, November 29.

Nahmias, Laura. 2011. "¿Si Se Puede?" *Politico*, October 17.

National Institute for Latino Policy. 2015. "Results of the New York City Latino Opinion Leaders Survey—March 23, 2015." NiLP Latino Policy & Politics Report. New York: National Institute for Latino Policy.

Navarro, Sharon A., and Armando Xavier Majia, eds. 2004. *Latino Americans and Political Participation: A Reference Handbook*. Santa Barbara, CA: ABC CLIO.

Negrón-Muntaner, Frances, ed. 2007. *None of the Above: Puerto Ricans in the Global Era*. New York: Palgrave Macmillan.

Nelson, William E., Jr., and Jessica Lavariega Monforti, eds. 2005. *Black and Latino/a Politics: Issues in Political Development in the United States*. Miami: Barnhardt & Ashe Publishing.

New York City, Department of Citywide Administrative Services. 2013. *2013 Workforce Profile Report*. New York: New York City, Department of Citywide Administrative Services.

New York State, Civil Service Commission. 2014. *Workforce Management Report*. Albany: NYS Civil Service Commission.

Opie, Frederick Douglass. 2014. *Upsetting the Apple Cart: Black-Latino Coalitions in New York City from Protest to Public Office*. New York: Columbia University Press.

Perez, Gina. 2004. *Near Northwest Side Story: Migration, Displacement, and Puerto Rican Families*. Berkeley: University of California Press.

Perez, Gina M., Frank A. Guridy, and Adrian Burgos Jr. 2010. *Beyond El Barrio: Everyday Life in Latina/o America*. New York: New York University Press.

Portes, Alejandro, Cristina Escobar, and Alexandria Walton Radford. 2007. "Immigrant Transnational Organizations and Development: A Comparative Study." *International Migration Review* 41 (1): 242–81.

Quiñones, Ernesto. 2008. "The Black-Brown Divide: For Every Race in America, There's Another Racial Barrier." *Esquire*, May 21.

Ramos-Zayas, Ana Y. 2003. *National Performances: The Politics of Class, Race, and Space in Puerto Rican Chicago*. Chicago: University of Chicago Press.

Remeseira, Claudio Iván. 2010. *Hispanic New York: A Sourcebook*. New York: Columbia University Press.

Reyes, Raul A. 2014. "Does NYC Mayor Bill De Blasio Have a 'Latino Problem'?" *NBC News*, December 11.

Ricourt, Milagros, and Ruby Danta. 2003. *Hispanas de Queens: Latino Panethnicity in a New York City Neighborhood*. Ithaca, NY: Cornell University Press.

Roberts, Sam. 2009. "For First Time, Minority Vote Was a Majority." *New York Times*, December 25.

Rodriguez, Orlando J. 2011. *Vote Thieves: Illegal Immigration, Redistricting, and Presidential Election*. Washington, DC: Potomac Books.

Saito, Leland T. 2009. *The Politics of Exclusion: The Failure of Race-Neutral Policies in Urban America*. Stanford, CA: Stanford University Press.

Sanchez, José Ramon. 2007. *Boricua Power: A Political History of Puerto Ricans in the United States*. New York: New York University Press.

Sharman, Russell Leigh. 2006. *The Tenants of East Harlem*. Berkeley: University of California Press.

Shear, Michael D. 2008. "Gasolina! Daddy Yankee Endorses McCain." *Washington Post*, August 25.

Slattery, Denis. 2015. "Assemblyman Marcos Crespo Replaces Carl Heastie as Chairman of Bronx Democratic Committee." *New York Daily News*, March 6.

Smith, Robert Courtney. 2006. *Mexican New York: Transnational Lives of New Immigrants*. Berkeley: University of California Press.

Sparrow, Bartholomew H. 2006. *The Insular Cases and the Emergence of American Empire*. Lawrence: University Press of Kansas.

Stokes-Brown, Atiya Kai. 2012. *The Politics of Race in Latino Communities: Walking the Color Line*. New York: Routledge.

Strom, Elizabeth J., and John H. Mollenkopf. 2007. *The Urban Politics Reader*. London: Routledge.

Subvervi-Velez, Federico, ed. 2008. *The Mass Media and Latino Politics: Studies of U.S. Media Content, Campaign Strategies and Survey Research, 1984–2004*. New York: Routledge.

Thomas, Lorrin. 2010. *Puerto Rican Citizen: History and Political Identity in Twentieth-Century New York City*. Chicago: University of Chicago Press.

Torres, Andres. 1995. *Between Melting Pot and Mosaic: African Americans and Puerto Ricans in the New York Political Economy*. Philadelphia: Temple University Press.

———, ed. 2006. *Latinos in New England*. Philadelphia: Temple University Press.

Torres, Andres, and José Velazquez, eds. 1998. *Puerto Rican Movement: Voices from the Diaspora*. Philadelphia: Temple University Press.

Torres-Saillant, Silvio, and Ramona Hernández. 1998. *The Dominican Americans*. Westport, CT: Greenwood Press.

Treschan, Lazar. 2010. *Latino Youth in New York City: School, Work, and Income Trends for New York's Largest Group of Young People*. New York: Community Service Society.

United States Census Bureau. 2009. *Current Population Survey*. Washington, DC: United States Census Bureau.

———. 2011. *2008–2010 American Community Survey*. Washington, DC: United States Census Bureau.

Urbano, Juan Luis, Jr. 2011. "All for One? Latino Group Consciousness and Partisanship." Paper presented at the Western Political Science Association 2011 Annual Meeting, April 21–23, San Antonio, Texas.

Vélez-Ibañez, Carlos G., and Anna Sampaio, eds. 2002. *Transnational Latina/o Communities: Politics, Processes, and Cultures*. Lanham, MD: Rowman & Littlefield.

Virtanen, Michael. 2011. "Espada Broke State Law by Hiring His Uncle; Panel: Ethics Panel Finds 'Reasonable Cause.'" *NBC New York*, December 27.

Whalen, Carmen Teresa, and Victor Vázquez-Hernández, eds. 2005. *The Puerto Rican Diaspora: Historical Perspectives*. Philadelphia: Temple University Press.

Conclusion

CHAPTER SIXTEEN

Nueva York, Diaspora City

Latinos Between and Beyond

JUAN FLORES

In the last few decades, there has been a proliferating turn to "diaspora" in the field of Latino Studies. Here, I characterize New York as a "diaspora city," and by that I mean an urban setting saturated by interacting and interlocking diasporic communities, including those among Latino populations from all over Latin America and the Caribbean.

Of all the huge Latino cities—Los Angeles, Houston, Miami, Chicago—Nueva York is the one with the greatest large-scale diversity. That is, it has the largest number of Latino nationalities with substantial populations: for over a generation now, five or more groups—Puerto Ricans, Dominicans, Mexicans, Colombians, and Ecuadoreans—have lived in New York in numbers exceeding one hundred thousand. And those striking numbers of people and groups refer only to New York City proper, not to the mammoth additional Latino populations in the tristate Greater New York area.

New York magazine was renamed *Nueva York*—at least for a week—as we entered the new millennium. The Spanish word on the cover of the September 6, 1999, issue was an eye-catcher for readers of the popular weekly, and attested to the currency of things, and words, "Latin" among the contemporary public in the United States. The theme of *Nueva York*, the issue's title, was "The Latin Explosion," those words being emblazoned in bold yellow-and-white lettering across the half-exposed midsection of Jennifer Lopez. The Nuyorican actress, singer, and pop idol is surely "Miss Nueva York" in recent times; her shapely body, a large crucifix dangling suggestively above her cleavage, provides the cover image, and the feature article, entitled "La Vida Lopez" (calling Ricky Martin to mind), sets out to explain "why Jennifer Lopez, Puerto Rican Day parade marshal, girlfriend (maybe) of Sean (Puffy) Combs, inspired by Selena, aspiring to be Barbara Streisand, and owner of America's most famous backside, might be the celebrity of the future." Before you know it, all New Yorkers, and all Americans, will be "living la vida loca" on the streets of Nueva York!

Still today, over a decade and a half into the new millennium, Latino fever is gripping US popular culture at a pitch unprecedented in the protracted history of that continental seduction. Hardly a week passes without still another media special, and hardly an area of entertainment and public life—sports, music, movies, television, advertising, fashion, food—is by now untouched by reference to that ubiquitous Hispanic presence. Only recently has that presence been matched by similar emergence in the political sphere, with both political parties foregrounding their campaign ads with Latino faces and with the appointment of Sonia Sotomayor to the Supreme Court in 2009.

Visibility is of course not new to the "Latin look" in American pop culture—think of Carmen Miranda, Ricardo Montalban, or Desi Arnaz—nor is the Latin "flavor," the *salsa y sabor*, a new ingredient in the proverbial melting pot, be it musical, sexual, or culinary. But those passing crazes and that subliminal sense of "otherness" have become in the present generation a veritable saturation of the pop public sphere, the "Latin" way attaining a ubiquity and prominence that has converted it into an active shaper of contemporary tastes and trends.

Underlying this spectacular cultural ascendancy are, of course, major demographic and economic changes, which have resulted in the incremental growth and enormous diversification of the Latino population in the United States. By now, all the Latin American and Caribbean countries are present in substantial numbers in many settings, especially in the global cities of Los Angeles, Miami, and New York. Already by the early 1990s, *New York Newsday* had titled a lengthy supplement "The New Nueva York," and with that phrase capsulized the momentous increase and dramatic recomposition of the city's

Latino community since the seventies. The swelling influx of Dominicans, Mexicans, Colombians, Ecuadoreans, and the numerous other Latin American nationalities has meant that "Latin New York," for decades synonymous with Puerto Rican, has become pan-ethnic to the point that Puerto Ricans have come to constitute less than half of the aggregate. By 1999, then, it was high time that New York became Nueva York, and that its burgeoning population of Spanish-language background be given its day in the glitz.

Visibility, though, can do as much to obscure as to illuminate, particularly when it remains so preponderantly concentrated in the image making of the commercial culture. In the case of US Latinos, celebrity status and the ceremonial fanfare are clearly part of the mirage, serving effectively to camouflage the structured inequality and domination which accounts for their diasporic reality in the first place. This deflects public attention from the decidedly unceremonious and unenviable social status of the majority of Latino peoples. The spectacular success stories of the few serve only to mask the ongoing reality of racism, economic misery, and political disenfranchisement endured by most Latinos, who moved northward from their homelands only because of persistent inequalities at global, regional, and national levels.

Nevertheless, it is clear by now that the Latino "sleeping giant" has awakened; it is a demographic and cultural monster whose immense commercial and electoral potential has only begun to be tapped and who, if roused, could well upset some of the delicate balances necessary for the prolongation of the "American Century." Typically, awe and fascination mingle with a sense of foreboding, an alarmism over the imminent threat Latinos are perceived to present to the presumed unity of American culture and to an unhampered control over the country's destiny. An integral component of this nervous prognosis, repeated with mantra-like predictability when public discussion turns to the "browning of America," is the identification of Latinos as the country's "fastest-growing minority," the group whose numbers have come to exceed those of African Americans. The fear of an "alien nation"—the title of a notoriously xenophobic book on immigration—veils, but thinly, an even deeper phobia, the fear of a nonwhite majority.[1] Dare I mention the next "sleeping giant"? In fact, the "brown peril" is soon to be eclipsed by another, "yellow peril," as Asian Americans are poised to outnumber both blacks and Hispanics by mid-century.

Such calculations, however, beg more questions than they answer when it comes to assessing the cultural and political relations that prevail in contemporary society. Most obviously, they take for granted the sociological equivalence of the various "minority" groups, in this case Latinos and African Americans, as though a diverse set of ethno-national diasporas constitute the same kind of collective association as a group which is unified, within the United States, on the basis of their common African ancestry and history of enslavement.

Of course African Americans, like all other groups, have long differed along class, gender, color, regional, and other lines, but the seams in the Latino patchwork stand out as soon as we go beyond the media hype and wishful census counts and undertake comparative analysis of any rigor. Even the obvious commonalities like language and religion, for example, turn out to be deceptive, at best, in light of the millions of Latinos who are neither Spanish-speaking nor of the Catholic faith. But beyond that, it is certainly a spurious sociological exercise to conjoin in one unit of discourse Puerto Ricans and Mexican Americans on the one hand, whose position in US society is fully conditioned by legacies of conquest and colonization, with, on the other hand, immigrant and exile nationalities of relatively recent arrival from varied national homelands in Latin America. Differences along the lines of economic class, educational attainment, and entrepreneurial capital are striking, as are those having to do with issues of race and national cultures.

At least one of the spokesmen cited in *Nueva York* voices sensitivity to the pitfalls of this pan-ethnic lumping and labeling process. Dominican writer Junot Díaz is skeptical about any and all ethnic generalizations; he states about "Latinos," "I'd rather have us start out as fractured so we don't commit the bullshit and erasures that trying to live under the banner of sameness entails." The most obvious of these erasures for Díaz, aside from the internal differentiation among the varied "Latino" groups already noted, is the reality of racism—being called a "spic" and reacting to that denigrating denomination. "And rare is the Latino kid who hasn't been called a spic." Discrimination regarding educational opportunities and at the hands of the criminal justice system, for example, is what unites Latinos beyond the multiple cultural variations, along with the strategies developed to confront these social inequalities. "This is a nightmarish place," Díaz concludes, "for people of color."

What is not mentioned in the pages of *Nueva York*, by Junot Díaz or any other commentator, is the most consequential of the "erasures" involved in pan-ethnic naming—the relation of Latinos to blackness, and to African Americans in particular. While the Latino concept does generally indicate "otherness," "people of color," and "nonwhite," the history of social categorization has selectively equivocated on the issue; and to this day, many media representations allow for, or foster, a sense of compatibility with whiteness. The Latino faces shown for broad public consumption, whether it is Daisy Fuentes, Keith Hernandez, or Christina Aguilera, tend to be decidedly from the lighter end of the spectrum. The unspoken agenda of the new Latino visibility, and of the surpassing of African Americans as the country's "largest minority," is the ascendancy of a nonblack minority. To mollify the fears of an invasion from south of the border is the consolation that at least the presence of this minority does not involve dealing with more souls of more black folk.

Yet social experience tells us otherwise; the rampant "racial profiling" and waves of police brutality are directed against both African American and Latino victims, with no color distinctions of this kind playing a decisive role. For the fact is that, in many inner-city situations, there is no such difference, and it is not possible to "tell them apart." What the hegemonic, consumer version of Latino ethnicity obscures is that many Latinos are black, especially according to the codes operative in the United States. And what is more, while this consumer version tends to racialize Latinos towards whiteness, much in tune with the racist baggage of Latin American and Caribbean home cultures, on the streets and in the dominant social institutions "brown" is close enough to black to be suspect.

In Nueva York in particular, where the prevalent Latino presence and sensibility remains Caribbean, this counterposition to blackness is often disconcerting at best, and many Puerto Rican and Dominican youth have responded by reaffirming a sense of belonging to an African diaspora. Indeed, for Puerto Ricans, this perspective entails not only emphasizing Afro-Boricua heritages but also, because of the decades-long experience of close social interaction with African Americans in New York, an identification and solidarity with American blacks perhaps unmatched by any other group (with the exception of English-speaking West Indians) in the history of the "nation of immigrants." Cultural expression in all areas—from language and music to literature and the visual arts—typically illustrates fusions and crossovers, mutual fascinations and emulations that have resulted in much of what we identify, for example, in the field of popular music, as jazz, rock and roll, and hip-hop. Collectively, and as a reflex of broader social experiences, this demographic reality and this intertwined cultural history show as a lie any wedge driven between Latino and black life and representation.

This Latino "double consciousness" among Puerto Ricans and other Caribbeans goes back generations, in intellectual life to the contributions of Puerto Rican collector and bibliophile Arturo Alfonso Schomburg during the Harlem Renaissance, in music history at least to the 1940s with the beginnings of Latin jazz, and in literature, to the writings of Jesús Colón in the 1950s and Piri Thomas in his 1967 novel *Down These Mean Streets*. In our own times, Latino youth find themselves in tight league with young African Americans in creating constantly shifting currents of hip-hop and other expressive styles. In a frequently cited poem, "Nigger-Reecan Blues," Nuyorican writer Willie Perdomo addresses once again the interracial dilemmas first articulated by Piri Thomas thirty years earlier, and concludes with the dramatic lines,

> I'm a Spic!
> I'm a Nigger!
> Spic! Spic! No different than a Nigger!
> Neglected, rejected, oppressed and depressed
> From banana boats to tenements
> Street gangs to regiments
> Spic! Spic! I ain't nooooo different than a Nigger.

In a similar vein, the spoken-word artist "Mariposa" (Maria Fernandez) objects to being called a "Latina writer," as present-day literary marketing would group her. She reminds her audience, "I myself feel more in common with my sistahs [African American women writers] than with, say, Chicana poets like Sandra Cisneros or Lorna Dee Cervantes."

Yet Mariposa does not consider this intense affiliation with African Americans to stand in any conflict with her Puerto Rican background. On the contrary, in her signature poem, "Ode to the DiaspoRican," she signals her "pelo vivo" ("lively hair") and her "manos trigueñas" ("dark hands") as evidence of her national identity, and rails against those who would deny it:

> Some people say that I am not the real thing
> Boricua, that is
> cuz I wasn't born on the enchanted island
> cuz I was born on the mainland . . .
> cuz my playground was a concrete jungle
> cuz my Rio Grande de Loiza was the Bronx River

cuz my Fajardo was City Island
my Luquillo Orchard Beach
and summer nights were filled with city noises instead of coquis
and Puerto Rico was just some paradise that we only saw in pictures
What does it mean to live in between . . . ?

In these memorable lines, Mariposa gives voice to the sentiments of many young Puerto Ricans, and of many Latinos in general, in their defiance of a territorially and socially confined understanding of cultural belonging. Place of birth and immediate lived experience do not wholly define cultural identification, which in this view has more to do with political and social experience, and with personally chosen ascription. "No nací en Puerto Rico," she exclaims in the poem's refrain, "Puerto Rico nació en mí." (I wasn't born in Puerto Rico, Puerto Rico was born in me.)

As these instances show, present-day social identities press simultaneously in varied directions, linking individuals and groups along lines that would appear mutually exclusive according to their representation in commercially and ideologically oriented media. *Nueva York, New York* magazine's momentary interlude as a Latino-focused publication, dwarfs the cultural horizons of Latino experience by postulating its categorical differentiation from blackness, and significantly by disengaging Latino culture in the United States from its moorings in Latin American and Caribbean realities. Not only are the featured Latino celebrities treated as interchangeable in their collective background, but in the entire issue no mention is made of Mexico, Puerto Rico, Cuba, the Dominican Republic, or Colombia, except as potential extensions of the US market. What is more, there is no discussion of the massive migrations from those home countries nor of those countries' historical relations with the United States, which have generated modern migration movements, as the transnational origin and setting for the very presence and position of Latinos in US society.

Today's global conditions impel us beyond these tidy, nationally constricted views of cultural identity, which might well be referred to as "consumer ethnicities." The Latino community is, if anything, a process rather than a circumscribed social entity, and its formation entails complex and often converging interactions with other, purportedly "non-Latino" groups such as African Americans and American Indians. But the idea of the pan-Latino necessarily implies the trans-Latino: the engagement of US-based Latinos in the composition of cultural and political diasporas of regional and global proportions. The interdependence of old and new "homes," the constant bearing of US policies and practices on the life circumstances in Latin America and the Caribbean, propel more and more Latinos across the hemispheric divide, and resonate loudly in the everyday lives of all Latinos. But beyond those direct geopolitical ties, awakened cultural heritages and congruencies also engage Latinos in more abstract but no less pronounced diasporic affiliations, notably transnational indigenous and "Black Atlantic" trajectories of identity formation.

Living multiple diasporic realities simultaneously is more common than not among the city's Latinos, as many find themselves sharing that reality with members of the Caribbean or African or broader "Latino" diasporas. "Diaspora City" *is* the "new Nueva York," a sociocultural location that is perhaps most accurately characterized as a demographic grid or matrix of transnational communities co-inhabiting a single geographically circumscribed polity.

The lives and writings of a new generation of writers like Mariposa, Willie Perdomo, and Junot Díaz are grounded in and dedicated to giving voice and image to this excitingly new and rapidly shifting reality. And a commercial publication like *New York* magazine does what it can to address this newness by adopting an assumed, non-English title, if only for a single week of innovation.

The term "diaspora" is so commonly used these days to refer to various Latino communities in the United States, and even to the Latino population as a whole, that it might appear to some that it has always been so. In fact, in earlier stages in Latino history, and in Latino studies, the word "diaspora" was generally not known or used. Among Mexican Americans the group terms for the community were Chicanos, La Raza, Aztlán, and "internal colonialism"; among Puerto Ricans it was "the migration" (*la migración*) or the "divided nation," while Cubans, especially after 1959, were "el exilio." Though "La Raza" was supposed to transcend its Mexican origin and embrace all Latinos, in reality other groups were never a comfortable fit, as they barely are today in the National Council of La Raza, or La Raza Unida Party. Until a generation ago there was no adequate designation for the entire pan-ethnicity; there was also no conceptual framework for accounting for the many Latino groups in all their diversity and commonalities.

The term "diaspora" came up in the writings of Samuel Betances in his journal *The Rican*,[2] and also in Adalberto López's anthology *The Puerto*

Ricans: Their Culture, History, and Society in 1975, but the widespread adoption of the term in reference to Latinos did not begin until the mid-to-late 1990s. Before that, it was the "African diaspora," which itself didn't emerge until the 1960s, and more conventionally, the "Jewish diaspora." But gradually and at first imperceptibly, we began to hear and speak of the Puerto Rican "diaspora," and then the term started getting applied to Dominicanos and other groups in New York and elsewhere.

"Diaspora" as a term in the Latino context came up in Glenn Hendricks's *Dominican Diaspora* (1974), in Edna Acosta Belén's edited volume *Adiós, Borinquen querida* (2000), and in *The Puerto Rican Diaspora*, edited by Carmen Teresa Whalen and Victor Vázquez Hernández (2005), whose experience and point of reference had been not New York but Philadelphia. More recently, books have appeared with similar usages in their titles, such as *Mexico and Its Diaspora* (Délano 2013), *The Dominican Diaspora* (Sagas and Molina 2004; Suarez 2006), *The Tejano Diaspora* (Rodriguez 2011), and *Woman Warriors of the Afro-Latina Diaspora* (Moreno-Vega, Alba, and Modestin 2012). Countless print and broadcast media specials about Latinos have also had recourse to this new, diverse, and complex "diaspora" or set of diasporas.

Mariposa's poem "Ode to a Diasporican" was an early instance of the usage in print, its playful conjunction with "Rican" suggesting more poetic license than a new conceptual vocabulary. It was a takeoff on the, by then, well-worn neologism "Nuyorican," intended to some degree as a way of broadening that group self-designation to include the nationwide dispersal of the stateside Puerto Rican population. With that same end in view, terms like "AmeRícan" and "Other Rican" have also surfaced over recent years. But "Diasporican" had the added advantage of tying the extended geographical reach of the word to a conceptually and historically grounded concept that was emerging in those years, as the notion of "new diasporas" came to apply the ancient Greek word to emergent migratory formations and unprecedented transnational experiences of peoples in many parts of the world.

The diaspora concept has proven to be an extremely useful and convenient one for taking account of multiple Latino realities in our times, especially as those realities have become more complex over the past generation of growth, dispersal, and internal diversity. For one thing, it helps disengage *Latinidad* from an automatic association with immigration, at least in the conventional understanding of that phenomenon as a one-way and permanent resettlement involving a disconnection from the background country and culture.

At least since the 1960s, the inadequacy of the immigrant analogy and assimilation paradigm had been widely observed and contested, but without an alternative terminology at hand to help redefine the new methodology and theoretical framework. It was clear that many Latina/os were not simply casting aside their inherited ways and accommodating themselves to the new setting, and that they were scattering and not limiting new homes to one location. Many were not even here to stay, and most retained strong affective ties to their home cultures, preserving them and reinventing them in highly creative ways.

The reality of massive return migration and circular geographical movement was turning out to be more the rule than the exception, as Latinos typically and willingly led bicultural and border-crossing lives. Latinos finding themselves in different locations faced diverse local particularities, but they were, at the same time, interlinked by congruent historical trajectories.

The idea of diaspora refers to exactly that kind of social experience, which is simply beyond the theoretical scope of the traditional study of immigration or exile. Diaspora is an eminently dynamic, situational category, demanding the analysis not so much of the "immigrant group" itself but of the ongoing relation or interaction between each group and its country or region of origin, and between that group and others with which it comes into close social contact. The more elaborated notion of "overlapping" or "multiple" diasporas accounts for the rich bridging between and among diasporic groupings and the frequent sense of an individual or community belonging to more than one diasporic configuration at the same time, for example, Dominican, Caribbean, Latino, and African.

The "new Nueva York" is rich with these innovative cultural possibilities, and as the newfound home of so many people from so many Latin American countries, it now serves as a seminal ground for the rethinking and reimagining of America. One hundred years after the prophetic ruminations of José Martí about the contours of "nuestra America," we are now in a position to conceptualize "America" itself in its world context, and the multiple lines of an "American" identity as coordinates of radical transnational remapping. The "Latin explosion" receiving so much coverage in the United States today, the hyperboles and hypes generated by "la vida loca," is but one index of a pervasive change in human affairs, leaving all of us asking, with Mariposa, "What does it mean to live in between?"

NOTES

1. The book referred to is Peter Brimelow, *Alien Nation: Common Sense about the America's Immigration Disaster* (New York: Random House, 1995).

2. "Rican" was used in the early 1970s by Samuel Betances as the title of his journal, *The Rican*, which only had a limited audience during its short life.

REFERENCES

Acosta-Belén, E., M. Benítez, J. E. Cruz, Y. González-Rodríguez, C. Rodríguez, C. E. Santiago, A. Santiago-Rivera, and B. R. Sjostrom. 2000. *"Adiós, Borinquen querida": La diáspora puertorriqueña, su historia y sus aportaciones.* Also published in English as *Adiós, Borinquen Querida: The Puerto Rican Diaspora, Its History, and Contributions.* Albany: Center for Latin American, Caribbean, and U.S. Latino Studies, State University of New York at Albany.

Betances, Samuel, ed. *The Rican: A Journal of Contemporary Puerto Rican Thought,* published from 1971 to 1974.

Délano, Alexandra. 2013. *Mexico and Its Diaspora in the United States: Policies of Emigration since 1848.* New York: Cambridge University Press.

Hendricks, Glenn. 1974. *Dominican Diaspora: From the Dominican Republic to New York City—Villagers in Transition.* New York: Columbia Teacher's College Press.

López, Adalberto. 1975. "The Puerto Rican Diaspora: A Survey." In *The Puerto Ricans: Their Culture, History, and Society,* edited by Adalberto López and James Petras, 313–43. Cambridge: Schenkman Publishing.

Moreno-Vega, Marta, Marinieves Alba, and Yvette Modestin, eds. 2012. *Women Warriors of the Afro-Latina Diaspora.* Houston: Arte Público Press.

Rodriguez, Marc Simon. 2011. *The Tejano Diaspora: Mexican Americanism and Ethnic Politics in Texas and Wisconsin.* Chapel Hill: University of North Carolina Press.

Sagas, Ernesto, and Sintia Molina, eds. 2004. *Dominican Migration: Transnational Perspectives.* New World Diasporas. Gainesville: University Press of Florida.

Suarez, Lucía. 2006. *The Tears of Hispaniola: Haitian and Dominican Diaspora Memory.* New World Diasporas. Gainesville: University Press of Florida.

Whalen, Carmen Teresa, and Victor Vázquez Hernández, eds. 2005. *The Puerto Rican Diaspora.* Philadelphia: Temple University Press.

CONTRIBUTORS

Sherrie Baver teaches political science and Latin American & Latino studies at The City College and The Graduate Center at the City University of New York. Her research interests focus on political institutions, environmental politics, and, especially, environmental justice struggles in the Caribbean, Latin America, and the diaspora. Among other awards, she has had two Fulbright Fellowships in the region. Along with articles and book chapters, she has published *The Political Economy of Colonialism: The State and Industrialization in Puerto Rico* (1993) and coedited *Latinos in New York: Communities in Transition*, 1st ed. (1996), and *Beyond Sun and Sand: Caribbean Environmentalisms* (2006).

Juan Cartagena, a constitutional and civil rights attorney, is president and general counsel of LatinoJustice / Puerto Rican Legal Defense and Education Fund (PRLDEF). Previously he served as general counsel and vice president for advocacy at the Community Service Society of New York. He has written widely on constitutional, human rights, and civil rights law and has been recognized for his work on the political representation of poor and marginalized communities.

Javier Castaño is founder and director of the digital/print news platform *QueensLatino.com*. Previously, he was managing editor of *El Diario–La Prensa* and editor-in-chief of *HOY*, two of the largest Spanish-language newspapers in the New York City area. Castaño has authored two books on Latino issues in New York City, one about the musician Luis Carlos Meyer (1998) and the other on Colombians in New York (2004).

Ana María Díaz-Stevens, a sociologist, is professor emerita of church and society, Union Theological Seminary, New York. Before beginning her teaching career, she held posts at the Office of the Spanish Apostolate at the Archdiocese of New York. Among her publications are *Oxcart Catholicism on Fifth*

Avenue: The Impact of the Puerto Rican Migration upon the Archdiocese of New York (1993) and *The Latino Resurgence in American Religion* (1997).

Angelo Falcón is president and founder of the National Institute for Latino Policy (NiLP). He is a nationally recognized expert on Latino politics and policy issues and edits the online *NiLP Latino Policy & Politics Report*. His writing has appeared in numerous publications, including *The Nation, New York Post, National Civic Review, El Diario–La Prensa, Social Policy,* the *Journal of American Politics,* and the *Hispanic Link News Service.* In addition to authoring numerous reports on the status of Latinos in the United States, he is coeditor of *Latino Voices: Mexican, Puerto Rican and Cuban Perspectives on American Politics* (1992) and *Boricuas in Gotham: Puerto Ricans in the Making of Modern New York City* (2005).

Juan Flores (1943–2014) was professor of Latino studies in the Department of Social and Cultural Analysis at New York University. During his long and distinguished career he taught, lectured, and wrote about Puerto Rican and Latino culture, theories of culture and popular culture, diaspora studies and transnational community, Latino literature and music, and Afro-Latino culture and history. Some of his best-known works are his translation of *The Memoirs of Bernardo Vega* (1984), *From Bomba to Hip-Hop* (2000), *The Diaspora Strikes Back* (2009), *Bugalú y otros guisos,* (2009), and *The Afro-Latin@ Reader* (2010). He was awarded the Casa de las Américas Prize in 1980 and again in 2009; and in 2008, he was honored with the Latino Legacy Award from the Latino Center at the Smithsonian Institution. Flores served on a range of advisory and editorial boards, and was a founding member of the Afrolatin@ Forum.

Gabriel Haslip-Viera is emeritus professor of social history in the Department of Sociology at the City College of New York. He is author or editor of several works, including *Race, Identity and Indigenous Politics: Puerto Rican Neo-Taínos in the Diaspora and the Island* (2014) and *Taíno Revival: Critical Perspectives on Puerto Rican Identity and Cultural Politics* (2001); and he was a coeditor of the first edition of *Latinos in New York: Communities in Transition* (1996), *Crime and Punishment in Late Colonial Mexico City, 1692–1810* (1999), and *Boricuas in Gotham: Puerto Ricans in the Making of Modern New York City* (2005).

Ramona Hernández, a native of the Dominican Republic, is professor of sociology at The City College of New York and The Graduate Center at the City

University of New York (CUNY). She also serves as director of the CUNY Dominican Studies Institute, housed at City College. She has published several books, reports, book chapters, and articles in both English and Spanish, and is on the editorial board of the *Latino Studies Journal* and *Encyclopedia Latina: History, Culture, and Society*. Two of her best-known works in English are *The Mobility of Workers under Advanced Capitalism* (2002) and *Dominican-Americans* (coauthor, 1998).

Luz Yadira Herrera received her PhD in urban education from the City University of New York (CUNY) Graduate Center and is assistant professor in the Department of Literacy, Early Bilingual, and Special Education in the Kremen School of Education at Fresno State University. Her teaching and research are in linguistically and culturally sustaining approaches to teaching emergent bilingual learners, engaging in translanguaging and critical pedagogy in the classroom, and bilingual education policy.

Gilbert Marzán is associate professor of sociology at Bronx Community College, City University of New York. His research interests include Latino sociology, race and ethnicity, urban sociology, and demography. Dr. Marzán has been researching gentrification in the South Bronx and the migration patterns of Puerto Rican New Yorkers for the last ten years. His latest project examines the socioeconomic incorporation of Salvadoran immigrants in the United States.

Ed Morales, an author and journalist, has written for publications such as *The Nation*, the *New York Times*, *The Los Angeles Times*, *Rolling Stone*, the *Guardian*, and *City Limits*, and is a contributing editor to *NACLA Report on the Americas*. He is a former *Village Voice* staff writer and *Newsday* columnist. Morales is author of two books, *Living in Spanglish* (2003) and *The Latin Beat* (2003). He is currently a lecturer at Columbia University's Center for the Study of Ethnicity and Race and at John Jay College, City University of New York.

Pedro A. Noguera, a sociologist, is distinguished professor of education in the Graduate School of Education and Information Sciences at University of California at Los Angeles and has held previous teaching appointments at New York University, Harvard University, and University of California at Berkeley. Dr. Noguera's teaching and scholarship focus on the ways schools are influenced by prevailing social and economic conditions as well as demographic trends. He has authored eleven books and over two hundred articles and monographs. He is the author of *The Trouble with Black Boys . . . and Other Reflections on Race, Equity and the Future of Public Education* (2008), and he is a coauthor of *Schooling for Resilience* (2014).

Rosalía Reyes, a career journalist, is an assistant producer on the literary program *El autor y su obra*, broadcast on the Hispanic Information and Telecommunications Network. A native of Monterrey, Mexico, she holds degrees from the Autonomous University of Nuevo León and the Universidad de Monterrey. She is the New York–based correspondent for RTV Nuevo Leon, a Mexican television network.

Clara E. Rodríguez is professor of sociology at Fordham University's College at Lincoln Center, where she previously served as dean of liberal studies. She is the author or coauthor of numerous books, including *The Culture and Commerce of Publishing in the 21st Century* (2007), *Heroes, Lovers and Others: The Story of Latinos in Hollywood* (2004), *Changing Race: Latinos, the Census and the History of Ethnicity in the United States* (2000), and *Latin Looks: Images of Latinas and Latinos in the Media* (1997). Rodríguez has received numerous research and teaching awards and has been a visiting professor at Columbia University, Massachusetts Institute of Technology, and Yale University; a visiting scholar at the Russell Sage Foundation; and a senior fellow at the Smithsonian Institution's National Museum of American History. Rodríguez has also served on the American Sociological Association's Governing Council.

José Ramón Sánchez is professor of political science and chair of urban studies at Long Island University–Brooklyn. He is a political theorist who has concentrated on urban political economy, American politics, and the nature of power and has published widely in those fields. Among his works are *Boricua Power: A Political History of Puerto Ricans in the United States* (2007), and he is coauthor of *The Iraq Papers* (2010). Sánchez has served on the boards of directors of a number of organizations, including the Institute for Puerto Rican Policy, the Center for Puerto Rican Studies, and the Puerto Rican Legal Defense and Education Fund.

Walker Simon was born in New York and raised in the Mexican city of Monterrey. He holds a BA in economics from Oberlin College and an MA in journalism from Columbia University. Simon has reported from fourteen countries in Latin America and the Caribbean, and in New York, he has covered Latin American art, culture, and ethnic communities; international diplomacy; and religious affairs.

Robert Courtney Smith is professor of sociology, immigration studies, and public affairs at Baruch College's School of Public Affairs and in the Sociology Department of the Graduate Center at City University of New York. His first book, *Mexican New York: Transnational Worlds of New Immigrants* (2006), won the American Sociological Association's 2008 overall Distinguished Book Award. His second book, *Horatio Alger Lives in Brooklyn, but Check His Papers*, is forthcoming. Smith has combined public advocacy with his intellectual work. He is the founding lead faculty for Baruch's Mexican Consulate Leadership Program and is also a cofounder and now board chair of Masa (masany.org), a fifteen-year-old nonprofit in New York promoting educational achievement and committed leadership with Mexican immigrants and their children. His work has been funded by the National Science Foundation, Social Science Research Council, Spencer Foundation, W. T. Grant Foundation, Guggenheim Foundation, and others.

Andrés Torres is distinguished lecturer in the Department of Latin American, Latino, and Puerto Rican Studies at Lehman College, City University of New York. He was previously professor of Latino studies and director of the Mauricio Gastón Institute for Latino Community Development and Public Policy at the University of Massachusetts at Boston. His book publications include *Between Melting Pot and Mosaic: African Americans and Puerto Ricans in the New York Political Economy* (1995), *The Puerto Rican Movement: Voices from the Diaspora* (coeditor 1998), *Latinos in New England* (2006), and *Signing in Puerto Rican: A Hearing Child and His Deaf Family* (2009).

Silvio Torres-Saillant, born in the Dominican Republic, is dean's professor in the humanities at Syracuse University, where he teaches English and Latino-Latin American studies. He was founding director of the CUNY Dominican Studies Institute. He publishes widely in both English and Spanish. Recent works are *An Intellectual History of the Caribbean* (2006), *El retorno de las yolas* (1999), and *Caribbean Poetics* (1997). His pathbreaking essay "An Introduction to Dominican Blackness" (1999) was reprinted in 2010. Torres-Saillant sits on several editorial boards publishing work on Latinos such as the *Oxford Encyclopedia of Latinos and Latinas in the United States*.

INDEX

Page numbers in italics signify tables or figures.

CPSIA information can be obtained
at www.ICGtesting.com
Printed in the USA
FFOW03n1623091017
40666FF